高等院校英语专业/翻译专业拓展阅读教材

The Selected Readings of Contemporary American Travel Writings

美国游记文学名篇导读与翻译

主　编　张慧芳　温秀颖
副主编　申彩红　杨　建
编　著　曲美茹　张小薪
　　　　王馨颐　杨少华

南开大学出版社
天　津

图书在版编目(CIP)数据

美国游记文学名篇导读与翻译 / 张慧芳,温秀颖主编.
—天津:南开大学出版社,2012.10
高等院校英语专业、翻译专业拓展阅读教材
ISBN 978-7-310-04043-8

Ⅰ.①美… Ⅱ.①张… ②温… Ⅲ.①英语－阅读教学－高等学校－教学参考资料 Ⅳ.①H319.4

中国版本图书馆 CIP 数据核字(2012)第 221784 号

版权所有　侵权必究

南开大学出版社出版发行
出版人:孙克强
地址:天津市南开区卫津路94号　邮政编码:300071
营销部电话:(022)23508339　23500755
营销部传真:(022)23508542　邮购部电话:(022)23502200

*

唐山天意印刷有限责任公司印刷
全国各地新华书店经销

*

2012 年 10 月第 1 版　2012 年 10 月第 1 次印刷
230×170 毫米　16 开本　28.875 印张　2 插页　541 千字
定价:55.00 元

如遇图书印装质量问题,请与本社营销部联系调换,电话:(022)23507125

编者的话

旅行，已经成为21世纪人类的一种重要生活方式。因之，游记创作成为现代人类表达自我、认知世界的重要精神诉述手段；而游记阅读不仅是一种单纯的阅读时尚，更是人们在文字图谱中饱尝山光水色、尽享异域风情、遭遇文化碰撞、驰骋想象、放飞心灵的高端文化活动；阅读旅者撰写的异域游记更能使我们从独特的视角和宽阔的视野去体验和感悟踽踽独行的旅者和大千世界的关联，深层次引发我们对"我"以何种方式存在于世的思考。这正是我们精心编选此书的初衷。

本书共分为五编，除"序曲"和"尾声"两编外，还有"沙漠游记"、"丛林游记"和"极地游记"三编主干内容。"序曲"包括编者撰写的《总序》和三篇哲思游记。其中的《旅行为哪般》从跨文化想象的视角把旅行看作"道德放假"，亦即旅者在旅行时需要暂时放下本土文化价值观和伦理道德观，以开放、开明、谦恭的姿态来体察异域生活状态和文化活动。《旅游双刃剑》更为注重现实问题：旅游开发固然能提升当地经济，旅游观光固然能提升旅者的自我境界，但二者却在不经意间合谋干扰和破坏了观光地的生活原态和文化原貌。而政府部门所标榜的"只开发不破坏"、"只观赏不践踏"就好比是"生龙活虎一男子躺在纯洁美丽之少女的身旁，不破坏和蹂躏又如何能享受少女之贞操？"这是典型的美国式幽默和讽刺，却鞭辟入里地揭露了旅游之双面效应。《魁北克最后的因纽特人》认为"一方水土一方人"，魁北克的因纽特人捕杀鲸鱼为生活习俗，而置身其外的所谓物种保护者们不能简单粗暴地对此种习俗说三道四，意在启发人们进一步思索：什么才是真正意义上的"人与自然和谐相处"？三编主干内容中的文章则启迪人们：沙漠、丛林和极地是生命存在于世的极端环境；只有沙漠才能彻底激发人对水彻骨的感念；只有丛林才能提供生命神秘的完整意义；只有极地才能宣告什么才是冰冷的美之真谛。"尾声"这一编是对全书的回顾以及对"序曲"的回应。《女孩子的沙特阿拉伯旅行指南》是对《旅行为哪般》的一种反讽，《正在消逝的尖端》和《鸟之年记》则为《旅游双刃剑》提出的旅游困境指明了出路。

本书的每一篇文章都有中英文双版，但其编排绝不同于一般的中英文对照。我们为英文版文章精心编著了或生动有趣或发人深省的导读，并为行文中的文化及语言难点做了详尽的注释，因而既适合英语水平较高的读者进行美文赏析式的休闲阅读，也适合作大中院校学生提升英语阅读水平、加强跨文化比较能力和提升人文素养之最佳素材。每一篇文章的中文版皆属上乘译作，既忠实于原文，又独立成篇，语言通畅，文笔自然，尤其适合广大读者用来进行赏析佳作、认识异域、开阔视野、提升境界等阅读活动。不同篇章的原文其语言也各具特色，或清丽、或深沉、或诙谐、或肃穆，各自的文化内涵丰富而又深邃，这些因素都给翻译活动带来很大的挑战。每一篇译文都倾注着译者对读者的尊重和热爱，翻译过程中字斟句酌、中西兼顾。因而，本书还特别适合作英中翻译实践的教材范本。

　　天津财经大学温秀颖教授负责全书的整体规划、选材取舍、终稿校订；天津财经大学张慧芳副教授编写了全书的阅读素材，注释和翻译了其中的 5 篇文章，撰写了总序、5 篇导读，校译了所有文章；天津财经大学申彩红老师注释和翻译了其中的 4 篇文章并撰写了 4 篇导读，参与了译稿校对工作；天津财经大学杨建老师注释和翻译了其中的 5 篇文章并撰写了 5 篇导读、后记，参与了译稿校对、篇目合成等工作；天津财经大学曲美茹老师注释和翻译了其中的 2 篇文章，并撰写了 2 篇导读、参与了校对；天津财经大学张小薪老师注释和翻译了其中的 2 篇文章，并撰写了两篇导读；天津财经大学王馨怡老师参与了资料查询和汇编等工作；天津财经大学人文学院外语系 2010 级研究生杨少华同学参与了资料查询、材料打印等工作。

　　尽管本书编者悉心谨慎并倾注全力，但终难免玉之瑕疵，若有纰漏和不当之处还望广大读者不吝赐教。

编　者

2012 年 5 月

总　序

21世纪美国游记文学中的生态文明景观。

这个命题包含着多重意思

21世纪，人类彼此交流互为理解的一个最为流行、也最为可靠的方式就是旅行。旅行是一个发现的过程。发现美丽，发现惊喜，发现新奇，发现自己。因为有了好奇和充满发现欲的眼睛，我们的旅程才不会单调乏味，才会不断让情绪升温。也正因如此，许多在身边习以为常视而不见的景物，才会在异国异地重新成为风景。然而，游而不记，旅行就不会圆满；记而不共享，旅行就太过私密，从而使旅行失去了应有的深度和影响。被记录了的旅行就是游记；语言有着文学性，主题充满思想性，对世界对人生对文化有所感悟，这样的游记就是游记文学。

21世纪，文学研究领域不断拓展其研究文类。除了在传统文类如诗歌、小说等中的坚守，传记文学等纪实类文学体裁方兴未艾。从美国文学研究角度看，游记文学受到关注肇始于对自传文学的探索，因为自传文学文本的核心主题就是天地之间、时代风云中的"自我"演变，而游记文学的客观叙述视角就是行走在世界中的"我"。美国学者嘉熙·布兰顿（Casey Blanton）如是说："游记是沟通手段，其目的是为了把自我介绍给他者，因而游记把自我与世界之间的契约典型化和戏剧化了。游记的核心就是展现作为观察者的我与异域世界产生共鸣的方式和手段。"[①] 换句话说，游记是"我"与世界发生对话的储存文本。中外学界已达成共识：游记不但是文学文本，也是文化文本。揭示游记文学中的文化乃至文明内涵是游记研究的实践意义所在。

美国思想者贝尔在上个世纪80年代末期提出"后工业社会"理念之后，美国对西方现代性的批判在整个思想界蔓延开来，很大程度上动摇了向来注重实用主义的美国民众对人与自然环境关系的认识，但是，直到2009年之后"生态文明"这一概念才散见于美国日常报端。在此前提下，美国旅者的生态环境价值观是潜意识的、散乱的，仍然受"美国文化优势论"的左右，因而，21世纪的美国游记文学所表现的生态景观也千差万别。然而，"千差万别"背后隐藏

[①] Blanton, Casey. *Travel Writing: the Self and the World*. New York: Routledge, 2002.

着相同的文化文明意识,那就是:在全世界都喧嚷国际化的 21 世纪,美国游记以绚丽多姿的文学文本、独特的俯视视角和悲悯情怀,透过其描述的几个景观世态,清晰地折射了世界各个角落的生态文明景观。

在学术层次上,美国生态文化价值观与游记文学渊源颇深。《花园里的机器:美国的技术与田园理想》[1]是一部影响甚广的生态批评理论著作。在这部名著里,作者探讨了美国人对自然环境的矛盾态度,认为这种态度反映在伊莉莎白时期的各种有关新大陆的游记文学作品之中。人是大自然的欣赏者,在大自然中畅游是人获得快乐的手段。这是游记文学的根本特征。而美国学者威廉·W·斯托[2]认为,美国游记文学中的风景记录或描述则是美国人构建自我身份和民族性格的一种特有的方式。这两个例证说明同一个问题:美国游记文学很大程度上反映着美国的自然观乃至生态观。

"作为一种特殊的文类,游记内容博杂,无所不包,一向是历史学、地理学、人类学、社会学等多种学科的有用材料。"[3] 如此说来,通过游记文学来透视一个民族对世界生态文明的建构理念也就顺理成章了。

从比较文学研究的角度看,具有不同文化体系的民族,其游记文学的核心审美观也是如此不同。中国游记文学,纵观古今,算上网络博客,无不"以构建人与自然审美关系为核心"。[4] 中国游记文学文本对山水花草树木等自然生态景物的关注似乎是一种本能,即便是对人文历史景观的游历记述也少不了自然景观的对比和观照。美国游记文学则不同,其核心是以优越的心态探奇、探险、探索未知。无论自然还是人文,美国旅者都会以二元论视角把景观作为人的对立面来审视、进而征服。而中国的旅者往往会身不由己地把自我与景观融为一体,以我之心体察景观之灵,进而感悟世界感悟生命之意义。中国游记历来以自然审美为核心,寄情山水以彰显人文情怀,而美国游记往往探险多于游历,哲思多于诗意,思辨多于感悟。中国旅者对景观采取的动作是"体察和感悟",而美国旅者则是"审视和征服"。

沙漠、丛林和极地是生命存在于世的极端环境,这些地方的生态之奇之险更能激发人的探索欲和征服欲。"沙漠之所以存在,是因为它们梦想着绿洲",沙漠之旅不在于欣赏风景,而在于对葱茏自然景色的反观;神秘,抑或是诡异?

---

[1] 利奥·马克斯.《花园里的机器:美国技术与田园理想》. 马海良 雷月梅 译. 北京:北京大学出版社,2011.

[2] Stowe, William W. "'Property in Horizon': Landscape and American Travel Writing". *The Cambridge Companion to American Travel Writing*. Alfred Bendixen ed. Cambridge: Cambridge University Press, 2009.

[3] 尹德翔.《跨文化旅行研究对游记文学的启迪》. 中国图书评论,2005 年第 11 期,21-23 页。

[4] 梅新林 俞樟华.《中国游记文学史》. 上海:学林出版社,2004.

难道生命的神秘只有在丛林才能得到淋漓尽致的绽放？极地苦寒的生活涤荡着人的灵魂，雪域人生中蕴含着胆识与智慧。只有沙漠才能彻底激发人对水彻骨的感念；只有丛林才能提供生命神秘的完整意义；只有极地才能宣告什么才是冰冷美之真谛。在沙漠、丛林和极地这样的极端环境，人类寻求着本原精神的复兴与超越之路。

21世纪美国游记文学中的生态文明景观。

在进一步追问之前，有必要先读上几篇吧？！

……

目 录

序 曲

旅行是一个发现的过程。发现美丽，发现惊喜，发现新奇，发现自己。然而，游而不记，旅行就会不圆满；记而不共享，旅行就太过于私密……

1. Why We Travel 旅行为哪般 ········ 3
2. The Two Faces of Tourism 旅游双刃剑 ········ 22
3. The Last Inuit of Quebec 魁北克最后的因纽特人 ········ 40

第一编　沙漠游记

"沙漠之所以存在，是因为它们梦想着绿洲。"沙漠之旅不在于欣赏风景，而在于对葱茏自然景色的反观。……

1. The Truck 撒哈拉的卡车 ········ 65
2. Thirteen Ways of Looking at a Void 沙漠无人区面面观 ········ 79
3. Stranger in the Dunes 沙丘来客 ········ 110
4. Slow Flying Stones 石光掠影 ········ 126

第二编　丛林游记

神秘，抑或是诡异？人对丛林的印象不外乎此。难道生命的神秘只有在丛林才能得到淋漓尽致的绽放？……

1. Lost in the Amazon 迷失亚马逊 ········ 165
2. The Vision Seekers 丛林灵巫 ········ 194
3. Eco-touring in Honduras 洪都拉斯生态游 ········ 207
4. The Cabin of My Dreams 我的梦想小屋 ········ 236

第三编　极地游记

极地苦寒的生活涤荡着人的灵魂，雪域人生中蕴含着胆识与智慧。在极地，人类寻求精神复兴与超越之路。……

1. The Endless Hunt 狩猎无极限 ········ 265

2. Lost in the Arctic 极地野生 296
3. Winter Rules 冬日独尊 318
4. The Very, very, very Big Chill 顶极酷寒 343

尾 声

  合书掩面，意犹未尽之时，仍有几篇美文翘首以待慰藉我们对自然美景自在自为之态的渴望……

1. A Girl's Guide to Saudi Arabia 一个女孩的沙特阿拉伯旅行指南 357
2. The Vanishing Point 正在消逝的端点 394
3. A Year of Birds 鸟之年鉴 409

  后　记 448

序　曲

　　旅行是一个发现的过程。发现美丽，发现惊喜，发现新奇，发现自己。然而，游而不记，旅行就会不圆满；记而不共享，旅行就太过于私密……

山 雨

Why We Travel

Pico Iyer

【导读】中国古语有云:"读万卷书,行万里路,"说的是读书丰富我们的知识,旅行开阔我们的视野。然而,旅行的意义还不止于此。旅行还是心灵开启之旅,美国当代游记作家匹克·艾雅就持如此观点。匹克·艾雅,1957年出生于英国,后随父母移民美国,是著名游记作家、小说家和散文家,在游记文学领域颇有建树,也颇有声望。《旅行为哪般》创作于21世纪初期,多年来被以各种形式转载或重印,受到旅行爱好者、散文爱好者、文化学者等的喜爱和好评。这篇游记散文探讨了旅行的特性,尤其是旅行的转变功能:旅行能打破旅行者以往的偏见和妄想;旅行的过程其实就是一个自我发现的过程;旅行还帮助旅行者架起了过去与将来、祖国乡土与异域他国之间联系的桥梁。本文指出,旅行是旅行者内在的自我发现之旅,其终极意义在于,跋涉之中,旅行者的内心逐渐变得强大和开阔。在旅行中,我们的灵魂如何被重新唤醒?我们的伦理道德遭遇到何种挑战?我们的视野和内心是怎样变得更为辽阔的?这篇文章探讨的并非旅行的物质过程,而是人行走在世界中的一种精神,是心灵与世界的一种高层次对话模式。文章旁征博引,涉及文化、文学、哲学、历史、地理等各个方面的知识,但读来却毫无堆砌之感,这是因为作者通过旅行与恋爱之间精辟的类比,以生动的语言、鲜活的意象和深邃的思想为读者娓娓道来旅行之美之妙之韵之灵。

We travel, initially, to lose ourselves; and we travel, next, to find ourselves. We travel to open our hearts and eyes and learn more about the world than our newspapers will accommodate. We travel to bring what little we can, in our ignorance and knowledge, to those parts of the globe whose riches are differently dispersed. And we travel, in essence, to become young fools again — to slow time down and get taken in, and fall in love once more. The beauty of this whole process was best described, perhaps, before people even took to frequent flying, by George Santayana in his lapidary essay, "The Philosophy of Travel." We "need sometimes," the Harvard philosopher wrote, "to escape into open solitudes, into aimlessness, into the moral holiday of running some pure hazard①, in order to sharpen the edge of life, to taste hardship, and to be compelled to work desperately for a moment at no matter what."

I like that stress on work, since never more than on the road are we shown how proportional our blessings are to the difficulty that precedes them; and I like the stress on a holiday that's "moral" since we fall into our ethical habits as easily as into our beds at night. Few of us ever forget the connection between "travel" and "travail," and I know that I travel in large part in search of hardship — both my own, which I want to feel, and others', which I need to see. Travel in that sense guides us toward a better balance of wisdom and compassion — of seeing the world clearly, and yet feeling it truly. For seeing without feeling can obviously be uncaring; while feeling without seeing can be blind.

Yet for me the first great joy of traveling is simply the luxury of leaving all my beliefs and certainties at home, and seeing everything I thought I knew in a different light, and from a crooked angle. In that regard, even a Kentucky Fried Chicken outlet (in Beijing) or a scratchy revival showing of *Wild Orchids* (on the Champs-Elysees) can be both novelty and revelation: In China, after all, people will pay a whole week's wages to eat with Colonel Sanders, and in Paris, Mickey Rourke is regarded as the greatest actor since Jerry Lewis.

If a Mongolian restaurant seems exotic to us in Evanston, Ill., it only follows that a McDonald's would seem equally exotic in Ulan Bator — or, at least, equally far from everything expected. Though it's fashionable nowadays to draw a distinction between the "tourist" and the "traveler," perhaps the real distinction lies between those who leave their assumptions at home, and those who don't: Among those who don't, a tourist is just someone who complains, "Nothing here is the way it is at home," while a traveler is one who grumbles, "Everything here is the same as it is in Cairo — or Cuzco or Kathmandu." It's all very much the same.

But for the rest of us, the sovereign freedom of traveling comes from the fact

---

① A moral holiday to run a pure hazard is a state of mind, when the traveler, (being alone in a strange place), makes a decision to cast off conventional standards of right, appropriate & safe behavior; in circumstances where only his personal well-being is at risk. The conventional, homespun, standard is clear & unambiguous: Don't expose oneself to dangerous bacteria in food that may not be clean. Cleanliness has become a mantra of Western (especially American) culture. A pure hazard exists in circumstances where there is no discernible benefit associated with the risk.

that it whirls you around and turns you upside down, and stands everything you took for granted on its head. If a diploma can famously be a passport (to a journey through hard realism), a passport can be a diploma (for a crash course in cultural relativism). And the first lesson we learn on the road, whether we like it or not, is how provisional and provincial are the things we imagine to be universal. When you go to North Korea, for example, you really do feel as if you've landed on a different planet — and the North Koreans doubtless feel that they're being visited by an extra-terrestrial, too (or else they simply assume that you, as they do, receive orders every morning from the Central Committee on what clothes to wear and what route to use when walking to work, and you, as they do, have loudspeakers in your bedroom broadcasting propaganda every morning at dawn, and you, as they do, have your radios fixed so as to receive only a single channel).

We travel, then, in part just to shake up our complacencies by seeing all the moral and political urgencies, the life-and-death dilemmas, that we seldom have to face at home. And we travel to fill in the gaps left by tomorrow's headlines: When you drive down the streets of Port-au-Prince, for example, where there is almost no paving and women relieve themselves next to mountains of trash, your notions of the Internet and a "one world order" grow usefully revised. Travel is the best way we have of rescuing the humanity of places, and saving them from abstraction and ideology.

And in the process, we also get saved from abstraction ourselves, and come to see how much we can bring to the places we visit, and how much we can become a kind of carrier pigeon — an anti-Federal Express, if you like — in transporting back and forth what every culture needs. I find that I always take Michael Jordan posters to Kyoto, and bring woven ikebana baskets back to California; I invariably travel to Cuba with a suitcase piled high with bottles of Tylenol and bars of soap, and come back with one piled high with salsa tapes, and hopes, and letters to long-lost brothers.

But more significantly, we carry values and beliefs and news to the places we go, and in many parts of the world, we become walking video screens and living newspapers, the only channels that can take people out of the censored limits of their homelands. In closed or impoverished places, like Pagan or Lhasa or Havana, we are the eyes and ears of the people we meet, their only contact with the world outside and, very often, the closest, quite literally, they will ever come to Michael Jackson or

Bill Clinton. Not the least of the challenges of travel, therefore, is learning how to import — and export — dreams with tenderness.

By now all of us have heard (too often) the old Proust line about how the real voyage of discovery consists not in seeing new places but in seeing with new eyes. Yet one of the subtler beauties of travel is that it enables you to bring new eyes to the people you encounter. Thus even as holidays help you appreciate your own home more — not least by seeing it through a distant admirer's eyes — they help you bring newly appreciative — distant — eyes to the places you visit. You can teach them what they have to celebrate as much as you celebrate what they have to teach. This, I think, is how tourism, which so obviously destroys cultures, can also resuscitate or revive them, how it has created new "traditional" dances in Bali, and caused craftsmen in India to pay new attention to their works. If the first thing we can bring the Cubans is a real and balanced sense of what contemporary America is like, the second — and perhaps more important — thing we can bring them is a fresh and renewed sense of how special are the warmth and beauty of their country, for those who can compare it with other places around the globe.

Thus travel spins us round in two ways at once: It shows us the sights and values and issues that we might ordinarily ignore; but it also, and more deeply, shows us all the parts of ourselves that might otherwise grow rusty. For in traveling to a truly foreign place, we inevitably travel to moods and states of mind and hidden inward passages that we'd otherwise seldom have cause to visit.

On the most basic level, when I'm in Thailand, though a teetotaler who usually goes to bed at 9 p.m., I stay up till dawn in the local bars; and in Tibet, though not a real Buddhist, I spend days on end in temples, listening to the chants of sutras. I go to Iceland to visit the lunar spaces within me, and, in the uncanny quietude and emptiness of that vast and treeless world, to tap parts of myself generally obscured by chatter and routine.

We travel, then, in search of both self and anonymity — and, of course, in finding the one we apprehend the other. Abroad, we are wonderfully free of caste and job and standing; we are, as Hazlitt puts it, just the "gentlemen in the parlour," and people cannot put a name or tag to us. And precisely because we are clarified in this way, and freed of inessential labels, we have the opportunity to come into contact with more essential parts of ourselves (which may begin to explain why we may feel most alive when far from home).

Abroad is the place where we stay up late, follow impulse and find ourselves as wide open as when we are in love. We live without a past or future, for a moment at least, and are ourselves up for grabs and open to interpretation. We even may become mysterious — to others, at first, and sometimes to ourselves — and, as no less a dignitary than Oliver Cromwell once noted, "A man never goes so far as when he doesn't know where he is going."

There are, of course, great dangers to this, as to every kind of freedom, but the great promise of it is that, traveling, we are born again, and able to return at moments to a younger and a more open kind of self. Traveling is a way to reverse time, to a small extent, and make a day last a year — or at least 45 hours — and traveling is an easy way of surrounding ourselves, as in childhood, with what we cannot understand. Language facilitates this cracking open, for when we go to France, we often migrate to French, and the more childlike self, simple and polite, that speaking a foreign language educes. Even when I'm not speaking pidgin English in Hanoi, I'm simplified in a positive way, and concerned not with expressing myself, but simply making sense.

So travel, for many of us, is a quest for not just the unknown, but the unknowing; I, at least, travel in search of an innocent eye that can return me to a more innocent self. I tend to believe more abroad than I do at home (which, though treacherous again, can at least help me to extend my vision), and I tend to be more easily excited abroad, and even kinder. And since no one I meet can "place" me — no one can fix me in my résumé — I can remake myself for better, as well as, of course, for worse (if travel is notoriously a cradle for false identities, it can also, at its best, be a crucible for truer ones). In this way, travel can be a kind of monasticism on the move: On the road, we often live more simply (even when staying in a luxury hotel), with no more possessions than we can carry, and surrendering ourselves to chance.

This is what Camus meant when he said that "what gives value to travel is fear" — disruption, in other words, (or emancipation) from circumstance, and all the habits behind which we hide. And that is why many of us travel not in search of answers, but of better questions. I, like many people, tend to ask questions of the places I visit, and relish most the ones that ask the most searching questions back of me: In Paraguay, for example, where one car in every two is stolen, and two-thirds of the goods on sale are smuggled, I have to rethink my every Californian assumption.

And in Thailand, where many young women give up their bodies in order to protect their families — to become better Buddhists — I have to question my own too-ready judgments. "The ideal travel book," Christopher Isherwood once said, "should be perhaps a little like a crime story in which you're in search of something." And it's the best kind of something, I would add, if it's one that you can never quite find.

I remember, in fact, after my first trips to Southeast Asia, more than a decade ago, how I would come back to my apartment in New York, and lie in my bed, kept up by something more than jet lag, playing back, in my memory, over and over, all that I had experienced, and paging wistfully though my photographs and reading and re-reading my diaries, as if to extract some mystery from them. Anyone witnessing this strange scene would have drawn the right conclusion: I was in love.

For if every true love affair can feel like a journey to a foreign country, where you can't quite speak the language, and you don't know where you're going, and you're pulled ever deeper into the inviting darkness, every trip to a foreign country can be a love affair, where you're left puzzling over who you are and whom you've fallen in love with. All the great travel books are love stories, by some reckoning — from the *Odyssey* and the *Aeneid* to the *Divine Comedy* and the New Testament — and all good trips are, like love, about being carried out of yourself and deposited in the midst of terror and wonder.

And what this metaphor also brings home to us is that all travel is a two-way transaction, as we too easily forget, and if warfare is one model of the meeting of nations, romance is another. For what we all too often ignore when we go abroad is that we are objects of scrutiny as much as the people we scrutinize, and we are being consumed by the cultures we consume, as much on the road as when we are at home. At the very least, we are objects of speculation (and even desire) who can seem as exotic to the people around us as they do to us.

We are the comic props in Japanese home-movies, the oddities Malian anecdotes and the fall-guys in Chinese jokes; we are the moving postcards or bizarre *objets trouvés*[①] that villagers in Peru will later tell their friends about. If travel is about the meeting of realities, it is no less about the mating of illusions: You give me my dreamed-of vision of Tibet, and I'll give you your wished-for California. And in truth, many of us, even (or especially) the ones who are fleeing America abroad, will

---

① Spanish words, natural art.

get taken, willy-nilly, as symbols of the American Dream.

That, in fact, is perhaps the most central and most wrenching of the questions travel proposes to us: how to respond to the dream that people tender to you? Do you encourage their notions of a Land of Milk and Honey across the horizon, even if it is the same land you've abandoned? Or do you try to dampen their enthusiasm for a place that exists only in the mind? To quicken their dreams may, after all, be to match-make them with an illusion; yet to dash them may be to strip them of the one possession that sustains them in adversity.

That whole complex interaction — not unlike the dilemmas we face with those we love (how do we balance truthfulness and tact?) — is partly the reason why so many of the great travel writers, by nature, are enthusiasts: not just Pierre Loti, who famously, infamously, fell in love wherever he alighted (an archetypal sailor leaving offspring in the form of *Madame Butterfly* myths), but also Henry Miller, D.H. Lawrence or Graham Greene, all of whom bore out the hidden truth that we are optimists abroad as readily as pessimists as home. None of them was by any means blind to the deficiencies of the places around them, but all, having chosen to go there, chose to find something to admire.

All, in that sense, believed in "being moved" as one of the points of taking trips, and "being transported" by private as well as public means; all saw that "ecstasy" ("ex-stasis") tells us that our highest moments come when we're not stationary, and that epiphany can follow movement as much as it precipitates it. I remember once asking the great travel writer Norman Lewis if he'd ever be interested in writing on apartheid South Africa. He looked at me astonished. "To write well about a thing," he said, "I've got to like it!"

At the same time, as all this is intrinsic to travel, from Ovid to O'Rourke, travel itself is changing as the world does, and with it, the mandate of the travel writer. It's not enough to go to the ends of the earth these days (not least because the ends of the earth are often coming to you); and where a writer like Jan Morris could, a few years ago, achieve something miraculous simply by voyaging to all the great cities of the globe, now anyone with a Visa card can do that. So where Morris, in effect, was chronicling the last days of the Empire, a younger travel writer is in a better position to chart the first days of a new Empire, post-national, global, mobile and yet as diligent as the Raj in transporting its props and its values around the world.

In the mid-19th century, the British famously sent the Bible and Shakespeare and cricket round the world; now a more international kind of Empire is sending Madonna and the Simpsons and Brad Pitt. And the way in which each culture takes in this common pool of references tells you as much about them as their indigenous products might. Madonna in an Islamic country, after all, sounds radically different from Madonna in a Confucian one, and neither begins to mean the same as Madonna on East 14th Street. When you go to a McDonald's outlet in Kyoto, you will find Teriyaki McBurgers and Bacon Potato Pies. The placemats offer maps of the great temples of the city, and the posters all around broadcast the wonders of San Francisco. And — most crucial of all — the young people eating their Big Macs, with baseball caps worn backwards, and tight 501 jeans, are still utterly and inalienably Japanese in the way they move, they nod, they sip their Oolong teas — and never to be mistaken for the patrons of a McDonald's outlet in Rio, Morocco or Managua. These days a whole new realm of exotica arises out of the way one culture colors and appropriates the products of another.

The other factor complicating and exciting all of this is people, who are, more and more, themselves as many-tongued and mongrel as cities like Sydney or Toronto or Hong Kong. I am, in many ways, an increasingly typical specimen, if only because I was born, as the son of Indian parents, in England, moved to America at 7 and cannot really call myself an Indian, an American or an Englishman. I was, in short, a traveler at birth, for whom even a visit to the candy store was a trip through a foreign world where no one I saw quite matched my parents' inheritance, or my own. And though some of this is involuntary and tragic — the number of refugees in the world, which came to just 2.5 million in 1970, is now at least 27.4 million — it does involve, for some of us, the chance to be transnational in a happier sense, able to adapt anywhere, used to being outsiders everywhere and forced to fashion our own rigorous sense of home. (And if nowhere is quite home, we can be optimists everywhere.)

Besides, even those who don't move around the world find the world moving more and more around them. Walk just six blocks, in Queens or Berkeley, and you're traveling through several cultures in as many minutes; get into a cab outside the White House, and you're often in a piece of Addis Ababa. And technology, too, compounds this (sometimes deceptive) sense of availability, so that many people feel they can travel around the world without leaving the room — through cyberspace or CD-ROMs, videos and virtual travel. There are many challenges in this, of course, in what it says about essential notions of family and community and loyalty, and in the worry that air-conditioned, purely synthetic versions of places may replace the real thing — not to mention the fact that the world seems increasingly in flux, a moving target quicker than our notions of it. But there is, for the traveler at least, the sense that learning about home and learning about a foreign world can be one and the same thing.

All of us feel this from the cradle, and know, in some sense, that all the significant movement we ever take is internal. We travel when we see a movie, strike up a new friendship, get held up. Novels are often journeys as much as travel books are fictions; and though this has been true since at least as long ago as Sir John Mandeville's colorful 14th century accounts of a Far East he'd never visited, it's an even more shadowy distinction now, as genre distinctions join other borders in collapsing.

In Mary Morris's *House Arrest*, a thinly disguised account of Castro's Cuba, the novelist reiterates, on the copyright page, "All dialogue is invented. Isabella, her family, the inhabitants and even *la isla* itself are creations of the author's imagination." On Page 172, however, we read, "*La isla*, of course, does exist. Don't let anyone fool you about that. It just feels as if it doesn't. But it does." No wonder the travel-writer narrator — a fictional construct (or not)? — confesses to devoting her travel magazine column to places that never existed. "Erewhon," after all, the undiscovered land in Samuel Butler's great travel novel, is just "nowhere" rearranged.

Travel, then, is a voyage into that famously subjective zone, the imagination, and what the traveler brings back is — and has to be — an ineffable compound of himself and the place, what's really there and what's only in him. Thus Bruce Chatwin's books seem to dance around the distinction between fact and fancy. V.S. Naipaul's recent book, *A Way in the World*, was published as a non-fictional "series" in England and a "novel" in the United States. And when some of the stories in Paul Theroux's half-invented memoir, *My Other Life*, were published in *The New Yorker*, they were slyly categorized as "Fact and Fiction."

And since travel is, in a sense, about the conspiracy of perception and imagination, the two great travel writers, for me, to whom I constantly return are Emerson and Thoreau (the one who famously advised that "traveling is a fool's paradise," and the other who "traveled a good deal in Concord"). Both of them insist on the fact that reality is our creation, and that we invent the places we see as much as we do the books that we read. What we find outside ourselves has to be inside ourselves for us to find it. Or, as Sir Thomas Browne sagely put it, "We carry within us the wonders we seek without us. There is Africa and her prodigies in us."

So, if more and more of us have to carry our sense of home inside us, we also — Emerson and Thoreau remind us — have to carry with us our sense of destination. The most valuable Pacifics we explore will always be the vast expanses within us, and the most important Northwest Crossings the thresholds we cross in the heart. The virtue of finding a gilded pavilion in Kyoto is that it allows you to take back a more lasting, private Golden Temple to your office in Rockefeller Center.

And even as the world seems to grow more exhausted, our travels do not, and some of the finest travel books in recent years have been those that undertake a parallel journey, matching the physical steps of a pilgrimage with the metaphysical steps of a questioning (as in Peter Matthiessen's great *The Snow Leopard*), or chronicling a trip to the farthest reaches of human strangeness (as in Oliver Sack's *Island of the Color-Blind*, which features a journey not just to a remote atoll in the Pacific, but to a realm where people actually see light differently). The most distant shores, we are constantly reminded, lie within the person asleep at our side.

So travel, at heart, is just a quick way to keeping our minds mobile and awake. As Santayana, the heir to Emerson and Thoreau with whom I began, wrote, "There is wisdom in turning as often as possible from the familiar to the unfamiliar; it keeps the mind nimble; it kills prejudice, and it fosters humor." Romantic poets inaugurated an era of travel because they were the great apostles of open eyes. Buddhist monks are often vagabonds, in part because they believe in wakefulness. And if travel is like love, it is, in the end, mostly because it's a heightened state of awareness, in which we are mindful, receptive, undimmed by familiarity and ready to be transformed. That is why the best trips, like the best love affairs, never really end.

旅行为哪般

匹克·艾雅

我们旅行，是为了自我迷失后的自我发现；我们旅行，是为了敞开心胸、放远视线，去更多地了解媒体之外的世界；我们旅行，是为了以微薄之力把自己的无知和所知传带到地球上某些独特而富饶的地方；我们旅行，从根本上说，是为了重返青涩年代——为了延缓时光的流逝，为了纵情光阴，为了再坠爱河。旅程的美妙或许在人们沉湎于频繁飞行之前就已在乔治·桑塔亚那的笔下得到了完美的诠释。这位哈佛哲学家在他论述精辟的《旅行哲学》一书中写道："有时，我们需要逃跑，逃到海阔天空的孤寥中，逃到漫无目的的无垠中；我们需要在休假中遭遇不可预料和控制的危险，从而陷入道德自省。只有这样，我们才能磨砺生活的锋刃，才能品尝千辛万苦工作之余的那片刻闲暇。"

我喜欢工作中的压力，因为压力之后的旅行能更加淋漓尽致地向我们展现：先前遭遇多大的困苦，之后就能得到多大的福报；我也喜欢"道德自省"休假所带来的压力，因为我们太容易陷入伦理道德的习以为常，容易得就像一到夜里就上床睡觉那样，因习惯而毫无感觉了。我们大多知道"旅行"（travel）与"旅途劳顿"（travail）之间的联系。① 而我自己旅行很大程度上是为了追寻艰辛与劳顿，既是为了感受自身的劳苦，也有必要体察他人的不易。在这个意义上，旅行引导我们更好地平衡智慧和博爱，使我们在更加清晰地认知世界的同时，也能真切地感知世界。因为，只认知而不感知，显而易见，就是冷漠；只感知而不认知，就是盲目。

不过，对我而言，旅行的第一乐事在于一种奢侈，奢侈到可以把自己的一切信仰与信念都撇舍身后，从而以不同的眼光、别样的角度来看待一切。因此不论是北京的肯德基快餐店，还是香榭丽舍的劣质电影《野兰花》的重播，这些都可能充满新奇和启示。在中国，人们会花上一周的工资和桑德斯上校一道用餐②，而在巴黎，米基·洛克③被公认为是继杰瑞·路易斯之后最棒的演员。

如果说，在伊利诺伊斯州的埃文斯顿市，蒙古餐馆极具异国情调，那么，

---

① 原文中 travel 与 travail 发音近似，且押头韵，但后者的真实意思是"煎熬；艰辛"；译文为了保持原文的押头韵修辞风格，故翻译为"旅行"与"旅途劳顿"，也符合汉语的表达习惯。

② Colonel Sanders 桑德斯上校，肯德基创始人，就是 KFC 店的招牌人物：一个和蔼的、笑眯眯的美国老头。

③ Mickey Rourke，美国影星，在色情电影《野兰花》中担任男主角。

人们完全可以认为麦当劳在乌兰巴托同样充满异域风情；或者，至少和当地人所预想的大相径庭。当下，把"旅者"（traveler）和"游客"（tourist）区别对待颇为盛行。或许真正的区别在于，有些人把主观臆断撇舍身后，以开放的心态周游四方，而有些人带着个人偏见打量周围的世界。后者中，游客会发牢骚："这儿的一切都和家里不是一回事。"在前者中，旅者会叨咕："这儿的一切都和埃及（或者库斯科，或者加德满都）一个意思。"不过如此而已。

但是，对于那二者之外的旅行者而言，旅行中最高境界的自由来自如下事实：旅程中的你好比跌入一股洪流，被卷入漩涡中，被浪头打得翻跟头，把曾经想当然的东西完全颠倒过来。如果一纸文凭可以作为通行护照（用以穿越显而易见的现实），那么一本护照完全可以成为一纸文凭（文化相对主义学科的速成毕业证）。也就是说，我们在旅程中所学的第一课，不管喜欢与否，就是我们原以为放之四海而皆准的一切是多么狭隘、多么不确定。举个例子。当你来到北朝鲜，就会真切地感觉到如同在另一个星球着陆；而北朝鲜人也毫不怀疑你是天外来客（否则，他们就想当然地认为，你和他们一样，每天早晨都会接到中央的命令，命令你今天穿什么衣服、走哪条路去上班；和他们一样，你每天天刚亮，就在卧室里听到扩音喇叭中传来的各类宣传；和他们一样，你安装无线电只是为了收听那个唯一的电台）。

那么，我们旅行，部分上是为了甩脱我们的自鸣得意，因为在旅程中我们看到了所有的道德上的、政治上的固守和生与死的困境，而在家乡和本土我们却很少遭遇如此的困境。而且，我们旅行也是为了填补新闻头条的遗漏：比方说，在海地首都太子港驱车前行，你会发现街道根本没有做任何铺设，而当地的女人们就在垃圾山旁边大小便，这个时候你的互联网及"大同世界"的理念都得全部改写，以使其更有益于人性的剖析。旅行是我们挽救和保留各地人文性的最好方式，以使其不至于淹没于抽象的意识形态。

同时，我们自身也从抽象理念中抽出身来，看看是否可为造访之地做些力所能及之事，是否能像信鸽而不是联邦快递那样为各种文化之间传递信息，使其互通有无。我总是把迈克·乔丹的海报带去京都，而把日本插花带回加州；到古巴旅行时，我总是在旅行箱里塞满泰诺感冒药和香皂，而带回的却是萨尔萨拉丁舞曲磁带，还有写给失散已久的弟兄的信，以及很多的希望和憧憬。

但更为重要的是，我们给造访之地带去了信息、信仰和价值观；在世界的很多地方，我们是当地人的放映机和活报纸，是使他们跳出当地政府对出版物、电影等的查禁的唯一渠道。在某些闭塞、赤贫的地方，如缅甸蒲甘城、古巴哈瓦那，我们就是所碰上的人的耳朵和眼睛，是他们与外面的世界唯一的联系，而且常常使得他们如此近距离地走近迈克·乔丹或者比尔·克林顿。因此，旅行中，我们要应对一个不小的挑战，那就是学会如何用温润之心来彼此传递梦想。

　　一直以来，普鲁斯特古色古香的诗句不断回荡在耳畔：真正的发现之旅不在于看到新奇的地方，而在于用新奇的眼光去看。① 然而，旅行还有更为精妙的美，那就是给萍水相逢的人带去新奇的目光。假期固然能让人更好地欣赏家园和故土，但这种欣赏的目光并非来自远道而来的仰慕者，异地旅行却能给游览之地的人们带去来自远方的新奇目光。你可以教给他们应该赞美的事物，反过来，你也要同样尽力去赞美他们教给你的事物。这样，旅游也就不再是破坏旅游地的文化，相反，它也能复苏或重振当地文化。旅游已然唤醒了巴厘岛的传统舞蹈，也促使印度手工艺品的复苏。如果我们首先要带给古巴的是真实的、公平的美国，那么接下来我们要带去的，或许是更为重要的，就是使当地人、尤其是那些关注世界的人，感觉到自己的国家如此与众不同的温暖和魅力。

　　因而，旅行改变了我们自身，可谓一举两得：一方面，旅行向我们展示了我们日常可能视而不见的景色、事物乃至价值观；另一方面，旅行使我们更加深刻地全面认识自我，没有旅行，我们内心深处的很多东西都可能会生锈变质。因为，在一个真正的异国他乡旅行，我们的情绪、心态，乃至内心深深隐藏的、暗流涌动的东西都必然显现无遗，而在日常生活中，我们少有缘由去注意这些潜在的东西。

　　从基本的说起吧。平常，我滴酒不沾，晚上九点就上床就寝，而在泰国旅行时，我总是在当地的酒吧待到曙光乍现；我并非真正的佛教徒，但在西藏，我一连数天在寺庙中流连，倾听喇嘛们诵经念佛；我去冰岛游览我心目中的月球空间：广袤的天地之间没有一棵树，有的只是无垠的空旷和无尽的寂寥；就在这空旷和寂寥中，我拍去凡俗世态的尘埃，身心涤荡。

　　我们旅行，既是为了寻找自我，也是为了隐匿自身——当然，找到了自我，也就隐匿了自身，反之亦然。在异国他乡，我们洒脱地甩掉工作、地位和立场的羁绊；正如赫兹里特②所说，我们是"客厅里的先生们，"人们既不知道我们的姓名，也无法判定我们的身份。恰恰因为我们如此净身在外，摆脱了不必

---

① Proust, 普鲁斯特，指法国小说家马塞尔·普鲁斯特，经典作品《追忆似水年华》；他的关于旅行的名句为世人津津乐道，原句为：The real voyage of discovery consists not in seeking new landscapes but in have new eyes. 而在本文的原文中，词语稍有出入：the real voyage of discovery consist not in seeing new places but in seeing with new eyes.

② 威廉·赫兹里特（William Hazlitt, 1778—1830）是浪漫主义时期英国大散文家，与兰姆齐名。他重感性和想象，张扬个性，反对权威和陈规陋习；主张多样和宽容，反对狭隘和专制；支持进步和革命，反对保守和停滞，是19世纪浪漫主义运动中的一位重要代表。

要的名签，才有机会接近内心更加本质的一些东西（这或许说明了为什么在离家万里之时我们才感觉到活在人世的无限美好。）

正是在异国他乡，我们才会深夜不眠，随心而动，心花怒放，如坠爱河。我们活着，既不用惦记过去，也不用挂虑将来，至少暂时如此。我们又拥有了自由之身，可供人任意争夺，任意阐释。甚或，我们变得很是神秘，起初别人觉得如此，有时连我们自己也觉得自己神秘起来。我们甚至成了尊贵的要人，好比是奥利弗·克伦威尔说得那样："一个不知道自己要去哪里的人可以走得很远很远。"①

当然，任何自由之路都危险重重，但旅行最大的诱惑是，旅行使我们获得重生，使我们能够时时变得更为年轻、更为开放。旅行，或多或少，使得时光流转，使得一天延续为一年——至少延为45个小时；旅行使得我们轻易地回到童年时代，被自己不知不懂的事物所包围。语言更是加宽了我们不知不懂的范围。比如，到了法国，我们小心翼翼地接近法国人，像小孩子一般，简单而有礼貌。说外语常常就是如此结果。在河内，我不说洋泾浜式的英语，而是直来直去；不再关心自己的言辞是否有水准，而只说简单而实在的词汇。

因而，对大多数人来说，旅行是一种追寻，不单单追寻那些我们所不知道的，也要追寻那些我们没有察觉的；至少我是如此，我带着纯真好奇和充满发现欲的眼睛旅行，这样能产生更为纯真的自我的回归。比起本土，在异国他乡，我往往相信更多的东西（尽管这可能有些背叛祖国，但至少帮我开阔了视野）；在异国他乡，我往往更容易激动，甚至会更加良善。既然没人能评判我的身份地位，没人知道我的来历，我就可以让自己变好，当然也可能变坏（如若旅行因是假扮身份者的摇篮而声名狼藉，那么旅行也可以因是真性情者的熔炉而威名远播）。如此说来，旅行差不多是移动修道院：旅途中，我们常常随遇而安，饮食起居都很简单（即便住在星级宾馆也是如此），财物也不过是随身的携带。

这正像加谬所说的："旅行的价值在于恐惧"——从环境中以及所有我们藏于其后的习惯中分离（或者解放）出来。而这也正是为什么大多数人旅行不是为了寻求答案而是为了寻求更好的发问。我亦如此。我喜欢思索游览之地所存在的问题，尤其喜欢琢磨那些耐人回味的问题。比方说，在巴拉圭，二分之一的车被偷窃，三分之二的商品是走私而来，这时我就不得不重新思考我原有的加利福尼亚式的意识和观念。在泰国，有很多年轻的女性靠出卖自己的身体来保护家人而成为优秀的佛教徒，我不得不质疑自己过于轻率的

---

① 奥利弗·克伦威尔（Oliver Cromwell, 1599——1658），英国政治家、军事家、宗教领袖。是英国清教徒革命的首脑人物，是议会军的指挥官。从1653年开始掌权并进行独裁统治。

评判。

"理想的游记应该有点像侦探小说，你得从中寻找点什么。"克里斯托弗·爱舍伍德[①]如是说。我再加上一句，如果你一直找不到，这就是最好的游记了。

记得十多年前，东南亚首次旅行归来，我躲在纽约的公寓里卧床不起，不仅仅是倒时差，也是一遍又一遍在脑海播放我所经历的一切，一张又一张地翻看照片，一读再读我的日记，仿佛要从中获取某些神秘之物。不管是谁看到如此奇怪的情景，都会不折不扣地得出如下结论：我恋爱了。

如果说一场真正的恋爱就像异国之旅，你不会说那里的话，也不知道自己要往哪里去，你被越来越深地拖入诱人的黑暗，那么异国之旅就像一场恋爱，你是谁、你爱上了谁；这一切你都茫然无知。粗粗估算一下，所有杰出的游记都是爱情故事，从《奥德赛》[②]到《埃涅阿斯纪》[③]到《神曲》到《圣经·新约》，所有美妙的旅行都像爱情一样，自我放逐却又被滞留在或险境或仙境。

这样的一个比喻也使我们深深懂得，所有的旅行都是双向交易。而我们常常忘记这一点。若说战争是国家之间打交道的一种模式，那么恋爱也是如此。我们常常忽视这种情形：在异国旅行，在我们审视端详当地人的同时，我们更是被当地人审视端详；在我们消费当地文化的同时，我们更被当地文化所消费，在家如此，在旅程中亦是如此。至少，我们成为当地人揣摩（甚至是渴望）的对象，因为不单对我们而言他们颇具异国情调，对他们来说我们同样也是充满来自别国的奇异。

我们是日本家庭电影中的漫画道具，是米兰奇闻轶事里的怪物，是中国笑话中的倒霉蛋，是秘鲁村民们事后对朋友们炫耀的活动明信片或者天然艺术品。说旅行是各国现实的汇集不亚于说旅行是各民族错觉的交融：你给我的是我梦想中的西藏，我给你的是你希冀的加利福尼亚。真实情况是，很多美国人，甚至（或者特别）那些逃离美国的美国人，都会被当作美国梦的象征，不管我们是否情愿如此。

旅行向我们揭示的最为核心的、也是最为纠结的问题就是：我们如何回应人们向我们抛出的梦想？你真的会助长他们的美国梦？你真的会对他们说，你自己弃之而去的美国是一个遍地流着牛奶与蜂蜜的地方？或者你试图浇灭他们

[①] 知名美国小说家。

[②] 《荷马史诗》第二部，讲述希腊与特洛伊战争结束后，希腊军首领之一奥德修斯的环绕世界的充满冒险的离奇经历，他的归乡之旅惊中有险，险中有奇，扣人心弦，趣味横生。

[③] 又译作《伊尼亚》，是古罗马诗人维吉尔的著名史诗，描述的是：希腊与特洛伊战争结束后，国破后逃离出特洛伊的一位英雄一路流浪，历经险境和奇迹，最终建立罗马。

的向往和热情？助长他们的梦想无非是加深他们的错觉，而浇灭他们的热情却可能剥夺了他们赖以在困苦中前行的安慰。

整个相互影响的过程颇为复杂，很像是我们面对爱人时的两难窘境：既要真心真意，又要乖巧机灵。这也是为什么很多游记大家们在本质上都是富有激情的性情中人：不管名声如何，皮埃尔·洛狄[①]，这位以《蝴蝶夫人》传奇故事的方式到处留情的典型水手，见一个地方就爱一个地方；洛狄之外，还有亨利·米勒，D. H. 劳伦斯，格雷厄姆·格林，他们都揭示了同一个深藏的事实——在自己国家我们都是悲观主义者，而到了国外我们全都成了乐观主义者。他们绝对不是看不见他们所去的地方的种种弊端和缺陷，但他们依然前往，力争发现一些让自己欣赏称颂的东西。

在这一点上，所有人都相信，旅行的意义之一就在于"被移动"，在于被私人的或公共交通工具"运输"；所有人都明白，服用"狂喜迷幻药"后，人们最亢奋的时刻在活动中来临，顿悟也是紧跟在活动之后，抑或是活动激发了顿悟的突然来临。记得我曾经问过极富盛名的游记作家诺曼·刘易斯是否有兴趣写一写南非的种族隔离。他颇为吃惊地看着我，说："要写好什么东西，首先我必须喜欢这个东西。"

这些都是旅行自身固有的特性。但在另一方面，从奥维德[②]时代到奥罗克[③]时代，旅行随着世界的改变而改变，而游记作家的写作权利也随之变化。对当代游记作家而言，单单旅行到天涯海角是不够的（绝非因为天涯海角常常出现在你的眼前）。前些年，像珍·莫里斯[④]这样的作家仅仅因为绕着世界各大城市航行了一圈就名声大噪，而现在，任何一个持有 Visa 信用卡的人都可以那样转上一圈。实际上，莫里斯是通过描绘大英帝国在各个城市的景象而把大英帝国的末日载入史册的。这样算来，现如今年轻一代的游记作家在记录一个新帝国的发展方面拥有更加有利的条件，这个新帝国是后民族主义的、全球性的、流

[①] Pierre Loti（1850-1923），十九世纪法国的一位海军军官，还是知名小说家。一生航行到很多国家和地区，并依据其旅行经历创作了很多小说，其中有讲述痴情日本少女的《菊子夫人》(Madame Chrysanthémé)。后来，意大利剧作家普契尼参考这部小说创作了歌剧《蝴蝶夫人》。

[②] 古罗马作家，其《变形记》是世界文学史上较早的一部流浪汉小说，后世很多文学大家如莎士比亚都从中汲取写作素材。

[③] 应该是指美国当代作家、政治讽刺家、记者 P. J. O'Rourke，生于 1947 年，自 1974 年起笔耕不辍，出版了各种引人关注的著作，近作有 2007 年的《国富论：改变世界的书》(On the Wealth of Nations: Books that Changed the World)，2010 年的《不要投票，那是哄骗混蛋的》(Don't Vote!—It Just Encourages the Bastards)。

[④] Jan Morris，1926 年生于英格兰，是一位威尔士民族主义者，也是历史学家，游记作家，尤以《和平不列颠》三部曲（the Pax Britannica trilogy）闻名于世。这是一部关于大英帝国历史的著作，特别记述了世界知名城市，如牛津、威尼斯、的里亚斯特、香港和纽约等。

动不居的,像大英帝国统治印度时那样勤奋地传输帝国的各种玩意和价值观。

众所周知,19世纪中期,英国向世界各地输出《圣经》、莎士比亚和板球;现在,一个更加国际性的帝国正向全球输出流行天后麦当娜、系列电影"辛普森一家"和最性感影星布拉德·皮特。然而,每种文化自身的产物所揭示的意义并不亚于他们对刚刚所提及事物的接纳。毕竟,穆斯林国家的麦当娜和儒教国家的麦当娜完全不同,而这两种文化中的麦当娜又和纽约东14大街的麦当娜是两回事。在东京的麦当劳店里卖的却是日本烧烤风味的汉堡包和培根土豆派。店里的榻榻米印的是东京城内最大的庙宇的地图,满墙张贴的却是圣弗朗西斯科著名景点的海报。至关重要的是,年轻人嘴里啃着巨无霸,倒戴着棒球帽,身穿着李维斯501紧身牛仔裤,然而他们的一举一动,他们的点头弓腰,他们的啜吸乌龙茶都不折不扣是完全日本式的,绝不混同于巴西里约、摩洛哥、尼加拉瓜等地的麦当劳店里的吃客。当今,真正称得上具有异国风情的奇异物品是那些两种文化混杂交融后的产物。

使得这一切变得更加复杂也更加刺激的另一因素则是人,那些说多种语言的混血儿。如今,这样的人越来越多,这样的城市也越来越多,如悉尼、多伦多、香港等。我自己在很多方面也越来越像这样的人,甚至是这类型的人的典型代表,因为我父母是印度人,而我却出生在英格兰,七岁时移居美国,我也说不上自己到底是印度人、美国人,还是英国人。简单地说,我生就一个旅人,去一趟糖果店就如同一次异国之旅,因为那里没有一个人和我父母、我自己属于同一类人。像我这种情形并非出于自愿,甚至是悲惨的,要知道,1970年世界难民有250万人,而现在难民至少有2,740万人。但是,对有些人来说,这种跨国旅行的机会并非坏事,反倒提升人的适应能力,习惯自己在哪儿都是外来者的身份,被迫养成对家的极度渴望感(如果没有地方可以称之为家,那么我们就乐观地处处为家)。

此外,即使那些不绕世界转的人也发现世界正绕着他们转。在纽约昆斯区或伯克利区走过六个街区,几分钟内就穿越了好几种文化;在白宫外乘坐一辆出租车,结果常常发现自己好像来到了埃塞俄比亚的首都亚的斯亚贝巴。网络空间、光碟、视频、虚拟旅行,诸如此类的科技更是加重了这种唾手可得的感觉,使得很多人感觉自己寸步未移却周游了世界。当然,这样的科技招来一片质疑之声,因为这些东西威胁到了有关家庭、社区和忠诚的基本内涵,人们担心这种装有空调的、纯人工合成的东西有朝一日会取代真实的事物,更不用说世界变动得越来越快,快得超出了我们对世界的理解。但是,这种变化至少对旅者来说是有意义的,其意义在于认知乡土和认知异域世界可以是一回事,可以一举两得。

从婴儿时期起，所有人就感觉到，甚至知道，我们经历的一切重要移动在某种意义上都是内在的。看一场电影，结识一个新朋友，路遇塞车，这都不失为一次次旅行。一篇小说常常就是一段旅程，同样，一部游记常常就是一篇小说，早在14世纪就已经如此了：当时约翰·曼德维尔爵士①为人们描绘了一个鲜明生动的"远东"，尽管他本人从没有去过那里。现如今，随着文学流派以分崩离析之势跨进其它领域，不同文学样式之间的界限也愈发地模糊了。

玛丽·莫里斯②的《软禁》以略微虚构的笔法讲述了卡斯特罗③时代的古巴。身为小说家的作者在这本书的版权页上一再重申："所有对话都是凭空虚构。伊莎贝拉，她的家人，还有当地居民，甚至连 La isla④ 都来自作者的想象。"但在书内172页，我们却读到这样的字句："当然，La isla 确实存在。关于此，可别让任何人愚弄你。感觉仿佛如此美丽的海岛并不存在，但事实却恰恰相反。"难怪小说里那位身为游记作家的讲述人——一个虚构人物（或许并非虚构？）——坦陈她所撰写的旅行杂志专栏文章是献给乌有之乡的。这大概是受了塞缪尔·巴特勒⑤的启发，巴特勒所著的优秀游记小说中的乌有之乡 Erewhon 只不过是把英语单词 nowhere 倒过来写罢了。

因此，旅行就是旅者到自己的梦想之地走上一遭，而所带回的是——也只能是——游览之地和自我相互混合的一种难以言喻的东西，是"我的到此一游"和"到此一游的我"的混杂。这也就是说为什么英国旅行家布鲁斯·查特文⑥的游记作品介于真实和虚构之间；也解释了为什么奈保尔的新作《世间之路》在英国是以"写实系列丛书"之名出版、而在美国却是以"一部小说"之名出版。同理，保罗·瑟鲁⑦真实与虚构参半的回忆录《我的另类生活》中的一些故事在《纽约客》杂志发表时，被巧妙地归类为"真实与虚构"。

在某种意义上，旅行是感知和想象的共谋。这正是我十分推崇艾默生和梭

---

① Sir John Mandeville，《曼德维尔游记》的作者。《曼德维尔游记》最初用古法语写成，在十四世纪中后期盛传，后被译成多种文字。这一著作其实是假托游记之名写成，其所谓旅途描述和记载充满假想，并无事实依据，但却产生了广泛影响，比如哥伦布就颇为相信此书。

② Mary Morris，生于1926年，美国作家，旅行家。

③ 菲德尔·卡斯特罗，古巴革命领导人。

④ 西班牙语，指"美丽的海岛"。

⑤ Samuel Butler, 1835-1902，英国小说家，他的《艾瑞璜》是一部讽刺小说，"艾瑞璜"是英文 nowhere 的倒写，通过一个游客在艾瑞璜的所见所闻，记述了这个乌托邦国家的生活，以此抨击和讽刺英国社会。在本文中，作者认为，玛丽·莫里斯受巴特勒影响，其《软禁》以所谓的虚构笔法真实再现了卡斯特罗统治下的古巴。

⑥ Bruce Chatwin，1940-1989，英国小说家，游记作家，其小说《黑山》曾获布莱克纪念奖。其游记作品以真实与虚构并存而著称。

⑦ Paul Theroux，生于1941年，当代美国小说家，游记作家。

罗两位伟大旅行家的原因（艾默生语破天惊地说"旅行是傻瓜的天堂"，梭罗则"多次旅行在康科德"）。这两位都坚持同一事实：现实是我们自己创造的，我们所看到的那些地方也是我们自己编造出来的，正如我们所读的书不过是我们自己的虚构。我们外在的发现其实存在于我们内心。或者，正如英国作家托马斯·布朗尼伯爵所说，"我们怀揣奇迹去寻找身外的奇迹。非洲固然存在，但非洲的奇观存在于我们内心。"

所以，如果说越来越多的人内心充满家国情怀，我们也要——艾默生和梭罗提醒我们——对旅行目的地充满情感。我们所探索的最为珍贵的太平洋来自我们内心的浩瀚，最重要的西北岔口是我们要跨过的内心的门槛。发现日本京都镀金凉亭的益处在于，你在洛克菲勒中心的办公室里拥有了一座你可以永远拜望的金色庙宇。

世界似乎变得更加枯竭，我们的旅行却不会如此。近些年来，堪称精品的一些游记著作要么是那些纪录朝圣旅途和哲学追问双重旅行的书（如彼得·马修森[①]的大作《雪豹》），要么是记载最不易到达的、最鲜为人知的地域习俗的行纪（如奥利弗·萨克[②]的《色盲之岛》，不但记述了在太平洋上一个偏远的环状珊瑚礁岛上的专门之旅，而且呈现了一个对光线有特别认识的奇异国度）。我们一再得到提醒，最偏远的海岸存在于睡在我们身边的那个人的心里。

所以，旅行在根本上是快速使我们的身心保持移动和清醒的方式。在本文一开始我提起的桑塔亚那，艾默生和梭罗精神的继承者，如此写道："尽可能多地从熟悉的地方到不熟悉的地方走一走不失为明智之举。这能使人头脑灵活，也能消除偏见，还能培养幽默感。"浪漫诗人开启了旅行之风潮，因为他们自身就是"睁眼看世界"的伟大倡导者。佛教僧人之所以经常云游四方，部分原因就在于他们信仰"清醒"。如若说旅行像恋爱，说到底，主要还是因为那是一种高度警醒的状态，在此状态中，我们充满惦念，我们乐意倾听，我们不会因为熟悉而麻木，反而随时准备转变自我。这就是为什么最出色的旅行永远不会真正地结束，恰如谈了一场绝佳的恋爱。

（张慧芳 译　杨建 校）

[①] Peter Matthiessen，生于1927年，美国小说家和纪实作家，环境活动家，两度荣获美国国家图书奖。
[②] Oliver Sack，1933年生于英国伦敦，现在旅居美国纽约，著名的神经学家，心理学家，同时还出版了多部畅销书。

The Two Faces of Tourism

Jonathan Tourtellot

【导读】开发旅游业固然可在经济上造福一方，但对所开发地的生态却是一种破坏，对本土文化的纯正也是一种玷污。这样的悖论早在20世纪中期已经出现，如今21世纪已经迈入它的第二个十年，世界全球化的进程促使旅游开发愈演愈烈，而对开发地的生态和文化的保护却效果甚微。从《圣经》开始直到18世纪的启蒙运动，西方文明对人与自然之间的关系提倡二元对立，自然站在人类的对立面，是人类探测、征服和盘剥的对象。《旅游双刃剑》对这种人与自然的对立关系的阐释却另有一番意味：优美的景色犹如洁白无瑕、青春年少的处女，而旅游业对风景胜地的开发如同与魅力处女同榻而眠，"没有破坏和蹂躏，就享受不了童贞"。尽管作者说这只不过是戏谑之辞，但对旅游开发之弊端却一语中的。这篇文章通过记述墨西哥政府对风景秀丽的峡谷群同时也是印第安人保留地的大规模开发而揭示了旅游开发所带来的利与弊，作者对其利似乎嗤之以鼻，对于其弊却痛心疾首。但作者并没有大声疾呼，也没有深情吁请，抑或鞭辟入里地批驳，而是以隐忍之笔为读者展示了一方净土在旅游开发前后的不同画面，留下足够的空间让读者自己去明辨是非。

At the lip of Batopilas Canyon, the Suburban van pulls off the narrow dirt track so that we can admire the view a mile down the road. Down, literally. The ponderosa highlands are behind us. In front, the land plummets away. Yucca, scrub, and raw rock line the giant gorge below. At the bottom, hazy with distance, a tiny, winding road leads, we've been told, into country you would hardly expect to find less than three hundred miles from the U. S. border – country long isolated from the modern world, where Tarahumara Indians[①] race each other up and down canyons, and where a town that I could be one of the last foreigners to see this road looking quite this way. Big plans are afoot.

---

① One of American-Indian tribes.

Skip McWilliams had phoned a month earlier to pose the problem. "It's like being with a charming maiden. How do we enjoy her without destroying" – McWilliams, prone to heterosexual analogies, tied to finesse this one – "her maidenness?"

The maiden is Mexico's Copper Canyon country, and the threatened defloration is the government's new program to attract more tourists to the area. Lots of them. McWilliams, a Detroit businessman, wanted me to go see for myself what's at stake. It was a biased plea: he owns two unusual small hotels in the area.

Now I'm in this van, gong from his lodge in the high country to his other trappings of "successful" tourism development.

Saving places from the ravages of mass tourism wasn't a major world until the late twentieth century. Now, with jet travel, superhighways, increasing world wealth, and exploding populations, tourism and travel are claimed to constitute the largest industry on Earth. The World Travel and Tourism Council predicts that people will be making one *billion* international trips annually by 2010. And, worldwide, four or five times as many domestic trips.

Try to imagine enough tour buses to hold a billion people. If parked end to end, the line would equal the length of every freeway in the 46,000-mile interstate system.

Triple-parked.

Hardly surprising, then, that tourism is transforming the world – in some ways for worse, in some ways for better.

As the Mexican government considers how to develop Copper Canyon country, it faces the classic dilemma confronting attractive places everywhere. Will the changes create a travel delight – or a tourism disaster? So far, indicators are mixed.

This region, in the sprawling state of Chihuahua, is known in the United States as the Copper Canyon. Actually, seven major canyon systems slice through this section of the Sierra Madre. The deepest systems slice through this section of the Sierra Madre. The deepest part of one is indeed named Copper Canyon, but the seven collectively are called *las Barrancas del Cobre* – the Copper Canyons, plural. They carve up an area more than half the size of Switzerland and constitute one of the most dramatic complexes of gorges anywhere, dropping more than six thousand feet – deeper than the Grand Canyon. They offer splendid adventure hiking, and their many microclimates support a wide variety of flora and fauna for ecotourists.

They also support the reclusive Tarahumara Indians, which accounts for the region's other names, Sierra Tarahumara①. Ever since the Spanish conquest four hundred years ago, the canyon's inaccessibility – limited until recent times to foot or hoof – has helped the Indians maintain one of the last semi-intact native cultures in North America. They have expressed little desire for company. Their own name for themselves, Raramuri, is said to mean "runners." Famed for fleetness of foot, they now have nowhere to run.

My first view of the area was from the east, a long afternoon's drive up into the Sierra from the city of Chihuahua. Rolling hills, ponderosa forests, colorful outcrops – you would never suspect the hugely ruptured terrain that lies ahead. At eight thousand feet, the climate is cool even in summer, with hints of wood smoke in the air.

The dusty sidewalks of Creel, the main town, were busy: mestizo men② in straw ranchero hats, Tarahumara women in traditional pleated skirts, European tourist in backpacks. Creel is becoming the regional tourist center – a needed boost, officials believe, for an economy too long dependent on logging, mining, and, in the back canyons, marijuana growing. The town is also becoming an architectural mishmash – new construction in stucco, cinder block, plate-glass. "Once the town was mostly log cabins," says Arturo Gutierrez, who runs a mountain-bike concession. "Creel's identity is already lost. It is very sad."

In a valley a few miles from Creel, I checked out Skip McWilliams's Sierra Lodge – long, low, and yes, all log. Each of the fifteen rooms has its own woodstove; there's no electricity, so illumination is by kerosene lamp; a sizable staff pampers guests with three meals, excursions, and margaritas. You can pay $250 per person nightly t stay there.

McWilliams, middle-aged and fit, was just in from Detroit, wearing his customary blue jeans and faintly mischievous expression③, as if he finds life generally amusing and is capable of creative tinkering when it isn't. Fluent in

---

① The Mother of Tarahumara.
② Mixed blood of Europeans and American Indian people.
③ 这里使用了异叙修辞格, 巧用一词多义的语法特点, 使得句子生动活泼。wear 后面接了两个宾语, 前一个 blue jeans, 后一个 mischievous expression; wear 因宾语不同而含义不同。

Spanish, he's been in and out of the canyons for eighteen years. Of his enterprises, the Copper Canyon lodges are his favorite.

That's why he's been trying to persuade tourism authorities that less is more. "I'd never build a hotel with more than fifteen rooms," he asserts. "No atmosphere." And look, he tells them: he can charge more for *not* having electricity! Locals are often baffled: surely rich foreign tourists would prefer smart new fluorescents and Formica. "The next thing you know," McWilliams fears, "people will be opening water slides and miniature golf courses, and playing colored lights on the rocks."

As in much of the world, distant officials make the major tourism decisions. The Chihuahua state government and local groups play a role in the Copper Canyons, but overall policy is set a thousand miles away in Mexico City, by the secretary of tourism and by FONATUR (Fomento Nacional de Turismo[①]), the federal tourism-development agency.

FONATUR's best-known accomplishment? Cancun.

Laid out on an uninhabited sand spit lined by a glorious beach, Cancun was planned as a utopian city of parks, low-rise hotels, and high-end tourists. But after the peso[②] crashed in 1982, Mexicans desperate for foreign exchanges relaxed the restrictions on Cancun. Hotel towers rose cheek by jowl[③]; shopping malls sprouted; sewage flooded into the lagoon, and drug money into the economy. Cheap package deals brought in the rowdy spring-break crowd.

In 1995 the rise of ecotourism and adventure travel inspired FONATUR to turn its sights on the Copper Canyons, launching a program strongly backed by the Mexican president, Ernesto Zedillo, himself. The goal by 2010 is to raise tourism in the canyons sixfold, to over 400,000 visitors a year.

New roads are already punching through the countryside, augmenting what has been the only mechanized transportation in the canyons: the dramatic Chihuahua-to-Pacific rail line, which is how most foreign visitors experience the place.

The train makes a fifteen-minute stop at Divisadero, an overlook that provides passengers with their only good view of Copper Canyon proper. To reach the rim,

---

① Spanish spelling.
② The Mexican currency.
③ Cheek by jowl is an idiom, which means side by side or close together.

tourists must thread through a gauntlet of craft and food vendors. Many visitors don't even make it to the overlook or to the pleasant two-story hotel whose glass-walled dining room commands a spectacular view. Outside, two pipes carry the establishment's septic runoff into the canyon, a watershed where several thousand people live. The manager told me matter-of-factly that the two other hotels on the rim do the same.

FONATUR nevertheless wants six hundred more hotel rooms up here, as well as some four hundred recreational-vehicle spaces in the region. Their idea, apparently, of what ecotourists and adventurers seek. "Enough to trigger it," FONATUR's assistant director Mario de la Vega, told me. "It" being the tourist boom.

An American guide, Marsha Green, blanches at the prospect, especially of RVs: "With RVs, the place isn't remote anymore; it turns into Disneyland." But Maria Barriga, who co-owns a hotel just down from the rim, can't wait. "It's going to be wonderful," she told me, eyes sparkling. A FONATUR man had been by, she added, urging her to expand to one hundred rooms. A state tourism official had assured me earlier that no hotel was to have more than fifty rooms.

We climb back in the Suburban and descend into Batopilas Canyon. It is thrilling. The narrow track loops downward hairpin after hairpin. The canyon sides rise, becoming peaks high above. Deeper still, the road notches into the cliffs, edging vertiginously above the Batopilas River. Side valleys provide glimpses into other canyons, compounding the massive play of light and shadow – yellows, hazy blues, dusty greens – all on a gargantuan scale, as if Maxfield Parrish[①] had painted the valleys of Brobdingnag. We are *descending* into a mountain range. No wonder this region has been so little known for so long.

In fact, startling discoveries are being made even now, largely by a balding, mild-mannered explorer named Carlos Lazcano, who has spent much of the past five years exploring the Sierra Tarahumara. In 1995, with the aid of back country locals, Lazcano identified Mexico's highest waterfall (at 1,486 feet the third highest in North America) in the canyons south of here. Just last year, up to the north, he found

---

[①] An American painter and illustrator active in the first half of the twentieth century. He is known for his distinctive saturated hues and idealized neo-classical imagery.

five-hundred-year-old, two-story Paquime Indian cliff-dwellings containing six intact mummies. All discoveries you would expect to have occurred back when the conquistadors came seeking gold.

Of course gold is not what drives governments to fund expeditions these days. Carlos Lazcano works for the Chihuahua state division of tourism. We who tour are the gold.

Continuing our descent, we round a bend and encounter a surveying crew. Road improvements. McWilliams doesn't like it, fearing it would diminish the travel experience and make access tempting for those RVs that FONATUR wants.

The funky former mining town of Batopilas straggles along the river at the bottom of the canyon. Built by silver, Batopilas reached a zenith of sorts in the late 1800s under the American mining baron Alexander Shepherd, who had previously governed Washington, D.C. By the 1900s, Batopilas's heyday was over, the town population in decline, the elegant mining houses in decay.

Yet the town didn't die, the remnant thousand or so residents carrying on in their remote canyon, accessible only by foot and by mule until the road was chiseled through in 1978. Down here the ranchero world survives, complete with ten-gallon straw hats and the occasional shootout, often over a woman or, these days, over drugs.

Adventure travelers have already discovered the town, and government tourism people have plans for it, as a hiking centre and historical site. The roofless, softly copper-toned adobe ruins of Shepherd's riverside hacienda form a major now-and-future tourist attraction.

There are already several small hotels in town, but none like McWilliams's. From ruins, he has built a dreamy re-recreation[①] of nineteenth-century Mexico: brilliantly painted rooms and passageways; garden courtyards; stenciled borders of blue curlicues on the walls; elegant kerosene lamps suspended everywhere; an eclectic collection of artwork and kitsch, antiques and knickknacks. In the big, eye-grabbing parlor, a faux-rococo painting covers the ceiling. The place is an *experience*. In the morning, you awake to the cooing of white-winged doves, the barking of town dogs, and the sight of sunlight touching the tips of the crags in the

---

① A dreamy relic.

other world far above.①

McWilliams wants to see the town not so much developed for tourism as restored for it. He's been urging locals to "return cobblestones to the streets, put back the old facades." He takes me into one of the abandoned, ruined houses from silver-boom days. Squatting over the rubble, he scrapes away a layer of grime on the wall with his penknife, revealing the same blue-curlicue stencil pattern now re-created in his hotel.

Being far from civilization, Batopilas lies close to unacculturated Tarahumara, often seen here in their traditional dress. Fro men, that's a billowy, balloon-sleeved shirt; a pale, triangular breechcloth called a *sitagora*; and a long-tailed headband. For women, it's brilliant, heavily pleated long skirts and full-sleeved blouses. Their clothes make the Trahumara intensely photogenic. They do not like being photographed.

The forty thousand Trahumara rank with Navajo and Cherokee ass one of the largest native nations in North America. The tourism industry deploys pictures of Tarahumara everywhere. In Creel, murals and paintings of the Indians, ranging from skilled to atrocious adorn hotel lobbies, shop signs, a motel water tank.

Ironically, Tarahumara value privacy even among themselves. They live apart, not in villages. They like silence, considering outsiders chatterboxes. They are loath to protest when wronged. It is through their lands that the envisioned legions of foreign hikers will pass.

I had to talk with them.

Her round, brown face small above the desk in the mission office in Creel, Felicitas Guanapani spoke hesitantly in the little-used English she picked up in a Jesuit school stateside: "When I was little, my other told me to run and hide from a *chabochi.*" *Chabochi,* whiskered one: any non-Indian. Trouble. Now, as a Tarahumara sophisticate, she could see the potential of tourism for her people, but she doesn't see it happening: "The white man takes all the money."

Except for crafts, especially violins. For over three centuries, the Indians have made violins to play at religious celebrations. Now there's a market for them. No varnish on them, though; the wood left unfinished by tradition.

---

① "the other world above" implies the heaven here.

In Batopilas, I buy one from Patrocinio Loptez, considered by some the Stradivarius[①] of the Tarahumara. By prearrangement, he jogs into town to sell it to me. The head is a delicately carved snake, a double loop. The Indians have found that this kind of embellishment boosts sales. Artistic corruptions? Or advance?

Loptez is an unusual Tarahumara; he enjoys slumming with *chabochis*. I ask about the prospect of many more tourists tramping through his country. Not so much a problem, he thinks. They come, they go. But most Indians make no distinctions among outsiders, lumping tourists in with evangelists – "*los aleluyas*" – who are a problem. "They stay, say we must wear pants, and change our ways. They marry Raramuri women."

I think of a McWilliams wisecrack: "The main tool of cultural change is impressing the girls."

Hikers in the quantities FONATUR wants would become a permanent phenomenon, too. The mountain-bike man, Arturo Gutierrez, also lead hikes but worries about crowds of independent trekkers. "What," I asked him, "if hikers had to have Tarahumara guides to keep them on acceptable paths?"

"Then it would not be the extreme experience that an adventure tourist wants."

Early one Saturday, the sound of helicopters drowns out the dogs and doves of Batopilas. Four times the choppers land, disgorging Mexico's technocratic elite. No ranchero hats in this lot. Crisp slacks, snappy weekend shirts, sunglasses. They are planners, architects, tourism specialists, officials, aides – yes, and even the governor of Chihuahua and the secretary of tourism for all Mexico.

The VIPs tour the town, then gather at McWilliams's hotel for a presentation by a high-powered Mexico City architectural firm. Handsome placards show the proposed restoration.

Not too bad, for Batopilas, at least. If – a big *if* – these plans come to pass, McWilliams would get almost everything he wants here, except the narrow road. Widened in some places, but not paved, they promise. In a region where tourism has triple din just the last three years? "It's like a guy getting into bed with a beautiful woman and promising not to touch her," he grumped. "How long will that promise

---

① an excellent craftsman of violins. The word "Stradivarius" has become a superlative associated with excellence in any field.

be kept?"

There's no mischievous look now. These canyonlands have carved themselves into Skip McWilliams's soul. He's not just protecting an investment; he's defending memories.

His own and those of his clients'. Memories of Batopilas inspired Cooper Young, a guest from Wichita Falls, Texas, to publish a story in the local paper when he got back home: See Batopilas now, he urged, "before electricity turns the stars off."

Some fell the tide of change need not be a flood. Electricity is spreading, but locals can mute the glare – especially if smart, revenue-bearing travelers request it. Tarahumara privacy is threatened, but there are ways to blunt the impact, like Indian cultural centers that provide visitors with museums, craft shops, dances, and events, located away from Indians' homes. North of the border several such centers provide models.

One, the Indian Pueblo Cultural Center in Albuquerque, provides a lesson, too. In the small museum there, a series of dioramas depicts Pueblo life over the centuries. In the last one, seated among several Indian figures, is a white man in casual shirt and sunglasses – the tourists. It's a frank acknowledgement of a growing worldwide truth: we visitors are woven into the fabric of the places we visit. The future of those placed – and the quality of the travel experience – depends not only on how we comport ourselves, but also on how well tourism entrepreneurs sustain the character of what we've come to see.

My last night in the canyons, I stop in at McWilliams's Sierra Lodge. The gracious manager, Mara Carrillo, is supervising dinner preparations. I join a table with a woman just from L.A.[①] – a return guest, happy to be back. "I had a dream before I left," she's telling tablemates, "that when I got here, I found the lodge had become some kind of sprawling, stuccoed[②] mega-resort. And to see Mara you had to make an appointment! But you could hear her voice on a loudspeaker: people with the red wristbands were to meet over there, and those with yellow wristbands over

---

① Los Angels.
② Stucco is a mixed material applied to decorate the walls of buildings. Here is used as a participle adjective.

here[①] ..."

　　She turns to me, thinking I might need clarification.

　　"It was a nightmare," she says.

[①] This refers to the dream the woman from L. A had dreamed. The woman is worried about the future of Copper Canyon and she dose not wish the present situation would change.

旅游双刃剑

乔纳森·托特洛特

在巴托皮拉斯峡谷的谷口，乡村大巴士从主干道上开下来，停在了 1 英里外的小土路上，为的是让我们欣赏优美的景色。"下来"，可不是说说而已。我们身后是长满北美黄松的高原，前面则是飞奔直下的悬崖峭壁，崖底的巨大峡谷两岸布满了古老的岩石，一丛丛的丝兰和灌木生长其间。在峡谷底部，我们被告知，在薄雾朦朦的远处，有条蜿蜒的小路通向一个出人意料的地方，距离美国边境不足 300 英里。这个地方长久以来与世隔绝，只有塔拉乌马拉印第安人[①]在峡谷峭壁间上下飞跃。这里有一个小镇，依旧保持着 19 世纪墨西哥的风貌。我也意识到，这条路现在这个样子将不复存在，我很可能是最后一批看到此路的外国人中的一个。庞大的计划正在进行中。

早在一个月前，斯科普·麦威廉在电话里提出同一问题："这好比是与一个魅力少女待在一起。没有毁坏，我们怎么能够享受——"麦威廉想通过异性关系的类比对这个问题做出精辟的解释，"她的童贞呢？"

这位少女就是墨西哥铜谷，而威胁到她的花季的正是政府要吸引大批游客的新计划。要吸引大批大批的游客。麦威廉，这位来自底特律的商人，请求我亲眼去看看风险何在。这个请求别有目的：他在那里有两家不同寻常的小旅馆。

现在，我正坐在大巴车上，从他那位于高海拔乡村地区的住所前往由于"成功的"旅游开发给他带来的其它建筑设施。

直到 20 世纪晚期，挽救某些地方免遭旅游带来的大肆破坏才成为全球性重大事件。飞机旅行和高速公路在发展，世界财富在增加，人口增多到爆炸的地步，旅游、旅行随之上升为地球上最大的产业。世界旅游旅行委员会预测，到 2010 年，每年的跨国旅行将突破 10 亿人次，而世界各国的本土旅行将增长 4 至 5 倍。

试想，得有多少辆旅行巴士来装运 10 亿人！如果这些巴士头接尾地挨个停放，其长度则等于绵延 46,000 英里的州际快速路总长。

停车场得建到 3 层了。

这样说来，也就没什么好惊讶的了。旅游正在改变世界，有些是变好，而有些则是变糟。

[①] Tarahumara Indians，北美印第安人的一支。

墨西哥政府考虑如何开发铜谷时所面临的两难境地是各个风景区的共同遭遇。开发带来的是旅游景观还是旅游灾难？目前为止，众说纷纭。

要开发的这个地方位于杂乱无章的吉华华州[①]，铜谷是这个地方在美国的叫法。事实上，这儿有七个较大的峡谷，把吉华华州境内的塞拉岭[②]切割开来，形成峡谷群。最深的一处叫做铜谷，但这七个峡谷合起来称为 *las Barrancas del Cobre*，意思是铜谷群。这个峡谷群切割下来的地方比瑞士的一半略大些，落差深达 6000 多英尺，比美国大峡谷还要深，形成世上最令人叹为观止的峡谷风光之一。这个地方成为探险远足的绝佳选择，多变的小型气候体系满足着各种动植物的生长，是生态旅游者的乐园。

这里也是塔拉乌马拉印第安人的隐遁之地，所以这个地方还有个别名，叫 Sierra Tarahumara，意思是"塔拉乌马拉之母"。四百年前西班牙占领墨西哥以来，这个地方因地势险要，不管是徒步还是骑马都难以侵入。这为印第安人在北美保持最后一处半完整的民族文化提供了条件。他们不想被外来者打扰。他们自己特有的称号为 Rarámuri，据说是"奔跑者"的意思。然而，以赤足速奔而闻名的他们，现在却无处可奔了。

我从东边进入，此地的优美景色初映眼帘。离开吉华华市，开了整整一下午的车才进入到母亲岭。起伏的丘陵，黄松林，五彩的岩石，实在让人难以想象前面会有断崖。在海拔 8000 英尺之地，即便是夏天也非常凉爽，空气中炊烟袅袅。

鱼篓镇是这个地方的大镇，尘土飞扬的边道上行人如织：戴着草帽的梅索蒂丝混血男人[③]，穿着传统褶皱裙的塔拉乌马拉女人，还有背包的欧洲游客。鱼篓镇正在成为地区旅游中心。政府部门相信，这是对当地经济一个必要的推动，因为长期以来这里的经济活动主要是矿业、伐木业，还有峡谷深处的大麻种植业。这个镇子现在也成了一个建筑大杂烩——刚盖好的房屋用的是粉饰灰泥、焦渣石、厚玻璃板。"原先，这个镇子差不多都是木头小屋，"经营着一个山地自行车商铺的阿图若·古铁拉斯说，"鱼篓镇的个性已经消失，实在悲哀。"

鱼篓镇几英里以外的一个山谷中，我找到了斯科普·麦威廉的小旅馆"塞

[①] Chihuahua，墨西哥北部的一个州，这里出产的一种名贵的狗，就是以 Chihuahua 命名的，中文翻译为吉娃娃狗。

[②] The Sierra Madre，西班牙语，意思是"母亲岭"(mother mountain range)，在墨西哥境内的几个州有好几处同名山岭，吉华华州有一处。

[③] 原文是 mestizo men（指欧洲人和印第安人的混血儿）。

拉小舍"——长长的，矮矮的，是的，全都是实木。一共15间房子，每间都有一座烧木柴的炉子；没有电，用煤油灯照明；工作人员充足，精心照料着客人的一日三餐，还提供远足旅行服务和鸡尾酒。每人每晚只需花250美元。

麦威廉人至中年，身体健硕，刚从底特律赶到这儿，身穿招牌式的蓝色牛仔裤，脸上挂着一丝顽皮的神情，仿佛发现生活总是那么有趣，即便没趣的时候，他也能颇有创建地做出补救。他说一口流利的西班牙语，在这片峡谷里出出进进已有18年了。在自己所有的实业中，他最喜欢的就是峡谷中的乡间小舍了。

这也正是为什么他一直力图使此地的旅游业主管相信：少一点就是多一点。"我决不会建造一座多于15个房间的宾馆，"他扬声说道，"没气氛。"他对那些旅游业官员说：看，因为没有电，所以我收费就会高一些！当地人就很迷惑不解：那些富有的外国游客肯定喜欢亮闪闪的东西。"下一步，"麦威廉很担忧地说，"人们就会修建水滑梯，迷你高尔夫球道，在岩石上挂满五颜六色的电灯。"

世界上很多地方都一样，虽然山高皇帝远，却由远在千万里之外的官员们对重大的旅游开发事件做出决定。吉华华州政府和地方组织在铜谷群开发中起到一定的作用，而大方针却来自1000英里之外的墨西哥城，由那里的旅游局长和联邦旅游开发部制定。

联邦旅游开发部最富有声誉的成就是什么？坎昆。

当初，坎昆是被规划建在一个无人居住、却拥有瑰丽海滩的沙嘴上，被设想成一座只有公园、低层宾馆和高端游客的乌托邦城。然而，1982年比索暴跌之后，墨西哥急需外汇，因而对坎昆的限制开始松动。宾馆冲天而起，鳞次栉比，大型购物中心不断涌现，污水大量排入濒海湖，毒品交易也融入经济活动。便宜的旅游一条龙服务招来大批度春假的闹哄哄的人群。

1995年，生态旅游和探险旅行的兴起促使墨西哥联邦旅游开发部把目光投向铜谷，由此发起了一个项目，得到了墨西哥总统埃内斯托·塞迪略本人的强力支持。这个项目的最终目标是，到2010年把铜谷的旅游业提高六倍，一年的游客大约40多万人次。

新公路已经开进了乡村，峡谷区唯一的机械化交通方式得到改变。之前，激动人心的吉华华至太平洋火车是外国游客欣赏峡谷风光的主要方式。

火车在一个名叫远景的小站停留15分钟，以供乘客眺望铜谷风光，因为这里是唯一可以俯瞰峡谷美景的绝佳视点。要想走进铜谷，游客们得穿过琳琅满目的手工艺品和各种各样的小吃摊。很多游客甚至根本到不了眺望地点或令人愉快的二层宾馆。透过宾馆餐厅的玻璃墙,峡谷的优美风光尽收眼底。而宾馆外面,两个粗粗的管子把宾馆的污秽废物排泄倾倒进峡谷的分水岭地带,而那里生活着好几千人。宾馆经理就事论事地告诉我,这里的其它两个宾馆也同样把污秽废物排到那里。

然而,墨西哥旅游开发部还要在这里增加 600 多个宾馆客房,同时建 400 多个野营车①泊车位。很明显,他们为的是吸引生态旅游和探险旅游的游客。旅游开发部的主任助理告诉我,"这就足可以拉动旅游业的繁荣了。"

一位名叫玛莎·格林的导游对这一前景感到忧虑,尤其担心野营车的开入:"如果野营车能够开进这个地方,那么这里就不再是偏远之地;这里就会变成迪斯尼乐园。"但是,在峡谷边上与人合伙经营一家宾馆的玛利亚·巴丽佳对此地的旅游开发已经迫不及待:"那样的话,就太棒了。"她满眼放光地如是说。她还说,一位旅游开发部的官员建议她把宾馆客房增加到 100 个房间。而早些时候,一位州属旅游官员非常肯定地告诉我,一家宾馆的客房数量不能超过 50 间。

我们回到乡村大巴士上,顺山势往下开进巴托皮拉斯峡谷。这段行程令人胆战心惊。狭窄的盘山路,一个急转弯接着另一个急转弯,一路向下,险象环生。峡谷侧峰拔地而起成为顶峰。再往下,路呈 V 字形直切悬崖,车窗外就是令人头晕目眩的巴托皮拉斯河陡峭的河岸。在方形山谷可以瞥见其它几座峡谷,那简直就是光与影的超大型合奏——黄色,雾朦朦的蓝色,灰朦朦的绿色,仿佛是马克斯菲尔德·帕里什②绘制的巨人国③的宏大山谷画卷。我们正在*降落*④进一道连绵的山脉。难怪这个地方长久以来不为人知。

事实上,即便是现在,这个地方也时有令人惊奇的新发现。这些发现大部分由一位名叫卡洛斯·拉兹卡诺的探险家完成。拉兹卡诺已经开始谢顶,但举止温和,五年来一直不断地探索铜鼓群。1995 年,在边陲村落的居民的帮助下,拉兹卡诺确认了墨西哥最高的瀑布(高达 1,486 英尺,在北美瀑布中排名第三)。这条墨西哥最高的瀑布就位于此地峡谷群的南部。就在去年,峡谷群正北,他发现了有 500 年之久的帕克美⑤印第安人的双层崖穴,其中有 6 具保存完整的

---

① Recreational-vehicle,简写为 RV。
② Maxfield Parrish,(1870-1966),美国画家,活跃在 20 世纪前半叶的艺坛,其画风以饱和明快的色调和理想化的新古典意象而闻名。
③ 英国作家斯威夫特名作《格列夫游记》中的巨人国。这里用来代指峡谷的巍峨宏大。
④ 斜体为原文作者所加。
⑤ Paquimé Indian,北美古老的印第安的一支。

木乃伊。你所期盼的所有发现都发生在征服者寻找金矿的时候。

当然,如今,金子并不是驱使墨西哥政府资助探索此地的因素。来此地观光旅游的我们就是金子。

我们继续下降,转了个弯,看见一批勘测队员。他们是改善路况的。麦威廉不喜欢他们这么做,担心这样就会减弱旅行的体验和感觉,也会把野营车招进来。而野营车的开入正是墨西哥联邦旅游开发部所希望的。

峡谷底部,巴托皮拉斯镇沿河岸凌乱地四散开来。巴托皮拉斯原是采矿小镇,盛极一时。巴托皮拉斯因银矿而建立起来,19世纪后期,在美国矿业大亨、管辖过华盛顿特区的亚历山大·夏伯特的扶植下达到鼎盛。到了20世纪,巴托皮拉斯繁华落尽,人口衰减,雅致的房子也败落了。

然而,这个镇子并没有销声匿迹。余下的一千来口居民在偏僻的峡谷继续着他们的生活,只有步行或者骑骡子才能进到这里来。然而,这种状况在1978年因道路的开凿而终止了。就在这深深的峡谷中,伐木工人倒是生活得很自在。他们头戴10加仑的大草帽,时常和女人鬼混,而眼下,时不时地嗑药过瘾。

探险旅行者已经发现了这个镇子。政府的旅游部门计划把这里开发成徒步旅行中心和历史遗迹胜地。那位矿业大亨夏伯特在河岸边的大庄园,房子已经没了屋顶,只剩下铜黄色的粘土砖块。这片庄园废墟却成为此地现在和将来的旅游胜地。

镇子的中心地带已经有了好几家小型宾馆,但都和麦威廉的不同。仿照废墟,他建造了一座宾馆,简直就是梦幻般的19世纪墨西哥的重现:房间和走廊都画着色彩鲜明的画;花园般的庭院;墙上有用模板印制的蓝色花体文字;到处都挂着精美的煤油灯;这里陈列着各种各样、别具一格的艺术收藏品,有真品,有赝品,有老古董,也有小摆设。宽敞的大堂极为吸引眼球,天花板上雕刻着仿制的洛可可式①壁画。这个地方就是一种感受。清晨,在白鸽咕咕的叫声中醒来,耳畔传来镇子里的犬吠,阳光洒照在仿佛来自天国的悬崖尖儿上。

麦威廉不愿看到镇子因旅游业而现代化,他更愿意看到镇子的复原。他敦请当地人"街道上仍然铺鹅卵石,恢复古旧的门楣。"他引领我走进一座废弃的、淘银热时代的房子里。他蹲在残砖烂瓦上,用小折刀从墙上刮下一层污垢,墙上露出了和他小型宾馆里同样的模板印制的蓝色花体文字图案。

---

① Rococo,洛可可式的,过分修饰的(用以描述装饰精巧的建筑、家具等,以及描写细腻入微的文学、音乐风格。洛可可风格盛行于18世纪)。

远离文明的巴托拉斯与民风古朴的塔拉乌马拉相邻。常有塔拉乌马拉人穿戴着传统的民族服饰：男人们穿的是大波浪的、灯笼袖的衬衫，腰上缠着一块叫作 *sitagora* 的灰白色三角形腰布，头上扎着留有长长飘带的束发带；女人们穿着色彩鲜艳的皱褶长裙，外面套着长袖罩衫。这样的衣着使塔拉乌马拉人极有镜头感，但他们并不喜欢被别人拍摄。

有着 4000 人的塔拉乌马拉族和纳瓦霍族、切罗基族并称北美最大的原住民族群。旅游宣传部门到处张贴拉乌马拉人的照片和图像。在鱼篓镇，有关印第安人的壁画和油画，从技法娴熟的到画笔拙劣的，不但装饰着宾馆的大厅、商店的招牌，甚至连汽车旅馆的水箱上贴的都是。

讽刺的是，塔拉乌马拉人非常珍视隐秘而讨厌他人的干扰，即便是自己人之间也是如此。他们散落而居，而不是以村落形式聚居。他们沉默少言，喜欢安静，觉得外来人全都是喋喋不休的话匣子。被冤枉或欺压时，他们也不喜欢大声抗议。然而，大批匪夷所思的外来远足者正践踏着他们的土地。

我得与他们谈一谈。

在鱼篓镇的布道所里，我见到了菲丽西塔丝·关娜佩妮。她圆圆的棕褐色的脸趴在办公桌上，显得小小的。她在美国边境的一家耶稣会学校学过英语，因为不常用，所以说得磕磕巴巴：" 小时候，我母亲告诉我说看见 *chabochi* 就跑开并藏起来。" *chabochi* 指的是长着络腮胡子的人、任何不是印第安的人，是大麻烦。现在，关娜佩妮在塔拉乌马拉人里面算是见多识广的，她明白旅游业开发会给她的民族带来好处，但结果却什么也没有："白人拿走了所有的钱。"

但手工艺品除外，尤其是小提琴。3 个世纪以来，印第安人一直制造宗教庆典演奏所需的小提琴。现在小提琴有了市场。他们的小提琴并不上漆。依据传统，所有的小提琴都是纯木的、不油漆的。

在巴托皮拉斯，我从帕特罗斯尼奥·洛佩斯手里买了一把。有人称洛佩斯是塔拉乌马拉的斯特拉迪瓦里[①]。按照事先约定好的，他一路小跑到镇子里卖给我这把琴。琴头被精心雕刻成双环蛇形。印第安人已经看出来了，有这种装饰的小提琴非常好卖。这究竟是艺术的堕落呢？抑或是艺术的进步？

洛佩斯是个非同寻常的塔拉乌马拉人，很乐意与 *chabochis* 穷聊。我问他怎么看待越来越多游客来践踏他的土地这件事。他认为这倒不是什么大问题。

---

① Stradivarius，是 17 世纪一个古老家族的名字，以制造小提琴闻名，特别是安东尼奥·斯特拉迪瓦里。据说，这个家族制造的小提琴用云杉木、柳木和枫木三种木头制造琴身的不同地方。

他们来了，但还会走的。但是，大多数印第安人对外来人不加任何区分，把游客和传道士混为一谈，而传道士——los aleluyas——才是问题所在。"他们留下不走，还说我们必须穿裤子，必须改变我们的生活方式。他们还与我们的女人结婚。"

我想起了麦威廉的俏皮话："促使文化发生改变的主要手段就是拉拢女孩子。"

墨西哥联邦旅游开发部所期冀的大批徒步旅行者也会成为一种长久的现象。阿图若·古铁拉斯，那个经营山地自行车的人也给徒步旅行者领路，可是特别担心那些拒绝领路人而自行其事的人群。我问他说："让徒步旅行者都跟随塔拉乌马拉向导走那些让走的路，这样行不行呢？"

"那样的话，探险游客们就得不到他们所向往的那种极致体验了。"

每个周六，直升飞机的嗡嗡声淹没了巴托皮拉斯的犬吠声和鸽子的咕咕声。这一天，直升机4次着陆，从中涌出来的是科技政治治国的墨西哥精英。在这批人里可没有什么伐木工大草帽。挺括的宽松长裤，漂亮时髦的周末衬衫，太阳镜。他们是城市规划者、建筑师、旅游业专家、政府官员、侍从武官——确实如此，甚至还有吉华华州的州长，来自墨西哥全国各地的旅游局局长。

这些要人们游览了全镇，然后聚在麦威廉的宾馆里参加墨西哥城一家极有实力的建筑公司举办的展示会。精美的海报和张贴展示了这家公司提出的复古样本。

至少对巴托皮拉斯来说，这还不算太糟。如果——一个大大的"如果"——这些计划通过的话，麦威廉就得到几乎一切他想要的东西，但不包括窄小的街道。他们保证说，只是把有些街道加宽，但绝不铺压成现代公路。在一个三年内旅游业增长三倍的地方，这可能吗？"这好比是一个小伙子和一个美丽的女人躺进同一个被窝，却保证不去碰她，"麦威廉嘟囔着，"这样的保证能遵守多久啊？"

现在麦威廉说这话时再也没有顽皮的神情了。这些峡谷的土地已经铸入了斯科普·麦威廉的灵魂。他不仅仅在保护投资，也是在守护记忆。

守护他自己和客人们的记忆。古博·杨格是一位来自德克萨斯威芝塔瀑市的房客。对巴托皮拉斯的记忆激发了他的灵感，回家后就写了一篇故事发表在当地的报纸上。看到巴托皮拉斯现在这个样子，他不无忧虑："电来了，星星没了。"

有些人觉得，不必把改变之潮看作洪水猛兽。电正在普及开来，但当地人能消除这刺眼的光芒——如果那些衣着光鲜、能带来税收的旅行者不希望有电，那就更好办了。塔拉乌马拉的隐秘受到了威胁，但并不是没有办法来减弱冲击，比如供游客参观的博物馆、手工艺品商店、舞蹈和庆典等各方面的印第安文化中心可以建在远离印第安人家园的地方。边境以北有几个类似的文化中心提供了参照样本。

在美国科罗拉多州的阿尔伯克基有一个普埃布罗文化中心，这个文化中心也给我们上了一课。在那里的一个小博物馆里，一组组的透视画描述了几个世纪以来普埃布罗人的生活状态。在最后一张画里，一个穿着普通衬衫、带着太阳镜的白人端坐在好几个印第安人中——这个白人是个游客。这是对一个正在全世界蔓延的事实毫不避讳的坦陈：我们这些游客已经被编织进游地的生活常态。那些游览地的未来——还有旅游感受的质量——不但取决于游客们的行为举止，也在于旅游开发商如何能维持游览地的游客们所喜闻乐见的品格。

在峡谷的最后一晚，我住进麦威廉开的"塞拉小舍"。殷勤和蔼的经理玛拉·卡里罗正在监督膳食的准备工作。我和一位刚从洛杉矶来的女客人坐在一桌——这是位回头客，重返此地很是高兴。"我上次离开前做了个梦"，她告诉一起就餐的客人说，"就是我到这里的时候，发现宾馆变成了那种乱糟糟的、拉毛粉饰的大型度假胜地。要想见见玛拉，还得预约。但能听见她在大喇叭里的声音：'戴红色腕带的在那边集合，戴黄色的在这边……'"

她转向我，觉得有必要跟我澄清一下。

"那真是一个噩梦，"她这样说道。

（张慧芳 译　杨建 校）

The Last Inuit[①] of Quebec

Justin Nobel

【导读】几千年前，人类的一支迁徙大军从亚洲出发跨过白令海峡向美洲腹地进发，但是有谁料到等待他们的是美洲印第安人的围追堵截和残忍杀戮！这支迁徙部队且战且退，最后退至北极圈内，时值寒冬，印第安人以为敌人不久便会被冻死，便停止了追杀。不料，他们不但在北极奇迹般生存了下来，而且还创造了独特的"白色文化"。这支部落就是北极土著居民中分布地域最广的民族——因纽特人。他们在恶劣环境中的生存奇迹使得他们的文化在形态各异的世界文化之林中闪耀着奇异的光芒，充满了神奇的魅力，不仅深深地吸引着社会学家和人类学家，也唤起了无数普通人的猜测和向往。有人说他们是吃生肉、捕鲸鱼的原始人，有人说他们是淳朴无邪、与世隔绝的世外人。然而，这些看法都早已与现实不符了。在政府的帮助下，现代因纽特人的生活已经发生了巨大变化。传统的渔猎生产方式转向现代城镇生活，具有传奇色彩的拱形圆顶小雪屋已经让位于设有暖气、水电齐全的房屋；传统的狗拉雪橇已大都被雪地车、越野车及各种汽车和卡车取代；然而，因纽特人的新生活也面临着严峻挑战：因为失去原有的生活方式，大多数人只能依赖政府的福利和救济生活；在因纽特社区，就业难、住房拥挤、年轻人自杀率高、文化断裂等社会问题突出。我们心中那片犹如世外桃源般的冰雪王国其实也和我们身处的大千世界一样，问题重重，曲折前行。历史前进的车轮无情碾过，没有哪片净土可以免俗。如何在继承传统和开创未来中寻求平衡是每个民族都亟需解决的问题，因纽特人尤为突出。本文讲述了当代因纽特人的真实生活，简单质朴的语言中流露出一丝忧伤，古老的传统不可避免地渐行渐远，多少会令人有些伤感，不过还好有文字可以帮助我们记住历史，记住传统，记住这最后的因纽特人。

THREE SUMMERS AGO, looking for adventure, I left New York City and

---

① A member of a people inhabiting the Arctic (northern Canada or Greenland or Alaska or eastern Siberia); the Algonquians called them Eskimo (`eaters of raw flesh') but they call themselves the Inuit (`the people').(编者注)。

drove to California for a newspaper job. One evening while jogging, I noticed a glowing rock high on a hill. A few weeks later, I pitched my tent beside it. After work, I'd trudge up my hill in the moonlight and sit for hours under the rock. On some nights, strange howls kept me awake. I wondered if there was a land where people still lived in skins, gathered around fire, and believed in magic and not God. Looking for that land, I quit the paper and traveled to Nunavik, an Inuit territory in Arctic Quebec.

On Canada Day[1], I landed in Kuujjuaq[2], a community of two thousand on the tree line. [3]An icy wind spat cold rain. On the shores of the Koksoak River[4], families picnicked beside their SUVs and Canadian flags flapped in the drizzle. "Things are changing so fast," said Allen Gordon, the head of the Nunavik Tourism Association. I later learned that his wife was the first one in town to ship north a Hummer[5]. We celebrated the holiday at the Ikkariqvik Bar, a cavernous dive without windows. There were darts and a disco ball. "If you're a woman, you'll win a sewing machine. If you're a man, you win nets. If you don't want either, you'll get four beers," shouted a lady selling raffle tickets. A teen dressed in black showed me a tiny silver pistol and someone collapsed on the edge of the dance floor. "We are drunk because it's Canada Day," said a man at the bar. When the raffle lady stumbled back onstage she was too drunk to announce who had won what.

Kuujjuaq is regarded as a *city*, severed from Inuit traditions. To find magic, I needed to go farther north, so I boarded a propeller plane for Ivujivik, a town of three hundred on the stormy coastline where Hudson Bay meets Hudson Strait. Trees disappeared then reappeared and then disappeared for good. This was tundra — a sopping, pitted landscape that shone brilliantly in the sun. Confused ribbons of water connected an endless splatter of lakes, some green, some yellow, some with red

---

[1] Canada Day is the national day of Canada, a federal statutory holiday celebrating the anniversary of the July 1, 1867, enactment of the British North America Act (today called the Constitution Act, 1867), which united three British colonies into a single country, called Canada, within the British Empire. Originally called Dominion Day, the name was changed in 1982 with the passing of Canada Act.

[2] Kuujjuaq is the largest Inuit village in Nunavik, Quebec, Canada.

[3] Tree line refers to the family tree line, which means all the community members belong to the same big family.

[4] The Koksoak River is a river in northern Quebec, Canada, the largest river in the Nunavik region.

[5] Hummer was a brand of trucks and SUVs, which were first designed and built by AM General Corporation but now belongs to GM General Motors Corporation.

edges and bright blue centers. Ancient channels were etched in the stone. We unloaded and picked up passengers in Inukjuak[①] and Puvirnituq[②]. Over Hudson Bay, a passenger spotted a pair of belugas.

A drunk woman named Saira showed up at the airport in a Bronco[③] packed with relatives and wanted me to live with her. We had met in Kuujjuaq at the home of a woman who peddled black-market booze. Saira was drunk on Smirnoff[④] at the time, but had somehow remembered my travel plans. I ignored her. A construction worker dropped me at a drab house on the edge of town occupied by a security guard named Chico who I had been told would have a free room. A man with a beat-up face came to the door. "Why are you here?" he asked. I explained. "I can't wait to get the hell out," he said. "I hate this place."

I was in e-mail contact with a nurse who supposedly had a room, but that too evaporated — her boss was in town. Reluctantly, I sought out Saira. She opened the door with a grin. "I'm drunk," she said, "but it's okay." I joined her and a niece with whittled teeth at a table covered with empty Budweiser[⑤] cans. The women looked at me and giggled harshly. They bantered in Inuktitut. Saira explained that she was getting evicted in a few days. "We will live in a tent in the back," she said, "and come in to take showers."

I stepped out to clear my head. A stiff wind whipped white caps from the cobalt[⑥] straight. I headed for it, walking over dinosaur egg-like rocks littered with ammo boxes and potato chip bags. At the edge of a headland, long rolling swells beat the boulders and blasted spray skyward. Beyond, the sea swirled. I stood there for some time, thinking about good meals and the New York subway. The strong wind dragged tears across my cheeks. I later learned this was the site where hunters once came to woo belugas into the bay so others could harpoon them.

Ivujivik had one store, a cooperative, which serves as a bank, post office,

---

① Inukjuak is an Inuit settlement located on Hudson Bay at the mouth of the Innuksuak River in the Nunavik region of northern Quebec, Canada.

② Puvirnituq is an Inuit settlement in Nunavik on the Povungnituk River near its mouth on the Hudson Bay in northern Quebec, Canada.

③ The Ford Bronco is a sport utility vehicle that was produced from 1966 to 1996.

④ Smirnoff is a brand of vodka owned and produced by the British company Diageo.

⑤ Budweiser is brand of beer which was created in 1876 in America.

⑥ Cobalt is a chemical element with symbol Co and atomic number 27. It is found naturally only in chemically combined form. The free element, produced by reductive smelting, is a hard, lustrous, silver-gray metal.

hardware store, and grocer. There were no bars and no restaurants. There was a school, a health center, a municipal building and a power plant that burned diesel fuel imported by a ship that comes twice a year. Homes were red, orange, blue, green, identical warehouse-like structures subsidized by the Quebec government. Each had a water tank and a sewage tank and trucks circled daily, refilling and relieving. All roads ended a few miles outside town. I was there in late July, and for children, who represent nearly half the population, these were the dog days[1] of summer.

Kids began the day in small groups that expanded as night neared. Afternoon activities included hide and seek, cavorting atop shipping containers, pouring buckets of water over slanted wooden planks and watching a bulldozer demolish a building. By nightfall, which lasts from 9 P.M. until well past midnight, children can be roaming the streets in groups of ten to twenty. Often, they get rowdy. The summer I was in Ivujivik, youths regularly broke into the youth center to steal video games. In an adjacent community, a posse comprised of kids as young as twelve pummeled a man with a hockey stick and golf clubs.

Teens had rosier options. Some worked at the co-op or for the municipality, driving the water and sewage trucks. Some wandered like the younger ones, but with more gadgets. Several tore around on dirt bikes and quite a few had iPods[2]. Gangsta Rap[3] was very popular in the north and there was even a local group — the North Coast Rappers, or NCR. One morning, I hung outside the co-op with a teen in black jeans named Lukasi who said he would introduce me to a member. Sure enough, a thuggish youth emerged to meet us. He wore a baggy T-shirt with a picture of Tupoc[4], his head in a bandana and bowed. Plastic diamonds protruded from the shirt, whose owner was also named Lukasi. He coolly lit a cigarette provided by the other Lukasi and discussed NCR, a three-man group that rapped over beats made by

---

[1] Dog days are the hottest, most sultry days of summer.

[2] IPod is a line of portable media players created and marketed by Apple Inc, which is very popular among the youth all over the world.

[3] Gangsta rap is a subgenre of hip hop music that evolved from hardcore hip hop and purports to reflect urban crime and the violent lifestyles of inner-city youths.

[4] Tupac Shakur was a highly-influential rapper, poet and actor who was murdered in 1996. He was born in New York but spent most of his adult life living in California where he became known as one of the founders of the west coast style of rap music. Tupac has sold more than 75 million albums worldwide and he is still considered one of the greatest rappers of all time.

a computer synthesizer program. When I asked what they rapped about Lukasi paused briefly, then said: "Bitches and ho's, mostly."

In August, I noticed a flier in the co-op about a bowhead whale hunt in the community of Kangiqsujuaq, several hundred miles down the coast. Bowheads can live for 150 years and weigh as much as five school buses. The Inuit of Nunavik had not landed one in more than a century, although locals had been pushing for a hunt since the mid-1980s. At that time, the Hudson Strait bowhead was designated as "endangered" and hunting was prohibited. The Inuit claimed that the whales were plentiful. In 2005, a study by Canada's Department of Fisheries and Oceans confirmed the Inuit's suspicions and in 2008, the Inuit of Nunavik were granted permission to hunt one bowhead. Kangiqsujuaq was chosen as the hunt site for its proximity to known bowhead grounds and the hunting prowess of its inhabitants. I e-mailed an editor at the *Nunatsiaq News*, a paper delivered across the Arctic by propeller plane. She said they'd pay for a story and photos. I hitched a ride on a canoe headed south.

Kangiqsujuaq, a town of six hundred, was bursting at the seams. The Inuit were delirious over the chance to eat bowhead *maktak*, or whale skin. On a blustery day I joined a group of Inuit at a sort of tailgate for the bowhead hunt. We picnicked on a barren knoll outside town that overlooked a rocky cove with several fishing boats and a dozen or more canoes. Tinned anchovies, sandwich pickles, Ritz crackers[①], Spam, and a jar of Miracle Whip [②]were spread over an impromptu plank table. A man with a buzz cut approached our group from the water's edge, his eyes hid by tinted shades, and the women shrieked. In each hand he grasped a fat, glistening Arctic char. Two ladies with buns of gray hair tucked beneath colorful bandanas laid the fish on a dismantled cardboard box. We squatted in the dirt and went at them with pocketknives and curved blades called *ulus*, slurping flesh from the skin as if spooning grapefruit. The meat was bright orange and sticky. "Chew the bones," the fisherman, whose name was Tiivi Qumaaluk, said. "They're the best."

The Inuit reached what is now northern Quebec more than two thousand years

---

① Ritz Crackers are a brand of snack cracker introduced by American Nabisco in 1934.

② Miracle Whip is a white salad dressing and sandwich spread manufactured by Kraft Foods, sold throughout the United States and Canada.

ago. In winter they dwelt in igloos along the coast, skewering seals and walruses at breathing holes in the ice with ivory-tipped harpoons. In summer they tracked caribou into the interior, ambushing them at river crossings or chasing the animals toward hidden archers. Whales were corralled in shallow bays with kayaks① made from sealskin stretched over bone. Polar bears were immobilized by dogs and then knifed. Still, famine was common. Elderly that slowed the group were left behind to die. Clans that settled near Kangiqsujuaq fared better than most. The large tides created caverns under the frozen sea that could be reached at low tide by chipping through the ice above. In times of hunger, hunters scavenged these caves for mussels and algae. "There are numerous indications that starvation and famines accompanied by infanticide and even cannibalism were not rare," writes Bernard Saladin D'Anglure, a twentieth-century anthropologist who spent time in Kangiqsujuaq.

By the late 1800s the Hudson Bay Company had built several trading posts in Nunavik, and in 1910 Révillon Frères②, a French fur company, opened one in Kangiqsujuaq. Inuit hunters stopped traveling with game and began searching for fox, which they traded at posts for nets, guns, and metal needles. Inuit began camping around stores rather than by hunting spots. They developed tastes for foods they had never eaten — flour, biscuits, molasses, tea, coffee. From the posts also came disease and dependence. "About 15 families camped in the settlement," reads the 1928 log from a Hudson Bay store operator in the Central Arctic; "they have no inclination to hunt or exert themselves but are content to sit around in a state of destitution."

By the 1960s, the north had become such a black eye ③that the Canadian government took steps to recuperate the region. Teachers, healthcare workers, and police were sent north. Homes and hospitals were built. Dogs were corralled by the police and shot. Some Inuit youth were shipped to southern schools against their will. The government's aim was to quell poverty and spur development, which to them meant providing Inuit with Western educations and eliminating sick dogs. But to many Inuit, these actions appeared to be part of a much more sinister agenda, the annihilation of their culture.

---

① A kayak is a small, relatively narrow, human-powered boat primarily designed to be manually propelled by by means of a double blade paddle.

② Révillon Frères(Revillon Brothers) was a French fur and luxury goods company, founded in 1723.

③ Black eye means the mark of humiliation.

In 1975, the Inuit and their native neighbors to the south, the Cree①, protested the Quebec government's seizure of their land for a massive hydroelectric project and received a settlement of nearly a quarter of a billion dollars in what was called the James Bay and Northern Quebec Agreement. The Inuit's share went toward the creation of the Makivik Corporation, a development agency charged with promoting economic growth and fostering Inuit-run businesses. Makivik is presently invested in construction, shipping, fishing, tanning, and air travel. They recently started a cruise ship company.

Kangiqsujuaq was trying to get itself on the adventure travel map. Much of the town's funding comes from a nearby nickel mine. Recent tourist-oriented projects have included an elder home, a community pool, a new hotel with a $400 suite, and a visitor center for a remote provincial park that protects a 2-million-year-old meteor crater said to contain the purest water on Earth.

When I entered the office of Lukasi Pilurtuut, who manages the Nunaturlik Landholding Corporation, which oversees development in Kangiqsujuaq, I found him alone at the end of a long table with his laptop, wearing a cap, jeans, and sneakers. Sunlight streamed through large windows, and the hilltops surrounding the town gleamed with freshly fallen summer snow. He was an ace student in high school but dropped out of a Montreal college after just three semesters, homesick. "It wasn't the problem of going to school," he said, "it was more the problem that I couldn't go hunting."

Dependence has made some people lazy, said Pilurtuut. The Canadian and Quebec governments subsidize housing and health care, and many Inuit also receive welfare checks. In 2007, high nickel prices helped the mine turn record profits, and each Inuit resident of Kangiqsujuaq received a check for $4,700. Some families got checks for $30,000. They bought ATV②s, SUVs, dirt bikes③, snowmobiles, motorized canoes, computers, and flat screen TVs.

Tourism money will be different, Pilurtuut said. Rather than destroying tradition, it could bring it back. In fact, this was already happening. As we spoke the

---

① A member of an Algonquian people living in central Canada.
② ATV stands for all-terrain vehicle. 全地形汽车.
③ Dirt Bike is a lightweight motorcycle equipped with rugged tires and suspension; an off-road motorcycle designed for riding cross country or over unpaved ground.

phone rang several times. "Yes!" he cried during one call, and then turned to me. "We have good news, four single kayaks coming in today." The Inuit invented the kayak but no one in Nunavik remembered how to operate one. Kangiqsujuaq had to order kayaks from southern Quebec and hire an outside guide to train locals.

On a crisp summer evening, I raced into the Strait to greet the bowhead hunters on a bright orange government speed boat. The sun sank through thin clouds and spilled across the horizon like paint. "This is so special for us," our navigator, a man named Tuumasi Pilurtuut, said to me, practically speechless with joy. "We're back with our ancestors."

The hunters fired flares to mark their position. A tremendous cheer went up as we arrived, and strips of *maktak*① were passed aboard. "Better than beluga," Pilurtuut said between chews. Lines of turquoise fire billowed in the night sky — the northern lights, in their first appearance of the season.

*The Nanuq*②, the boat to which the whale was secured, motored through the night and reached the cove near town where I had tailgated the week before shortly after dawn. The bowhead was moored to three orange buoys on the edge of the bay, where it bobbed, with a long knife called a *tuuq* stuck in its top, until early afternoon, when the tide lowered. Canoes ferried hungry onlookers to the site and the slicing of *maktak* began. Naalak Nappaaluk, a revered elder and the only man alive who remembered stories about the bowhead hunts of yesteryear, sat on a rock with a pad of *maktak* nearby and tears in his eyes. Nappaaluk had a shot at a bowhead as a teen, but it escaped through a lead in the ice. "Today, I have seen people standing on the bowhead for the first time," he told me through a translator. "It's overwhelming." A bulldozer that had intended to flip the whale had trouble making it to the site, and the majority of the meat rotted. When I returned three days later, the stench was so potent that men were vomiting uncontrollably.

One tradition that had survived intact was the caribou hunt. Nearly a million caribou dwell in Nunavik and when a herd nears towns, offices empty. By

---

① whale skin with blubber.

② In Inuit mythology, Nanook or Nanuq which is from the Inuit language for polar bear, was the master of bears, meaning he decided if hunters had followed all applicable taboos and if they deserved success in hunting bears. here, it is the name of one boat.

mid-August the chatter around Kangiqsujuaq was that the animals were close. One morning at the grocery store I ran into Tiivi, the man who had caught the char at the tailgate party. He invited me to go hunting with him the following day.

Tiivi killed his first caribou at age nine while looking for bird eggs with his five-year-old brother. Unable to cut the carcass themselves, the boys rushed back to tell their mother. "She was so excited," Tiivi said, "she was like shouting of joy." In his teens he worked as a garbage man and at twenty-one he took a job pulverizing rock at the nickel mine, earning a $2,500 paycheck twice a month.

Tiivi married a janitor from the mine and they moved in together, living in a town on the Hudson Strait called Salluit. The marriage was a nightmare. Fights were frequent; in one she bit him, leaving a knotty scar over his bicep. Another time she plunged a steak knife into his chest. He was medevaced to a hospital on the other side of Nunavik for a tetanus shot. "The next day I couldn't lift my arm because all the muscles were cut," he said. One night, while she was asleep, he snuck out with just the clothes on his back. While visiting cousins in Puvirnituq, he met a second cousin named Elisapie. "A lot of different girls tried to be with me but I refused them all because I saw Elisapie and I wanted only her," said Tiivi. "She was so fine looking." They recently married.

I met Tiivi at his home just after 9 A.M. He wore muck boots, grease-stained pants, and a hunting cap. He carried a rifle for caribou and a shotgun for geese. We were joined by his aunt, Qialak, and his brother, Jimmy, who trailed us on a second ATV. On a ridge patterned with jackknifed rocks Tiivi signaled a shiny outcrop where carvers come for soapstone[①]. Cumulus clouds splotched the sky and sunbursts lit mats of lichen red and orange. "There might be some gold particles," Tiivi said, as we crossed a stream. "Our land is full of minerals."

With mud splattering from the tires, we descended a spongy slope then looped around a lake where the week before Jimmy and Qialak had strung nets. Tiivi and Qialak reeled them in, half a dozen flapping Arctic char. "So fresh the heart is still beating," Tiivi said. Qialak sliced open the bellies of the females and wailed — two had eggs. I held a sandwich baggy open while she scooped in the long slimy packets.

We sat at the water's edge and slurped the bright orange flesh from flaps of

---

① Soapstone is a soft heavy compact variety of talc having a soapy feel; used to make hearths and tabletops and ornaments.

skin. The meat was sticky and chewy, like a fatty piece of steak. The fresh blood tasted sweet. We drank tea from a thermos and ate packaged biscuits. Tiivi smoked two cigarettes and then we left. A muddy track led above the lake to the next ridge. Arctic poppies bobbed in the breeze. Jimmy spotted snow geese.

"They're going to land because of the wind," said Tiivi. We abandoned the ATVs and crouched low. Jimmy and I followed Tiivi along a sliver of wet land behind a low rock ridge. We crawled close on our bellies. When the geese took flight the men bolted upright and fired. Two birds fell. One goose lay sprawled in the tundra with wings still beating. Its handsome white coat was ruined by a single red smear. Tiivi pinned its chest with his arms. The long neck slowly lifted and the head cocked sideways and gasped. "Now it's dying because I'm holding the lungs," he said.

With a soft thud the head dropped. "Hurray!" Tiivi said and peeled a Clementine①. He tossed the squiggled rind aside and gave me half. Qialak looked at me beaming, "You're probably getting the experience of a lifetime."

On a ridge above a river, under a sunset the color of skinned knees, Qialak spotted a large buck. Tiivi slowly extended his arms above his head, bent his elbows out, and pointed his fingers skyward, imitating antlers. The buck stared at us intently then resumed foraging. A smaller buck beside him followed suit. We splashed across the river and sped, sheltered by the ridge, towards the buck. Its impressive rack was just visible above the hill's crest in the grainy light.

"Stay low," Tiivi said. He crept up the ridge, rested on a rock, and fired several shots. The buck rushed forward frantically then halted. It seemed not to know where to step next. Tiivi fired again and it swayed. Its massive head lowered to the ground, eyes still opened. The body slumped. Labored, spastic breaths rose from the ground. The younger buck remained for a moment then darted.

Everyone produced knives; Tiivi held one in each hand. The buck lay on its side, its chest heaving. Tiivi approached from behind, and it kicked the air violently. He jabbed a knife into its neck, then jostled the blade back and forth. As darkness fell the three Inuit dismembered the carcass. Everything was taken but the head and intestines. Tiivi tied his parts in a bundle — heart, hindquarters, filet, stomach, ribs. Recrossing the river we washed our hands and drank cold river water from our

---

① Clementine is a variety of mandarin orange that is grown around the Mediterranean and in South Africa.

palms. "I'm all clean," Tiivi said.

During my last week in Kangiqsujuaq, I met with Father Dion, a Catholic priest originally from Belgium who had been in Nunavik for nearly five decades. He was a tiny, puckered man whose congregation was dwindling, but he was a bull. He laughed loudly, spoke with a thick French accent, and commanded respect from everyone in town, young and old, Inuit and non-. His church was a pint-sized building in the center of town and he lived inside. When I knocked one drizzly day he didn't hear me. I entered. He was on the couch, in leather sandals with socks and a sky-blue sweater, watching CNN[①].

He shook my hand with a strong grip and heated a cup of tea in an old microwave, then served it to me with the last two of a package of biscuits. He handed me a pair of ivory binoculars wider than they were long and suggested I view the Hudson Strait, which he had a clear shot of. When he was nineteen, the Germans invaded Belgium. Father Dion was in the seminary and went to war. When it ended he was given the choice of working in a hospital in his home country or being sent as a missionary to the Congo. He chose Congo, a dreadful two years. "It was hot," he said. "A lot of animals, a lot of sickness." Afterward, he requested to be sent to the Arctic, where Belgium had some missionaries stationed. He arrived in Nunavik in 1964, and spent his first nine years in a community of three hundred called Quaqtaq. He survived a famine and a fall through the ice on a snow mobile. "I have a very strong esteem for these people and how they survived in such harsh conditions," he said. "I appreciate them very, very much."

Father Dion addressed some misconceptions. The dogs were shot because they were starving and had been eating Inuit babies. The schooling the government imposed on the Inuit helped create a generation of bright leaders. A change he wasn't fond of concerned the church. Newer community members were now following the Pentecostal church[②], whose loud hectic services made some think the group was a

---

[①] Cable News Network.美国有线电视新闻网络。

[②] Pentecostal church believes in Pentecostalism which is a renewal movement within Christianity that places special emphasis on a direct personal experience of God through the baptism in the Holy Spirit, has an eschatological focus, and is an experiential religion.

revival of shamanism[1]. Inuit once depended on shamans to bring good results in a hunt or lift them out of famine, but shamans could also bring death. "It was a kind of liberation when they disappeared," said Father Dion. Shamans were replaced by the Catholic Church.

I asked Father Dion if the Inuit would be better off as Nunavik modernized. He chewed his cheek and looked out the window at the gray town. The tide was going out, leaving black pools of water between the rocks. A septic truck passed. "When I arrived, this land was empty," he said. "Nothing. No houses, nothing. People were living in tents in the summer and igloos in the winter. Now, they have enough to eat, warm houses, transportation, communication. They don't fight for survival."

Just before I left, Tiivi began a job managing the new elder home. I stopped in to stay good-bye. A hefty woman in a pink nightgown was working on a puzzle of a snowy European forest. The place smelled of new furniture and cleaning agents. Tiivi led me into his office. The walls were bare, and he had taped a black trash bag over the window to keep the sun out. On his desk was a flat-screen computer; the screensaver was a shot of his son taken during the bowhead whale hunt. "So," said Tiivi, indicating his office items. "I have a good job."

Summer ended and I returned to Kuujjuaq days before the first blizzard hit. In mid-September, I flew to Montreal and boarded a Greyhound[2] bound for the border. My bus crossed into the U.S. at midnight and by dawn I was in New York City. The day was warm and breezy, the city still smelled of summer. I began an internship at *Audubon*[3] magazine but without enough money to get an apartment, I moved back in with my parents, in the suburbs. Unable to sleep in my teenage room, still lined with posters of conspiracy and aliens, I set up the tent in a wooded spot near where my childhood dog was buried.

I imagine that in a far-off land, harbored by the heartwood of a massive forest,

---

[1] An animistic religion of northern Asia having the belief that the mediation between the visible and the spirit worlds is effected by shamans.

[2] Greyhound Canada is the largest provider of intercity bus transportation in Canada, serving nearly 1,100 locations.

[3] The National Audubon Society (Audubon) is an American non-profit environmental organization dedicated to conservation. Incorporated in 1905, Audubon is one of the oldest of such organizations in the world .The society's flagship journal is the profusely illustrated magazine, Audubon, on subjects related to nature, with a special emphasis on birds.

there are a people who still remember how to do the things their ancestors did and there are still shamans and nobody has ever heard of God. I don't know how long that place will last or even if it deserves to, but surely it will soon enough be gone.

　　The leaves turned crisp yellows and oranges and fell to make large colored mats on the forest floor. Holes formed in the tent and spiders moved in. It got cold and I moved out. I had saved enough money from the internship for a cheap spot in Brooklyn.

魁北克最后的因纽特人[①]

贾斯廷·诺贝尔

三年前，为了寻求冒险，我驱车前往加州，在那里找了一份报社的工作。一天晚上，在慢跑的时候，我注意到一座山上有块闪闪发亮的石头。几周之后，我在这块石头旁边扎了个帐篷。工作之余，我会借着月色，登山跋涉，在岩石下坐上几个小时。有几个晚上，奇怪的嚎叫声令我无法入睡。我揣测附近是不是还有某片区域仍然生活着一批原始部落的人，他们兽皮遮体，篝火取暖，相信魔力而不是上帝。为了寻找这样的地区，我辞掉了报社的工作，前往努纳维克[②]去旅行。努纳维克地区是因纽特人的领土，位于北极圈内的魁北克省。

在加拿大日[③]那天，我到达了库朱阿克[④]。这是一个拥有2000人口的社区，社区成员都来自于同一家族。那天寒风冷雨交加，在科克索克河[⑤]的两岸，很多家庭在他们的SUV[⑥]旁边野餐，加拿大国旗在细雨中迎风飘动。"天气变化得太快了，"努纳维克旅游协会的负责人艾伦·戈登说道。后来，我得知他的妻子是第一个把悍马[⑦]运到北部的人。我们在伊卡瑞维克酒吧庆祝节日，这是一个没有窗户的洞穴式酒吧。酒吧里有飞镖游戏和迪斯科霓虹灯。"如果你是位女士，你能赢得缝纫机。如果你是个男人，你能赢得网子。如果这两样你都不想要，还可以赢得四瓶啤酒，"一个卖彩票的女人大声叫喊。一位黑衣少年向我展示一把微型银质手枪，还有个人瘫倒在舞池边上。酒吧里的一个男人说："我们为国庆而醉酒。"彩票女郎跄跄跄跄地返回舞台时，已酩酊大醉，根本无法宣布谁赢了什么。

[①] 因纽特人是北美原住民族之一，分布于北极圈周围，包括加拿大魁北克、西北地区、育空地区等地，说因纽特语。因纽特人属于爱斯基摩人（Eskimos）的一支。有人认为爱斯基摩人是当地其他印第安人部落对他们的称呼，意思是"吃生肉的人"，带有贬义，因此他们称自己为因纽特人。

[②] 努纳维克地区由加拿大第三大省魁北克省构成，是魁北克因纽特人的家园。

[③] 加拿大日是加拿大的全国公众假日，定于每年的7月1日。此假日是庆祝1867年7月1日加拿大自治领籍《英属北美条约》将英国在北美的三块领地合并为一个联邦，包括加拿大省（今安大略和魁北克省南部）、新斯科舍省和新不伦瑞克省。1879年此日被正式定为节日，最初被称为"自治领日"，纪念代表政治联盟的加拿大自治领。1982年10月27日根据《加拿大法案》改名为加拿大日。

[④] 库朱阿克是加拿大魁北克省最大的因纽特村。

[⑤] 科克索克河是加拿大魁北克省北部努纳维克地区最大的河流。

[⑥] SUV代表Sports Utility Vehicle，多功能箱式跑车。

[⑦] 悍马是轻型多用途军车的品牌，诞生于1985年，由美国AM General公司（AMG）生产，现商标使用权和生产权归美国通用汽车公司所有。

库朱阿克被视为一座*城市*，一座与因纽特传统割裂开来的城市。为了寻获魔力，我还得继续北行。因此我登上了一架飞往伊武吉维克镇的螺旋桨飞机。伊武吉维克镇只有三百来口人，位于哈得逊湾与哈得逊海峡交汇、频受风暴袭击的海岸线上。远方的树木忽隐忽现，最后完全从视线中消失。这就是寒漠风光——湿漉漉、坑坑洼洼，在阳光下熠熠生辉。缎带般的水流相互交织，无数的湖泊星罗棋布，有的水面是绿色的，有的是黄色的，有的是明蓝色的水心镶嵌在红色湖濒之间。古老的海峡蚀刻在乱石之中。我们的飞机在伊努爪克和皮维尼克[①]两起两落，乘客有上有下。在哈得逊湾上空，有位乘客瞄见了一对白鲸。

一位名叫萨莉娜的女士现身机场，一幅醉醺醺的样子。她开了辆烈马牌多用车，里面塞满了亲戚。她想让我住到她那里去。我们曾经在一个倒卖黑市酒水的女人家里见过面，萨莉娜因为喝多了司木露[②]而醉倒，但是不知怎么地却记住了我的旅行计划。我没有理睬她，而是搭乘一个建筑工人的车来到城郊一所土褐色房屋前。一个叫奇科的保安住在这所房子里，之前他告诉我能分给我一间闲置的房间。一个蓬头垢面的男人来应门。"你为什么到这儿来？"他问我。我向他解释了一番我此行的目的。"我都等不及要离开这个鬼地方了，"他说，"我讨厌这个地方。"

此前，我也一直和一位护士保持电邮联系，她本来应该有一个房间，但是这个备份也泡汤了——她的老板来镇上了。我只好很不情愿地又找到萨莉娜。她面带微笑地打开大门。"我有点醉了，"她说，"不过没问题。"我和萨莉娜以及她的一个牙齿参差不齐的侄女一起坐到桌边，桌子上摆满了空空的百威啤酒瓶。两个女人看着我，咯咯笑起来，很刺耳。她们用因纽特语逗乐打趣。萨莉娜解释说过几天她就会出去住。"我们会住到后面的帐篷里去，"她说，"冲淋浴时再进来。"

我走出去，想清醒一下头脑。从含有钴[③]元素的海峡吹来强劲的风，猛烈地抽打着白色的冠岩。我朝着海峡走去，跨过恐龙蛋般的岩石，岩石上到处都是人们胡乱丢弃的弹药盒子和土豆片包装袋。在一处岬角的边缘，滚滚波涛拍打着岩石，激起飞溅的浪花。远处，大海卷曲盘旋。我在这里站了一会，想起了可口的饭菜和纽约的地铁。强劲的风吹得我泪流满面。后来我得知，猎人们

---

① 伊努爪克和皮维尼克都是加拿大魁北克省北部的因纽特人居住区。
② 司木露是一种伏特加酒的商标名，为英国迪阿吉奥饮料公司所有。
③ 钴是一种过渡元素，化学符号 Co，原子序数 27。以微量形式存在于许多矿物和矿石中，这种具有磁性、稍带淡蓝的银白色金属大部分用于精密科技的特种合金（如铝镍钴合金和工具钢）。

曾经把白鲸引诱到这片海湾，用鱼叉进行捕捉。

伊武吉维克有一个综合性商店，同时兼具银行、邮局、五金店和杂货店的功能。镇子上没有酒吧和餐馆，却有一所学校、一个医疗中心、一所市政大楼和一座发电厂。发电厂所需要的柴油燃料由轮船每年分两次运送进来。房屋的颜色丰富多彩，红色，橙色，蓝色，绿色的；房屋结构极为相似，均为魁北克政府资助建造的仓库式。每家都有一个净水池和一个污水池，卡车每日巡回，给池子重新注入新水并取走脏水。所有的道路在镇外几公里处就到了尽头。我在那里的时候是七月下旬。对于孩子们来说，这正是夏天最热的时候，孩子几乎占了全镇人口的一半之多。

孩子们总是在夜晚快来临时才成群结伙地开始这一天。下午的游戏活动包括捉迷藏、在集装箱上嬉戏打闹、往倾斜的木板上倒水，或者是观看推土机推倒大楼。夜幕降临时分，从晚上9点来钟一直持续到午夜之后，孩子们聚集成团，10个一群，20个一伙儿，在街上闲逛，吵吵闹闹。我在伊武吉维克的那个夏天，年轻人常常闯入青年活动中心，偷取电子游戏机。在一处相邻的社区，一个少年犯罪集团用曲棍球和高尔夫球杆把一个男人痛打了一顿，而这个团伙中最年轻的孩子才12岁。

年纪大些的孩子有较好的选择。一些人在合作社或者市政局工作，负责开水车和污水车。一些像小孩一样游荡，但是带有更多的小玩意。有几个青年骑着脏兮兮的自行车到处乱窜，还有好几个带着苹果音乐播放器。冈斯特说唱音乐[1]在北部非常流行，甚至当地也有一支乐队，叫NCR（North Coast Rappers）——"北方海岸说唱歌手"。一天早上，我在合作社外面和一个穿着黑色牛仔叫卢卡斯的青年闲聊，他说可以介绍我认识乐队的一名成员。不出所料，我们见到的是一个面色凶恶的年轻人。他穿着一件宽松的T恤衫，上面印有说唱歌手图帕茨[2]的照片，头上系着块大头巾，弓着腰，塑料饰品从T恤衫里显露出来，他的名字也叫卢卡斯。这个卢卡斯淡定地点燃另一个卢卡斯奉上的香烟，谈论起NCR这个三人组合，这个组合通常跟随电脑合成的音乐节奏进行说唱。当我问他们说唱的内容时，卢卡斯沉思片刻，然后说："婊子和妓女，主要就是这些。"

---

[1] 冈斯特说唱音乐是嘻哈文化的分支，试图反映城市犯罪和城市青年人的暴力生活方式。也叫"暴徒"说唱乐。

[2] 图帕茨·沙库尔是一位很有影响力的说唱歌手、诗人和演员，1986年被谋杀。他是西海岸风格的说唱音乐创始人之一。

八月份的时候,我在合作社看到关于捕捉弓头鲸的宣传单,捕捉地点在距离海岸线几百公里的康吉苏爪克社区。弓头鲸可以活150多年,有5辆校车那么重。虽然努纳维克的因纽特人在长达一个世纪的时间里都没有捕到过一条,但是当地人从20世纪80年代中期就开始为之努力。在那个时候,哈得逊海峡的弓头鲸已经被列为"濒危物种",禁止捕捉。但因纽特人声称鲸鱼的数量众多。2005年,加拿大渔业和海洋部门的一项研究证实了因纽特人的观点。2008年,努纳维克的因纽特人获准捕捉一头弓头鲸。康吉苏爪克被选为捕捉地点,因为这里离弓头鲸的活动区域最近,而且当地居民捕捉能力也很出色。我给《努那斯克新闻》的编辑发了封电子邮件,这是一份用螺旋桨飞机在北极圈递送的报纸。编辑回复说他们愿意为这个故事和图片支付酬劳,于是我便搭上了一艘向南行驶的独木舟。

康吉苏爪克是一个有600人口的镇子,此时已经被挤得水泄不通。因纽特人因为有机会吃到弓头鲸的鲸皮而欣喜若狂。在一个狂风大作的日子,我加入了对弓头鲸追捕的尾随队伍。我们在镇外一个光秃秃的小山上野餐,从山上可以俯瞰到岩石丛生的海湾里停泊着几艘渔船和十几艘或者更多的独木舟。在用木板临时充当的桌子上面摆放着沙丁鱼罐头,三明治泡菜,乐之饼干①和猪肉罐头,还有一瓶奇妙酱②。一个留着时髦寸头的男人从水边向我们走来,他的双眼用遮光板挡着,女人们尖叫起来。他的两只手里各抓着一只肥硕闪亮的北极鲑鱼。两位戴着彩色大头巾以遮掩白发的妇女将鱼放在拆解了的硬纸盒上。我们蹲在泥土中,拿着随身携带的小刀和被称为乌卢刀的弯刃刀扑向鲑鱼,从鱼皮上取下鲜鱼肉吧嗒吧嗒地吃起来,就好像用汤匙舀葡萄柚吃一样。鱼肉是明橙色的,而且黏糊糊的。"嚼嚼骨头,"这位叫提维·曲马路克的渔夫说,"骨头是最好吃的。"

因纽特人2000多年前就来到了魁北克北部。冬天,他们在海岸边的冰屋里生活,用象牙尖的鱼叉在冰孔里刺穿海豹和海象。夏日,他们一路追踪驯鹿到内陆,在河流交叉处进行埋伏或者将动物驱赶到埋伏的弓箭手处。鲸鱼被多个海豹皮骨制成的独木舟围堵在浅水海湾里。猎狗制服北极熊后猎人们再用上刀子。但是,饥荒仍然是普遍现象。拖累群体的老年人被丢弃等死。在康吉苏爪克附近定居的部族比其他大部分部落情况要好一些。大潮汐在冰冻的海面下形成很多洞穴。通过凿穿表层的冰冻,人们可以在低潮时接近海水。在饥饿的时

---

① 乐之饼干是美国美国纳贝斯克食品公司在1934年创建的饼干品牌。
② 奇妙酱是美国卡夫食品公司生产的一种白色沙拉酱和三明治伴侣,主要在美国和加拿大出售。

候，猎人们在这些洞穴里找寻蚌类和藻类。"无数迹象表明，饥饿和饥荒总是伴随着杀婴的残忍行为，甚至连食人行为也不罕见。"20世纪的人类学家伯纳德·萨拉丁·德安格鲁尔写道，他曾经在康吉苏爪克呆过一段时间。

到19世纪晚期，哈德逊湾公司已经在努纳维克建立了若干个贸易站；1910年，一家法国皮毛公司"莱维安兄弟"（Révillon Frères）①在康吉苏爪克也开办了一个贸易站。因纽特猎人不再追捕猎物，而是开始寻找狐狸，因为他们可以用狐狸在贸易站交换渔网、猎枪和金属针。因纽特人开始在商店周围安营扎寨而不是在狩猎地点。他们也开始喜欢以前从未吃过的食物——面粉、饼干、糖蜜、茶和咖啡。但贸易站也带来了疾病和依赖性。北极圈中央的一位哈德逊湾商店经营者在1928的日志记载："大概15个家庭在此安营定居，他们不愿意打猎或者付出什么努力，满足于自己的贫穷状态，终日无所事事。"

到20世纪60年代，北部地区已经过于落后，加拿大政府开始采取措施逐步发展该片地区。教师、医疗工作者和警察被派往北部。政府建造起房屋和医院；警察将野狗围堵射杀；一些因纽特青少年不情愿地被送到南方学校去。政府的目的是要消除贫困，促进发展。因此对于他们来说，他们要做的就是给因纽特人提供西式教育和清除有病的狗。但是对因纽特人来说，这些举措似乎更像是阴险计划的一部分，是要毁灭他们的文化。

1975年，因纽特人和他们在南方的本土邻居克里族②共同抗议魁北克政府因为一项巨大的水电工程而占有他们的土地，并从所谓的"詹姆士湾和魁北克北部的协议"中获得了将近2.5亿元的收入。因纽特人应得的那份收入都用来创立马克维克公司了，这个公司是负责推动经济增长和培养因纽特自营生意的发展机构。马克维克公司现在广泛投资于建筑、运输、渔业、制革和航空等行业。他们最近还创建了一家游轮公司。

康吉苏爪克过去一直努力让自己被纳入冒险旅游地图之内。镇子的大部分资金都来自于附近的一家镍矿。最近以旅游为导向的项目包括一所养老院、一个社区游泳池和一个新酒店，酒店里的套房高达400元一晚，以及为一座遥远的省立公园而建的游客中心，这座公园保护着一个200万年历史的陨石坑，据说这个坑里存有地球上最纯净的水。

卢卡斯·皮鲁徒特是努那特利克地产公司的管理人，这家地产公司负责监督康吉苏爪克的发展。当我走进皮鲁徒特的办公室时，发现他独自一人坐在长长的办公桌的一端，用着笔记本电脑，戴着帽子，穿着牛仔裤和运动鞋。阳光

---

① Révillon Frères，英文名称为Revillon Brothers，是创建于1723的法国皮毛和奢侈品公司。
② 克里族是生活在加拿大中部的阿耳冈昆人的分支。

透过巨大的窗户照射进来,环绕镇子的山顶因为被刚降的夏雪所覆盖而隐约闪烁。他在高中时是个讨人喜欢的学生,但是在蒙特利尔学院念了三个学期后因为想家而辍学。他对我说:"问题不在于我是否去上学,而在于我因此不能去打猎了。"

皮鲁徒特还说,依赖性已经让一些人变的懒惰。加拿大和魁北克政府资助住房和医疗,很多因纽特人也收到了福利金。在2007年,镍的高价格使得矿厂获得了创纪录的利润,每个康吉苏爪克的因纽特居民都得到了4700美金。有的家庭一共得到了3万美金。他们购买了全地形汽车、轻型摩托车、雪上汽车、电动独木舟、电脑和平板电视。

但是靠旅游业挣钱则是另当别论,皮鲁徒特说。旅游业可以回归传统,而不是破坏传统。事实上,这样的事情正在发生。我们在谈话时,电话响了好几次。"太好了!"他在一次电话里大喊,然后转向我说,"我们接到个好消息,今天四艘橡皮船就到了。"当初是因纽特人发明了橡皮船,但是现在却没有一个努纳维克人知道如何操作这种船。康吉苏爪克地区不得不从魁北克南部订购橡皮艇,并从外面雇一个教练训练当地人。

在一个凉爽的夏日傍晚,我乘坐一艘政府的明橙色快艇进入海峡迎接弓头鲸的捕猎者们。太阳在薄云中慢慢降落,落日的余晖洒在地平线上犹如图画一般。"这对我们来说太特别了,"我们的领航员,一个叫徒马斯.皮鲁徒特的男人和我说,他欣喜地几乎说不出话来。"我们和祖先在一起了。"

猎人们放出火焰以表明自己的位置。当我们到达时,一条条的带脂鲸皮被送上船来,人们爆发出热烈的欢呼。"比白鲸味道好,"皮鲁徒特边嚼边说。很多道翠绿色的火焰在夜晚的天空翻滚——这是北极光在这个季节的首次出现。

鲸鱼被妥善地放置在纳努奇号上,船连夜航行,在晨光初露后不久到达了一个小镇附近的海湾。上周我曾跟捕鲸船来过这个小镇。弓头鲸被系在海湾边上三个橙色的浮标上,一把长刀插在它的头部,鲸鱼不断地摆动,直到下午潮水退去的时候。独木舟载来饥饿的观看者们,对鲸皮的切割开始了。那阿拉克.那帕阿鲁克是位备受尊敬的老人,也是唯一一位能记得过去关于弓头鲸猎人传说的在世老人。他坐在一块岩石上,身旁放了一块鲸皮,眼中饱含泪水。那帕阿鲁克在少年时曾射中了一头弓头鲸,但是那头鲸从冰中的水道逃跑了。"今天,我第一次看到人站在弓头鲸上,"他通过翻译告诉我。"这个场景令人无法自已。"本来打算用来翻转鲸鱼的推土机因故没有来到,大部分鲸鱼肉都腐烂了。当我三天后返回这里时,恶臭强烈刺鼻,以至于人们不禁呕吐起来。

　　捕捉驯鹿是一项完整无损地保留下来的传统。大约一百万只驯鹿栖息在努纳维克地区。当鹿群靠近镇子时，人们都从办公室跑出去了。到了八月中旬，康吉苏爪克的居民纷纷议论，说鹿群已经靠近。一天早上，我在杂货店遇到了那个抓到北极鲑鱼的男人提维，他邀请我第二天和他一起去打猎。

　　提维在小时候与哥哥一起寻找鸟蛋时，猎杀了第一头驯鹿，那时候他还只有9岁，哥哥长他5岁。因为无法独自拆解尸体，两个男孩子跑回去告诉母亲。"她非常兴奋，"提维说，"她好像高兴地都叫了出来。"在提维青少年时期，他做过垃圾工；在21岁时，他在镍矿里找了份粉碎岩石的工作，每半个月能挣到2500元。

　　提维娶了矿上的一位清洁工，他们搬到一起生活，住在哈得逊海峡上一个叫做沙鲁伊的镇子。但是这场婚姻却是场噩梦。他们经常打架；有一次她还咬了他，在他的二头肌上留下了一个明显的伤疤。还有一次她将一个牛排餐刀插进了他的胸膛。为了打破伤风针，提维被用直升飞机护送到位于努纳维克另一端的一家医院。一天晚上，当她熟睡时，提维只是带了几件衣服就偷偷溜走了。在拜访住在普维瑞尼克的表妹时，他认识了另一个叫伊莉萨皮的表妹。"很多不同的女孩都想和我在一起，但是我都拒绝了，因为见到了伊莉萨皮，而我只喜欢她，"提维说。"她非常漂亮。"他们最近结婚了。

　　上午九点我在提维的家里见到他。他穿着淤泥靴和浸满油渍的裤子，戴着一顶猎帽。提维扛着一把来福步枪用来打驯鹿，一把鸟枪用来打鹅。一起同行的还有他的阿姨奇拉克，他的弟弟吉米。吉米开着辆二手的全地形车尾随在后。在一处有弯折岩石图案的山脊上，提维指着一片露出地面的闪闪发光的岩层，原来这里是雕刻工来取皂石①的地方。积云笼罩了天空，从云隙射下的阳光将青苔映照得呈红色和橘色。"可能是有一些金子微粒，"我们在跨越一条河流时提维说。"我们的土地里到处是矿物质。"

　　我们从一处松软的斜坡下来，泥水从轮胎上四处飞溅，然后围着一个湖绕了几圈。上周吉米和奇拉克在这里撒下了渔网，现在提维和奇拉克将渔网卷起，大概有半打活蹦乱跳的北极鲑。"非常新鲜，心脏还在跳呢，"提维说。奇拉克将雌鱼的肚子划开，哀叹起来——原来两只都有了卵。我把宽大的三明治袋子撑开大口，奇拉克把一个又长又黏的小包裹放进去。

　　我们坐在水边，吧嗒吧嗒地吃着鱼翼上的橘色鲜肉。鱼肉很黏也很有嚼劲，

---

① 皂石是一种软质、重而紧密的滑石，有光滑手感，用做炉边、桌面和装饰物。

像一块肥牛排。新鲜的鱼血是甜甜的。我们从暖水瓶里倒些茶喝，还吃了袋装的饼干。提维抽了两支烟后我们就离开了。湖上方一条泥泞的小路将我们带到下一个山脊。北极罂粟在微风中摇曳。吉米发现了雪雁。

"因为有风，所以它们会降落的，"提维说。我们都下车蹲在地上。吉米和我跟随着提维沿着低矮的岩石山脊后面的一条狭长的湿地前行，我们几乎是匍匐前进。当大雁飞起时，他们马上开火射击。两只鸟从天而落。一只大雁四肢平躺在冻土上，两只翅膀还在扑腾。它那美丽的白色外衣般的羽毛被一片红色血污弄脏了。提维用双臂压住它的胸膛，大雁的脖子慢慢抬起，头部向一边翘起，大口喘气。"现在，它马上就要死了，因为我按着它的肺了。"提维说。

砰，轻轻地响了一声，大雁的脑袋垂了下来。"好哇！"提维一边剥着克莱门氏小柑橘①一边说。他把果皮随便一扔，给了我半个橘子。奇拉克笑容满面地看着我，"这次的经历会让你终生难忘的。"

河里的一条山脊在夕阳下呈现出裸色，奇拉克发现了一只大公鹿。提维慢慢地把胳膊伸到头上，弯曲肘部，手指向上指，模仿鹿角的样子。大公鹿先是专心地盯着我们看了一会，然后继续觅食。它身旁的一只小公鹿亦步亦趋。我们溅着水花趟过河流，在山脊的掩护下不断加速接近公鹿。那一对硕大的鹿角在山顶上的有纹理的光线下清晰可见。

"低下身子，"提维说。他悄悄爬上山脊，躲在一块岩石后面，射了几枪。公鹿疯了一般向前狂奔然后停了下来，似乎不知道下一步该去往何方。提维又射了一枪，公鹿开始摇晃，它那巨大的头颅垂到了地上，但是眼睛仍然睁着。随后身体轰然倒下，艰难的、痉挛式的呼吸从地上传来。小公鹿停留了片刻后一溜烟地跑掉了。

每个人都拿出了刀子；提维则是一手一个。公鹿侧躺着，胸膛还在起伏。提维用刀子从后面戳进去，公鹿狠狠地踢了几下蹄子。提维将刀刺入公鹿的脖子，然后来回搅动刀片。当夜幕降临时，三个因纽特人已经肢解了尸体。除了头部和肠子，一切都被取走了。提维把他的那份包在一个包裹里——心脏、两条后腿、里脊、胃和肋骨。在重新越过河流时，我们洗了手，用手掌捧了点冰冷的河水喝。"我都洗干净了。"提维说。

在康吉苏爪克停留的最后一周，我结识了迪昂神父，一位来自于比利时的天主教神父，他已经在努纳维克居住了将近50年。迪昂神父身材矮小，满脸皱纹，而且他主持的集会规模也在日渐缩小，但是他却是个声粗如牛的人。他总

---

① 克莱门氏小柑橘是一种生长在地中海或者南非的蜜橘品种。

是高声大笑，说话带着浓厚的法国口音。他要求镇上的所有人都要对他恭敬有加，不管是年轻的还是年老的，因纽特人还是非因纽特人。他的教堂是位于镇子中心的一座微型建筑，迪昂神父就住在这里。我在飘着蒙蒙细雨的一天去敲门，他没有听到敲门声。我便径直走了进来，看到迪昂神父坐在躺椅上，穿着袜子和皮凉鞋，上身穿了件天蓝色毛衣，正在看 CNN① 的节目。

　　神父用力地与我握手，用一个老式微波炉给我热了杯茶，与茶一起端来的还有一包饼干里的最后两块。神父递给我一副宽度超过长度的象牙望远镜，建议我眺望哈得逊海峡，他在这里是可以清楚看到的。在神父 19 岁时，德国人入侵比利时。那时他还在神学院读书，也参加了战争。当战争结束时，神父面临两个选择：一是留在自己的国家，在一所医院工作；一是作为传教士前往刚果。他选择了刚果，两年可怕的时光。"那里很热，"神父说。"很多动物，很多疾病。"之后，他要求被派往北极圈，比利时在这里也驻扎了一些传教士。神父于 1964 年到达努纳维克，并在一个叫做夸克塔克的 300 人小社区度过了最初的 9 年。他在一场饥荒中幸存下来，曾经从一辆机动雪橇摔到冰上却大难不死。"我对这里的人们充满敬意，佩服他们能在这样恶劣的环境中生存下来，"神父说。"我非常非常欣赏他们。"

　　迪昂神父向我解释了一些普遍的错误看法。比如狗被射杀是因为它们过于饥饿并吃过因纽特婴儿；政府强加给因纽特人的教育其实有助于培养更聪明的下一代领导人。他不喜欢的一个变化是牵涉到教堂的。较新的社区成员现在信奉五旬节派教会②，这个教会吵闹而狂热的宗教仪式使一些人认为这个教会是萨满教③的复苏。因纽特人曾经依赖于萨满教僧给他们的打猎带来好结果或者帮助他们摆脱饥荒，但是萨满教僧也会带来死亡。"当萨满教僧消失时，是一种解放，"迪昂神父说，后来萨满教僧被罗马天主教所取代。

　　我问迪昂神父，随着努纳维克的现代化，因纽特人是不是生活的更好。迪昂神父肃穆沉吟，望向窗外灰色的镇子：此时潮水正在退去，在岩石之间留下黑色的水坑，外面一辆垃圾车经过。"我刚到这里时，这片土地还是一片空旷，"他说道，"什么都没有。没有房屋，什么都没有。人们夏天住在帐篷里，冬天住在冰屋里。现在，他们有足够的食物，温暖的房子，运输，交流。他们不再为生存而打斗。"

　　在我即将离开之前，提维开始了一份管理养老院的新工作。我前去和他道

---

　　① Cable News Network；美国有线电视新闻网络。
　　② 五旬节派教会是基督教新教宗派之一，19 世纪发源于美国，强调直接灵感，信奉信仰治疗。
　　③ 萨满教是亚洲北部的原始宗教，是一类涉及到诊断、治疗与引发病等能力的传统信仰及实践，有时因为与灵魂的特殊的关系、或对灵魂的控制而造成人们的苦难。

别，在养老院看到一个穿着粉色睡袍的胖女人正在研究一块欧洲雪景森林的拼图。这个地方还能闻到新家具和清洁剂的味道。提维把我带到他的办公室，四面墙都是光秃秃的，提维用胶布在窗户上粘了个黑色垃圾袋来遮挡阳光。他的办公桌上有一个平板电脑；屏保是他儿子在捕弓头鲸时拍的一张照片。"所以呢，"提维指着办公室里的物件说，"我有了份好工作。"

夏天结束了，我在第一场暴风雪来临的前几天返回了库朱阿克。九月中旬，我飞往蒙特利尔，随后登上一辆驶往边境的长途公共汽车。我乘坐的公共汽车在午夜时分到达美国，黎明时分我已身在纽约。这里天气温暖，微风徐徐，城市里依旧充满了夏日的味道。我开始了在《奥杜邦》①杂志的实习工作，但挣得钱还不够租间公寓的，因此我搬去与郊区的父母同住。我的房间还是青少年时的装饰，墙上贴着海报，都是一些关于阴谋或者外星人的影片。在这样的房间里我无法入睡，我就在一片树林里支起了帐篷，我童年时代养过的一条狗就埋葬于此。

我想象着，一片辽远的土地掩映在广袤的森林里，那里有这样一个民族：他们仍然记得祖先生活和劳作的方式，仍然有萨满教众，从没有人听说过上帝。我不知道那个地方还能延续多久，或者即使值得延续，但无疑也会很快逝去。

枯黄的树叶和橙子掉落下来，给森林的地面铺上了一层彩色的垫子。帐篷破了洞，蜘蛛搬了进来。天气变冷了，我要搬走了。我的实习工作为我挣了些钱，够在布鲁克林找个便宜住处的了。

（张小薪 译　张慧芳 校）

---

① 奥杜邦学会（Audubon 学会）是美国的一个非赢利性民间环保组织，这一组织以美国著名画家、博物学家奥杜邦来命名，专注于自然保育。奥杜邦学会建立于 1886 年，是世界上同类组织中历史最悠久的。取名为奥杜邦学会旨在纪念美国鸟类学家、博物学家和画家约翰·詹姆斯·奥杜邦。奥杜邦学会出版一本名叫奥杜邦的画报，这本杂志以自然为主要主题，专注于鸟类研究。

第一编　沙漠游记

"沙漠之所以存在,是因为它们梦想着绿洲。"沙漠之旅不在于欣赏风景,而在于对葱茏自然景色的反观。……

The Truck

Ryszard Kapuscinski
Translated by Klara Glowczweska

【导读】18 世纪感伤主义诗歌代表作《墓园挽歌》里有一句传诵千古的名句："多少花儿寂然绽放，枉费芬芳在荒漠。"（Many a flower were born unseen; waste its sweetness on the desert air.）诗句中的伤感、惆怅、悲怆、凄美正是《撒哈拉的卡车》一文的基调。这篇文章有极强的画面感：广漠浩瀚寂寥、杳无人烟的撒哈拉沙漠也了无其它生命的痕迹，一辆试图穿越沙漠的卡车抛锚难行；两个来自不同世界、语言不通的男人，一个是对西方文明产物——卡车——捉摸不透的大漠司机，一个是来自西方、却对荒漠生活毫无经验的、搭乘顺风车的大漠旅者；司机高大威武、体格健壮，拥有生命之水，而旅者疲惫虚弱、焦渴难耐，却滴水未带；旅者在焦渴之中对"生命与水"这一永恒母题进行了天马行空般的思索；在他因缺水而生命垂危之时，眼前出现了美丽的幻境：葱茏的棕榈林，波光淼淼的蓝色湖泊。文章的点睛之笔颇耐人寻味："肮脏的沙漠之水延长了我的生命，却夺走了我的天堂美景。"（在极端的生存环境中，与陌路人分享生命之水的卡车司机、放弃优势文化与文明而甘愿备尝沙漠生活的原始和艰辛的踽踽行者、乃至传说中与干燥酷热抗争而自创生命之水的沙漠小甲虫，他们都是寂然绽放的荒漠之花。）热爱生命，尊重生命，创造生命，不管是在绿洲，还是在荒漠，不管人间，还是天堂，花儿虽然寂然绽放，但其芬芳却不会枉费。但，永远牢记，荒漠的存在是因着对绿洲的渴望！

In the darkness, I spotted two glaring lights. They were far away and moved about violently, as if they were the eyes of a wild animal thrashing in its cage. I was sitting on a stone at the edge of the Ouadane oasis in the Sahara, northeast of Nouakchott, the Mauritanian capital. For an entire week now, I had been trying to leave this place – to no avail. It is difficult to get to Ouadane, but even more difficult to depart. No marked or paved road leads to it, and there is no scheduled transport. Every few days – or weeks – a truck will pass, and if the driver agrees to take you with him you go; if not, you simply stay, waiting who knows how long for the next opportunity.

The Mauritanians who were sitting beside me stirred. The night chill had set in, a chill that descends abruptly and, after the burning hell of the sun-filled days, can be almost piercingly painful. It is a cold from which no sheepskin or quilt can adequately protect you. These people had nothing but old, frayed blankets, in which they sat tightly wrapped, motionless, like statues.

A black pipe poked out of the ground nearby. This was the region's sole gas station, and passing vehicles always stopped here. There was no other attraction in the oasis. Ordinarily, the days went by uneventfully and unchangeably, resembling in this the monotony of the desert climate: the same sun always shone, hot and solitary, in the same empty, cloudless sky.

At the sight of the still distant headlights, the Mauritanians began talking among themselves. I didn't understand a word of their languages. It's quite possible that they were saying, "At last! It's finally coming! We have lived to see it!"

It was recompense for the long days spent waiting, gazing patiently at the inert horizon, on which no moving object, no living thing that might rouse you from the numbness of hopeless anticipation, had appeared for a long time. The arrival of a truck – cars are too fragile for this terrain – didn't' fundamentally alter the lives of the people. The vehicle usually stopped for a moment and then quickly drove on. Yet even this brief sojourn was vital to them: it injected variety into their lives, provided a subject for later conversation, and, above all, was both material proof of the existence of another world and a bracing confirmation that that world, since it had sent them a mechanical envoy, must know that they existed.

Perhaps they were also engaged in a routine debate: Will it – or won't it – get here? Travelling in these corners of the Sahara is a risky, unending lottery, perpetual uncertainty. Along these roadless expanse full of crevices, sinkholes, protruding boulders, sand dunes and rocky mounds, loose stones and fields of slippery gravel, a vehicle advances at a snail's pace – several kilometers an hour. Each wheel has its own drive, and each one, meter by meter, turning here, stopping there, going up, down, or around, searches for something to grip. Most of the time, the sum of these persistent efforts and exertions, which are accompanied by the roar of the straining and overheated engine and by the bone-bruising lunges of the swaying platform, finally results in the truck's moving forward.

But the Mauritanians also knew that a truck could get hopelessly stuck – sometimes just a step away from the oasis, on its very threshold. This can happen when a storm moves mountains of sand onto the track. Either the truck's occupants manage to dig out the road or the driver finds a detour – or he simply turns around and goes back where he came from. Another storm will eventually move the dunes farther, and clear the way once more.

This time, however, the electric lights were drawing nearer and nearer. At a certain moment, their glow started to pick out the crowns of date palms that had been hidden in darkness, and the shabby walls of much huts, and the goats and cows asleep by the side of the road, until, finally, tailing clouds of dust behind it, an enormous Berliet[①] truck drew to a stop in front of us, with a clang and a thud of metal. Berliets are French-made trucks adapted for roadless desert terrain. They have large wheels with wide tires, and air filters mounted high atop their hoods. Because of their great size and the prominent shape of the air filter, from a distance they resemble the fronts of old steam engines.

The driver climbed down from the cab using a ladder – a dark skinned, barefoot Mauritanian in an ankle-length indigo djellabah. He was, like the majority of his countrymen, tall and powerfully built. People and animals with substantial body weight endure tropical heat better.

The Mauritanians from the oasis surrounded the driver. A cacophony of greetings, questions, and well-wishings erupted. This went on and on. Everybody was shouting and gesticulating, as if haggling in a noisy marketplace. After a while, they began to point at me. I was a pitiful sight – dirty, unshaved, and, above all, wasted by the nightmarish heat of the Sahara summer. An experienced Frenchman had warned me earlier: It will feel as if someone were sticking a knife into you. Into your back. Into your head. At noon, the rays of the sun beat down with the force of a knife.

The driver looked at me and at first said nothing. Then he motioned toward the truck with his hand and called out to me – "*Yallah!*" ("Let's go ! We are off!") I climbed into the cab and slammed the door shut. We set off immediately.

---

① A French automobile company.

I had no sense of where we were going. Sand flashed by in the glow of the headlights, shimmering with different shades, laced with strips of gravel and shards of rock. The wheels reared up on granite ledges or sank down into hollows and stony fissures. In the deep, black night, one could see only two spots of light – two bright, clearly outlined orbs, sliding over the surface of the desert. Nothing else was visible.

Before long, I began to suspect that we were driving blindly, on a shortcut to somewhere, because there were no demarcation points, no signs, posts, or any other traces of a roadway. I tried to question the driver. I gestured at the darkness around us and asked, "Nouakchott?"

He looked at me and laughed. "Nouakchott?" He repeated this dreamily, as if it were the Hanging Gardens of Semiramis[①] that I was asking him about – so beautiful, but for us lowly ones too high to reach. I concluded from this that we were not headed in the direction I desired, but I did not know how to ask him where, in that case, we were going. I desperately wanted to establish some contact with him, to get to know him even a little. "Ryszard," I said, pointing at myself. Then I pointed at him. He understood. "Salim," he said, and laughed again. Silence fell. We must have come upon a smooth stretch of desert, for the Berliet began to roll along more gently and quickly (exactly how fast I don't know, since all the instruments were broken). We drove on for a time without speaking, until finally I fell asleep.

A sudden silence awoke me. The engine had stopped. The truck stood still. Salim was pressing on the gas pedal and turning the key in the ignition. The battery was working – the starter, too – but the engine emitted no sound. It was morning, and already light outside. He began searching around the cab for the lever that opens the hood. This struck me at once as odd and suspicious: a driver who doesn't know how to open the hood? Eventually, he figured out that the latches that needed to be released were on the outside. He then stood on a fender and began to inspect the engine, but he peered at its intricate construction as if he were seeing it for the first time. He would touch something, try to move it, but his gestures were those of an amateur. Every now and then, he would climb into the cab and turn the key in the ignition, but the engine remained dead silent. He located the toolbox, but there wasn't much in it. He pulled out a hammer, several wrenches, screwdrivers. Then he

---

① The Hanging Gardens of Babylon. Semiramis refers to one of several legendary queens in the ancient Assyrian kingdom, and the Hanging Gardens of Babylon were built for Semiramis Ⅱ.

started to take the engine apart.

I stepped down from the cab. All around us was desert. Sand, with dark stones scattered about. Nearby, a large black oval rock. (In the hours following noon, after it had been warmed by the sun, it would radiate heat like a steel-mill oven.) A moonscape, delineated by a level horizon – the earth ends, and then there's nothing but sky and more sky. No hills. No dunes. Not a single leaf. And, of course, no water. Water! It's what instantly comes to mind in such circumstances. In the desert, the first thing a man sees when he opens his eyes in the morning is the face of his enemy – the flaming visage of the sun. The sight elicits in him a reflexive gesture of self-preservation: he reaches for water. Drink! Drink! Only by doing so can he ever so slightly improve his odds in the desert's eternal struggle – the desperate duel with the sun.

I resolved to look around for water, for I had none with me. I found nothing in the cab. But I did discover some: attached with ropes to the bed of the truck, near the rear, underneath, were four goatskins, two on the left side and two on the right. The hides had been rather poorly cured, then sewed together in such a way that they retained the animal's shape. A goat's leg served as a drinking spout.

I sighed with relief, but only momentarily. I began to calculate. Without water, you can survive in the desert for twenty-four hours; with great difficulty, for forty-eight or so. The math is simple. Under these conditions, you secrete in one day approximately ten liters of sweat, and to survive you must drink a similar amount of water. Deprived of it, you will immediately start to feel thirsty. Genuine, prolonged thirst in a hot and dry climate is an exhausting, ravaging sensation, harder to control than hunger. After a few hours, you become lethargic and limp, weak and disoriented. Instead of speaking, you babble, ever less cogently. That same evening, or the next day, you get a high fever and quickly die.

If Salim doesn't share his water, I thought, I will die today. Even if he does, we will have only enough left for one more day – which means we will both die tomorrow, or the day after, at the latest.

Trying to stop these thoughts, I began to observe him closely. Covered with grease and sweating, Salim was still taking the engine apart, unscrewing screws and removing cables, but with no rhyme or reason, like a child furiously destroying a toy that won't work. On the fenders, on the bumper, lay countless springs, valves, compression rings, and wires, some had already fallen to the ground. I left him and went around to the other side of the truck, where there was still some shade. I sat down on the ground and leaned on back against the wheel.

Salim.

I knew nothing about the man who held my life in his hands. Or, at least, who held it for this one day. I thought, If Salim chases me away from the truck and the water – after all, he has a hammer in his hand and probably a knife in his pocket, and, on top of that, enjoys a significant physical advantage – if he orders me to leave and march off into the desert, I won't last even until the nightfall. And it seemed to me that that was precisely what he might choose to do. He would thereby extend his life, after all – or, if help arrived in time, he might even save it.

Clearly Salim was not a professional driver, or, at any rate, not a driver of a Berliet truck. He also didn't know the area well. (On the other hand, can one really know the desert, where successive storms and tempests constantly alter the landscape, moving mountains of sand to ever-different sites and transporting the natural features?) It was common practice in these parts for someone – perhaps after a small financial windfall – to hire another person with less money to carry out his tasks for him. Maybe the rightful driver of this truck had hired Salim to take it in his stead. And in Mauritania no one will ever admit to not knowing or not being capable of something. If you approach a taxi driver in the city, show him an address, and ask him if he knows where it is, he will say yes without a second's hesitation. And only later, when you are driving all over the city, round and round, do you fully realize that he has no idea where to go.

The sun was climbing higher. The desert, that motionless, petrified ocean, absorbed its rays, grew hotter, and began to burn. The Yoruba[①] are said to believe that if a man's shadow abandons him he will die. All the shadows were beginning to shrink, dwindle, fade. The dread afternoon hours were almost upon us – the time of day when people and objects have no shade, exist and yet do not exist, reduced to a glowing, incandescent whiteness.

I thought that this moment had arrived, but suddenly I noticed before me an utter different sight. The lifeless, still horizon – so crushed by the heat that it seemed

---

① One of the largest ethnic groups in West Africa.

nothing could ever issue forth from it – all at once sprang to life and became green. As far as the eye could see stood tall, magnificent palm trees, entire groves of them along the horizon, growing thickly, without interruption. I also saw lakes – yes, enormous blue lakes, with animated, undulating surface. Gorgeous shrubs grew there, with wide-spreading branches of a fresh, intense, succulent deep green. All this shimmered continuously, sparkled, pulsated – as if it were wreathed in a light mist, soft-edged and elusive.

"Salim!" I called. "Salim!"

A head emerged from under the hood. He looked at me.

"Salim!" I repeated once more, and pointed.

Salim glanced where I had shown him, unimpressed. In my dirty, sweat face he must have read wonder, bewilderment, and rapture – and something else besides, which clearly alarmed him, for he walked up to the side of the truck, untied one of the goatskins, took a few sips, and wordlessly handed me the rest. I grabbed the rough leather sack and began to drink. Suddenly dizzy, I leaned my shoulder against the truck bed so as not to fall. I drank and drank, sucking fiercely on the goat's leg and still staring at the horizon. But as I felt my thirst subsiding, and the madness within me dying down, the green vista began to vanish. Its colors paled, its contours blurred. By the time I had emptied the goatskin, the horizon was once again that, empty, and lifeless. The water, disgusting Sahara water – warm, dirty, thick with sand and sludge – extended my life but took away my vision of paradise. The crucial thing, though, was the fact that Salim himself had given me the water to drink. I stopped being afraid of him. I felt that I was safe – if only until we were down to our last sip.

We spent the second half of the day lying underneath the truck, in its faint, bleached shade. In this world circled all about with flaming horizons, Salim and I were the only life. I inspected the ground within my arm's reach, the nearest stones, searching for some living thing, anything that might twitch, move, slither. I remembered that somewhere in the Sahara there lives a small beetle that the Tuareg[①] call Ngubi. When it is very hot, according to legend, Ngubi is tormented by thirst, desperate to drink. Unfortunately, there is no water anywhere, and only burning sand

---

① The *Tuareg* people are nomads of the Sahara who speak various *Tuareg* languages.

all around. So the small beetle chooses an incline – this can be a sloping fold of sand – and with determination begins to climb to the summit. It is an enormous effort, a Sisyphean task[①], because the hot and loose sand constantly gives way, carrying the beetle down with it, right back to where he began his toils. Which is why, before long, the beetle starts to sweat. A drop of moisture collects at the end of his abdomen, and swells. Then Ngubi stops climbing, curls up, and plunges his mouth into that very bead.

He drinks.

Salim has several biscuits in a paper bag. We drink the second goatskin of water. Two remain. I consider writing something. (It occurs to me that this is often done at such moments.) But I don't have the strength. I'm not really in pain. It's just that everything is becoming empty. And within this emptiness another one is growing.

Then, in the darkness, two glaring lights. They are far away and move about violently. Soon the sound of a motor draws near, and I see the truck, hear voices in a language I do not understand. "Salim!" I say. Several dark faces, resembling his, lean over me.

---

① An endless and meaningless task. In Greek mythology Sisyphus was a king punished by being compelled to roll an immense boulder up a hill, only to watch it roll back down, and to repeat this throughout eternity.

撒哈拉的卡车[①]

雷沙德·卡普钦斯基

卡拉拉·葛洛齐斯卡译

  黑暗中，我看见两盏耀眼的灯。灯光还离得很远，剧烈地晃动着，如同拼命挣扎的困兽的眼睛。撒哈拉沙漠中的绿洲瓦丹位于毛里塔尼亚首都努瓦克肖特的东北部。此刻，我正坐在瓦丹边界的一块石头上。整整一个星期，我一直在设法离开这里——但白费力气。抵达瓦丹很难，离开瓦丹更是难上加难。没有任何路标指向这里，没有铺设好的路通向这里，也没有按时准点的班车抵达这里。每隔几天——或者几周——有辆卡车会路过这里，而且是，如果司机同意带上你，你就跟他走；如果不同意，那你只得待着，等下一次机会，至于等多久就没人知道了。

  坐在我旁边的毛里塔尼亚人骚动起来。夜间的寒冷袭来。白天阳光暴晒，灼热得像地狱，到了夜里，寒冷骤然而至，冷得刺骨疼。这种冷，不管是羊皮还是被子都难以抵御。这里的人没什么别的，只有磨损坏的旧毯子；他们把毯子紧紧地包裹在身上，就那么一动不动地坐着，雕塑一般。不远处，一条黑色的管道翘出地面。这是当地唯一的一处加油站，路过的车辆总是在这里停靠。绿洲里没有其它引人注意的东西。通常情况下，日子波澜不惊、一成不变地过着，极像沙漠气候的单一：天空总是那么空旷，那么万里无云，同样的日头总是那么照耀着，热烈而寥落。

  一看到尚在远处的大灯，毛里塔尼亚人就开始自顾自地说起话来。我对他们的语言一窍不通。很可能，他们是在说："终于！它总算是来了！我们总算是在有生之年看到它了！"

  这是对你的回报：数日以来，漫长的等待，耐心地注视着了无生气的地平线；就这么无望地期待着，长久地等着，等得麻木起来；而地平线上没有任何移动着的东西、没有任何可以把你从麻木中唤醒的活物。卡车的到来——在这样的地区，汽车太过于娇贵了——并没有从根本上改变这里的人们的生活。车辆通常只停一会儿，之后很快就又上路了。然而，即便这短暂的停留对他们也

  [①] 本文的英语原文是译文，由美国知名杂志人 Klara Glowczewska 由 Ryszard Kapuscinski 撰写的波兰语原文翻译而来。

是至关重要的：它给他们的生活注入了变化，为他们提供了谈资，最为重要的是，它既不折不扣地证明着另外一个世界的存在，又令人振奋地证实了那个世界也肯定知道他们的存在，因为那个世界给他们派来个机械信使。

或许他们也乐此不疲地重复着一场辩论：它会——还是不会——到这里来？在撒哈拉如此偏远的角落旅行是一种危险的、永不知道结果的博彩，不确定性永远存在。在无路可走的浩瀚沙漠中，到处都是裂缝、陷坑、沙丘、巨砾、石头堆、松动的石块、滑溜的砾石地，在这样的地面上，车辆开起来如同蜗牛爬——一小时走不了几公里。每一个轮子都在艰难前行，每一个轮子，一米一米地，在这里转弯，在那里停下，爬上，爬下，打转，寻找着可以抓握的东西。大多数时间里，这些坚持不懈的努力和挣扎，伴随着使用过度、热得发烫的引擎的呼号，还有左摇右晃的车身使人骨裂的猛冲。所有的这些加在一起才最终使得卡车朝前移动。

但是，毛里塔尼亚人也知道，卡车很可能会抛锚，令人无计可施——有时离绿洲只有一步之遥，就停在绿洲的门槛上。这种情况会发生在风暴把成座成座的沙山搬移到行车路线上的时候。这时候，要么是卡车的乘客下去挖路，要么是司机绕道行驶——或者干脆调转车头，从哪儿来回哪儿去。再来一场风暴，沙丘最终会被搬移走，道路就会重新出现。

然而，这一次，灯光越来越近。慢慢地，灯光开始照在藏在黑暗中的沙枣树的树冠上，接着照在棚屋破败的墙上，然后照在睡在路边的山羊和母牛的身上，直到最后，车尾带着团团尘雾，一辆巨大的贝利埃①卡车叮叮哐哐地停在我们面前。贝利埃是法国制造的卡车，经过改装以适应无路可行的沙漠。这种卡车的轮子很大，车胎很宽，空气过滤器高高地架在前机盖上面。这种车的体型过大，空气过滤器的形状过于突出，远远看去，很像古老的蒸汽机的前部。

司机借助一架梯子从司机室里爬了下来——是位黑皮肤、打赤脚的毛里塔尼亚人，穿一件长及脚踝的靛青色带帽风衣。和他的大多数同胞们一样，这位司机身材高大、体格健壮。不管是人，还是牲畜，拥有足够的体重才能更好地忍耐热带地区的酷热。

绿洲里的毛里塔尼亚人把司机团团围住。人们七嘴八舌地打着招呼，问着问题，送着祝福，一发而不可收。人人都叫嚷着，比划着，好似在嘈杂的市场讨价还价。过了一会儿，他们开始指着我说了。我的光景实在令人可怜——脏兮兮的，胡子拉碴，更为显眼的是，受尽撒哈拉夏季梦魇般的酷热而衰弱不堪。早些时候，一位经验丰富的法国人警告过我：那感觉仿佛是有人拿刀捅你，捅

---

① 一家法国汽车公司。

你的背，捅你的头。中午时分，太阳光刀一样地刺射着。

司机看了看我，开始什么也没说。过了会儿，他指指卡车，向我喊道——"Yallah"（"走吧！我们出发了！"）我爬进司机室，砰地关上门。我们立刻就出发了。

我们要去哪儿，我毫无感觉。在卡车大灯的光线里，沙子飞闪而过，明暗不定，夹带着砾石条和岩石片。车轮子一会儿被花岗岩岩礁撬起来，一会儿陷进沙沟里或石头缝里。在深沉漆黑的夜里，人所能看到的只有两个光圈——两个明亮的、轮廓清晰的圆圈，划过沙漠的地表。除此之外，什么都隐而不现。

没过多久，我就开始怀疑我们只是盲目前行，抄近道开往某个地方，因为根本没有任何的地界，没有任何标牌，没有任何标杆，或者其它任何路的痕迹。我尝试着问一问司机。我向着四周的黑暗比划着，问道："努瓦克肖特？"

他看了看我，笑了起来。"努瓦克肖特？"他梦幻般地重复着这个词，仿佛我问他的是塞米勒米斯的空中花园①——美丽如斯，但对我们这些卑微的人来说，那花园高得难以企及。我以此判定我们并不是朝着我想去的方向行走，但我不知道怎么问他我们到底是往哪儿走。我玩儿命地想与他做些沟通，了解他一点儿是一点儿。"莱斯萨尔德，"我指着我自己说到。然后，我又指指他。他懂了。"萨利姆，"他说，又笑了起来。又是一阵沉默。我们肯定走在一片平缓的沙地上，因为贝利埃卡车此刻行驶得比较温和也比较快（到底有多快，我不知道，因为所有的仪表盘都是坏的）。我们行驶着，谁也不说话，后来，我就睡着了。

突如其来的沉寂把我惊醒。引擎不转了。卡车动不了了。萨利姆使劲踩油门、转动钥匙打火。电池没问题——起动机也没问题——但引擎一点动静没有。已经是清晨了，外面已经有了天光。他在司机室里查找打开前机盖的拉杆。这立即使我感到奇怪和怀疑：一位司机却不知道怎么打开前机盖？后来，他总算弄明白，需要打开的阀门在车外面。然后，他站在一个挡泥板上查看引擎，但他大眼瞪小眼地看着她复杂的构造，那样子仿佛是第一次见到这玩意儿。他这儿摸摸，那儿弄弄，但完全一副外行的架势。他时不时地爬回到司机室，转动钥匙打火，然而引擎依然毫无动静。他找到了工具箱，但里面也没什么可用的东西。他拿出一把锤子，几把扳手，几把螺丝刀。然后就开始拆卸引擎。

---

① 就是古巴比伦空中花园。塞米勒米斯指的是古亚述王朝的王后，据说巴比伦空中花园是为塞米勒米斯二世所建造。

我从司机室里走了出来。四周全是沙漠。沙子，还有散落在沙子上的深色石头。不远处，有一大块黑色的椭圆形岩石。（在接近中午的几个小时内，被太阳晒热后，这块岩石就会像炼钢炉一样释放出热量。）一派月球风光，周边勾画着平直的地平线——土地消失了，除了天空还是天空，一无它物。没有山丘。没有沙丘。连一片叶子也没有。而且，当然，没有水。水！在如此情形下，第一时间跃入脑海的就是它了。在沙漠中，清晨，人们睁开眼睛看见的第一件东西就是敌人的脸——太阳那火光四射的脸庞。这一照面立即引发了人体内自我保护的条件反射：要水。喝呀！喝！只有这样才能略微改善人们在沙漠中永久抗争的力量悬殊——与太阳的拼死决斗。

我下定决心四下找水，因为我一滴水也没带。在司机室里什么也没找到。但我还是找到了一些：在卡车车身底部靠近后面的地方，用绳子绑缚着四个山羊皮口袋，左边两个，右边两个。羊皮加工得非常粗糙，然后又缝合成山羊的形状。一条羊腿用作喝水的喷口。

我得救般地出了口长气，不过只那么一小会儿。我计算起来。没有水，你在沙漠中能存活 24 小时；再挣扎着坚持一下，大约能活 48 小时。算起来很简单。在这样的条件下，你一天分泌大约十升汗液，而要活下去你务必要喝同等容积的水。喝不到水，你会立即感到干渴。在炎热干燥的气候中，真正的、长久的干渴让人精疲力竭，对人的损害很大，这种感觉比饥饿更难控制。数小时后，你就变得昏昏欲睡，软弱无力，神志不清。这时，你言语不清，梦言呓语，语意模糊。当天晚上，抑或转天，你就会高烧不退，快速死去。

如果萨利姆不给我水喝，我暗自思忖，今天我就会死掉。即便是他给我水喝，我们也只够多撑一天——也就是说，明天我们两个双双死去，或者，至多活到后天。

为了阻止自己的这些念头，我开始仔细打量他。萨利姆浑身油污，满身是汗，还在拆卸引擎，松螺丝，拔电线，但干得毫无头绪，像个小孩子恼怒地毁坏着一个不能玩的玩具。挡泥板上，保险杠上，乱七八糟地放着弹簧、阀门、螺丝垫圈、电线，掉得地上都是。我离开他，走到卡车的另一边，那儿还有点阴凉地儿。我坐在地上，往后靠着车轮。

萨利姆。

我对这个人一无所知，而我的命却掌控在他的手中。或者说，至少，就这一天，他掌控着我的生命。我不禁想到，如果萨利姆撵我走，让我远离卡车和水——毕竟，他手里有锤子，口袋里可能还有刀子，何况，他还有体格上的优势——如果他命令我走开，把我赶到沙漠深处，我可能都活不到夜里。嘿，此刻，在我看来，这或许正是他的选择。毕竟这么做能延长他的生命——或者，如果援救及时到达，他能得活。

很明显，萨利姆不是专业司机，或者，不管从哪点看，他都不是开贝利埃卡车的司机。他对这一带也不熟悉。（另一方面，又有谁真正了解沙漠呢？沙漠里，一波接一波的狂风暴风不断地改变着地貌，不断地把座座沙山四处搬运，不断地改变着自然特征。）有人——或许是发一笔意外小财——花些小钱雇别人来替他执行任务，这种情况在这一带很常见。或许这辆卡车真正的司机雇了萨利姆代他的班。而且，在毛里塔尼亚，从没有人会承认自己有什么不知道或者有什么事不能做。在城市里，如果你找到一位出租车司机，给他看一个地址，问他知不知道这个地方，他会说知道，连一秒钟的犹豫都没有。只是到后来，他载着你转遍全城，转了一圈又一圈，你才彻底明白，他根本就不知道要去哪里。

太阳升得更高了。沙漠，这片纹丝不动、被吓得呆头呆脑的沙海，吸收了太阳的光线，变得更热了，热得烫人。据说，约鲁巴族[①]的人认为，如果一个人的影子弃他而去，那这个人就会死去。此刻，所有的影子都在缩小，变弱，消退。可怕的午后时光就要降临在我们身上——在这段时光里，不管是人还是物都没有了阴影，似有还无地存在着，都被缩减为白花花的一片，灼烧而又炙热。

我正想着，这一刻到来了，但是，突然间，我注意到我的前方的景象发生了变化。毫无生机的、寂静的地平线——被热浪逼压得好像什么东西也不会从中涌出——刹那间焕发了勃勃生机，变得葱茏一片。目之所及的地方生长着高大巍峨的棕榈树，沿着地平线，一丛丛的，连绵不断，茂密而紧凑。我还看到了湖泊——是的，广袤的蓝色湖泊，湖面波浪滚滚，栩栩如生。那里生长着美丽无比的灌木丛，宽阔延展的枝条鲜嫩多汁、生机盎然。这一切都熠熠生辉，活力无限，令人悸动——如若轻雾缭绕，柔和得让人无从捉摸。

"萨利姆！"我大喊。"萨利姆！"

一个头从前机盖下面探了出来。他看看我。

"萨利姆！"我又重复一次，用手指着。

萨利姆往我指的方向瞥了一眼，无动于衷。从我脏兮兮、汗津津的脸上，他一定看到了惊异、迷惑、狂喜——还有其它别的什么，这显然让他机警起来，因为他走到卡车的一边，解下一个羊皮口袋，喝了几小口，然后无言地把剩下的递给了我。我一把抓过粗糙的皮口袋，喝了起来。突然间一阵晕眩，我把肩

[①] 西非最大的部落之一。

膀斜靠在车身上才不致栽倒在地。我喝呀喝，疯狂地吮吸着羊腿，却依然注视着地平线。然而，我的干渴感消退下去，体内的疯狂也平息下来，随之，那片绿色风景也开始消失。它的颜色变淡了，它的轮廓模糊了。等我喝光了羊皮袋里的水，地平线又恢复如初，空旷而又死寂。水，让人作呕的撒哈拉之水——温乎乎，脏兮兮，混浊得半是沙子半是泥——延长了我的生命，却夺去了我的天堂美景。然而，紧要的事实是，萨利姆亲自给了我水喝。我不再害怕他了。我感觉自己是安全的——哪怕是到了我们只剩下最后一小口水的时候。

后半天，我们就躺在卡车下面，躺在它那稀薄的、漂晒了的阴凉处。在周遭都是灼烧的地平线的世界里，我和萨利姆是仅有的活物。我审视着臂长所及的地面，审视着离我最近的石头，搜寻着活着的东西，任何可能抽动、移动、滑动的东西。我记得，在撒哈拉的某个地方生活着一种小甲虫，图阿雷格人把这种小甲虫叫做 Ngubi。传说，当天气特别热的时候，Ngubi 受尽干渴的折磨，拼命想喝到水。不幸的是，四下里哪儿也没有水，有的只是滚热的沙子。这样一来，小甲虫就选取一个斜坡——可能就是一抔沙子的凹斜处——然后坚定不移地开始爬向顶峰。这需要艰苦卓绝的努力，简直就是一项希绪弗斯①式的工程，因为灼热而松散的沙子不断滚落，把甲虫也给带了下来；然而，一回到起始之地，甲虫又开始了它的艰辛之旅。如此这般，不多久，甲虫开始出汗。一小团湿气在它的腹尾部聚集，然后变大。接下来，Ngubi 停止爬动，蜷起身，一嘴扎进那个小水珠。

他喝到水了。

萨利姆的一个纸袋子里有几块饼干。我们喝掉第二个羊皮袋里的水。还剩下两个。我考虑要不要写些什么。（我想到，这种情形下通常要写些东西。）但我没有力气。倒不是真的疼痛，就是觉得一切都变得空虚起来。一个套着一个，空虚不断增长。

接下来，黑暗中闪出两盏耀眼的灯。灯光还离得很远，剧烈晃动着。很快，马达声临近了，我看到了卡车，听到了人声，说的是一种我不懂的语言。"萨利姆！"我说。几张和他相似的黑黝黝的脸朝着我俯了下来。

（张慧芳 译 温秀颖 校）

---

① 希绪弗斯是希腊神话里的一个国王，遭受天神惩罚，把一块巨石推上山顶，眼看巨石滚落，然后再推，再滚落，无休止地循环重复推巨石的任务。希绪弗斯式任务就是劳而无功、永不休止的任务或工程。

Thirteen Ways of Looking at a Void

Michael Finkel

　　【导读】地处西非的尼日尔特内雷地区是一片沙漠。这里气候条件非常恶劣，终年干旱，日夜温差极大，而且天气状况很难预测，几分钟之前还是骄阳似火，转眼间就可能狂风暴雨，有时还夹带着冰雹和风沙。这个地区被当地人称为"沙漠无人区"。本文就讲述了作者在试图穿越该地区的过程中遇到的人和事。

　　这里有为了糊口不得不往返于沙漠和利比亚之间的莫萨卡，"沙漠就是地狱"；为沙漠的曼妙美丽所折服的美国老妪莫尼克，"是特内雷给了我信念"；以做导游为生，会讲7种语言的27岁小伙艾哈迈德，"等我有钱了会找像这样的女人"；靠一颗枣子过活3天的钓行，"关于无人区我真的从来没思考过"；贪污腐化的尼日尔警察穆斯塔法，"你只要付钱就行了"；经营着一间酒吧兼妓院的老板娘格雷斯，"啤酒和女人"；坚信万物皆有灵性的沃阿迪果乌，"沙漠里到处都是灵魂"；为了争取民族权力而随时准备战斗的汤布，"把枪拿回来也是轻而易举的事"；为了实现足球梦险些丧命的凯文，"我想到了死亡"……

　　本文字里行间反映着大沙漠独有的地形地貌与风土人情，犹如一幅充满异国风情的画卷。清新、细腻的文字里，一种情愫在萦绕，一种鲜活在流淌，一种震撼心灵的人性开始浸润。作者以极大勇气和灵明智慧行走在沙漠里，讲述了一个个生动离奇的故事。他笔下这些小人物犹如开在沙漠里的繁花，到处绽放美丽，将生命高高举在尘俗之上，那份浓浓的温暖流淌在沙漠里。

　　"Hell," says Mousaka. He raises a forefinger and circles it in the air to indicate that he is referring to the whole of the void. I am sitting on Mousaka's lap. Mousaka is sitting on Osiman's lap. Osiman is sitting on someone else's lap. And so on — everyone sitting on another's lap. We are on a truck, crossing the void. The truck looks like a dump truck, though it doesn't dump. It is twenty feet long and six feet wide, diesel-powered, painted white. One hundred and ninety passengers are aboard, tossed atop one another like a pile of laundry. People are on the roof of the cab, and straddling the rail of the bed, and pressed into the bed itself. There is no room for carry-on bags; water jugs and other belongings must be tied to the truck's rail and hung over the sides. Fistfights have broken out over half an inch of contested space. Beyond the truck, the void encompasses 154,440 square miles, at last count, and is virtually uninhabited.

Like many of the people on board, Mousaka makes his living by harvesting crops — oranges or potatoes or dates. His facial scars, patterned like whiskers, indicate that he is a member of the Hausa① culture, from southern Niger②. Mousaka has two wives and four children and no way to provide for them, except to get on a truck. Also on the truck are Tuareg and Songhai and Zerma and Fulani and Kanuri and Wodaabe. Everyone is headed to Libya, where the drought that has gripped much of North Africa has been less severe and there are still crops to pick. Libya has become the new promised land. Mousaka plans to stay through the harvest season, January to July, and then return to his family. To get to Libya from the south, though, one must first cross the void.

The void is the giant sand sea at the center of the Sahara. It covers half of Niger and some of Algeria and a little of Libya and a corner of Chad. On maps of the Sahara, it is labeled, in large, spaced letters, "Ténéré③" — a term taken from the

---

① The Hausa are one of the largest ethnic groups in West Africa. They are a Sahelian people chiefly located in northern Nigeria and southeastern Niger, but having significant numbers living in regions of Cameroon, Ghana, Cote d'Ivoire, Chad and Sudan. Predominantly Hausa communities are scattered throughout West Africa and on the traditional Hajj route across the Sahara Desert, especially around the town of Agadez. A few Hausa have moved to large coastal cities in the region such as Lagos, Accra, Kumasi and Cotonou, as well as to countries such as Libya. However, most Hausa remain in small villages and towns, where they grow crops and raise livestock, including cattle. They speak the Hausa language, an Afro-Asiatic language of the Chadic group.

② Niger, officially named the Republic of Niger, is a landlocked country in Western Africa, named after the Niger River. It borders Nigeria and Benin to the south, Burkina Faso and Mali to the west, Algeria and Libya to the north and Chad to the east. Niger covers a land area of almost 1,270,000 km², making it the largest nation in West Africa, with over 80 percent of its land area covered by the Sahara desert. The country's predominantly Islamic population of just above 15,000,000 is mostly clustered in the far south and west of the nation. The capital city is Niamey, located in the far southwest corner of Niger.

③ The Ténéré is a desert region in the south central Sahara. It comprises a vast plain of sand stretching from northeastern Niger into western Chad, occupying an area of over 154,440 square miles (400,000 km²). Its boundaries are said to be the Aïr Mountains in the west, the Hoggar Mountains in the north, the Djado Plateau in the northeast, the Tibesti Mountains in the east, and the basin of Lake Chad in the south.

Tuareg[①] language that means "nothing" or "emptiness" or "void." The Ténéré is Earth at its least hospitable, a chunk of the planet gone dead. Even the word itself, "Ténéré," looks vaguely ominous, barbed as it is with accents. In the heart of the void there is not a scrap of shade nor a bead of water nor a blade of grass. Most parts, even bacteria can't survive.

    The void is freezing by night and scorching by day and wind-scoured always. Its center is as flat and featureless as the head of a drum. There is not so much as a large rock. Mousaka has been crossing the void for four days; he has at least a week to go. Except for prayer breaks, the truck does not stop. Since entering the void, Mousaka has hardly slept, or eaten, or drunk. He has no shoes, no sunglasses, no blanket. His ears are plugged with sand. His clothing is tattered. His feet are swollen. This morning, I asked him what comes to mind when he thinks about the void. For two weeks now, as I've been crossing the Sahara myself, using all manner of transportation, I have asked this question to almost every person I've met. When the truck rides over a bump and everybody is jounced, elbows colliding with sternums, heads hammering heads, Mousaka leans forward and tells me his answer again. "The desert is disgusting," he says, in French. "The desert is hell." Then he spits over the side of the truck, and spits again, trying to rid himself of the sand that has collected in his mouth.

    "Faith," says Monique. "The Ténéré gives me faith." Monique has been crossing and recrossing the void for four weeks. We've met at the small market in the Algerian town of Djanet, at the northern hem of the Ténéré. Monique is here with her travel partners, re-supplying. She's Swiss, though she's lived in the United States for a good part of her life. Her group is traversing the void in a convoy of

---

    [①] The Tuareg people are predominently nomadic people of the sahara desert. The Tuareg are often referred to as "Blue Men of the desert" — because their robes are dyed indigo blue. They live in small tribes with between 30 and 100 family members and keep camels, goats, cattle and chicken which graze the land. They are a proud race of people, famous for their fighting abilities and artwork, now staring urbanisation and resettlement in the face. The sword is a Tuareg's most valued possession. Many are passed from generation to generation and said to be protected by the victories of its past owners.

Pinzgauers[①] — six-wheel-drive, moon-rover[②]-looking vehicles, made in Austria, that are apparently undaunted by even the softest of sands.

Monique is in her early seventies. A few years ago, not long after her husband passed away, she fulfilled a lifelong fantasy and visited the Sahara. The desert changed her. She witnessed sunrises that turned the sand the color of lipstick. She saw starfish-shaped dunes, miles across, whose curving forms left her breathless with wonder. She heard the fizzy hum known as the singing of the sands. She reveled in the silence and the openness. She slept outside. She let the wind braid her hair and the sand sit under her fingernails and the sun bake her skin. She shared meals with desert nomads. She learned that not every place on Earth is crowded and greed-filled and tamed. She stayed three months. Now she's back for another extended visit.

Her story is not unusual. Tourism in the Ténéré is suddenly popular. Outfitters in Paris and London and Geneva and Berlin are chartering flights to the edge of the void and then arranging for vehicles that will take you to the middle. Look at the map, the brochures say: You're going to the heart of the Sahara, to the famous Ténéré. Doesn't the word itself, exotic with accents, roll off the tongue like a tiny poem?

Many of the tourists are on spiritual quests. They live hectic[③] lives, and they want a nice dose of nothing — and there is nothing more nothing than the void. The void is so blank that a point-and-shoot camera will often refuse to work, the auto-focus finding nothing to focus on. This is good. By offering nothing, I've been

---

① The Pinzgauer is a family of high-mobility all-terrain 4WD (4x4) and 6WD (6x6) military utility vehicles. They were manufactured in Guildford, Surrey, United Kingdom, by BAE Systems Land & Armaments. The vehicle was originally developed in the late 1960s by Steyr-Daimler-Puch of Graz, Austria, and was named after the Pinzgauer, an Austrian breed of horse. It was popular amongst military buyers, and continued in production throughout the rest of the century. In 2000 the rights were sold to Automotive Technik Ltd (ATL) in the UK. ATL was subsequently acquired by Stewart & Stevenson Services, Inc. in 2005; in May 2006, Stewart & Stevenson became a subsidiary of the aerospace and defence group Armor Holdings, Inc.. One year later, Armor Holdings was itself acquired by BAE Systems plc, who discontinued the UK-production of the Pinzgauer, which was proving to be vulnerable to mines and improvised explosive devices in Afghanistan. Development work (done in the UK) on the planned Pinzgauer II was evaluated by BAE subsidiary in Benoni, Gauteng, South Africa but no vehicle was ever manufactured.

② A lunar rover or Moon rover is a space exploration vehicle designed to move across the surface of the Moon. Some rovers have been designed to transport members of a human spaceflight crew; others have been partially or fully autonomous robots.

③ adj. Characterized by intense activity, confusion, or haste.

told, the void tacitly accepts everything. Whatever you want to find seems to be there. Not long after I met Monique, I spoke with another American. Her name is Beth. She had been in the Ténéré for two and a half weeks, and she told me that the point of her trip was to feel the wind in her face. After a fortnight of wind, Beth came to a profound decision. She said she now realized what her life was missing. She said that the moment she returned home she was quitting her Internet job and opening up her own business. She said she was going to bake apple pies.

"Money," says Ahmed. "Money, money, money, money, money." Ahmed has no money. But he does have a plan. His plan is to meet every plane that lands in his hometown of Agadez①, in central Niger, one of the hubs of Ténéré tourism. During the cooler months, and when the runway is not too potholed, a flight arrives in Agadez as often as once a week. When my plane landed, from Paris, Ahmed was there. The flight was packed with French vacationers, but all of them had planned their trips with European full-service agencies.

No one needed to hire a freelance guide. This is why Ahmed is stuck talking with me.

Ahmed speaks French and English and German and Arabic and Hausa and Toubou②, as well as his mother tongue, the Tuareg language called Tamashek. He's twenty-seven years old. He has typical Tuareg hair, jet black and wild with curls, and a habit of glancing every so often at his wrist, like a busy executive, which is a tic he must have picked up from tourists, for Ahmed does not own a watch, and, he tells me, he never has. He says he's learned all these languages because he doesn't want to get on a truck to Libya. He tells me he can help tourists rent quality Land Cruisers, and he can cook for them — his specialty is tagela, a bread that is baked in the sand — and he can guide them across the void without a worry of getting lost. Tourism, he says, is the only way to make money in the void.

Inside his shirt pocket, Ahmed keeps a brochure that was once attached to a

---

① Agadez (also Agades) is the largest city in northern Niger, with a population of 88,569 (2005 census). It lies in the Sahara and is the capital of Aïr, one of the traditional Tuareg-Berber federations. The city is also the capital of the Agadez Region, with a population of 347,330 (2005).

② The Tubu (Toubou) are an ethnic group that live mainly in northern Chad, but also in Libya, Niger and Sudan. The majority of Toubou live in the north of Chad around the Tibesti mountains. Numbering roughly 350,000, they are mostly Muslim. Most Toubou are herders and nomads, though many are now semi-nomadic. Their society is clan-based, with each clan having certain oases, pastures and wells. They are divided in two closely associated people, the Teda and the Daza.

bottle of shampoo. The brochure features photos of very pretty models, white women with perfect hair and polished teeth, and Ahmed has opened and closed the brochure so many times that it is as brittle and wrinkled as an old dollar bill. "When I have money," he says, "I will have women like this."

"But," I point out, "the plane landed, and you didn't get a client."

"Maybe next week," he says.

"So how will you make money this week?"

"I just told you all about me," he says. "Doesn't that deserve a tip?"

"Salt," says Choukou. He tips his chin to the south, toward a place called Bilma, in eastern Niger, where he's going to gather salt. Choukou is on his camel. He's sitting cross-legged, his head wrapped loosely in a long white cloth, his body shrouded in a billowy tan robe, and there is an air about him of exquisite levity — a mood he always seems to project when he is atop his camel. Often, he breaks into song, a warbling chant in the Toubou tongue, a language whose syllables are as rounded as river stones. I am riding another of his camels, a blue-eyed female that emits the sort of noises that make me think of calling a plumber. A half dozen other camels are following us, riderless. We are crossing the void.

Choukou is a Toubou, a member of one of the last seminomadic peoples to live along the edges of the void. At its periphery[①], the void is not particularly voidlike; it's surrounded on three sides by craggy mountains — the Massif de l'Aïr, the Ahaggar, the Plateau du Djado, the Tibesti — and, to the south, the Lake Chad Basin. Choukou can ride his camel sitting frontward or backward or side-saddle or standing, and he can command his camel, never raising his voice above a whisper, to squat down or rise up or spin in circles. His knife is strapped high on his right arm; his goatskin, filled with water, is hooked to his saddle; a few dried dates are in the breast pocket of his robe, along with a pouch of tobacco and some scraps of rolling paper. He is sitting on his blanket. This is all he has with him. It has been said that a Toubou can live for three days on a single date: the first day on its skin, the second on its fruit, the third on its pit. My guess is that this is truer than you might imagine. In two days of difficult travel with Choukou, I saw him eat one meal.

If you ask Choukou how old he is, he'll say he doesn't know. He's willing to guess (twenty, he supposes), but he can't say for sure. It doesn't matter. His sense of

---

① noun. The outermost part or region within a precise boundary.

time is not divided into years or seasons or months. It's divided into directions. Either he is headed to Bilma①, to gather salt, or he is headed away from Bilma, to sell his salt. It has been this way for the Toubous for two thousand years. No one has yet discovered a more economical method of transporting salt across the void — engines and sand are an unhappy mix — and so camels are still in use. Camels can survive two weeks between water stops and then, in a single prolonged drink, can down twenty-five gallons of water, none of which happens to be stored in the hump. When Choukou arrives at the salt mines of Bilma, he will load each of his camels with six fifty-pound pillars of salt, then join with other Toubous to form a caravan — a hundred or more camels striding single file across the sands — and set out for Agadez. In the best of conditions, the trek can take nearly a month.

Choukou occasionally encounters tourists, and he sometimes sees the overloaded trucks, but he is only mildly curious. He does not have to seek solace from a hectic life. He has no need to pick crops in Libya. He travels with the minimum he requires to survive, and he knows that if even one well along the route has suddenly run dry — it happens — then he will probably die. He knows that there are bandits in the void and sandstorms in the void. He is not married. A good wife, he tells me, costs five camels, and he can't yet afford one. If he makes it to Agadez, he will sell his salt and then immediately start back to Bilma. He navigates by the dunes and the colors of the soil and the direction of the wind. He can study a set of camel tracks and determine which breed of camel left them, and therefore the tribe to which they belong, and how many days old the tracks are, and how heavy a load the camels are carrying, and how many animals are in the caravan. He was born in the void, and he has never left the void. This is perhaps why he looks at me oddly when I ask him what comes to mind when he contemplates his homeland. I ask him the question, and his face becomes passive. He mentions salt, but then he is quiet for a few seconds. "I really don't think about the void," he says.

"Cameras," says Mustafa. "Also videos and watches and Walkman and jewelry and GPS units." Mustafa has an M-i6 rifle slung over his shoulder. He is trying to

---

① Bilma is an oasis town in north east Niger with a population of around 2,500 people. It lies protected from the desert dunes under the Kaouar Cliffs and is the largest town along the Kaouar escarpment. It is known for its gardens, for salt and natron production through evaporation ponds, date cultivation, and as the destination of one of the last Saharan caravan routes (the Azalai, from Agadez). On June 23, 2010 in Bilma was recorded the highest temperature ever in Niger with 48.2 °C (118.8 °F).

sell me the items he has taken from other tourists. I am at a police checkpoint in the tiny outpost of Chirfa①, along the northeastern border of the void. I've hired a desert taxi — a daredevil driver and a beater Land Cruiser — to take me to Algeria. Now we've been stopped.

Mustafa is fat. He is fat, and he is wearing a police uniform. This is a bad combination. In the void, only the wealthy are fat. Police in Niger do not make enough money to become wealthy; a fat police officer is therefore a corrupt police officer. And a corrupt officer inevitably means trouble. When I refuse to even look at his wares, Mustafa becomes angry. He asks to see my travel documents. The void is a fascinating place — there exist, at once, both no rules and strict rules. To cross the void legally, you are supposed to carry very specific travel documents, and I actually have them. But the documents are open to interpretation. You must, for example, list your exact route of travel. It is difficult to do this when you are crossing an expanse of sand that has no real roads. So of course Mustafa finds a mistake.

"It is easy to correct," he says. "You just have to return to Agadez." Agadez is a four-day drive in the opposite direction. "Or I can correct it here," he adds. "Just give me your GPS unit." He does not even bother to pretend that it isn't a bribe. Mustafa is the leader of this outpost, the dictator of a thousand square miles of desert. There is no one to appeal to.

"I don't have a GPS unit," I say.

"Then your watch."

"No," I say.

"A payment will do."

"No," I say.

"Fine," he says. Then he says nothing. He folds his arms and rests them on the shelf formed by his belly. He stands there for a long time. The driver turns off the car. We wait. Mustafa has all day, all week, all month, all year. He has no schedule. He has no meetings. If we try to drive away, he will shoot us. It is a losing battle.

I hand him a sheaf of Central African francs, and we continue on.

"Beer," says Grace. "Beer and women." Grace is maybe thirty-five years old and wears a dress brilliant with yellow sunflowers. She has a theory: Crossing the void, she insists, seeing all that nothing, she posits, produces within a man a certain

---

① Chirfa is a populated place in Agadez, Niger, Africa. Chirfa is also known as Chirfa Driga.

kind of emptiness. It is her divine duty, she's decided, to fill that emptiness. And so Grace has opened a bar in Dirkou①. A bar and brothel②.

Dirkou is an unusual town. It's in Niger, at the northeastern rim of the Ténéré, built in what is known as a wadi —an ancient river-bed, now dry, but where water exists not too far below the surface, reachable by digging wells. The underground water allows date palms to grow in Dirkou. Whether you are traveling by truck, camel, or 4x4, it is nearly impossible to cross the void without stopping in Dirkou for fuel or provisions or water or emptiness-filling.

Apparently, it is popular to inform newcomers to Dirkou that they are now as close as they can get to the end of the earth. My first hour in town, I was told this five or six times; it must be a sort of civic slogan. This proves only that a visit to the end of the earth should not be on one's to-do list. Dirkou is possibly the most unredeeming place I have ever visited, Los Angeles included. The town is essentially one large bus station, except that it lacks electricity, plumbing, television, newspapers, and telephones. Locals say that it has not rained here in more than two years. The streets are heavy with beggars and con artists and thieves and migrants and drifters③ and soldiers and prostitutes. Almost everyone is male, except the prostitutes. The place is literally a dump: When you want to throw something away, you just toss it in the street. Grace's emptiness theory has a certain truth. I arrived in Dirkou after riding on the Libya-bound truck for three days. Of the 190 passengers, 186 were male. Those with a bit of money went straight to Grace's bar. The bar was like every structure in Dirkou: mud walls, palm-frond roof, sand floors. I sat at a scrap-wood table, on a milk-crate chair. A battery-powered radio emitted 90 percent static and 10 percent Arabic music from a station in Chad. I drank a Niger beer, which had been stored in the shade and was, by Saharan standards, cold. I drank two more.

My emptiness, it seems, was not as profound as those of my truck mates. In the Ténéré, there exists the odd but pervasive belief that alcohol hydrates④ you — and not only hydrates you but hydrates you more efficiently than water. Some people on

---

① Dirkou is a town in the Bilma Department, Agadez Region of north-eastern Niger. It lies in the northern Kaouar escarpment, a north-south line of cliffs which form an isolated oasis in the Sahara desert.

② noun. a house or other place where men pay to have sexual intercourse with prostitutes.

③ noun. One that drifts, especially a person who moves aimlessly from place to place or from job to job.

④ verb. To supply water to (a person, for example) in order to restore or maintain fluid balance.

the truck did not drink at all the last day of the trip, for they knew Grace's bar was approaching. Many of these same men were soon passed out in the back of the bar. There is also the belief that a man cannot catch AIDS from a prostitute so long as she is less than eighteen years old.

One other item that Dirkou lacks is bathrooms. After eating a bit of camel sausage and drinking my fourth beer, I ask Grace where the bathroom is. She tells me it is in the street. I explain, delicately, that I'm hoping to produce a different sort of waste. She says it doesn't matter, the bathroom is in the street. I walk out of the bar, seeking a private spot, and in the process I witness three men doing what I am planning to do. This explains much about the unfortunate odor that permeates Dirkou.

"Spirits," says Wordigou. He is sitting on a blanket and holding his supper bowl, which at one time was a sardine tin. His face is illuminated by a kerosene lamp. Wordigou has joined us for dinner, some rice and a bit of mutton. He is a cousin of Choukou's, the young salt trader who told me that he does not think about the void. Choukou allowed me to join his camel trek for two days, and now, in the middle of our journey, we have stopped for the evening at a Toubou encampment. Wordigou lives in the camp, which consists of a handful of dome-shaped grass huts, two dozen camels, an extended family of Toubous, and a herd of goats. In the hut I've been lent for the night, a cassette tape is displayed on the wall as a sort of curious knickknack. Certainly there is no tape player in the camp. Here, the chief form of entertainment is the same as it is almost everywhere in the void — talking. Wordigou, who guesses that he is a little less than thirty years old, leads the mealtime discussion. He is a sharp and insightful conversationalist. The topic is religion. The Toubous are nominally Muslim, but most, including Wordigou, have combined Islam with traditional animist[①] beliefs.

"The desert," says Wordigou, "is filled with spirits. I talk with them all the time. They tell me things. They tell me news. Some spirits you see, and some you don't

---

① noun. Animism encompasses philosophical, religious, and/or spiritual beliefs that souls or spirits exist not only in humans but also in all other animals, plants, rocks, natural phenomena such as thunder, geographic features such as mountains or rivers, or other entities of the natural environment. Animism may further attribute souls to abstract concepts such as words, true names or metaphors in mythology. Animism is particularly widely found in the religions of indigenous peoples, although it is also found in Shinto, and some forms of Hinduism, Sikhism, Buddhism, Pantheism, Islam, Christianity, and Neopaganism.

see, and some are nice, and some are not nice, and some pretend to be nice but really aren't. I ask the nice ones to send me strong camels. And also to lead me to hidden treasures."

Wordigou catches my eye, and he knows immediately that I do not share his beliefs. Still, he is magnanimous. "Even if you do not see my spirits," he says, "you must see someone's. Everyone does. How else could Christianity and Judaism and Islam all have begun in the very same desert?"

"Work," says Bilit. "It ties me to the desert." Bilit is the driver of the overloaded truck that is headed to Libya. He has stopped his vehicle, climbed out of the front seat, and genuflected① in the direction of Mecca. Sand is stuck to his forehead. The passengers who've gotten off are piling aboard. Only their turbans② can be seen through the swirling sand. Everyone wears a turban in the void — it protects against sun and wind and provides the wearer with a degree of anonymity③ which can be valuable if one is attempting a dubiously legal maneuver, like sneaking into Libya. Turbans are about the only splashes of color in the desert. They come in a handful of bold, basic hues, like gumballs. Bilit's is green. I ask him how far we have to go.

"Two days," says Bilit. "*Inshallah*," he adds — God willing. He says it again: "*Inshallah*." This is, by far, the void's most utilized expression, the oral equivalent of punctuation. God willing. It emphasizes the daunting fact that, no matter the degree of one's preparation, traveling the void always involves relinquishing control. Bilit has driven this route — Agadez to Dirkou, four hundred miles of void — for eight years. When conditions allow, he drives twenty to twenty-two hours a day. Where the sand is firm, Bilit can drive as fast as fifteen miles an hour. Where it is soft, the passengers have to get out and push. Everywhere, the engine sounds as though it is continually trying to clear its throat.

His route is one of the busiest in the Ténéré – sometimes he sees three or even four other vehicles a day. This means that Bilit doesn't need to rely on compass

---

① verb. To bend the knee or touch one knee to the floor or ground, as in worship.

② Turban is an English word used to refer to several sorts of headwear. A commonly used synonym is a Pagri, the Indian word for turban. Turbans are a popular form of headgear worn in the Middle East, North Africa and Southwest Asia. They are designed to help keep the user cool in hot desert environments such as the Sahara.

③ Anonymity is derived from the Greek word anonymia, meaning "without a name" or "namelessness". In colloquial use, anonymity typically refers to the state of an individual's personal identity, or personally identifiable information, being publicly unknown.

bearings or star readings to determine if he is headed in the correct direction. There are actually other tire tracks in the sand to follow. Not all tracks, however, are reliable. A "road" in the Ténéré can be twenty miles wide, with tracks braiding about one another where the drivers detoured around signs of softness, seeking firmer sand. Inexperienced drivers have followed braided tracks and ended up confounding themselves. In a place with a blank horizon, it is impossible to tell if you're headed in a gradual arc or going straight. Drivers have followed bad braids until they've run out of gas.

Worse is when there are no tracks at all. This happens after every major sandstorm, when the swirling sands return the void to blankness, shaken clean like an Etch-A-Sketch[①]. A sandstorm occurs, on average, about once a week. During a storm, Bilit stops the truck. Sometimes he'll be stopped for two days. Sometimes three. The passengers, of course, must suffer through it; they are too crowded to move. The trucks are so crowded because the more people aboard, the more money the truck's owner makes. The void is a place where crude economics rule. Comfort is rarely a consideration.

One time, Bilit did not stop in a sandstorm. He got lost. Getting lost in the void is a frightening situation. Even with a compass and the stars, you can easily be off by half a degree and bypass an entire town. Bilit managed to find his way. But recently on the same route, a truck was severely lost. There are few rescue services in the Ténéré, and by the time an army vehicle located the truck, only eight people were alive. Thirty-six corpses were discovered, all victims of dehydration. The rest of the passengers — six at least, and possibly many more — were likely buried beneath the sands and have never been found.

"War," says Tombu. Where I see dunes, Tombu sees bunkers. Tombu is a soldier, a former leader of the Tuareg during the armed rebellion that erupted in Niger in 1990. Warring is in his blood. For more than three thousand years, until the French overran North Africa in the late 1800s, the Tuaregs were known as the bandits of the Ténéré, robbing camel caravans as they headed across the void.

The fighting that began in 1990, however, was over civil rights. Many Tuaregs felt like second-class citizens in Niger — it was the majority Hausas and other ethnic

---

① "Etch A Sketch" is a registered trademark for a mechanical drawing toy manufactured by the Ohio Art Company.

groups, they claimed, who were given all the good jobs, the government positions, the college scholarships. And so these Tuaregs decided to try to gain autonomy① over their homeland, which is essentially the whole of the Ténéré. They were fighting for an Independent Republic of the Void. Hundreds of people were killed before a compromise was reached in 1995: The Tuaregs would be treated with greater respect, and in return they would agree to drop their fight for independence. Though isolated skirmishes continued until 1998, the void is quiet, at least for now. This is a main reason why there has been a sudden upswing in tourism.

Tombu is no longer a fighter; he now drives a desert taxi, though he drives like a soldier, which is to say as recklessly as possible. I have hired him to take me north, through the center of the void, into Algeria — a four-day drive. We were together when the police officer forced me to pay him a bribe. During rest stops, Tombu draws diagrams in the sand, showing me how he attacked a post high in the Massif de l'Aïr and how he ambushed a convoy of jeeps in the open void. "But now there is peace," he says. He looks disappointed. I ask him if anything has changed for the Tuaregs.

"No," he says. "Except that we have given up our guns." He looks even more disappointed. "But," he adds, visibly brightening, "it will be very easy to get them back."

"Speed," says Joel. He has just pulled his motorbike up to the place I've rented in Dirkou, a furnitureless, sand-floored room for a dollar a night. Joel is in the desert for one primary reason: to go fast. He is here for two months, from Israel, to ride his motorbike, a red-and-white Yamaha, and the void is his playground. Speed and the void have a storied relationship; each winter for thirteen years, the famous Paris-to-Dakar rally cut through the Ténéré — a few hundred foreigners in roadsters and pickup trucks and motorbikes tearing hell-bent across the sand. The race was rerouted in 1997, but its wrecks are still on display, each one visible from miles away, the vehicles' paint scoured by the windblown sand and the steel baked to a smooth chocolate brown.

Joel reveres the Paris-to-Dakar. He talks about sand the way skiers talk about snow — in a language unintelligible to outsiders. Sand, it turns out, is not merely

---

① noun. Self-government or the right of self-government; self-determination.

sand. There are *chotts*[①] and *regs*[②] and *oueds* and *ergs* and *barchans*[③] and *feche-feche* and *gassis*[④] and *bull* dust[⑤]. The sand around Dirkou, Joel tells me, is just about perfect. "Would you like to borrow my bike?" he asks.

I would. I snap on his helmet and straddle the seat and set out across the sand. The world before me is an absolute plane, nothing at all, and I throttle the bike and soon I'm in fifth and the engine is screaming and sand is tornadoing about. I know, on some level, that I'm going fast and that it's dangerous, but the feeling is absent of fear. The dimensions are so skewed it's more like skydiving — I've committed myself, and now I'm hurtling through space, and there is nothing that can hurt me. It's euphoric, a pure sense of motion and G-force[⑥] and lawlessness, and I want more, of course, so I pull on the throttle and the world is a blur and the horizon is empty, and it is here, it is right now, that I suddenly realize what I need to do. And I do it. I shut my eyes. I pinch them shut, and the bike bullets on, and I override my panic because I know that there's nothing to hit, not a thing in my way, and soon, with my eyes closed, I find that my head has gone silent and I have discovered a crystalline form of freedom.

"Death," says Kevin. "I think about dying." Kevin is not alone. Everyone who crosses the void, whether tourist or Toubou or truck passenger, is witness to the Ténéré's ruthlessness. There are the bones, for example —so many bones that a good way to navigate the void is to follow the skeletons, which are scattered beside every

---

① In geology, chott or shebka (of the former the spelling is French, it is pronounced, and sometimes spelled, shott) is a dry (salt) lake in the Saharan area of Africa that stays dry in the summer, but receives some water in the winter. This water may come as a groundwater discharge, for example from the Bas Saharan Basin.

② The Sahara Desert has many different landforms. Parts have sand dunes. A sand dune is a mountain of sand. Some dunes can be as high as 600 feet. These dunes are found in huge areas of shifting sand called ergs. Regs are another type of landform found in the desert. Regs are broad plains covered with sand and gravel. Regs make up most of the Sahara.

③ barchan, also spelled Barkhan, crescent-shaped sand dune produced by the action of wind predominately from one direction. One of the commonest types of dunes, it occurs in sandy deserts all over the world.

④ bare rock of the Western Sahara.

⑤ Bull dust is a fine talcum powder-like dust. It often occurs in areas where the track gets wet then dries and breaks up into fine dust. It is particularly prevalent in areas in the far north where it is boggy in the wet season and bone dry in the dry. Bull dust is very deceptive. Looking out your front windscreen it looks like smooth hard patches but in fact it usually is a fine covering of dust over a deep hole. Driving through bull dust at speed is very dangerous - try to avoid bull dust at all times. It can cause damage if sucked into engines too.

⑥ noun. the force of gravity.

main route like cairns① on a hiking trail. They're mostly goat bones. Goats are common freight in the Ténéré, and there are always a couple of animals that do not survive the crossing. Dead goats are tossed off the trucks. In the center of the void, the carcasses become sun-dried and leathery, like mummies②. At the edges of the void, where jackals roam, the bones are picked clean and sunbleached white as alabaster. Some of the skeletons are of camels; a couple are human. People die every year in the Ténéré, but few travelers have experienced such deaths as directly as Kevin.

Kevin is also on the Libya-bound truck, crossing with the crop pickers, though he is different from most other passengers. He has no interest in poking crops. He wants to play soccer. He's a midfielder, seeking a spot with a professional team in either Libya or Tunisia. Kevin was born in South Africa, under apartheid, then later fled to Senegal, where he lived in a refugee camp. His voice is warm and calm, and his eyes, peering through a pair of metalframed glasses, register the sort of deep-seated thoughtfulness one might look for in a physician or religious leader. Whenever a fight breaks out on the truck, he assumes the role of mediator, gently persuading both parties to compromise on the level of uncomfortableness. He tells me that he would like to study philosophy and that he has been inspired by the writings of Thomas Jefferson. He says that his favorite musician is Phil Collins. "When I listen to his music," he says, "it makes me cry." I tell him, deadpan, that it makes me cry, too. This is Kevin's second attempt at reaching the soccer fields across the sands. The first trip, a year previous, ended in disaster.

He was riding with his friend Silman in a dilapidated Land Cruiser in the northern part of the void. Both of them dreamed of playing soccer. There were six other passengers in the car and a driver, and for safety they were following another Land Cruiser, creating a shortcut across the Ténéré. The car Kevin and Silman were in broke down. There was no room in the second Land Cruiser, so only the driver of the first car squeezed in. He told his passengers to wait. He said he'd go to the nearest town, a day's drive away, and then return with another car.

After three days, there was still no sign of the driver. Water was running low. It was the middle of summer. Temperatures in the void often reach 115 degrees

---

① noun. A mound of stones erected as a memorial or marker.
② noun. The dead body of a human or animal that has been embalmed and prepared for burial, as according to the practices of the ancient Egyptians.

Fahrenheit and have gone as high as 130 degrees. The sky turns white with heat; the sand shimmers and appears molten. Kevin and Silman decided they would rather walk than wait. The other six passengers decided to remain with the broken vehicle. Kevin and Silman set out across the desert, following the tracks of the second Land Cruiser. Merely sitting in the shade in the Sahara, a person can produce two gallons of sweat per day. Walking, Kevin and Silman probably produced twice that amount. They carried what water they had, but there was no way they could replace a quarter of the loss.

Humans are adaptable creatures, but finely calibrated. Even a gallon loss — about 5 percent of one's body fluid — results in dizziness and headache and circulatory problems. Saliva glands dry up. Speech is garbled. Kevin and Silman reached this state in less than a day. At a two-gallon deficit, walking is nearly impossible. The tongue swells, vision and hearing are diminished, and one's urine is the color of dark rust. It is difficult to form cogent thoughts. Recovery is not possible without medical assistance. People who approach this state often take desperate measures. Urine is the first thing to be drunk. Kevin and Silman did this. "You would've done it, too," Kevin tells me. People who have waited by stranded can have drunk gasoline and radiator fluid and battery acid. There have been instances in which people dying of thirst have killed others and drunk their blood.

Kevin and Silman managed to walk for three days. Then Silman collapsed. Kevin pushed on alone, crawling at times. The next day, the driver returned. He came upon Kevin, who at this point was scarcely conscious. The driver had no explanation for his weeklong delay. He gave Kevin water, and they rushed to find Silman. It was too late. Silman was dead. They returned to the broken Land Cruiser. Nobody was there. Evidently, the other passengers had also tried to walk. Their footprints had been covered by blowing sand. After hours of searching, there was no trace of anyone else. Kevin was the only survivor.

"History," says Hamoud. Hamoud is an old man — though "old" is a relative term in Niger, where the life expectancy is forty-one. I have hired a desert taxi to take me to a place called Djado, in eastern Niger, where Hamoud works as a guide. Djado is, by far, the nicest city I have seen in the Ténéré. It is built on a small hill beside an oasis thick with date palms and looks a bit like a wattle-and-daub① version of Mont-St-Michel. The homes, unlike any others I've seen in the void, are multistoried, spacious, and cool. Thought has been given to the architecture; walls are elliptical, and turrets have been built to provide views of the surrounding desert. There is not a scrap of garbage.

One problem: Nobody lives in Djado. The city is several thousand years old and has been abandoned for more than two centuries. At one time, there may have been a half million people living along Djado's oasis. Now it is part of a national reserve and off-limits to development. A handful of families are clustered in mud shanties a couple of miles away, hoping to earn a few dollars from the trickle of tourists.

Nobody knows exactly why Djado was deserted; the final blows were most likely a malaria epidemic and the changing patterns of trade routes. But Hamoud suggests that the city's decline was initiated by a dramatic shift in the climate. Ten thousand years ago, the Sahara was green. Giraffes and elephants and hippos roamed the land. Crocodiles lived in the rivers. On cliffs not far from Djado, ancient paintings depict an elaborate society of cattle herders and fishermen and bow hunters. Around 4000 B.C., the weather began to change. The game animals left. The rivers dried. One of the last completed cliff paintings is of a cow that appears to be weeping, perhaps symbolic of the prevailing mood. When Djado was at its prime, its oasis may have covered dozens of square miles. Now there is little more than a stagnant pond. Hamoud says that he found walking through Djado to be "mesmerizing" and "thrilling" and "magnificent" and "beautiful." I do not tell him this, but my overwhelming feeling is of sadness. In the void, it seems clear, people's lives were better a millennium ago than they are today.

"Destiny," says Akly. He shrugs his shoulders in a way designed to imply that he could care less, but his words have already belied his gesture. Akly does care, but he is powerless to do anything — and maybe this, in truth, is what his shrug is attempting to express. Akly is a Tuareg, a native of Agadez who was educated in

---

① Wattle and daub (or wattle-and-daub) is a building material used for making walls, in which a woven lattice of wooden strips called wattle is daubed with a sticky material usually made of some combination of wet soil, clay, sand, animal dung and straw. Wattle and daub has been used for at least 6,000 years, and is still an important construction material in many parts of the world. Many historic buildings include wattle and daub construction, and the technique is becoming popular again in more developed areas as a low-impact sustainable building technique.

Paris. He has returned to Niger, with his French wife, to run a small guest house. Agadez is a poor city in a poor nation beset by a brutal desert. It is not a place to foster optimism.

Akly is worried about the Sahara. He is concerned about its expansion. Most scientific evidence appears to show that the Sahara is on the march. In three decades, the desert has advanced more than sixty miles to the south, devouring grasslands and crops, drying up wells, creating refugees. The Sahara is expanding north, too, piling up at the foothills of the Atlas Mountains, as if preparing to ambush the Mediterranean.

Desertification is a force as powerful as plate tectonics. If the Sahara wants to grow, it will grow. Akly says he has witnessed, just in his lifetime, profound changes. He believes that the desert's growth is due both to the Sahara's own forces and to human influences. "We cut down all the trees," he says, "and put a hole in the ozone. The earth is warming. There are too many people. But what can we do? Everyone needs to eat. everyone wants a family." He shrugs again, that same shrug.

"It has gotten harder and harder to live here," he says. "I am glad that you are here to see how hard it is. I hope you can get accustomed to it."

I shake my head no and point to the sweat beading my face, and to the heat rash that has pimpled my neck, and to the blotches of sunburn that have left dead skin flaking off my nose and cheeks and arms.

"I think you'd better get used to it," Akly says. "I think everyone should get used to it. Because one day, maybe not that far away, all of the deserts are going to grow. They are going to grow like the Sahara is growing. And then everyone is going to live in the void."

沙漠无人区面面观

迈克尔·芬克尔

"地狱,"莫萨卡说道。他举起食指在空中比划了一圈,他指的是整个无人区。我正坐在莫萨卡的大腿上。莫萨卡正坐在奥斯曼的大腿上。奥斯曼正坐在另一个人的大腿上。以此类推——每个人都是坐在其他人的大腿上。我们正在一辆卡车上面,穿越这所谓的沙漠无人区。我们的卡车酷似垃圾车,区别是它并不倾倒垃圾。它 20 英尺长,6 英尺宽,柴油驱动,车身漆成了白色。搭载了 190 名乘客,一个堆在另一个之上,就像一大堆待洗的衣物。驾驶室的顶上都有乘客,也有人跨坐在底座的围栏上,而且被压进了底座里面。根本没有放随身行李的地方;水壶以及其他物品必须绑在卡车的围栏上悬在外面。就连半英寸的狭小空间都会引发一场斗殴。在卡车以外,据最新统计,沙漠无人区面积为 154,440 平方英里,并且根本无人居住。

和许多乘客一样,莫萨卡以务农为生——种植橘子、马铃薯或者枣子。他面部的胡须状疤痕说明他是豪萨[①]族的一员,来自尼日尔南部地区。莫萨卡有两位妻子,四个孩子。他无力供养家庭,只能坐上卡车出外谋生。卡车上还有图阿雷格、桑海、骁马、富拉尼、卡努力和沃达比。所有人的目的地都是利比亚。在利比亚,席卷非洲北部的干旱形势不那么严峻,仍然能够收获庄稼。因而利比亚成为了新的乐土。莫萨卡计划从 1 月到 7 月整个收获季节都呆在那里,然后才回家。然而从南部到达利比亚,必须首先要穿越这无人区。

所谓的无人区其实是位于撒哈拉沙漠中心的巨大沙海。它覆盖了尼日尔的一半疆土,阿尔及利亚的一部分,利比亚的少部分地区,以及乍得的一角。在撒哈拉沙漠的地图上,它被隔开的字母大大的标注成"特内雷[②]"——这是从

[①] 在豪萨语中,Hau 表示骑,Sa 表示牛。因此,现在学术上比较倾向于的关于豪萨人的起源的说法是:豪萨人过去为游牧民族,而且常常带着牛迁移,所以被称为牛背上的民族。当今我们所说的豪萨有两个含义:即一种语言和说此语言的民族的集合。豪萨语是非洲三大语言(即北非的阿拉伯语、东非的斯瓦西里语、西非的豪萨语)之一。使用该语言的国家主要有尼日利亚和尼日尔。喀麦隆、乍得、加纳、塞拉利昂的一些地区也使用该语言。豪萨语还作为商业用语,通用于西非几内亚湾沿岸各国。使用该语言的人口达 6000 万以上。由于豪萨人常常与弗拉尼人混居,且通婚情况非常普遍,所以我们在说豪萨的时候常常带上弗拉尼,即豪萨-弗拉尼。

[②] 特内雷,世界第一大沙漠的中部地域,一直延长到尼日利亚,被人称为"沙漠中的沙漠"。

图阿雷格①部族的语言中借用的一个词，意思是"无"或"空虚"或"空洞"。特内雷是地球上最不适宜人类居住的地方，是这个星球死掉的一大块。即使是这个词本身，"特内雷"看上去也隐约不祥，因为带有重音而听上去有讽刺意味。在无人区的中心地带，既没有一丝阴凉，也没有一滴水珠，更没有一棵小草。在其大部分地区，甚至连细菌都无法生存。

无人区晚上冰冷刺骨，白天热气灼人，常年狂风冲刷腐蚀。其中心地带犹如鼓面一样平坦无奇，连一块大点的岩石都没有。莫萨卡穿越无人区已经是第四天了；他至少还需要一周的时间才能走出去。除了祈祷的间歇，卡车根本不会停下来。自从进入无人区以来，莫萨卡几乎没有睡过觉，没有吃过东西，更没喝过酒。他没有鞋子，没有墨镜，也没有毯子。他的耳朵已经被沙土堵塞了，衣衫褴褛，双脚红肿。今天早上，我问他，当想到无人区的时候，头脑中最先出现什么。最近2个星期，因为我自己一直在利用各种交通方式横越撒哈拉沙漠，因此我几乎向每一个我遇到的人提出同样的问题。卡车偶然压过一块石头，所有乘客随之颠簸，臂肘磕碰胸口，头撞着头，莫萨卡向前倾着身子，再次回答我的问题。"沙漠真令人厌恶，"他用法语说道，"沙漠就是地狱。"然后他冲车外吐唾沫，再吐，试图摆脱嘴里的沙子。

"信念，"莫尼克说道。"是特内雷给了我信念。"4个星期以来，莫尼克一直反复穿越无人区。我们在阿尔及利亚的贾奈特小镇的小集市上见过，这个小集市位于特内雷北部的边缘。莫尼克与她的旅行伙伴来到这里是为了重新补充给养。她是瑞士人，但大部分时间都在美国生活。她的小组在平茨高尔②车队的护送下穿越无人区——六轮驱动，月球漫游者模样的车辆，奥地利制造，即使在最细柔的沙子面前仍然勇敢无畏。

莫尼克70岁出头。几年前，她的丈夫去世后不久，莫尼克终于完成了一生的梦想，来到了撒哈拉。沙漠改变了她。她亲眼目睹了日出的光辉将漫漫黄沙染成了唇彩的颜色，看到了海星形状的沙丘，绵延数英里，其弯曲的形状令她叹为观止。她听到嘶嘶的声音，这正是金色的沙粒在唱歌。她陶醉在万籁俱寂和广袤空旷之中。她睡在户外，任风儿为她编织发辫，沙儿藏在指甲缝中，太

---

① 图阿雷格族（Tuareg 或 Touareg）是一支主要分布于非洲撒哈拉沙漠周边地带的游牧民族，是散布在非洲北部广大地区的柏柏尔（Berber）部族中的一支。以迥异于周边民族的文字、语言与独特的游牧生活出名，今日的图瓦雷克主要分布在包括马里共和国、尼日尔共和国、阿尔及利亚民主人民共和国、大阿拉伯利比亚人民社会主义民众国与布基纳法索在内，原本是法属殖民地的北非与西非国家境内。

② 平茨高尔（Pinzgauer）原由奥地利斯太尔-戴姆勒-普赫公司生产，现由英国车辆技术（Automotive Technik,ALT）公司在英国进行生产。在1965年研制并于1971年投入量产，独特的底盘结构使平茨高尔在越野能力上堪称一流。

阳炙烤她的肌肤。她与沙漠牧民一同风餐露宿。她了解到，不是地球上的每一个地方都拥挤不堪，不是地球上的每个地方都充满贪婪无耻和逆来顺受。她当时呆了三个月。现在，她回来了，这次预计呆的时间更久。

她的故事并不少见。特内雷的旅游业几乎是一夜之间名扬万里。在巴黎和伦敦，日内瓦和柏林，旅行用品商纷纷包下整个航班搭载游客来到无人区的边缘地带，然后安排专车将你带到核心地带。宣传小册子提到：看一看地图吧，你即将要去的地方是撒哈拉的心脏，著名的特内雷。这个词本身，带有异国情调的重音，难道不会让你像读一首小小的诗一样卷舌吗？

许多游客来到这里都是出于精神上的追求。他们平日里过着忙碌的生活，他们希望得到一种虚空——然而有什么能比无人区的虚空更虚空的呢。无人区空空如也，就连傻瓜照相机都拒绝工作，自动对焦的照相机也找不到聚焦的对象。这是好事。有人告诉我，因为不给予任何东西，所以无人区也默默地接受一切。不管你想找什么，似乎都能在那里找到。遇见莫尼卡后没多久，我又遇到了另一位美国人并且与她攀谈起来。她的名字叫贝丝。她在特内雷已经呆了两个半星期了，她告诉我，她此行的重点是感受沙漠之风吹拂在脸上的感觉。吹了两周的风后，贝丝做出了一个意义深远的决定。她说，她刚刚回到家就马上辞去网络方面的工作，自己创业了。她说，她打算烘焙苹果派。

"钱，"艾哈迈德说，"钱，钱，钱，钱，钱。"艾哈迈德身无分文。但他的确有个计划。他的家乡是阿加德兹，在尼日尔的中部地区，也是特内雷的核心旅游区之一，他的计划就是去为每一架降落在阿加德兹的飞机乘客接机。较凉爽的几个月，机场跑道较平坦时，每周都有航班到达。当我从巴黎乘坐飞机降落到这里时，艾哈迈德就来了。当时的飞机搭载了太多的法国度假者，但所有人都早已与欧洲一条龙服务机构安排好了他们的旅程。

没有人需要聘请一名自由职业的导游。这也就是艾哈迈德一直跟我交谈的原因。

艾哈迈德会讲法语、英语、德语、阿拉伯语、豪萨语和图布语，以及他的母语，即图阿雷格人的语言，称为塔马奇克语。他今年27岁。头发是典型的图阿雷格人的头发，乌黑蓬乱，卷曲浓密。他经常习惯性地抬起胳膊扫一眼手腕，活脱脱一个繁忙的管理人员，这肯定是他从游客那里学来的小动作，因为艾哈迈德根本就没有自己的手表，并且他告诉我，他从来就没有过手表。他说，他之所以学习了各种语言，正是因为他不想坐卡车去利比亚谋生。他告诉我，他可以帮助游客租到高级越野车，可以为游客烹调——他的拿手好菜是塔格拉，一种大漠烤面包——最重要的是他能够带领游客穿越无人区，不用担心迷路。他说，旅游是在无人区唯一赚钱的方法。

艾哈迈德在他的上衣口袋里一直保留着一本小宣传册，是买洗发香波时赠送的。这本小册子里面全印着漂亮模特，都是白人美女，秀发皓齿。艾哈迈德反复翻阅小册子，皱得像一张张旧美钞一样。"等我有钱了，"他说，"我会找像这样的女人。"

"但是，"我指出来，"飞机已经降落了，而你却没有一个客户。"

"也许下周能有呢，"他说。

"那这个星期你要靠什么挣钱呢？"

"我把我所有的事都告诉你了，"他说。"这还不值点小费？"

"盐，"钓行说道。他的下巴冲着南边努着，朝着一个叫比尔马的地方，在尼日尔的东部，他将在那里收盐。钓行骑着他的骆驼。他盘腿而坐，头上松松垮垮地裹着一条长长的白布，身着棕褐色的宽大长袍，表情优雅泰然而飘忽不定——这是一种心境，每当他骑在驼背上的时候，似乎总能表达出来的一种心境。他时常哼唱小曲，用图布语婉转地诵扬，图布语的音节犹如圆润的鹅卵石一般。我骑着的骆驼也是他的，蓝色眼睛的母骆驼，发出的低低的声响，使我想起了管道工人。另外还有六只无人骑乘的骆驼跟随着我们。我们正行走在无人区的路上。

钓行是图布族人，也是最后的半游牧民族的一员，生活在广袤的无人区的边缘地带。在其周边，无人区也并不是完全空空如也；它三面环山，山路崎岖多峭壁——阿伊尔高原、阿哈加尔山、加多高原、提贝斯提高原——南部是乍得湖流域。钓行骑着他的骆驼，可以朝前坐、朝后坐、侧坐在驼鞍上或站在上面，而且他可以通过耳语命令他的骆驼蹲下或立起来或转圈。他的刀高高的绑在右臂上；装满了水的山羊皮水壶勾在马鞍上；几颗干枣和一小袋烟叶，几撮烟卷纸塞在长袍胸前的口袋里。他正坐在毯子上。这便是他的全部家当。据说，图布族的人可以靠一颗枣活3天：第一天吃枣皮，第二天吃枣肉，第三天吃枣核儿。据我的猜测，这可是比你想象的真实得多。和钓行艰难旅行的两天时间里，我看到他真地只吃了一顿饭。

如果你问钓行多大年纪，他会说不知道。他很愿意猜测（他认为20岁吧），但他并不能确定。这也没关系。他对时间的概念不是按照年或季节或月份来分的而是按照方向分的。要么他奔赴比尔马收盐，要么他离开比尔马卖盐。两千年来，这一直是图布人的生活方式。至今还没有任何人发现一个比骆驼更经济高效的方法跨越无人区运送盐——发动机和沙子的组合并不理想——因而骆驼仍然派得上用场。骆驼可以在无水供给的情况下存活两周，然后，一次长时间的饮水，可在驼峰中储存25加仑水。钓行到达比尔马盐矿之后，给每一头骆驼都加载六个50磅的柱状盐袋，然后和其他图布人组成驼队——100多头骆驼一字排开，纵队大步跨越大漠——朝阿加德兹行进。最好的情况下，长途跋涉需要近一个月的时间。

钓行偶尔也会遇到游客，他有时会看到超载的卡车，但他只是略微好奇而已。他不需要从忙碌的生活中寻求任何慰藉。他也不需要去利比亚收获庄稼。他带着仅能维持生命的必需品旅行，并且他知道，沿途哪怕有一口井突然干涸了——确实会发生这样的事——那么他也很可能会命丧于此。他知道，无人区里有土匪，有沙尘暴。他还没有结婚。他告诉我，需要5头骆驼才能娶一位贤妻，但他目前连一头骆驼都买不起。如果能顺利到达阿加德兹，他将把盐卖出，然后立即赶回比尔马。他通过沙丘、土壤的颜色和风向辨别路线。通过观察骆驼的连串足迹，他能断定骆驼的品种，进而推断它们所属的部落，行程的天数，负重情况，以及驼队中骆驼的数量。他在沙漠中出生，一生从未离开过这里。这也许就是当我问及他对家乡的看法时他奇怪地望着我的原因。我问他那个问题时，他的脸色变得被动。他提到了盐，但后来沉默了几秒钟。"关于无人区我真的从来没思考过，"他说。

"相机，"穆斯塔法说，"还有摄像机、手表、随身听、珠宝和GPS。"穆斯塔法肩膀上挎着一支M-16步枪。他正试图向我兜售从其他游客那里弄来的东西。我正身处位于希尔法小型哨站的一个警察检查站里，临近无人区的东北边界。我已雇了沙漠出租车——一名超胆侠司机和一辆无敌越野车——带我到阿尔及利亚。然而现在，我们却被阻止前进了。

穆斯塔法很胖。他真是胖，并且身穿警服。这是一个糟糕的搭配。在无人区，只有富人才会胖。尼日尔的警察不能赚足够的钱而变胖，因此，胖警察就一定是贪污腐化的。贪污腐化的官员必然意味着麻烦。当我连看都不看他的商品时，穆斯塔法非常恼怒。他要求看我的旅行证件。无人区是一个有趣的地方——同时可以既没有规则又有严格的规则。为了能够合法地穿越无人区，你应该携带非常特殊的旅行证件，而我实际上有这些证件。但对这些证件的解释又是因人而异的。例如，你必须列出旅行的确切路线。这一点很难做到，因为你穿越的是一片辽阔的沙漠，根本就没有真正的道路。所以，穆斯塔法轻而易举就找到了一个错误。

"错误很容易纠正，"他说，"你只需要返回阿加德兹。"返回阿加德兹需要向相反的方向开四天的车。"或者我可以在这里改正错误，"他补充说，"只要把您的GPS装置给我就行。"他对受贿甚至都不屑于假装一下。穆斯塔法是这座哨站的头目，掌管1000平方英里沙漠的独裁领导人。根本没有上诉的对象。

"我没有GPS装置，"我说。

"那你的手表也行。"

"不,"我说。

"付钱就行了。"

"不,"我说。

"好,"他说道。然后,他什么也没说。他交叉双臂放在腹部赘肉上。他在那里站了很长时间。司机将车熄火。我们等着。穆斯塔法有的是时间,整天、整周、整月、整年。他有没有其他安排。他没有会要开。如果我们试图把车开走,他就会朝我们开枪。这注定是一场败仗。

我给了他一捆中非法郎,于是我们能继续上路了。

"啤酒,"格雷斯说。"啤酒和女人。"格雷斯大概35岁,穿着一条带有黄色向日葵图案的颜色鲜艳的连衣裙。她有这样一条理论:她坚信,跨越无人区并且亲眼目睹所有的空无,她断定,会在一个人内心产生某种空虚。她下定决心要填补这种空虚,这是她的神圣职责。所以格雷斯在迪尔库开了一家酒吧,既是酒吧也是妓院。

迪尔库是一个不同寻常的小镇。它位于尼日尔,在特内雷的东北部边缘,建在一个旧河道里面——一个古老的河床,现在已经干涸了,但地表以下不远处就有水源,打井即可有水。地下水为椰枣树在迪尔库的生长提供了保障。无论你驾乘卡车、骆驼,还是四驱越野车,所有穿越无人区的人几乎不可能不在迪尔库停下,要么补充燃料,要么补充给养,要么补充水或其他缺乏的东西。

显然,这里流行的说法是,一定要告知每位新来迪尔库的人,他们现在所在的地方,其实是大地的尽头。我刚到镇上才1个小时,就被五六个人告知这事了;那肯定是一句市民口号。这仅仅能证明到大地的尽头来旅行不应该列在每个人的任务列表上。迪尔库大概是我所游览过的最无法赎罪的地方,包括洛杉矶在内。这座小镇本质上是一个大型公交车站,但它缺乏电、水暖、电视、报纸和电话等基本设施。据当地人说,这里两年多以来一直没有下过雨。街道上到处是乞丐、骗子、盗贼、移民、流浪汉、士兵和妓女。除了妓女几乎都是男人。说这个地方是真正的垃圾场一点也不过分:只要你想扔东西,就直接扔在街上就行了。格雷斯的空虚理论确有一定道理。我在从利比亚回来的卡车上坐了3天才到达迪尔库。190名乘客中,有186名是男性乘客。那些有点钱的直奔格雷斯开的酒吧。酒吧和迪尔库的其他地方一样:泥做的墙,棕榈树叶搭的屋顶,沙子地板。我坐在一个用零碎木板搭成的桌子旁,用牛奶货柜当做椅子。电池供电的收音机播放着某个乍得电台的音乐,只是90%都是干扰音,只有10%才是阿拉伯音乐。我喝了一杯尼日尔啤酒,这啤酒一直被储存在阴凉处,以撒哈拉的标准来说,就算冰镇啤酒啦。于是我又多喝了两杯。

似乎我的空虚并不如卡车上其他朋友的空虚那么深刻。在特内雷，存在这样一种奇怪但又很普遍的信念，就是酒精能够给你补充水分——不仅是给你补水，而且补水的效果比水更强。卡车上有些人在最后一天的行程里滴水未沾，因为他们知道格雷斯的酒吧正一步一步接近他们。这些男人中的许多都很快在酒吧喝醉了。人们也相信，只要妓女未年满18岁，客人就不会从她那里感染艾滋病。

在迪尔库，另一个缺乏的东西就是卫生间。吃完一些骆驼肉香肠，喝完第四杯啤酒之后，我问格雷斯卫生间在哪里。她告诉我在街上。我非常委婉地向她解释，我将要生产一种不同类型的废物。她说，不要紧，卫生间的确就是在大街上。我走出酒吧，试图寻找一个隐蔽点的地方，在这个过程中我亲眼目睹了3名男子正在做我打算做的事情。这就解释了弥漫在迪尔库空气中的那股不幸的气味。

"灵魂，"沃阿迪果乌说道。他正坐在毯子上，抱着饭碗，所谓的饭碗不过是个沙丁鱼罐头盒。他的脸被一盏煤油灯照亮着。沃阿迪果乌和我们共进晚餐，吃了米饭和一点羊肉。他是钓行的一个表兄弟，钓行就是那个年轻的盐商，曾经告诉过我，他对沙漠无人区没什么想法。钓行允许我加入他的驼队，我们已经跋涉了两天，而现在，在旅途过程中，我们在一个图布人的营地借宿。沃阿迪果乌便生活在这个营地里，这个营地由几处圆顶草屋组成，还包括24头骆驼，一个图布族的大家庭和一群山羊。在我借宿的小屋里，一盘盒式磁带居然作为一件有意思的小摆设挂在墙壁上。当然，营地里可没有录音机。在这里，娱乐的主要形式和无人区的所有地方的娱乐形式是相同的——谈天说地。沃阿迪果乌猜他自己不到30岁，他组织大家在进餐时间进行讨论。他是一个尖锐并有见地的健谈者。讨论的主题是宗教。图布族名义上是穆斯林，但大多数人，包括沃阿迪果乌在内，都将伊斯兰教和传统的万物有灵信仰结合起来。

"沙漠里，"沃阿迪果乌说，"到处都是灵魂。我总是与他们交谈，他们告诉我一些事情，他们告诉我一些消息，有的灵魂你是可以看到的，但有的你看不到，一些是好的，一些是不好的，一些假装是好的，但事实正好相反。我向那些好的灵魂请求得到强壮的骆驼，也请求指引我找到隐匿的宝藏。"

沃阿迪果乌吸引了我的注意力，他马上看出来，我并不赞同他的信仰。不过，他很宽宏大量。"即使你没有看到我的灵魂，"他说，"你肯定能看到某个其他人的。每个人都是如此。否则的话，为什么基督教、犹太教和伊斯兰教都缘起于这同一片沙漠？"

"工作，"比利特说道。"这工作使我和沙漠紧密连在了一起。"比利特正是前往利比亚的超载卡车的司机。他停下车，从驾驶座爬出来，向着麦加的方向施跪拜礼，额头上沾满了沙子。刚从车上下来的乘客正在返回卡车，一个摞在另一个上面。透过飞旋的黄沙只能看见他们的头巾。沙漠无人区里每个人都戴着头巾——既可以防止风吹日晒也可以为人们提供匿名身份，如果一个人想偷渡到利比亚或试图做其他有违法嫌疑的举动时，这点尤其宝贵。头巾是沙漠中仅有的色调。色调中有些是醒目的基本色，就像色彩鲜艳的口香糖球一样。比利特的头巾是绿色的。我问他，我们还要走多远。

"还有两天，"比利特说。"听天由命吧，"他补充道——但愿一切顺利吧。他又说了一遍："听天由命。"到目前为止，这句话是沙漠无人区里使用率最高的表达方式，作用就相当于口语中的标点符号。但愿一切顺利。这强调了一个严峻的事实，那就是无论准备得有多细致入微，在无人区的旅行，总是会遇到失控的状态。比利特已经开这条线路——从阿加德兹到迪尔库，绵延400英里的沙漠无人区——有8年时间了。条件允许的情况下，他每天开20到22个小时。在沙子相对坚硬的地方，比利特可以达到每小时15英里的速度。如果遇到软沙地，乘客不得不下来推车。不管开到哪里，发动机的响声，就好像它在不断地清喉咙。

他这条路线是特内雷地区最为繁忙的路线之一——有的时候，他一天能看到三至四辆其它的车。这就意味着比利特并不需要依靠指南针或北斗七星来确定他是否向着正确的方向前进。沙漠里实际上也有其它的轮胎痕迹。然而，并非所有的痕迹都是可靠的。在特内雷，一条"道"的宽度可以是20英里，上面布满了交错的轮胎痕迹，因为有的司机需要绕过软沙，寻找更稳固的沙道。经验不足的司机有可能遵循交错的车辙，最终误入歧途。在一个只能看到空白的地平线的地方，不可能分辨出来你究竟是沿着一个渐进的弧线在行进还是直着往前走。有的司机就这样沿着错误的交错路线行驶，直到汽油耗尽。

更糟糕的是没有任何痕迹。每次大沙尘暴过后便会这样，纷飞的沙砾将无人区变成一片空白，仿佛神奇画板一样，轻轻一摇，又是一张空白的画布。沙尘暴大概平均每星期发生一次。沙尘暴期间，比利特停止开车。有时，他将被迫停2天，有时甚至3天。乘客当然必须受这种苦，由于太过拥挤动弹不得。车太拥挤，是因为乘客越多，车主挣钱越多。在沙漠无人区里，原始经济主宰一切，舒适性是很少被考虑的因素。

有一次，沙尘暴来临的时候比利特没有停车，结果他迷路了。在无人区迷失是非常可怕的。即使有指南针和星星，也很容易偏离半度，错过一个镇。那一次比利特成功地找到了正确的路。但是，就在最近，就在同一路线上，一辆卡车彻底迷路了。在特内雷几乎没有救援服务，直到一辆军车定位到卡车时，只有八人还活着。人们发现了36具尸体，都是脱水而死。其余的乘客——至少有六名，很可能有更多的乘客——被埋在黄沙之下，至今未被发现。

"战争，"汤布说。我看到的是沙丘，汤布看到的却是掩体。汤布是一名士兵，曾经在 1990 年尼日尔爆发的图阿雷格人武装叛乱中做过领导人。战斗已经融化在他的血液里了。3000 余年以来，直到法国在 19 世纪末期占领了北非，图阿雷格人一直被视为特内雷地区的土匪，他们在穿越沙漠无人区的时候抢劫骆驼篷车。

然而，从 1990 年开始的战斗是为了争夺公民权利。许多图阿雷格人在尼日尔觉得自己像二等公民——他们声称，是那些人口占多数的豪萨族人和其它族群的人得到了良好的就业机会，政府的职位，以及大学奖学金。因此图阿雷格人决定通过武力获得对自己家园的自治权，而他们所谓的家园，实质上就是整个特内雷地区。他们争取建立一个沙漠无人区独立共和国。数百人死于这场争斗，直到 1995 年双方才达成了妥协：图阿雷格人将得到更多的尊重；作为回报，他们必须同意放弃独立。虽然零星的小规模战争一直持续到 1998 年，无人区还算安静，至少现在是这样。这也是本地区旅游业突然回暖的一个主要原因。

汤布不再是一名战士；虽然现在开沙漠出租车，但他仍像一名士兵一样，开起车来横冲直撞。我雇他将我带向北部，穿越无人区的中心，到达阿尔及利亚——总共为期 4 天的车程。当一名警方人员强迫我行贿时，他就在我身旁。休息时，汤布在沙子上绘出地形图，指给我，他如何攻击一处阿伊尔高原上的高高的岗哨，以及如何在广阔的无人区伏击了整个吉普车队。"但现在是和平时期，"他说道。他看上去挺失望。我问他，图阿雷格人的情况是否有所改变。

"没有，"他说。"唯一的改变就是我们已经缴枪投降了。"他看起来更加失望了。"但是，"他的脸色突然由阴转晴，并补充说，"把枪拿回来也是轻而易举的事。"

"速度，"乔尔说。他刚刚把摩托车停在房子前面，这是我在迪尔库租的地方，一间无家具陈设的小屋，租金是 1 夜 1 美元，沙子做的地板。乔尔来到沙漠只为一个原因：提高速度。他在这里呆了两个月，从以色列来到这里为的是骑摩托车练习，一辆红白相间的雅马哈牌摩托车，沙漠无人区便是他的训练场。速度和沙漠无人区是由故事相互联系的；13 年以来，每年的冬天，特内雷都是著名的巴黎-达喀尔拉力赛的必经之路——几百名外国人乘坐跑车、小货车或摩托车撕心裂肺一般从沙漠呼啸而过。1997 年，比赛改变了路线，但之前的残骸仍然清晰可见，每隔几英里都能见到，车辆的油漆被风沙侵蚀，钢铁被烤成均匀的巧克力棕色。

乔尔对巴黎-达喀尔拉力赛有种敬畏之情。他谈到沙地的感觉就仿佛滑雪者谈到对雪的感情——以一种外人无法理解的语言。事实证明，沙子，并不仅仅是沙子。有浅盐水湖、沙海、旱谷①、尔格、新月形沙丘、流沙、裸岩和粉末灰尘。乔尔告诉我，迪尔库周边的沙子是再好不过的了。"你想借用我的车吗？"他问道。

　　我当然想。我啪的一声戴上他的头盔，跨腿坐在车座上，向一片黄沙奔去。世界在我面前是绝对的平坦，什么都没有，我拼命加油，很快挂到5档，引擎惊声尖叫，沙子四下咆哮。一定程度上，我知道，我的速度太快，极为危险，但感觉却是毫无恐惧。坐标开始变得扭曲，更像是跳伞——我已经下定决心，此刻正在天际飞驰，一切都无法伤害我。这是一种欣快、纯粹的感情，纯粹的重力和无法无天的快感，我当然想得到更多的愉快，所以我猛拉油门，世界变得一片模糊，地平线消失了，正是在这时，在这里，我突然意识到，我需要做些什么。我就这样做了。我闭上眼睛。紧紧地闭上，摩托车子弹上膛，顾不上恐慌，因为我知道，根本不会遇到障碍，很快，我紧闭双眼，感觉大脑一片空白寂静，一种水晶般剔透的自由。

　　"死亡，"凯文说。"我想到了死亡。"并不只凯文这样想。每个横跨沙漠无人区的人，无论游客，图布族人还是卡车的乘客，都亲眼见证了特内雷的残酷无情。例如，骸骨——许多具骸骨，在沙漠无人区行驶的一个好方法就是遵循尸骨的痕迹，这些尸骨散落在每条主要线路的旁边，如同徒步旅行小径上的堆石标。大多是山羊的骨头。山羊是特内雷地区比较常见的货运工具，在跨越无人区的过程中，总有一两只会死掉。死掉的山羊都被抛出车外。在沙漠无人区的中心地带，尸体都被晒干，变得坚韧，像木乃伊一样。在无人区的边缘地带，黑背豺四处流浪，骨头都被它们啃得精光，白骨被太阳晒得褪色，酷似雪花石膏。有的尸骨是骆驼的，有一两具是人的。每年在特内雷都有人送命，但几乎没有旅客像凯文这样直接经历死亡。

　　凯文也坐在开往利比亚方向的卡车上，和采摘作物的人们一同跨越无人区。但他和大多数其他乘客有所不同，他对摘作物没什么兴趣，他想踢足球。他是一名中场球员，打算在利比亚或突尼斯的专业队里找到一个位置。凯文出生在南非，成长在种族隔离制度下，后来逃到了塞内加尔，生活在那里的难民营中。他的声音富有温暖和平静的气息，他带着一副金属架眼镜，深邃的眼眸中透露出一种深层次的思虑，看起来像一位医生或宗教领袖。每次卡车上发生争斗的时候，他便担任调停者的角色，温和地说服双方在求同存异的基础上做出妥协。他告诉我，他想研习哲学，并且一直深受托马斯·杰斐逊著作的启发。

---

① 旱谷是干旱区的干河谷，为干燥的沟壑或陡壁的峡谷。暂时性的洪流侵蚀形成的沟壑或河床，有的还参与改造，使谷道加深展宽，形状极不规则，主谷、支谷难以分辨。平时河床干涸，只在暴雨洪流时河床中才有水。

他说，他最喜欢的音乐家是菲尔·柯林斯。"听他的音乐，能让我动容。"他说，我面无表情的告诉他，菲尔·柯林斯的音乐也会让我落泪。这是凯文第二次尝试跨越沙漠到达足球场。1年以前的第一次旅行，以灾难结束。

他和朋友西尔曼乘坐在一部破旧的越野车上，行驶在无人区的北部。他们两个都梦想着有朝一日能够踢足球。车上还有另外6名乘客和1名司机，为了安全起见，他们跟着另一部越野车，试图找到穿越特内雷的一条捷径。凯文和西尔曼坐的车突然抛锚了。第二辆越野车上已经没什么空间了，所以只有第一辆车的司机挤上了车。他告诉其他乘客等着他。他说，他会去距离最近的城镇，大概1天的车程，然后开另一辆车返回。

然而3天过去了，仍然不见司机的踪影。饮用水已经所剩无几了。当时正是仲夏期间，无人区的气温经常达到华氏115度，最高能够达到130度。热气腾空，将天空染成了白色；黄沙闪闪发光，几近熔化。凯文和西尔曼决定，与其坐以待毙不如徒步而行。其他6名乘客决定继续呆在破车上。凯文和西尔曼继续穿越沙漠，跟随着第二辆越野车的印记。即使坐在撒哈拉的树荫下，一个人每天都会散出2加仑的汗水。凯文和西尔曼在徒步的情况下很可能散出两倍的汗水。他们把所有的水都带在身上，但仍然连四分之一的消耗量都不可能补上。

人类是适应性很强的动物，但精准性也很高。即使丧失1加仑水分——约5%的体液——都会导致头晕、头痛和血液循环问题。唾液腺会干涸，语言会混乱。凯文和西尔曼不到一天就变成了这种状态。如果有2加仑的水分赤字，走路几乎是不可能的。舌头肿胀，视力和听力减弱，尿液变成深锈色。就连清醒的思想都难以形成。没有医疗援助的话，恢复体力是不可能的。接近这种状态的人往往会采取孤注一掷的措施。尿液首当其冲会被喝掉。凯文和西尔曼就是这样做的。"如果换做你，你也会这么做的，"凯文告诉我。被迫滞留的人们会喝掉汽油、散热器液，甚至蓄电池酸液。也有真实的例子，讲由于干渴，濒临死亡的人杀死别人为的就是饮血。

凯文和西尔曼徒步行走了3天。最终西尔曼崩溃了。凯文独自继续前行，有时甚至爬行。第二天，司机回来了。他突然出现在凯文面前，这一时刻，凯文已经几乎没有了知觉。司机并没有解释他为期一周的耽搁。他给了凯文水，而后赶去寻找西尔曼。但为时已晚。西尔曼已经死了。他们又返回到破旧的越野车附近，却一个人也没看见。显而易见，其他的乘客也试图徒步离开。他们的足迹已经被扬沙覆盖了。经过几个小时的搜索，还是没有其他人的踪迹。凯文是唯一的幸存者。

"历史，"哈穆德说。哈穆德是一个老头——尽管"老"在尼日尔是相对的，尼日尔人的平均寿命是 41 岁。我雇了一辆沙漠出租车到尼日尔东部的一个叫贾多城①的地方，哈穆德是贾多城的导游。到目前为止，贾多城是我在特内雷见到过的最好的城市。它建在一座小山丘上，山丘的旁边是长满枣椰树的绿洲，小山丘看起来有点像抹过灰涂满泥的圣米歇尔山②。这里的家不像我在沙漠无人区中看到的其它任何建筑，它是多层的，宽敞凉爽的。建筑师的煞费苦心也可见一斑；墙被建成椭圆形，并已建成角楼供人环视四周的沙漠。一点垃圾也没有。

一个问题：并没有人生活在贾多城。这座城有几千年的历史，并被废弃了两个多世纪。这里曾经一度居住着 50 万人，他们沿着贾多城的绿洲生活。现在它成为了国家保护区的一部分并禁止发展。少数家庭聚居在几英里之遥的泥窝棚里，依靠从稀稀落落的游客身上赚取几美元过活。

到底贾多城为什么会被遗弃，没有一个人知道究竟；最有可能的致命打击就是疟疾的传播以及贸易路线的变化。但据哈穆德分析，城市的衰落是剧烈的气候变化引发的。1 万年前，撒哈拉还是一片绿色。长颈鹿、大象、河马在这片土地上繁衍畅行。鳄鱼在河流中生活。距离贾多城不远处的悬崖峭壁上，一些古老的岩画描绘了当时繁荣的社会，牧民、渔民、弓箭猎人等。大约公元前 4000 年，天气开始发生变化。狩猎动物逐渐离开。河流渐渐干涸。最后一幅完整的悬崖岩画是一头似乎正在哭泣的母牛，这也许象征着笼罩在当时的气氛。贾多城繁荣之时，它的绿洲面积或许覆盖几十平方英里，而现在的面积只相当于一口淤污的池塘。哈穆德说，他发现走在贾多城的道路上感觉"催人入眠"、"惊心动魄"、"金碧辉煌"和"楚楚动人。"我没有告诉他，我的强烈感觉却是悲伤。在沙漠无人区，似乎再清楚不过的一个事实就是，1000 年以前人们的生活比今天要好一些。

"是命运啊，"艾克里说。他耸了耸肩，暗示他本应不在乎，但他的话已经背叛了他的身体语言。艾克里的确很在乎，但他无能为力——也许，说实话，这正是他耸肩所试图表达的含义。艾克里是图阿雷格人，一个在巴黎接受过教育的阿加德兹本地人。他返回了尼日尔，带着他的法国妻子，经营着一间小小

---

① 在撒哈拉沙漠中，曾经有一座城市叫做贾多城。它的存在证明了横贯撒哈拉沙漠的卡沃尔地区在古代曾有人类居住。自从罗马人在公元三世纪从小亚细亚引进了骆驼以来，成千上万的旅行者都到过这个沙漠贸易的控制据点。在一位古代作家的笔下，五世纪时的贾多城有充足的食盐和用盐块垒成的房子，人们在此过着穴居的生活。

② 圣米歇尔山是法国著名古迹和基督教圣地，位于芒什省一小岛上，距海岸两公里。小岛呈圆锥形，周长 900 米，由耸立的花岗石构成。海拔 88 米，经常被大片沙岸包围，仅涨潮时才成岛。圣米歇尔山及其海湾，文化遗产，1979 年列入世界遗产名录。

的招待所。阿加德兹是一个被暴虐的沙漠所包围的贫穷国家的贫穷城市。这不是一个培养乐观精神的地方。

  艾克里非常担心撒哈拉。他非常关注其扩张的情况。多数科学证据似乎都显示，撒哈拉大沙漠依然在行进之中。在过去的30年中，沙漠向南部挺进了超过60英里，吞噬了大片的草原和农作物，一口口水井干涸，大量难民流离失所。撒哈拉也在向北延伸，逼近阿特拉斯山脉的山麓，仿佛准备伏击地中海。

  荒漠化具有和板块构造一样强大的力量。撒哈拉如果想要生长，它就会生长。艾克里说，仅仅他生活的这些年里，就见证了深刻的变化。他认为，沙漠的扩张是由于撒哈拉自身的力量和人类的影响。"我们砍掉所有的树木，"他说，"臭氧层被我们戳了一个洞，地球正在变暖，人口数量过多，但我们又能做些什么呢？每个人都需要吃饭，每个人都想要一个家庭。"他再次耸了耸肩，和之前一样。

  "住在这里已经变得越来越困难，"他说，"我很高兴，你能来到这里，看到这些困难的情况，希望你能够逐渐习惯。"

  我摇摇头，指了指脸上成串的汗珠，指了指脖子上猩红的痱子，又指了指造成鼻子、脸颊和手臂上死皮剥落的晒斑。

  "我想你最好习惯它，"艾克里说。"我认为，每个人都应该习惯它。因为早晚有一天，也许不会很远，所有的沙漠都将扩大。它们都会像撒哈拉大沙漠一样成长。那么每个人都会生活在无人区里。"

（杨建 译　申彩红 校）

Stranger in the Dunes①

Graham Brink

【导读】心中有岸,不怕远航。当代著名诗人汪国真曾说:"我不去想是否能够成功,既然选择了远方,便只顾风雨兼程;我不去想身后会不会袭来寒风冷雨,既然目标是地平线,留给世界的只能是背影。"本文作者带着无比虔诚、勇敢而充满好奇的心走进了摩洛哥的这片沙漠,作为美国人的他,特别是"9·11"恐怖袭击之后,需要多么大的勇气。作者笔下的摩洛哥人是单纯可爱的,对于普普通通的穆斯林来说,他们从未见过真正的高楼大厦,却因发达国家造成的环境污染,生活在这片荒漠中,艰难度日。小伙子说着蹩脚的英语,却也挡不住他与来客的交谈,连骆驼都被赋予了人的灵性,作者所接触的穆斯林,对于恐怖这个名词,似乎都从未听过。他们对于恐怖的概念,也仅限于"炸毁建筑就像偷窃——偷钱、偷物、偷窃他人生命,而任何偷窃都是不应该的",他们朴素的观念的确给人以震撼。"摩洛哥人希望被看作世界上最友好的人们",这是他们发自内心的愿望。标榜富足的美国人对陌生人是冷漠的,恐惧的,而这群生活在简单中的穆斯林人似乎有着一种与生俱来的热情,你一旦被当作客人,做客家中,便自然而然的被主人热情地招待着、保护着、照顾着。信任一个素未相识的人,这的确有些让人难以置信。这便是他们的逻辑:笑对生活,不怕烦恼来敲门。

MERZOUGA, Morocco — The sand slams into Zahid's full-length white robe, flattening it against his chest and thighs, blowing the extra material up behind him like a cape. A heavily wrapped scarf covers his head, leaving only a slit for his dark eyes.

He leads the riderless② camel through the low-rolling dunes between two ranges of 600-foot peaks. Our footprints begin disappearing, first in minutes, then in

---

① The Sahara Desert has many different landforms. Parts have sand dunes. A sand dune is a mountain of sand. Some dunes can be as high as 600 feet.

② adj. Having no rider; as, a riderless horse.

seconds. The grains penetrate zippers and chafe exposed skin. Throats scratch. Eyes slowly close with grit.

Gait slowed and head bent low, Zahid pushes on. In comic contrast, the camel seems to smile through his thick lips and bat his huge lashes. We are a couple of hours into a four-day trek through the giant dunes. Four days? I think. Only if we make it through the next four minutes.

Then, the wind vanishes.

No big deal, Zahid announces while shaking a pailful of sand out of his scarf. In the summers, the flying sand blots out the sky, he says. Camels get lost. Nomads sometimes die.

The dunes, named Erg Chebbi[①], rest in the middle of a plain on the western edge of the Sahara. Chebbi is the largest erg, or sand sea, in Morocco. At about 150 square miles, it's small compared to the Grand Ergs in Algeria and Libya.

Zahid wonders why anyone would travel so far to visit his country's super-sized sandbox. He's not complaining; he just doesn't get it.

"Sandstorms. Not fun. No, no, no," Zahid says.

When I first thought about flying to Morocco last summer, it seemed a convenient location to live out my desert fantasies — camels, sand, nomads, brutal weather — my own sanitized version of *Lawrence of Arabia*[②].

After Sept. 11, the trip took on new allure. It became what you don't do. You don't vacation alone in a Muslim country in the middle of a war on terrorism when many people are scared to visit grandparents in Omaha. You don't insist on talking religion and politics in a strange and sometimes volatile land.

In America, we are taught to keep strangers at arm's length. In recent months, that lesson has grown to "suspect everyone," especially anyone who looks Arab. This was a chance to turn the tables, to be the stranger, the one suspicion is cast

---

① 尔格谢比沙峰位于撒哈拉沙漠的西部边缘，富于层次感，是骆驼队长途跋涉的好去处。

② *Lawrence of Arabia* is a 1962 British epic film based on the life of T. E. Lawrence. It was directed by David Lean and produced by Sam Spiegel through his British company, Horizon Pictures from a script by Robert Bolt and Michael Wilson. The film stars Peter O'Toole in the title role. It is widely considered one of the greatest and most influential films in the history of cinema. The dramatic score by Maurice Jarre and the Super Panavision 70 cinematography by Freddie Young are also highly acclaimed. The film depicts Lawrence's experiences in Arabia during World War I, in particular his attacks on Aqaba and Damascus and his involvement in the Arab National Council. Its themes include Lawrence's emotional struggles with the personal violence inherent in war, his personal identity, and his divided allegiance between his native Britain and its army and his newfound comrades within the Arabian desert tribes.

upon.

'I married my father'

"You ready to walk?" Zahid asks as I pull my shoes back on and wipe the remnants of the sandstorm from my cords and long-sleeved shirt.

Zahid's casual cool is bred from a lifetime of struggle. At 55, Zahid (like many Moroccans, he uses no last name) has overcome sun blindness, 130-degree temperatures, camel thieves, tribal disputes, disease and those hellish sandstorms, just to name the most obvious.

A prolonged drought forced Zahid and his wife off the plains four years ago and into a remote hamlet called Taboumiat, population 30. They bought a small house with a view of the dunes, and Zahid took up handling camels for tourists.

He hasn't had much to do lately.

Even in the desert, Zahid has had to deal with the fallout① from the collapse of the "grand buildings." He wonders if he will have to return to his life as a herder on the plains, with little money to buy new camels. Will his wife be forced to give up her new loves — her stove, her friends, the lights that come on with a flick of a switch?

For Zahid the choice is between convenience and hardship. The dunes are a living. Me? I'm entranced by the eerie② beauty.

Throughout the day, the color of the sand ranges from pink to red to brown to black. Look one way and the dunes are a washed-out canvas. Turn around and the sun has transformed them into a masterpiece of shadows and contrast. With the rising heat, the smaller dunes appear to move like slow waves.

The wind shapes the dunes quickly, shearing and building peaks, bending razor-straight ridges into S's. The worst storms kick sand high into the sky, sometimes carrying it as far as the Caribbean islands.

The only other person on our trek is Zahid's 18-year-old assistant, Hassan. He can cook a tangy Moroccan stew, carry a tune and speak parts of seven languages. The part of English he knows doesn't include many pronouns. So whether he is talking about the camel or his mother, the sentence begins with "I." As in, "I eat a lot

---

① noun. The slow descent of minute particles of debris in the atmosphere following an explosion, especially the descent of radioactive debris after a nuclear explosion.

② adj. Inspiring inexplicable fear, dread, or uneasiness; strange and frightening.

of desert plants" or "I married my father in a ceremony near the dunes."

On the first day, he keeps saying we are headed for a "weesis." A weesis? It sounds more like a stifled sneeze than the palm tree-lined "oasis" where we wind up for the first night.

Of terrorists and thieves

That evening, we bundle under camel-hair blankets and stoke the fire as the temperature drops into the low 40s. A full moon backlights Zahid's every breath. With his sinewy frame, well-trimmed black mustache and chiseled features, he looks like a slightly darker version of Burt Reynolds.

The conversation gets going with stupid tourist stories — the winner being Hassan's yarn about a Dutch guy who thought it would be funny to brush his camel's teeth until it bit down, swallowing the brush and the tip of the man's middle finger.

Hassan recalls a myth about how the dunes were created thousands of years ago when the local people refused to help a woman and child who needed food and shelter during a festival. Incensed①, God buried the town and its inhabitants in sand.

The story illustrates the importance many Moroccans place on hospitality. In the time it takes to travel only a few miles, a stranger on a bus will offer up a small cup of milk and some smoked sardines, then invite me to his sister's wedding.

At first all the attention makes me suspicious. What scam are they trying to pull? I check my pockets for my money and make sure my bag is still where it should be. Despite my obvious skepticism, the invitations keep coming. I figure the whole country cannot be after my wallet. My guard starts to come down.

Moroccans, it turns out, consider guests to be gifts from Allah.

"We need more gifts," Zahid tells me in Arabic. "Why'd they all go away?"

I'm not sure what to tell him other than that Westerners aren't comfortable and, in some cases, are downright② angry with the Arab world. I begin to tell him about the Israeli-Palestinian debacle③ and Middle Eastern politics, but he gets a perplexed look. It's tough to explain new global realities to someone who has never seen a globe.

A few minutes later, Zahid quietly moves to a flat patch 20 yards away to pray.

---

① adj. extremely angry.

② adj. frank or straightforward.

③ noun. A sudden, disastrous collapse, downfall, or defeat.

Zahid is Berber, an indigenous tribe introduced to Islam in the 7th century by the invading Arabs.

Praying is common in a country with 29-million Muslims, 98 percent of the population. No one complains when taxi drivers pull to the side of the highway and drop to their knees on the gravel shoulder. Train passengers switch seats so they face Mecca and quietly whisper "Allahu akbar" (Allah is the greatest).

Zahid doffs his sandals and socks. With the dry sand, he washes his hands, forearms, feet and ankles and runs his hands over his head. He faces east and prays, standing, then kneeling, four times.

Zahid knows that five times a day Osama bin Laden prays the same way to the same God. He smiles when he considers what possible ties a camel herder in the middle of nowhere could have with a Saudi Arabian heir turned terrorist mastermind.

"Are you a terrorist?" I ask jokingly.

No, but you look like you could be, he shoots back with a smile.

The only thing Zahid knows about terrorism is what he's heard from tourists. He knows of the Basques in northern Spain and remembers a Japanese group telling him about poisonous gas in the Tokyo subway.

Zahid has never visited a city. Four months ago, he didn't know what a skyscraper was. But he remembers feeling sad and then angered when he heard about the Sept. 11 attacks. He said toppling a building is like stealing — property, money and lives — and stealing is never justified.

In the desert when a camel died, any Berber could leave it and the load it was carrying where it fell by simply marking the camel with his brand, Zahid says. No other Berber who happened along would take the load.

Whether it's a dead camel in the desert or a 110-story building, it doesn't matter to Zahid.

"Bin Laden took the load," he said. "There is never an excuse for that."

'Hard to relax'

Each morning after making tea and toast, Zahid gathers the saddle bags and ropes and begins a daily battle with our 1,000-pound camel, named Jimi Hendrix after the rock star who once visited Morocco.

With 8-foot-tall Jimi lying on his belly, Zahid plops the saddle bags over the hump, then digs away the sand under Jimi's belly to affix a rope. He skillfully lassos another rope through Jimi's mouth. With each addition to the load — 50 pounds of bottled water or a towel —Jimi turns his long neck to stare at Zahid, baring his yellowing teeth and mucusy[①] tongue, and lets out a series of long, wet, guttural bellows that echo off the dunes.

In the uneven landscape, Jimi is an uncomfortable, butt-numbing ride. So for most of the trip, he acts as a beast of burden, carrying all the gear as we walk.

With the load secured, our caravan moves out of the dunes onto the hard rocky pan that makes up most of the Sahara. The buttes[②] that mark the Algerian border lie a few miles to our right. Keeping the dunes to our left, we walk past a herd of goats. A big-eared Fennec[③] fox eyes us from a distance.

An hour later, we run into a Berber[④] family, their black camel-hair tent pitched on level ground about a mile from the dunes. The family has 30 camels and 50 goats grazing nearby. Two boys kick a soft soccer ball high in the air and give chase barefoot across shards of fossilized rock.

A man dressed in a flowing black and orange robe waves hello.

"As-salaam 'alaikum (Peace upon you)," he says.

His name is Abdullah, and while pouring tea for me he explains in so-so English that he is not a nomad, although he was born in the desert. He left when he was 15 in search of steadier work. Now he sells carpets in Rabat, Morocco's capital city of 1.3-million people, a full day's journey by bus. He has come to visit his sister's family, who own the herds.

He invites us into the tent, which is tall enough to stand up in. In a back corner two baby goats keep warm under the tent flaps. Lately in Rabat, the "worries are more," Abdullah says. In the desert, the rest of the world seems so distant, less important in a way.

"Hard to relax in the city right now," he says. "Don't know what will happen next. What Morocco's role will be."

Abdullah had little formal schooling, but he can read the daily newspapers. He

---

① adj. of or related to mucus. Mucus means: the viscous, slippery substance that consists chiefly of mucin, water, cells, and inorganic salts and is secreted as a protective lubricant coating by cells and glands of the mucous membranes.

② noun. A hill that rises abruptly from the surrounding area and has sloping sides and a flat top.

③ noun. A small nocturnal fox of desert regions of northern Africa, having fawn-colored fur and large pointed ears.

④ A member of a North African, primarily Muslim people living in settled or nomadic tribes from Morocco to Egypt.

hopes the world situation doesn't destabilize the country, making it even harder for young people to find work. He's read about violent clashes at universities between Islamist student movements and government troops. He wonders how the country's allies will react if terrorist cells are found in Morocco, a country with a reputation as a bridge between Arab and western countries.

Moroccans like to be thought of as the friendliest people on earth, Abdullah says.

"Everyone is a brother," he says. "But I fear some will take advantage of that."

The welcoming committee

The next day, we've been walking for an hour toward the next "weesis" when Jimi starts munching on a shrub. We all stop for a rest.

Hassan wants to know who worked in the World Trade Center and the size of the hijacked planes. His family doesn't have a TV, and he hasn't seen the footage. He's having difficulty fathoming the height of the Twin Towers.

"See that," I say, pointing to a 600-foot dune. "Twice as tall as that."

He pauses a second, looking into the sky above the sandy peak. The tallest building in the biggest town he's visited is just a few stories high.

"How did they not fall down earlier?" he asks.

We arrive at the oasis just after noon. Zahid starts making lunch just for me. Zahid and Hassan cannot eat. Not yet, at least.

We are traveling in the middle of Ramadan, the holy month when Muslims are asked to renew their relationship with God through prayer and fasting. From dawn to dusk, Zahid and Hassan do not eat or drink, not even water.

Zahid seems at ease with the rigor. The younger Hassan, on the other hand, spends the day talking about water, drinking and thirst.

He asks if Americans drink water right from the tap. What's the biggest lake I've ever seen? Could I drink from it? He explains, with a hint of envy, that a camel's kidneys can concentrate urine until it becomes thick like syrup and saltier than the ocean. Camels also extract so much water from their fecal pellets that they can be used right away for fuel, he says.

In the late afternoon, he wraps himself in a blanket and sleeps away a couple of hours. He says he dreams of eggs and toast and sardines.

Rejuvenated after eating the evening meal of dates, bread and apples, Hassan convinces us to climb the big dune behind the oasis. With each step up the steep slope, the sand slides away underfoot. It's like climbing on a Stairmaster; our hearts pound and our thighs burn, but we don't really go anywhere. We change to a zigzag pattern and 15 minutes later reach the peak.

A few lights from Taboumiat and neighboring Merzouga shine in the distance. Behind us, we can see the Algerian desert. The dunes seem dark and moody, all blues and blacks. As the moon rises, long shadows stretch across the sand.

Zahid asks about the mood in the big cities like Casablanca[1], Fes[2] and Marrakesh[3]. Are there lots of military patrols? (No.) Do people seem worried? (A little.) Have I been harassed or threatened when people find out I live in the United States? (No.)

The next day we walk back into town, past the makeshift soccer field and the smattering of sand-colored homes with bright blue doors. I'm the one the locals will peer out their windows to see. They smile. I smile back. Are they suspicious, afraid? I have no way to know, but I don't think so. It seems more like curiosity, more like "How was the trip?" than "Don't cause any trouble." They have felt their own reverberations from Sept. 11 but still want to share dinner and tea.

It has become clear to me that they live by a less suspicious ethos. Here, they presume I am okay. Back home, we demand proof.

I say goodbye to my two companions. In the days that follow, Hassan will help buy food for his family by selling some of the fossilized rocks he finds in the desert and later polishes to a shine. Zahid will hope for the knock on his door that signals the start of another trip.

I will cross back over the Atlas Mountains to Casablanca and fly home through New York City, the "grand buildings" missing from the skyline. Before the plane to

---

[1] A city of northwest Morocco on the Atlantic Ocean south-southwest of Tangier. Founded by the Portuguese in the 16th century, it became a center of French influence in Africa after 1907. It is now Morocco's largest city. Population: 2,930,000.

[2] A city in north central Morocco.

[3] A city of west-central Morocco in the foothills of the Atlas Mountains. Founded in 1062, it is a commercial center and a popular resort noted for its leatherwork. Population: 823,000.

Tampa takes off, a flight attendant asks if anyone onboard knows how to speak Turkish. The heads in front of me pop up or crane down the aisle, eyeballing the tall, dark-skinned man near the door.

The looks say it all. Stranger, don't cause any trouble.

沙丘来客

格雷厄姆·布林克

摩洛哥的梅如卡——扎海德身着白色的齐脚长袍，沙子如狂风般朝里灌，长袍紧贴在身上，显出胸部和大腿的清晰轮廓，长袍的其余部分被风沙甩在身后，仿佛披肩一般。头上严严实实的包裹着头巾，只留出一条细细的缝隙，黑色的眼睛滴溜直转。

他牵着骆驼穿过缓慢移动的沙丘，这些沙丘的两侧绵延着两条平均海拔600英尺的山脉。我们身后的脚印开始变得模糊，一开始是几分钟，后来，几秒钟就消失得无影无踪了。沙子简直无孔不入，一粒粒，一颗颗，透过拉链打在裸露的皮肤上，灼灼逼人。我们的喉咙干渴难忍。我们的眼睛几乎闭上，以躲避沙砾。

扎海德放慢了脚步，低着头，一步一个脚印的往前挪。与他相映成趣的是，那头骆驼仿佛通过厚厚的嘴唇微笑着，扑眨着硕大的睫毛。再过两三个小时，我们即将开始四天的艰苦跋涉，穿过这巨人般的沙漠。四天？我想大概如此。只要我们再坚持四分钟。

而后，狂风戛然而止。

"这没什么大不了的，"扎海德一边宣告，一边解下头巾，抖掉几乎一桶沙子。"在夏天，"他说："飞沙能遮天蔽日。连骆驼都会迷路。游牧民有时也会命丧于此。"

这些沙丘被命名为尔格谢比，位于撒哈拉沙漠西部边上一个平原的中间地带。谢比是最大的一个尔格，在摩洛哥语就是沙海的意思。谢比的面积大约150平方英里，然而与阿尔及利亚和利比亚的大尔格相比，这还不算什么。

扎海德一直闹不懂，为什么有人愿意长途旅行来到他的国家，为的只是游览这些超级大沙箱。他并不是抱怨，而是无法理解个中缘由。

"沙尘暴。不是开玩笑的。不，不，不。"扎海德说。

去年夏天，我产生了飞赴摩洛哥的念头。打从有了这个念头，摩洛哥似乎就是我体验并完成沙漠梦想的最理想的地点——骆驼、沙子、游牧民、恶劣的天气——是一部我自己的《阿拉伯的劳伦斯》[①]，只不过"口味"比较纯净。

[①] 一部经典的英国电影，该片1962年上映，反映了阿拉伯民族反抗土耳其统治的斗争，也凸现了西方国家的背信弃义和贪婪的本质。

"911"恐怖袭击之后，这一沙漠之旅增添了一层新的魅力。它成了你不可以做的事情。举国上下笼罩在反恐战争阴影中的时候，你不会独自一人在一个穆斯林国家度假，很多人甚至连探望住在奥马哈市的祖父母都害怕呢。在这样一个陌生且时而反复动荡的地方，最好不要轻易谈论宗教和政治。

在美国，我们被教导要与陌生人保持至少一臂的距离。最近几个月来，教导的内容居然升级为"怀疑每个人"，尤其阿拉伯人模样的。做个陌生人，成为被怀疑的对象，这在过去却是扭转人生败局的机会。

"我和我的父亲结婚了"

"能走了吗？"扎海德问道。那会儿，我正重新穿上鞋，并擦掉灯芯绒裤和长袖衬衫上剩余的沙尘。

扎海德的随意和从容之中透着一种酷酷的感觉。这种酷是从一生的挣扎痛苦中孕育出来的。55岁的扎海德（和许多摩洛哥人一样，他不用姓氏）克服了日盲症的困扰，顶着130度的高温，在偷骆驼的盗贼、部落的纷争、来自地狱的沙尘暴之间周旋闪躲。而这些只不过是表面上的困难。

4年前，一次干旱持续了很长时间。扎海德和他的妻子迫不得已离开了他们居住的平原地区，来到一个叫做塔布米埃特的只有30口人的小村庄。他们买下一座小小的房子，从房子里可以看到沙丘，后来，扎海德干起了为游客提供骆驼服务的营生。

他最近都没什么生意。

甚至远在沙漠，扎海德都不得不面对来自那些"富丽堂皇的大厦"的土崩瓦解所带来的放射性尘埃。他不知道自己是否有朝一日还要回到以前的生活：在平原上放牧，依然买不起新骆驼。难道妻子还要被迫放弃她的"新欢"吗——她的火炉、她的朋友、以及啪嗒两声就能开关的电灯？

对扎海德来说，这样的选择是介于便利和困苦之间的。沙丘是一种生活。那我呢？不过是被一种怪异的美所迷倒罢了。

一天之中，从拂晓到傍晚，沙海的颜色从粉红变成鲜红，再变成棕色，最后成了黑色。从一侧观察，这些沙丘宛如一块褪色的帆布。从另一侧看，太阳把他们变成了一幅杰作，明暗恍然、对比鲜明。温度逐渐升高，小一点的沙丘看上去像缓慢的波浪在移动。

风急速地吹动着沙子，沙堆平了又起，笔直的沙丘被吹成了S形。大风挟裹着沙子吹向天空，吹向遥远的加勒比群岛。

我们一行之中还有扎海德18岁的助理哈桑。这个男孩会做味道浓郁的摩洛哥风味的炖汤，会唱歌，而且可以讲7种语言，当然都只会一点。他知道的英语代词有限，所以无论是讲骆驼或者他的妈妈，他都用代词"我"，例如他会说"我（指骆驼）吃了很多沙漠植物"或者"我（指妈妈）在沙丘附近举行婚礼嫁给了我爸爸。"

第一天，他一直说我们是朝着一个"唔洲"的方向去。一个"唔洲"？听起来像是想打喷嚏没打出来，而不是指我们第一晚要歇息的地方，那个长满棕榈树的"绿洲"。

有关恐怖分子和窃贼

那天晚上，气温下降到零下40度，我们紧紧裹住骆驼毛的毛毯，把火烧得旺旺的。天上一轮满月，从背后照亮了扎海德因呼吸而起伏不已的身体。强壮的身形，精心修剪的黑胡须，轮廓分明的容貌，看起来像伯特·雷诺兹[①]，只是肤色稍黑一些。

我们后来开始讲述各自知道的那些愚蠢的旅游观光故事，结果哈桑赢了。他讲到一个来自荷兰的家伙，竟然认为如果给骆驼刷牙应该会很有趣，结果骆驼一口咬下来，吞掉了牙刷，也吞掉了那个家伙中指的指尖。

哈桑讲了一个关于沙丘的神话。几千年前，在节日期间，有一个女人和孩子饥寒交迫，需要帮助，而当地人却拒绝帮助她们。这惹恼了真主，真主一气之下就把这个小镇和镇上的居民全都埋在了沙子里。

这个故事也说明了为什么很多摩洛哥人都很好客。乘公共汽车短短几英里的旅途，就有陌生人给我一小杯牛奶和一些烟熏沙丁鱼，还邀请我参加他姐姐的婚礼。

起初，这让我很狐疑，他们是不是想骗我。于是赶快检查我的口袋，看钱是不是还在，包丢了没有。尽管我的疑心十分明显，但还是有人不断的邀请我。我想总不可能整个国家的人都想骗我的钱吧，于是戒心也就松了下来。

结果原来是摩洛哥人把客人看作是真主阿拉赐予的礼物。

"我们需要更多的礼物，"扎海德用阿拉伯语告诉我说，"可为什么他们都走了呢？"

事实上西方人不喜欢甚至于有时候非常讨厌阿拉伯世界，我不知道除了告诉他这个真相之外，还能说什么。我试着给他讲巴以冲突和中东的政治局势，但他显得很茫然，露出困惑的表情。很难向一个从未见过世界的人解释新的世界现实和全球局势。

---

① 伯特·雷诺兹1936年2月11日生于美国乔治亚州。曾就读于佛罗里达州立，在校时曾是橄榄球队的明星球员。大学毕业后，由于车祸受伤而不得不放弃做一名职业球员的打算，转而投身演艺圈。

几分钟后,扎海德悄悄挪到 20 码外的一处平地上,开始祈祷。扎海德是柏柏尔人,这是一个土著的宗族,在公元 7 世纪的时候从入侵的阿拉伯人那里接触到了伊斯兰教。

这个国家有 2900 万穆斯林,占总人口的 98%,祈祷是很平常的事情。因此出租车司机将车停在公路边,下车跪在碎石铺就的路肩上开始祈祷时,没有任何人抱怨。火车上的乘客也会调整座位,朝着圣地麦加的方向,默念"伟哉真主"(真主最伟大)。

扎海德脱掉他的草鞋和袜子,用干沙子洗手、小臂、脚和足踝,双手抚过头顶。他转朝东方,开始祈祷,先站立,后跪下,如此反复 4 次。

扎海德知道,奥萨马·本·拉登也是如此,跟他一样,每天祈祷五次。他这样一个在前不着村后不着店的地方放骆驼的小人物能和沙特阿拉伯裔的恐怖大亨有什么联系呢?想到这里,他笑了。

"你是恐怖分子吗?"我开玩笑地问他。

我不是,但是你看起来像,他笑着回击我。

从游客的只言片语中,扎海德对于恐怖主义有了些许的了解。他知道西班牙北部的巴斯克人,还有一群日本游客告诉他东京地铁中的毒气事件。

扎海德从未去过城市。就在四个月前,他还不知道摩天大楼是什么。但是在听说"9.11"恐怖袭击后,他感到很伤心、很愤怒。他说炸毁建筑就像偷窃——偷钱、偷物、偷窃他人生命,而任何偷窃都是不应该的。

他说,在沙漠中,骆驼死后,柏柏尔人只要把它做上标记,就可以把它和货物都留在原地,其他路过的任何柏柏尔人都不会拿走货物。

对于扎海德来说,死亡和骆驼和 110 层的大楼都一样,没有什么区别。

"本·拉登把别人的货物拿走了,"扎海德说,"他无论如何都不应该这么做。"

"难以放松"

每天早晨,泡好茶、烤好面包后,扎海德就收拾马鞍袋和绳索,然后开始和重达 1000 磅的骆驼奋战,这是他每天的工作。这只骆驼名叫吉米·亨德里克斯[①],在这位摇滚明星访问摩洛哥后,这只骆驼就有了这个名字。

8 英尺高的吉米卧在地上,"扑通一声",扎海德先把马鞍袋放在驼峰上,然后把吉米身下的沙子挖开,把绳子穿过去,固定住。他很灵巧地把另一根绳子穿过吉米的嘴。每次往骆驼身上添加东西——比如重达 50 磅的瓶装水或者一

---

① 一位著名的美国吉他演奏家,歌手,和作曲人,被公认是流行音乐史中最重要的电吉他演奏者。

条毛巾,吉米都会转动它长长的脖颈,盯着扎海德,张开嘴,露出它泛黄的牙齿和黏糊糊的舌头,从喉咙处发出一串长长的、湿漉漉的呼呼声,在沙丘间回荡着。

在崎岖的地方,骑骆驼并不舒服,整个屁股都会麻木。所以在大部分的行程中,吉米都是用来驮行李,我们步行,它驮着我们所有的装备。

行李固定好之后,我们一行走出了沙丘,进入坚硬的、岩石遍布的地区,撒哈拉多数地方都是这种地形。我们右边几英里处,立着一些孤立的山丘,那是阿尔及利亚的边境,沙丘在我们的左侧。路上,我们遇到一群山羊,一只耳廓狐①从远处注视着我们。

一个小时后,我们遇到一个柏柏尔家庭。他们的黑驼毛帐篷立在平地上,距沙丘约一英里远。这个家庭有30头骆驼和50只山羊,在附近放牧。两个男孩光着脚,把一个软绵绵的足球踢到空中,然后在碎石间追逐、跑闹。

一个男子,穿着顺滑的黑橙色相间的长袍,向我们挥手问好。

"愿平安归于你们,"他说。

这个男子名叫阿卜杜拉,他边给我们倒茶,边磕磕巴巴地用英语给我们解释说他虽然出生在沙漠中,可并不是牧民。现在他在拉巴特卖地毯。拉巴特是摩洛哥的首都,那里的人口有130万,距这里一天的车程。他来这里是来探望他妹妹一家,那些骆驼和羊都是他妹妹家的。

他邀请我们进入帐篷。帐篷很高,在里面可以站起来。在帐篷后面的一个角落里,有两只小山羊缩在帐篷的帘布下取暖。阿卜杜拉说,最近拉巴特总是让人"忧心忡忡"。在沙漠中,感觉其他地方都那么遥远,也不那么重要了。

"现在城市里面总是很紧张,很难放松,"他说,"不知道接下来会发生什么事情,也不知道摩洛哥的角色又将是什么。"

阿卜杜拉几乎没有接受过正规的学校教育,但他可以阅读日常的报纸。他希望世界局势不会破坏他们国家的稳定,否则年轻人就更难找到工作了。他读报了解到,在大学里伊斯兰学生运动和政府军之间发生了暴力冲突。他想知道,如果在摩洛哥,这个被誉为阿拉伯世界和西方国家之间桥梁的国家,发现了恐怖组织,那么该国的盟国会作何反应。

阿卜杜拉说,摩洛哥人希望被看作世界上最友好的人们。

"四海之内皆兄弟,"他说,"但是我怕有人不怀好意,会利用这一点。"

---

① 耳廓狐又翻译为"非洲小狐"、"大耳狐"、"沙漠小狐"。生活于北非、阿拉伯半岛的干旱沙漠,具有挖掘地洞的本领,奔跑速度也极快。

迎宾委员会

第二天，我们向着下一个"唔洲"出发了，走了一个小时后，吉米停下来，开始大嚼灌木，我们也停下来歇歇脚。

哈桑问我，什么人在世界贸易中心里面工作，那个被劫持的飞机有多大。因为他家里面没有电视，所以他没有看到那个报道的画面。他无法想象双子塔的高度。

"看那里，"我指着一个 600 英尺高的沙丘说，"有那个的两个高。"

他停顿了一下，看向那个沙峰高处的天空。他去过的最大的城里面最高的建筑也仅仅几层楼而已。

"那么高，它们之前怎么没倒塌呢？"他问道。

刚过中午，我们就走到了那块绿洲。扎海德亲手给我做午饭，他和哈桑不能吃，至少现在不能吃。

因为那时候正是斋月，在斋月里，穆斯林要通过祈祷和禁食来更新他们与真主的联系。从黎明到黄昏，扎海德和哈桑都不吃东西、不喝东西，连水也不喝。

对于这严苛的要求，扎海德似乎非常习惯。但是年轻的哈桑，却不习惯这样，一整天都嚷着要喝水。

他问我，美国人是不是直接喝自来水？我见过的最大的湖泊是哪个，有没有喝过里面的水？他带着一丝羡慕说，骆驼的肾脏可以集中尿液，直到尿液变得像糖浆一样浓稠，像海水一样咸。他还说，骆驼能够从它们的粪粒中提取水分，以至于它们的粪便很干燥，可以直接用来当做燃料。

下午的晚些时候，他把自己裹在毯子里，睡了几个小时。醒来后他说自己梦到了鸡蛋、烤面包片和沙丁鱼。

晚饭吃了枣子、面包和苹果后，哈桑恢复了活力，他劝说我们去爬绿洲背后的大沙丘。在陡峭的斜坡上爬一步，脚下的沙子就往下滑一步，就像在爬梯机上面一样。一会我们的心跳开始加速、大腿酸痛，但是其实根本还没爬上多高。之后我们改变策略，改走之字形路线，结果 15 分钟后就爬到了顶峰。

远处塔布米埃特和邻近的梅如卡闪耀着几处灯光。在我们身后，可以看到阿尔及利亚的沙漠。沙丘看起来黝黑、阴郁，呈现一片蓝黑色。月亮升起来后，长长的影子蔓延至整片沙地。

扎海德问我在卡萨布兰卡、非斯和马拉喀什这样的大城市中感觉如何。问我：

在这些地方是不是有很多军队巡逻？没有。

人们是不是看起来很焦虑？有一点。

别人发现你来自美国,有没有骚扰或威胁你?没有。

第二天,我们步行回镇里,经过一个临时的足球场,还有零零落落的镶着蓝门的沙色房子。我经过的时候,当地人会透过他们的窗子看我。他们朝我笑笑,我也向他们笑笑。他们是不是怀疑我甚至害怕我,我无从知晓,但是我认为他们不会。他们看起来更像是好奇,像是在说"旅途如何?"而不是"可千万别惹麻烦"。9.11事件后,他们的确受到了影响,但是他们还是愿意请我们喝茶、共进晚餐。

我很清楚地认识到他们没有那么多疑。在这里,他们认为我并无恶意。但是回去之后,我却需要证明这一点。

我跟我的两个同伴道别。接下来的日子里,汉森可能将那些在沙漠里捡到的岩石进行打磨,然后卖掉,帮助家里买食物。扎海德可能期待有人再次敲他的门,请他陪伴旅行。

我将折回,穿过阿特拉斯山脉,到达卡萨布兰卡,然后经纽约市飞回家,那些"宏伟的建筑"消失在天际线处。飞往坦帕市的飞机起飞前,一个乘务员问机上是否有人会讲土耳其语。坐在我前面的那些人探出脑袋,伸长脖子看向过道尽头,看着门口那个身材高大、皮肤黝黑的男士。

他们的表情很明显:陌生人,可别惹什么麻烦。

(杨建 译 张慧芳 校)

Slow Flying Stones

Kate Hennessy

【导读】长久以来,沙漠总是和广阔、孤寂、贫穷、落后联系在一起,在沙漠中旅行是对人的体力和智力的挑战,需要旅者历尽艰难,可是过程却充满刺激。凯特·亨尼西正是以这样的心态游走在辽阔的撒哈拉沙漠中,她不仅感受到撒哈拉的浩瀚无际而且体会到生活于其中的生命的奥秘。正是撒哈拉无可抗拒的自然力打开了她的心扉,使她在接下来的雨林的庇护下尽情地思索,并最终下定决心选择徒步穿越沙漠。非洲的贫瘠唤起了凯特心中对于童年时代所经历的贫穷的刻骨铭心的记忆,令她对贫穷有了新的感悟和体验。凯特将自己比作一块缓慢飞行的石头,通过到非洲的朝圣之旅学会了去领悟和感受所见所闻,然而这片苦难的土地即便在她离开后也无时不令她牵挂。本文中凯特把细腻的景物描写和浓厚的情感表达交织在一起,构成一幅独特的风景人文图画,而这一切无不归功于作者深厚的语言功底,长句和短句错落有致,各种修辞穿插其中,呈现出独有的沙漠风貌和给人以启迪的人生感悟。阅读此文就如同与凯特·亨尼西一起穿越时光,掠过非洲广袤的大地,感受这片土地的苦难,回想人生所经历的点点滴滴,使得心灵得到净化和升华。

IN THE FOURTH CENTURY, tens of thousands of men and women headed to the desert looking for religion; asceticism was breaking out everywhere. I could understand why as we drove south from Oujda[①], where we crossed into Algeria, and camped in Taghit[②] at the edge of the Grand Erg Occidental[③], a sand dune larger than Ireland. I watched the sunrise over dunes that rose like mountains outside the door of my tent, and felt tension and unhappiness recede before sand so fine it flowed like water.

---

① a city in eastern Morocco with an estimated population of 1 million.

② a town in western Algeria.

③ also known as the Western Sand Sea, the second largest erg in northern Algeria, behind the Grand Erg Oriental, which contains no human villages and no roads through it.

They say the shifting sands of the Sahara often shift themselves onto entire villages. People move out when the sand advances — bone-dry tidal waves often a thousand feet high that move foot by foot, as far as twenty yards in a year — and move back when it recedes. Land on the move in a country of nomads, land formed and ruled by the wind with ripples and eddies, whirls, crests, and troughs of an ocean marked by nothing but the wind and the faint trails of lizards, beetles, camel spiders, and larks.

The Sahara is 3 million square miles and growing. At its center in the Ahaggar Mountains[①] are volcanic plugs and mountains of rock reaching 9,000 feet. These are surrounded by gravel plains larger than France and Italy combined, which in turn are bordered by the *erg,* or sand dunes. It is a world of sand, gravel, and rock shaped by water, sun, and wind. A world where, on the maps, "*eau potable*" and "*eau bonne*"[②] are meticulously marked in the middle of blank expanses, and swallows fly across twice yearly on their way between Britain and South Africa, traveling 30,000 miles per year. It is a world where blind guides go by the smell of the sand, and the sand has been heard to speak in a low, penetrating boom.

The Sahara is deceptive, for you think you are seeing all there is, but the elements cover with their simplicity a secret life of the desert. It is a land where the animals lie buried under the sand and come out only at night. Horned vipers, poisonous and square-headed, hide under the sand wailing for prey. Large black scorpions hide under delicately perched granite boulders. The mouflon, or wild sheep, and addax, or antelope, seldom if ever drink water and are rarely seen. Seeds can wait for ten years for the perfect moment when they will germinate within three days after a rainfall and sow seeds ten days after that. Water hides, revealed sometimes by the presence of oleander bushes. The people hide, too. Moslem women completely cover themselves, leaving only one eye showing, and Tuareg[③] men cover their faces with black or indigo veils. The granite boulders are a dull brown at midday but contain secret colors, turning orange in the late-afternoon sun and purple at twilight. There are hidden remnants of a secret past, three-thousand-year-old olive trees in the mountains, ancient cypresses fifty feet tall, rock carvings of elephants, giraffes, and zebras, and fossilized trees and fish bones.

---

① also known as the Hoggar, a highland region in central Sahara, or southern Algeria.
② eau potable and eau bonne, French, drinkable and good water.
③ a Berber nomadic pastoralist people, who are the principal inhabitants of the Saharan interior of North Africa.

After some days in the desert, you begin to feel the Sahara's secret life, for it forces you to look closely. Perhaps that is why the desert fathers and mothers came in droves. Sand, gravel, and sky, texture and color, took on an intensity I wouldn't have thought possible, and in my inspection I backed off from the self-inspection and self-consciousness that were in danger of suffocating me. The overwhelming immensity of the Sahara could sink you. Perhaps the reason the best Saharan guides are blind is that they aren't caught and unsettled by the immensity. There is no distraction of insignificance.

What sent me to Africa I'll never know. In 1989, I joined up with a British overland tour company whose glossy Mercedes-Benz truck matched their glossy brochure. We started in London with plans to reach Zimbabwe[①] seven months later. The truck — that orange-and-white monstrosity that was our wheels, our pantry, our refuge — made it to Zimbabwe, as did most of the people on it. I did not, for I got lost along the way, deliberately so, and in the getting lost found my independence, but it was a hard, hard fight.

There were twenty-five of us: Brits, Aussies, an Irishman, a Dutchman, a Fijian[②], and me, the lone American. We left London and hurtled south past a blur of flat French farms and Spanish olive groves, then rode the ferry across the Strait of Gibraltar to Ceuta[③], Morocco, where we slept on our first African soil. It didn't seem to want us; our tents were almost swept away in a torrential downpour.

After three weeks on the road, I knew I had made a terrible mistake. I felt trapped by that orange-and-white monster of a Mercedes-Benz truck, outfitted as it was to keep twenty-five people secure and in splendid comfort with Pink Floyd[④] on the tape deck, cases of Marmite[⑤] and canned cream-of-mushroom soup on the roof, and one long video of Africa playing across our windows. The atmosphere on the

---

① a landlocked country located in the southern part of the African continent, which won its internationally recognized independence in 1980 and whose capital city is Harare.

② Fijian people are the major indigenous people of the Fiji Islands. Fiji, is a Melanesian country in the South Pacific Ocean.

③ an autonomous city of Spain and an exclave located on the north coast of North Africa surrounded by Morocco.

④ an English rock band that achieved worldwide success with their progressive and psychedelic rock music.

⑤ a nutritious savory spread that contains B vitamins, enjoyable in a sandwich, on toast, bread or even as a cooking ingredient.

truck was claustrophobic and raucous①. The air reeked of② alcohol and volatile group dynamics. I spent my time day-dreaming, sometimes eight or nine hours at a stretch③.

Under the influence of the Sahara, we all quieted down, although this may have been due to the lack of alcohol. Nouas, the Algerian beer, was hard to find and not very good when we did find it. Even the truck's tape deck, which had been playing nonstop since London, quieted down. Camping night after night, the sun setting over purple mountains rising straight up from the gravel plains turning the scattered boulders a warm orange, reduced me to a state of pure pleasure. I was content with clean clothes, clean body, and a good spot to pitch the tent. Going for a pee meant squatting in the middle of nowhere with nothing to hide behind, but who cared? We played boccie ④ in the shadow of timeless stucco walls. I saw seven-thousand-year-old rock carvings of elephants at Timimoun⑤ and wandered through the tamarisks and date palms and found a boy twenty feet up in the trees knocking dates to the ground. His mother gave me a handful so sweet and moist I was sure I'd never find such dates again, not even in Sahadi's on Atlantic Avenue in Brooklyn.

I spent every moment I could away from the truck, listening to the silence, watching the colors change, always feeling slightly on edge because of the scorpions, who like sleeping bags. Intolerance and impatience abated as I listened to the silence; I finally felt caught up in the adventure of crossing the Sahara, which, through its elemental abundance, began to bring me out of myself. In the Sahara, nothing is in your face. All space is given to you with nothing but seas of sand, followed by mountains of rock, and then there were no sand dunes or mountains at all, just a wide, unbroken expanse of blue sky, brown earth, and the line where they met.

Arab travelers called the Ahaggar Mountains the country of fear. Riding in a

---

① Claustrophobic: causing an abnormal fear of being in narrow or enclosed spaces; raucous: noisy and disorderly.

② reek of: give off a bad smell.

③ at a stretch: continuously, without stopping.

④ a ball sport belonging to the boules sport family and developed into its present form in Italy , which is played around Europe and also in overseas areas that have received Italian migrants.

⑤ Timimoun: a little oasis town in Adrar Province, Algeria.

rented Land Rover up to the hermitage of Charles de Foucauld[1] at Assekrem[2], our driver, a young Tuareg dressed in a white head veil, stone-washed jeans, and a fake Rolex, called me Amereeka and drove so fast he left the other vehicles in the dust. This isn't easy in a region of Tuaregs with heavy feet on the gas pedal. Pere Foucauld (the Brits in my group pronounced it "FUCK-all"[3]) had at one time been a surveyor-spy traveling through Morocco disguised as a rabbi and carrying a sextant and compass. He had come to the Ahaggar Mountains in 1906 to create a new model of a contemplative, religious life, and was killed ten years later in the revolt against the French. He died alone and left behind a hermitage and the world's best Tuareg-French dictionary. The hermitage was a fifteen-minute walk up a rise beyond a hotel that was nothing more than several empty concrete rooms without windows or beds. The chapel was one of a small cluster of small stone buildings that shared a spectacular view of volcanic plugs and jagged mountains of rock and rubble, basaltic lava that was left lying around like gravel piles for giants. In the chapel, a Little Brother of Jesus[4] led vespers in French.

That night, after watching the sunset turn the mountains purple, we slept on the floor of a room carpeted wall-to-wall with snoring and rustling people. There was intermittent traffic to and from the loo, which was filthy, but the moon was so brilliant I didn't care. Kicked, cramped, and cold, I spent the wee hours of the night lying awake wondering why the monks were so tenacious. What were they doing here, these French Catholic mystics perched on top of a mountain in the middle of a country of Moslems and pastoral nomads? Chewing on this mystery, I missed the sunrise by ten minutes.

The only route from Bangassou[5] to Kisangani[6] — across the Ubangui River[1]

---

[1] a French Catholic religious and priest living among the Tuareg in the Sahara in Algeria, who was assassinated in 1916 outside the door of the fort he built for protection of the Tuareg and is considered by the Catholic Church to be a martyr.

[2] a spectacular collection of narrow mountain peaks forming part of the Ahaggar Mountains.

[3] Due to the similar pronunciations of Foucauld and FUCK all, Foucauld was jokingly called by the Brits as Fuck all.

[4] The Little Brothers of Jesus is a religious congregation of brothers within the Catholic Church; it is inspired by the life and writings of Blessed Charles de Foucauld. Founded in 1933 in France.

[5] a city in the south eastern Central African Republic, lying on the north bank of the Mbomou River, the capital of the Mbomou prefecture.

[6] the capital of Orientale Province in the Democratic Republic of the Congo, the 3rd largest urbanized city in the country and the largest of the cities that lie in the tropical woodlands of the Congo.

and through the forests of northern Zaire — is at a snail's pace, seven miles one day, ten the next. It's a good way to see every single flower, tree, and mud hole of the rainforest. The road was a river of mud, and the bridges a handful of uneven, rotting logs. We passed through tiny villages surrounded by banana trees and pockets of sweet-smelling white coffee blossoms.

"*Mbote*," I called out as I walked ahead of the truck, smelling the whiff of independence.

The villagers smiled and waved. "*Merci*," they replied. A few asked for cigarettes or a Bic pen.

We bartered glass and plastic containers for bananas, pineapples, sweet potatoes, pumpkins, butternut squash, and eggs. (There wasn't much money left after crossing the border and dealing with its predictably rapacious border officials.)

The second night, near the border village of Ndu, women sang and danced outside our truck as Bob Marley played on the tape deck. The older women, who could have been either forty-something or eighty (it was hard to tell), sat on stools in the light of the campfire, laughing at the younger women, who were dancing and singing. An old man shouted now and again. The only word I understood was "Mobutu[2]." We had barely crossed into Zaire, and already Mobutu's name and face cropped up everywhere you turned.

"Hey!" we all shouted in reply, raising our fists.

I have no idea what praise we were giving to that wonder of wonders, one of the wealthiest men in the world, leader of some of the poorest people in the world, but I shouted along anyway, just as energetically and enthusiastically as the next guy.

Days of parasol trees and bamboo stands thirty feet high. I was in love with parasol trees and bamboo stands and the sound of the hyrax screaming in the night. I never saw a hyrax; no one sees them. They are shy. I still don't know what they look like. I've been told they are a rabbit-sized relation of the elephant, and that they can also live in the Sahara. Definitely a mythical creature with a nerve-racking cry in the dead of night.

We met a Red Cross worker who was riding a bicycle on his way to visit his

---

[1] also spelled Oubangui, the largest right-bank tributary of the Congo River of Central Africa.

[2] Mobutu (1930 – 1997), born Joseph-Désiré Mobutu, the former President of the Democratic Republic of the Congo, who, in his office, formed an authoritarian regime, amassed vast personal wealth, and attempted to purge the country of all colonial cultural influence and maintained an anti-communist stance.

parents. His village was twenty-five miles from his job, but he hadn't seen his family in six years.

Coffee and banana trees, young people with goiters, entire villages of people with goiters, and small thatched houses in random clearings kept immaculate; not one speck of garbage to be seen.

"It's because of the snakes," our driver told me. I began to check for vipers before crawling into my sleeping bag; I hadn't yet recovered from my Saharan scorpion scares.

Days of digging the truck out of potholes the size of ponds, navigating across moss-covered log bridges, and nights of bush camping in churchyards where the churches were simple thatched canopies over log benches. There we sat huddled around a tiny shortwave radio, listening to news of the fall of the Berlin Wall. Times were changing, and we were stuck outside them. Off the clock in Zaire.

Zaire was my dream of Africa — the Africa I had wanted to imagine but couldn't yet. It wasn't the spectacular Africa of seas of flamingos and waves of wildebeests; of the Masai in full dress, greeting me from a good foot and a half above with a nicely clipped "Good morning"; or of the women of Lomé①, Togo, who were dressed to kill, their hair small works of art. It was an Africa much harder to define. The road from Ndu to Kisangani is one of the greatest roads I've been on. It's a road for walking, a road for dreaming. I regained some of my peace of mind on that endless muck of a road, walking past liana vines and ferns and protected by the green, sun-speckled canopy above. You must look up in a rainforest; the eye is drawn to the canopy as compellingly as to a cathedral vault, to a higher world, inaccessible, unknown, and unexplored.

Day after day, mile after mile, of being God only knew where. The desert in Africa goes on for weeks, and the semidesert Sahel, too, and the rainforest. All of Africa goes on for a very long time. It was clearly marked on my Michelin map, of course, my pen mark moving steadily south, stars to indicate where we camped each night, but this was no real point of reference at all.

My days of canopied reverie ended abruptly in Buta②, the first sizable town since Bangassou. In the only bar there, we partied hard, drinking them dry of Primus

---

① the capital and largest city of Togo, one of the smallest countries in Africa.

② a town and seat of Buta Territory in the northern Democratic Republic of the Congo.

and Skol, the local beer, with our dancing and drunken idiocies after those long forest days and nights. It all deteriorated into streaks of nastiness from too much time spent together, group dynamics hitting a low point, hostility going wild in all directions, particularly toward Africa and the Africans.

Here I am again, I thought, and went to bed. The protection of the rainforest canopy was proving to be false.

We arrived in Kisangani, my city of hope, of dreams, of desires (this should amuse anyone who knows Kisangani), thirteen days and three hundred miles after crossing the Ubangui River. I sat in the bar of the Hotel Olympia, a large bottle of Primus in my hand. Providing cheap and plentiful beer, I had discovered, was the ex-tent of Mobutu's social welfare policy. I found my bottle of Primus extremely helpful as a waiter dug away at the jiggers in my toes. Jiggers are hideous. They look like a cross between a tick and a grub, and I didn't like the idea of them living in my tender flesh. The waiter was quite good at digging jiggers out from even the pinkest of American toes, and he laughed when I hollered and tried to yank my foot away. But I let the fellow continue, for there was a story making the rounds among travelers, about a man, English, they said, who had decided to wait and bring his jiggers back home for his mates to see, only the jiggers stayed in his foot too long and multiplied so wondrously he had to have his foot amputated. There were quite a few cautionary tales like this floating about. No one ever claimed to believe them ... but I wanted those creatures out of my toes, and fast.

Not bad beer, that Primus. Comes in a nice big bottle, too.

Sitting at the bar in the Hotel Olympia after more than three months of shame as an overland truck traveler, the village of the goiters was somehow the last straw, though little did the villagers know it: I said to myself, "This is it. Off I go."

This was quite easy to say while drinking Primus in the shelter of a hotel, but it would take another two weeks before I finally walked free of the life of an overland truck traveler.

There was a select group of things to fear. Malaria. Being robbed while in the middle of a malaria attack. Bilharzia, yellow fever, hepatitis, meningitis, dysentery, AIDS, insect bites gone septic, flies that lay eggs under your skin if you don't iron your shirts. Damn, I didn't bring my iron. I hadn't even come close to hearing all the horror stories, some rumor, some true.

And then there was the language barrier. I didn't speak French, which is the official language of Zaire, or Lingala, the language of the army, or Swahili, which they spoke in the eastern mountains. Obtaining food, rides, and shelter should be interesting, I thought. I didn't even have a guidebook.

Could I cross that line from having it all taken care of to not having a blessed thing done for me? I had traveled overseas quite a bit before Africa — in Europe, the Soviet Union, India, and Nepal — but I had never traveled alone. This tormented me. There were things I was sure I wouldn't see unless I was on my own. There would never be any sense that this journey was my journey and not as thoroughly canned as the truck's vast supply of canned soups. This illusory notion of traveling through Africa, this delusion that I was understanding anything of what I was glimpsing through the truck windows, had to be punctured with a good dose of adrenaline, which only throwing myself out into the world alone would provide.

Of course, leave it to me to choose Zaire as the birthplace of my independence. Italy might have sufficed. Or Ireland, if I really wanted to live dangerously.

Three days later, the orange-and-white monster, my home for the past three months, left Kisangani without me. But I wasn't alone — yet; hoping to blur the line a bit, postponing independence slightly, I agreed to travel with Simon, an Englishman who spoke fluent French, which I felt would make up for any flaws in his character. We settled down to wait for the riverboat to Kinshasa[①].

Kisangani is a place where people wait. For what, I don't know, for the riverboat. for any ride out. It is hot, wet, overcast, isolated, surrounded by the bush, with streets of red mud and crumbling sidewalks and an evil history as an Arab slave depot and Belgian killing fields. The air was so oppressive that I rarely stepped out into the streets. No one else seemed to be moving, either. The markets were unsettling, full of smoked monkey hands and bowls of caterpillars, palm grubs, and other larvae, large, small, white, black, fresh or deep-fried. I stuck with manioc and peanut butter served on banana leaves.

I spent seven days in Kisangani, seven long days, but I never made it onto the riverboat, for by the fourth day Simon had begun to deteriorate, rotting like a fallen tree in the rainforest, sinking into the torpor of Kisangani and the poison of Primus. I woke up in the middle of the night to see him stark naked and pissing by the light of the moon into the corner of the room. He then climbed on top of the table and

---

① the capital and largest city of the Democratic Republic of the Congo.

crouched there on all fours, being eaten alive by mosquitoes, too drunk to notice he hadn't quite made it back to his bed safely under the mosquito netting. It wasn't the first time he'd been this plastered. He'd been plastered for about three months straight, having begun this journey on the heels of a divorce — as good a reason as any, perhaps, to sell the house and head to Africa, but my sympathy had run dry.

"Forget it," I told him the next morning as he drank his third cup of coffee and dug away at his bleeding mosquito bites. "I'm going east."

I joined up with Ena, an Irish lady I had met several weeks earlier in Bangui. For two days, we sat in the Hotel Olympia watching the only eastbound trucks pass through — more overland trucks that had taken on the feeling of termites crawling out of the bush and into the mud of Kisangani.

I had plenty of time to think in Kisangani. There are images that you can't get out of your mind, that are left to fester in the heavy heat — Henry Morton Stanley[1] looking for fame, fortune, and a doomed Livingston[2]; Conrad's Marlowe[3] traveling up the Congo River; the tens of thousands of severed hands left by the Belgians. I thought about the three months I had spent in Africa so far. I had been treading on awfully thin ice, trying desperately to keep Africa at bay[4], trying to keep at a distance this sense of it perched on the edge of a chasm.

I come from poverty, I thought. I should know something of what I am seeing here, but I'm not. Who am I seeing, then? Myself, of course, reflected in the truck's window, Africa turning my gaze back upon myself.

Each of us hears and sees something different when we speak of poverty, depending upon which spot of wealth, or lack of it, we stand on. We all think we know poverty when we see it, those of us looking at it from our middle-class doorsteps, those of us who have been welfare recipients, those of us who find ourselves traveling through Africa and gazing at the lives of others who may or may not be poor. We don't know what we are looking at, for we are too far removed from the only signs we have been taught to recognize, and which in Africa are

---

[1] a Welsh journalist and explorer famous for his exploration of Africa and his search for David Livingstone.

[2] a Scottish Congregationalist pioneer medical missionary with the London Missionary Society and an explorer in Africa.

[3] Marlowe, the protagonist of Heart of Darkness, a novella written by Joseph Conrad, the English novelist of Polish ethnicity, is an Englishman who takes a foreign assignment from a Belgian trading company as a river-boat captain in Africa.

[4] at bay: at a distance.

extraordinarily inadequate to the job. Split-level houses? Family minivans? Bob Marley① tapes? Goiters? How confusing it can get when you are neither in Beverly Hills② nor in a Sudanese refugee camp. I knew I wasn't seeing the whole truth, just as people did not see the whole truth when they looked at me as a child of poverty.

My childhood was in many ways a painful affair, so I avoided for years the memories and any attempt at understanding them. But Africa was sending me back.

My mother was a single mother of nine. A simple statement anda minefield of memories. The story of my parents is a simple story of good, practicing Catholics making a bad marriage. As a child, primed to take things personally, I got caught by the physical manifestations of the poverty that resulted from my parents' separation. The most apparent sign, the one that showed us to the neighbors, the one that reflected back judgment and anger, was our house, our sad shambles of a house that had once been beautiful, now with its buckled and stained hardwood floors and peeling wallpaper that depicted elegant ladies in carriages, ghosts of a more successful and welcoming era. The house was a long, continuous New England farmhouse of white clapboard with peeling paint, surrounded by a yard gone amok with ragweed and burdock and a green Datsun rusting under the butternut tree. It was a home nestled in a lovely, bucolic valley, though. The only photo of the house I can bear to look at, even now, is a black-and-white shot taken from the hill behind it. All you can see is the flow of the roof from the main house to the ell and its three gables and on to the barn. From that distance and angle, there's no rot visible, no details of neglect, just a beautifully simple line that flows with the line of the hill and is framed by butternut and maple trees. I was saved by that valley and the hills around it; by August afternoons picking blackberries warmed by the sun; by dreaming in the hemlock and beech woods, listening to the velvet echoes of the wood thrush; by sitting in the apple tree near the spring well, reading *The Complete Sherlock Holmes*③ three times, in three consecutive Septembers when I could reach over my shoulder to pick a crisp, clean apple.

"Sad house, poor house." my mother would say. It was over a hundred years

---

① a Jamaican singer-songwriter and musician, whose music was heavily influenced by the social issues of his homeland, and who is considered to have given voice to the specific political and cultural nexus of Jamaica.

② one of the most affluent cities in the world, and is located in the western part of Los Angeles County, California, United States.

③ the classic crime fiction about the detective Sherlock Holmes written by Sir Arthur Conan Doyle.

old; it deserved better. It burned down in 1979, when I was nineteen, and I was glad. It seemed the only way to cleanse it, to rid it of the years of neglect and abuse. It seemed the only way to cleanse my own feelings of shame.

You grasp on to these physical aspects of poverty because it is what the world sees of you and it is how the world judges you. But I quickly learned how twisted that world could be.

My parents separated when I was one and my oldest sister was sixteen. Neighbors told my mother to send some of us kids to foster homes.

"We'll take the older girls," they offered thoughtfully, "and why don't you sell your house."

What they meant was, Sell your house and move to where all the other poor people live, like you're supposed to. My mother kept the house and kept us kids. How, then, can I continue to loathe our house? It kept us together and out of Westview, the local low-income housing project.

Our house was a nightmare, but it wasn't what sent me reeling into the world. The everyday details of growing up with little money seem unremarkable to me now. They are mere facts of life. Sure, I was mortified when visitors saw how we lived, but houses can be left behind. It's the unseen things that eat away at you, the real poverty I had inhaled for far too long, a slow intake of toxicity. Deep down I knew the fallacy of the judgment this house brought down on us. I knew I was something much more than this, but who would recognize it? Who could recognize this, taught as we are what poverty is — rusty cars, couches that sag, clothes that shout "donation!"?

My mother received less than two hundred dollars a month from Aid to Dependent Children[①]. In the early years, she would on occasion pile us kids into the red Corvair or the green Volkswagen or whatever piece of junk she was currently driving, and head to the local ice cream stand. The neighbors complained furiously to the welfare office: "We don't want our tax money spent on ice cream for those kids." The harassment became so severe that my mother's caseworker commented, "You don't have very nice neighbors, do you?"

---

① a federal assistance program in effect from 1935 to 1996 created by the Social Security Act and administered by the United States Department of Health and Human Services that provided financial assistance to children of single parents or whose families had low or no income, which was later replaced by the more restrictive Temporary Assistance for Needy Families (TANF) program.

It took a toll on me as a child. One of my sisters recently discovered an undeveloped roll of film that contained photos of me when 1 was about eight. I looked at them without recognition. Who is that pale, sad-faced waif? Sweet, unkempt, and burdened. Was that really me? What was 1 burdened by? 1 wondered, knowing the answer before I'd finished the question. Poor children grow up intently watching their parents. I watched my mother bear the brunt of our poverty as she kept things together.

As a teenager, I didn't know how to envision a future and plan for it, how to take stock of my resources, and certainly not how to consider myself as my greatest resource. I didn't know that life requires constant self-evaluation; I didn't know I was a project worthy of the best investment. I had no sense that there were any strengths or skills to build upon, or even that there were ways to shore up weaknesses without despairing over them. Instead, I wandered about in confusion, knowing something had been given to me but not having a clue how to pursue it, unable to discern what was worth struggling for, what details made me happy, or how to care for them. Poverty isn't supposed to have details, it isn't supposed to have value, and welfare brats certainly aren't supposed to be valuable. I felt my family's poverty was a statement of my self-worth. I felt it meant something much more than simple unfortunate circumstance; it was a reflection of what I deserved for being poor in value and in human potential, physically, intellectually, and emotionally.

In Africa, I paid good money to see the poverty others lived in, and I thought I could see it well, for I had grown up poor, but I was hiding behind my window, pretending either that I knew all about it or that I knew nothing about it. I was protected from all that I feared, but how, then, would I ever know what it was I had come to see? I needed to move beyond the careless cruelty of using other people's poverty as something to observe, as just another video to watch casually and without consequence; beyond traveling in a way that wasn't much more than following marks on a map and being rewarded with stamps in a passport; beyond a tawdry sort of exploration that easily slipped into exploitation. Replace a consonant and add a vowel, and there you are[①].

I had been unable to move beyond the reflection of myself in that truck window, and Africa, home of us all, was flinging me back to my own beginnings. It had thrown my beliefs and private myths back in my face. The victim of poverty was now the woman of wealth, staring with those middle-class eyes at "the poor," and God, did I need to be saved. I had at the time no money in the bank, no couch at all, sagging or not; but as a stationery-store owner reminded me, "You had the money for the plane ticket, and you have the time to come to Africa." I had time, loads of time, precious time to spend in Africa, and thus 1 had wealth beyond compare. This wealth, though, was tricky. I could use it to remain behind the truck window, peering out, or I could lace up my Timberlands, adjust my backpack, check my malaria prophylactics, open my eyes, and, with the bruises of my own history of childhood poverty and the blessing of shame and the grace that came from it, step out of that truck and into the roads of Zaire, woman of wealth drawing upon the strength of an American poverty.

After seven days in Kisangani, I gave in to the inevitable, and, sick with frustration and heat, Ena and I arranged a lift to eastern Zaire on another overland truck. A bitter, bitter pill[②]. It was smaller and poorer, the shoestring version of overland traveling with ten Australians who called every African they met Trevor.

I hated it and despised myself for not getting off and walking. I despised myself every single moment I held back from making the leap, but now 1 see it had to be done in these small stages, that this leap of courage required baby steps. Still, there is only so far you can go before you reach that last step, the one that makes all the difference in the world, the difference between standing on the edge of the cliff and jumping off it.

I made that step ten days later, on a busy intersection in Goma[③], when I jumped down from the truck with nothing but my backpack. I understood none of the local languages and had no guidebook, but I was happier than a pig in shit, even if breathless. I who went to New York City at age twenty and spent a painful year there

---

① Here the author plays a word game about the two words exploration and exploitation, which are very similar in spelling and will become identical with a slight change of a consonant and a vowel, but she emphasizes the sharp contrast of their meaning, indicating the different ways of exploring Africa.

② a bitter pill: an unbearable experience.

③ a city in the eastern Democratic Republic of the Congo and the capital of North Kivu province.

before I felt at ease walking down Second Avenue in the East Village — now jumping out on that muddy, noisy, chaotic African intersection. Evolution at its zenith, my life hitting the summit of Mount Everest. All those long lines of Hennessys, Days, Batterhams, all coming to this — their child, Kate. free, alone, and unwashed in Goma, Zaire.

I had a revelation, or perhaps it was altitude sickness, in the sulfur mists rising from the hardened lava on top of Nyiragongo Crater[①]. I was eleven thousand feet up. King in a tin hut, my muscles collapsed from the climb, in the bitter cold, the first cold I'd felt in a long time. The wind was furiously worrying a loose piece of tin, which, accompanied by the rain hitting the roof, made a racket that kept me awake.

Africa was irrevocably changing my traveling ways. Sniveling fear was yielding to happy cluelessness and rampant idiocies. I became foolish and thickheaded, never knowing what to do or where to go or how to get there or how to ask, and was delighted to be so. Let me make a fool of myself daily; I shall be daily forgiven. Zaire freed me from bad traveling, a clear lesson in learning that what I had most feared, namely jumping out alone into Africa, was what I was coming to love.

I learned that as long as I was part of a large group, we all, travelers and locals, remained faceless to each other. Stepping off that truck gave a face to me and to those I met, which was all that I could hope for. There wasn't much more to it than a never-ending flow of strangers and the effort of navigating through the days without too many foolish mistakes and wrong turns, getting from one place to another, finding food and lodging. Being on the road is a daily lesson in asking for help, and a lesson in how to greet the world — *mbote*, *jambo*, hello, *bonjour*, It's a lesson in being a beginner every step of the way. It's never knowing where you are in any detail, with any certainty. Being on the road whittles away at everything you believe about yourself. Everything you have been applauded for and recognized for, falls away. On the road, no one has heard you sing "Hard Hearted Hannah" or knows about your 3.9 GPA at Yale or that you were the national woodcarving champion at the age of fifteen. No one knows your motivations or intentions. No one knows if you are a good person or not.

I had begun the journey as a spectator, sometimes with lucky moments of

---

① Mount Nyiragongo is a stratovolcano in the Virunga Mountains associated with the Albertine Rift. It is located inside Virunga National Park, in the Democratic Republic of the Congo. The crater presently has two distinct cooled lava benches within the crater walls.

connection and peace of mind, but most often irritated, fearful, and judgmental. Traveling alone, I was still a spectator, wandering from town to town, watching people as they went about the real business of living — brief glimpses of lives I would never see again. It was much like a silent movie, and I heard very little for a while, still too far removed, even though I walked side by side or sat hip-to-hip with others in a *matatu*①, I on my odd journey, they on their way home or to the market, for we were not on the same road by any stretch of the imagination.

Then I was overtaken by the dust-covered days on the backs of trucks so full there was nowhere to put your feet if you sat down, and if you stood up there was nothing to hold on to. Days where there were immediate consequences, and different worlds encountered on a whim. Shall I go west or east? Hop on this truck or that one? Help! There are just too many roads. Which one am I on? I traveled thousands of miles to get here, and whaddya know? I am bouncing about on a pothole-ridden road, trying to avoid sitting on overripe avocados. I was overtaken by a feeling that anything was possible and nothing was going to stop me — not that I knew what I was doing.

On top of Nyiragongo Crater, I couldn't imagine the route beyond the Zaire border. I had been in the country for five weeks, not that much lime at all, and yet I felt so disconnected from the rest of the world that I was reluctant to leave, as if it meant risking all that I had gained. My mind and lungs had been stretched into shapes they had never known before, but now I was sure to remain loose, like a deflated balloon, and willing to be blown back up again.

I spent the last two weeks of my trip in Lamu, a Moslem fishing village on an island north of Mombasa②, in the Indian Ocean. It was my first sight of an ocean since the Gulf of Guinea at Lomè, Togo, and seven months had passed since landing at Ceuta, where the torrential rain had almost swept our tents right back into the Strait of Gibraltar.

Having begun my trip in the Moslem countries of Morocco and Algeria, I ended it in a Moslem region, yet it might as well have been another religion, another continent, another Kate.

Lamu was a tourist trap, but a peaceful one where everyone knows you within

---

① privately owned minibuses in Kenya and neighboring nations.
② the second-largest city in Kenya lying next to the Indian Ocean and serving as the centre of the coastal tourism industry.

your first day. I wrote in my journal during the cool early mornings and drank fresh mango juice. I watched children play hide-and-seek in Swahili① as dhows sailed in and out of the bay. On Manda Island② I ate freshly caught fish cooked over an open fire, eating with my fingers and silting amid garbage and acacia trees. I walked on the empty beach, a three-mile walk along the shore, or took a ten-shilling ride in a dhow. There was no schedule; the boats left when full, as with all African transportation. The beach was clean and empty, and the sea was full of jellyfish. One afternoon, a Western couple walked hand in hand, buck naked. The next afternoon, several Lamuian women, completely covered in their *bui bui*③, sat on the beach. There must have been a schedule for that sort of thing — naked couples on Tuesdays and Thursdays, women in *bui bui* on Mondays and Wednesdays.

I would wait for the afternoon heat to pass in Peponi's, a high-priced restaurant that sold canned mango juice. Mango season had just passed, and I had to search from one end of town to the other for a glass of freshly squeezed juice. On the lucky days, a few restaurants, Hapa Hapa, the Yogurt Inn, or the Coconut Juice Bar, were able to buy a few mangoes off the daily boat from the mainland. You had to be at the right place at the right lime, ahead of all the other mango juice fanatics. There was no shortage of limes, coco-nuts, and bananas, though. No matter where you go in the world, you can never escape from bananas.

At Peponi's I drank Bitter Lemon before walking the three miles back into town.

"*Jambo, habari?*" the young men called out to me. It was the Rasta boys' last three days with their dreadlocks before a police decree forced them to cut their hair.

"*Mzuri,*" I mumbled, sweaty, salty, and tired. You always reply "*Mzuri,*" or "Fine," no matter how tough a day on the beach it had been. I didn't trust the boys. Were they coming on to me? I was soon exchanging safer greetings with the older men in traditional dress.

"*Jambo, karibu,*" people called out as I walked down the streets. Swahili is a marvelous language. You can spend five minutes throwing one-word greetings to one another, making it easy to be polite.

It was Ramadan, so there wasn't much point in returning to town before six.

---

① a kind of robe(usu. white) worn by Bantu males.

② a quiet island near Lamu.

③ the traditional black veil worn by Kenyan females.

Everything closed during the day, and the town came alive an hour before dinner when every child and adult male was out in the streets. The older men waited for the call to prayer; the children played under the care of their fathers. Women strode down the street like black clouds, *bui bui* billowing about them, flashes of bright colors underneath, and hurrying as only the women do. On the waterfront, travelers sat on the cement wall, waiting for the restaurants to open. Vendors set up their stands of big pots of iced passion fruit juice, *samosas*, *bhajias*, and pancakes. Prayers blasted out of the mosques' many loudspeakers. Men wearing *khanzus*, or long robes, and *kofia*① caps flowed in and out of the mosques; some sat on the steps listening. At 6:28 or 6:30, according to exactly when the sun set, which you could find out in the daily newspaper, everyone disappeared. Dinnertime.

Streets that were teeming with people one moment emptied out the next until there were only the donkeys and cats left. The donkeys, free to wander, jogged down the main street or stood listlessly in the shade, heads in the doorways as if hoping for an invitation to dinner. (They say the cats are descendants of the royal cats of Egypt. Some are well cared for, most are starving.)

Many Lamuians stayed up all night for Ramadan②, during which they are permitted to eat until 5:30 A.M., followed by another day of rest, prayer, and fasting. Nonetheless the market was always full of women shopping. Non-Moslems ate indoors, away from fasting eyes. I ate my lunch, bread and peanut butter, in my bedroom, furtively, guiltily, with the door closed.

Africa changed my traveling ways. Here, spots of erosion, crumbled stones, and small trees sprouting from fissures appeared in the wall that was the image I had had of myself. Thoroughly stuck in the "I," I had flung myself out into Africa, and though I remained still firmly ensconced in that "I," it had become something less poverty-molded and something much more vast, much more awake, much more uncertain. But it was the sort of uncertainty that breeds courage and leads you to look more closely and calmly at those sorry bits of your own life, and at the scary bits of those around you.

Poverty can be a bitter, bitter way of moving through the world. It can be a life

---

① a brimless cylindrical cap with a flat crown, worn by men in East Africa, especially Swahili-speaking cultures.

② Ramadan is the ninth month of the Islamic calendar, which lasts 29 or 30 days. It is the Islamic month of fasting, in which participating Muslims refrain from eating, drinking, smoking and sex during daylight hours and is intended to teach Muslims about patience, spirituality, humility and submissiveness to God.

of reaction, of only coming from and never moving toward, no matter how far from it you come. Peace is rarely made with the past, for it is populated with too many ghosts, and with too much heartbreak.

I still look longingly through the windows of those whose lives seem full of impossibly ordered beauty, who live with immaculate carpets, unmarred walls, groomed gardens, and working televisions and toilets. I'm still drawn to the look of a person whose sofa doesn't sag. But thank God for my lessons in shame, for how else would I have learned to travel alone through Africa? There was no automatic commonality, for this was another continent, another world, but I had learned to see the details of people's lives a little more clearly than if I hadn't grown up poor. There wasn't as much to fear, and I didn't have as compelling an instinct to close my eyes. And yet it also made it all a little more raw. I knew too much. How close could I look?

Africa taught me to love glimpses of strange things that would never be explained, to love that sense of the secret life of the desert, of the rainforest canopy, and of those whom I met briefly. Love for the open road that helps the imagination flow, that breaks down the boundaries of thought and emotion with chance encounters and changing languages, customs, faces, and predicaments. My mind goes elsewhere on a road unhampered by what I think I know or expect to see.

I doubt, though, that I will ever get back on an overland truck.

From the terrace of my Lamuian guesthouse, I looked out to the east, to the Indian Ocean, toward Bombay, thinking of the Ugandan road sign that said SLOW FLYING STONES and feeling like a slow flying stone myself. But I had gotten things going. I was in the air. I had skimmed across Africa like a water spider shooting across a pond that was no pond at all but deep, dark, and unfathomable, like the flooded granite quarry we went swimming in as kids, nervously, for who knew how deep it was or what strange things you could find at the bottom. I flitted across this continent, sensing great pools of disaster lurking beneath, riptides and tidal waves about to destroy it all; sensing a fragility that made me want to weep. Humans and creatures, the Masai and the Turkana[①], the gorillas and the hyraxes, all going through hard times and poised on the razor's edge. Soon after I returned to the United States, Algeria descended into a brutal civil war. The Tuaregs revolted and

---

① a Nilotic people native to the Turkana District in northwest Kenya.

scattered, losing their nomadic ways. Refugees from the Rwandan genocide flooded Goma. Five countries, including Zaire, were pulled into war. And I just missed it all, having perfectly timed my passage between droughts and genocide.

There was a saying that was making the rounds among backpackers in Nairobi[①]: "You go to Latin America to learn politics, you go to Asia to learn philosophy, and you go to Africa to learn how to laugh."

I'm soft in the head about Africa, this land of still, moist twilight scented with jasmine and silhouettes of acacia trees and giraffe necks; this continent of endless, pothole-ridden roads; this land of shifting, golden Saharan sand and sticky, red Zairian mud, all pulling you into going nowhere yet sending you off to places you never imagined.

---

① the capital and largest city of Kenya.

石光掠影

凯特·亨尼西[1]

  公元四世纪，成千上万的男男女女前往沙漠寻找宗教信仰，那时到处盛行苦修主义。我可以理解为什么我们穿过乌杰达[2]向南进入阿尔及利亚时要在比爱尔兰还要大的沙丘——西部大沙漠[3]边缘的塔吉特[4]——宿营了。清晨我看着太阳从帐篷外像山峰一样高大的沙丘上升起，面对着似水般流动的细沙，紧张和不快的感觉渐渐褪去了。

  据说撒哈拉沙漠的流沙经常覆盖住整个村庄。流沙前进时——经常掀起一千英尺高的极干燥[5]的沙浪，慢慢地移动着，一年里最远可移动 20 码——人们在流沙到来时搬走，又在流沙退却后搬回来。那片由游牧民族居住的移动国土，那片由风掀动沙海泛起涟漪、产生洄流、形成漩涡、隆起成堆、低陷成槽而形成并主宰着的国土。沙海上只有风吹过的痕迹以及蜥蜴、甲壳虫、驼蛛[6]和百灵鸟留下的隐约的印迹。

  撒哈拉沙漠方圆 300 万平方英里，并且还在继续扩大。位于其中心的阿哈加尔山脉[7]到处都是火山塞[8]和高达 9 千英尺的石头山，周围则是面积比法国和意大利加起来还要大的砂砾平原；毗连 *erg*[9] 或沙丘。这是一个在水、阳光和风的作用下形成的由沙子、砾石和岩石构成的世界。这个世界在地图上大片空白处的中央被细致地标记为 "*eau potable*" 和 "*eau bonne*"[10]。燕子每年在英国和南非之间飞越 3 万英里时会两次经过这片土地。在这个世界里盲人向导通过沙

---

  [1] Kate Hennessy，凯特·亨尼西，专栏作家。

  [2] Oujda，乌杰达，摩洛哥东北部城市，人口大约 100 万。

  [3] Grand Erg Occidental，西部大沙漠。撒哈拉沙漠的一部分，位于阿尔及利亚西部，面积 8 万平方公里。沙丘呈蜂房状分布，高达 300 米，受禾草和灌木固定。地下水较丰富，南部接近地表，椰枣树无需灌溉即可以生长。

  [4] Taghit，塔吉特，阿尔及利亚西部城镇。

  [5] bone-dry，极干燥的。

  [6] camel spiders，驼蛛，又称避日蛛，生活在干热地区，腹部有毛，圆形，甚似蜘蛛；前面的附肢似蝎。极贪食，体型最大的种类甚至可杀死小型脊椎动物。

  [7] Ahaggar Mountains，阿哈加尔山脉，又称霍加尔山脉，位于撒哈拉沙漠的中心、阿尔及利亚的阿尔及尔市以南。

  [8] volcanic plug，火山塞，指充填在火山通道呈圆柱形的熔岩或火山碎屑。

  [9] erg，沙海。

  [10] *eau potable*，饮用水。*eau bonne*，好水。

砾的气味来辨别方向，还能听见沙子发出的低沉而极具穿透力的轰鸣声。

撒哈拉沙漠是捉摸不定的，你认为看到了全部，但实际上在所有元素的简单外表之下隐藏的是沙漠的神秘生命。在这片土地上动物们都深藏在沙砾之下，只有晚上才出来活动：有着方形脑袋的剧毒角蝰潜伏在沙子底下等待猎物；巨大的黑蝎隐藏在巍然耸立着的花岗岩巨石下；欧洲盘羊①或野羊，以及曲角羚羊②或羚羊非常罕见，即便它们要喝水也很少出现。种子可能要等 10 年才能等到一个合适的时机，在雨后 3 天内发芽并于 10 天后播撒种子。水埋藏于地表以下，偶尔通过夹竹桃丛的出现显露出来。甚至连人们也躲藏起来，穆斯林妇女们把自己包裹得严严实实，只露出一只眼在外面，图阿雷格③男人用黑色或深蓝色的面罩把脸部遮起来。花岗岩巨石在正午呈现出带有神秘色彩的暗褐色，在傍晚的阳光下变成橙色，到了黄昏时分则变成紫色。还有神秘过往遗留下来的隐秘痕迹，山中有着 3000 年树龄的橄榄树，50 英尺高的古柏，大象、长颈鹿和斑马的石雕，以及树木和鱼骨的化石。

在沙漠中待上几天，你就会感受到撒哈拉神奇的生命，因为在这里，你禁不住仔细地观察，或许这是为什么沙漠教父教母成群迁徙的原因。沙砾、碎石、天空、纹理和色彩，呈现出一种超乎想象的饱和度，观察这些时我不再感受到那种几乎使我窒息的自我审视和自我意识。撒哈拉那无可抗拒的辽阔无垠可能压垮你，或许这就是为什么撒哈拉最好的向导是盲人，因为他们不会对这种无垠感到困扰和不安，因而也不会受到自视渺小的干扰。

我不知道到底是什么驱使我来到非洲。1989 年我加入一家有着精美宣传手册和炫目④梅塞德斯-奔驰卡车的英国陆路旅行团。我们从伦敦出发计划 7 个月后到达津巴布韦⑤，那辆卡车——那个充当着我们的座驾、食物储藏间和庇护所的橙白相间的庞然大物——成功抵达了津巴布韦，乘坐卡车的人大部分也如此，而我却没有到达，我在路上故意让自己迷失了方向，但在这迷失里我找到了独立的自我，虽然那是一场艰苦的斗争。

---

① mouflon，欧洲盘羊，是欧洲濒危野生动物之一，原产于科西嘉、萨丁尼亚和塞浦路斯。形小，似绵羊，野生，浅红褐色，腹部白色。雄体背部有浅色马鞍形斑块，有尖端向外转的大而弯曲的角，雌体无角。

② addax，曲角羚羊，一种非洲羚羊，生活在撒哈拉沙漠的中部和南部。生有一对卷曲的角，毛皮为浅棕色，夏天比冬天颜色淡一些，腹部和脸部有白色斑纹，额毛为黑色。

③ Tuareg，图阿雷格人，撒哈拉中的一个半游牧的伊斯兰民族，居住在阿尔及利亚、利比亚、尼日尔和马里几个北非国家中，有近百万人。他们是柏柏尔族的支系，属欧罗巴人种地中海类型，其语言提菲纳格语属于柏柏尔语的一种。

④ glossy 在这里用来修饰 brochure 和 truck，分别译为精美和炫目。

⑤ Zimbabwe，津巴布韦，是非洲南部的内陆国家，1980 年 4 月 18 日独立建国，国土面积为 39.058 万平方公里，首都哈拉雷（Harare）。

我们一行共有25人：有英国人、澳洲人、1个北爱尔兰人、1个荷兰人、1名斐济群岛人①，还有我——孤独的美国人。我们离开伦敦，向南疾驰驶过平坦的法国农场和西班牙橄榄树丛模糊不清的交界，然后乘船横渡直布罗陀海峡到达摩洛哥的休达②，在那里度过来到非洲土地上的第一夜。但是这块土地似乎并不欢迎我们；那天晚上我们的帐篷几乎被滂沱大雨卷走。

上路3周后，我意识到自己犯了一个严重的错误。我感觉困在了那个橙白相间的庞然大物——我们的梅塞德斯-奔驰卡车里。尽管卡车装备精良，足以使我们25个人安全舒适地享受旅程：磁带舱里装着平克·弗洛伊德③乐队的磁带，车顶上放着马麦酱和罐装奶油蘑菇汤，还有窗户对面一直不停播放着的非洲电视节目。卡车里气氛压抑，声音嘈杂，空气中弥漫着酒精的味道和反复无常的群体的躁动。但我大部分时间都在胡思乱想，有时一想就是八九个小时。

在撒哈拉沙漠的影响下我们都安静下来，尽管这有可能是由于缺乏酒精引起的，很难找到阿尔及利亚啤酒努阿斯④，即使找到也品质欠佳。卡车上从伦敦开始一直不停播放着的磁带也悄无声息了。夜夜宿营，夕阳西沉在砾原上高高耸立的紫色山脉上方，给散落一地的卵石披上了温暖的橘黄色，使我处于纯粹的欢乐中。我满足于拥有干净的衣服，洁净的身体和用来支起帐篷的好地点。去撒尿就意味着蹲在某个无名之地的中央，没有什么东西可以遮挡，但是又有谁在乎呢？我们在亘古不变的灰泥墙的阴影里玩博西球⑤。我在提米蒙⑥看到了7000年之久的大象石刻，漫步在撑柳和椰枣树林间，发现一个男孩正在树上20英尺高的地方把枣子晃到地上。他母亲递给我一大捧味道香甜、水分十足的椰枣，我确信再也找不到这样的椰枣了，即便是在位于布鲁克林区的大西洋大道的萨哈迪店。

我尽可能地远离卡车，倾听着寂静，观看着色彩的变幻，还一边担心着爱钻进睡袋的蝎子。倾听寂静时，我变得更宽容更有耐心了；最终我感觉被穿越撒哈拉的探险之旅征服了，撒哈拉以它强大的自然力使我开始显露真实的自我。撒哈拉里没有什么东西挡着你，所有的空间都留给你自己，只有沙海、岩

---

① Fijian，斐济群岛人，斐济群岛共和国位于南太平洋，瓦努阿图以东、汤加以西、图瓦卢以南，首都苏瓦（Suva）。

② Ceuta，休达，摩洛哥北部港市，西班牙位于海外的自治市。

③ Pink Floyd，平克·弗洛伊德，英国摇滚乐队，以哲学的歌词、音速实验、创新的专辑封面艺术与精致的现场表演闻名。

④ Nouas，努阿斯，阿尔及利亚啤酒品牌。

⑤ Bocci，博西球，也称地掷球，意大利式保龄球，流行于意大利皮埃蒙特和利古里亚（Liguria）以及居住在美国、澳大利亚和南美的意大利裔中间。

⑥ Timimoun，提米蒙，阿尔及利亚阿德拉尔省的一个镇。

石山，然后连沙丘或山脉都消失了，剩下的只是辽阔无垠的蓝色天空、一望无际的褐色土地以及它们交接的地平线。

阿拉伯旅行者将阿哈加尔山脉称为恐惧之乡。我们的司机——一个披着白色头纱，穿着砂洗牛仔裤，戴着假劳力士的图阿雷格年轻人，开着租来的陆虎驶向位于阿塞克赖姆山[①]的查尔斯·德·富考德[②]的修道院。他叫我美国佬，开着快车很快把其它车辆远远抛在后面，这在习惯猛踩油门的图阿雷格地区相当不容易。富考德（旅行团中的英国人戏称为"FUCK ALL"）[③]曾经做过测量员间谍，当时他假扮成犹太法学博士，手持六分仪和指南针，长途跋涉穿越摩洛哥。他于1906年来到阿哈加尔山脉并创建了一种冥想式宗教生活的新典范，10年后死于反对法国人的叛乱中。他一个人孤零零地死了，留在身后的是一个修道院和世界上最好的图阿雷格语-法语词典。从仅仅由几间没有窗户或床的空水泥屋子组成的旅馆向上走15分钟就到了修道院，这个小教堂是一片小型石屋群中的一个，这些石屋外都有着壮观的火山塞以及由岩石和碎石形成的高低不一的山脉，玄武熔岩四处散落着，像巨人们使用的碎石柱。礼拜堂里，一位耶稣小兄弟会的成员用法语引导人们进行晚祷。

那天晚上，我们看着夕阳将山脉熏染成紫色之后，便与打着鼾窸窣作响的人们一起躺在铺满地毯的房间地板上睡觉，晚上不时有人出入脏兮兮的厕所，月色皎洁，但我无心赏月。我感觉又冷又挤还被蹬了几脚，前半夜躺在那里睁着眼睛思考为什么那些修道士如此坚韧不拔。这些法国天主教神秘主义者栖身于一个由穆斯林和游牧民族组成的国家，在它正中央的山巅做些什么呢？我思考着其中的奥秘，以至于以10分钟之差错过了日出。

从班加苏[④]到基桑加尼[⑤]的唯一路线——跨过乌班吉河[⑥]，穿过北扎伊尔的森林——走起来如蜗牛般缓慢，一天7英里或10英里。这是一个观察每一朵花、每一颗树和每一个热带雨林的泥坑的好方法。路是一条泥河，桥则是一捆长短不一破烂不堪的圆木。我们穿过周围满是香蕉树和一簇簇芳香扑鼻的白色咖啡花的小村庄。

---

① Assekrem，阿塞克赖姆山，位于阿尔及利亚境内撒哈拉沙漠的中部。

② Charles de Faucauld，查尔斯·德·富考德（1858—1916），居住在阿尔及利亚撒哈拉沙漠图阿雷格人中的法国天主教神父，1916年被刺杀于他建造的庇护图阿雷格的城堡门外。

③ Faucauld 与 FUCK ALL 读音相似，因而旅行团中的英国人开玩笑称富考德为"FUCK ALL"。

④ Bangassou，班加苏，中非共和国东南边境城市，姆博穆省首府。在姆博穆河右岸的热带雨林地带，人口1.9万。

⑤ Kisangani，基桑加尼，旧称"斯坦利维尔"。"刚果民主共和国"第三大城市，东方省首府，该国东北部最大的工商业城市。

⑥ the Ubangui River，乌班吉河，中部非洲刚果河的主要支流。

"Mbote[①]，"我大声喊道，走在卡车前面，嗅到了独立的味道。

村民们笑着挥了挥手，回答着"Merci[②]，"有几个人过来索要香烟或比克笔[③]。

我们用玻璃和塑料器皿换来香蕉、菠萝、红薯、南瓜、冬南瓜和鸡蛋。（过边境时和意料之中贪婪的边境官员打完交道后钱已经所剩无几了）。

次日晚上，在边境村庄恩杜[④]附近，鲍勃·马力打开磁带机，妇女们在我们的卡车外唱歌跳舞。老一点的妇女，可能有40多岁或80岁（这一点很难判断），在篝火的映照下坐在板凳上，嘲笑着正在唱着跳着的年轻妇女。一位老人不时高声喊叫，我唯一听懂的词是"蒙博托[⑤]"，自从我们踏上扎伊尔的土地，无论去何处都可以看见蒙博托的名字和脸庞。

"嗨！"我们都举起拳头应声答道。

我不知道要如何赞扬那位奇迹中的奇迹，世界上最富有的人之一，世界上一部分最穷的人的领袖，但无论如何我一直在喊着，同旁边的家伙一样积极热情。

那些伴着梧桐树和30英尺高的竹株的日子。我喜欢梧桐树、竹株和夜里蹄兔的尖叫声。我从未见过蹄兔；没有人见过。它们胆小羞怯，我仍然不知道它们长什么样，听说它们是大象的亲戚，只是大小如兔子，可以在撒哈拉沙漠里生存，在深夜里发出令人心神不安的叫声，它无疑是沙漠中的神秘动物。

我们遇见一位红十字会工人正骑着自行车去看望父母，他住的村庄离上班的地方只有25英里远，但6年来他一直没有见过父母。

咖啡树，香蕉树，甲状腺肿大的年轻人，所有村民都甲状腺肿大的一个个村庄，空地上随意建造的收拾得一尘不染的茅草小屋；垃圾已不见踪迹。

"这是因为蛇的缘故，"司机告诉我们。我在爬进睡袋前检查看有没有毒蛇；我还没有从对撒哈拉的蝎子的恐惧中恢复过来。

那些日子，我们将卡车从池塘大小的坑洞里拖出来，驶过长满青苔的圆木桥，夜里则宿营在教堂庭院的灌木丛中。教堂只是遮住木板凳的简陋的茅草棚，在那里我们围着一个小小的短波收音机蜷坐着，听着柏林墙倒塌的消息。时代在变化，我们却游离在时代之外。在扎伊尔脱离时代。

---

① Mbote，你好。
② Merci，谢谢。
③ Bic pen，比可笔，法国老牌优质笔。
④ Ndu，恩杜，位于刚果民主共和国和喀麦隆交界处。
⑤ Mobutu，蒙博托（1930—1997），原名约瑟夫·德西雷·蒙博托，扎伊尔前总统、人民革命运动主席。1997年5月29日被赶下台，在他掌权32年中，巧取豪夺，聚敛了40亿美元的家产。

扎伊尔才是我梦想中的非洲——我一直试图想象却难以想象的非洲。它不是那个红鹳成群角马成批的场面壮观的非洲；也不是那个衣着盛装，比我足足高出一英尺半的马赛人清晰地说着"早上好"表示欢迎的非洲；也不是那个多哥的洛美①妇女梳着小小艺术品般的头发，穿着色彩绚丽衣服的非洲。这是一个难以言说的非洲。从恩杜到基桑加尼的路是我所走过的最惬意的一条路。这是一条用来行走的路，是一条用来梦想的路。走在那条杂乱的无止尽的小路上，我重获宁静的心境，我掠过藤蔓植物和蕨类植物，绿色的树冠上洒下斑驳的光影，给我以庇护。在雨林里你必须抬头仰望；眼球被吸引到像教堂的穹顶一样高高在上的树冠上，被引领到一个更高的世界，一个难以企及的、不为人知的、尚未被探索过的世界。

一天又一天，一英里又一英里，行走在只有上帝才知道是哪里的地方。走在非洲的沙漠上，一走就是几周，在半沙漠化的萨赫勒②行走也一样，穿行雨林同样费时。整个非洲的行走都持续很久，这在我的米其林地图上都清楚地做了标记，当然我钢笔的痕迹一直在向南移动，星号则标明每晚宿营的地点，但这并不是真正的参照点。

我在树荫下狂想的日子终结于布塔③，班加苏之后第一个小有规模的城镇。我们在那儿唯一的酒吧里举杯狂饮，喝光了酒吧里的当地啤酒普利姆斯和狮威④，在林中度过漫长日夜的我们跳着舞，说着醉话。在一起呆的太久就会生出几分龃龉，团体影响力降到了最低点，敌意四处蔓延，尤其针对非洲和非洲人。

我又回到了原点，我想着，上床睡觉了。雨林树荫的庇护只是假象而已。

我们跨过乌班吉河行走了13天300英里之后到达基桑加尼，我的希望之城，梦想之城，欲望之城（这应该很吸引那些知道基桑加尼的人）。我坐在奥林匹亚酒店的酒吧里，手里拿着一大瓶普利姆斯。我发现供给便宜充裕的啤酒属于蒙博托的社会福利政策范围。我发觉在服务员从我的脚趾里挖出沙蚤时，那瓶普利姆斯特别管用。沙蚤很讨厌，看起来像蜱和蛆交配而生的杂种，我不喜欢任由它们寄生在我鲜嫩的肉里。那个服务员很善于挑出沙蚤，即便是从美国人最粉嫩的脚趾里，当我号叫着竭力想把脚拉走时他大笑着，但我还是让那个小伙子继续下去。在旅行者中流传着一个故事：据说一个英国人决定把沙蚤带回家

---

① Lomé，洛美，非洲最小的国家之一多哥（Togo）共和国的首都，位于多哥的西南角。

② Sahel，萨赫勒，阿拉伯语意为"沙漠之边"。指非洲苏丹草原带北部一条宽 320-480 公里的地带(包括非洲塞内加尔北部、毛里塔尼亚南部、马里中部、布基纳法索北部、尼日耳南部、乍得中部)，是由典型的热带草原向撒哈拉沙漠过度的干旱、半干旱地带。

③ Buta，布塔，刚果北部城镇。

④ Primus 普利姆斯，Skol 狮威，都是啤酒品牌。

让他老婆看看，但是沙蚤们在他脚里待的时间太长，开始大量繁殖，最后他被迫截肢。像这样的警世的故事广为流传。没有人说过相信这些：……但是我想把那些生物弄出来，越迅速越好。

不错的啤酒，那种普利姆斯。又送来一大瓶。

3 个多月来，乘坐陆路卡车旅行的经历让我羞愧难当。此刻，我坐在奥林匹史酒店的小酒吧里，这个村子里的所有人都患甲状腺肿大，这使我无法忍受，而村民们却对此一无所知。我对自己说，"就这样了，我得离开。"

呆在酒店里喝着普利姆斯这样说说是很容易的事情，但是又过了 2 星期我才最终摆脱陆路卡车旅行者的生活。

有很多令人惧怕的事物：疟疾；疟疾发作时被抢劫。血吸虫，黄热病，肝炎，脑膜炎，痢疾，艾滋病，昆虫咬伤溃烂，如果你不熨烫衣服就会在皮下产卵的苍蝇。该死的，我没带熨斗，我甚至几乎没听说过所有这些恐怖的说法，一些是道听途说，一些是真实情况。

然后就是语言障碍，我不会说扎伊尔的官方语言法语，也不会讲林加拉语[①]——军方用的语言，更不会说斯瓦西里语[②]——东部山区的方言。找寻食物、搭车和借宿应该是有趣的事情，我想。我甚至连旅行指南都没有。

从完全被人照顾，到什么事都没人帮忙，我能够适应这种变化吗？来非洲之前我已经多次在海外游历——欧洲、苏联、印度和尼泊尔——但我从未单独旅行过，这一点一直折磨着我，有些东西我确定如果不是独自旅行就不会看到。我的这次旅行如果不能像卡车上提供的大量罐装汤那样被精心保存的话就没有任何意义了。这种正在非洲旅行的幻觉，这种我能了解透过卡车车窗瞥见的一切事物的错觉，必须得使用适当剂量的肾上腺素来戳穿，而这只有让我一个人独自行动才能做到。

那么就让我来选择扎伊尔作为我独立自由的诞生地吧，意大利也可以。或者爱尔兰，如果我真想生活在危险中的话。

3 天后，那个橙白相间的庞然大物，过去 3 个月里我的家，离开了基桑加尼，留下了我，但我不是一个人——还不是；我希望模糊一下那条界线，稍微延迟一下独立，就同意和一个名叫西蒙的英国人一起旅行，他讲一口流利的法

---

① Lingala，林加拉语，是班图语支的一种语言，主要分布在刚果民主共和国（刚果-金沙萨）的西北部和刚果共和国（刚果-布拉柴维尔）的大部，安哥拉和中非共和国局部。

② Swahili，斯瓦西里语，属于班图语族，是非洲语言当中使用人口最多的一种（5500 万多人），是坦桑尼亚的唯一官方语言，肯尼亚和刚果民主共和国的国家语言之一，和赞比亚、马拉维、布隆迪、卢旺达、乌干达、莫桑比克等国的重要交际语。

语，这一点我感觉弥补了他性格中的任何缺陷。我们安顿下来等待开往金沙萨[①]的河船。

基桑加尼是一个人们用来等待的地方，等待什么，我不清楚，等待河船，等待外出旅行。这里炎热、潮湿、阴沉、孤立，四周都是灌木丛，街道上布满红泥，人行道残破不堪，有着作为阿拉伯奴隶关押地和比利时杀戮场的罪恶历史。这里空气压抑，我很少到街上去，也没有其他什么人出去走动。市场让人感觉不大舒服，摆满了熏制的猴爪、满碗的毛毛虫、鸡母虫和其它幼虫，大的、小的、白的、黑的、生的或油炸的。我用裹着香蕉叶的木薯和花生奶油填饱了肚子。

我在基桑加尼度过了7天，漫长的7天，但并没有设法登上河船，因为到第四天时西蒙就开始堕落，像雨林里的落叶一样在腐烂，沉沦于基桑加尼的懒散和普利姆斯的毒害里。我半夜醒来看见他裸着全身乘着月光在房间的角落撒尿，然后爬上桌子，手脚并用，蹲伏在上面，任凭蚊虫叮咬，烂醉如泥的他没有意识到自己并没有成功地返回床上的蚊帐里。这不是他第一次喝醉，他已经一连醉了大约3个月了，自离婚以来一直这样——这也许是一个卖掉房子前往非洲的再好不过的理由，但是我的同情心已经耗尽了。

第二天早上，我告诉他："算了吧，我要向东走了。"这时他正在喝第三杯咖啡，并随手把蚊子叮咬的地方抠得血淋淋的。

我和几周前在班吉见到的爱尔兰女士伊娜一起旅行。两天来我们坐在奥林匹亚酒店看着向东行驶的卡车经过——更多的陆路卡车感觉好像爬出灌木丛钻进泥泞的基桑加尼的白蚁。

在基桑加尼我有充裕的时间进行思考，有些形象是挥之不去的，留在那里在酷热中恶化——追寻名誉、财产和命丧非洲的利文斯通[②]的亨利·莫顿·史丹利[③]；沿着刚果河旅行的康拉德的马洛[④]；比利时人留下的成千上万的被砍掉的手。我思考着迄今为止在非洲度过的3个月，我一直如履薄冰，拼命地不让非洲逼近，竭力摒弃非洲岌岌可危的这种感觉。

---

① Kinshasa，金沙萨，扎伊尔的首都，中部非洲的最大城市，是个拥有300多万人口的现代化非洲都城，是全国政治、经济、交通和文化中心。

② Livingston，利文斯通（1813～1873），英国传教士，非洲地理考察家，从1852年开始，为了传教和开辟内陆的贸易通道，对非洲中南部进行了3次长途考察。

③ Henry Morton Stanley，亨利·莫顿·史丹利（1841～1904），英裔美籍探险家与记者，以他在非洲的冒险及搜索戴维·利文斯通（David Livingston）的事迹而闻名于世。

④ Conrad's Marlowe，康拉德的马洛，马洛是生于波兰的英国小说家约瑟夫·康拉德（Joseph Conrad 1857—1924）的中篇小说《黑暗之心》（1899年）的主人公，一位被一家比利时贸易公司雇佣担任非洲河船船长的英国人，该书通过马洛的旅行揭露了人性和比利时殖民的黑暗。

我自认为出身贫寒，应该能了解这里所见到的一切，但是我没有。那么我看见了谁？当然是我自己，车窗里反射出的我，非洲使我开始审视自己。

我们每个人在提及贫穷时听到和看到的东西都不尽相同，这取决于我们处于什么样的富裕或者贫穷状况。我们都认为自己看见贫穷时会理解它，那些从中产阶级的门阶看待贫穷的我们，那些曾经接受过福利的我们，那些穿越非洲目睹其他或穷或不穷的人的生活的我们。我们不理解所看到的事物，因为我们太不熟悉自己学到的辨别贫穷的唯一标志了，而这些标志在非洲完全不适用。错层式房子？家用小货车？鲍勃·马利①的录音带？甲状腺肿大？当你既不在贝弗利山庄②也不在苏丹难民营时一切都变得那么令人困惑。我知道自己并没有看到全部真相，正像人们将我看成穷孩子时没有看到全部真相一样。

我的童年在很多方面都是一场痛苦的经历，因此多年来我都避免回忆童年时代，也尽量不去试图理解那些记忆。但非洲唤回了我的记忆。

我的母亲是一位有着9个孩子的单身母亲。简单的一句话却蕴涵着许多艰难的回忆。我父母的故事是一个善良虔诚的天主教徒造就一场不幸婚姻的简单故事。作为一个易于感情用事的孩子，我对父母离异引起的贫穷的实质表现感到不安。最明显的标志，那个将我们曝露给邻居们的标志，那个反映评价和愤怒的标志，是我们的房子，我们那个曾经美丽后来却变得令人悲哀的乱糟糟的房子。房子里的硬木地板弯曲变形，布满污迹，剥落的墙纸描绘出乘坐马车的举止优雅的女士，但那只是一个更为成功令人愉快的时代的幻影。我们的房子是一座由白色墙板建成的长排连续型的新英格兰式农舍，墙漆剥落，院子里豚草和牛蒡肆意生长，一辆绿色的德森汽车在灰胡桃树下锈迹斑斑。即使它是一个坐落在美丽乡村山谷中的家，但直到现在我唯一能够看得下去的关于它的照片，是一张从房子后面的小山拍摄的黑白照。照片上你能看到的是从正屋到厢房及其3个三角墙再到谷仓的绵延不断的屋顶。从那个距离和角度看不见腐烂，也看不见疏于照料的细节，能看见的只是一个与小山一同起伏、由灰胡桃树和枫树衬托的美丽简单的轮廓。那个山谷和周围的小山挽救了我；在8月的下午去采摘被太阳晒得温热的黑莓；在铁杉和山毛榉林中遐想，倾听林中画眉鸟悦

---

① Bob Marley 鲍勃·马利（1945-1981）牙买加的民族英雄。他正直的品格、对理想的执着、和对牙买加以及世界流行音乐的贡献，使他站到了最伟大的音乐家的行列里。

② Beverly Hills，贝弗利山庄，是一座位于美国加利福尼亚州洛杉矶县西边的城市，和邻近的西好莱坞被洛杉矶市完全包围，是美国乃至世界知名的高级住宅区。大多数好莱坞的明星们以及众多的富豪住在这里。

耳的叫声；连续三年的 9 月坐在涌泉旁的苹果树下，将《福尔摩斯探案全集》[①]看了 3 遍，那时我伸手就能够到鲜脆干净的苹果。

"悲伤之家，贫穷之家，"我母亲这样说道。房子有 100 多年的历史；它值得有更好的归宿。1979 年我 19 岁时房子烧毁了，我很高兴，这似乎是唯一除掉它的方法，清除掉多年的疏忽和侮辱，也是洗去我羞耻感的唯一方法。

你之所以对贫穷的物质层面耿耿于怀，是因为贫穷是这个世界从你身上所看到的东西，是这个世界对你做出的评判。但是我很快知道这是一个怎样扭曲的世界。

我父母离异时，我 1 岁，我最大的姐姐 16 岁。邻居们劝母亲把一些孩子送到寄养家庭。

"我们会领养大一点的女孩，"他们考虑周到地主动献策，"为何不卖掉房子。"

他们的意思是，卖掉房子搬到你们该去的所有其他穷人们居住的地方吧。我母亲留下了房子也留住了我们，那么我又怎么会一直讨厌我们的房子呢？它使我们能够生活在一起，而不用去考虑那些专为低收入者建造的经济适用房。

我们的房子是个恶梦，但并不是它令我跟跟跄跄地步入这个世界。靠着一丁点钱成长的日常细节在我现在看来似乎不值一提，它们只是生活的现实。我的确为访客看见我们如何生活而感到羞辱，但是房子是可以抛诸脑后的。反而正是看不见的东西侵蚀着你，我浸透其中太久的真正的贫穷，一个慢性中毒的过程。内心深处我清楚，由于这座房子别人对我们做出了错误的推断，我知道自己远不是他们想的那样，但是又有谁会承认这一点呢？谁能认识到这个，像我们一样被教导什么是贫穷——生锈的车子、塌陷的沙发、明显标示着"捐赠物"的衣服？

我母亲每月从未成年儿童援助项目[②]那里得到不足 200 美元的救助。小时候，她有时会把我们塞到红色的科威尔或绿色大众或任何她当时驾驶的破车里，开往当地的冰淇淋店。邻居们向福利办公室强烈投诉："我们不想把交纳的税金用来给那些孩子买冰淇淋。"他们后来更加变本加厉，以致我母亲的生活调查员做出这样的评论，"你们的邻居很不友好，是吗？"

[①] The Complete Sherlock Holmes，《福尔摩斯探案全集》，阿瑟·柯南道尔经典的探案小说，其中包括《冒险史》系列、《新探案》系列、《回忆录》系列、《归来记》系列、《血字的研究》、《恐怖谷》、《巴斯克维尔的猎犬》、《四签名》。

[②] Aid to Dependent Children，未成年儿童援助项目，1935 年由作为罗斯福新政一部分的社会安全法案（Social Security Act）所创立，1960 年改名为抚养未成年儿童家庭援助（Aid to Families with Dependent Children，简称 AFDC），1997 年被困难家庭临时援助（TANF）被替代。

这深深地影响了我的童年。最近我的一个姐姐发现了一个未冲洗的胶卷，里面有我八岁时的照片。我看着那些照片一点都没认出来那就是自己。那个面色苍白、一脸悲哀的孤儿是谁啊？长相可爱却头发蓬乱，心事重重，那真的是我吗？我到底在担忧些什么呢？我问自己，其实在问题提完之前我就知道了答案。穷人的孩子在成长过程中一心关注着他们的父母，而我看到了母亲在维持全家人生活时所承受的贫穷带来的压力。

青少年时期的我不知道如何展望并筹划未来，如何评价自己所拥有的资源，当然也不知道怎样把本身视为最大的资源。我不知道生活需要不断的自我评价；我不知道自己是一个很值得投资的项目；我不知道有些优点或技能可以依靠，或者甚至有些方法可以弥补缺点而不必感到绝望。我懵懵懂懂地四处游荡，知道自己被赋予了一些东西却一点也不知道如何去追寻它们，无法甄别什么值得奋斗，哪些细节使我快乐，或者如何计较这些细节。贫穷不应该有细节，不应该有价值，接受救济的小家伙当然也不应该被珍视了。我感觉家里的贫穷标明我的自我价值。我感觉贫穷并不仅仅意味着不幸的境况；它反映出我无论在体力、智力还是情感上都应该没什么价值和潜力。

在非洲，我花了大笔钱来看别人过着的清贫生活，我以为我能看清楚，因为我就是在贫穷中长大的，但是我躲在窗户后面，假装要么非常了解贫穷，要么对它一无所知。我避开自己惧怕的所有东西，但是这样我又怎么知道到底来这里看些什么东西呢？我想要的不只是冷漠残酷地把他人的贫穷当作观察的对象，当作随意观看、不顾后果的又一段视频录像；不只是沿着地图上的标志赢得护照上的一个个印章的旅行方式；不只是进行一场华而不实容易沦为广告的探险①。换掉一个辅音，加上一个元音就变成那样了。

我无法超越车窗里自己的映像。非洲，我们所有人的家，把我推回到起点，唤起我对信仰和个人神话的记忆。那个贫穷的受害者此刻成了一个富有的女人，以中产阶级的眼光看着"穷人"，上帝啊，我真的需要得到救赎。当时我银行里没有存款，没有长沙发，不管是凹陷还是不凹陷的；但是正像一个文具店老板提醒我的，"你有钱买机票，有时间来非洲。"我有时间，有大量宝贵的时间在非洲度过，因此我拥有无与伦比的财富。然而，这种财富带有欺骗性。我

---

① 这里 exploration 和 exploitation 只有一个元音和一个辅音之差，在这里作者玩起了文字游戏，表示自己不愿意把此次探险当作利用的工具哗众取宠，分别译为"探险"和"广告"。

能够利用这种财富待在卡车窗后，凝视窗外，或者可以系好天伯伦①鞋的鞋带，打好背包，带好疟疾预防药，睁大双眼，带着穷苦的童年时代留下的创伤和伴着贫穷而生的经受羞耻的福分和恩泽，跨出卡车，走到扎伊尔的路上，拥有财富的女人在这里动用美国式贫穷产生的力量。

在基桑加尼呆了7天后，我不得不屈服于不可避免的事情。我和伊娜无法忍受挫折和炎热，计划搭乘另一辆陆路卡车前往东扎伊尔，那是一段不堪的经历，微不足道又可怜兮兮，一次小规模的陆路旅行，同伴是10位澳大利亚人，它们称呼遇见的所有非洲人为特雷弗。

我讨厌这样的事情，恨自己没有下车步行。每当我忍住没跳车的时候我都恨自己，但是现在我明白这个决定得一步一步地来做，鼓足勇气跳车需要像婴儿学步一样，你只有走那么远才能到最后一步，那产生巨大差异的一步，那是站在悬崖边上和跳下悬崖的差异。

10天后我在戈马②的一个繁忙的交叉路口走出了那最后一步，除了背包什么都没带的我从卡车上跳了下去。我不懂任何当地的语言，也没带旅行指南，但是我比满身臭粪的猪还快乐，即便是走得气喘吁吁。我在20岁的时候去了纽约，在那里度过了痛苦的一年后才能在东村区③的第二大道上自在地行走——现在我跳出那里来到这个泥泞、吵闹、混乱的非洲十字路口。这是我发展的全盛期，我的人生在此刻到达了珠穆朗玛峰的顶点。所有那些亨尼西、戴、巴特汉姆④世家都集中到这儿——他们的孩子，凯特，自由地，孤单地，脏兮兮地待在扎伊尔的戈马。

我在尼拉贡戈火山口⑤顶上变硬的火山熔岩挥发形成的硫化雾里突然得到一个神示，或者也许只是高原反应。我躺在位于11,000英尺高处的锡制小屋里，肌肉由于在严寒中攀爬已经疲惫不堪，那是长期以来第一次感到严寒。风猛烈地吹打着一块松掉的锡板，伴随着雨敲打屋顶的声音，发出巨大的声响，

---

① Timberlands，天伯伦，是全球领先的户外品牌，通过提供高质量、讲究细节的工艺制品，来满足不同户外环境下的需求。这家成立于1918年的美国波士顿的公司创业初期是一家专业制鞋公司。从80年代起，Timberland逐渐成长为一家国际品牌，并开始生产服装，女鞋，背包等，经过近30年的努力，Timberland已遍及世界90多个国家，Timberland制作的鞋无论是在设计，质量，坚固耐用还是功能性方面堪称世界一流。

② Goma，戈马，刚果民主共和国东部旅游城市，北基伍省省会。在基伍湖北岸，近卢旺达边界。

③ The East Village，东村区，又称曼哈顿东村，位于Houston街上方，曾经是嬉皮士出没的地区，也是众多音乐家、艺术家云集的地方。

④ Hennessy, Day, Batterham都是爱尔兰姓氏，在这里指作者所属的族系。

⑤ Nyiragongo Crater，尼拉贡戈火山口。尼拉贡戈火山是非洲中东部维龙加山脉的活火山。在刚果民主共和国靠近乌干达边境的维龙加国家公园的火山区内。火山口最大直径2千米(1.3英里)，深约250米(820英尺)，里面有一个熔岩湖。山上一些旧的喷火口以珍奇植物出名。

使我清醒过来。

非洲正无可挽回地改变着我的旅行方式，软弱的恐惧正让位于快乐的无知和蔓延的愚蠢。我变得愚蠢无知，不知道该做些什么、去什么地方、怎么到要去的地方或者如何问询，但是我乐于如此。让我每天都那么无知吧；每天我都会得到宽恕。扎伊尔使我摆脱了糟糕的旅行，这是一个显而易见的教训，从中我知道我最惧怕的，即单枪匹马闯非洲，也正是我逐渐喜欢上的。

我知道只要是一大群人中的一员，我们所有人，不论是旅行者还是当地人，彼此都是陌生的。步出卡车使我和所见到的人都显露出来，这正是我所希望看到的，再也不用看永无休止、川流不息的陌生人，也不用担心在一天天的寻道问路中犯下很多愚蠢的错误，错拐了很多弯，从一个地方奔到另一个地方寻找食物和住处。旅行意味着每天都要学习寻求帮助，学习问候这个世界——*mbote*, *jambo*, hello, *bonjour*①，学习如何开始旅行中的每一步，它并不要求确定你具体所处的位置。旅行渐渐吞噬掉你关于自己的一切想法，你赞成和认可的一切都逐渐消失了。在旅途中，没有人听你唱过"狠心汉娜"，了解你在耶鲁拿到3.9分的平均成绩，或者知道你在15岁时获得全国木雕冠军。没有人知道你的动力或企图，也没有人知道你是好人还是坏人。

我作为旁观者开始了这次旅行，有时幸运地与之产生联系获得平静的心态，但更常见的是烦忧、恐惧和偏见。一个人旅行时我仍然是个旁观者，从一个城镇游荡到另一个，看着人们忙着生活中的日常事务——这种匆匆掠过的生活我永远也不会再见到了。这很像一部无声电影，一段时间以来我听到的很少，还是隔得太远，即便我和其他人肩并肩地行走着，或者臀贴臀地坐在马他突②上，我在进行一次非同寻常的旅行，而他们正在回家或去往市场的途中，无论怎么想我们都不是同一条路上的人。

接着我在卡车车斗里度过了那些灰尘满天的日子，车斗里挤满了人，坐下无处放脚，站着又无东西可抓。那些产生直接后果的日子，那些随意遭遇不同世界的日子。我该向西走还是向东走？上这辆卡车还是那辆？帮帮忙吧！路太多了，我应该选择哪条啊？我行走了几千英里到这儿，你知道吗？我在坑坑洼洼的路上颠簸行驶，尽量避免坐在熟透的鳄梨上。我突然感觉一切皆有可能，没有什么可以阻止我——并不是因为我知道自己在干什么。

站在尼拉贡戈火山口峰顶，我无法想像扎伊尔边界以外的路线，来到这个国家已经5周了，时间并不长，但是我感觉已脱离了世界上其它地方，我不愿

---

① 这里是林加拉语、东非语、英语和法语打招呼的用语，表示"你好"。
② Matatu，马他突，非洲特别是肯尼亚颇受欢迎的一种小巴士。

意离开这里，似乎离开就意味着失去自己所获得的所有东西。我的心灵和肺脏曾经被拉伸成前所未知的形状，但现在肯定很松弛，就像一个泄了气的气球，准备再次充满气。

我旅程的最后两周是在拉穆①度过的，那是一个穆斯林渔村，坐落在位于印度洋的蒙巴萨②北部的岛屿上。这是我离开位于多哥洛美的几内亚海湾后第一眼看到大海，自从在休达登陆后已过了7个月，在那里滂沱大雨几乎把我们的帐篷卷进了直布罗陀海峡。

我的旅行开始于穆斯林国家摩洛哥和阿尔及利亚，终结于穆斯林地区，但是也有可能会是另一种宗教，另一个洲，另一个凯特。

拉穆是一个通过和平方式敲旅客竹杠的地方，在那里所有人在你到达的第一天就认识你了。凉爽的早晨里我写着日记喝着新鲜的芒果汁，看着身穿斯瓦西里衣服③的孩子们玩捉迷藏，独桅三角帆船在海湾驶进驶出。在曼达岛④我坐在垃圾和金合欢树间用手指夹着吃在明火上做好的鲜鱼。我走在空无一人的海滩上，沿着海岸有3英里的行程，或者掏10个先令乘坐独桅三角帆船。这里没有日程表；像所有非洲交通工具一样，船满即刻扬帆启程。海滩洁净空旷，海里满是水母。一天下午，一对西方夫妇一丝不挂地手牵手漫步，隔天下午，几位拉穆女人，全身罩着 *bui bui*⑤坐在沙滩上。那样的事肯定有个日程表——周二周四是赤身裸体的夫妻，周一和周三是穿着 *bui bui* 的女人。

我会在价格昂贵的佩伯尼饭店躲避下午的酷热。这家饭店出售罐装芒果汁。芒果上市的季节刚结束，我不得不从城镇的一头跑到另一头去寻找一杯鲜榨的芒果汁。幸运的时候有几家餐馆，像哈帕哈帕，酸奶酒店，或者椰子汁吧，能在每天从大陆来的船只上买到一些芒果。你得先于其他芒果汁爱好者在合适的时机出现在合适的地方。但是从来不会缺少酸橙、椰果和香蕉，无论你去世界上任何地方，永远摆脱不了香蕉。

我在佩伯尼餐馆喝了苦柠檬水，然后步行3英里回到镇上。

"*Jambo*, *habari*?⑥"年轻人朝我大声喊道。这是拉斯特法里派⑦男孩们披

---

① Lamu，拉穆，肯尼亚最古老的居住城镇，现已成为旅游名镇。
② Mombasa，蒙巴萨，位于肯尼亚东南部，滨海省省会，是肯尼亚最大的港口城市和第二大城市。
③ Swahili，这里指班图人的一种长袖衣服（通常为白色），通常东非男子穿着这样的衣服。
④ Manda Island 曼达岛，拉穆附近的一个遍布沙丘和红树林的安静小岛，海滩上堆满被海水冲上来的垃圾。
⑤ *bui bui*，肯尼亚女人传统的黑色面纱。
⑥ *Jambo*, *habari*? 斯瓦西里语，您好，你好吗？
⑦ Rasta，拉斯特法里信徒，拉斯特法里运动(Rastafari movement)，又称为拉斯特法里教(Rastafarianism)，是1930年代起自牙买加兴起的一个黑人基督教宗教运动。该运动信徒相信埃塞俄比亚皇帝海尔·塞拉西一世是上帝在现代的转世，是圣经中预言的弥赛亚重临人间。

着拉斯塔法里发绺的最后3天，警察发布命令让剪掉头发。

"Mzuri①，"我咕哝着，浑身散发着汗味，疲惫不堪。你总是回答"Mzuri"，或"很好"，不论你在海滩上度过了多么艰难的一天。我不相信那些男孩，他们是在对我示好吗？我很快与穿着传统服饰的年长男子小心地打招呼。

"Jambo，karibu，②"我沿着街走的时候人们高声喊道。斯瓦西里语是一门绝妙的语言，你们能花5分钟时间相互致以一个词的问候，礼貌很容易就能做到。

正值斋月③，因而六点之前返回城里毫无意义。白天所有的商店都关门，城镇在晚餐前1小时所有孩子和成年男子来到街上时就活跃起来了。上了年纪的人等着有人叫他们去祈祷；孩子们在父亲的照料下玩耍。妇女们像黑云般走过街道，身上的bui bui飘动着，闪现出里面鲜艳的颜色，以只有女性才有的姿态匆忙走着。在湖边区域，游客们坐在水泥墙上等待饭店开门。小商贩们支起了大锅卖冰镇西番莲汁、萨莫萨三角饺、油炸蔬菜馅饼和薄煎饼。清真寺的音箱里发出响亮的祈祷声。男人们穿着Khanzus或长袍，戴着Kofia④帽子进进出出清真寺；有些人坐在台阶上倾听。根据每天报纸上刊登的日落的准确时间，在6：28或6：30，所有人都消失了，这是就餐时间。

此刻人潮汹涌的街道下一刻便空无一人了，留下的只有驴和猫。随意闲逛的驴子沿着主街缓步前行或者懒洋洋地呆在树荫下，头伸进门廊里，似乎希望有人请它们共进晚餐。（他们说那些猫是埃及神猫的后代。它们中有些得到了很好的照顾，大多数却是忍饥挨饿。）

许多拉穆人为斋月守夜，在此期间他们直到次日早晨5：30才能进食，接下来又是休息、祈祷和斋戒的一天。尽管如此，市场里还是挤满了购物的女人。非穆斯林信徒避开斋戒者的眼光在家里进食。我关着门，心怀内疚地在卧室里偷偷地吃午饭，有面包和花生奶油。

非洲改变了我的旅行方式。这里那蚀迹斑斑、布满碎石、裂缝里长出了小树的墙就是我心目中的自我形象。完全困在那个"我"中的我突然闯入非洲，尽管我仍然坚定地安守于自己那时的状态，但已经不那么受到贫穷的影响，而是变得更加心胸开阔、清醒和不确定。但正是这种不确定性所孕育的勇气引导你更加认真平静地看待你自己生活中那些令人难过的和周围那些令人惊慌的点点滴滴。

---

① Mzuri，很好。
② Jambo，karibu，你好，欢迎。
③ Ramadan，斋月，伊斯兰教历的9月伊斯兰教徒每日从黎明到日落禁食。
④ Kofia，当地男人戴的绣花无边软帽。

穿行于世间，贫穷可能令人难以忍受。它可能是一种倒退的生活，可能是一种只看来处不管去处的生活，无论你来自多远的地方。过往很少是平静的，因为过去有太多的可怕回忆，太多的伤心往事。

我仍然渴望透过窗户观察那些生活中充满了不可思议的有序美的人，他们拥有洁净无暇的地毯，完整无损的墙面，精心修饰的花园以及正常工作的电视和抽水马桶。我仍然为那些沙发不塌陷的人的外表所吸引。但是感谢上帝教给我羞耻，因为除此之外我又能学会以怎样的方式独自穿越非洲呢？没有自然而然就存在的共性，因为这是另一个洲，另一个世界，但是如果我不是在贫穷中长大的话，我不会比现在能更清楚地看到这里人们生活中的细节。没什么可怕的，我也没有像闭眼那样的强烈本能。但这也使这一切变得更真实。我知道的已经够多了，还要怎样看得更仔细呢？

非洲让我喜欢去领悟那些无法解释的奇特的东西，喜欢去感受沙漠生活的神秘、遮天蔽日的雨林以及萍水相逢的人们。喜欢那让我驰骋想象的公路，路上偶然的相遇及变化着的语言、风俗、面孔和困境打破了思绪和情感的界限。我的思绪飘向路上的任何地方，不受自认为知道或期待看到的东西的阻碍。

然而我怀疑自己是否会返回陆用载货汽车上。

我从所住的拉穆宾馆的房顶向东眺望，望向印度洋，望向孟买，想起乌干达的路标指示牌上用大写字母写着"缓慢飞行的石头"，感觉自己就像一块缓慢飞行的石头。我匆匆掠过非洲，就像水蛛迅速游过池塘一样，当然那不是一个池塘，而是幽暗、深不见底的水域，如同我们小时候游泳去的那个被水淹没的花岗岩采石场，那时我们很紧张，因为没人知道那儿到底有多深或在水底会遇到什么奇怪的东西。我飞快地穿过这片大陆，感受其深处潜伏着的种种灾难以及即将到来的摧毁一切的怒潮和海啸；感到使我想要哭泣的软弱。在那里人类和生物，马赛人和图尔卡纳人①，猩猩和蹄兔，都在经历艰难的岁月，处于岌岌可危的状态。我返回美国后不久，阿尔及利亚突然爆发残酷的内战，图阿雷格人发起了叛乱，四处流窜，失去了游牧的生活方式。卢旺达种族灭绝的难民们涌到了戈马。包括扎伊尔在内的5个国家都卷入了战争。我只是避开了这一切，将我的旅行恰巧安排在旱灾和种族灭绝之间。

在内罗毕②背包客中流传着这样一句话："你去拉美学会政治，去亚洲学会哲学，去非洲学会笑对人生。"

我内心对非洲充满同情，这片有着充满茉莉花香的宁静湿润的黎明以及金

---

① the Turkana，图尔卡纳人，东非民族之一，主要分布在乌干达、肯尼亚西北部和苏丹共和国东南部（7万）。属尼格罗人种苏丹类型，为尼罗特人南支之一，使用图尔卡纳语。

② Nairobi，内罗毕，是东非国家肯尼亚的首都，也是非洲的大城市之一。

合欢树和长颈鹿剪影的土地；这片有着连绵不断坑坑洼洼道路的大陆；这片有着变幻莫测的撒哈拉金黄色沙子和粘乎乎的扎伊尔红泥土的土地，所有这一切都不知会把你引向何处，而那些地方是你过去从未想象过的。

（申彩红 译 杨建 校）

第二编　丛林游记

神秘，抑或是诡异？人对丛林的印象不外乎此。难道生命的神秘只有在丛林中才能得到淋漓尽致的绽放？……

Lost in the Amazon

Matthew Power

【导读】"人最宝贵的是生命，生命对于每个人来说只有一次。人的一生应该这样度过：回首往事，他不会因为虚度年华而悔恨，也不会因为碌碌无为而羞愧。"《钢铁是怎样炼成的》里的这段名言包含着深刻的哲学命题和高度的道德期许。然而，我们还要进一步追问：在气象万千、人生价值观多元化的当今世界，怎样才算年华不虚度、碌碌不无为？从古至今，热衷于"世上第一人"称号、以此留名于世的举动不绝于史，比如"世上游泳横渡欧亚两大洲第一人"、"世上徒步横跨南极第一人"，诸如此类。这些不为科学考察、也不为游山玩水的、纯粹是个人冒险的行为究竟意义何在？挑战人力的最终极限？证明人性的勇猛？这正是《迷失亚马逊》一文的追问并试图寻找到答案。在各种交通手段如此发达先进的21世纪，却偏偏要以两人微薄之力，徒步纵跨整个亚马逊流域，从攀爬巍峨险峻的高山寻找其源头开始，抛开阳关大道不走，偏偏选取人迹罕至、洪涝不已的茫茫丛林，跋山涉水，遭遇虫叮蚊咬、蟒蛇电鳗、土著追杀、毒贩灭口等各种预料之中或预料之外的各种危险，简直就是流行一时的网络游戏"迷失亚马逊"真人版。而这样做的真正缘由却是"还从来没人这么做过，"遵循的逻辑也荒唐透顶："明知这么做毫无意义，但无论如何都要做。"本文作者和我们读者一样，实在不明白这种"世上第一人"的探险究竟意义何在，干脆设身处地陪同那位"傻瓜探险者"傻走了10天，结果弄得"双脚一天12小时地浸泡在水里，此时已变得如同死人的脚一样灰白；我渴望喝到没有碘坑味道的水。我浑身都是蚂蚁咬的伤痕，脚踝上嵌满了寄生蚤。"寻找的答案似乎是"不问结果，尽享过程"的一种超脱的宿命论人生观："让自己漂浮起来，感受这一时刻的宁静，"同时对时间的认识也发生了重大改变：不要行色匆匆，不要拼命完成时间表；要从容地走完探险之路，时间"有多久算多久"。这就是年华不虚度、碌碌不无为么？

Iquitos, Peru, population 360,000, bills[①] itself as the largest city in the world that cannot be reached by road. The capital of the Peruvian Amazon, it is an island in a vast ocean of jungle, a seaport two thousand miles from the sea, linked to the outside world only by air or by the roiling wasters of the Amazon River. At the height of the rubber trade in the late nineteenth century, Iquitos was one of the richest cities in South America, a boomtown that could afford to ship in a prefab mansion designed by Gustave Eiffe[②]l or ship out dirty linens to be laundered in Paris. Today it is a filthy, crumbling frontier town, choked with motorcars, three-wheeled taxis that turn the dusty streets into a buzzing and honking chaos. Iquitos is also a launching point for exploration of the two-million-square-mile rainforest that spreads across the Amazon basin, home to a tenth of the world's known species, several of which I can see as I walk along the waterfront, where hawkers sell stuffed piranhas, mounted butterflies the size of paperbacks, and twelve-foot anaconda skins unrolled with a theatrical flourish. [③]But I have no time to barter for souvenirs. It's the rainy season, and black-bellied thunderheads are piling up on the horizon as the pressure drops in the soupy tropical air. I am hurrying to the port to catch a boat heading downriver, through the vast unsettled territory that lies between Iquitios and Peru's frontier with Brazil and Colombia.

If all goes according to plan, somewhere on the banks of the mile-wide river I will rendezvous with a thirty-three-year-old former British army captain named Ed Stafford. But Stafford has warned me that in the Amazon things rarely go according to plan. He should know: since April 2008 he has been on an expedition to be the first person in history to travel the entire four-thousand-mile length of the Amazon River on foot, through the heart of the largest jungle on earth. He's attempting to walk every step of the river's route from source to sea, wherever it is possible to walk. There are also several hundred tributaries he will need to cross using an inflatable raft he carries with him, and he must traverse three countries and the

---

① Bill here is used as a verb, describing someone or something in a particular, usually promotional, way, esp. as a means of advertisement. 中文大意为：号称，标榜。

② a French structural engineer, an accomplished architect, particularly specializing in metallic structure in the late 19th century and early 20th century.

③ The meaning of "stuff", used as a past participle adjective in the text, is to fill out the skin of (a dead animal or bird) with material to restore the original shape and appearance. The meaning of "mount", also used as a past participle adjective, is to set in or attach to a backing or setting. stuff 和 mount 在本文都指制作标本的一种方式，前者是把动物的皮囊里填充起来使其形状和生前一模一样，而后者是把昆虫标本固定在标本夹上。

territories of dozens of indigenous tribes. In his expedition blog, Stafford writes: "Walking from the source to the sea is one of the last great feats of exploration."

We live in an age of diminishing firsts, so those wishing to find fame or notoriety through adventure are forced into increasingly baroque categories: summiting Everest① on prosthetic legs, or climbing Kilimanjaro② on Rollerblades③. The Amazon has been run several times by kayaking④ expeditions, and a Slovenian named Martin Strel has even swum most of its length, but nobody has ever crossed it on foot. When I first read about Stafford's mission I immediately wondered what made Stafford believe he could actually make it.

Perhaps more than any other landscape, the Amazon jungle is steeped in myth and mystery, looming over the human imagination as a symbol of both untamed wilderness and environmental vulnerability. The mind⑤ shudders at its enormity. The river that begins as a trickle of glacial melt water at 20,000 feet in the Andes discharge 32 million gallons a second. Twenty percent of all fresh water flowing into the world's oceans passes through its mouth, which gapes 150 miles wide. For five centuries the river has been the obsession (and undoing) of countless outsiders, from the lunatic conquistador Lope de Aguirre⑥ to the vanished 1920s explorer Percy Fawcett⑦. The lore of Amazon exploration is filled with starvation, madness, disease, and murder.

I understood the region's undeniable allure, but I was still curious why anyone

---

① Mount Everest, the world's highest mountain, with a peak at 8,848 meters (29,029 ft) above sea level. It is located in the Mahalangur section of the Himalayas. 珠穆拉马蜂。

② a dormant volcano in Kilimanjaro National Park, Tanzania and the highest mountain in Africa at 5,895 metres or 19,341 feet above sea level. 乞力马扎罗山。

③ An Italian brand of inline skates. 一种意大利牌子的轮滑鞋。

④ Paddling with a kind of canoe coated with seal skin, originated from Eskimos.

⑤ A person identified with their intellectual faculties.

⑥ a Spanish conqueror present during much of the infighting among the Spanish in and around Peru in the mid sixteenth century. Best known for his final expedition, he went mad with paranoia. He was considered a symbol of cruelty and treachery in colonial Spanish America, and has become an antihero in literature, cinema and other arts. (for more please referring to online Wiki).

⑦ a British artillery officer, archaeologist and South American explorer. Along with his eldest son, Fawcett disappeared under unknown circumstances in 1925 during an expedition to find "Z" – his name for what he believed to be an ancient lost city in the uncharted jungles of Brazil.

would subject himself to two years cr0ssing a landscape largely populated① by anacondas, jaguars, vampire bats, pit vipers, scorpions, wasps, army ants, electric eels, piranhas②, drug smugglers, hostile tribes, dengue *and* yellow fever, malaria, fifteen-foot black caimans, and eighteen-inch leeches. Not to mention the candiru, a pin-size catfish that has the ability to swim up a stream of urine and lodge itself irretrievably in the urethra. There are almost no roads along Stafford's route, and since the most common way of traveling is by boat, even trails are scarce. So to try to understand whatever impulse inspires Stafford onward, I arranged to join him for a few weeks of his journey. But first I had to find him.

At the Iquitos docks I board a rusting double-decker ferry, whose every inch of deck space is strung with hammocks. I am the only gringo aboard, and everything I do meets with stares. The sky is flame orange: cumulonimbus clouds boil over the forest as the boat noses out into the current. The water is the color of cappuccino, and putting green-size mats③ of floating vegetation drift along in it. Dugouts with outboards hug the banks and beat their way upstream against the flow. The ferry steams along swiftly with the current, the river lashing in broad meanders between the unbroken walls of jungle.

As darkness falls and most of the passengers climb into their hammocks, I stand by the wheelhouse, watching as the pilot navigates around huge floating logs. After several hours of staring into the blackness, we see a tiny cluster of lights on the far bank. As we get closer, I see two men, and the taller one, wearing a baseball cap, waves to men. The big boat grounds itself against the muddy bank, and I jump down, the only passenger disembarking at this stop. The two men approach. I can't resist: "Mr. Stafford, I presume?"

"Have a beer," he replies, laughing.

---

① With double meanings: a. form the population of an area. b. Fill or be present in (a place, environment, or domain). Here "populated" is used as a syllepsis, a kind of rhetorical device in which one word (usually a <u>verb</u>) is understood differently in relation to two or more other words, which it modifies or governs. (异叙修辞格，巧用一词多义的语法特点)。

② All of these are dangerous or poisonous species particular in South America.

③ Putting green refers to a smooth area of short grass surrounding a hole, either as part of a golf course or as a separate area for putting. Putting green 指的是高尔夫球的轻击地区，中文直译为"果岭"，高尔夫球运动中的一个术语，是指球洞所在的小山丘，该山丘上通常会将草修剪得较短。果岭二字即为英文 green 英音译而来。选手在打球时，第一个目标即是将球打上果岭，再进一步以推杆来进球。果岭的草比球场其他区域的草更为娇贵、细嫩。在这里指有果岭面积大小的绿色水生植物像席子一样漂浮在亚马逊河面上。

Ed Stafford stands about six feet tall, wearing flip-flops[1], tattered cargo pants, and a filthy T-shirt, and walks with the bouncy gait of someone who has just set down a heavy load. He has two weeks' growth of beard, an easy laugh, and dark glimmering eyes. He introduces me to his expedition partner, Gadiel Sanchez Rivera, a twenty-eight-year old Peruvian nicknamed Cho. It is 3 A.M., and percussive cumbia music[2] blasts from the town's only bar, where we drink beer as Stafford fills me in on his story so far. In more than ten months of walking he has faced poisonous snakes, navigated perilous footpaths above Class V rapids[3], and had his life threatened by angry tribesmen. He has traveled about two thousand miles so far and is almost halfway to the Atlantic. "Unfortunately, this has been the easy half," he says.

Inauspiciously expelled from his posh British private school at age seventeen for chopping down a tree planted by the queen, Stafford spent four years in the British army, making the rank of captain. He was once a competitive rugby player and has a false incisor in place of the one he lost on the cricket field. He organized security logistics[4] for the UN during Afghanistan's 2004 elections[5] and led an expedition for a BBC nature documentary in Guyana. He wanted a life of adventure,

---

[1] A light sandal, typically of plastic or rubber, with a thong between the big and second toe.

[2] Cumbia music is a Colombian music genre popular across Latin America, originated from Africa, and its major instrument is drum.

[3] Skill Level in International Scale of River Difficulty, means extremely difficult, Exceedingly difficult, long and violent rapids, following each other almost without interruption; riverbed extremely obstructed; or, whitewater, large waves, continuous rapids, large rocks and hazards, maybe a large drop.

[4] Both "security" and "logistics" here are military terms, the former one referring to the military goods for defense and the latter one the organization of moving, housing, and supplying troops and equipment.

[5] Though Afghanistan has had democratic elections throughout the 20th century, the election institutions have varied as changes in regimes have disrupted political continuity. Presidential elections in 2009, raised doubts about the legitimacy and power of the current electoral system, established in the 2003 constitution, in both the national political environment and the international community. Under the 2001 Bonn Agreement, Afghanistan was scheduled to hold presidential and parliamentary elections in 2004 in order to replace the transitional government led by American-backed Hamid Karzai since his appointment in December 2001. Presidential elections were held in 2004, but parliamentary elections were not held until mid-September 2005. In March 2005 UN Security Council issued a report on parliamentary elections delay.

like that of his hero Sir Ranulph Fiennes①, so he and a colleague named Luke Collyer brainstormed possible expeditions they could undertake. Stafford's jungle experience in Belize② and Borneo③ – expeditions he led to raise money for charity – gave him the idea of walking the length of the Amazon. To their surprise, it had never been done.

The expedition began on Peru's Pacific coast in April 2008, with Collyer. The pair hiked up the Colca Canyon and into the Andes, traversing several of the possible sources of the Amazon to cover all their bases. They crossed the mountains with pack burros, and from eighteen thousand feet began their long descent into the Amazon basin.

As Stafford sees it, there was an imbalance from the beginning. During the months of planning, securing sponsors, permits, and equipment, Collyer was busy with work, so Stafford handled most of the logistics himself. When Collyer arrived in Peru he was out of shape, didn't speak a word of Spanish, and had gotten engaged a few weeks before. "He was totally unprepared for what we were about to do," Stafford tells me. "And that became more and more apparent as we went on. His heart just wasn't in it."

Three months in, Collyer placed a supply order that contained just one MP3 player. Stafford got angry and asked why Collyer hadn't also gotten one for him. Collyer announced that the player was for Stafford and that he was quitting the expedition. The breakdown had been a long time coming. "The MP3 player was just the final straw," says Stafford. "He claimed he was leaving because our friendship was more important to him than the expedition. For me the expedition is more important than anything." The two men haven't spoken in five months.

When I later contacted Collyer for his side of the story, he e-mailed a polite "no comment": "A lot of time has passed and I've removed myself from anything to do with the expedition," he wrote. "And I'm happy to keep it that way."

Stafford continued on alone, walking with a succession of local guides. Then, in

---

① Born in March 1944, a British <u>adventurer</u> and holder of several endurance records. Fiennes served in the British Army for eight years. He later undertook numerous expeditions and was the first person to visit both the <u>North</u> and <u>South</u> Poles by surface means and the first to completely cross <u>Antarctica</u> on foot. In May 2009, at the age of 65, he climbed to the summit of <u>Mount Everest</u>. He wrote many well-accepted books based on his expeditions.

② a country located on the north eastern coast of Central America; the only country in Central America where <u>English</u> is the official language.

③ the third <u>largest island in the world</u> and is located in <u>Indonesia</u>.

August 2008, he met Cho in the town of Satipo, Peru. Cho had worked some time as a forester, hiking deep into the jungle to find large specimens of the most desirable timber hardwoods: mahogany, cedar, tornillo. He had initially agreed to walk with Stafford for five days. The two didn't get along at first, but Cho grew enthusiastic about the mission and proved a tireless and loyal companion, and so Stafford brought him on as paid partner for the remainder of the expedition.

"He's got balls of steel①, and he's as keen as I am to complete this expedition," says Stafford. "He's taken the whole thing on as a sort of personal challenges as much as I have. And to find someone like that has been a real key. You just can't do something like this alone." Stafford now has someone to share the weight of food and gear and help bridge the language gap, but Cho's greatest value is psychological: the sheer relief of having someone to watch your back. They have been walking together for seven months now, and Cho has committed to ticking with Stafford until they reach the Atlantic, however long that takes.

Which may be very long time. Stafford originally planned to travel about ten miles a day, which he soon realized was "vastly overoptimistic." At that rate he would have reached the Colombia-Brazil border by Christmas. But it was already February, and Colombia is more than one hundred miles east of us. The rainy season is in full swing②, and the forests alongside the main channel have begun to flood. Stafford and Cho have gotten a taste of that in the last two weeks, crossing the wide delta where the Rio Napo③ joins the Amazon. "The forests were completely flooded, waist-high, sometimes head-high," Stafford tells me. "We were scrambling over three trunks under the water. There's a species of palm here where the entire trunk is covered with three-inch spikes. They were like needles driving straight into our knees."

In the morning the children of the village sit in a hut to watch a badly dubbed version of Jean-Claude Van Damme's *Kickboxer*, and then spill out into the intense sunlight to practice their new moves. They watch raptly as Stafford, Cho, and I organize our gear. My frame pack is stuffed with a waterproof canoe bag; within that are smaller dry bags and zip locks, a system that keeps things dry while making

---

① Balls of steel: strong will.
② In full swing: at the strongest moment.
③ A branch river.

them impossible to find. Stafford's bag, a battered one-hundred-liter monster that weight in at seventy-five pounds, contains everything he needs to be a self-documenting, one-man twenty-first-century expedition. "My kit would be a lot lighter if I wasn't trying to blog this whole thing," he says, as he double- and triple-bags the sensitive electronic that are his only link to the outside world.

Part of Stafford's mission statement is to document the customs and perceptions of the tribes he encounters and the environmental issues facing the region, as well as raise $200,000 for a host of charities. Yet he is the first to admit that he is doing this mainly because it has never been done, and because he wants to have an extraordinary life and support himself with adventures. There's something anachronistic about the project, a "because it's there" attitude that could be criticized as a risky ego trip. I ask Stafford if he feels as if he belongs in an earlier era, perhaps that of Captain Cook[①] or Admiral Byrd[②]. "I feel like I was born at exactly the right time," he says. "I don't think a middle-class individual would have been able to do this sort of thing before." And he admits to an "element of pride about the whole thing," adding, "If anyone has got a problem with it, they should come try it themselves."

Stafford has acquired a full set of forty-year-old National Geographic Institute of Peru 1:100,000 topographical maps, still the most accurate available. In conjunction with his handheld GPS, they actually provide fairly decent route finding. He shows me his new route, tracing a band of altitude that should – he hopes – help us avoid walking through a swamp and make for faster travel. "One of the odd things about *walking* the length of the Amazon," he says, "is that you don't actually see the river very much."

For each leg of his walk, Stafford tries to hire a local guide, someone with knowledge of the forest who can help pick the most efficient route. In Oran he has engaged the services of Mario, a sixty-two-year-old farmer and father of twelve, who has been hunting these forests for five decades. Mario doesn't stand an inch above five feet, and his gear is the minimalist opposite of Stafford's: everything he needs is

---

① (1728 – 1779), a British explorer, navigator.

② (1888 – 1957), a naval officer in USA, who specialized in feats of exploration. Aircraft flights, in which he served as a navigator and expedition leader, crossed the Atlantic Ocean, a segment of the Arctic Ocean, and a segment of the Antarctic Plateau. Byrd claimed that his expeditions had been the first to reach the North Pole and the South Pole by air. Byrd was a recipient of the Medal of Honor, the highest honor for heroism given by the United States.

stuffed into a small flour sack that he carries by a cloth strap across his forehead. The only other items he has are rubber boots, a machete, and an ancient rusting shotgun, in case he stumbles across dinner[①].

Shouldering our packs, we turn away from the river and cross a cow field behind the village, the tropical sun crushing down on us. A few one-hundred-foot shade trees have been left standing alone, a sobering indication of the original height of the rainforest's triple canopy. This part of the Amazon, too remote and flood-prone to be easily exploited, still offers glimpses of the devastation wrought elsewhere.

We make our way up a slope, and within minutes we plunge into the tangled green wall that closes off the edge of the forest, leaving the bright world behind. Even at noon on the equator, the jungle is dim, the filtered green sunlight offering little sense of direction or time. The air is cooler, sounds are muffled, and the line of sight is reduced to a dozen yards through the dense understory tangle of creeping vines, lianas, and sprawling root systems. Huge trunks shoot up through the canopy, clung to by vines and strangler figs, giant bromeliads hanging like chandeliers. An astonishing amount of biomass claws upward, trying to bridge the gap between the limitless water of the ground and the limitless sunshine of the forest roof. You can almost hear it growing. The leaf litter on the ground is a foot-deep cushion, and there is no sound but the drone of insects and the distant calls of birds.

Mario leads the way along a barely perceptible path. His machete seems to be an extension of his body, and he parts the jungle with deft ease, using only the tip of the blade to slice thick vines and huge leaves. Stafford has also become adept with the indispensable machete but still relies on brute force to hack his way through obstacles. The diminutive Mario doesn't even sweat and seems to expend almost no effort as the trail parts before him with a flick of his wrist.

Taking up the rear, I'm already soaked through with sweat as we balance our way across mossy logs spanning tea-colored streams and scramble over waist-high buttress roots. Mosquitoes swarm around us, and hordes of stinging ants brush off from overhanging leaves or the trunks of trees. Even the vegetation has evolved with its own aggressive microspecialization. There are spike-covered roots that seem to grow exactly where a handhold is required, vines like rubber bands that wrap around

---

① During his guiding, perhaps he can hunt some animals or birds as their dinner.

my ankles, and thorny tendrils that snatch the hat right off my head. The worst by far is serrated razor grass, which slices through clothing and skin with the lightest touch. Stafford has been told there are endless stretches of razor grass downriver in Brazil, another obstacle to add to the preposterously overfull roster that stands between him and the mouth of the Amazon.

A few times Mario stops dead and points off into the underbrush. I see nothing moving at all. "Pit viper," Stafford tells me. I've researched enough about the variety of horrible deaths on offer in the Amazon to know that a pit viper's hemotoxin causes massive hemorrhaging, bleeding from the eyes and ears, necrosis, then death. "Oh, don't worry," Stafford says cheerfully. "We've got six doses of dry antivenin, enough to last eighteen hours, and there's a military rescue helicopter in Iquitos. The worst-case scenario is if you were bit at sunset, because the helicopter can't fly at night. But we'd be able to keep you alive until dawn." Well, then. No worries. The expedition has already come across ten pit vipers, all but one of which have been quickly dispatched by their guide's machetes. In stark contrast to our own conservation dogma, no local guide would let a poisonous snake escape if he could help it.

The only anaconda they had come across while walking was a beautiful twelve-footer that Stafford stopped to film. When he'd finished, his native guide hacked the creature into pieces. "He said it was to feed to his dog," Stafford tells me. "But one of the things I learned early on was that here was no point in trying to impose my Western sensibility on the people who live here. They do what they do to survive. They don't think of animals as having any value except food."

In late afternoon we find a small stream and stop for the night. After months of sleeping out, Stafford and Cho have reduced setting up a camp to a science[①]. I have not reached that point and very nearly dismember myself with the machete while trying to clear an area of underbrush. Eventually I get a tent fly strung between two trees as a shelter. This way camp can be made even in a driving rain. The key piece of equipment is the expedition hammock, enclosed by mosquito netting and entered via a Velcro-sealed slit in its bottom.

Cho and Stafford assemble a structure of damp green wood on which to build a fire and support the cook pot, gathering standing deadwood from the forest for fuel.

---

① They have become very skilled in setting up a neat and comfortable camp.

It's a miracle the fire will catch with wood that is drenched daily, but Cho soon has a crackling blaze and puts on a pot of stream water. Dinner is boiled rice with canned tuna bought from a supply store in the last village we'd passed through. "When I first began, I thought there would be much more of a survivalist element, fishing and living off the land," says Stafford. "But as it's happened, we come across villages often enough that we can resupply or pay villagers to cook for us. That's been the most surprising aspect: how much we've had to deal with people. I had imagined it would be emptier, more man versus nature." He realized that the cultural interchange with the people of the Amazon was an integral part of the expedition. He also realized that it was easier to start a fire with a cheap plastic lighter than with flint and steel.

Even though we're coated with deet① the mosquitoes are swarming around us, and as the equatorial night drops fast I crawl into my hammock and close myself in. A symphony of insects performs, multilayered, shockingly loud. Thousands of mosquitoes tap against the netting, probing for an entrance. The cough-like whoops of howler monkeys echo in the distance. Then a low hiss builds and builds, until the temperature drops and the rain opens up like a jet taking off, drowning all other sound, enshrouding the night.

In the morning I put on all my still-wet clothes from the previous day. Wrung-out is as dry as any of us ever gets, and Stafford tells me to look out for foot rot②, staph-infected cuts, and all the other bacterial and fungal delights of the Amazon's petri-dish environment. In an uncaffeinated haze I remember that you are supposed to shake your boots out before putting them back on in the jungle. I tap one upside down and a cricket the size of a sparrow cambers out and hops away.

The Amazon has a keen sense of irony. Mention how easy it is to cross a log bridge, and you will do a gainer into a stream; praise the quality of the trail, and it will disappear into a swamp; comment on the fine weather, and a Wagnerian③ thunderstorm will ensue. Stafford has gotten used to the frequent mishaps and come to see them, afterward, as a kind of comic relief. One afternoon he left the map

---

① a colorless oily liquid with a mild odor, used as an insect repellent.
② Foot rot is a bacterial disease of the feet in hoofed animals, and here refers to the disease in the travelers' feet.
③ Having the enormous dramatic scale and intensity of a Wagner opera. Wagner is a famous French musician and dramatist.

behind when we stopped for lunch. Mario, far faster than any of us and more certain of his direction, dashed off to retrieve it and returned at nightfall. Months earlier Stafford dropped his only machete during a river crossing and had to push on to the next village with his bare hands. Self-deprecation seems to be a key to his success so far, and he has the ability to take the expedition seriously and recognize its absurdities at the same time. Plunging up to our necks in a creek crossing, he mutters, "Bloody silly expedition," and soldiers on.

For days we continue slogging along the contours of the chart, differently only in scale from the columns of leaf-cutter ants that march alongside us. It is exhausting, dirty work, and I am covered with mud, scratches, and bruises. The prospect of doing this with no clear end date would be daunting. Stafford stops periodically to check our progress with the GPS. Mario looks on politely, though he has no idea how to read a map and the GPS is an impenetrable mystery to him. Stafford defers to Mario's local knowledge but likes to double-check against modern technology. "I know with this I'd be able to make it without a local guide," says Stafford, "but it would be much slower, and much more work." The GPS show that Mario has taken us almost exactly along the planned route.

It's disheartening to see indisputable data on how slow our progress has been. On a good trail, two or three miles an hour is reasonable, but in trackless jungle, scrambling over or under fallen trees, hacking through vines or wading through mud, forward movement can slow to an agonizing crawl. After struggling with the frustration of slow progress for much of the trip, Stafford has finally reached some sort of peace with it. In the slog through the Napo delta, he noticed that in chest-deep water his heavy pack became buoyant, and there was a "bizarre sort of serenity" as he made his way through the silent flooded forest. "For some reason my default mode is military, 'we've got to get there,'" Stafford explains to me. "Cho takes his time walking through water. Suddenly, I wasn't getting frustrated walking only 2.5 kilometers a day. It was tranquil, and I realize it's going to take as long as it takes."

Although Stafford has become accustomed to the physical hardships of the jungle, encounters with tribes remain Stafford's greatest challenge. Many villages speak unique dialects, using only rudimentary Spanish. There is a long history of exploitation of tribes by oil and gold prospectors, and thousands of indigenous and rural Peruvians were murdered during the years of insurgency by the Shining Path guerrillas①. So it's for good reason that many indigenous communities harbor a deep suspicion of outsiders.

One of the most pervasive fears is that white people are *pela cara*②; literally it means "face peeler," but the term has become a myth among many native communities that outsiders will steal their organs. "The last thing you want after an exhausting day of walking is to arrive someplace and have the whole community be scared of you," Stafford says, but he has learned how to stay calm, how to de-escalate tensions.

Once, upon entering a village back along the Apurimac③, Stafford was immediately confronted by an angry mob of Indians. They poured water on him, shoved dirt in his mouth, and smeared his face with red paint. He was scared but did his best to stay calm. "I just shook hands with their chief, turned around, and walked out of the village," he recalls. Not long after that incident he and Cho were crossing a tributary in the pack rafts. Cho looked over his shoulder and saw that they were followed by five canoes filled with furious Ashaninka Indians. The men were armed with bows and arrows and shotguns; the women carried machetes. "I was pretty sure we were going to die," says Stafford. Even Cho, normally unflappable, thought they were done for. They were surrounded, and the leaders of the tribe approached them, screaming, blind with rage. Stafford showed them their permits from the regional authorities, but nothing helped. The women seemed ready to hack them into pieces. Finally, speaking slowly and quietly and holding hands open, he managed to get them to calm down. Andreas and Alfonso, the leaders of the tribe, ended up joining them as guides for six weeks. Stafford was astonished. "The people I was most afraid of on the entire expedition turned out to be the most kind, helpful, and loyal people I've met."

That experience has convinced Stafford that he'll be able to handle whatever situation arises downriver. But Brazil presents even greater risks. When Stafford applied for permits through a fixing agency in Manaus④, he initially got no response. "When I finally reached them," he says, "they said they didn't respond because I was

---

① A insurgent organization in Peru, active in 1970s-1980s.

② A kind of Spanish dialect word.

③ A source river of the Amazon in Peru.

④ a city in Brazil, the capital of the state of Amazonas. It is situated at the confluence of the Negro and Solimões rivers.

going to die. 'It's a suicide mission. The indigenous reserve on the other side of the border in Brazil is the fiercest in the Amazon basin. Colonial Brazilians don't even go there. You're white, don't speak Portuguese, and are wandering around with a video camera.'" All salient points, he thought, but decided he'd "just go in and be very friendly and very calm." He still believes that with the right guides and the right approach, he'll make it. "But I have yet to meet a Brazilian who thinks it's possible," he concedes. "The only people who say 'Yeah, you'll be fine' are your friends back home, who haven't a fucking clue."

While Stafford measures the risks rationally, Cho has a more mystical outlook. A deeply religious Christian, he believes that God is protecting them. Stafford is more fatalistic. "I am either going to make it, or I am going to die trying," he says in a way that is almost cocky, confident that he can manage the risks and come out the other end alive and victorious.

We stay in a Yawa① village for a day, where I entertain the children with my Buster Keaton② antics, smacking my head on five-foot-high door frames and falling out of hammocks. A boy in a dugout paddles us across the tributary Rio Apicuyu, loaded high with our gear. Drifting, watching toucans and scarlet macaws alight in the trees by the riverbank and huge iridescent blue morpho butterflies rising on the breeze, I am struck by the folly of Stafford's "bloody silly expedition." The Yawas paddle up and down the river in dugout canoes, slipping easily with the current wherever they wish. All the cultures in the Amazon make use of the thousands of miles of waterways. Walking the Amazon seems analogous to crossing the Sahara on snowshoes: you could do it, but it's certainly not the way the locals go. There's a reason nobody has ever done this before.

I bring this up to Stafford, and he laughs. "A friend of mine once said, 'I fucking love your expedition because it's pointless.' It's a real British mentality: it's fucking pointless but we'll do it anyway." Like Livingstone③ and Scott④ before

---

① A native tribe.

② A famous American comic actor.

③ David Livingstone, a Scottish explorer in Africa in 19th century. His fame as an explorer helped drive forward the obsession with discovering the sources of the River Nile that formed the culmination of the classic period of European geographical discovery and colonial penetration of the African continent.

④ Robert Falcon Scott, (1868 – 1912) was a Royal Navy officer and explorer who led two expeditions to the Antarctic regions: the Discovery Expedition, 1901–04, and the ill-fated Terra Nova Expedition, 1910–13.

him, Stafford has completely bought into the stiff-upper-lip[①] masochistic absurdity of his endeavor, and he's proud of it.

Sore and scraped up after three more days of hacking our way through maze-like jungle, we finally reach the next village. Porvenir is an idyllic scattering of thatch houses on stilts set on a bluff above the Rio Ampicuyu, another small tributary of the Amazon. From here we must temporarily leave the route of the expedition to rendezvous with Pete McBride, a photographer from Colorado. We spend five hours in a dugout canoes, motoring downstream to the ramshackle market town of Pevas, right on the Amazon itself, where we meet up with McBride, resupply our stocks of tuna and ramen noodles, and return to the spot where we'd left off.

This is one of the self-created regulations of the expedition: whenever Stafford leaves the route, he sets a GPS marker so he can return to the exact spot and pick up where he left off. It's what makes the game of walking the Amazon fun, a stickler of a rule that presents all sorts of logistical challenges. There is, of course, nobody to enforce this except Stafford and Cho, but the idea of cutting corners is unfathomable to them. "I wouldn't bother suffering this much if I were going to cheat on the small things," says Stafford."If we're going to do this, we're going to do it right."

Mario returns home to his family and village, and for the next leg of the journey we will travel with a guide named Bernobe Sancha, a thirty-eight-year-old Ocaina Indian. I wake up in the morning to find Bernobe standing perfectly still, perched on a root above the edge of the river, holding a machete. With a quick flick and a splash, he hacks downward. A fish, hits head surgically cut in half, drifts up to the surface of the water. We gut it and split it for breakfast, five ways.

When we walk out through the fields behind Porvenir, I stumble across a well-tended little plot of coca[②] bushes. We are only fifty miles south of the Colombian border, and a huge amount of drug trafficking passes through the region. Peru is the world's second-largest producer of coca, whose leaves are refined into paste before being trekked to drug labs across Colombia's border for further processing. Encounters with nervous traffickers, the vast majority of them poor

---

① A idiom, meaning strong-willed, never-surrender.
② A sort of herb plant particular in South America.

Peruvians, will be a serious risk as Stafford and Cho approach the "Triangle of Death" at the Peru-Brazil-Colombia frontier. In Pevas I read an account of a Peruvian village that had been burned to the ground in a turf war between rival drug gangs. It was right along Stafford's planned route.

  The jungle life is beginning to wear on me after ten days of trekking. As my willpower flags, my astonishment at Stafford's determination grows. My feet, soaked for twelve hours a day, look cadaverous. I long for water that doesn't taste like an iodized puddle. I am covered with ant bites, and my ankles are embedded with parasitic fleas. At one point Stafford stumbles into a swarm of wasps, and the four of us sprint in a panic back down the trail. Then, while crossing through waist-deep water, McBride looks down and shouts, "What the hell is that thing?" This is not something anybody wants to hear while standing in an Amazonian swamp.

  The creature has a huge whiskered head like a catfish, but a bright red mouth and tail that winds off behind a stump and breaks the water six feet away. It swims slowly toward McBride and then vanishes below the surface in the murk. Bernobe tries to explain in broken Spanish, repeating the word *anguila*, but none of us knows what it means. Only later do we realize that the thing was an enormous electric eel, which could have generated enough of a shock to knock us all unconscious, facedown in the water.

  On the day McBride and I are to leave, we have to make our way to the bank of the Ampicuyu to meet with a boat down toward the Amazon. According to Stafford's GPS, the river is eight hundred yards away. We strike out toward it, hacking through vines and undergrowth, but after just a few yards there is nothing but flooded forest as far as I can see. The only way to the river is straight ahead. We are knee-deep, then waist-deep, and the dry bag in my pack begins to float and the weight is lifted off my aching shoulders. Our footsteps are silent, and we glide around enormous root buttresses in the light-dappled water. The flooded forest is other-worldly, literally: an exact replica of the forest, the sky, and ourselves moving in reflection over the still black water. When it is too deep we load our bags in the pack rafts and push them through the water, swimming in our heavy boots, laughing, spiders and ants on every branch. The water is too murky to even see a hand below the surface – or an electric eel.

  The flooded forest is the epitome of all childhood nightmares, and yet I'm not afraid. I now understand the realization Stafford came to while crossing the Napo delta: he learned to let himself float, to feel the tranquility of the moment he was in. Stafford has a long way to go, perhaps eighteen more months, but you can't rush an expedition like this. It will take as long as it takes.

迷失亚马逊

马修·鲍尔

秘鲁的爱奎托斯人口有 36 万，自我标榜为世界上不能由陆路抵达的最大城市。这座城市是秘鲁境内亚马逊地区的首府，其实是丛林之洋中的一座岛屿，还是一个离海两千英里远的海口，依靠航空或者亚马逊滚滚河水与外界相通。在 19 世纪晚期的橡胶贸易高峰期，爱奎托斯曾是南美最富有的城市之一，暴富的人们摆阔，不是从巴黎海运来鼎鼎大名的设计师卡斯塔夫·埃菲尔设计的活动豪宅，就是把脏亚麻床单之类海运到巴黎的洗衣房去洗。如今，这里却是一个肮脏破败的边境小镇，充斥着摩托车、三轮出租车，使得灰尘飞荡的街道变得轰轰锵锵得一片嘈杂。爱奎托斯还是亚马逊盆地 200 万平方英里的雨林探险的聚散地。全世界十分之一的知名物种生长在这片雨林里，我沿着镇上的河边散步时就看到了好几种。河边的小商贩叫卖着食人鱼标本、平装版书籍大小的蝴蝶标本册、一张张的展开来足有 12 英尺长的、光怪陆离①的水蟒蛇皮。不过我可没时间倒腾旅游纪念品。现在正是热带地区的雨季，空气因水汽饱和而让人感觉黏糊糊的；随着气压的降低，地平线上乌黑的雷雨云层层堆积。我脚步匆匆，赶着搭乘顺流而来的船只，然后乘船穿越广袤的无人区。我要穿越的这片区域位于爱奎托斯和秘鲁与巴西、哥伦比亚交界处之间。

如果一切都能照计划顺利进行，那么在一英里宽的亚马逊河河岸的某个地方我将会如约相见 33 岁的英国退役陆军上尉艾德·斯达福德。但是，斯达福德警告我说，在亚马逊，事情往往不会依照计划行进。他应该知道：自 2008 年 4 月以来，他徒步探索全长 4000 英里的亚马逊河，穿过了地球上最大丛林的心脏地区，这在历史上还是头一次。从亚马逊河源头到入海口，只要有下脚的地方，他都要走上一走。此外，他不但要用随身携带的充气筏跨过好几百条支流，还要跋山涉水穿过 3 个国家以及几十个土著部落的领域。在自己的探险博客里，斯达福德写道："从源头到入海口，一路徒步走来，这是探险活动中尚存的最大魅力之一。"

我们生活的这个时代，出人头地的机会越来越少，因此，那些希望通过探险以求流芳百世或遗臭万年的人被强行归入愈演愈烈的怪异之流：用义肢登顶

---

① 原文 unrolled with a theatrical flourish 用来修饰 anaconda skins。水蟒活着的时候一般盘蜷起来，而把蟒蛇皮剥离下来并铺展开来，其图案、其形状看起来很夸张，很奇异。Flourish 做动词时，其比喻意义之一就是"用各种颜色或图案做盛装装饰"。

珠穆朗玛峰；穿着轮滑鞋攀登乞力马扎罗山。已经有好几拨人划着小筏子探索过亚马逊河了，甚至有位名叫马·斯特尔的斯洛文尼亚人游过了大部分河段，但还真没有人徒步穿越过这条河。我第一次读到关于斯达福德这次行动的时候，就特好奇到底是什么让他相信自己能成事。

或许，与其它任何景观相比，亚马逊丛林饱含神话和神秘，是荒蛮旷野和脆弱环境的象征，影影绰绰地挑动着人类的想象。这片丛林的巨大让有胆识者也不寒而栗。亚马逊河在其源头不过是海拔两万英尺的安第斯山上冰雪融水的一条细流，却有着每秒钟3200万加仑的排水量。在所有流入世界各大洋的淡水中，有20%流经亚马逊河宽达150英里的入海口。5个世纪以来，从"疯狂征服者"洛浦·德·阿吉雷[①]到20世纪20年代"消失了的探险者"珀西·法奥希德[②]，亚马逊河成为多少个外来者魂牵梦绕之地（抑或葬身之地）。有关探险亚马逊河的民间传说无不充斥着饥饿、疯狂、疾病以及谋杀。

我懂得，这个地域有着不可否认的诱惑，但我依然百思不得其解，为什么总有人不惜花上两年的时间来穿越如此一块土地——遍布着蟒蛇、虎豹、吸血蝙蝠、蝎子、黄蜂、蚂蚁军团、电鳗、食人鱼、毒品走私贩、充满敌意的部落、登革热、黄热病、疟疾、15英尺长的黑色凯门鳄和18英寸长的水蛭。这还没有算上candiru，一种针一样大小的鲶鱼；这种微型鲶鱼有一种特殊本领，能攀沿着人的小便流往上游，一直游到尿道并寄住在那里，无论人怎么除也除不掉。在斯达福德的行走路线里几乎无路可行，甚至连小径都了无痕迹，因为这里最普遍的旅行方式是乘船。所以，为了深入了解斯达福德为何心血来潮地如此前行，我计划着加入他的行程，和他一起走上几周。但，首先我得找到他。

在爱奎托斯码头，我登上一艘锈迹斑斑的双层轮渡。轮渡的甲板上到处都挂着吊床，而我是轮渡上唯一的外国佬，我的一举一动都会引来别人注目。天空一片火红，森林上空积雨云滚滚翻腾，而船只小心翼翼地穿行在浪涛里。河水是卡布奇诺咖啡的颜色，却有柔软细嫩的水生植被像席子一样漂浮在水面上。带有推进机的独木舟环拥着河岸，破浪逆流而行。我们乘坐的轮渡顺流快速航行，大河宽阔而蜿蜒，后浪有力地抽打着前浪，两岸尽是密实不透的茫茫丛林。

黑暗降临，大部分乘客都爬进各自的吊床，而我站在操舵室旁观看舵手在巨大的滚木中间绕来绕去地前行。好几个小时我们一直盯着黑乎乎的前方，这时候才刚看见远处的岸上有一小簇灯光。等到驶近些，我看到一高一矮两个男人，高的那个戴着一顶棒球帽，正冲着渡船上的男人们挥手。大船在泥糊糊的

[①] 16世纪的一位西班牙探险者。在他最后一次探险亚马逊河时，得了失心疯，所以有"疯狂征服者"的名号。

[②] 英国考古学者和探险家。1925年在亚马逊探险时失踪。

岸边抛了锚，我跳下船，是唯一在这一站上岸的乘客。那两个男人走了过来。我不禁叫道："斯达福德先生，我没弄错吧？"

"喝杯啤酒吧，"他回答道，同时大笑起来。

艾德·斯达福德身高6英尺①，穿着橡胶便鞋，破破烂烂的工装裤，脏兮兮的T恤衫，步态轻盈弹跳，好似刚卸去重负。两周没刮的胡子，轻松的笑声，闪亮幽黑的眼睛。他向他的探险伙伴介绍了我。这位伙伴名叫贾德尔·桑彻兹·里维拉，秘鲁人，今年28岁，绰号町。下午3点，小镇上唯一的酒吧里传出震耳欲聋的锣鼓喧天般的格姆比亚音乐②。在酒吧里，我们边喝啤酒，边听斯达福德一股脑地把他自己的来历倾倒给我。在10个多月的徒步行走中，他与毒蛇面对面，在V级难度③的激流中择路划行，生命时刻受到愤怒的部落族人的威胁。迄今为止，他已行走了2000英里，距离大西洋入海口处差不多一半的路程。"不幸的是，走完的这一半还是容易的一半，"他说。

17岁的时候，斯达福德倒了霉运，因为砍了一棵女王栽种的树，被学校开除。那学校可是英国一流的私立学校。之后，他在英国军队待了4年，混成了上尉。他曾经是位极具实力的橄榄球球手，而且在一次板球比赛中磕掉一颗门牙而装了颗假牙。在2004年阿富汗选举中他曾负责联合国方面的防御物资后勤保障，也曾为英国广播公司BBC的大自然纪录节目而率领探险队远赴圭亚那。他渴望冒险刺激，想像他心目中的英雄蓝阿尔夫·费恩斯爵士④那样去生活。因此，他和一个名叫鲁克·克里尔的同事挖空心思想尽了所有可能实施的探险。斯达福德曾为慈善筹款而率队到伯利兹⑤和婆罗洲⑥探险。这一丛林探险的经历给他带来灵感，促使他进行全程徒步探索亚马逊河。让他和同事吃惊的是，还从来没人这么做过。

2008年4月，和克里尔一起，斯达福德从秘鲁的太平洋海岸开始了这次探

---

① 一英尺等于0.3048米，6英尺约1米8几。一英寸等于2.54厘米。本文有多处以英尺与英寸为单位的重要数据。

② cumbia music，这种音乐最初来源于非洲，由西班牙殖民者贩卖的黑奴带入拉丁美洲，是拉丁音乐的一种，其主要乐器是鼓。

③ Class V. 指国际上河流探险的技术难度系数，V级是极其高难度的一级，其情形是：独身一人划着橡皮筏子行进在激流湍进、乱石险滩、垂直而下的瀑布之中，危险系数极高。

④ 英国著名冒险家，出生于1944年三月。是以陆路或海路方式探索南极和北极的第一人，也是徒步穿越整个南极大陆的第一人。在2009年，以65岁高龄登顶珠穆朗玛峰。他以自身的探险经历为基础创作了很多为人喜爱的文学作品和纪实作品。

⑤ 是中美洲的一个国家，是中美洲唯一以英文为官方语言的国家。

⑥ 世界第三大海岛，位于印度尼西亚境内。

险。这对伙伴攀沿着科尔卡大峡谷徒步而行，一直走进安第斯山脉，横越了好几个可能是亚马逊河源头之流的地方，以使他们的探索基点覆盖全面。赶着驮运行装的小毛驴，他们跨越了好几座大山，然后从 18,000 英尺高度开始漫漫下山之旅，直到亚马逊盆地。

在斯达福德看来，这次探险从一开始就任务分配不公。在几个月的准备工作中，克里尔一直忙于他自己的工作，策划、弄妥资助、获得探险许可、置办探险设备等一系列的后勤保障事宜大都由斯达福德一人操办。抵达秘鲁的时候，克里尔已经溃败不堪，一句西班牙语也不会说，好几周前就开始打退堂鼓。"他对我们要做的事根本毫无准备，"斯达福德告诉我说。"随着我们的前进，这已经变得越来越明显。他的心思根本就没在这件事上。"

3 个月后，克里尔订购了一些补给物品，其中只有一部 MP3 播放器。斯达福德特别生气，质问克里尔为什么不帮他也买一部。克里尔郑重其事地宣告，这部就是给斯达福德买的，他自己要退出这次探险。他们迟早是要闹翻的，"MP3 不过是最后一击，"斯达福德如是说。"他声言他=要离开是因为我们的友谊要比探险重要得多，而对我，什么事也没有探险重要。"这两个人五个月内没再说话。

后来，我联系到了克里尔，想听听他对此事的说词。他写了一封很礼貌的"无可奉告"的电子邮件："时间已经过去很久了，我已经撇清了与那探险的任何关系，"他写道，"我很高兴事情是这个样子。"

斯达福德独自一人继续前行，一连雇佣了好几个当地向导。接下来，2008 年 8 月，在秘鲁的萨蒂扑镇，他遇见了町。有段时间，町做林务员工作，徒步深入丛林寻找理想的硬木标本：红木、雪松木、牧豆树。一开始，町答应陪斯达福德一起走上 5 天。最初的时候两个人合不来，但町对这次探险任务的热情越来越高涨，也证明自己是一位不知疲倦的、忠实的陪伴，所以斯达福德带上了他，成为其在余下的旅程的带薪合作伙伴。

"他有着钢铁般的意志，和我同样有着完成这次探险的热忱，"斯达福德说道。"和我一样，他把整个事态看作一种个人极限挑战。找到这样一个人物确实是关键所在，因为你不可能独自一人进行如此的探险。"现在斯达福德有人帮他分担食物和用具的重负，帮他架起语言鸿沟的桥梁，但町真正的价值是心理方面的：有人守望着你的纯粹慰藉。他们已经一起走了 7 个月，町已经承诺，要和斯达福德亦步亦趋直至抵达大西洋，不管这将走上多久。

或许真的会很久。斯达福德最初计划一天走 10 英里，可很快就明白"这简直是太乐观了。"按原定速度，圣诞节前夕有望抵达哥伦比亚和巴西交界处。但现在已是 2 月份了，而哥伦比亚还在我们东面 100 英里开外的地方。雨季正酣，主干河流沿岸的森林已经开始被洪水淹没。在上两周,在穿过里约纳波河与亚马逊河交汇的宽阔的三角洲地带的时候,斯达福德和町已经尝到了那种洪水泛滥的滋味。"森林陷入一片汪洋,水漫过腰部,有时还漫过头顶,"斯达福德告诉我说。"我们曾攀爬过水下的3个大树干。这个地方有种棕榈树,树干上布满了3英寸长的穗,这些穗像钢针一样直插我们的膝盖。"

早晨,村子里的孩子们坐在一间棚屋里观看让-克劳德·范达美演的、译制粗糙的电影《搏击》,接着就飞散到毒日头下演练他们新学的招式。他们全神贯注地看着我和斯达福德、町收拾东西。我的帧包里塞有一个防水皮筏子袋,里面装着小一些的干袋子和拉链锁,还有一个使东西保持干燥却也让东西难以找到的设备。斯达福德的行囊则是一个破旧的、容积100升、重达75磅的庞然大物,里面装着21世纪自行自录的探险活动所需要的一切物品。"要不是我打算把整个过程发到博客上,我的行囊要轻得多,"他边说,边把那台使行囊重了两三倍的精密电子设备装进去。这台电子设备是他与外界的唯一联系。

斯达福德此次行动的任务包括:为好几个慈善团体筹集 20 万美元慈善基金,此外,还要记录沿途所遇的各个部族的风俗观念以及当地所面临的环境问题。然而,他是第一个承认之所以这么做主要是因为从来没人这么做过,因为他想过一种非同寻常的生活,靠冒险来养活自己。此项计划中有些不合时宜的东西,一种"因为它就在那儿"的态度,这可能被指责为出风头的冒险旅行。我问斯达福德,他是不是觉得自己属于早先哪个时代的人,或许就是库克船长[①]或者伯德上将[②]那个时代。"我觉得生逢其时,"他说道:"我认为,在以前,一个中产阶级出身的人是不能够做这类事情的。"而且,他承认:"整个事件中也有尊严的因素,"他补充说,"任何一个人碰见问题都应当尝试着自己去解决。"

斯达福德得到了一整套40年前国家地理机构印制的1:100,000 的秘鲁地形图,依旧是目前最为精确的一套地形图。这套地形图和他的手控 GPS(全球卫星定位系统)能够提供相当准确的路线导航。他向我展示了他的新路线,就是沿着一条地势高的夹层前进,他希望这能够帮我们避开沼泽地而加快旅行进度。"徒步探索亚马逊河的怪事之一,"他说,"就是事实上你不大看得见这条河。"

每走一步,斯达福德都恨不得雇用一名当地向导,亦即一个熟知森林、能帮着找出最有效的路线的人。在奥兰,他得到马里奥的尽心尽力的服务。马里奥是个农夫,今年62岁,有12个孩子,在附近的森林里打猎已有50个年头了。

[①] 18 世纪英国探险家和航海家。
[②] 二十世纪初美国海军上将,著名航海家和探险记,据说是以飞行方式环游南极与北极的第一人。

他身高不过 5 英尺，所用的家伙也是最少的，与斯达福德的庞然大背包形成鲜明的对比：他所需要的所有东西都装在一个小面粉袋里，用一布条绕过前额而绑在脑后。所需其它物件就是一双橡胶靴、一把大砍刀和一把古老的生了锈的手枪，以便碰见猎物时好射杀来当晚餐。

我们背起行囊，离开大河，穿过村子后面的一片奶牛牧场。热带地区的太阳光浓烈得像是要把我们击垮。几棵足有 100 英尺高的阴凉大树寥落站在那里，不动声色地昭示着雨林原有的华盖擎天。这一带的亚马逊流域区极为偏僻，也是极易发生洪涝灾害的地方，很不利于开发利用。即便如此，依然可以瞥见遭到人类蹂躏破坏的痕迹。

我们顺着斜坡向上攀行，不过几分钟，我们就钻进一道枝桠交错的绿色高墙。这道绿色墙壁正是森林的边界，把明亮的世界挡在身后。在赤道地区，即使是正午，丛林也是阴暗无光的。透过绿荫照进来的斑驳阳光也难以让人辨别方向或时间。空气凉爽了些，声音却被压抑了，视线也被压缩在几码之内，因为眼前尽是纵横交错的攀生藤、蔓生藤以及到处窜长的各种根系，这些都是丛林里的低层植物群。巨大的树干拔地而起直冲树冠，而树身却被各种藤蔓死死缠住；凤梨科植物如同枝形吊灯一样倒垂而下。数量惊人的各种生物玩命向上攀爬，下要覆盖地面之上漫漫水波，上要遮蔽森林穹顶无尽日光。你几乎能够听到它的生长。地面上的落叶形成 1 英尺厚的软垫，除却各类昆虫的嗡嗡、远处鸟儿的鸣叫，丛林里再无其它声音。

马里奥引领我们走在一条几乎不可辨认的小道上。他的大砍刀就像是他身体延伸出来的一部分，他身形矫捷，轻松自如地分开丛林，用刀锋片开粗藤和硕大的叶子。斯达福德也能熟练地使用不可或缺的大砍刀了，但依旧靠蛮力来劈开拦路的枝蔓。矮小的马里奥甚至都不出汗，只见他手腕轻抖，小径自开，似乎毫不费力。

我们跟跟跄跄地跨过横在茶色溪水上的、长满青苔的滚木，在齐腰高的树桩子上爬上又爬下。由我殿后，却走得我汗流如雨、浑身湿透。蚊子成群结队地簇拥在我们周围，叮咬人的蚂蚁也成群结队，或从垂悬的树叶或从树干倾泻而下。甚至连植物都进化得有了各自特有的攻击本领。树根上长满钉刺，好像是你要抓扶哪里，钉刺就长在哪里；藤蔓就像橡皮筋，紧紧裹缠着我的脚踝；带刺的植物卷须不偏不倚地抓去我头上的帽子。眼下最麻烦的是锯齿状的剃刀草，人只要轻轻一碰，那草叶子就割透衣服直切皮肤。斯达福德被告知，巴西境内的亚马逊河沿岸生长着绵延无穷尽的剃刀草。横亘在他与亚马逊河口的乖戾的障碍原本已经多不胜数，这种剃刀草成为又一项横亘在他与亚马逊河口之间的多不胜数的荒谬可笑的障碍。

有好几次，马里奥像死去一样呆在原地，手指向乱丛棵子。我什么也没看见。"蝮蛇，"斯达福德告诉我。来之前，我对亚马逊河指南手册上提到的各类恐怖死因做了足够的研究，因而知道蝮蛇的厉害：蝮蛇的血毒素能引发大出血，先是耳朵、眼睛都会流血，然后血液坏死，最后会让你毙命。"哦，不用担心，"斯达福德给我打气。"我们带了 6 剂抗蛇毒素药粉，其药效能持续 18 小时，而且在爱奎托斯有军用救援直升飞机。最糟糕的情形是你在日落时分被蛇咬，因为直升飞机夜间不能飞行。但我们依然有办法让你活到天亮。"那么，好吧，不用担心。这次探险已经 10 次遭遇到蝮蛇，有 9 次蛇都被向导的大砍刀当场砍死。与我们刻板的物种保护教条相反，当地的向导们只要有办法就绝不会放走任何一条毒蛇。

徒步过程中，他们遇见的唯一一条蟒蛇有 12 英尺长，很是漂亮，斯达福德驻足拍摄。拍完后，他那位土著向导就把这东西给剁成好几段。"他说要拿来喂狗，"斯达福德告诉我说。"但我先前学会的事情之一就是，把我的西方理念强加给生活在这片土地上的人毫无意义。他们所做的一切都是为了生存。除了当做食物，他们不认为动物还有其它什么价值。"

傍晚之前，我们发现一条小溪，就停下来过夜。数月以来，斯达福德和町风餐露宿，他们已经非常精于搭建帐篷。我还没修炼到那个程度，我挥动砍刀割除乱丛棵子而清理一块搭帐篷的空地，结果却险些把自己肢解了。最终，我把一幅帐篷的门帘绑在两棵树之间搭成一个屏障。这样一来，即便是下瓢泼大雨，帐篷也能抵挡得住。装备中的关键物品是探险用的吊床，外面用蚊帐包裹严实，从底部的尼龙拉带封口处进入。

町和斯达福德用一些潮湿的青木做了一个火架子，在上面支起一口锅，又捡了一些枯木当柴火。可是这些柴火白天已经浸泡得透湿，现在想烧着简直就是奇迹。但町很快就把柴烧得噼里啪啦作响。晚餐是蒸米饭加金枪鱼罐头。罐头是我们经过上一个村子时从那里的供销社买来的。"刚开始的时候，我认为会有很多野外生存的事要做，比如捕鱼啦、摘野果啦什么的，"斯达福德说道，"可事实是，我们常常碰上村落，从那里我们能得到补给，或者付钱给村民让他们给我们做饭。这是最令人惊奇的方面：人与人打交道得到什么程度呢。我原本想象的是，这个地方人烟稀少，更多的是人与自然的直接对抗。"他最后明白了，与亚马逊河流域的人进行文化交流是这次探险的一个主要部分。他也明白了，用一个廉价的塑料打火机来生火比燧石打火镰容易得多。

即便是我们全身都涂着厚厚的驱蚊液，蚊子依然成群结队地绕着我们飞。赤道地区的夜色很快降临，我爬进吊床把自己封了起来。昆虫交响乐开始上演，层次丰富，声音出奇地大。几千只蚊子敲打着蚊帐，想方设法找一个入口。远处，吼猴像咳嗽一样的叫声彼此呼应。然后，一种低低的嘶嘶声越来越大，直到温度下降，大雨喷破而下，像一架起飞的喷气式飞机，淹没了所有的声音，笼罩着深沉的夜色。

  早晨，我穿上前一天的衣服。衣服还是湿乎乎的，我们能做的也就是尽可能拧干。斯达福德提醒我当心脚溃烂、葡萄球菌感染的伤口，以及其它亚马逊流域这个大培养皿里所有细菌真菌疾病。半信半疑中，我想起来一个忠告：在丛林里，一定先把靴子摇一摇倒一倒，然后再穿上。我把一只靴子倒过来敲了敲，结果麻雀那么大的一只蟋蟀掉出来蹦走了。

  亚马逊河有着强烈的讽刺感。刚一说过独木桥很容易，你立马就来个后空翻跌进溪水里；刚一夸赞小径很好走，结果它就消失在一片沼泽地里不见了踪影；刚一评论说天气不错，一场华格纳戏剧般热闹的雷雨就前来报到。斯达福德对这些倒霉事已经司空见惯了，逐渐学会了把这些烂事看成一种有趣的调剂。一天下午，斯达福德把地图落在了我们停下吃午饭的地方。马里奥比我们熟悉方向，也比我们快，就飞跑着去找，到夜色降临时才回来。几个月前，斯达福德过河时把他那唯一一把大砍刀掉进了河里，不得不赤手空拳地往前推进直到下一个村落。自我贬损是他目前成功的关键，他能够既认真对待探险又同时认清探险的荒诞。我们跳进一条齐脖子深的溪水，要蹚水过河，他一边低声骂："这倒霉催的傻帽探险，"一边雄赳赳地前进。

  几天以来，我们一直沿着地形图的指示吃力前行，只是在规模上不同于和我们一道前进的食叶蚂蚁纵队。这实在是又累又脏的差事，我浑身都是泥巴、擦伤和淤青。就这么一直走着，不知道走到哪天才是个头，这才是让人害怕的。斯达福德隔一段时间就停下来用 GPS 来检测我们的行程。马里奥礼貌地在旁边看着，尽管他丝毫不知怎么看地图，GPS 对他来说更是不可逾越的神秘之物。斯达福德信从马里奥对当地的了解，但喜欢依靠现代科技来个双重保险。"我知道，有了这个，就算不用本地向导也能行，"斯达福德说，"但这样一来就会慢很多，而且也会多出来很多事。"GPS 表明，马里奥领我们走的路几乎和原计划的路线分毫不差。

  无可争辩的数据表明我们的进程太慢了，这实在让人沮丧。路好走的时候，一小时走上两三英里不成问题，但在根本无路可走的丛林里，时而要从倒下的树上爬过去，时而又要从下面钻过去，时而要在藤蔓丛中砍出路来，时而要蹚过泥巴地，前进的步伐慢得如同令人苦痛的爬行一般。斯达福德为如此缓慢的行程着实感到气馁，也着实为这气馁纠结了一番，最后总算心平气和地接受了。吃力地穿过纳波河三角洲的时候，他注意到，在齐胸深的水中，他那沉重的行囊变得轻盈起来；穿行在沉寂的被洪水淹没的森林里，他感到一种"奇异的静谧。""或许可以从军事角度来看这次探险的行程迟缓，亦即'不管怎么样，我们一定会抵达'，"斯达福德向我解释道。"町不慌不忙地涉水而行。突然间，我不再为一天才走 2.5 公里感到气馁。我从容不迫起来，因为我已明白，该多久就多久。"

尽管斯达福德对丛林中自然存在的艰难习以为常，但与当地部族的遭遇依然是他最大的挑战。很多村落说的都是独一无二的方言，只使用基本的西班牙词汇。历史上很长一段时间，这些部族受到勘探石油或者金矿者的盘剥，在暴动年代，数千秘鲁土著和农人被"光辉道路游击队"①杀害。所以，很多土著居民区有足够的理由对外来者抱有极度的怀疑。

其中，一种最为普遍的恐惧四下蔓延，说白人都是 *pela cara*，其字面意思是"剥脸皮的人"，但这个词在当地很多区域已经演变成一种荒诞的传言，说外来者会偷去他们的器官。"走了一天，精疲力竭地到达了某个地方，那里所有的人却都害怕你，这是我最不愿意看到的事，"斯达福德说。但他已经学会如何保持镇定，如何去化解紧张不安。

有一次，斯达福德走近阿普里马克河②沿岸的一个村落。刚一进村，立刻就遭遇到一群愤怒的印第安人。他们往他身上浇水，往他嘴里塞脏东西，还涂抹得他满脸都是红漆。他很害怕，但尽力保持镇定。"我只是和他们的头人握了握手，就转身离开了村庄，"他回忆道。那件事情之后不久，他和町乘坐驮运木筏穿过一条支流。町不经意回头一望，却看见 5 只独木舟追踪他们，独木舟上挤满了咆哮着的阿莎林卡印第安人。男人们拿着弓箭和手枪，女人们则手持大砍刀。"那时候，我确信我们必死无疑，"斯达福德说。就连平时镇定自若的町也认为他们要玩儿完了。他们被包围起来，部落首领们向他们逼近，嘶叫着，怒不可遏。斯达福德向他们出示了当局的许可证，但一点用没有。女人们似乎已经准备好要将他们碎尸万段。后来，他语速缓慢，语调平和，双手摊开，设法让那些印第安人平静下来。结果是，部落首领安德烈亚斯和阿方索给他们当了 6 个星期的向导。斯达福德很是震惊："原本是整个探险中我最惧怕的人却成了我所遇见的最和气、最有益、最忠诚的人。"

那次经历让斯达福德确信，他将能应对下游出现的任何状况。但是，巴西却呈献给他更大的风险。斯达福德在玛瑙斯③一家驻地机构申请许可证，刚开始没有得到任何回音。"后来我找到他们，"他说，"他们说之所以不给我回音是

---

① 秘鲁历史上的一只反政府武装，活跃在在 20 世纪七八十年代。
② 秘鲁境内的亚马逊河之源头河。
③ 巴西亚马逊州首府，地处黑河和索里芒斯河（亚马逊河支流）交汇处。

因为我就要死了。'那就是去找死。巴西境内的交界处是整个亚马逊盆地中土著保留地闹得最凶猛的地方。殖民地的巴西人根本不去那里。你是白人,又不会说葡萄牙语,还抗着个摄像机到处转悠。'"他把所有不利因素都考虑了个遍,但还是决定他"就是进去走走,保持友好也保持镇定。"他依然相信只要有合适的向导,合适的路径,他就成事。"但我首先得找到一个认为这事可行的巴西人,"他做出了让步。"会说'是的,你肯定行'的唯一的人是家里的朋友,但他们对此一无所知。"

斯达福德理智地权衡风险,而町所展望的未来却充满神秘。町是位非常虔诚的基督徒,相信上帝一直都在保护着他们。斯达福德比较听天由命。"要么成事,要么死磕,"他说话的口气有点趾高气扬,有信心搞定所有风险,有信心活着走出亚马逊河的另一端,凯旋而归。

我们在一个雅瓦①村落待了1天。我学巴斯特·基顿②的滑稽动作逗村子里的孩子们开心,一会儿一头撞在5英尺高的门楣上,一会儿从吊床上摔出来。一个男孩划着独木舟把我们送过支流里约阿皮库约,舟上高高地堆着我们的行囊。一边漂流在河面上,一面观望着河岸上的巨嘴鸟和猩红色的金刚鹦鹉飞落在树上,还有那巨大的拟态蝴蝶闪着熠熠蓝光在微风中飞起,斯达福德竟然愚蠢地说什么"倒霉的傻帽探险",我对他的说法不以为然。雅瓦人划着独木舟或逆流而上,或顺流而下,轻松自如,随心所欲。亚马逊流域的所有文化文明都充分利用了长达数千英里的水路。徒步穿越亚马逊好比是穿着雪地靴横跨撒哈拉:行倒是行,但绝对不是当地人的走法。原因就是以前没人这么干过。

我把这一想法透露给斯达福德,他大笑道:"我的一个朋友曾这么说,'我爱死你的探险了,因为它毫无意义。'这是不折不扣的英国式思维:这事毫无意义,但是不管怎么样我们都要做。"就像他以前的利维斯顿③和司各特④,斯达福德所付出的努力之中含有一种顽强的自虐式的荒谬,可他却为此感到骄傲。

用大砍刀开路,我们在迷宫一般的丛林里又走了3天,浑身酸痛,伤痕累累,终于抵达了下一个村落。里约阿姆皮库约是亚马逊的又一条小支流。我们抵达的村落波韦尼尔就坐落在这条支流上游的一处高地上。波韦尼尔的吊脚茅草屋疏落分散在村落各处,颇具田园风光。从这里,我们务必要暂时离开原定探险路线,因为要与来自卡罗拉多的一名叫皮特·麦布莱德的摄像师汇合。我

---

① 当地的一个土著部落。
② 美国著名喜剧演员。
③ 19世纪英国的一位苏格兰探险家,以在非洲的探险闻名于欧洲。
④ 19世纪末期的一位英国皇家海军军官,两次领军到北极地区探险。

们开动一艘带马达的游艇向下游驶去，5个小时后抵达皮瓦斯，一座破烂不堪的集市小镇，就坐落在亚马逊河河岸。在这里我们与麦布莱德碰头，补给金枪鱼罐头、拉面，然后原路返回。

这是本次探险自创的规则之一：不管什么时候，只要离开原定探险路线，斯达福德就在 GPS 上做个定位记号，这样他就能返回原点，找到原来的路。这使徒步穿越亚马逊河来不得半点马虎，也是一条必须要恪守的规则，用来应对后勤保障上的所有挑战。当然，除了斯达福德和町，没有人会强制这条规则的实施，但他们绝不敢贸然抄近路走捷径。"如果我耍些小花招，我也不会受这么多的罪，"斯达福德说道，"但既然我们要做这件事，那么我们就要好好做。"

马里奥回他自己的村子找家人去了，下一段行程给我们领路的向导名叫柏诺波·桑卡，是位 38 岁的奥凯纳印第安人。早上醒来，我发现柏诺波纹丝不动地站在河边的一条树根上，手握大砍刀。快速一挥，水花飞溅，他砍了下去。一条鱼荡出水面，头部却如同动了手术般一分为二。我们把鱼开膛破肚，5 人 5 份 5 种吃法，早餐就这样解决了。

我们走出波韦尼尔后面的田地时，不经意间我看见一小块得到精心照料的古柯①林。我们离哥伦比亚南部边境只有 50 英里，看到数量巨大的贩毒活动在这一地区进行。秘鲁是世界上第二大古柯产地。古柯树叶被精炼成软膏，然后穿过哥伦比亚边境被运送到药厂进行进一步加工。毒贩绝大多数是贫穷的秘鲁人。斯达福德和町很快就要抵达地处秘鲁-巴西-哥伦比亚边境的"死亡三角"，如若碰见精神紧张的毒贩将是一种严重的风险。在皮瓦斯的时候，我读到过一则报道，说是两个敌对贩毒团伙为争夺势力范围打了起来，在战斗中，一个秘鲁村庄被夷为平地。那个村庄就在斯达福德所计划的路线上。

跋山涉水走了 10 天，丛林生活开始使我感到厌烦。我的意志力逐渐衰退，而斯达福德的决心却更加坚定，这让我震惊不已。我的双脚一天 12 小时地浸泡在水里，此时已变得如同死人的脚一样灰白。我渴望喝到没有碘坑味道的水。我浑身都是蚂蚁咬的伤痕，脚踝上嵌满了寄生蚤。有一次，斯达福德不小心捅了黄蜂窝，吓得我们四人全速后退。接着，蹚过齐腰深的水时，麦布莱德低头一看，大声叫嚷："那是什么鬼东西？"站在亚马逊沼泽地里，可没有谁乐意听到这样的问题。

那东西长着巨大的头，像鲶鱼一样有触须，但嘴巴和尾巴都是鲜亮的红色，在一个树桩后面弯弯曲曲地游动，拍打着 6 英尺开外的水浪。它慢慢地向麦布莱德游去，随后消失在一片黑暗的水中。柏诺波用磕磕巴巴的西班牙语费力地

---

① 一种南美药用植物。

解释着，反复重复一个词 *anguila*，但我们谁也不知道那是什么意思。直到后来我们才明白那东西是一条巨大的电鳗，很可能会释放出一阵电波，足以把我们五个人全都电晕，脸朝下泡在水里。

在我和麦布莱德离开的那一天，我们不得不设法到阿姆皮库约河岸去，在那里搭乘顺流而下到亚马逊去的船只。斯达福德的 GPS 显示，阿姆皮库约河远在在 800 码①开外的地方。我们全力开进，砍断藤蔓和乱丛棵子，但只走了几码，我们就发现，前面尽是一眼望不到头的被洪水淹没的森林。可这是到达阿姆皮库约河唯一的路。我们只得涉水而行，水先是齐膝深，后是齐腰深，我背包里的干袋子开始漂浮起来，重负离开了我疼痛难忍的双肩。我们的脚步寂静无声，在光影斑驳的水里，我们滑过硕大的树根。被淹没的森林简直别有洞天：逼真的森林复制品，天空，还有移动着的我们在静静的黑色水面上的倒影。水太深的时候，我们就把背包装在充气皮筏子上，穿着沉重的靴子游着泳，说说笑笑地推着皮筏子前进，每一个枝条上都是蜘蛛和蚂蚁。水太浑浊了，甚至连水下面的手都看不到，就更别说电鳗了。

被洪水淹没的森林简直就是孩童时代所有噩梦的缩影，可我并不害怕。现在我理解了斯达福德在穿过纳波三角洲时所悟到的东西：让自己漂浮起来，去感受这一时刻的宁静。斯达福德有很长的路要走，或许还要走上 18 个月，但像这样的探险，你却不能赶路急行。有多久算多久。

（张慧芳 译 杨建 校）

---

① 一码约合三英尺，约等于 91.4 厘米；一英尺等于 0.3084 米。

The Vision Seekers

Kira Salak

【导读】《论语》中写道:"子不语怪、力、乱、神。"细读《论语》,我们发现,孔子专注的是解读人事,但也并没有否定鬼神的存在,只是没工夫去钻研灵异神怪之事,之所谓"未能事人,焉能事鬼"。西方启蒙思想以来,人们逐渐摒弃了对灵异神怪的迷信,但创立了另一种迷信:科学迷信。正是对科学的极度崇拜,人类丢弃了对大自然的敬畏之心,而是借科学之名对自然滥加开发和剥削,导致人类居住环境日益恶化,最终引得大自然的疯狂报复。站在高远之处洞察人类历史,"科学地认识世界"不过是人类探索世界和解读生命的一种方式,原始宗教迷信则是另外一种,不能简单粗暴地加以否定。盛行于南美洲亚马逊流域的萨满教就是这样一种带有原始迷信色彩的认知世界的方式,试图借自然之药手打通人类此岸世界和灵异神怪的彼岸世界。在不残害人类和破坏自然的前提下,我们对任何信仰都应该持一种尊敬的态度,不管信与不信、理解与不理解。本文讲述了萨满人如何利用从植物中提取的一种叫"死藤水"的灵药治愈了一位美国作家病因不明、久治不愈的偏头痛。其医药原理是否科学、服药者所感所见是否有心理因素,这都无关紧要。重要的是萨满人对大自然的敬畏、与其它物种和谐相处的精神,这正是 21 世纪人类文明延续和发展的指路明灯。

Here's the truth: I have traveled more than 4,000 miles to the middle of the Peruvian Amazon to be "cured" by shamans.[①] It's nighttime. The riverboat I'm on plies dark waters, the jungle thick on either side, emitting loud reptilian sounds that drone on like police sirens. I see no lights, no villages anywhere.

My companions are Kevin, a pan-flute maker from Canada; Wendy, an

---

① Shamans are spiritual beings with the ability to heal, work with energies and 'see' visions. The essential characteristics of shaman are mastery of energy and fire as a medium of transformation. (编者注)

acupuncturist and energetic healer① from Massachusetts, and her husband, Joe, a burly carpenter who wants nothing to do with us or shamanism, who has said upward of five words so far and who busily reads *Chomsky on MisEducation*② as the jungle slides by.

Hamilton Souther, our shamanic guide, sits with long, burnished legs on the guardrail of the boat. "Our greatest fear is the fear of death," he's telling us. "During the *ayahuasca*③ ceremony, you'll be taken to the edge of that fear, taught to surrender to it, release it." He has the classic good looks of a *Baywatch* actor. Hamilton is 26 years old, a native of California who has practiced shamanism for several years. His company, Blue Morpho Tours, features a "shamanic healing center" in a remote area of the Amazon. Listening to him is like listening to the newest Castaneda. He talks constantly about spirit friends and alternative realms of reality.

I discovered Blue Morpho Tours while investigating the huge variety of New Age trips offered on the Web, many stressing shamanism in various cultures as a means of reaching spiritual "transformation." Skeptical but curious, I wondered what that meant, and how it worked. Not quite sure what to expect, I signed up for the trip.

Our boat ride will take 14 hours from the Peruvian town of Iquitos, followed by another river journey to reach our destination. On the deck below, passengers' hammocks crowd together like rows of cocoons, bodies swinging and bumping into one another, frenetic guitar music rupturing the mosquito-filled night.

It's midday. We're all in a dugout, heading up a narrow river into the depth of the jungle. Giant butterflies with wings of blue satin fly sluggishly over the water. Nests of parakeets let off raucous squawks, rivaling the boat's motor. The sun and its sticky heat burrows into my skin, exhausting me.

---

① Energetic Healing is an umbrella term for any therapy that manipulates the energy circuits in our physical or subtle bodies to regain balance and facilitate our body's innate healing mechanisms. A medical worker who takes up energetic healing is an energetic healer.

② Noam Chomsky, (1928-), American linguist and linguistic philosopher. *Chomsky on Mis-education* is the first book edited to systematically present Chomsky's influential writings on education. In this book, Noam Chomsky encourages a larger understanding of our educational needs, starting with the changing role of schools today, and broadening our view of new models of public education.

③ 巴西产的蔓生植物，也指此种蔓藤泡制成的致幻饮料。

In our boat are two local shamans we picked up this morning from the tiny river town of Genaro Herrerra. Don Julio, 86, is widely considered by locals to be one the greatest living shamans in the Amazon; his only baggage consists of a small woven pouch full of *mapacho* (sacred tobacco) cigars, which Peruvian shamans smoke to secure the favor of spirits. The second shaman, Don Alberto, 46, Hamilton's current shamanic mentor, rests on the gunwale and winces at the sun-dappled waters.

The sun vies with the clouds; large flies land painlessly on me, swelled with blood before I notice them. Joe has stuck the Chomsky book, now dog-eared and smudged, in the back of his jeans. His wife, Wendy, on this trip in part to try to improve her energetic healing abilities, has her camcorder out, recording our journey up the river. Kevin, who said he chose to go on this tour to "hopefully release issues," sits silently beside me. He is middle-aged, shy, unmarried. I tell Hamilton about the inexplicable daily migraines that started in just the past year and how they leave me temporarily blind in one eye.

The motor is killed. We pass through a swamplike area of low branches into a small lagoon. High on a nearby slope sits Hamilton's healing center: a large hut made of rain-forest planks and palm-leaf thatch, with the jungle imposing on all sides. A single family acts as caretakers. Hamilton introduces us to their youngest girl, Carlita, only 5, a budding shaman who already knows the sacred *icaros*, or shamanic power songs. Carrying a Barbie purse around her arm, she gives us all a deep, penetrating stare that unhinges me.

Shamans don't cut down medicinal plants in the jungle without first asking the spirits' permission and giving thanks. Victor, our jungle guide, teaches us about this as he takes our group on an afternoon trek, stopping abruptly before a fresh skeleton on the ground.

"Bushmaster," Victor says, beaming like a proud father.

The bushmaster is the largest venomous snake in the New World. Victor has also introduced us to a large wasp whose venom kills tarantulas and incapacitates humans. And now, overhead, he taps his machete against a vine that, if severed, he says, will leak a fluid that easily burns through human flesh.

These are only a few of the dry-ground threats, which don't include the fare of the waterways: piranhas, electric eels, alligators It's a shaman's paradise, shot① full of formidable creatures and the spirits that command them.

I return to the hut with another of my migraines. Kevin and I decide to attend Hamilton's energetic healing class, Hamilton taking us on a guided visualization. The idea, he explains, is to feel connected to the earth's center and the universe. "See yourself heading to the stars," he says. "Tell me when you see the planet Mercury."

It's hard to concentrate. Joe has been lecturing Victor on the uncanny similarities between George W. Bush② and Genghis Khan③.

"Thank the emerald light for taking you to the golden arc of the sun and the eternal flame," Hamilton is saying.

I'm starting to hope that I'm not stranded in the middle of the Amazon with a bunch of lunatics. Little Carlita sits nearby, staring at us from the crook of a rocking chair. She takes slow puffs from a shaman's cigar, her eyes narrow, face expressionless.

Last night, Kevin, Wendy and I met in the hut to participate in the first of our three shamanic ceremonies. We drank the "sacred visionary medicine" called *ayahuasca*, which had been prepared by Don Alberto earlier that day. Perhaps because it had been burned accidentally, we felt nothing.

Today, a new batch is being prepared, and tonight's ceremony promises to give us a real shamanic experience — whatever that will entail. Anxiety settles in my gut. "*Ayahuasca*" itself is the name of a jungle vine, but the word is used as shorthand for a concoction of boiled plant essences that, when drunk, allow for — as Hamilton puts it — "journeys into the realm of spirit."

Our group joins Don Alberto in collecting and preparing the fixings for the special brew. Any would-be Peruvian shaman must master an extensive knowledge of Amazonian plant species, each of which, the shamans believe, has a spirit that contributes protection or guidance to the ceremony. Don Alberto puts several different ingredients into a large cooking pot to be repeatedly boiled for the next

---

① shot 有"镜头、景"的意思，在这里用作 paradise 的同位语，用来形容 paradise 是为了更形象化，可译为"满是……的一派景色"，或译为"尽是……"。

② The former American president.

③ A Chinese emperor in Yuan Dynasty. 成吉思汗。

several hours: pieces of tree bark, crushed ayahuasca and fresh, green chacruna[①] leaves.

"Once you take ayahuasca, you can meet any spirit you'd like — deceased loved ones, guardian angels, power animals," Hamilton tells us seriously. "Just call upon them, and they'll come."

"I've always wanted to meet Walt Whitman[②]," I muse out loud.

The hour arrives — 9 p.m. Having fasted for seven hours, Kevin, Wendy and I take our seats in the middle of the hut. We each get a plastic bucket and a roll of toilet paper for wiping our faces. Shamans believe that the inevitable vomiting — "purging" — caused by the ayahuasca mixture is a physical manifestation of negative energy being dispelled from the body. The more disgorged, the better.

Hamilton, Don Alberto and the ancient Don Julio sit before us, lighting their cigars. When they yawn, which is frequently, they make undulating sounds like horses neighing. Don Alberto blows tobacco smoke into the bottle of thick, brown ayahuasca, then whistles under his breath. Spirits, Hamilton says, are now filling the hut. All manner of wholesome, positive spirits. Don Alberto begins pouring out cups of ayahuasca, blessing our serving[③] before we drink; the ayahuasca has the taste and consistency of Bailey's Irish Cream.[④] The shamans are last to drink.

I wait. Ten minutes. Twenty. It looks as if the rafters of the hut are swaying. Someone extinguishes the kerosene lamp and there's complete darkness. The shamans start shaking their *shacapa*s[⑤], leaf rattles, and singing loudly. I lie down, eyes closed, a pleasant vibration coursing through my body to the beat of the shamans' songs.

A piercing scream tears through the hut. I hear violent gurgling and retching. "Hamilton!" Wendy yells. "Get this out of my head! Make it stop!"

Hamilton stops singing for a moment. "Wendy," he says soothingly, "that's just your fear speaking. Ask God to take your fear away."

Now Kevin lets out a loud wail. "Oh, God! Help me! No! No!" He throws up,

---

① A kind of plant whose leaves can be used as herbs.

② An American poet, essayist and journalist. Whitman is among the most influential poets in the American canon, often called the father of free verse. His poetry collection *Leaves of Grass* praises American compassion and freedom.

③ A kind of religious manner, making drinking or food holy by saying prayer over them.

④ An Irish liqueur, a beautiful blend of whiskey and cream.

⑤ A sort of traditional Peruvian musical instrument, whose shape looks like a long flute.

and I hear the loud, mysterious plop of something large landing in the bucket.

The shamans get up to perform healing songs over Kevin and Wendy, who are vomiting now. "Don't resist," Hamilton tells them. "Surrender to your fear. Surrender. Let it all out." He comes over to me. "The spirits tell me that your migraines are caused by worry energy trapped in your head. I'm going to take that energy out for you now." He puts his lips to my temple, sucking hard several times and spitting the unsavory energy over his shoulder.

I start to see geometric patterns. Colorful realms. Shapes and forms coalesce into an endless stream of beauty and perfection. An old man in a white robe walks toward me, smiling. He greets me with a long hug, kissing the top of my head. Walt Whitman!

Wendy and Kevin's desperate bellows retreat into distant space. The visions end. I feel an awful, painful ball of nausea in my gut and vomit prodigiously into the bucket.

Kevin has stopped screaming and sobs now. "I see angels," he chimes. "It's so beautiful."

The shamans fall silent. Don Julio announces that he's called back the spirits and ended the ceremony early because the forces were too strong for Wendy and Kevin. A light goes on. I open my eyes to see Hamilton holding Kevin in his arms like a small child. "You're back," he's cooing to him. "Welcome back."

Kevin looks around him in wonder, smiling. "I've never been so happy," he says.

We all received a day of downtime after the ceremony. Wendy had met me outside the hut, crying and distraught, and I didn't know what to do for her. Hamilton assured us that she'd soon feel better, that she was still "resisting the experience." Luckily, Victor had taken her and Joe to see some pink dolphins, which seemed to calm her. Ignoring her protestations, Kevin and I went ahead with our final scheduled *ayahuasca* ceremony on the last night; we both had little vomiting and our visions were pleasant ones.

It's almost the end of the trip. Wendy sits before Don Julio and Don Alberto, reading their palms. Joe passes me a bumper sticker: "Bush Lies — Who Dies?"① I catch Kevin smiling. He initiates a conversation with me for the first time, and takes out his pan flute to serenade us.

"How are you feeling today?" he asks me.

I try to be scientific about it. My migraines are completely gone, I tell him. I'm enjoying a bizarre, inexplicable feeling of happiness and peace that actually transcends my usual writer's angst.

The others leave. A few days later, on my own overnight journey back to Iquitos, I lie beside Hamilton on the roof of the riverboat and discuss what has happened. "O.K.," I say, "so how do I know if any of this was real?"

He chuckles knowingly, putting his hands behind his head and staring up at stars so bright that they burn afterimages on my retinas. "It doesn't matter if you think it's real or not," he says, "just as long as it works."

---

① A bumper sticker is an adhesive label or sticker with a message, intended to be attached to the bumper of an automobile and to be read by the occupants of other vehicles. Most bumper stickers are very humorous although cover different subjects such as politics, religions or marriage, etc. "Bush lies, who dies" was once a popular bumper sticker, which was inspired by the hen political phenomenon that the Bush administration's lies about Iraq's problems and Iraq War and American people felt hurt by those lies. This sentence employs a figurative device called assonance: Lies vs. Dies; "Who" is a smart word here, and can be replaced by any word, and many parody sentences are coined, for example, Bush Lies, New Orleans Dies; Bush Lied, I Died; Bush Lies, Democracy Dies.

丛林灵巫

凯拉·萨拉克

　　事情的真相就是：我跋山涉水 4000 多英里来到秘鲁境内的亚马逊河畔，让那里的萨满①来给我"祛病"。更深夜半，我乘坐的船只划过黑沉沉的水面，两岸浓密的丛林中传来爬虫响亮的叫声，如同警笛般持续不断。四下望去，既不见任何光亮，也没有任何村落。

　　与我同行的有：科文，来自加拿大，制作排笛的能手；雯迪，来自马塞诸塞州，针灸医师，也是能量平衡治疗医师②；还有雯迪的老公乔，一位魁梧的木匠。乔不愿意掺和我们的事，也不想和萨满教有什么瓜葛，到目前为止，他说的话没有多过 5 个字。丛林在两岸滑过，而乔忙着阅读《乔姆斯基论教育的误区》③。

　　汉密尔顿·扫塞尔是我们的萨满向导。此刻，他坐在那里，长长的、亮闪闪的双腿翘在船的护栏上。"我们最大的恐惧就是对死亡的恐惧，"他告诉我们说，"在'死藤水'仪式期间，你就会被带到那种恐惧的边缘，你会被教导去屈从于那种恐惧，进而释放那种恐惧。"这位向导的长相很正派，酷似电视剧《海岸救生队》④里的男主角。汉密尔顿 26 岁，土生土长的加州人，修炼萨满教义有几个年头了。他所在的旅游公司名叫"蓝色形态之旅"，其特色服务项目就是在亚马逊河的偏僻之地设有"萨满治疗中心"。听他说话就像是在听 Castaneda 乐队的新唱片。他一会儿谈论灵界，一会儿又跳转到现实王国，不断地这么讲着。

　　我是在网页上查询"新时代"旅行的时候发现"蓝色形态之旅"旅游公司的。有关"新时代"旅行的信息量非常大，种类也特别多，其中有很多都强调

---

① 萨满人，指有灵异能力的人，据言，萨满人能通过操控"精气"和火焰为人驱病祛邪、沟通灵魂和创制幻象。

② 英语中的 energy 在医疗语境下相当于中医中的"气"、"气血"等，指在人体内流通循环的一种东西等，一般译作"能量"。Energetic Healing 是对调节人体内"能量"平衡疗法的总称，针灸就是其中的一种疗法；energetic healer 是从事这种疗法的医师。

③ 诺姆·乔姆斯基，（1928-），美国语言学家和语言哲学家。本书系统地介绍了乔姆斯基对教育的观点和看法。"学校充当着教化和驯服民众的机构。纵观历史，学校远非在培养独立思考者，反而在控制和胁迫民众制度中扮演着机构性的角色。"乔姆斯基在书中说道。

④ 美国动作电视剧，讲述加利福尼亚洛杉矶海岸救生的故事，扮演男主角的是 David Hasselhoff，高大健壮，沉稳冷峻。

不同文化背景下的萨满教却都是一种通灵之术。我对此很是怀疑，但又充满好奇，很想知道那种通灵术意味着什么，又是如何运行的。结果会如何，我并没有十足的把握，就这么着，我报名参加了这次旅行。

从秘鲁小镇爱奎托斯出发，乘船而行，要走上14个小时，然后再走一段水路，才能到达目的地。在下层的甲板上，乘客们的吊床像一排排蚕茧拥挤在一起，躺在里面的身体荡荡悠悠，碰来撞去；狂乱的吉他乐声打破了满是蚊子的夜空。

正午时分，我们全都上了一个独木舟，划进一条窄窄的河，逆流而上，进入丛林深处。巨大的蝴蝶扑打着蓝色缎面一样的翅膀，慵懒地飞行在水面上。长尾小鹦鹉的巢里传出嘎嘎的鸟叫，声音大得简直盖过了机动船的引擎。太阳直射，温度高，湿度大，我浑身的皮肤黏糊糊的，真是让人精疲力竭。

今天早上，在河岸边一个叫基纳罗·何烈拉的微型小镇上，我们接上2位当地的萨满人。唐·朱里奥，86岁，被当地人尊为亚马逊当代最了不起的萨满。这位老人唯一的行李就是一个小小的编织褡裢，里面装满了"莫巴克"（圣烟草）雪茄。秘鲁萨满抽这种雪茄来获得灵魂对自己的喜爱。另一位萨满是唐·阿尔伯特，46岁，是汉密尔顿的现任萨满师父。阿尔伯特背靠船舷，对着阳光斑驳的水面不断地抽搐着。

太阳和乌云在博弈；硕大的苍蝇落在身上，不痛不痒的，但不一会儿就吸饱了血。乔把乔姆斯基的书插在牛仔裤屁股口袋里，书已经卷了角，脏兮兮的。对乔的妻子雯迪来说，此次旅行部分原因是为了提高自己的能量平衡医疗技术。此刻，她正拿着摄影机摄录我们逆流而上的旅程。科文说他之所以选择此次旅行是为了"成功地排解忧烦"。这会儿，他正安静地坐在我身后。科文人到中年，很腼腆的一个人，还没有结婚。我告诉汉密尔顿，从去年开始我患了不明缘由的偏头痛，而且每天如此，导致一只眼睛暂时性失明。

船的发动机熄了火。我们穿过一片枝桠蔓延的、类似沼泽的水域，然后进入一个小小的淡水湖。汉密尔顿的治疗中心就坐落在附近的一个斜坡顶部。治疗中心是一座用雨林木板条搭建而成的大棚屋，茅屋顶上铺着棕榈叶，四周尽是强势狂野的丛林。一个家庭的全家人齐上阵，充当医护人员。汉密尔顿把我们引见给了这家最小的女儿卡莉达。别看卡莉达只有5岁，却是位崭露头角的小萨满，已会唱萨满神力圣歌 icaros 了。她胳膊上挎着个芭比手提袋，给我们每个人深沉的一盯，直穿我们的内心。这一盯让我胆颤心惊。

萨满人在采割药草之前必定先求得神灵的允许并表示感谢。我们的丛林向导维克多给我们讲述了这些情况。下午，他带领我们游逛的时候，突然间停下，原来地上有一副新骷髅。

"巨蝮，"维克多满面笑容地说，如同一位自豪的父亲。

巨蝮是新大陆上最大的毒蛇。维克多还让我们认识了一种硕大的黄蜂，这种黄蜂的毒液能杀死多毛毒蜘蛛，还能致人伤残。这会儿，他用那把大砍刀碰了碰头顶的一种藤。他说，把藤条切割开后，就会流出一种汁液，而这种汁液能毫不费劲地烫透人的皮肤。

这些不过是陆路上的几种毒害物种，而水域中还有比拉鱼、电鳗和短嘴鳄鱼。这里可真是萨满的伊甸园，里面尽是可怕的生灵，还有掌控这些生灵的神灵。

我的偏头痛又犯了，只得返回棚屋。我和科文决定加入汉密尔顿的能量治疗。在治疗中，汉密尔顿会引导我们进入视觉幻象，按他的解释，也就是感受与地心及宇宙的关联。"想象自己正飞向其它星球"，他说，"看到水星的时候告诉我一声。"

很难聚精会神地这么做。乔在一旁正向维克多宣讲乔治·W·布什和成吉思汗之间奇特的相似之处。

"感谢翠绿之光把你带到太阳的金色拱柱和永恒之焰，"汉密尔顿也在说。

现在，我有点希望我不是和一群疯子一起被困在亚马逊腹地。小卡莉达坐在一旁，透过摇椅的弯曲靠背栏盯着我们看。她缓慢地抽着萨满雪茄，眯缝着眼睛，脸上毫无表情。

昨夜，科文、雯迪、还有我，聚在棚屋里参加第一次萨满仪式。这样的仪式共3次。我们饮下一种叫"死藤水"的"神圣的幻象之药"。这药是唐·阿尔伯特在当天早些时候备下的。或许是因为这药被意外地熬糊了，我们喝下后没有任何感觉。

今天又新熬了一些药，说是今夜的仪式保证能带给我们真正的萨满体验——不管这体验牵扯到什么。我内心充满焦虑。"死藤"本身是一种丛林藤本植物，但这里却被用来代称用植物精华液熬煮调配的药物。按汉密尔顿的说法，喝了这种药水，人就会"踏上通向神灵王国的旅程"。

我们一行人加入了唐·阿尔伯特的采集、熬煮那种特别药物的劳动。任何想成为秘鲁萨满的人都必须精通亚马逊植物种类的各种知识，因为萨满相信每一种植物都有一位神灵保护或引导着用药仪式。唐·阿尔伯特把好几种不同的材料放进一口大锅里，烧开后一直滚煮了好几个小时。放在一起煮的材料有：树皮、捣碎的死藤和新鲜翠绿的贻贝叶。

"一旦喝下死藤水，你想见什么神灵就能见到什么神灵——已逝的至爱，守护天使,动物神,"汉密尔顿神情严肃地告诉我们说,"你只要呼唤他们,他们就会出现。"

"我一直都想见见沃尔特·惠特曼①,"我若有所思,不由得说出声来。

那一时刻到来了——晚上9点钟。科文、雯迪和我已经斋戒了7个小时,然后在棚屋的中间就座。我们每人发了一只塑料桶,还有一卷用来擦脸的卫生纸。饮下这种死藤水混合物势必引起呕吐,萨满管这种呕吐叫"净化",认为呕吐出的东西是从体内排除的恶性能量的物质性体现。吐出的越多就越好。

汉密尔顿、唐·阿尔伯特,还有上了年岁的唐·朱里奥坐在我们面前,点燃了萨满雪茄。他们不断地打哈欠,发出像马鸣一般高低起伏的声响。唐·阿尔伯特把烟雾吹进装着粘稠的棕褐色死藤水的瓶子里,接着发出深沉的哨音。汉密尔顿说,现在神灵正进到棚屋里来。全都是有益健康的善心的神灵。唐·阿尔伯特倒出几杯死藤水,把我们那几份祝圣②后才给我们喝下。死藤水喝起来有爱尔兰利口甜酒③的味道,粘稠度也和这种酒类似。萨满是最后喝的。

我在等。10分钟。20分钟。棚屋的橡栋好像在晃动。有人熄灭了煤油灯,顿时漆黑一片。萨满们开始挥舞他们手中的 *shacapas*④,这种乐器顶端的叶状物发出咔哒咔哒的声音,伴随着萨满们大声的歌唱。我躺下来,闭上眼睛,一种令人愉悦的震颤应和着萨满歌声的节奏流遍了我的全身。

一声刺耳的尖叫穿透棚屋。我听到了剧烈的汩汩声和干呕。"汉密尔顿!"雯迪大声叫嚷,"把这种东西从我脑子里弄走!快让它停下!"

有那么一会儿汉密尔顿停下来不唱。"雯迪,"他安慰道,"那东西就是你的恐惧在说话。恳请上帝把你的恐惧带走。"

这个时候,科文大放悲声:"哦,上帝啊,救我!不!不!"他呕吐起来,我听到有某种神秘的东西"噗咚"一声重重地落到塑料桶里。

萨满站起身来对着正呕吐的科文和雯迪演唱医治灵歌。"别抗拒,"汉密尔顿告诉她们,"顺从你们的恐惧。顺从。释放出所有的恐惧。"他向我走过来。"神灵们告诉我说你的偏头痛是由困在你头脑里的担忧之气引起的。现在我要为你把那股气放出来。"他把嘴唇对着我的太阳穴狠狠地吮吸了几次,回头吐出那股难闻之气。

---

① 十九世纪美国浪漫主义诗人,弘扬了自由体诗歌,著有诗集《草叶集》,讴歌了美国人民自由奔放的精神。

② 一种宗教或祭祀仪式,即对食物或酒水之类的做祈祷或念咒语,这样这些食物或酒水就成了圣餐或圣水。

③ 一种淡褐色的酒,含有奶油、爱尔兰威士忌和一些调味香料(香草和巧克力)甜酒。

④ 一种传统的秘鲁乐器,长的一端像长笛,但短的一端类似尖尖长长的树叶。

我开始看到几何图案。色彩斑斓的王国。各种形状和样式汇聚成连绵无尽的完美至极的光流。一个身穿白袍的老人向我走来，笑眯眯的。他长拥着我，吻了吻我的额头。沃尔特·惠特曼！

雯迪和科文歇斯底里的嚎叫变得飘渺遥远。灵异幻象结束了。我感到胸口拥堵一团，又恶心又疼痛，接着就对着塑料桶狂吐起来。

这会儿科文已经不再尖叫，而是抽抽搭搭地哭泣着。"我看见天使了，"他幽然地说道，"简直是太美了！"

萨满们也复于沉静。唐·朱里奥宣布说他已召回神灵，提早结束了治疗仪式，因为冲击力对科文和雯迪来说太强大了，他们难以承受。一盏灯点亮了。我看见汉密尔顿把科文抱在怀里，好似抱着一个婴孩。"你回来了，"他抚慰道，"欢迎回来。"

科文茫然四顾，面带微笑。"我从来没有如此幸福，"他说。

这次治疗仪式结束后，我们每人的治疗都停了一天。雯迪在棚屋外面遇见了我，哭喊不已，情绪极为波动，而我也不知道该为她做些什么。汉密尔顿请我们放心，说她很快就会好起来，只不过现在还依旧"抗拒那种体验"。幸好维克多带着她和乔去看了一些粉红色海豚，这多少使她平静了一些。不顾她的反对和阻挠，我和科文继续我们的治疗，依照先前的安排，在最后一晚进行了我们的第三次死藤水仪式；这次我们两个都没怎么吐，各自的灵异幻象也都是令人愉悦的。

旅行接近尾声。雯迪坐在唐·朱里奥和唐·阿尔伯特面前，给他们看手相。乔递给我一张汽车贴纸，上面写道："布什撒谎，谁会死亡？"[1] 我捕捉到科文的浓浓笑意。他第一次主动和我说话，拿出他的排笛为大家吹奏了小夜曲。

"今天感觉如何？"他问我。

我力图实事求是。我告诉他说，我的偏头疼完全消失了。我体验到一种怪异的、莫名的快乐和平静，完全超度了我作为作家通常感到的焦虑。

其他人都离开了。几天后，我自己也乘船连夜返回爱奎托斯。我和汉密尔顿并排躺在船屋顶上，谈论着死藤水治疗仪式。"好吧，"我说道，"那么我怎么知道这是否是真的？"

---

[1] 这是汽车贴纸上的一句广告词，在乔治·布什担任美国总统期间流传颇广。当时，布什政府对伊拉克所谓核武器威胁做了手脚，说了谎言，后来发动的伊拉克战争及石油问题伤害了美国民众的情感，美军在伊拉克也时有伤亡。美国民众以其惯有的幽默讽刺来指责当时的布什政府。lies, dies 两词，在英语读音中谐音押韵，又拼写相近，是一种特别的修辞手段；who 也颇耐人寻味，任何人或地方感觉受到谎言欺骗，都可以自己之名来替换 who，比如有：Bush Lies, New Orleans Dies，Bush Lied, I Died，Bush Lies, Democracy Dies。

他头枕双手，仰望星空，发出会意的笑声。星空如此明亮，照在我眼球上的残影都仿佛在灼烧。"真实与否无关紧要，"他说道："只要管用就行了呗。"

（张慧芳 译　曲美茹 校）

Eco-Touring in Honduras

Elisabeth Eaves

【导读】关乎"生态旅游",在于"无为和倾听",即在旅游地,除了摄影,什么也别取;除了脚印,一切勿留;行进途中,不妨驻足片刻,静静聆听,倾听这里一切"居民"的声音,听听环境的呼喊与细语,与自然进行灵性上的交流,唤醒人类对遗忘的本源的回忆,最终使人进入一种境界:人类诗意般生活在地球村内,这便是生态游的根本。本文起始于"生态游",归落于"生态破坏",作者将他在洪都拉斯的所见所闻展现给读者,一幅饱含关切与遗憾的图景,是是非非生态游!

一、岛,岛,岛。

每个人心中都有一个岛之梦,桃花岛、菊花岛,抑或是喇叭花岛。在岛上,看风,看海,与世隔绝,有船可以登岛或者离岛。静静的。然而洪都拉斯人的"岛之梦"却是截然相反的,这里的"岛之梦"是旅游业的繁荣所造成的假象,岛上到处都是待遇优厚的工作机会,因此很多人被这种假象所吸引,从本土来到岛上捞金,结果加速了植被的消失。

二、鲨鱼无罪,"怀璧"其罪(鲨鱼本没有罪,因其具市场价值而"获罪",招致杀身之祸——译者注)。

鲨鱼本是海中之王,海洋食物链的顶端,基本无天敌可言,仅仅是由于"美味营养"的"鱼翅",频遭人类毒手。作者在洪都拉斯潜水时亲眼见到带着伤疤的鲨鱼从身边游过,不禁想起鲨鱼在拼命挣扎中被割去鱼鳍,活生生被抛入大海,鲜血染红了海水……

三、文明的痕迹,逝去的自然。

溪水流过涧渠,流星划过夜空,牛羚穿过草原,痕迹记录着自然的变迁。痕迹有着自己的方向:遗失、湮灭。痕迹总会凑成文明,然而,文明也总在遗失、湮灭。作者说:"期望留下痕迹的欲望是无法抑制的。"昨日的哥伦布航线正是今日的洪都拉斯的痕迹。那么今日人类文明的痕迹又会给明日的大自然带来什么?

四、脆弱的香蕉。

洪都拉斯的经济命脉一度受制于人，国人曾经依靠向美国出口香蕉维持生计。然而时至今日，作者亲历，该国依然依靠水果出口，脆弱不堪，与此同时，一味仰仗旅游业过活之势愈演愈烈，不禁令人隐忧。

五、还有多少玛雅在哭泣？！

作者游览了玛雅古城。这是世界上唯一一个诞生于热带丛林而不是大河流域的古代文明，也是一株一夜之间神秘消失的人类奇葩。当众人还沉迷于猎奇玛雅"活人祭祀"的古代陋习时，又能有多少双关注的眼睛探寻环境退化逼迫玛雅抛弃了持续600多年的繁荣？

Island Dreams

Colonia Balfate[①] and Colonia Policarpo Galindo are not in the guidebooks, and for good reason. They are conjoined shantytowns[②] that spill upward along two steep tropical gullies[③] into the green jungle above. A few of the 2,300 residents have homes made of cinder block or cement, but the rest make do with scavenged wood planks, corrugated tin, or sheets of plastic. Tawny dirt roads, raw as open wounds and lined with garbage, climb sharply from the entrance to the settlement. Water delivery to the community is sporadic[④], residents lack a sewage system or a health clinic, and neighbors complain that the colonias are crime-ridden. In March, the owner of a nearby botanical garden called them "a haven for thieves and robbers" in the local press after two hikers were robbed on his grounds.

Balfate and Policarpo Galindo are among the faces of modern tourism. These fast-growing slums are located not on the outskirts of some Third World city but on a resort-dotted island in the Caribbean — one peddling sun, sea, and piña colada[⑤] dreams to a richer, colder world. Here on Roatán, one of the Bay Islands of Honduras, direct flights from the United States are on the rise, a new ferryboat speeds crossings to the mainland, and cruise-ship traffic is ramping up[⑥]. A terminal

---

① Balfate is a municipality in the Honduran department of Colón. Balfate itself is a town of about 2500 but the municipality includes the towns of Lucinda (600) Lis Lis (1200) and several others. Balfate was the first port in Honduras from which banana shipments left to the United States, however the rail lines were dismantled in the mid 1950's and the pier demolished.

② A town or section of a town or city inhabited by very poor people living in huts and shanties.

③ A deep ditch or channel cut in the earth by running water after a prolonged downpour.

④ Appearing singly or at widely scattered localities, as a plant or disease.

⑤ A mixed drink made of rum, coconut cream, and unsweetened pineapple juice.

⑥ to increase or cause to increase.

slated to open in 2009 will be able to handle 7,000 cruise-ship passengers a day. Cement trucks, feeding a construction boom in new hotels, rumble along the two-lane jungle road that serves as the island's main thoroughfare. As tourism grows, though, the island is killing off the flora and fauna that lured the foreigners in the first place while failing to enrich many Hondurans. From cruise shipper to backpacker, every traveler who sets foot on the island, including me, is contributing to this process.

I came to Honduras hoping to unravel① some of the effects of travel — because I travel and don't intend to stop and because, as a child of my time, I'm cursed with the burden of knowing I live in a planet-sized web of cause and effect. I can't abstain from this web anymore than a butterfly can refrain from moving its wings, but I feel drawn, nevertheless, to follow a few of its strands.

We hear a lot about eco-tourism these days, a term rendered nearly meaningless by travel-industry hype, but which the International Ecotourism Society defines as "responsible travel to natural areas that conserves the environment and improves the welfare of local peoples." That's the kind of definition that begs more questions: Improves how much? Which local people? But it's safe to say that the businesses and well-meaning organizations promoting eco-tourism agree on one thing: If developing countries conserve their natural areas, revenue from tourism can make up for foregone income from other uses of the same land, such as logging, fishing, and farming. That income, in turn, will reinforce the will to conserve.

Often, though, this theory isn't borne out in real life. Consider Ecuador's Galápagos Islands②, long the poster child for eco-travel, now turning into an eco-disaster. Between 1999 and 2005, the islands' GDP grew by a stunning 78 percent, two-thirds of which was due to tourism, according to a new study by J. Edward Taylor of the University of California, Davis. But individual welfare barely improved. GDP per head grew by a paltry 1.8 percent in the same period because the islands' population — drawn by the business engine of eco-tourism — grew by 60 percent. That ballooning population is taking an ever-higher toll on the fragile

---

① To separate and clarify the elements of (something mysterious or baffling); solve.

② A group of volcanic islands lying along the equator in the Pacific Ocean west of the mainland of Ecuador. The islands are famous for their rare species of fauna, including the giant tortoises for which they are named. Charles Darwin visited the islands in 1835 and collected a wealth of scientific data that contributed to his theory of natural selection. Tourism is now strictly regulated to protect the endangered species unknown outside the archipelago.

ecosystem.

In addition to being endowed with fertile jungle and turquoise① sea, Honduras is a good testing ground for eco-tourism's central proposition. It's poor. It wants tourism, or indeed anything that will supplement an economy based on remittance payments, maquiladoras, and fruit. There appears to be an official will to conserve: The government has designated, at least on paper, 107 protected areas in which hunting and development are either limited or banned outright. Together, they make up an impressive 24 percent of Honduran territory and are home to endangered creatures, like the howler monkey and the manatee, and spectacular ones, like the scarlet macaw. My plan was to visit several of the national parks, meeting up with my parents along the way and ending our trip at the ancient Mayan ruins of Copán.

On a map published by the government-affiliated Honduras Institute of Tourism, nearly the entire 80-square-mile island of Roatán is part of a national marine park. But a staffer at a local conservation organization told me that while that was the plan, it wasn't actually the case. At the moment, only eight miles of shoreline, stretching little more than a mile out to sea, are officially protected.

Diving in that area earlier in the day, I had seen a hawksbill turtle, two and a half feet long, beating its flippers as it glided by like a prehistoric shadow. The hawksbill — locally called carey — is critically endangered, still hunted for its dark-and-light patterned shell. Some locals make jewelry out of it—a barefoot man had already tried to sell me a carey necklace on the beach. "One of the sad side effects of the tourism and cruise-ship industry is that it has generated a lot of illegal activity," said James Foley, director of research and development for Roatán Marine Park, which maintains a tiny beachfront office in the village of West End.

The colonias, a handful of which are scattered around the island, are another disturbing side effect.

"See those houses?" Rosa Danelia Hendrix asked me, gesturing to some 15 shacks scattered high on the hills, the latest expansions to Balfate and Policarpo Galindo. We were standing in the yard of the three-room yellow schoolhouse where she is principal.

"Three months ago, they weren't there. They don't have septic tanks. When the rains come, the waste will run down the hill and cause diseases," she said. The

---

① A light to brilliant bluish green.

human waste, garbage, and sediment from the torn-up jungle also wash into the sea and onto nearby coral reefs, which are inside the supposed eight-mile protected area and which are home to hawksbill[①]s, bottlenose dolphins, and myriad[②] fish. The sediment reduces the amount of sunlight that reaches the coral, killing it, which, in turn, slowly kills the fish that live there.

The residents of the colonias come to the island from mainland Honduras because the tourism boom shimmers with the illusion of plentiful, well-paid jobs. "The island dream," mainlanders call it. "They confront reality when they realize they don't speak English, or don't have construction skills, and they can't get good jobs," Hendrix said.

To leave the colonias, I hopped in a minibus, and in 10 minutes I was back in West End, which is far from swanky but still a world away. It was my own island dream: a single dirt road running along a palm-fringed waterfront, lined with low-key restaurants, hotels, and dive shops. I stepped into an open-air beach bar called Sundowners and ordered a piña colada, and in no time the man on the next stool was telling me he hadn't paid federal taxes since 1967. The bar filled up, and as the sun moved closer to the sea, everyone turned to watch. It slipped over the edge of the earth, streaks of orange and pink filled the sky, and the black silhouette of a cruise ship sailed across the horizon.

Beware, shark

Not so much swimming as hovering, I slipped into the school of sharks. There were 18 of them, some as long as 8 feet. "These are big girls," the dive master had warned us; many were pregnant and thicker than usual. They swam above, below, and around me, so close I could have reached out and touched them. The dive master had advised us not to, a warning that had struck me as bizarre. I mean, really. What idiot would do such a thing?

But now I saw the problem. These Caribbean reef sharks had skin like velvet, dark and rich in the shadows, shiny and pale when it caught the light. They shimmered hypnotically as they moved. I noticed scars, dark healed gashes on their sides and around their jaws, telling stories I couldn't read — of feeding frenzies,

---

① 玳瑁。

② Constituting a very large, indefinite number; innumerable.

mating rituals, and fishermen. I wanted to touch. The sharks, meanwhile, seemed to register me as an uninteresting object. They came disquietingly close but always turned away from me at the last second. As they swerved①, I found myself wishing one would shimmy② along my body as she did, gliding in tandem with me for a few moments.

The sharks gave me butterflies, but the truth was that I was probably more of a danger to them than they were to me. For one thing, I was with 14 other humans, some of them fatter and slower than me, giving the sharks considerable choice should they choose to nibble. For another, as sharks go, the Caribbean reef shark is not especially threatening. Just four species of the 410 or so known to science account for most shark attacks on humans, and this wasn't one of them.

The sharks, on the other hand, would have had a lot to worry about had they been half as anxiety-prone as humans. Our group was shark baiting, one of the most controversial eco-tourism practices in the Caribbean. Sharks, being wild animals, are difficult to procure on command. So many of the hundreds of shark-dive operators around the world tempt the animals with food. At Waihuka Diving, Roatán's sole shark operation, the dive master took a plastic bucket with holes punctured in the lid and filled it with a small amount of chopped-up fish. The dive master planted the bucket in the sand 20 feet from the coral wall where we kneeled, and the sweet smell of fish guts lured the sharks to school③ right in front of us. They kept schooling as, at the dive master's signal, we moved into the fray. My excitement was pure, more real and visceral④ than I had expected. And, fortunately, immune to the presence of other humans and the artificiality of the setup.

Which brings me back to the bait. In 2001, Florida banned shark feeding in its waters, a move hailed by public-safety officials but also by conservationists. Feeding sharks lowers their natural fear of humans, which makes them easier prey for fishermen. And repeatedly luring them to the same spot makes them easy for fishermen to find.

This is a problem, because more than 100 million sharks are killed by humans every year. Several species are critically endangered, and some have gone extinct

---

① To turn aside or be turned aside from a straight course.
② To vibrate or wobble abnormally; To shake the body in or as if in dancing the shimmy.
③ To swim in.
④ Instinctive.

within specific regions. Sharks are frequently killed as collateral① damage — for instance, by tuna boats in the Pacific. (Your dolphin-safe tuna is not necessarily shark-safe.) Sharks are also a direct target of fishermen, especially for their fins, with escalating demand for shark-fin soup in China and Taiwan. The fins are so valuable that fishermen often cut them off and throw the shark back into the ocean, where it bleeds and sinks to its death.

We humans returned to our places in front of the coral wall, and the dive master, wearing a chain-mail gauntlet②, ripped the lid off the bucket of chopped fish. The effect was instantaneous. These lazily graceful creatures were suddenly bullets of muscle. In a matter of seconds they became a writhing, food-focused mass. A single thrash by a single shark looked powerful enough to knock me out.

As the melee ended, the sharks dispersed, trolling the area in wider and wider curves until a few disappeared into the blue. The divers reluctantly began to swim up the anchor line. At 15 feet below the surface, I paused and hung onto the line, floating like a windsock in the current while the nitrogen left my body. For a few minutes, I was able to watch the sharks from above, now just gray silhouettes but still recognizable by the S-curve of their swim.

A fisherman on Roatán can get about $40 for one of these sharks, or $720 for 18. Waihuka gets about $80 per diver, so $960 on this 12-customer dive. They can charge $960 for those same sharks again and again, and the sharks don't have to die: The resource is renewable. Assuming similar overhead (a boat, an outboard engine, gasoline), shark-watching is more profitable for the locals than shark-fishing, and it conserves nature rather than decimating it.

Doesn't that make shark diving a good thing? The rosy view of eco-tourism would say we should exploit shark viewing to stop shark fishing. Hire the fishermen as dive masters, and you've got a win-win-win for locals, tourists, and sharks. Shark-watch businesses further argue that the more people have happy encounters with the animal, the more public support there will be for researching and protecting it. (The whale-watching industry plausibly advances a similar argument.)

Unfortunately, ecology is a little more complicated. The day before my dive, I had asked James Foley of Roatán Marine Park what he thought about shark baiting.

---

① Situated or running side by side; parallel.
② A protective glove worn with medieval armor.

"If you feed sharks, you're interfering with their natural feeding cycle," he said. Since they're the top predators, that messes with the entire food chain. If they eat less of their usual prey, the prey population balloons and eats more of the creatures below it, and so on and so forth. "It sends shock waves through the whole ecosystem," Foley said. Masses of data and very sophisticated computing are required to get an idea of the ultimate impact, but the point is this: Feed wild beasts with utmost caution, not because of some selfish concern over getting your hand bitten off, but for their sake.

Even knowing what Foley had told me about the food chain, I wanted, post-dive, to side with proponents of shark diving, the ones who say that such cara-a-cara[①] encounters will teach man to love the beast. After I surfaced, and for some time afterward, I would close my eyes and try to re-imagine myself back down to the reef, envisioning their skin and their scars and re-tasting the frisson. Not many experiences in adult life make me want to do that.

Signs of Civilization

Parks, reserves, and wildlife refuges dot the northern coast of Honduras like a string of emeralds, starting in the west at the Barra del Rio Motagua National Park, tucked away on the Guatemalan border, and reaching the vast expanse of the Rio Plátano Biosphere Reserve in the east. The reserve cuts off the easternmost province of Gracias a Dios[②] from the rest of the country and is covered with the largest remaining expanse of virgin tropical jungle in Central America.

I approached the north coast of mainland Honduras by ferryboat from Roatán, thinking of two antecedents: Christopher Columbus, who was real, and Allie Fox, who was not. Columbus passed this way by ship in 1502 and claimed the shore for Spain. The existing human residents, the Tolupan[③], Pech[①], and Tawahka[②], lived in

---

① "卡拉一个卡拉",西班牙语意为"面对面"。

② Gracias a Dios (Spanish: Thank God) is one of the 18 departments into which the Central American nation of Honduras is divided. Gracias a Dios department covers a total surface area of 16,630 km² and, in 2005, had an estimated population of 76,278. Though it is the second largest department in the country, it is sparsely populated, and contains extensive pine savannas, swamps, and rainforests. However, the expansion of the agricultural frontier is a perennial threat to the natural bounty of the department.

③ The Tolupan or Jicaque people is an indigenous ethnic group of Honduras primarily inhabiting the community La Montaña del Flor in central Honduras.

hidden jungle settlements, so Columbus would have seen an unbroken wall of green rising from the sandy beach up to the 8,000-foot peak of Pico Bonito. As my ferryboat approached, the peak loomed over the coast, first hazy in the bright morning sun, then greener as we got closer to the shore.

As the wilderness has become a place that humans visit by choice rather than necessity, the "leave no trace" credo has evolved into a mantra for outdoor enthusiasts. In my case, it's been ingrained since grade-school day hikes. So it's odd to think just how new this philosophy is to Western thinking. Columbus, I'm guessing, would have considered the idea of leaving no trace incomprehensible. Every Spanish name, every cathedral, every empty silver mine in Central America is testament to the belief that the bigger the trace, the better. Or consider the Babylonians, the Romans, the Mayans — the entire history of civilization is one of bending the earth to the needs and wants of humans. Today, we might worship at the altar of low-impact living, but I'll wager that our brains have not yet adapted. On a purely psychological level, impact is good. Who wants to be forgotten? We have families, make art, and build McMansions[3] precisely so that we leave a trace.

Allie Fox and his family also approached the north coast by ship in The Mosquito Coast, a novel by Paul Theroux[4], who seems to have chosen the region as a metaphor for the opposite of civilization. Fox wants to escape a corrupt and materialistic modern United States, and he has notions that the Mosquito Coast savages, as he sees them, are a purer version of mankind. But once in the jungle, he is desperate to civilize it. He plants neat rows of beans and builds a giant ice

---

[1] Pech (Paya) were the original inhabitants of the Bay Island of Roatan but were removed to the mining areas of the mainland by the Spanish during the early colonial period. There are now about 2,000 Pech confined to a few small communities in Olancho, Colón and Gracias a Dios. They have resisted total assimilation and, under the national bilingual programme, have developed Pech-language courses and Pech teachers.

[2] The Tawahka are the smallest of the Honduran indigenous groups. The population totals about 1,000 people. Tawahka occupy an area of 233 hectares in the centre of the Mosquitia, rainforest. Presently the group is struggling to have this area declared an indigenous reservation, and to be considered as one of the main biological areas of Mesoamerica. Many Tawahka communities have abandoned their language in the face of pressures to assimilate.

[3] McMansion is a pejorative term for a large new house which is judged as pretentious, tasteless, or badly designed for its neighborhood.

[4] Paul Edward Theroux (born April 10, 1941) is an American travel writer and novelist, whose best known work of travel writing is perhaps The Great Railway Bazaar (1975). He has also published numerous works of fiction, some of which were made into feature films. He was awarded the 1981 James Tait Black Memorial Prize for his novel The Mosquito Coast.

machine.

My parents met me at the ferry terminal with Mark, a guide from a local company that specializes in aventuras ecológicas. The outfit is called Garífuna① Tours, after an African-Indian ethnic group that lives along the north coast. This was supposed to be a group tour, but we were the only customers. We felt a bit decadent.

We drove through the modern, low-rise② city of La Ceiba③, which, despite its banks and restaurants and grid-patterned streets, looked bleached and weathered, as though it were still trying to assert itself against nature. The impact of humans on the north coast accelerated considerably after 1502, culminating in today's cultural peak, which comes complete with Dunkin' Donuts and KFC. Mark whisked us west of the city, turned off the paved road, and drove through a field of pineapples. A mechanical conveyor with a green-painted metal boom sat idle in the field.

The low, spiky pineapple plants grew right up to the edge of Pico Bonito National Park④, 414 square miles of mountain and jungle encompassing Pico Bonito itself, the jutting peak I had seen from the sea. Entering the jungle was like stepping into a yawning palace, one made of ceiba and mahogany and rosewood trees, lit only by a few sunbeams that penetrated a latticework high above. Up there — 30 or 40 yards up in the trees — existed a whole world of insects and animals that never

---

① A member of a people of mixed Carib and African ancestry living along the Caribbean coast of Honduras, Guatemala, Belize, and Nicaragua. The Garifuna were deported to the area in the late 18th century after their defeat by the British on the island of St. Vincent, where shipwrecked and escaped African slaves had intermarried with the indigenous Carib population beginning in the early 17th century.

② Of or relating to a building having few stories and often no elevators.

③ La Ceiba is a port city on the northern coast of Honduras in Central America. It is located on the southern edge of the Caribbean, forming part of the south eastern boundary of the Gulf of Honduras. With an estimated population of over 174,000 living in approximately 170 residential areas (called colonias or barrios), it is the third largest city in the country and the capital of the Honduran department of Atlántida. La Ceiba was officially founded on August 23, 1877. The city was named after a giant ceiba trees which grew near the old dock, which itself finally fell into the sea in late 2007. The city has been officially proclaimed the "Eco-Tourism Capital of Honduras" as well as the "Entertainment Capital of Honduras". Every year, on the third or fourth Saturday of May, the city holds its famous carnival to commemorate Isidore the Laborer (Spanish San Isidro Labrador). During this time, the city is host to approximately 500,000 tourists.

④ Pico Bonito National Park (PBNP) is located on the north coast of Honduras, in the mountain range called Cordillera Nombre de Dios, to the southwest of the city La Ceiba. It is part of the Mesoamerican Biological Corridor (MBC). It has a surface area of 1,073 square kilometres including its buffer zone - i.e. approximately 20 x 20 miles or 30 x 35 km. This area is very popular for the practice of rafting, kayaking and hiking, and a number of tour operators offer transportation, tours and lodging.

deigned to touch the ground. The trail began to climb, and small unseen creatures rustled and were gone before I could get a look. When we came upon a termite nest, Mark urged me to eat one of the insects, and when I refused, he told me that at least I knew now that they were edible, in case I got lost in the forest. We passed a sign that banned venturing off-trail into the pathless woods beyond. Mark said a group of Spaniards had recently headed that-a-way, gotten lost for six days, and had to be rescued.

In an hour, we arrived at a waterfall. A foamy white feather spewed out of the jungle, down vine-covered rock, and eddied and churned its way to the deep, calm pool that spread out at our feet.

Outside the air-conditioned rooms, the heat had been constant since I arrived in Honduras. It was the kind that pressed on your body like a physical force, barely lessened by an evening breeze or a dip in the bath-water sea. During our short jungle climb, it seemed to have grown even thicker. Now here was a chance to be cool. I dove under the water and felt the blood rush to the surface of my skin.

As I was drying off, a troop of teenagers from the town of Tela arrived at the fall. They were on a Sunday hike with a lone American friend, a redheaded Peace Corps volunteer from Texas. Honduras is host to 192 volunteers—the Peace Corps' second-largest deployment in the world (only Ukraine has more) — who are scattered around the country on their vague but benign mission to be of use. Jonathan was at the end of his two-year tour, which he had spent advising the Tela mayor's office on business development. "The Peace Corps has been in Honduras for 40 years," he told us. "So you might well ask, just how much good are we doing?"

Perhaps not much. But the urge to leave a trace is irrepressible.

Pineapple Fields Forever
American short-story writer O·Henry, exiled to Honduras in the 1890s, coined a term to describe the country that was so perfectly evocative of colonial horrors, bad government, tropical weather, ripe fruit, and lush bougainvillea vines creeping up the

patio[1] railing that it's in wide circulation more than a century later. The term was banana republic. That piece of poetry conjures an entire period of history. For the first half of the 20th century, large swaths of Honduras were more or less run by the Standard Fruit Co. (now Dole) and the United Fruit Co. (now Chiquita). They bribed the politicians and summoned the U.S. military when things got out of hand. They built and owned the railways, which tended to run from the fields to the ports but not to anywhere useful to Hondurans, such as the capital.

Of course, the country has come a long way since then. Or has it? During my visit, Honduras This Week ran the front-page headline "President Zelaya Addresses Melon Crisis." The photographic evidence showed the mustachioed president sitting at his desk, Honduran flag visible to one side, biting into a juicy cantaloupe. The power of big fruit has diminished in recent decades, but pineapples, bananas, and melons are still export staples. A relatively minor U.S. Food and Drug Administration warning — that melons from a particular Honduran farm might contain salmonella — can become a flash point for a fragile economy.

Now a lot of people are hitching hopes for Honduras' economy to tourism. Plans for at least two new resorts are under way on the north coast, one of them adjacent to a national park. Signs in the protected areas I visited bore the logos of donor organizations — USAID[2], WWF[3], the Honduras-Canada Fund for Environmental Management. Even the Peace Corps[4] was onboard. Since running into Jonathan at the waterfall, I had met a second Peace Corps volunteer, Nicole,

---

[1] A patio (from the Spanish: patio meaning 'back garden' or 'backyard') is an outdoor space generally used for dining or recreation that adjoins a residence and is typically paved. It may refer to a roofless inner courtyard of the sort found in Spanish-style dwellings or a paved area between a residence and a garden.

[2] U.S. Agency for International Development. An agency of the U.S. federal government that provides foreign aid and financial assistance to other countries. It helps after natural disasters and conducts anti-poverty programs in various parts of the world. It was established in 1961.

[3] World Wide Fund for Nature, a nature conservation organisation previously named World Wildlife Fund.

[4] The Peace Corps is an American volunteer program run by the United States Government, as well as a government agency of the same name. The mission of the Peace Corps includes three goals: providing technical assistance, helping people outside the United States to understand U.S. culture, and helping Americans understand the cultures of other countries. Generally, the work is related to social and economic development. Each program participant, (aka Peace Corps Volunteer), is an American citizen, typically with a college degree, who works abroad for a period of 24 months after three months of training. Volunteers work with governments, schools, non-profit organizations, non-government organizations, and entrepreneurs in education, hunger, business, information technology, agriculture, and the environment.

who was visiting the Cuero y Salado wildlife reserve with her father. Nicole was stationed in the south, in a small town in the department of Valle. I asked her what went on there, economically speaking. She furrowed her brow and thought for a minute. Finally, she said that there were a lot of armed security guards. She was working with a women's cooperative, trying to come up with things its members could sell to foreigners. They made attractive pottery, but it didn't ship well. Nicole had hit upon the idea of making small, bright-colored purses woven from old potato-chip bags, an item she had seen for sale in other parts of Central America. There were no tourists where she lived to buy such things, but she thought that maybe the townsfolk could lure travelers from the Pan-American Highway, which passed nearby.

Tourism was clearly a popular cause, but was it smart? Does it make sense, in the long term, to sell natural charms that will be steadily worn down by the buyers? A city can renew itself with man-made attractions. I wasn't sure that jungles and coral reefs had that kind of staying power.

On our last day on the coast, I floated facedown in the Caribbean, toting up my sins. I had flown in an airplane, taken taxis instead of buses, requested air conditioning, run the air conditioning even after I realized I couldn't shut one of my windows, and bought small plastic bottles of water. That was all before sundown on my first day. Subsequently, I had participated in the feeding of wild animals, been driven around in gasoline-powered cars and boats, eaten conch (I didn't know it was threatened), and — this one hadn't even occurred to me until I read it in a guidebook — worn sunscreen and DEET[①]-laden bug repellent while swimming above the delicate corals. But I had no idea how to weigh all that against whatever minuscule[②] economic benefit I might have been bringing to Honduras.

We were in Cayos Cochinos[③] Marine National Park, a collection of cays northeast of La Ceiba. That morning, snorkeling off a deserted cay, I had seen parrotfish, jacks, schools of blue tang, and one fat, lazy barracuda, motionless except

---

① A colorless, oily liquid, that has a mild odor and is used as an insect repellent.

② Very small; tiny.

③ The Cayos Cochinos or Cochinos Cays are a group of two small islands and 13 more small coral cays situated 30 kilometers northeast of La Ceiba on the northern shores of Honduras. Although geographically separate, they belong to the Bay Islands department and are part of Roatán municipality. The population numbered 108 at the 2001 census. The total land area measures about 2 km². The islands are a Marine Protected Area and are managed by the Honduran Coral Reef Foundation.

for its snapping jaw. The reef life was more vivid and abundant than anything I had seen off Roatán, probably because of all the diving and development there.

Now I was floating off Cayo Chachauate, a coral cay just a few hundred feet long that was home to a Garífuna village of about 30 families. The Garífuna, who descend from escaped slaves and Carib Indians, lived on the island of St. Vincent until 1797, when the British deported[①] the entire population to Honduras, where they established fishing villages. Chachauate's wooden huts were strung out along the sand just yards above the high-water mark. An assortment of canoes, makeshift sailboats, and outboards sat on the beach. The big news in the village was that it had recently acquired a diesel generator, which ran every evening from 6 to 8. Any villager who invested in his own power line was free to share. Until the generator, only one ambitious family had had electricity, provided by a solar panel on their roof.

I watched a purple fan coral sway with the movement of the tide. The sea stretched away turquoise in three directions and grew pale where it rose up to the beach. Up there, a woman in a hut was making me fried chicken for lunch. I swam in closer to shore, gliding over sea grass and rippled sand. I saw a few tiny fish and a corroded soda can. And then I saw the bearded face of José Trinidad Cabañas, a long-ago president of Honduras. He was decorating a 10-lempira bill, which lay flat and motionless on the sand. Struck by this oddity, I dove for the bottom, but when I picked up the money, it felt so slippery and fragile that I thought it would disintegrate in my hand, so I let it flutter back down to the seabed again.

Mel Gibson and the Demise of Civilization

"Forget about the movie," Gustavo told Denise.

She ignored him.

"They took the heart out, and it was still beating," she said. "And they held it up like this!" She raised one pale, triumphant arm above her head.

"Let the movie go," we said in chorus, my mother and I now joining Gustavo. He was our portly[②], scholarly guide to the ancient Mayan city of Copán, an urban center of 24,000 people during its heyday, which was sometime between A.D. 400

---

① To expel from a country.

② Comfortably stout; corpulent.

and 800. He carried a stick with a bird feather attached to one end to point out archeological details, and he had the slightly aggrieved air of a man who had to be patient a lot.

Gustavo was unhappy with Mel Gibson and, in particular, with what he referred to as "that stupid movie," Apocalypto[①]. In case you missed it, the 2006 film was a revisionist and gruesomely violent retelling of history. No surprise there, but this movie happened to be set among the ancient Maya. There were beheadings, impalings, and human sacrifices performed by drug-addled priests. Not that the real Mayans didn't perform the odd human sacrifice. But Gustavo was at pains to contextualize.

At the entrance to Copán, my parents and I had teamed up with Diane and Denise, two middle-aged women from New York City, both with strong Brooklyn accents. Denise, who had short black hair and wore bright red lipstick, was a Gibson fan. To Gustavo's consternation, she kept asking where the sacrifices were performed.

And now, finally, we were in the middle of the Grand Plaza, once quite a hub, open to all members of the ancient Copán public and used for both commerce and worship. There was a small pyramid at the center of the plaza, and steles[②] scattered around, each one intricately carved in honor of one king or another. And there, right in front of us, was a large stone object made for the express purpose of sacrificing humans.

It was dome-shaped, about 4 feet wide and 3 feet tall, with a depression hollowed out of the top just big enough to cup a human head. Two channels ran down the sides to drain the blood away. Gustavo grabbed my arm and told me to lean backward over the dome with my head in the depression — kind of comfy, if you must be sacrificed — and made as though to cut off my head with his feather-stick. That was when Denise got excited and started recounting the Apocalypto sacrifice scene, thrusting her hand into the air as though holding a

---

① *Apocalypto* is a 2006 American film directed by Mel Gibson. Set in Yucatan, Mexico, during the declining period of the Mayan civilization, *Apocalypto* depicts the journey of a Mesoamerican tribesman who must escape human sacrifice and rescue his family after the capture and destruction of his village. The film, similar to Cornel Wilde's 1966 *The Naked Prey* features a cast of Mexicans and some Native Americans, and its Yucatec Maya dialogue is accompanied by subtitles.

② An upright stone or slab with an inscribed or sculptured surface, used as a monument or as a commemorative tablet in the face of a building.

beating heart. "And the people were still alive!" she said.

She reluctantly followed as the rest of us moved away across the plaza to the city's ball court. Relief-carved macaw heads decorated the walls. Mayan ball courts, it turns out, were not for playing ball in the Western sense of a game, as an earlier generation of archeologists believed. "The idea of the ball ceremony was not to please a human audience, but to please the gods," Gustavo explained. Performed correctly, the ball "game," conducted by specially trained young men, was believed to make the sun and moon come up on time.

Today, though much of ancient Copán still lies buried, you can wander among its carvings and pyramids, tombs and temples, halls of government and homes, visualizing the bright-colored stucco① that once adorned them. Until the 19th century, however, they were completely invisible. Some time in the 800s, the civilization of the Classic Maya period began a collapse so complete that by the time the Spaniards began to arrive, there was no trace of it. Descendants of the ancient Maya scattered and survived, but the great painted cities, with their pyramids and temples, were gone, swallowed whole by the jungle. The last date found on a Mayan monument corresponds to the year 909, as though time just stopped one day.

Archeologists still debate what happened. It's clear, though, that environmental degradation played a role in the collapse. In the Copán valley in particular, studies show that as the population grew, the people stripped the hillsides of trees. Major soil erosion preceded the city's downfall. Copán also suffered droughts, which may have been partly brought on by the deforestation. The Mayans cut down the trees to plant corn, and for firewood to burn limestone, a key ingredient in their bright pigments②. Why didn't they pull themselves out of this ecological tailspin? Presumably they could see the trees disappearing and the mud running down the hills. In Collapse: How Societies Choose To Fail or Succeed, Jared Diamond suggests that the elites who might have led the way out of this mess had insulated themselves from the problems of the people. So as the poor began to suffer — infant mortality was probably 50 percent toward the end — the kings kept demanding tribute.

---

① A durable finish for exterior walls, usually composed of cement, sand, and lime, and applied while wet.

② Dry coloring matter, usually an insoluble powder, to be mixed with water, oil, or another base to produce paint and similar products.

We stood in front of the hieroglyphic[①] stairway, an inscription covering 72 steps that make up one face of the acropolis[②]. It's the longest hieroglyphic inscription found in the Americas, and no one has completely deciphered it. Archeologists know that it tells a history of ancient Copán and that it was created by a ruler named Smoke Shell in 753, when the city was already in decline. When the staircase is eventually decoded, maybe Smoke Shell will have something more to tell us about his doomed metropolis.

In the meantime, Honduras is still being deforested. Central America has lost more than 70 percent of its forest cover since 1960, mostly to make way for cattle ranches, sugar-cane fields, and coffee plantations. Between 1990 and 2005, Honduras lost 10,567 square miles of forest —an area about the size of Massachusetts. But that's just another scary environmental statistic. Taken together, all the bad news is enough to make you turn to irrational beliefs about planetary control. Or to mindless entertainment.

Gustavo began to tell us the story of the Mayan codices, manuscripts that could help decode the hieroglyphics. Denise cut in.

"Did they sacrifice people up there?"

Gustavo sighed. "Yes, and then they let the head roll down the steps and gave it to the victim's son," he said. "Too much Mel Gibson for you."

---

① Of, relating to, or being a system of writing, such as that of ancient Egypt, in which pictorial symbols are used to represent meaning or sounds or a combination of meaning and sound.象形文字的。

② A citadel or elevated fortification of a settlement.卫城，城堡。

洪都拉斯生态游[1]

伊丽莎白·伊芙斯

岛之梦

旅游指南中找不到巴尔法特和波利卡波加林多这两个垦殖区的踪迹，这也没什么奇怪的。它们只是两片相连的棚户区，沿着两条陡峭的热带沟渠向上蔓延至顶部的绿色丛林中。那里2300户居民中，只有少数的房子是用煤渣砖或者水泥建成的，其余的都是用捡来的废弃木板、凹凸不平的白铁板或者塑料布凑合着搭起来的棚子。黄褐色的土路，非常自然原始，像开裂的伤口一样，路两旁都是垃圾。这些路从入口处直直地、陡峭地通向垦殖区。在那里，供水时断时续，没有下水道系统，也没有卫生所。周围其他区域的居民经常抱怨，这两个垦殖区犯罪猖獗。3月份，附近的一个植物园园主在当地的报纸上称这两个垦殖区为"鼠窃狗盗之徒的避风港"，此前有两个背包客在他的园子里遭遇劫匪。

巴尔法特和波利卡波加林多是现代旅游新开发出来的区域。这两个迅速增长的贫民区并非位于某些第三世界城市的郊区，相反，它们坐落于加勒比海中一个度假村星罗棋布的岛屿上，这个岛屿向比它更为富有、更为寒冷的世界兜售那些充满阳光、海浪和菠萝鸡尾酒的美梦。罗丹岛是洪都拉斯的海湾群岛中的一个，美国直飞这里的航班数量一直在增加，新开通的渡轮加快了它与本土之间的来往，游船的数量也一直在增加。一个新的交通枢纽站，计划于2009年开始使用，之后每天将能够容纳7000位搭载游船的乘客。水泥搅拌车轰隆隆地驶过双车道的丛林路，为日益增多的新酒店的建设提供材料，这条两车道的丛林路是罗丹岛的交通要道。旅游业的增长使得该岛上那些最初吸引外国人来此的动植物群正在慢慢消失，而且也未能让多数洪都拉斯人富起来。无论是游船主还是背包客，每一个踏上该岛的旅客，包括我，都间接地加快了这些动植物消失的过程。

我来到洪都拉斯，希望能够揭开旅行的某些意义。我一直在旅游，而且没打算停下脚步，因为在童年的时候，我像被一种认知所诅咒，那就是我生活在一张星球大小的因果关系网中。我无法从这张网中挣脱，就如同蝴蝶无法停止

---

[1] "生态旅游"或"生态游"这一术语，最早由世界自然保护联盟（IUCN）于1983年首先提出，1993年国际生态旅游协会把其定义为：具有保护自然环境和维护当地人民生活双重责任的旅游活动。生态旅游的内涵更强调的是对自然景观的保护，是可持续发展的旅游。

震动它的翅膀。但是，我被吸引着去探索织成这张网的一些脉络线路。

现在我们常常听到人们谈论生态旅游，这个词几乎已经被旅游业的大肆炒作宣传搞得毫无意义，但是国际生态旅游协会将其定义为一种"自然地区的负责任的旅游，它可以保护当地的环境，改善当地居民的福利。"这种定义引出了更多问题：从多大程度上改善当地人的福利？改善哪些当地人的福利？但是可以肯定的一点就是，旅游企业和善意的组织机构在推行生态旅游时有一点是一致的：如果发展中国家保护他们的自然区，那么发展旅游业的收入可以弥补之前本可用作它途的土地带来的收益，如伐木、捕鱼、农耕等。而且旅游业的收入反过来可以进一步增强人们保护自然的意愿。

不过，现实情况通常并非如此。想想厄瓜多尔的加拉帕戈斯群岛，长久以来一直是生态旅游的典范，但是现在它变成了生态灾难。1999至2005年间，岛上的GDP增长了78%，着实惊人，据美国加州大学戴维斯分校的J·爱德华·泰勒新的研究显示，三分之二的增长来自旅游业。但是民众个人的福利却几乎没有任何改善，同期人均GDP增长不足1.8%。这是因为岛上的人口在生态旅游业的带动下增长了60%，急速膨胀的人口给原本脆弱的生态系统带来了更为沉重的压力。

洪都拉斯拥有丰富的丛林和蔚蓝的大海，正是验证生态旅游的中心观点的好地方。那里很穷，需要发展旅游业或者说需要任何能够增强其以汇款支付、边境加工厂和水果为基础的经济的事情。看起来似乎官方有意保护其资源，因为政府已经指定了（至少书面上是）107个保护区，这些保护区限制或者完全禁止狩猎和开发。它们的面积加起来总共占洪都拉斯领土的24%，一个比较惊人的数字。这些保护区是诸多濒危物种的家园，如吼猴、海牛，还有其他更为惊人的物种，如绯红金刚鹦鹉。我的计划是参观几个国家公园，在途中与我父母会合，然后去参观位于科潘①的古老的玛雅遗址，之后结束此行。

政府下属的洪都拉斯旅游协会出版的地图显示，面积为80平方英里的整个罗丹岛几乎都成为了国家海洋公园的一部分。但是，当地的一个自然保护组织的职员告诉我，那只是计划而已，事实并非如此。目前，只有8英里的海岸线，延伸到海面1英里的地方，属于正式的保护区域。

当天早些时候我在那个区域里潜水，看到一只玳瑁，有2.5英尺长，拍打

---

① 科潘玛雅遗址位于洪都拉斯首都特古西加尔巴西北部科潘省，距特古西加尔巴西北约225千米处。靠近危地马拉边境。科潘玛雅遗址坐落在13公里长、2.5公里宽的峡谷地带，面积0.15平方千米，海拔600米。科潘玛雅遗址是公元前7—1世纪洪都拉斯玛雅古城的遗址。科潘是玛雅文明最重要的地点之一，直到19世纪才被挖掘出来。它的中心地带和壮丽的公共大广场体现了它三个主要发展时期，早在10世纪初期的时候，这座城市就被遗弃了。

着脚蹼像史前的影子一样滑走了。当地人把玳瑁称为凯里,这是一种极度濒危的物种,但是人们仍然为了获取其黑白相间的外壳而对其进行猎杀。一些当地人用它的壳制作首饰,在海滩上的时候就有一个光脚的男子试图向我兜售玳瑁壳制作的项链。詹姆斯·福利是罗丹海洋公园的研究和发展总监,在西尾的村里有一间小小的靠海的办公室,他说:"发展旅游业和游船行业引发了大量的非法活动,这一点很让人忧心。"

有一些垦殖区散乱地分布于整个岛上,这是另一个让人烦恼的地方。

罗萨·达娜莉·亨德里克斯是一所学校的校长,我们站在她那个有3间房屋的黄色校舍的院子里时,她指着高处山上散布的大约15间窝棚,这些是新近才在巴尔法特和波利卡波林多搭起的窝棚,"看到那些房子没有?"她问我。

"3个月前还没有那些窝棚,那里没有化粪池。一旦下雨,废弃物将会顺山坡流下,引发疾病,"她接着说。人的排泄物、垃圾和丛林破坏引发的泥沙沉积也会被冲到海里,附着到附近的珊瑚礁上面,这些珊瑚礁应该是在8英里的保护区范围里面,它们是玳瑁、宽吻海豚和各种鱼类的生存地。沉积物减少了能够到达珊瑚的日照量,导致珊瑚死掉,这样也就等于慢慢杀死了生存在那里的鱼类。

旅游业的繁荣造成了一种假象,那就是岛上到处都是待遇优厚的工作机会,因此很多人被这种假象所吸引,从洪都拉斯本土来到这个岛上,这些垦殖区的居民也是这样。洪都拉斯本土的居民将这种现象称之为"岛之梦"。"但是他们过来后,意识到因为自己不会讲英语或者没有建筑技能,不可能找到好工作的时候,他们就要面对现实了。"亨德里克斯说。

要离开这些垦殖区了,我跳上一辆面包车,10分钟就回到了西尾。西尾虽然远远称不上多么繁华和现代,但是它仍然是一个很遥远而不同的世界。我自己的岛屿梦是这样的:一条土路顺着边缘长满棕榈树的海滨延伸,两旁是低调的餐厅、酒店和潜水商店。我迈进一家叫做夕阳西下的露天沙滩酒吧,点了一杯菠萝鸡尾酒,很快坐在旁边凳子上的人就跟我攀谈起来,告诉我他自1967年就没有再缴过联邦税。这个酒吧很快坐满了人,太阳沉到海面的时候,每个人都转过头观看。太阳慢慢地落到了地平线之下,天上到处都是粉色、橙色的条纹,远处天边一条游船的黑色影子驶过地平线。

小心,鲨鱼

说是游泳,我徘徊好久之后,才滑入鲨鱼群。总共有18只,有一些身长达8英尺。潜水师已经警告过我们说,"这些都是大的母鲨";有一些已经怀孕,所以看起来要比平时粗壮的多。它们上下、前后、左右地在我身边游动,离我那么近，我只要伸手就可以碰到它们，但是之前潜水师就曾警告过我们不要碰它们，他的警告曾让我觉得很奇怪，真的，我当时真的是这么想的。哪个傻瓜会去做这种事情呢？

但是现在我明白了，他为什么要这么警告我们。这些加勒比礁鲨的皮肤像天鹅绒一样，在阴影中显得黝黑、饱满，在光线照耀之下则变得嫩白而富有光泽。它们游动的时候，身体闪着微光，让人感觉眩晕。我看到它们身体两侧和嘴巴周围有疤痕和黑色的已经愈合的伤口，这些都代表着我无法知晓的曾经发生的事情——鲨鱼群争食、交配仪式以及渔民的捕捞。我想摸一摸它们，但是这些鲨鱼却似乎对我不感兴趣。它们总是游到离我很近的地方，近的甚至有点让我不安，但是却又在最后一刻转身离开了。它们掉头游走后，我发现自己其实希望能有一只围着我摆动，跟我一起游几分钟。

这些鲨鱼让我神经紧张、心惊胆颤，但事实是，它们对我的危险性其实可能不如我对于它们的危险性大。因为，首先，我是和其他 14 个人一起的，他们中有些比我胖、比我游得慢，所以鲨鱼如果想要捕食的话，应该更可能会选择他们；其次，就鲨鱼种类来说，加勒比礁鲨并不是特别危险的一种。就科学已知的约 410 种鲨鱼种类中，只有 4 种常袭击人类，而加勒比礁鲨并不在其中。

另一方面，鲨鱼如果能有人类一半的焦虑敏感度，那么就该有许多需要担心的事情了。我们这一组是在进行海底大冒险游戏，这是加勒比海地区最具争议的生态旅游项目之一。鲨鱼作为一种野生动物，很难听从控制、指挥。所以世界各地数百个鲨鱼潜水项目经营者中，许多都是用食物来引诱鲨鱼。外呼卡潜水中心是罗丹岛唯一一家鲨鱼潜水项目经营者,这里的潜水师用一个塑料桶，桶盖上扎了许多小孔，桶内装了一些切碎的鱼，然后把桶埋在距离珊瑚墙 20 英尺远的沙子里，我们就跪在珊瑚墙那里。鱼的香味吸引来鲨鱼，就在我们前面受训。它们在按照潜水师的信号受训的时候，我们就游到争抢食物的这群鲨鱼中。对我来说，这种刺激很单纯，但是也比我原来想象的更为真实和本能。而且，幸亏我已经习惯了有其他人在场，以及这种故意的人为安排。

想起另一件事也是关于用饵引诱鲨鱼的。2001 年的时候，佛罗里达州下令禁止在鲨鱼活动区给它们喂食，此举不仅为公共安全官员所赞成，自然资源保护主义者也十分拥护。给鲨鱼喂食会降低它们原本对于人类的害怕，这就会导致它们更容易被渔民所捕获。而且多次把它们引诱到同一个地点后，它们会更容易被渔民发现。

这是个很严重的问题，因为每年有超过 1 亿只鲨鱼被人类杀死。有一些种类已经濒临灭绝，还有一些种类在某个区域已经灭绝了。鲨鱼经常被渔船等无意中间接杀死，例如，太平洋中的金枪鱼捕捞船经常会间接杀死鲨鱼。（不会伤害到海豚的金枪鱼捕捞船并不一定就不会伤害到鲨鱼。）同时也有渔民为了获取鲨鱼的鳍专门捕捞鲨鱼，因为中国大陆、台湾等地的鱼翅汤的需求量越来越大。鲨鱼鳍的价值很高，所以有渔民捕到鲨鱼后，切下它们的鳍，然后把它们重新扔回海里，以至它们在海里不停的流血、虚弱，直至死亡。

我们回到之前待的珊瑚墙前面的位置后，手上带着锁子护手套的潜水师扯开那只装着切碎的鱼的水桶的桶盖。瞬间，情况发生了变化，这些之前还懒懒的、优雅的鲨鱼突然之间像变成肌肉子弹一样。短短几秒钟内，这群生物就激烈翻滚扭动着去争抢食物。一条鲨鱼拍打一下的力道足以把我击倒。

混乱的争抢结束后，鲨鱼群散开了，搅起越来越宽的波纹，直到最后几只消失在蓝色的海水中。潜水的人们不情愿地开始朝着上面的锚线游去。上升到距水面 15 英尺的地方时，我停了下来，抓住锚线，随着氮气从我身体飘开，我像涌流中飘着的一个风向标一样。有几分钟时间，我从上面看不到下面的鲨鱼，只能看见灰色的轮廓，但是它们游动时搅起的 S 形波纹仍然能让我认出，那是它们。

罗丹岛的渔民捕到这样一只鲨鱼可以卖 40 美元，18 只总共就是 720 美元。外呼卡潜水中心向每位参加鲨鱼潜水游戏的人收取 80 美元，这样一次 12 个人的潜水活动就可以收 960 美元。有了这样一群鲨鱼，它们每次活动都可以收 960 元，而且还不用杀死鲨鱼：这就成了可再生资源。算上类似的日常开支费用（船、舷外机、汽油），对于当地人来说，鲨鱼观赏活动要比鲨鱼捕猎更具利润，而且还能保护自然，而非摧毁它。

这样鲨鱼潜水不就是一件好事吗？对生态旅游抱乐观看法的人们就可能说，我们应该开发鲨鱼观赏活动来阻止鲨鱼捕捞。可以雇佣渔民担任潜水师，这样当地人、游客和鲨鱼就能达到三赢的局面。鲨鱼观赏行业进一步辩称如果更多的人能够有和鲨鱼同乐的经历，那么就会有更多的公众支持它的研究和保护。（赏鲸行业似乎也提出过类似的说法。）

不幸的是，生态系统要比我们想象的复杂一些。潜水前一天，我问过罗丹海洋公园的詹姆斯·福利，对于用饵引诱鲨鱼他怎么看。"喂食鲨鱼会干扰它们自然的食物链循环，"他这样回答我。因为鲨鱼是食物链顶端的捕食者，所以这样就破坏了整个食物链。如果鲨鱼减少了捕食，那么它们原本的捕食对象数量就会剧增，这些捕食对象就会吃掉更多食物链中处于它们下端的生物，等等。"这样会严重地冲击整个生态系统，"福利说。要得出这种行为的最终影响，需要大量数据和非常复杂的计算，但是有一点却很清楚，那就是，喂食野兽需要非常谨慎，并不只是自私地考虑如何防止被它们咬掉手，而是为了动物本身着想理应如此。

虽然明白了福利跟我说的食物链的重要性，但是在潜水后，我仍然愿意和那些鲨鱼潜水支持者站在一边，就如他们说的，这种与鲨鱼面对面的接触可以教导人们爱护这种动物。浮出水面后，以及那之后的一些时候，我会闭上双眼，尝试想象我又回到水下的珊瑚墙那里，想象着鲨鱼的皮肤和它们身上的疤痕，重温那种因为兴奋和害怕而颤抖的感觉。成年后的生活中，并没有太多事情能够让我这样乐于回忆。

文明的标志

公园、保护区和野生动物保护点像一串绿宝石一样，散布于洪都拉斯的北部海岸，西起莫塔瓜河国家公园，到与危地马拉接壤处有所减少，东达广阔的雷奥普拉塔诺生物圈保留地[1]。这个保护区把该国最东部的格拉西亚斯-阿迪奥斯角[2]省隔了开来，区内覆盖着中美洲保留下来的最大的原始热带雨林。

我从罗丹岛乘渡船到洪都拉斯本土的北海岸，这让我想起了两位前辈：真实的克里斯托弗·哥伦布和虚构的阿利·福克斯。哥伦布1502年乘船经过这里，宣布该海岸为西班牙所有。那里的人们，希卡克人、帕亚人和苏莫人[3]都居住在隐秘的丛林中，所以估计哥伦布当时应该只能看到一条绵延不断的绿墙从沙滩一直延伸至8000英尺高的皮科波尼多峰。我乘坐的渡船逐渐前行，山峰隐约浮现在海岸上空，一开始在早晨明亮的太阳光里，看起来只是一个朦胧的影子，随着我们的船靠近海岸，就变得越来越绿。

既然旷野是人们可以选择参观而非必须参观的地方，那么"不留痕迹"这个信条已成为户外运动爱好者的口头禅。就我而言，还是小学生远足的时候，我就已经深知这一点。所以现在再思考这条信念对于西方思想是如何新鲜未免有些奇怪。我猜想哥伦布肯定会认为不留痕迹这一想法难以理解。中美洲的每

---

[1] 雷奥普拉塔诺生物圈保留地是洪都拉斯加勒比海岸的一个保护区，保护区囊括了普拉塔诺河流域以及其他河流，草木和流水从山坡上奔流而下，奔向加勒比海的红树林、泻湖、沿海草地和海滩。面积5,250平方公里，全区大致沿雷奥普拉塔诺河分布。该地有许多濒临灭绝的物种，1982年列入联合国教科文组织世界遗产名录，后两次列入濒危世界遗产名录。保护区是山区和低地组成的热带雨林，动植物超过2000种。本区也是从墨西哥向南至中美洲的中美洲生物走廊的一部分。

[2] 格拉西亚斯-阿迪奥斯角是中美洲东岸中部蚊子海岸的海岬，也是尼加拉瓜北大西洋自治区和洪都拉斯格拉西亚斯-阿迪奥斯省的界河——科科河（Río Coco）汇入加勒比海的地方。

[3] 洪都拉斯土著族名。洪都拉斯居民中印第安人与西班牙人混血种人约占91%，其中一部分是从危地马拉迁来的印第安人、西班牙人混血种人的后裔，肤色较黑，在各省几乎均占多数。印第安人占6%，主要有帕亚人、伦卡人、希卡克人、米斯基托人、苏莫人和玛雅人。部分印第安人仍保留着本民族的一些传统生活习俗。黑人占2%（其祖先来自西印度群岛），集中在加勒比沿海一带，以农业为主。白人占1%，主要来自美国和西班牙，多居住在工矿业和种植业发达地区。土生白人居住城市，居统治地位。此外居民中还有极少数印度人、华人、阿拉伯人等，分散各地，以经商为生。

一个西班牙语名称、每一个教堂、以及每一个挖空的银矿无不表明这样一种信念，那就是，痕迹越大越好。或者再想想巴比伦人、罗马人以及玛雅人，会发现整个文明史就是按照人类的需求和需要改造世界的过程。今天，我们也许会在圣坛前祈求，崇拜一种简单、低影响的生活方式，但是我可以打赌，我们的头脑还不能适应这样的生活。单纯从心理层面来讲，施加影响是好事。谁愿意自己被遗忘掉呢？我们建立家庭、创造艺术、精准地建设大厦，留下我们的痕迹。

在保罗·瑟鲁①的小说中，阿利·福克斯也是和他的家人一起乘船到达北部的莫斯基托海岸，作者似乎是将这一地区比作文明的对立面。福克斯想逃离腐败和物欲横流的现代美国，他见到莫斯基托海岸的野人后，就觉得他们是更为纯净的人类。但是到了丛林之后，他就迫不及待地开始开发那里。他种了齐整的一畦畦的豆子，还造了一台巨型制冰机。

我父母和一个导游在渡轮码头那里等待与我会合，那个导游名叫马克，来自当地一家专业开发经营生态探险的公司。此行叫做加里富纳②之行，得名于沿北海岸居住的非洲-印度族群。这本该是个团体游，但是游客却只有我们三人，这让我们觉得有点失落。

我们驱车穿过拉塞瓦市，这是一个有着低矮建筑的现代城市，这里尽管有银行、餐馆和纵横交错的街道，但是整个城市看起来有些褪色、风化的感觉，仿佛仍然在努力摆脱自然的束缚并肯定自己。1502 年后，人类对北海岸的影响大大加快，在今天的文化高峰入侵下达到了顶峰，这种文化高峰带来了顿金甜甜圈和肯德基。马克载我们飞速掠过城市的西部，拐出公路，穿过一块菠萝地。地里有一台闲置的机械输送机，机上的金属吊杆刷着绿漆。

矮矮的、尖尖的菠萝树丛一直延伸到皮科波尼多国家公园的边缘。414 平方英里的山脉和丛林环绕着皮科波尼多峰，那座我们在海上就已经看见的山峰。进入丛林，就像步入了一个巨大的宫殿，一个长满了木棉、红木树的宫殿，只有头顶上阳光透过树木照出的格子，星星点点照亮丛林。上面 30 或 40 码高的树上，生活着许多昆虫和动物，它们从不屑于到地面上来。林中小径逐渐陡起来了，一些看不见的生物发出簌簌的声音，在我看到它们之前，它们就已经不见了。我们遇到一个白蚁穴，马克劝我吃一只白蚁试试，我拒绝了，他告诉我，虽然我没吃，但是至少我现在知道了这种白蚁是可以吃的，在森林里迷路的时候可以用它们充饥。我们在路上还看到一个标志牌，上面写着禁止进入无路的

---

① 保罗·瑟鲁（Paul Theroux, 1941—），美国作家，在小说、游记两种文体写作中成就卓著。
② 加里富纳人是非洲、阿拉瓦克和加勒比血统、以及中美洲加勒比海岸本地人的混血儿。

林区。马克说最近有一群西班牙人进入了无路的林区,失踪了六天之后,才被救了出来。

一小时后,我们到达一条瀑布前面。羽毛般带着泡沫的白色水柱从丛林中喷薄而出,沿着长满青藤的岩石,冒着漩涡,翻腾着流入下面平静、幽深的水池,这个水池一直延伸到我们脚边。

抵达洪都拉斯后,只要出了装着空调的屋子,我就一直感觉非常炎热。那种热就像是一种物理力量施加在身上,即使傍晚的微风或者浸泡在浴场的海水中也丝毫不能缓解这种炎热。在丛林里攀爬一会后,似乎感到更热了。现在终于有机会清凉一下了,我潜入水底,感觉浑身的血都涌到了皮肤表面。

从水中出来后,等待身体晒干的时候有一群少年来到了瀑布这里,他们来自于特拉市,陪一位美国朋友进行周日徒步旅行,这位红头发的美国朋友是来自于得克萨斯州的和平队志愿者。洪都拉斯总共有192名这种和平队志愿者,数量位居全球第二(乌克兰最多),这些志愿者分布于全国各地,怀抱着一种能够给予当地帮助的使命,虽然不知道怎样帮,但是想法是好的。这位名叫乔纳森的美国志愿者即将结束他为期两年的志愿期,在这两年里,他就商业开发给特拉市市长办公室提出各种建议。"和平队已经在洪都拉斯待了40年,"他告诉我们。"所以你可能会问,我们到底做了多少事情?"

也许并没有多少。但是期望留下痕迹的欲望却无法抑制。

永远的菠萝田

美国短篇小说作家欧·亨利在19世纪90年代被流放到洪都拉斯,他造了一个词用来形容这个国家。这个词总是能够很形象地让人想起殖民的恐怖、糟糕的政府、热带气候、成熟的水果和爬到楼台栏杆上面的茂密的九重葛藤蔓,以至于这个词在当时流传很广,比现在还要广。这个词就是香蕉共和国。这首诗呈现了一段完整的历史时期。20世纪的前50年,洪都拉斯的大部分地带或多或少都为美国标准水果公司(现在的都乐)和美国联合水果公司(现在的奇基塔)所管理。这些公司贿赂、收买官员,在事情失控的时候就召来美国军队帮忙。他们修建归自己所有的铁路,这些铁路往往都是从地头到港口,他们从不会将铁路修建到其它对洪都拉斯人有用的地方,例如首都。

当然,自那时以来,洪都拉斯已经取得了很大进展,或者说真的有进展了吗?我在此旅行期间,《本周洪都拉斯》头版的大标题写着"塞拉亚总统就甜瓜危机发表演讲。"照片上长着大胡子的总统坐在他的办公桌旁边,咬着一个多汁的甜瓜,一旁可以看见洪都拉斯国旗。近几十年来,大水果的形势不好,但是菠萝、香蕉和瓜类仍然是主要的出口产品。哪怕美国食品和药物管理局发布一个轻微的警告，声明来自洪都拉斯某个农场的瓜可能含有沙门氏菌，这点星星之火都足以燎原，毁掉原本就很脆弱的洪都拉斯的经济。

现在有很多人把洪都拉斯的经济希望寄托在发展旅游业上面。目前北部海岸正计划修建至少两个新的度假村，其中一个紧邻国家公园。我参观的保护区里面都有各个捐助组织的标识，包括美国国际开发署、世界自然基金会和洪都拉斯-加拿大环境管理基金，甚至还有和平队的标识。在瀑布那里遇见和平队志愿者乔纳森之后，我又遇到了另一个志愿者尼科尔，她当时正和她的父亲一起参观洪都拉斯库埃罗辐萨拉多野生动物保护区。尼科尔的驻地在南部山谷区的一个小城镇。我问她那里的经济发展怎么样，她皱起眉头，想了一下，然后说那里有很多武装警卫。她在一个妇女合作社工作，希望帮助合作社的成员找到她们能够向外国人出售的东西。她们曾经做过很漂亮的陶器，但是这些陶器不适合船运。尼科尔偶尔想到一个好主意，可以用旧的装薯片的袋子来编织颜色鲜艳的小钱包，她曾经在中美洲其它地方见过有卖这种钱包。她住的地方没有游客买这种东西，但是她想也许小镇的居民可以向经过泛美公路的旅客出售这种东西，因为公路正好穿过她们镇子附近。

旅游业明显是一个很受欢迎的项目，但是发展旅游业是否是明智的做法呢？从长远来看，向游客出售这种终将被他们破坏掉的自然魅力是否有意义？城市可以不断地增建人造景点，但是我不知道丛林和珊瑚礁是否也能这么具有持久力。

在北海岸的最后一天，我脸朝下漂在加勒比海中，清算我所犯下的"罪"。我搭乘飞机，能做公车的时候反而去搭出租车，要求房间里面有空调，甚至在发现房间里的一扇窗户无法关上的时候，我还开空调，而且买小的塑料瓶装水，这些都是在我到这里的第一天日落前发生的事情。之后，我还参加喂食野生动物的活动，乘坐汽油驱动的汽车和船只到处闲逛，还吃了海螺（吃之前我不知道它是濒危物种），而且在精致的珊瑚上空游泳的时候，我还涂了防晒霜和含有避蚊胺的驱虫剂，这一点是直到看了旅游指南的时候，才发现不应该这么做。来这里旅游，我可能会给洪都拉斯带来一点微乎其微的经济收益，但是与我所犯下的这些罪相比，不知道这个国家是不是得不偿失。

我们去了位于拉塞巴东北部的科奇诺斯群岛国家海洋公园，那里到处都是珊瑚礁。那天早晨，我浮潜到一个荒僻的珊瑚礁，看到了鹦嘴鱼、狗鱼、一群蓝色刺猬鱼，还有一条胖胖的、懒洋洋的梭鱼，它除了下巴在动，身体一动不动。我在罗丹岛之外的地方，从未见过如此生动、丰富的珊瑚礁生物种类，可能是因为那里的潜水活动和开发。

现在我漂浮在 Chachauate 岛上，这是一个只有几百英尺长的珊瑚岛，这里是一个加里富纳人村庄的所在地，村里大约有30户人家。加里富纳人是逃脱的奴隶和加勒比印第安人的后代，他们之前一直住在圣文森特岛，直到1797年，英国人把他们全部驱逐到了洪都拉斯，在这里，他们建了渔村。Chachauate 的木屋绵延在沙滩上，距离最高水位线只有几码。沙滩上散落着一些独木舟、临时帆船和舷外挂机艇。村子里的一个大新闻是最近买了1台柴油发电机，每天傍晚6点到8点工作。任何村民只要自己买电线，就可以免费用发电机发的电。在有这台发电机之前，整个村子只有一户人家用安装在屋顶上的太阳能电池板来获取电力。

一个紫色的扇柳珊瑚随着潮水摇摆。蓝绿色的大海向着3个方向延伸，到了海滩的时候慢慢呈现出苍白色。在海滩那里，木屋里有一个女子正在给我做午饭要吃的炸鸡。我慢慢地朝海边游过去，划过海草和波纹状的沙子，看到了一些小鱼和一个已经腐蚀掉的苏打水易拉罐。接着我就看到了洪都拉斯的前总统何塞·特里尼达德那长着大胡子的脸，他是在一张10伦皮拉[①]的钞票上面，这张钞票静静地躺在沙子上面。好奇心使然，我潜到水底，捡起这张钱，但是它看起来如此光滑易碎，好像要在我手中碎掉一样，所以我松开了手，它又漂回到了海底。

梅尔·吉布森[②]和文明的消亡

"别再说电影了，"古斯塔沃对丹尼斯说。

丹尼斯没理他。

"他们把心挖出来的时候都还在跳动，"她说。"他们就这样把它举起来！"说着高高的举起她苍白的手臂。

"别再说了，"我妈和我以及古斯塔沃异口同声地说。古斯塔沃是我们的导游，大腹便便，有些学者派头，他带我们参观位于科潘的玛雅古城，在公元400年和800年之间的鼎盛时期，那里曾有24,000人口。古斯塔沃拿着一根棍子，棍子的一头上装饰有鸟的羽毛，他用这个棍子来指点那些详细的考古地点，他看起来好像有点愤愤不平的样子，一副极力忍耐的样子。

---

① 洪都拉斯流通铸币。币值换算1伦皮拉=100分。币值：1、2、5、10、20、50分。辅币名称：分。

② 梅尔·吉布森，1956年1月3日出生于美国纽约，因浓重澳洲口音被当成澳洲人，父母是爱尔兰天主教徒，在纽约长大的吉布森从小就对电影产生巨大浓厚的兴趣。1968年他随家庭迁至澳大利亚居住，并且在悉尼学习专业表演技术，随后进入影坛。1995年在《勇敢的心》中为世人塑造了一个传奇般的爱国英雄——威廉·华莱士，今年他又为世人带来了另一位伟大的《爱国者》——本杰明·马丁。他棱角分明的脸庞、英俊刚毅的气质、至刚至阳的男人血性，使他完美地为世人奉献了二位用生命捍卫神圣家园的伟大的爱国者，凭着自身的实力成为好莱坞顶级的电影巨星。

古斯塔沃对梅尔·吉布森非常不满，尤其不喜欢《绝代启示录》，他说这部电影非常愚蠢。如果你没看过这部电影，那么我来说明一下，这部2006年上映的电影是关于历史修正主义的，是对历史的恐怖暴力的复述。这本没有什么值得大惊小怪，但是这部电影碰巧将剧情设定在古玛雅城。电影里有斩首、刺刑，还有由于药物而头脑混乱的祭司执行的活人祭祀。并不是说真正的玛雅人没有进行过这种活人祭祀，只是古斯塔沃无法接受这一点而已。

在科潘城的入口处，我们遇到了两位中年女士——戴安和丹尼斯，她们俩都来自于纽约市，有着浓重的布鲁克林口音。丹尼斯留着黑色短发，涂着鲜艳的口红，是吉布森的粉丝。她不停地问当年活人祭祀是在什么地方进行的，这让古斯塔沃非常惊愕，有点招架不住。

最后我们一行终于到了大广场的中央，这里以前曾是个中心区域，对所有的科潘公众开放，是个商业集散地，同时也是祭祀的地方。在广场的中央有一个小金字塔，周围散布着一些石碑，每一块都雕刻得很精致，用来纪念某位国王或者其他什么人。在我们正前方那里，有一块大的石头物体，很明显那就是用来进行活人祭祀的地方。

这块石头有个圆顶，大约4英尺宽，3英尺高，顶上有一个挖空的凹窝，大小正好可以放下一个人的头部，两边有两条凹槽，可以让血顺流而下。古斯塔沃抓住我的胳膊，让我往后躺到圆顶之上，头正好落在那个凹窝里面，如果作为祭祀品，这个姿势还有点舒服，他用他装着羽毛的棍子，做出砍我脑袋的样子。就是在这时候，丹尼斯兴奋起来，开始描述电影《绝代启示录》里的活人祭祀场景，她把手举到空中，好像真的握着一颗跳动的心脏那样。"那个祭祀的人还活着呢！"她说。

丹尼斯很不情愿的跟我们一起离开，穿过广场，到了城市的球场，那里的墙上刻着鹦鹉头的浮雕。早期的考古学家认为，玛雅的球场并不是西方意义上的那种用来进行球类游戏的场所。古斯塔沃给我们解释说"举行球类仪式并不是为了娱乐大众，而是为了取悦神灵。"人们认为由专门受过培训的青年男子按照特定规则表演的球类"游戏"是为了让太阳和月亮准时升起。

现在，虽然大部分的科潘古城仍然埋于地下，但是可以漫步于那些雕刻和金字塔中、陵墓和寺庙里、政府和房屋的门厅前，仿佛可以看见曾经的那些明亮的粉饰。但是在19世纪之前，这些都是无法见到的。大约在800到899年间的某个时间，古典的玛雅文明开始塌陷，这种塌陷如此彻底，以至于西班牙人到这里的时候，没有发现任何关于它的痕迹。古玛雅人的后裔分散于各地、存活了下来，但是那些伟大的、色彩鲜艳的城市和金字塔、庙宇一道消失了，被整个丛林吞噬掉了。玛雅纪念碑上发现的最后日期是909年，好像时间突然停止在了某一天。

考古学家们仍在争论那时到底发生了什么事情。但是很明显，环境退化一定程度上导致了城市的塌陷。尤其是在科潘山谷地区，研究显示，随着人口的增长，人们砍掉了山坡上的树木。在城市毁灭之前，水土流失已经很严重。科潘还遭受旱灾的影响，这可能在一定程度上也是由于砍伐森林引起的。玛雅人砍掉树木，种植玉米，烧石灰来获取燃材，这是他们明亮的染料的主要成分。他们为什么没有把自己拉出这种生态的深渊？假如他们能够看到树木消失，看到泥土冲下山坡。在《大崩溃：社会如何选择失败或成功》一书中，作者贾雷德·戴蒙德说那些本可找到逃出这种混乱的途径的精英们置这些问题于不顾。所以穷人就开始受苦，最后婴儿的死亡率几乎达到了50%，国王们还在不停地要求朝贡。

我们站在刻有象形文字的阶梯前，这些铭文覆盖了72级阶梯，组成了卫城的一面。这是美洲发现的最长的象形文字铭文，到目前为止还没有人完全破译它。考古学家知道，这些铭文讲述了古城科潘的历史，是由一个名叫"烟壳王"[①]的统治者在753年创建的，那时候这个城市已经开始衰退。等这个阶梯上的铭文完全破译后，也许这位"烟壳王"可以告诉我们更多关于这座注定会陷落的大城市的信息。

与此同时，洪都拉斯仍在继续砍伐森林。自1960年以来，中美洲已经失去了超过70%的森林，多数森林被砍掉是为了建养牛场、甘蔗和咖啡种植园。1990年至2005年间，洪都拉斯失去了10,567平方英里的森林，这几乎是整个马萨诸塞州的面积。但这只是另一个让人恐慌的环境统计数据而已，如果所有的坏消息放到一起，足以让你震惊到宁愿去相信能够控制行星，或者转向那些不需动脑筋的娱乐活动。

古斯塔沃开始给我们讲关于玛雅古抄本的故事，这些手稿可以帮助破译象形文字。丹尼斯突然打断他说：

"他们是在那里进行活人祭祀的吗？"

古斯塔沃叹了口气，无奈地说："是的，然后他们就让祭祀人的脑袋滚下楼梯，滚到他的儿子面前，你真是太迷梅尔·吉布森了。"

（杨建 译　申彩红 校）

[①] "烟壳王"于公元749年继位后，努力挽救政权，他同玛雅西部的大城邦帕伦克联姻，并且在科潘大兴土木，兴建了大量的纪念碑。今天的考古学家正是通过这些纪念碑，得以了解科潘的历史。

The Cabin of My Dreams

Patrick Symmes[1]

【导读】远离纷繁复杂的生活,追求生命的本真,这似乎是现代人的一个梦想,而对这种梦想孜孜不倦的追求可以追溯到美国超验主义作家梭罗。早在1845年,他就拿起斧头孤身一人跑进无人居住的瓦尔登湖畔的山林里建造小木屋并居住了两年多的时间,并将这种自给自足宁静简朴的生活记录在他的散文名作《瓦尔登湖》中。毫无疑问,《我的梦想小屋》的作者帕特里克·西麦斯也怀揣这样的梦想,在历尽十多年的渴望之后才得以在阿根廷巍峨壮丽的安第斯山麓建造他的梦想小屋。所不同的是梭罗运用了细腻而自然的文字以作家的敏感和哲人的深刻表达了对大自然的至诚的感受和感动,而帕特里克则以简洁凝练幽默风趣的笔法记述了小屋的筹划、选址、前期准备和建造,特别突出了身为美国记者的帕特里克眼中的阿根廷人的独特的价值观,从最初的愤怒不解到最后的宽容接受乃至感同身受,拉美的异域风情和文化表露无遗。阿根廷是拉美仅次于巴西的第二大国,其广袤的土地、肥沃的土壤、丰茂的草原和良好的气候赋予这块土地(阿根廷在拉丁文中意为白银)滚滚而来的财富,也赋予了阿根廷人热情快乐的性格特征,他们凡事都从容不迫,以快乐的心情享受工作和生活中的琐碎小事,这一点体现在本文中以朱利多为代表的小屋建造者的身上。帕特里克最终也意识到阿根廷人跟他一样也在逃离世事的烦扰,不同的是他选择了远在千里之外的世外桃源般的安第斯山麓小屋,而小屋建造者们则在建造小屋的过程中成功地做到了这一点。

COMEDY IS TRAGEDY plus time, and I'm telling you, not enough time has passed. Two years now and my friends automatically start cracking up when anyone says, "How's your cabin?"

I just get mad. I don't get the joke, presumably because I am the joke. All I wanted to do was stop talking about, and finally build, a cabin. Yet when you reach

---

[1] Patrick Symmes, a journalist whose work focus on Latin America.

the end of this story, I won't have driven one nail.

It's not really my fault, this boondoggle①. Real estate is more or less the male biological clock. There is some hardwired imperative that kicks in at a certain point, the way caribou migrate and birds sing. Around the start of their fifth decade, men suddenly discover gardening. They plant trees. They lay down fence lines. They construct and hold. Like a spoiled child, we say, This is mine. Mine, mine, mine.

Building a cabin in the wilderness is a nearly universal dream. Honestly, if you haven't had it at some point, there's something wrong with you. In college, I wasted hours with my buddy Tim arguing over where we would build our dream shack. Montana? Oregon? Hawaii? Years later, he came back from New Zealand, raving about how we could build it there.

Reality intrudes on such plans. Tim went into finance and worked long hours to support his five kids. I spent those years wandering everywhere without coming to roost anywhere. I never found that piece of peace and quiet I'd been imagining.

And then the clock started ticking②. In my late thirties, my only assets — a tiny Manhattan sublet and a rusting motorcycle — came to feel inadequate. The dream cabin, with its imaginary forest, grew slowly into a compulsion. Certainly, it was an inversion of the real life I was leading with a press card in my pocket, working in war zones and Third World quagmires. Whenever something went wrong, which was often, I would catch myself dreaming about the cabin again. A cozy little bolthole③. Some gentle spot where no one would point a gun at me. A "crucible of calm," as Teddy Roosevelt's place in the Badlands was called.

I started skimming from paychecks. The worse the place or the experience, the more I set aside: one thousand dollars after a nasty brush with the guerrillas in Colombia; two thousand dollars for walking into a minefield in Afghanistan; a drug gang in Brazil; teenage muggers in Havana; several Asian insurgencies. All I wanted was the basics: some running water — as in a trout stream — and a star-strewn sky. But after five years, I'd saved twenty thousand dollars, which wouldn't buy a garden shed in Montana's Paradise Valley.

I looked elsewhere, out of necessity. Oregon had been bid up by Californians; West Virginia colonized by D.C. weekenders; the Adirondacks cheap only in their

---

① boondoggle: (sl) unnecessary and wasteful work.
② 这句话原意指时钟滴答作响，这里引申为时光就一分一秒地在流逝。
③ Bolthole: a means of escape，在这里译为"庇护所"。

boggiest, northernmost reaches, five or six hours from New York City. Since anything I could afford was beyond the reach of weekend use anyway, I began to accept what my heart had been screaming all along: Go south, young man!

As in way south. Just short of my fortieth birthday, I told my wife, Beth, I was going to build us a little weekend place in…well, in the, uh, Southern Hemisphere. The deep Southern Hemisphere, actually. New Zealand, maybe. Or Argentina. Possibly Chile. She suggested medication.

I knew this was insane. My friends scoffed. My father-in-law called it "the most ridiculous thing I have ever heard."

But for me, the cabin was as necessary as it was preposterous[①]. Enormously far away, these wide-open lands, which share a lonely vigil in the deepest realms of the world's emptiest hemisphere, had long ago infused me with their clean skies, eerily pure water, and deep forests. I ruled out Chile, which had too much rain and, with apologies, too many Chileans. New Zealand seemed ideal, but a visit on my honeymoon showed me how much the *Lord of the Rings* effect had changed the country, with every millionaire priced out of Napa planting grapes in Nelson[②].

Like at all good parties, I was left with my original date: Argentina. A lovely, unstable land, it had dug hooks into me during a hitchhiking trip in 1991. With its dry flatlands and green mountains, cowboys, rambling old cars, and lack of fences, Patagonia[③] seemed at times like Wyoming in 1950. When the Argentine economy collapsed in 2002, the prices also retreated by a few decades. Though far away (two flights, totaling fourteen hours, plus a drive), it was still a lot closer than New Zealand, and the time zone—two hours ahead of EST — was close, close enough to stay in touch by telephone and come and go without jet lag. Despite an old-fashioned attachment to crime and the occasional run of five presidents in two weeks, Argentina had infrastructure, people, and wines that were all decent and getting better.

---

① 这里"as…as"结构译为"既……又……"。

② Napa is a city of western California north of Oakland. It is a center of the Napa Valley, a mountainous region that is famous for its vineyards. Nelson is the second oldest city in New Zealand, named after the Admiral Horatio Nelson who defeated both the French and Spanish fleets at the Battle of Trafalgar in 1805.这里指《指环王》的风靡给这里带来的巨大的广告效应。

③ Patagonia is a region located at the southern end of South America, territory shared by Argentina and Chile.

I was looking at northern Patagonia, a far gentler land than Tierra del Fuego①, some seven hundred miles to the south. I wasn't alone in this interest: everything from Bariloche②, an alpine gateway to the forests and parks of the region, south to Esquel③ was enjoying a real estate boom. My predecessors were Ted Turner④, Sylvester Stallone⑤, and Sharon Stone⑥. The Benetton⑦ family owned a huge spread outside of Esquel. The flag bearers in this foreign invasion, conservationists Kris and Douglas Tompkins⑧, now have some two million acres in Argentina and Chile.

Big names created big expectations. "I have the perfect place for you," one broker told me over a crackling connection: "fifteen thousand acres, fourteen buildings, and five hundred head of cattle already on the land." It was "priced to move" at seven million dollars. I couldn't bear to tell him I'd be happy with half an acre.

In the end, I made the search the old-fashioned way, mano a mano⑨. I flew to Bariloche with Beth, and we worked our way southward in a rental car, poking up gravel roads in the mountains, following tips from hitchhikers or small signs that read LOT FOR SALE. Near the town of El Bolsón⑩, we saw a fifty-acre place — too big for us but considered puny in Patagonia—while another lot, near the sensitive border with Chile, was forbidden to foreigners. Price depended on

---

① an archipelago off the southernmost tip of the South American mainland.

② a city in the province of Río Negro, Argentina, situated in the foothills of the Andes on the southern shores of Nahuel Huapi Lake and is surrounded by the Nahuel Huapi National Park.

③ a town in the northwest of the province of Chubut, in the Argentine Patagonia.

④ an American media mogul and philanthropist, the founder of the cable news network CNN—the first dedicated 24-hour cable news channel.

⑤ an American actor, filmmaker, screenwriter, film director and occasional painter, who is known for his machismo and Hollywood action roles. 史泰龙。

⑥ an American actress, film producer, and former fashion model, who achieved international recognition for her role in the erotic thriller Basic Instinct 莎朗·斯通。

⑦ The Benetton family founded Benetton Group, a global luxury fashion brand, based in Treviso, Italy, which has a network of around 6,000 stores in 120 countries and generate a total turnover of over 2 billion euro.

⑧ Douglas Tompkins, an American environmentalist, prominent landowner, conservationist and a former businessman, co-founded and ran two clothing companies: the outdoor clothing company The North Face; and with his then-wife Susie, the ESPRIT clothing company. Later the couple dedicated themselves to environmental activism and land conservation, having conserved over 2 million acres of wilderness in Chile and Argentina.

⑨ Mano a mano is used originally for bullfights where two matadors alternate competing for the admiration of the audience. Here it means "one on one" or "a single combat".

⑩ a town situated in the southwest of Río Negro Province, Argentina.

amenities. A hundred acres in the dry, windswept flatlands where the Benettons grazed sheep came cheap. But two acres on a trout-packed river, lined with willows, in a perfect green valley near Cholila were offered up at a price that made even the toothless old cowboy saying it giggle. May Ted Turner find and bless him.

Finally, we ran out of pavement in Trevelín[①], a kind of Argentine Bozeman[②] near Los Alerces National Park[③]. We sat beside a gray-haired Argentine couple at dinner. At the mention of the word *cabin*, they looked up.

"We have more land than we can farm," the woman said. Successful in the fruit and alfalfa business, they had picked up neighboring plots cheap over the years. With prices for land and everything else rising, they were looking to raise some cash. "Come have a look tomorrow," the husband said.

We drove two miles up a dirt road, into the foothills of the Andes, and walked the parcel. It was on a mild slope overlooking a valley, thickly forested with young ponderosa and Oregon pines, with deep grass in the clearings, a few apple trees, and a flock of colorful Patagonian parakeets bursting through the trees. It was miles from electricity. The only water was a rivulet, fouled by cows. At ten acres, it was twice the size I wanted, and at forty thousand dollars, it was twice what I had in the bank.

My wife is tolerant, in a long-range way. The plan was absurd, she reminded me. But Beth knew there was something deeper than the rational at work in me. She loved the view over the valley. And the Argentines were fun, she agreed: "The joie de vivre[④] you only get in a place that survived military dictatorship."

"Just buy it," she finally said, shaking her head.

Easier said than done, alas. I had only half the money I needed. I called up Tim, my old colleague in cabin dreams. New Zealand was now in Patagonia, I told him. Before I could even spit out a plan to go fifty-fifty, he blurted out "Yes." As long as there was room to store his kayak, he didn't care about design—and became my silent partner when matching funds arrived a week later.

The actual purchase was held up nine months by paperwork, bilingual

---

① a town in the Patagonian Argentine province of Chubut.

② Bozeman is a city located in the heart of southwestern Montana's Rocky Mountains, just 90 miles north of Yellowstone National Park, just as Trevelín in Argentina is situated near Los Alerces National Park. 这里把具有相似地理位置的阿根廷的特雷弗林和美国的波兹曼做了类比，使美国读者更了解特雷弗林的情况。

③ a national park in Chubut Province, Argentina, best known for the alerce trees.

④ French, literally joy of living.

wrangling, and lost wire transfers. All of which was merely prologue. Eventually, when I was high in the mountains of Lebanon, interviewing a warlord, the fax in my old Ottoman hotel ground out the news that a small piece of quiet was mine.

You can buy books on the tribulations and techniques of building a cabin, the benefits of feng shui, and the sublime pleasures of Norwegian framing techniques. I checked one on basic framing out of the New York Public Library, bought some graph paper, and headed south.

This kind of overconfidence is occasionally useful. Since I had helped build a house once before—sort of, partly, briefly, a long time ago—I figured I was qualified. In Argentina, I hired a local carpenter named Flaco ("Skinny"), who outlined glorious plans and then quit a few weeks before the start; he'd met a woman in Chile and simultaneously discovered I wasn't Ted Turner. His replacement was a disturbingly young carpenter called Julito ("Little Julio[①]"). He'd never actually built a house before, but Julito looked over my amateurish sketches for a five-hundred-square-foot one-room cabin with a shed roof. "Fast and easy to build," he assured me. He told me that it could be framed up in 30 days of hard work. He promised to bring the tools, the expertise, and extra hands. We shook on it.

I'd be bringing my own "toolbox[②]" to the site—a band of volunteers who'd cleared two weeks of vacation and paid their own way to Patagonia for some romantic labor. Along with my wife came her twin sister, Amy, who'd built refugee camps for Doctors Without Borders[③]. Even better, her husband, Simon, was a civil engineer and former house builder. My side of the aisle contained more enthusiasts than engineers: my sister, Deebie, and a friend from Buenos Aires[④], Colin. These were the people I cruelly (and secretly) referred to as Team Sawyer[⑤], since they would paint my picket fence for me. Meanwhile I expected to engage in more executive-level pursuits, like Tom himself — supervising, translating, doodling on graph paper. There was no architect, of course, or even a genuine blueprint. We

---

① Skinny 和 Little Julio 是对作者所雇佣的阿根廷木匠的幽默的称呼。

② 这里 "toolbox" 是作者对自己即将同往阿根廷帮助建造小屋亲戚朋友的幽默的说法。

③ Doctors Without Borders/Médecins Sans Frontières (MSF) is an international medical humanitarian organization working in nearly 70 countries to assist people whose survival is threatened by violence, neglect, or catastrophe.

④ the capital and largest city of Argentina, and the second-largest metropolitan area in South America.

⑤ Here Team Sawyer is humorously named after Tom Sawyer, the leading character of Mark Twain's masterpiece *The Adventures of Tom Sawyer*, which conveys the author's witty and humorous style of writing.

would buy everything locally and use what architects call "vernacular" methods. I called it Taoist nonplanning and actually thought it would work.

Three Argentines, all named Charley[①], agreed to give me advice, if not labor. The first was the owner of Casa Verde ("Green House"), a local hostel where Team Sawyer and I would all be sleeping, so I called him Green Charley. Then there was the farmer who'd sold me the lot; he was Welsh Charley, after his heritage. Gaucho Charley was a sinewy little cowboy in his sixties who ran cattle on the hillside and had the hard-won insights gained by actually living there.

I had spent ten years dreaming, three years shopping for land, and now almost two years arranging the construction, which I planned to spend thirty days supervising. Months before the planned January 2007 start, I flew down for ten days to line up a sawmill, open accounts at hardware stores, and coordinate a tight schedule of just-in-time deliveries. Julito vowed to have the site prepped and the foundation built before I returned with Team Sawyer in January, the height of Patagonian summer. We would go straight to the barn-raising scene in *Witness* where Harrison Ford[②] is clambering all over the roof beams.

Cut to reality. In January, Beth and I found the site green and lovely — and completely undisturbed. Not a single board, beam, nail, tile, or bolt had arrived, not a clod of dirt had been moved, and Julito and his crew were nowhere to be found — and wouldn't show up until a week later. Team Sawyer drifted in over the next few days. At sunset every night, we marveled at Trevelín's view of the Andes and toasted the coming endeavor. Mornings, we stood around the grassy clearing scuffing our heels. Right away an argument broke out over where to put the hot tub.

Who said anything about a hot tub? But building, I soon realized, is about ambition. Flee to the simple life if you want. Your dreams, friends, and family will still have their say. Deebie insisted on relocating the cabin to the highest point, for the view. Beth argued for a lower point, where a large meadow could accommodate the family house she imagined. ("One room?" she whispered accusingly. "What

---

① 作者对三位 Charley 的命名再次凸显了他的幽默文风。第一位是 Casa Verde（西班牙语，意为绿房子）的主人，因此叫绿色查利；第二位因其血统是被称为韦尔士·查利；第三位则因他是一位牛仔而命名为加乌乔牧人查利。

② Henry Ford is an American film actor and producer, famous for his performances as Han Solo in the original Star Wars trilogy. He once starred the 1985 thriller movie Witness，in which he had clambered over the roof beams in a barn-raising scene.这里作者幽默地表达了他和索亚团队对小屋很快就能建好的强烈愿望，然而现实总是与期望背离。

were you thinking?") Amy and Simon urged me to add a second story so I wouldn't have to expand later.

I gave speeches on Thoreauvian[①] self-sufficiency, which were ignored, and then conceded several points. We would build where we were, in the small upper clearing, but expand the floor plan to 850 square feet, making space for a separate bedroom, a larger deck, and other bourgeois sellouts. Each change meant more graph-paper calculations, more wood, more delays, more costs, and more hours of carpentry.

My dream was entering the spiral of geometric expansion, and the design suggestions came pouring in. Amy came back from a rafting detour in Chile and said, hopefully, "I saw these nice railings at the camp there, made from stripped and seasoned saplings."

"Recycled barn doors," my wife suggested.

"Mapuche[②] carvings would look nice," Colin offered.

Walls stuffed with hay bales? Why not a $1,300 propane refrigerator shipped down from California? Green Charley visited the site one morning and waved his hands in the air as he described a passive water heater made from black hoses and old wine bottles, although he admitted he'd never actually seen such a thing. Julito suggested energy-efficient sawdust insulation, until I pointed out that in a forest fire the cabin would go up like a Roman candle. Hadn't I heard about the new double-paned, helium-filled, nano-coated, electricity-generating windows my sister knew about? "You could make a windmill," Amy offered; she'd seen a Peace Corps design on the Internet. I swatted down as many of these ideas as I could, but Team Sawyer continued to fight a quiet insurgency, and one morning I found the stakes for the outhouse moved to a new location.

Necessity is the mother of compromise. A wind turbine was impractical, water power absurd, but in the bright Andean summer months of December through February, I often had twelve hours of sunshine on site. In Afghanistan a few years ago, I'd seen the Special Forces carrying solar panels that folded up like a map. I'd brought one, which charged my cell phone in forty-five minutes (I could get a weak signal on the highest bump of my land) and my laptop in an afternoon. Green

---

① Henry David Thoreau (July 12, 1817 – May 6, 1862) was an American author, poet, philosopher, and leading transcendentalist. He is best known for his book Walden, a reflection upon simple living in natural surroundings.

② a group of indigenous inhabitants of south-central Chile and southwestern Argentina.

Charley lent me a car battery, Julito wired up some twelve-volt light bulbs, and suddenly we had illumination. Propane tanks would run a standard kitchen range and even a hot-water tank. For less than a thousand dollars, I soon owned all modern conveniences, though I still had no cabin to put them in.

Water was the issue that made my wife groan in frustration. A Californian, Beth expected to die of thirst on the hillside, given that the trickling stream seemed to be 50 percent cow urine. On an almost daily basis, I scrounged in the supply shops of local towns, until I came up with 420 meters of black hose to bear the water from the stream's source, a spring buried in a cleft of the hill above my land, to the cabin. After twelve days of constant promises, none of the wood for the cabin had yet arrived, so the appearance of a delivery truck carrying the hose, on the day scheduled, was such a shock that everyone pulled out their cameras.

We rolled the coiled hose uphill, to the spring. Julito built an improvised filter, and we jammed the hose into a point where no cow could reach; pure, icy spring water now gushed through the hose at one liter per second. Back home, we'd have run a Ditch Witch down to the cabin, digging a trench to bury the hose. Here, Gaucho Charley turned up at dawn with a pair of bellowing oxen, which dragged an ancient iron plow up the hill and back down, drooling.

Meanwhile, Julito's camp was getting nicer and nicer. He and his three assistants had built an outdoor shower, a barbecue pit, and a huge earthen larder filled with sausages, noodles, and wine. They dammed a bend in my little stream with logs, making a plunge pool for the ninety-degree afternoons.

The only things missing were beams, boards, nails, brackets, and a roof.

There was work, actually. We cleared the ground, felling a single Oregon pine to free up space for the theoretical cabin. We leveled hillocks and pruned branches to create an entry for the lumber truck, which was due any minute. We designed a tower for the water tank and then abandoned the idea. We argued over different spots for the cabin. We feuded over how to build a gate, and then built it, but Gaucho Charley was so appalled by the result that he remade the whole thing with a pair of pliers. I made a courtesy call on the crusty old cowboy, to thank him, but instead of hot tea he offered a cold shoulder. I wanted a buddy; he wanted a patron.

Temperatures, and tempers, were rising①. Team Sawyer was burning vacation time with nothing to show for it but a blank meadow. Delays, disagreements, and confusion ruled the site; my hardware-store accounts sat unused. Julito would drive into town and return hours later beaming with confidence: "*Ciao, problema*②*!*" he'd call out. Whatever the problem was, he'd fixed it, solved it, or arranged it. The foundation materials were definitely coming tomorrow. The framing lumber would arrive on Friday, for sure. We'd start building any minute.

Guido at the sawmill failed to deliver boards on yet another deadline. Julito's own support beams, supposedly ready weeks ago, disappeared. The hardware stores promised me everything and delivered nothing. Julito threw his hands up. Guido at the sawmill threw his hands up. "This is the reality of a subdeveloped country," he said fatalistically, pouring me another shot of bitter tea. Julito tried yelling at him and also pleading and begging. This produced no boards.

But Argentines know how to take a break. With summer light running from 6 A.M. to 10 P.M., it was possible to get two days of work out of one. We'd start early, at least by Argentine standards, and call it quits at two, before rousing ourselves at four or five for another three hours of work on the outhouse, or the fencing, anything but the nonexistent cabin. In the sunstruck heat of those early afternoons, I'd retreat to a hammock I'd strung between two ponderosas. Here, I'd engage in Big Picture Thinking, with a cowboy hat over my face. The boys would spend the siesta eating, drinking red wine, gossiping, sleeping hard, debating soccer, or bird watching. With a series of squawks and whistles, Julito could summon the Patagonian parakeets, which perched in the very top branches of the pines, aloof.

My father could make such birdcalls, and I'd lie in the hammock recalling the way he'd taken us one summer from Virginia to New Hampshire to build his dream cabin in the woods. I was 16. A couple of months of building walls, laying floors, putting up paneling, and then wiring and plumbing had given us a ski house. It also gave me a bad case of resentment. I thought him a fool for wanting a cabin so far away that we would use it only once a year, at most.

So this splendid idiocy was a family tradition, which I could now repeat board for board.

---

① 这里 temperatures 和 tempers 读起来颇有一种语言的韵律在里面，两者的谓语相同都用了 were rising，翻译时需要分译，译为温度在升高，怒火在激增。

② Italian, with the meaning of "bye bye, problem".

It is important to have some failures in life, so this one was working out great. And as everything unraveled, my wife never once said, "I told you so," God bless her.

By aiming my hammer at a hillside in one of the most remote regions on earth, I'd simplified my tasks in some ways — no building codes! no disapproving neighbors! — but complicated almost everything else. This was no *A Year in Provence*①, in which Peter Mayle drank his way to the keyboard every day, lifting no tool heavier than a corkscrew while contractors rebuilt his house around him. Mayle, for all his famous quibbling with French stonemasons, admitted that he'd never been happier. My mood was blacker than a coal mine, preoccupied by the missing lumber, money problems, and the growing frustration of friends and family, who, two weeks in, somehow stayed sweaty and dirty yet never got to build the cabin they'd been promised. The wheels were coming off, our weeks in Patagonia expiring as a busted play.

Mayle's architect compared building to trench warfare, with long periods of boredom interrupted by sudden fits of violence. The Latin sense of time, he said, was elastic. A "quarter of an hour" really meant "today." "Tomorrow" meant "this week." Any estimate of time preceded by the word *normally*, or followed by a hand gesture that involved fluttering the palm, was real trouble. Julito spoke this language. On at least half of the thirty days I was to spend on the hillside, he promised me something that turned out not to be true — the wood was coming today or being cut to the right lengths today or delivered to the sawmill today or chopped down today. The roofing materials were coming. The telephone poles for the foundation were coming. The cement or gravel or tools or provisions were coming. Tomorrow. Definitely. *Ciao, problema.*

In America, these same delays were completely normal, according to Simon, the engineer. Builders divided all delays into three categories. First was "mobilization," which covered everyone showing up late or a lack of supplies. "Contingencies" meant any setback or unexpected development, like snow. And then there was "mañana②," meaning any day in the future.

The mañanas and contingencies mounted. The sawmill truck broke down. The

---

① a 1989 bestselling autobiographical novel by the British author Peter Mayle about his first year in Provence, and the local events and customs, which has started a fashion of pursuing a kind of tranquil, casual but quality life.

② Spanish, some other day.

guy who was going to fix the sawmill truck ("Monday!") had a breakdown himself, and two Mondays later it still hadn't been fixed. (Indeed, the sawmill truck was never fixed and, to this day, sits rusting in the lumberyard.) Wire transfers from America wandered off, lost in various Patagonian banks. Every male in Argentina fell in love with my sister-in-law, Amy, and if I looked away for a moment I'd turn back to find the three assistant carpenters offering her advice in a rustic mixture of Spanish, Italian, English, and hand gestures. She meanwhile dug a giant latrine, lined it with bricks, then reinforced it with concrete. It was more like a bomb shelter than a crapper, surpassed National Park Service requirements, and could serve three thousand Boy Scouts[1].

At the height of summer, it snowed. It was only a light dusting before dawn, and melted quickly, but my carpenters declared the road to be endangered, descended to town, and didn't return for days. I stalked around, fuming and bitter, practicing my tirades in Spanish. I didn't fire them, only because hiring someone else would put me a year behind schedule.

Only while peering into the carpenters' larder of sausages and noodles, their tent packed with cheese and Cruz de Malta[2] mate tea, did I finally appreciate their utter lack of urgency. I'd never understood why they'd set up a tent camp when their homes, with hot showers, were just half an hour away. Only after studying the careful construction of their fire pit — a two-day job — did I realize their true agenda: They were on vacation.

I wasn't paying them by the day, the week, or the month. They were paid the same amount whether they finished the job in three weeks or three years. From the Argentine point of view, this was not an incentive to hurry but an opportunity to linger — employment was essentially guaranteed for as long as they stayed on the hillside. Why not enjoy it? They would rhapsodize about the stars at night, the red sunsets, the jagged peaks of the Andes. They were, I realized with a shudder, hiding. Hiding from wives, girlfriends, bills, obligations. In that sense, they were like me; the cabin had become their refuge, too. They weren't building a house in the woods; they were on a camping trip that happened to involve a little digging.

Everything I loved about Argentina — the willingness to linger over a meal, the

---

[1] Here the author uses an exaggerating and humorous way to describe the hugeness of the latrine.
[2] Cruz de Malta is Argentina's famous mate tea brand. Mate tea is typical of Argentine's tea drinks.

care brought to a cup of coffee, the enthusiasm for new ventures — was doubling back to haunt me. These men were talented, skilled, and hardworking when they needed to be, and happy, even when they needed to be unhappy. The cabin existed only in an idealized, future condition; the best had become the enemy of the good[①].

After filling another page of graph paper with scratch calculations of my mounting bills, I moved out of the Green House and pitched my tent next to Julito's camp. One member of Team Sawyer blew up and walked off the job. Two marriages went rocky for a few minutes. I was denying reality, becoming irrational, yelling at the locals. Family dysfunction, broken promises, missed deadlines — all darkened the mood.

"You could write an article about this cabin for *Psychology Today*," Julito volunteered at one point. That same night, Oscar, the cheeriest of the assistants, openly compared our doomed encampment to "*El Projecto Blair Witch*.[②]"

Time ran out, and we began a set of runs to the airport. Day by day, Team Sawyer broke up. They departed smiling, rapt by the Andes and, from the safety of the departure lounge, amused by the fiasco back on the hillside. There was not one board in place. Not even a foundation.

It took Mark Twain only a few pages to tell the story of Tom Sawyer's picket fence and the crew that assembled to paint it. I had interpreted that tale as a challenge, an invitation to let others build my house for me. Now, at the end of my designated thirty days, I looked at the barren hillside and saw I had been not Tom but one of his victims. I bought a bottle of *vino tinto*[③] that day and, near midnight, drove back to my tent on the hillside, where the carpenters were snoring away; forty-eight hours later I was back in the U.S.

Twain would say that in attempting you get things done, that small failures do eventually add up to something. So here's the bottom line: I did get my cabin built, sort of. Just not by me or by Team Sawyer. In the end, long after I'd gone home and dried out my soul, boards from the sawmill began trickling up the hillside. The boys spent the entire summer up there and, gradually, at their own happy pace, built the

---

① This sentence means that to attain a perfect thing, whatever it is, will become infinitely more difficult as you near it.

② a 1999 American psychological horror film titled The Blair Witch Project.

③ famous wine originally produced in Argentina.

floor, the walls, and the roof. Like every other yuppie[①], I paid someone else to take my splinters for me.

They did a shockingly good job, though. A year after the monthlong folly, I rolled up the hill again and found the trees swaying in the breeze just as I remembered, the parakeets still flitting overhead, and a beautiful cabin, standing by itself, utterly quiet. It is filled with Julito's skilled detailing and Oscar's thoughtful little adaptations of my design. The modern conveniences worked out better than expected — there's even a flush toilet leading to Amy's massive septic bunker. The price got a little out of hand, but not by too much. I don't have any furniture yet, so I ate and slept on the floor. I didn't drive a single nail, but it still felt like my refuge, the place where absolutely nothing could go wrong. Peace, at last!

There was, of course, a huge forest fire raging right then, and it barely missed my land. And a couple of months after I left, a volcano over in Chile blew up, scattering a rain of hot ash on the little building. But other than that, it all worked out perfectly.

---

① Short for "young urban professional", a term that refers to a member of the upper middle class or upper class in their 20s or 30s. It first came into use in the early-1980s and largely faded from American popular culture in the late-1980s, due to the 1987 stock market crash and the early 1990s recession.

我的梦想小屋

帕特里克·西麦斯[①]

喜剧是悲剧加时间。我告诉你们，时间过去的还不够久。到现在有两年了，每当有人问起"你的小屋怎么样了？"时，我的朋友们就会自然而然地开起玩笑来。

我只会生气，我不觉得有什么好笑，也许因为我自己就是个笑话。我想做的是不再空谈，建成自己的小屋。然而当你读完这个故事时会发现我连一个钉子都没钉过。

想做这种无聊的事真不是我的过错。房屋差不多是男性的生物钟。某个无法改变的规则在特定的时刻会介入进来，比如北美驯鹿迁徙的方式和鸟类歌唱的方式。男人大约在50岁开始时，会突然发现园艺的价值和乐趣，他们栽种树木，建造篱笆墙，就这样不断地建造、维护，像一个被宠坏的孩子。我们说，这是我的，我的，我的，我的。

在荒野建造一个小屋几乎是大家共同的梦想。坦白说，倘若你在某个时候没有这样的梦想，那肯定有问题。大学时我和好兄弟蒂姆花费好几个小时争论要在那里建造我们的梦想小屋。蒙大拿？俄勒冈？还是夏威夷？多年后，从新西兰归来的他热切地谈论我们如何能在那儿建造小屋。

现实总是打乱这样的计划。蒂姆从事了金融业，每天工作很长时间以养活5个小孩，那些年我四处游荡，无意安顿在任何地方，我从未找到一直以来想像中的那块和平静谧之地。

然后时光就一分一秒地在流逝。我快40岁时对自己仅有的资产——一间小小的曼哈顿转租屋和一辆生锈的摩托车——感觉到不足了。梦想小屋以及想像中的树林慢慢地成为一种欲望。当然这是对我口袋里揣着记者证工作在战区和第三世界泥潭中的真实生活的逆转。每当有问题出现时，这经常发生，我就会发现自己又做起有关小木屋的梦。那是一个舒适的小庇护所，某个没人拿枪指着我的温和的地方。一个平静的考验之地，位于蛮荒之地[②]的泰迪·罗斯

[①] Patrick Symmes，帕特里克·西麦斯，美国作家、新闻记者，现居住在纽约。主要报道叛乱、环境问题、旅游和地缘政治学，为《户外》、《纽约时报》等报刊杂志撰写稿件。

[②] the Badlands，蛮荒之地，这里指北达科他的牧场，青年时代的罗斯福在第一任妻子和母亲去世后前往那里学会了骑马拳击等技能，他的个性也得到了锤炼，这为他后来的政治生涯打好了基础。

福①的住处就是这么叫的。

我开始翻看支付薪水的支票。去的地方或经历的事情越糟糕,我攒的钱就越多;在哥伦比亚与游击队员发生激烈冲突后拿到 1000 美元;走进阿富汗布雷区得到 2000 美元;巴西遭遇贩毒团伙;哈瓦那遇到青少年强盗;亚洲发生的多次暴乱。我想要的是最基本的生活:流动的水——比如有鳟鱼的溪水——和缀满星星的天空。但是 5 年后,我只攒了 2 万美元,在蒙大拿的天堂谷连 1 个花园棚都买不到。

出于需要我看了看其它地方。俄勒冈已经由加州人竞出高价;西弗吉尼亚被哥伦比亚特区②周末度假的人占据;阿迪朗达克山脉③只有潮湿的最北部地区便宜,离纽约市有五六个小时远。既然我能买的起的无论怎样都不能作为周末度假的地方,我开始听从自己一直在呼喊着的心:去南方吧,年轻人!

要去往南方。就在我 40 岁生日前夕,我告诉妻子贝思要建造一个小小的周末度假屋,在……呃,在南半球。事实上是南半球南部腹地。或许是新西兰,或者阿根廷;也许是智利。她建议我吃药。

我知道这个想法很疯狂,朋友们嘲笑我,岳父称之为"我听过的最荒谬的事情"。

但是在我看来,小屋既荒谬可笑,又必不可少。非常遥远的地方,这些完全开放的土地,都孤独地守护在处于世界上最空旷半球的最神秘的王国,很久之前我就了解到那里有着澄净的天空,极其纯净的水,和幽深的森林。我排除了智利,那里雨水太多,抱歉的是人口也太多。新西兰似乎是个理想的地方,但是我的蜜月之行向我展示了《指环王》效应在多大程度上改变了这个国家,每个百万富翁对在纳尔逊④种植的纳帕⑤葡萄定出天价。

像所有精彩的舞会一样,我和最初的约会对象留在一起:阿根廷,一片可爱动荡的土地,早在 1991 年搭便车旅行时就吸引了我。巴塔哥尼亚⑥有着干燥的平原、郁郁葱葱的山脉、牛仔和杂乱无章的老式轿车,没有边界,有时看起

---

① Teddy Roosevelt(1858-1919),泰迪·罗斯福,即狄奥多·罗斯福,美国军事家、政治家,第 26 任总统(1901-1909)。美国历史上最伟大的总统之一。

② D.C.美国的哥伦比亚特区。

③ the Adirondacks,阿迪朗达克山脉,美国纽约州东北部的山脉。面积 240 万公顷,是纽约州最高的山峰。介于圣劳伦斯河、尚普伦湖、安大略湖与莫霍克谷地之间,属广义的阿巴拉契亚山系的一部分。

④ Nelson,纳尔逊,又译"尼尔森",这是新西兰南岛北岸港的一个城市。

⑤ Napa,纳帕,美国加利福尼亚州西部一城市,位于奥克兰以北。是纳帕山谷的中心,此山区是有名的葡萄园地区。

⑥ Patagonia,巴塔哥尼亚地区,几乎包括阿根廷本土南部的所有土地,面积约 673,000 平方公里,由广阔的草原和沙漠组成,西抵安地斯山脉,北滨科罗拉多河,东临大西洋,南濒麦哲伦海峡。

来像 1950 年的怀俄明州。2002 年阿根廷经济崩溃时物价也跌回到几十年前。虽然地处偏远（两个航班，共计 14 小时，再加上一段路程的驾车），阿根廷比起新西兰还是近多了，而且时区——比东部时间早 2 个小时——很接近，可以用电话联系，来去不用担心时差问题。尽管阿根廷仍像过去一样犯罪频发，有时两周内连换 5 任总统，它还是有着相当不错且越来越好的基础设施、人和葡萄酒。

我正在探察巴塔哥尼亚北部，远比位于约 700 英里以南的火地岛[①]要温和的多。我并不是唯一对此有兴趣的人：从这个地区的森林和公园的高山入口巴里洛切[②]，南到埃斯克尔[③]的所有地方都在经历不动产的迅速发展。在我之前有特德·特纳[④]、西尔维斯特·史泰龙[⑤]和莎朗·斯通[⑥]都做出了这样的选择。贝纳通[⑦]家族在埃斯克尔外围拥有一大片土地。这次外国人入侵中的旗手、自然资源保护主义者道格拉斯·汤普金斯和妻子克里斯[⑧]现在在阿根廷和智利拥有约 200 万英亩的土地。

这些知名人士引起了过高的期望。"我这里有最适合您的地方，"一个地产经纪人通过杂音很大的电话告诉我："这块 15000 英亩的土地上已经有 14 栋建筑和 500 头牛了。"价格在 700 万美元上下。我禁不住告诉他我有半英亩大的地就很满足了。

最终我采取古老的方式单枪匹马地[⑨]去寻找合适的地方。我和贝思乘飞机到巴里洛切，驾着租来的车沿着山中的沙石路颠簸，遵从搭便车旅行者的建议

---

① Tierra del Fuego，火地岛，位于南美洲的最南端，是拉丁美洲最大的岛屿，东部属阿根廷，西部属智利。

② Bariloche，巴里洛切风景区，坐落在阿根廷西部安第斯山麓，这里依山傍水，风景秀丽，自然环境酷似欧洲的阿尔卑斯山地区，有"小瑞士"的美称。

③ Esquel，埃斯克尔，阿根廷南方丘布特省的一个城市。

④ Ted Turner，特德·特纳，全美最大的有线电视新闻网——CNN 的创办者，开创了世界上第一个全天候 24 小时滚动播送新闻的频道，也是世界上最早出现的国际电视频道。

⑤ Sylvester Stallone，西尔维斯特·史泰龙，美国演员、导演及制作人，生于美国纽约曼哈顿。父亲是意大利人，母亲是歌舞团演员。在《洛奇》和《第一滴血》电影系列中，奠定他在好莱坞武打动作巨星的地位。

⑥ Sharon Stone，莎朗·斯通，美国演员。1958 年生于宾夕法尼亚州的一个小镇。在 1992 年的法国戛纳电影节上，凭借在《本能》中的大胆演出，被人们熟知。

⑦ Benetton，贝纳通公司成立于 1965 年，最初以生产手工编织套衫为主，后陆续推出休闲服、化妆品、玩具、泳装、眼镜、手表、文具、内衣、鞋、居家用品等。主要针对大众消费者，特别是年轻人和儿童，由总设计师朱丽安娜·贝纳通（1938 年—）及 200 多名设计师共同设计、制作。

⑧ Kris and Douglas Tompkins，道格拉斯·汤普金斯和妻子克里斯，服装品牌 North Face 和 Esprit 的创始人。他们创办的一个基金会在巴塔哥尼亚拥有 200 万英亩土地，在上面建起了重要动物保护区，但允许搞一些狩猎活动。

⑨ mano a mano，西班牙语，来自斗牛语，意为"手对手地"，后指"单打独斗地"、"肉搏"等，这里译为单枪匹马地。

或写着"土地出售"的小牌子的指示一直向南行驶。在埃尔博尔松市①附近，我们看见一块50英亩的地方——对我们而言太大了，但在巴塔哥尼亚被认为微不足道——而另一块地皮靠近阿根廷和智利的敏感边界区域，不对外国人开放。价格取决于舒适度，在贝纳通家族放牧绵羊的地方，这是一片干燥风大的平原，100英亩大小的地皮非常便宜，而乔利拉②附近的绿意盎然的山谷中2英亩的土地，临着满是鳟鱼的小河，两岸清风拂柳，其要价足以让老掉牙的牛仔傻笑着说，"但愿特德·特纳找到这块地并保佑他"。

最后我们在特雷弗林③——这里就像阿根廷的波兹曼④，位于卢斯阿莱尔塞斯国家公园⑤附近——走完了公路。我们就餐时坐在一对头发花白的阿根廷夫妇旁边，当提到"小屋"的字眼时，他们抬起头来。

"我们有耕种不完的土地，"女人说道。他们在水果和紫花苜蓿生意上大获成功，多年来以便宜的价格购买邻近的小块土地。由于土地和其它东西价格在上涨，他们想要筹集一些现金。"明天来看看吧，"丈夫说。

我们沿着一条土路行驶了2英里，进入了安第斯山脉的山麓小丘，走过那块土地。那块地坐落在俯瞰着山谷的缓坡上，坡上覆盖着茂密如林的北美黄松幼苗和俄勒冈松树，林中空地上长着长草和几棵苹果树，一群色彩鲜艳的巴塔哥尼亚长尾小鹦鹉突然穿过树林，这里离通电的地方有几里之遥，唯一的水源是被牛群弄脏的小溪。这块地有10英亩大，两倍于我想要的土地，要价四万美元，两倍于我的银行存款。

我的妻子贝思从长远来看是宽容的。这个计划很荒谬，她提醒我，但是她知道有某种比理性更深层次的东西影响着我。她喜欢山谷上方的景色。阿根廷人很有趣，她赞同这一点："这是你能在军事独裁下幸存的地方里获得的唯一的生活乐趣⑥。"

"买吧，"她最后摇头说道。

哎呀，说得比做得容易，我仅仅有所需钱数的一半，打电话给一同拥有小屋梦想的老伙伴蒂姆，告诉他新西兰现在在巴塔哥尼亚，我还没能说出一半的计划之前，他就脱口而出"好的"。只要有地方容纳他的皮划艇，他不在乎设

---

① El Bolsón，埃尔博尔松市，位于阿根廷的内格罗河省西南部。
② Cholila，乔利拉，阿根廷地名。
③ Trevelín，特雷弗林，位于阿根廷的丘布特省。
④ Bozeman，波兹曼，落基山脉一个宁静安谧的小城镇。
⑤ Los Alerces National Park，卢斯阿莱尔塞斯国家公园，位于阿根廷丘布特省（Chubut）的西边，主要景点是它无与伦比的美丽和数百岁的落叶松。
⑥ joie de vivre，法语，人生的极大乐趣。

计——然后就成了我无声的合伙人，一周后同等数额的资金到帐。

实际购买由于书面工作、双语纠纷和遗失的电汇延续了 9 个月，所有这一切都只是开始。最终当我身处黎巴嫩的高山区域采访一位将军时，所住的古老的土耳其酒店的传真机传出消息，那一小块宁静的土地属于我了。

你可以购买有关建造小屋的困难和技术的书籍、有关风水的益处以及挪威构架技术的崇高的乐趣的书籍。我从纽约公共图书馆借了一本有关基本构架的书，买了一些图纸，就前往南方了。

这种过度的自信有时很有用。由于我以前曾经帮忙建过一座房子——类似的、部分的、短暂的、很久以前——我想我能胜任这工作。我在阿根廷雇佣了一个名为弗莱克（"极瘦的"）的当地木匠，他制定了宏伟的计划，然后在开工前几周离开了；他在智利见到一个女人，与此同时发现我竟然不是特德·特纳。代替他的是一个名叫朱利多（"小胡里奥"）的令人不安的年轻木匠，他之前从未实际建造过房子，但是他浏览完我所画的面积为 500 平方英尺的包括一个房间并带有屋顶的木屋的业余水平的草图后，就向我保证："很快很容易就能建好。"他告诉我只要 30 天的辛勤劳动就能使小屋成形，并许诺带来工具、技术和帮手。我们就此握手达成协议。

我会把自己的"工具箱"带到工地——一伙自告奋勇者利用 2 周的假期自己付钱前往巴塔哥尼亚进行富有浪漫色彩的劳动。和我妻子一起来的有她的双胞胎妹妹艾米，她曾为无国界医生组织[①]建造难民营，更好的是她带来了身为土木工程师和以前曾是房屋建造者的丈夫西蒙。我这边热心者多于工程师：我妹妹黛比以及一位来自布宜诺斯艾利斯[②]的朋友科林。我残忍地（秘密地）将这些人称为索亚团队[③]，因为他们会为我油漆尖板条栅栏。同时我期待像汤姆那样从事更多的管理活动——监督、翻译、在图纸上胡乱涂鸦。当然并没有建筑师，或者甚至一张真正的蓝图。我们会在当地购买所有的东西，运用建筑师所说的"本土"建筑方法，我把它称为道家的清静无为，并确实认为它会起作用。

3 个名叫查利的阿根廷人同意，即使不为我劳动也会给我提出建议。第一

[①] Doctors Without Borders，无国界医生组织，于 1971 年 12 月 20 日在巴黎成立，是一个由各国专业医学人员组成的国际性的志愿者组织，专门从事医疗援助的人道主义非政府组织，是全球最大的独立人道医疗救援组织。1999 年获得诺贝尔和平奖。

[②] Buenos Aires，布宜诺斯艾利斯，是阿根廷最大城市、首都和政治、经济、文化中心，素有"南美巴黎"的美誉。

[③] Team Sawyer，索亚团队，这里仿照马克·吐温的《汤姆·索亚历险记》中 Tom Sawyer 名字而来，透露出作者的幽默。

个是我和索亚团队居住的当地旅馆绿房子①（"Green House"）的老板，因此我称他为绿色查利。然后是卖给我这块土地的农民；他是韦尔士·查利②，以他的血统命名。加乌乔牧人查利③则是一位60多岁身体强壮个子矮小的牛仔，他在山坡上放牛而且长期居住在那里使他获得来之不易的眼光。

我花了10年时间做梦，3年买地，现在又花了近2年时间安排建房，并计划花30天监工。在原计划2007年1月开工前数月我飞到南方待了10天，联系锯木厂，在五金工具店开通账户，和准时递送业务协调紧凑的日程表。朱利多许诺会在我和索亚团队在巴塔哥尼亚的盛夏时节1月份返回之前准备好工地，打好地基。我们会直接见证类似哈里森·福特④在《目击者》⑤中爬上屋顶的大梁建造房屋的场景。

画面切换到现实。一月我和贝思来到工地发现那里郁郁葱葱、非常可爱——而且毫无动静。一块木板，一根大梁，一个钉子，一片瓦，一个插销都没到货，连一块土都未曾动过，朱利多和他的团队不见踪影——直到一周后才出现。索亚团队在接下来的几天里闲逛。每天晚上日落时，我们看着特雷弗林的安第斯山脉的景观感到惊叹不已，并为即将到来的努力干杯庆祝。早晨我们站在绿草茵茵的空地上磨着鞋跟，立刻就掀起一场关于在哪儿建热水浴盆的争论。

谁谈论起热水澡盆的事情？但是我很快意识到建造房子事关理想抱负。倘若你愿意就逃回简单的生活。你的梦想、朋友和家庭仍然有机会发表意见。黛比坚持应该把小屋建到最高处，这样就能眺望美丽的风景。贝思争辩说应该选择较低处，这样辽阔的草地就能容纳想象中的房子。（"一个房间？"她带着谴责的口气低语，"你到底在想些什么呢？"）艾米和西蒙力劝加建第二层，这样以后就不必再扩建了。

我就被忽视的梭罗⑥式的自给自足的生活方式发表了一通演说，然后又承认有几点是合理的。我们将在所给地方的较高的小片空地上建造房子，但会把房屋面积扩大到850平方英尺，腾出空间建一个单独的卧室、一个较大的露天平台和其他中产阶级需要的设施。每个变化都意味着更多的图纸计算、更多木

---

① Casa Verde，西班牙语，意为绿房子。
② Welsh Charley，韦尔士·查利，韦尔士是英格兰姓氏，因而这里说以他的血统命名。
③ Gaucho Charley，加乌乔牧人查利，Gaucho指南美草原地区的牛仔。
④ Harrison Ford，哈里森·福特，美国男演员。曾担任《星球大战》男主角，塑造了银幕超级英雄形象。1981年，福特接演了由斯蒂文·斯皮尔伯格导演、卢卡斯担任制片的《夺宝奇兵》(Raiders of the Lost Ark)，因而名垂影史。
⑤ Witness，《目击者》，美国1985年发行的电影，由哈里森·福特主演。
⑥ Thoreauvian，梭罗（式）的。梭罗是美国作家、哲学家，代表作有著名散文集《瓦尔登湖》，反映出作家倡导自给自足的生活方式。

料、更长时间的拖延、更大的费用和更多的木工活。

我的梦想正进入几何级数扩展的螺旋形上升阶段，设计建议源源不断。艾米刚结束在智利的竹筏漂流回来，充满期望地说到："我看到那里的营地栅栏的很好看，由剥了皮的风干的树苗制成。"

"谷仓门可以回收利用，"妻子建议。

"马普切①雕刻看上去不错，"科林提出。

用干草捆填充而成的墙？为什么不用从加州海运过来价值1300美元的丙烷冰箱呢？一天早上，绿色查利来参观工地，挥动着双手描述一种由黑色胶皮管和旧酒瓶做成的被动热水器，不过他承认自己实际上从未见过这种东西。朱利多提议用节能锯末绝热材料，直到我指出森林大火中小屋会像罗马焰火筒一样被付之一炬。难道我没听说过妹妹知道的双层玻璃的、充满氩气的、具有纳米涂层的、能发电的新型窗户吗？"你可以制作风车，"艾米建议，她曾在网上见过和平部队②的设计。我尽可能地强烈反对许多这样的建议，但索亚团队继续进行着无声的叛乱，一天早上我发现户外厕所的木桩被移到了新的地方。

需要是妥协之母。风力涡轮机不太现实，水力发电有些荒谬，但是安第斯山脉从12月到2月的夏季阳光充足，经常有12小时的日照。几年前我在阿富汗看见特种部队带着折叠成地图样子的太阳能板，就带回来一个，45分钟就给手机充满了电（在我买的土地的最高处可以收到微弱的手机信号），下午给笔记本电脑充满了电。绿色查利借给我一块汽车电池，朱利多给一些12伏的灯泡接通电，顷刻间我们有了照明。丙烷气罐会支持一个标准炉灶甚至还有一个热水箱的运作。我花了不到1000美元，很快就拥有了所有现代便利设施，尽管我还没有建起小屋存放它们。

水的问题使我妻子感到挫败叹息不已。贝思来自加利福尼亚，考虑到流动的溪水有50%似乎都是牛尿，她以为在山上会干渴而死。我几乎每天都到当地镇上的供应店搜寻，直到最后找到长达420米的黑色胶皮管从小溪的源头把水运到小屋。小溪源自隐蔽在我买的土地上方山上的裂缝里的泉水。12天以来不断听到许诺，说会送来建造小屋的木料，但是连一块木头都没送到，因而当送货卡车拉着胶皮管在定好的日子到达时，所有人都感到震惊，掏出相机记录下这一时刻。

我们把盘好的胶皮管滚到山上的源泉。朱利多临时制作了过滤器，我们把

---

① Mapuche，马普切人，又名巴塔哥尼亚人（Patagonian），南美洲南部主要印第安部落之一，智利和阿根廷最大的印第安部族，操马普切语，人口约为100万人左右。

② Peace Corps，和平部队，由美国肯尼迪总统发起的将受过训练的志愿人士送到发展中国家提供技术服务。

胶皮管塞进牛够不着的地方；此刻纯净凉爽的泉水以每秒一升的速度流过胶皮管。回去后，我们会开一辆地威挖沟机到小屋，挖掘沟渠以深埋胶皮管。加乌乔牧人查利牵着一对牛于黎明时分出现在这里，牛哞哞叫着，刚把古老的铁犁拉上山又拉下来，嘴里涎着口水。

与此同时，朱利多的营地变得越来越好，他和 3 位助手建起了户外淋浴设备、烧烤炉和一个巨大的土制食品贮藏处，里面装满了香肠、面条和葡萄酒。他们用圆木在我的小溪的拐弯处围成堤坝，为华氏 90 度的炎热下午建成了一个游泳池。

唯独大梁、木板、钉子、托架和房顶仍不见踪影。

事实上我们在忙碌着。我们清空场地，砍伐一棵俄勒冈松树为理论上的小屋腾出空间。我们铲平小丘，修剪枝条，为随时可能到来的运送木材的卡车营造入口。我们设计一个塔作为水箱，然后又否决了这个想法。我们为建造小屋的不同地点而争论。我们就如何建造大门争吵了很长时间，接着建了它，但是加乌乔牧人查利被此吓坏了，用老虎钳又重做了整个门。我礼貌性地拜访了那个顽固的老牛仔表示感谢，但是他没有以热茶待我，对我很冷淡。我想要一个伙伴；他却想要一个顾客。

温度在升高，怒火在激增。索亚团队耗尽假期，除了一块空旷的草地之外一无所获。延迟、争论和混乱主宰了整个工地；我在五金店开的账户尚未动用过。朱利多驾车进城几小时后返回来，脸上露出自信的笑容："Ciao，Problema!①"他大叫着。不论是什么问题他都搞定了，解决了或安排好了。地基所需的材料明天肯定会来，构建框架的木料周五肯定到货，我们随时可以开始建屋。

锯木厂的吉多到又一个最后期限还没有送来木板。本来几周前就该到货的朱利多的支撑梁消失了。五金店许给我所有东西，但什么都没送来。朱利多绝望了。锯木厂的吉多也无可奈何。"这就是不发达国家的现实，"他听天由命地说道，这无疑又给我泼了盆冷水。朱利多朝他大声喊着，祈求并恳求着，但也造不出木板。

但是阿根廷人知道如何休息。当夏季日光从早晨 6 点持续到晚上 10 点时，一天可能当成两天来用。我们会早早起床，至少根据阿根廷标准来看是这样的，两点结束，然后 4 点或 5 点醒来再工作 3 个小时，主要是户外厕所或栅栏，除了不存在的小屋之外的任何东西。在那些烈日炎炎的午后时分，我就退避到系在两棵美国黄松间的吊床上歇息。在这里我会脸上遮着一顶牛仔帽忙着思考全

---

① Ciao，Problema，意大利用语，意思为再见了，问题。

局，男孩们会在午休时间吃些东西，喝着红酒，闲谈，难以入睡，讨论足球或观察鸟类。朱利多发出一阵咯咯声和口哨声，召唤那些远远栖息在松树梢上的巴塔哥尼亚长尾小鹦鹉。

我的父亲也能发出这样的鸟叫声，我躺在吊床上回忆着，一年夏天他把我们从弗吉尼亚带到新罕布夏州，在林中建造他的梦想小屋，那年我16岁。我们花了几个月的时间筑墙，铺地板，搭建镶板，然后通电通水，最终拥有了一座滑雪小屋，这也成为我不满的糟糕的理由。我认为父亲很傻，竟然渴望在那么远的地方建造一个小屋，我们一年中至多用一次而已。

因而这种绝妙的蠢事是家族传统，我现在在一板一板地重复着同样的事情。

在生活中经历一些失败尤为重要，因而这次失败产生了很好的结果。直到一切事情得到解决时，我妻子从未说过，"我早跟你说过会这样的。"愿上帝保佑她。

我用铁锤瞄准处于地球上最偏远的地区之一的山坡，这在一些方面简化了我的工作——没有建筑规范！没有难缠的邻居！——但使其它事情复杂化了。这不是《普罗旺斯的一年》[①]，那本书中彼得·梅尔每天喝着酒到键盘前，承造商在他周围改建房子时，他从未拿起过比螺丝锥更重的工具。尽管梅尔与法国石匠的争论广为人知，他还是承认从来没有那么快乐过。我的情绪比煤矿还要幽暗，成天想着不见踪影的木材、资金问题以及朋友家人与日俱增的挫折感，两周以来他们又累又脏却从未得以建造曾被许诺过的小屋。一切都乱套了，我们在巴塔哥尼亚度过的几周以演砸的戏剧而告终。

梅尔的建筑师把建房比作堑壕战，整个过程中长时间的无聊被突发的阵阵暴行所打断。他说拉丁民族的时间概念是极具弹性的，"一刻钟"真正指的是"今天"，而"明天"实际指的是"这周"。任何对时间的估计如果前面加了单词 normally（通常）或者后面做出挥动手掌的手势，就意味着陷入了真正的麻烦中。朱利多用的就是这种语言，我在山坡上呆的30天中至少有一半的时间里，他许下的诺言结果都未成真——今天木材会到或会被切割成适当的长度，或送到锯木厂或者被砍伐。屋顶材料即将到货，地基的电线杆就要来了，水泥或沙石，或工具，或粮食会送到。明天。确定无疑。Ciao，Problema。

据工程师西蒙看来，这些同样的延误在美国是完全正常的。建房者把所有

[①] *A Year in Provence*，《普罗旺斯的一年》，英籍知名作家彼得·梅尔的作品，曾获英国书卷奖"年度最佳旅游书"奖。该书雅致而幽默地记录了梅尔隐居乡野第一年的闲情逸趣和悠然自在，传递出一种豁然安宁的生活态度。作者彼得·梅尔曾是资深广告人。在纽约麦迪逊大街从事广告业15年后，淡出喧嚣，于1975年开始专事写作。1987年移居法国普罗旺斯，难抑对当地风情民俗的喜爱，写下《普罗旺斯的一年》，随意之举也成就经典，在全球掀起一股追求质感生活的风尚。此后笔耕不辍，创作出很多同类作品。

的延迟分为 3 类，第一种是"调动"，涉及所有人员的迟到或供应的缺乏。然后是"突发状况"，指任何挫折或者意外事件，比如下雪。最后是"改期①"，指未来中任意一天。

事件改期和其它突发状况越来越多。锯木厂的卡车出了故障，将要修卡车（"周一！"）的家伙自己也出了问题，两个周一之后卡车还没修好。（事实上，锯木厂卡车再也没有修好，而且到今天为止，仍然在废物场生着锈）。来自美国的电汇汇错了，遗失在巴塔哥尼亚的各家银行。阿根廷的所有男性都爱上了我的妻妹艾米，假如我有片刻朝别处看看，我就会返回去找那 3 个助理木匠，他们用西班牙语、意大利语、英语和手势合成的带有乡村气息的混和语给她提出建议。在此期间她挖了一个硕大的沟形厕所，里面铺好砖并用水泥加固，这更像防空洞而不像厕所，超出了国家公园服务设施的要求,可供 3000 童子军来使用。

盛夏时分下雪了，这仅仅是一场黎明前的粉尘状的小雪，很快就融化了，但是我的木匠们宣告道路危险，就下山回城，多日来没有返回。我四处走动，既愤怒又伤心，用西班牙语对此一通谴责。我没有解雇他们，仅仅因为雇佣其他人会使我的工期又推后一年。

只有当我看到木匠们存放香肠和面条的食品贮藏处以及装满乳酪和克鲁兹迪马尔塔马黛茶②的帐篷时，我才最终意识到他们缺乏紧迫感。我从不明白他们装有热水淋浴的家仅有半小时的路程却要支起露营的帐篷。只有在观察他们如何精心地建造火坑后——2 天完成的工作——我才意识到他们真正的日常工作：他们在度假。

我没有按日，按周或者按月付给他们工资，无论在 3 周或者 3 年内完成这项工作他们都得到同样的报酬。在阿根廷人看来，这不是加快进度的动力而是拖延磨蹭的机会——反正不管他们在山上滞留多长时间就业都有保障。为什么不好好享受呢？他们会痴狂于夜晚的星辰，红色的夕阳，还有安第斯山脉参差不齐的山峰。我全身一震，突然意识到他们在逃避。逃避妻子、女朋友、帐单还有义务。从那种意义上来讲他们像我；小屋也成了他们的庇护所。他们并不是在林中建造房屋；而是在进行一次碰巧需要挖挖填填的营地旅行。

我所喜爱的关于阿根廷的一切——对一餐饭的恋恋不舍，对一杯咖啡的关注，对新事物的热情——萦回在我的脑际。需要时这些人有天赋，有技能且勤劳能干，即便需要他们不快乐时他们依然很快乐。小屋仅仅以理想化的未来的

---

① Mañana，西班牙语，改期。
② Cruz de Malta mate tea，克鲁兹迪马尔塔，阿根廷著名的马黛茶品牌。马黛茶是阿根廷的一大特产。

状况而存在；要求太高反而很难取得成功①。

我在另一张图纸上写满了日益增多的帐单的粗略的计算结果，之后我搬出了绿房子在朱利多营地边支起帐篷。索亚团队的一个成员勃然大怒，扔下工作掉头走了。两桩婚姻一时之间濒于破裂。我拒绝接受现实，变得不可理喻，对着当地人大吼大叫。破裂的家庭、打破的诺言、错过的最后期限——所有这些都使我情绪低落。

"你可以为《今日心理学》写一篇有关建造这个小屋的文章，"朱利多当时提出建议。就在那个晚上，奥斯卡，木匠助手中最开心的一位，公然将我们命中注定的营地比作"《女巫布莱尔》②"。

时间耗尽了，我们纷纷前往机场。一天一天地索亚团队散伙了，他们笑着离开候机室的庇护，为安第斯山脉心醉神迷，对山上毫无进展的情况感到有趣可笑。没有一块木板到位，甚至连地基都没建好。

马克·吐温仅仅用几页就讲述汤姆·索亚的尖木桩栅栏及其聚集起来油漆栅栏的所有人员的故事。我把这个故事视为鞭策，敦促我让其他人帮我修建房子。现在原先定好的30天期限即将结束，我看着光秃秃的山坡，明白了我不是汤姆，而是他的一个牺牲品。那天我买了一瓶威豪品味葡萄酒③将近午夜时分驱车赶回山坡上的帐篷，在那里木匠们鼾声如雷；48小时后我回到了美国。

吐温说事情在尝试中做好，多次小小的失败最终会有所成就。因而这里的基本要点是：在某种程度上我的小屋确实建成了，只是不是由我或索亚团队建造的。最后，在我回到美国耗尽心神后很久，来自锯木厂的木板开始慢慢地被送上山。男孩们整个夏天都在山上度过，逐渐地以他们自己乐意的速度建造地板、墙和屋顶。像所有其他雅皮士一样，我付钱给人帮我处理了些微不足道的事情。

然而，他们的工作干得令人震惊的好。那次长达1个月的愚蠢行为后1年，我又驾车上山，发现树林正像我记忆中那样随微风摇摆，长尾小鹦鹉仍然从空中轻快掠过，一座漂亮的小屋静静地独自矗立在那里。它充满了朱利多技能高超的细致装饰以及奥斯卡对我的设计进行的精心修补。现代便利设施比预想的运行地更好——甚至装了冲水马桶通往艾米巨大无比的化粪池。花费有点失控，但并不过分。我还没有任何家具，因而吃住在地板上。我甚至连一个钉子都没有钉过，但小屋仍感觉像是我的庇护所，绝对不会出任何问题的地方，终于平静了。

---

① The best had become the enemy of the good. 要求太高反而很难取得成功。
② EL Projecto Blair Witch,《女巫布莱尔》，美国好莱坞制作的一部恐怖电影。
③ Vino tinto, 产自阿根廷的威豪品味葡萄酒。

当然那时一场森林大火正在肆虐蔓延,我的土地勉强幸免于难。我离开后几个月,远在智利的一座火山喷发,炙热的灰尘如雨点般散落在小小的木屋上,但是除此之外,小屋一切安好。

(申彩红 译　杨建 校)

第三编　极地游记

　　极地苦寒的生活涤荡着人的灵魂，雪域人生中蕴含着胆识与智慧。在极地，人类寻求精神复兴与超越之路。……

The Endless Hunt

Gretel Ehrlich[①]

【导读】格陵兰是一个充满神秘感和无穷想象力的国度，这座以白色而不是绿色为基调的名不副实的岛屿常常唤起人们无尽的遐想和向往。其炫目的极光、辽阔的苔原、闪烁的冰柱、奇特的冰山以及超乎想象的寒冷无一不是美丽的童话故事中不可或缺的元素。然而这一幅幅美妙图景下却是极其恶劣的自然环境，生活在这些区域的人们是如何存活下来的？他们有没有受到现代科技的同化？冰河时代的文化又披着怎样的神秘外纱？格蕾特尔·埃利希在其游记《狩猎无极限》中探讨了这些问题。埃利希是美国游记作家、诗人和散文家。1946年出生在加州圣巴巴拉市，1978年开始全职写作生涯，1993年自雷击康复的埃利希踏上前往中国西部和格陵兰的旅行征程，为后来的小说和散文创作积累了大量素材。她的作品经常被各大媒体引用，曾被译为法语、意大利语、德语、日语、丹麦语等多种语言。美国艺术文学院曾授予她杰出散文奖。埃利希善于将关于自然的生动细致的描写与冷漠神秘的个人叙述视角结合起来。《狩猎无极限》中埃利希以细腻生动的笔触再现了她和因纽特人一同北上狩猎的惊险而独特的经历，从而刻画了勤劳能干、乐观向上、恪守传统的因纽特人形象。文中简洁的叙事、逼真的景色描写、离奇的传说的呈现、人和动物之间矛盾情感的剖析以及字里行间蕴含的人文关怀错综复杂地交织在一起，给我们带来感官的享受和心灵的震撼。

A YOUNG INUIT[②] FRIEND asked if I had come to Greenland[③] from California by dogsled. He had never traveled any other way and didn't realize that

---

[①] an American travel writer, poet, and essayist.

[②] a group of culturally similar indigenous peoples inhabiting the Arctic regions of Alaska, Greenland, and Canada, and Siberia.

[③] Greenland is an autonomous country within the Kingdom of Denmark, located between the Arctic and Atlantic Oceans, east of the Canadian Arctic Archipelago. Greenland is, by area, the world's largest island. In 1979 Denmark granted home rule to Greenland, and in 2008 Greenland voted to transfer more power from the Danish royal government to the local Greenlandic government.

the entire world wasn't covered by ice. At age seven, he had never seen a car or a highway or been in an airplane, and he assumed the world was flat. He is part of a group of Polar Eskimos in northwest Greenland who still share in an ice-age culture that began more than four thousand years ago, when nomadic boreal① hunters began walking from Ellesmere Island② across the ice to Greenland. Many of their ancient practices — hunting with harpoons, wearing skins, and traveling by dogsled — have survived despite modernizing influences that began at the turn of the century, when the explorer Robert Peary③ gave them rifles. The Arctic cold and ice have kept these hardy and efficient people isolated even today.

I began going to Greenland in 1993 to get above tree line④. I was still recovering from being struck by lightning, which had affected my heart and made it impossible to go to altitude, where I feel most at home. In Greenland, I experienced tree line as a product of latitude, not just altitude. I had already read the ten volumes of expedition notes of Arctic explorer and national hero Knud Rasmussen⑤, and when I met the Greenlandic people, my summer idyll turned into seven years of Arctic peregrinations that may never end.

This latest journey is taking place in April; I am traveling to Qaanaaq⑥, the northernmost town in the world, where I will join two Inuit subsistence hunters — Jens Danielsen and Mikile Kristiansen, friends with whom I have been traveling since I first came to Greenland — on their spring trip up the coast to hunt seal, walrus, small birds called dovekies, and polar bear.

Despite their Danish names (Greenland, once a Danish colony, is now largely self-governing), Jens and Mikile are Eskimos, descendants of hunters who walked the Bering Land Bridge⑦ from Siberia to Alaska, across the Canadian Arctic, and,

---

① boreal: of the north.

② part of the Qikiqtaaluk Region of the Canadian territory of Nunavut, the world's tenth largest island and Canada's third largest island.

③ an American explorer who claimed to have led the first expedition, on April 6, 1909, to reach the geographic North Pole.

④ The tree line is the edge of the habitat at which trees are capable of growing. Beyond the tree line, they are unable to grow because of inappropriate environmental conditions (usually cold temperatures or lack of moisture).

⑤ a Danish polar explorer and anthropologist, who has been called the "father of Eskimology" and was the first European to cross the Northwest Passage via dog sled.

⑥ the main town in the northern part of the Qaasuitsup municipality in northwestern Greenland.

⑦ a land bridge roughly 1,000 miles (1,600km) wide (north to south) at its greatest extent, which joined present-day Alaska and eastern Siberia at various times during the Pleistocene ice ages.

finally, to Greenland, following the tracks of polar bears, the migration of caribou and birds, the breathing holes of seals, the cracks in the ice where walrus and whales were found.

Greenland is 1,500 miles long and is crowned by a 700,000-square-mile sheet of ice whose summit is 11,000 feet high. The habitable fringe of land that peeks out from this icy mass is mostly rock, to which houses are bolted[1]. No roads connect villages; transportation is by dogsled or boat, or the occasional helicopter taxi that can be summoned at a formidable price, weather permitting. The closest town to the south would lake one and a half months to reach by dogsled from Qaanaaq.

The ice came in October and now paves the entire polar north — rivers, oceans, and fjords arc all solid white. Like old skin, it is pinched, pocked, and nicked[2], pressed up into lowering hummocks and bejeweled by stranded calf ice[3] sticking up here and there like hunks of beveled glass.

The arrival of a helicopter is still an event in any Arctic village. Snow flies as we land, and families and friends press forward to greet their loved ones. Qaanaaq, a town of 650 people and 2.000 dogs in the northwestern corner of Greenland, is built on a hill facing a fjord. Down on the ice, there is always activity: Sleds are lined up, dogs are being fed or harnessed, hunters are coming home from a day's or month's journey or arc just taking off. It's said that the Polar Eskimo begins and ends life with traveling. Even at home, they are always preparing for the next journey.

Jens Danielsen comes for me in the morning. Tall and rotund, he has a deep, gentle voice and a belly laugh that can make the ice shake. He wears sweatpants and tennis shoes despite biting cold. Almost forty, he's already beginning to gray at the temples. Jens estimates that he travels more than 3,500 miles a year by dogsled while hunting for food for his family. When not on the ice, he is a politician, heading up the Avanersuaq[4] hunting council, a job that requires him to go below the Arctic Circle to Nuuk, Greenland's capital city. There, he testifies in front of Parliament in an effort to preserve the traditional lifestyle of northern hunters. So far, they've been able to restrict the use of snowmobiles (in Qaanaaq, one is owned by the hospital for emergencies), limit the number of motorized boats in the summer so as not to disrupt

---

[1] bolt: to secure as if with a bolt.
[2] pinched: withered;　pocked: covered with marks or scars;　nicked: with a shallow cut.
[3] calf ice: a small floating chunk of ice split off from the iceberg.
[4] Northern Greenland.

the hunting of narwhals using kayaks, and dictate the means by which animals are to be killed. Rifles are used to hunt seals and polar bears. Harpoons are used on narwhals and walrus.

A northern hunter's year could be said to begin when the new ice comes in late September or early October. They hunt walrus by dogsled in the fall. After the sun goes below the horizon on October 24, the dark months last until February. By moonlight, seals are hunted with nets set under the ice. Spring means bearded and ringed seals, polar bears, narwhals, rabbits, and foxes, and when the dovekie migration begins around May 10, hunters climb talus slopes and catch the birds with nets. In summer, narwhals are harpooned from kayaks.

To say that Jens, Mikile, and the other villagers are subsistence hunters is perhaps stretching the truth. A couple times a year, in late summer when it can make it through the ice, a supply boat comes and delivers goods from Denmark: wood, building supplies, paint, heating oil, and other necessities. It is also possible to buy small quantities of imported Danish foods — brought in by helicopter — at the tiny, sparsely stocked grocery store, but most villagers can't afford to live on Danish lamb and chicken, and, furthermore, prefer not to. During bouts of bad weather, no supplies come at all. These are hunters who, at the end of the twentieth century, have chosen to stay put and live by the harpoon, gun, and sled.

At the last minute, Jens's wife, Ilaitsuk, a strong, handsome woman a few years older than her husband, decides to come with us. "*Issi,*" she says, rubbing her arms. Cold. Before getting on the sled, she and I change into *annuraat ammit* — skins. We pull on *nannuk,* polar bear pants: *kapatak,* fox-skin anoraks; *kamikpak,* polar bear boots lined with *ukaleq,* arctic hare; and *aiqqatit,* sealskin mittens. Then we prepare to head north in search of animals whose meat we will live on and whose skins Jens, Mikile, and their families will wear.

Mikile has joined the hunting trip because he needs a new pair of polar bear pants. He has already packed his sled and has begun harnessing his dogs. In his mid-thirties, Mikile is small and wiry, with a gentle demeanor and face. He is traveling light and carries only one passenger, photographer Chris Anderson.

Thule-style sleds are twelve to fourteen feet long, with upturned front runners and a bed lashed onto the frame. Jens lays our duffels on a tarp, and Ilaitsuk places caribou hides on top. The load is tied down, and a rifle is shoved under the lash-rope. The Danielsens' five-year-old grandson, Merseqaq, who is going with us, lies on the skins with a big smile. The dogs, which are chained on long lines when not being used, are eager to get to work. Jens bends at the waist to untangle the trace lines — something he will do hundreds of times during our journey. As soon as the dogs feel the lines being hooked to the sled, they charge off out of sheer excitement — there is no way to stop them — and the wild ride begins.

We careen[1] down narrow paths through the village. Bystanders, children, and dogs jump out of the way. Jens leaps off as we approach the rough ice at the shoreline. Walking in front of the team, he whistles so they will follow him as Ilaitsuk steadies the sled from behind. We tip, tilt, and bump[2]. The dogs are not harnessed two by two as they are in Alaska but fan out on lines of varying lengths. This way, they can position themselves however they want, rest when they need to, or align themselves with a friend. Ilaitsuk and Jens run hard and jump on the sled. I've been holding the little boy. Soon, we bump down onto smooth ice. Jens snaps the *iparautaq* (whip) over the dogs' heads as they trot across the frozen sea.

We head west, then straight north past a long line of stranded icebergs that, in summer, when there is open water, will eventually be taken south by the Labrador current[3] from Baffin Bay[4] to Davis Strait[5], then into the North Atlantic. In winter, the icebergs are frozen in place. They stand like small cities with glinting towers, natural arches that bridge gaping portholes through which more icebergs can be seen.

Jens snaps the whip above the dogs' backs. "*Ai, ai, ai, ai.. .,*" he sings out in a high falsetto, urging them to go faster. Snow-covered ice rolls beneath us, and the coastline, a walled fortress, slides by. On a dogsled, there is no physical control — no rudder, no brakes, no reins. Only voice commands and the sound of the whip and the promise of food if the hunt is good, which is perhaps why these half-wild, halt-starved dogs obey. A dogtrot — the speed at which we move up Greenland's northwest coast — is about four miles an hour. Dog farts float by, and the sound of

---

[1] careen: rush headlong or carelessly.

[2] tip or tilt: move to a slanting position; bump: shake up and down.

[3] a cold current in the North Atlantic Ocean which flows from the Arctic Ocean south along the coast of Labrador and passes around Newfoundland, continuing south along the east coast of Nova Scotia.

[4] Located between Baffin Island and the southwest coast of Greenland, Baffin Bay is a marginal sea of the North Atlantic Ocean.

[5] a strait of the northern Atlantic Ocean between southeast Baffin Island and southwest Greenland, which separates Baffin Bay to the north from the Labrador Sea to the south, and forms part of the Northwest Passage.

panting is the one rhythm that seems to keep our minds from flying away.

Half an hour north of Qaanaaq, the snow deepens, and the dogs slow down. They are already pulling seven hundred pounds. We follow the track of a sled that is carrying a coffin. Earlier this week, a young hunter died in an accident on the ice in front of Qaanaaq where schoolchildren were playing. Now his body is being taken home to Siorapaluk[①], a subsistence hunting village of a few dozen people up the coast from here. Some say the hunter was suicidal. "There are troubles everywhere. Even here," Jens says, clasping his tiny grandson on his lap at the front of the sled. "*Harru, harru.*" (go left), he yells to the dogs. "*Atsuk, atsuk!*" *(Go* right.) When his grandson mimics the commands, Jens turns and smiles.

We stop twice to make tea. The old Primus stove[②] is lit and placed inside a wooden box to shelter the flame from the wind. Hunks of ice are chipped off an iceberg, stuffed into the pot, and melted for water. Danish cookies are passed. A whole frozen halibut, brought from home, is stuck headfirst into the snow. Mikile, Ilaitsuk, and Jens begin hacking at its side and eating chunks of "frozen sushi." The dogs roll in the snow to cool themselves, while we stand and shiver.

The closer we get to Siorapaluk, the colder it gets. Jens unties a dog, which had become lame, from the front of the sled, and throws him back into the pack. Appearances count: It wouldn't look right to arrive in a village with an injured dog. We slide around a bend, and Robertson Fjord opens up. Three glaciers lap at the frozen fjord, and the ice cap rises pale and still behind snowy mountains. Where one begins and the other ends is hard to tell. On the far, east-facing side of the fjord, the village comes into view. It has taken us eight hours to get here.

We make camp out on the ice in front of the village, pushing the two sleds together to serve as our *igliq* (sleeping platform) and raising a crude, bloodstained canvas tent over them. When I look up, something catches my eye: The funeral procession is winding up the snowy path above the houses. Six men are carrying the hunter's coffin. We hear faint singing — hymns — then the mourners gather in a knot as the wooden casket is laid down on the snow, blessed, and stored in a shed, where it will stay until the ground thaws enough for burial.

---

① a settlement in the Qaanaaq area of the Qaasuitsup municipality, in northern Greenland.

② the first pressurized-burner kerosene (paraffin) stove, was developed in 1892 by Frans Wilhelm Lindqvist, a factory mechanic in Stockholm, Sweden.

When the sun slips behind the mountains, the temperature plummets[①] to eighteen degrees below zero. All six of us crowd into the tent. Shoulder to shoulder, leg to leg, we are bodies seeking other bodies for warmth. With our feet on the ice floor, we sip tea and eat cookies and go to bed with no dinner. When we live on the ice, we eat what we hunt — in the spring, that means ringed seals, walrus, or polar bears. But we did not hunt today.

The sound of thirty dogs crooning and howling wakes me. I look across the row of bodies stuffed into sleeping bags. Jens is holding his grandson against his barrel chest. They open their eyes: two moon faces smiling at the canine chorus. There are gunshots. Mikile sticks his head out of the tent, then falls back on the *igliq,* grunting. "They shot at something but missed," he says. "At what?" I ask. "*Nanoq, immaqa*" (a polar bear, maybe), he says, smiling mischievously.

Bright sun, frigid breeze. It must be midday. We sit in silence, watching ice melt for tea water. "*Issi,*" Ilaitsuk says again. Cold. My companions speak very little English, and my Greenlandic is, well, rudimentary. Some days we talk hardly at all. Other times we pool our dictionaries and enjoy a feast of words. I try to memorize such useful phrases as "*nauk tupilaghuunnguaju,*" which means "you fool": and "*taquliktooq,*" "dark-colored dog with a white blaze over its eye." But often, I fail, which just makes for more merriment.

Today, we break camp quietly. The pace of the preparations is deceptive: It looks laid-back because Inuit hunters don't waste energy with theatrics or melodrama. Instead, they work quietly, steadily, and quickly. Before I know it, Jens is hooking the trace lines to the sled. I grab the little boy and make a flying leap as Ilaitsuk and Jens jump aboard the already fast-moving sled. Jens laughs at his grandson for not being ready, and the boy cries, which makes Jens laugh harder. This is the Eskimo way of teaching children to have a sense of humor and to pay attention and act with precision — lessons that will later preserve their lives.

Snow begins pelting us. "The weather and the hunter are not such good friends," Jens says. "If a hunter waits for good weather, well, he may starve. He may starve anyway. But if he goes out when conditions are bad, he may fall through the ice and never be seen again. That's how it is here."

Snow deepens, and the dogtrot slows to a walk. On our right, brown cliffs rise

---

① plummet: decline suddenly and steeply.

in sheer folds striped with avalanche chutes crisscrossed by the tracks of arctic hares. "*Ukaleq, ukaleq.*" Ilaitsuk cries out. Jens whistles the dogs to a stop. Ilaitsuk points excitedly. The rabbits' hides provide liners for *kamiks* (boots), and their flesh is eaten. We look: They are white against a white slope and bounce behind outcrops of boulders. No luck. On the ice, there are no seals. What will the six of us plus thirty dogs eat tonight?

As we round a bend and a rocky knob, a large bay opens up. We travel slowly across its wide mouth. Looking inward, I see a field of talcum powder, then a cliff of ice: the snout of an enormous glacier made of turquoise, light, and rock, carrying streambed debris like rooftop ornaments. My eyes move from the ice cap above to the frozen fjord below. Bands of color reveal the rhythm of ablation and accumulation for what it is: the noise and silence of lime — Arctic time — which is all light or all dark and has no hours or days. When you're on a dogsled, the twenty-four-hour day turns into something elastic, and our human habits move all the way around the clock; we find ourselves eating dinner at breakfast lime, sleeping in the all-day light, and traveling in the all-light night. What we care about is not a schedule but warmth and food and good weather as we push far north of the last village and see ahead only cold and snow and a growing hunger that makes us ache.

We change course. The going has been torturously slow. Instead of following the coastline straight north, we now veer out onto the frozen ocean; we follow a lead in the ice, looking for seals. The snow comes on harder. The cowl of a storm approaches, crossing Ellesmere Island, pulling over the hundred-mile-wide face of Humboldt glacier[①]. Wind whips the storm's dark edge; it fibrillates like a raven's wing feathers, and as it pulls over, the great dome light of inland ice goes dark.

There are breathing holes all along the crack, but no *uuttuq* — seals that have hauled themselves out on ice — which are usually common in the spring. We keep going in a westward direction, away from the historic camping sites of Neqi[②], where we will sleep tonight, and Etah[③].

All afternoon and evening, we travel in a storm. I remember a hunter once telling me about getting vertigo. "Sometimes when we are on our dogsleds and there

---

[①] the widest tidewater glacier in the Northern Hemisphere, which borders the Kane Basin in North West Greenland and is named after German naturalist Alexander von Humboldt.

[②] a settlement in northern Greenland.

[③] an abandoned settlement in northern Greenland, once serving as the starting point of the Arctic expedition.

is bad fog or snow, we feel lost. We can't tell where the sky is, where the ice. It feels like we are moving upside down." But today we aren't lost. "We can tell by wind direction," the same hunter told me. "and if we keep traveling at the same angle to the drifting snow, we're okay."

All is white. We stop for tea, pulling the two sleds close together and lashing a tarp between for a windbreak. We scrounge through our duffels for food. Chris finds a jar of peanut butter. I'm dismayed to see the words REDUCED FAT on the label. Never mind. We spread it on crackers, then drink tea and share a bittersweet chocolate bar. Bittersweet is what I am feeling right now: happy to be in Greenland among old friends but getting hungrier with each bite I take.

It's easy to see how episodes of famine have frequently swept through the Arctic, how quickly hunting can go bad, how hunger dominates. Before stores and helicopters, pan-Arctic cannibalism was common. After people ate their dogs and boiled sealskins, they ate human flesh — almost always the bodies of those who had already died. It was the key to survival, repellent as it was. Peter Freuchen, a Danish explorer who traveled with Knud Rasmussen for fourteen years, wrote of the practice: "At Pingerqaling I met a remarkable woman, Atakutaluk. I had heard of her before as being the foremost lady of Fury and Hecla Strait[①] — she was important because she had once eaten her husband and three of her children."

Freuchen went on to describe the ordeal. Atakutaluk's tribe had been traveling across Baffin Island when a warm spell hit and it became impossible to use a sled. There were no animals in the area. When they ran out of food, they ate their dogs, then the weaker people in their hunting party. When Freuchen met Atakutaluk, she said, "Look here. Pita. Don't let your face be narrow for this. I got a new husband, and I got with him three new children. They are all named for the dead ones that only served to keep me alive so they could be reborn."

We head north again, crossing back over a large piece of frozen ocean. Rabbit tracks crisscross in front of us, but we see no animals. The edge of the storm frays, letting light flood through. Snow, ice, and air glisten. Ilaitsuk and I tip our faces up to the sun. Its warmth is a blessing, and for a few moments, we close our eyes and doze.

---

① a narrow channel of water located in the Qikiqtaaluk Region of Nunavut, Canada, which connects Foxe Basin, to the east, with the Gulf of Boothia, to the west.

There's a yell. Ilaitsuk scrambles to her knees and looks around. It is Mikile far ahead of us. He's up on his knees on his fast-moving sled: "*Nanoq! Nanoq!*" he yells, pointing, and then we see: A polar bear is trotting across the head of a wide fjord.

Jens's dogs take off in that direction. Mikile has already cut two of his dogs loose, and they chase the bear. He releases two more. "*Pequoq, pequoq.*" Jens yells, urging his dogs to go faster. It is then that we see that there is a cub, struggling in deep snow to keep up. The mother stops, wheels around, and runs back. Mikile's loose dogs catch up and hold the bear at bay. Because she has a young one, she will not be killed; an abandoned cub would never survive.

Now we are between the cub and the she-bear. Repeatedly, she stops, stands, and whirls around to go back to her cub. The dogs close in: She paws, snarls, and runs again. Then something goes terribly wrong: One of the dogs spies the cub. Before we can get there, the dog is on the cub and goes for his jugular. We rush to the young bear's rescue, but the distances are so great and the going is so slow that by the time we make it, the dog is shaking the cub by his neck and has been joined by other dogs. Mikile and Jens leap off their sleds and beat the dogs away with their whip handles, but it is too late. The cub is badly hurt.

We stay with the cub while Mikile catches up with the mother. The cub is alive but weak. A large flap of skin and flesh hangs down. Even though he's dazed and unsteady, he's still feisty. He snarls and paws at us as we approach. Jens throws a soft loop around his leg and pulls him behind the sled to keep him out of the fray; then we let him rest. Maybe he will recover enough for us to send him back to his mother.

Far ahead, the mother bear starts to get away, but the loose dogs catch up and slow her progress. Near the far side of the fjord, the bear darts west, taking refuge behind a broken, stranded iceberg. Mikile cuts more dogs loose when the first ones begin to tire. The bear stands in her icy enclosure, coming out to charge the dogs as they approach. She doesn't look for her cub; she is fighting for her own life.

The sun is out, and the bear is hot. She scoops up a pawful of snow and eats it. The slab of ice against which she rests is blue and shaped in a wide V, like an open book whose sides are melting in the spring sun. The dogs surround her in a semicircle, jumping forward to snap at her, testing their own courage, but leaping back when she charges them.

Five hundred yards behind Mikile, we watch over the cub. If we get too close, he snaps. Sometimes he stands, but he's weak. He begins panting. His eyes roll back; he staggers and is dead.

Jens ties a loop around his neck, and we pull the cub like a toy behind the sled. Mikile turns as we approach. "Is the cub dead?" he asks. Jens says that he is. The decision is made: Mikile will shoot the mother. I ask if killing her is necessary — after all, she is a young bear that can have more cubs — but my Greenlandic is unintelligible. I plead for her life using English verbs and Greenlandic nouns. Jens says, "It is up to Mikile."

Mikile, whose polar bear pants are worn almost all the way through, listens, then quietly loads his rifle. We are standing close to the bear, close enough for her to attack us, but she has eyes only for the dogs. Standing on her toes, she lays her elbow on top of the berg and looks out.

Silently, I root for her: Go, go. These are the last moments of her life, and I'm watching them tick by. Does she know she is doomed? Once again I plead for her life, but I get only questioning looks from the hunters. I feel sick. Peeking over the top of the ice, the bear slumps back halfheartedly. She is tired, her cub is gone, and there is no escape.

Ilaitsuk covers Merseqaq's ears as Mikile raises his rifle. The boy is frightened. He has seen the cub die, and he doesn't want to see any more.

The bear's nose, eyes, and claws are black dots in a world of white, a world that, for her, holds no clues about human ambivalence. She gives me the same hard stare she would give a seal — after all, I'm just part of the food chain. It is the same stare Mikile gives her now, not hard from lack of feeling but from the necessity to survive. I understand how important it is for a hunter to get a polar bear. She will be the source of food, and her skin will be used for much-needed winter clothing. It is solely because of the polar bear pants and boots that we don't freeze to death. Nevertheless, I feel that I am a witness to an execution.

The bear's fur is pale yellow, and the ice wall is blue. The sun is hot. Time melts. What I know about life and death, cold and hunger, seems irrelevant. There are three gunshots. A paw goes up in agony and scratches the ice wall. She rolls on her back and is dead.

I kneel down by her. The fur is thick between her claws. There is the sound of gurgling. It's too early in the year for running water. Then I see that it is her blood pouring from the gunshot wound that killed her.

Mikile ties his dogs back in with the others. Knives are sharpened. Tea water is put on to boil. We roll up our sleeves in the late afternoon sun. Ilaitsuk glasses the ice for other animals; Merseqaq is on the snow beside the bear and puts his tiny hand on her large paw.

The bear is laid out on her back. Jens puts the tip of his knife on her umbilicus and makes an upward cut to her neck. The fine tip travels up under her chin and through her black lip as if to keep her from talking.

Soon enough she is disrobed. The skin is laid out on the snow, and, after the blood is wiped off, it is folded in quarters and laid carefully in a gunnysack on the sled. Then her body is dismembered, and the pieces are also stowed under the tarp, so when we put away our teacups and start northwest toward Neqi, she is beneath us in pieces and we are riding her, this bear that, according to Inuit legends, can hear and understand everything human beings say. We travel the rest of the day in silence.

We cross the wide mouth of the fjord and continue on to Neqi, a camp used by Inuit hunters and European explorers for hundreds of years. There is no village, only a cabin, low and wide, set at the tip of a long thumb of land sticking out from between two glaciers. The cabin looks down on the frozen Smith Sound[①]. The word *neqi* means "meat," and this was a place where meat caches were laid in for hunters and explorers on their way to the far north of Greenland or to the North Pole. We push our sleds up through the hummocks to the cabin. The meat racks are crowded with walrus flippers, dead dogs, and bits of hacked-up seals. Half sanctuary, half charnel ground.

We stand on the ice terrace in front of the cabin. Looking out at the wide expanse of frozen ocean, we salute the rarely seen sun. Its warmth drives into us, and for the first time, we relax. A hidden beer emerges from Jens's duffel bag and is passed around.

The strangled cry of a fox floats out over the frozen bay where we shot the bear. Now a band of fog rises from that place, a blindfold covering the labanotations[②] — the script of the bear's death dance: where she stopped, wheeled around, attacked,

---

[①] an uninhabited Arctic sea passage between Greenland and Canada's northernmost island, Ellesmere Island, which links Baffin Bay with Kane Basin and forms part of the Nares Strait.

[②] a system of movement notation for dance that employs various symbols to record the points of a dancer's body, the direction of a dancer's movement, the tempo, and the dynamics.

and kept running; the hieroglyphics of blood and tracks; and the hollows in the snow where the dogs rested after the chase. I'm glad I can't see.

A Primus is lit, and water is put on to boil. Then the backstrap of the polar bear — the most tender part — is thrown in the pot. It's so warm, we take off our anoraks and hats. Jens passes paper plates. "*Nanoq. Nanoq,*" he says in a low voice. "The polar bear is king. We have to eat her in a special way. We boil her like the seal, but we pay special respects to her so her soul shall not have too much difficulty getting home."

After twenty minutes, chunks of meat are doled out. They steam on our plates. "*Qujanaq,*" I say, thanking Mikile, Jens, and, most of all, the bear. The meat is tender and good, almost like buffalo.

Later, we get into our sleeping bags and lie on the *igliq*. It is still warm, and no one can sleep. Jens and Ilaitsuk hold their grandson between them as Jens begins a story: "A long time ago, when shamans still flew underwater and animals could talk, there was a woman named Anoritoq who lived on that point of land north of Etah. The name Anoritoq means 'windswept one.' This woman had no husband, and her only son was killed by a hunter out of jealousy, because the young boy had no father but was becoming a great hunter anyway. After her son died, a hunter brought the woman a polar bear cub, which she raised just like a son. The bear learned the language of the Eskimo and played with the other children. When he grew up, he hunted seals and was very successful. But she worried about him. She was afraid a hunter might kill him, because he was, after all, a bear, and his skin was needed for clothing. She tried covering him with soot to make him dark, but one day, when some of his white fur was showing, a hunter killed him. She was so sad, she stopped eating and went outside and stayed there all the time and looked at the sea. Then, she changed into a stone. Now when we go bear hunting in that area, we put a piece of seal fat on the rock and pray for a good hunt."

Morning. We follow the coast north to Pitoravik[①]. It's not a long trip. From there, we will determine our route to Etah — either up and over part of the inland ice or following the coast if there is no open water or pressure ice. A wind begins to blow as Jens and Mikile take off to investigate the trail over the glacier. They are gone several hours, and when they come back, they shake their heads. "The drifts are

---

① the Greenland's ancient relic.

too deep and the crevasses too wide, and the snow hides them," Jens says. "Down below, the ice is badly broken with open water. Too dangerous. We'll wait until morning. If the weather is good, we'll try to go over the top. If not, then we'll go to the ice edge out there, toward Canada, and hunt walrus and narwhal."

In the morning, the weather is no better. A continuous, mesmerizing snow falls. "I think the hunting will be better out there," Jens says, using our vantage point to look out over Smith Sound. Beyond, Ellesmere Island is a blue line of mountains with a ruffle of white clouds. We descend and go in a southwesterly direction toward the island of Kiatak[①].

For three or four days, we travel in weather that keeps closing down on us. When we stop to rest the dogs, Ilaitsuk, Merseqaq, and I play tag on the ice to keep warm. The child never complains. When his feet get cold, he merely points to his toes, and Ilaitsuk puts on the overboots she sewed together when we were in the cabin at Neqi. Then he sits at the front of the sled, wind-blasted and happy, echoing his grandfather's commands, snapping the long whip, already becoming a man.

Patience and strength of mind are the hunter's virtues. Also, flexibility and humor. Jens shoots at a seal and misses. Another one catches his scent and dives down into its hole. He returns to the sled, laughing at his failures, explaining to Mikile exactly what he did wrong. Later, he reverts to winter-style seal hunting called *agluhiutuq*, hunting at the *agluq* (breathing hole). But even this fails.

We continue on. "*Hikup hinaa*," Jens says. The ice edge. That's what we are now looking for. There we will find plentiful seal, walrus, and narwhal. My stomach growls, and I think of the legend of the Great Famine, when winters followed one after the other, with no spring, summer, or fall in between. Jens says that this last winter and spring have been the coldest in his memory. Ironically, colder weather in the Arctic may be a side effect of global warming. As pieces of the ice cap melt and calve into the ocean, the water temperature in parts of the far north cools, as, in turn, does the air. Maybe global warming will cancel itself out, I say. Jens doesn't understand my "Greenenglish." "Issi," he says, rubbing his arms. Cold. "Maybe we will have to eat each other like they did in the old days," he says, smiling sweetly.

For the Eskimo, solitude is a sign of sheer unhappiness. It is thought to be a perversion and absolutely undesirable. Packed tightly together on the sled, we are

---

① an abandoned small island of Greenland.

fur-wrapped, rendered motionless by cold. It's good to be pressed between human bodies. We scan the ice for animals. Shadows made by standing bits of ice look like seals.

Then we do see one, a black comma lying on the alabaster extravagance.

Jens and Mikile stop their dogs. Jens mounts his rifle on a movable blind — a small stand with a white sailcloth to hide his face. The snow is shin-deep, but the wind is right. He creeps forward, then lies down on his belly, sighting in his rifle. All thirty dogs sit at attention, with ears pricked. When they stop panting, the world goes silent. As soon as they hear the muffled crack of the gun, off they go, running toward Jens as they have been trained to do.

We stand in a semicircle around a pool of blood, backs to the wind. Quickly and quietly, Jens flenses the seal. He cuts out the liver, warm and steaming, holds it on the end of his knife, and offers it to us. This is an Inuit delicacy. Eating the steaming liver has helped to save starving hunters. In gratitude, we all have a bite. Our mouths and chins drip with blood. There is a slightly salty taste to the lukewarm meat.

Ilaitsuk folds the sealskin and lays it under the tarp alongside the polar bear skin. Jens cuts a notch through the back flipper for a handhold and drags the pink body, looking ever more diminutive, over the front of the sled. Lash lines are pulled tight, and we take off as snow swirls.

We are still traveling at 10:30 in the evening when the storm breaks. We watch the dark edge pull past, moving faster than the sled. Under clear skies, the temperature plummets to somewhere near twenty degrees below zero.

One seal for thirty dogs and six humans isn't very much meat. We stop at an iceberg and hack out slabs of ice, then make camp. As Ilaitsuk and I unload the sleds. Jens and Mikile cut up seal meat. The dogs line up in rows, avidly waiting for food. It has been two days since they've eaten fresh meat. A chunk is flung through the air, then another and another. Jens's and Mikile's aims are so perfect, every dog gets its share, and the faster they eat, the more they get.

Jens cuts up the remaining seal for our dinner. Inside the tent, we watch as lumps of meat churn in brown water. As the hut warms up. we strip down. Merseqaq's tiny red T-shirt reads: I LOVE ELEPHANTS, though he has never seen one and probably never will.

We eat in silence, using our pocketknives and fingers. A loaf of bread is passed. We each have a slice, then drink tea and share a handful of cookies. After, Ilaitsuk sets a piece of plywood in a plastic bucket and stretches the sealskin over the top edge. With her *ulu*— a curved knife with a wooden handle — she scrapes the blubber from the skin in strong, downward thrusts. When the hide is clean, she turns to her *kiliutaq* —a small, square knife used to scrape the brownish pink oil out of a fur.

Ilaitsuk lets me have a try at scraping. I'm so afraid I'll cut through and ruin the skin, I barely scratch the surface.

Later, lying in my sleeping bag, I listen to wind. Jens tells stories about the woman who adopted a bear, the hunter who married a fox, and the origin of fog. His voice goes soft, and the words drone, putting us into a sweet trance of sleep so pleasurable that I don't know if I'll ever be able to sleep again without those stories.

In the next days, we search for the ice edge, camping on the ice wherever we find ourselves at the end of the night. We travel straight west from the tip of Kiatak Island out onto the frozen ocean between Greenland and Ellesmere Island. On the way, Jens teaches his grandson voice commands and how to use the whip without touching the backs of the animals. "Will Merseqaq be a hunter, too?" I ask. Jens says, "I am teaching him what he needs to know. Then the decision will be up to him. He has to love this more than anything."

When we reach a line of icebergs, Jens and Mikile clamber to the top and glass the entire expanse of ice to the west. It feels as if we're already halfway across Smith Sound. Jens comes back shaking his head. "There is no open water," he says incredulously. "It is ice all the way to Canada." This has never happened before in any spring in memory. It is May 8.

We turn south to an area where sea currents churn at the ice. Maybe there will be an ice edge there. Down the coast at Kap Parry[①], we meet two hunters who are coming from the other direction. As usual, there is a long silence, then a casual question about open water. They shake their heads. No ice edge this way, either.

That night, I lie in my sleeping bag, squeezed tightly between Mikile and Ilaitsuk. "I feel as if we are stuck in winter," Mikile said earlier, looking frustrated. He has a big family to feed. Along with Jens, he is considered one of the best hunters in Qaanaaq, but even he can't kill enough game if spring never comes. We lie awake listening to wind.

---

① a cape of Greenland.

At midday, we climb an iceberg that is shaped like the Sydney Opera House, to see if the ice edge has appeared. Jens shakes his head no. As we climb down, Mikile yells and points: "Nanoq." Far out, a polar bear dances across the silvered horizon, blessedly too distant for us to hunt. A mirage takes him instead of a bullet, a band of mirrored light floating up from the ice floor. It takes his dancing legs and turns them into waves of spring heat still trying to make its way past the frigid tail end of winter.

Finally we head for home, traveling along the east side of Kiatak. Walls of red rock rise in amphitheaters; arctic hares race across snow-dappled turf and grass. A raven swoops by, and a fox floats its gray tail along the steep sidehill. Near the bottom of the cliff, icicles hang at odd angles from beds of rock. We pass over a floor of broken platelets that look as if they'd been held up like mirrors, then tossed down and broken, making the sled tip this way and that. Some pieces of ice are so exquisite that I ask Jens to stop so I can stare at them: a finely etched surface overlaid with another layer of ice punctured by what look like stars.

The dogs bring me back. They fight and fart and snarl and pant. One of them, Pappi, is in heat, and the Other dogs can think of nothing except getting to her. Pappi slinks behind the others, clamping her tail down and refusing to pull. Then the males fall back, too, fighting one another, and the sled eventually comes to a stop. Jens unties Pappi and fastens her behind the sled, but this doesn't work, either. She falls and is dragged and can't get up.

Finally Jens cuts Pappi loose. There's a moment of relief, as if she had been freed from a tight world of ice and cold and discipline. Ilaitsuk looks at me and smiles. Her face is strong in the late evening sun. The boy is ensconced[①] in his grandfather's lap, wearing dark glasses. We have failed to bring home much meat, but Jens shrugs it off, reminding me that worrying has no place in the Arctic. He and all those before him have survived day by day for four thousand years, and one bad hunting trip won't set him back. There is always tomorrow.

Now Pappi is running free and happy. Jens urges her to go on ahead. The snow is hard and icy, and the sled careens as the dogs give chase. Sometimes when we are airborne, flying over moguls, little Merseqaq gets on his hands and knees and squeals with delight. The cold and hunger and terrible hunting conditions are behind us now, and as we near Qaanaaq, the dogs, ever optimistic, run very fast.

---

① ensconce: settle oneself securely or comfortably.

狩猎无极限

格蕾特尔·埃利希[①]

一位来自因纽特[②]的年轻朋友曾问我是否是乘着狗拉雪橇从加利福尼亚来到格陵兰岛[③]的。他以前出远门无一例外是乘雪橇，因而没有想到这个世界上还有地方没有雪。7岁之前他从未见过汽车和高速公路，也没乘坐过飞机，认为这个世界是平的。这位朋友是生活在格陵兰岛西北部的北极爱斯基摩人。早在4000多年前，这些北部游牧狩猎者徒步从埃尔斯米尔岛[④]穿越冰川到达格陵兰岛，开启了他们延续至今的独特的冰川纪文化。尽管在世纪之交探险家罗伯特·皮瑞[⑤]赠与他们步枪从而带来现代化的影响，他们的许多古老的习俗——用鱼叉狩猎，以动物毛皮做衣，以雪橇代步——还是保留下来了。即便在今日，极地的寒冷和冰川依然使这些勇敢能干的人生活在与世隔绝中。

我于1993年开始前往格陵兰岛并到达林木线[⑥]以上的区域。那时我刚从雷击中康复，那次雷击影响到我的心脏，使我无法再轻松自如地到达高海拔的地方。在格陵兰我体验到林木线不仅仅是高海拔，而且也是高纬度的产物。我已经阅读了北极探险者和民族英雄库纳德·拉斯穆森[⑦]的10卷探险笔记。当我看到格陵兰人时，我的夏日田园之旅就变成漫长的7年北极游历。

最近的一次旅程发生在4月；我跋涉到世界上最北的城市卡纳克[⑧]，与两位以打猎为生的因纽特猎人叶恩斯·丹尼尔森和米基里·克里斯蒂安森汇合，一同沿着海岸线进行春季狩猎之旅，主要猎取海豹、海象、小海鸟和北极熊。

[①] Gretel Ehrlich，格蕾特尔·埃利希是美国著名的旅行作家，小说家和散文家。美国艺术文学院曾授予她杰出散文奖。她的作品经常被各大媒体所引用。

[②] Inuit，爱斯基摩人（Eskimo）北极地区的土著民族。自称因纽特人，分布在从西伯利亚、阿拉斯加到格陵兰的北极圈内外。

[③] Greenland 格陵兰岛，世界最大岛，面积2,166,086平方公里（836,330平方哩），在北美洲东北，北冰洋和大西洋之间。丹麦属地，1979年实现自治，2009年通过公投获得更多自治权。首府努克（Nuuk，又名戈特霍布〔Godthab〕）。

[④] Ellemere Island 埃尔斯米尔岛，世界第十大岛，加拿大北极群岛最北端岛屿，东北紧临格陵兰岛。

[⑤] Robert Peary，罗伯特·皮瑞，美国探险家（1856–1920），1909年率领探险队到达北极点。

[⑥] tree line，林木线，为生态学、环境学及地理学的一个概念，乃指分隔植物因气候、环境等因素而能否生长的界线。

[⑦] Knud Rasmussen（1879–1933），库纳德·拉斯穆森，丹麦北极探险家、人类学家，被称为"爱斯基摩之父"，是乘狗拉雪橇穿越西北行道的第一个欧洲人。

[⑧] Qaanaaq，卡纳克，格陵兰西北岸的城市。

这两位朋友从我初次来到格陵兰就一直是我的旅友。

叶恩斯和米基里两人虽然有着丹麦名字（格陵兰曾经是丹麦的殖民地，现在基本实现了自治），却是爱斯基摩人，他们是狩猎者的后代，他们的先人曾经追循着北极熊的痕迹、驯鹿和鸟类的迁徙、海豹的透气孔以及海象和鲸鱼所处的冰川缝隙，曾经徒步翻过白令陆桥[①]从西伯利亚来到阿拉斯加，再穿过加拿大北极群岛最终到达格陵兰。

格陵兰长1500英里，为最高达11,000英尺、面积700,000平方英里的冰川所覆盖。这片辽阔的冰川延伸出去了一小块可供居住的土地，主要由岩石构成，房屋均建筑在这些岩石上。村庄之间没有公路连接；交通主要靠狗拉雪橇或船，天气状况允许的情况下偶尔可以高价租乘直升机。乘坐狗拉雪橇从卡纳克到南部最近的城市要花1个半月才能到达。

10月份格陵兰就迎来了冰冻时节，这个时候冰已布满整个北极地区——河流、海洋、和峡湾都是冰雪皑皑，整个地区像苍老的皮肤一样皱皱巴巴，坑坑洼洼[②]，挤压成一座座高大的雪丘，而搁浅的小块浮冰则像一块块斜边玻璃一样插满其上[③]。

直升机的到来在北极的每个村庄都是一件众人瞩目的事情。我们降落时雪花飞溅，家人和朋友们纷纷围上来问候自己的亲人。卡纳克位于格陵兰西北角，这个拥有650口人和2000只狗的小城建在面朝峡湾的山上。小城下方的冰川上总是忙碌的：雪橇排成一排，狗儿们在被喂食或套上挽具，猎人们正结束1天或1个月的旅程归来或者正要出发。据说北极爱斯基摩人以旅行作为生命的开始和终结。即使是呆在家中，他们也总是准备着下一段旅程。

叶恩斯·丹尼尔森早晨来找我，他身材高大壮实，声音深沉而温柔，捧腹大笑时能将冰块震裂。叶恩斯不顾刺骨的严寒只穿着宽松的运动长裤和网球鞋，他快40岁了，两鬓已开始斑白，一年中大概需要乘狗拉雪橇行驶3500多英里为家人猎取食物。不在冰上时他是一个政治人物，领导北部格陵兰狩猎委员会。这个工作要求他到位于北极圈以南的格陵兰首府努克。在那里，他在国会发誓要竭力维护北部狩猎者传统的生活方式。迄今为止这些狩猎者已经能够限制雪地车的使用（卡纳克只有医院拥有一辆雪地车以处理紧急状况），在夏日限定机动船只的数量以防止它们干扰猎人乘坐海豹皮艇猎杀独角鲸的狩猎活动，他们还规定以何种方式捕杀动物：步枪用来猎杀海豹和北极熊；鱼叉则用来猎取独

---

① Bering Land Bridge，白令陆桥，位于白令海，连接现今的美国阿拉斯加西岸和俄罗斯西伯利亚东岸。

② 原文中pinched, pocked, and nicked 都有留下刻痕的意思，在这里根据苍老皮肤的比喻，译为"皱皱巴巴，坑坑洼洼"。

③ 原文中calf ice 指"小块冰"，beveled glass 意为"斜边玻璃"。

角鲸和海象。

每年 9 月末或 10 月初新的冰封期来临时就是北部猎人们开始狩猎的季节。他们在秋天乘坐狗拉雪橇猎杀海象。每年 10 月 24 日，太阳落下海平面后就开始了漫长的极夜期，一直持续到来年的 2 月。在月光的照射下，海豹们被冰下设置的渔网所捕获。春季则是猎杀髯海豹和环斑海豹、北极熊、独角鲸、北极兔以及北极狐的季节。而到了 5 月 10 日左右鸟儿迁徙时，猎人们攀上岩石的侧面张网捕捉它们，夏季里他们登上皮艇用鱼叉猎杀鲸鱼。

说叶恩斯、米基里和其他村民靠打猎维持生计也许有些言过其实。每年中有好几次，特别是晚夏时节，船可以通过冰面的时候，就会从丹麦驶来补给船。它们会带来木材、建筑材料、涂料、燃油和其它的必需品。村民们还有可能在零星分布的小型杂货铺里买到少许丹麦进口的食物——由直升机空运而来，不过他们负担不起或者说没指望靠这些丹麦羊肉和鸡肉过活，因为天气恶劣的时候根本就没有补给到来。这些就是猎人们的生活方式，他们在 20 世纪末选择停滞不前，仍然靠鱼叉、猎枪和雪橇来生活。

叶恩斯的妻子伊莱特苏克比他大几岁，健壮而美丽。她决定跟我们一起出发。"Issi,"她摩擦着手臂说。 冷。在坐上雪橇之前我们都换上了 annuraat ammit ——毛皮。我们穿上 nannuk，北极熊皮裤；kapatak，狐皮夹克；用北极兔毛 ukaleq 连接的 kamikpak，北极熊皮靴子；以及 aiqqatit，海豹皮制成的连指手套。然后我们向着北方去搜寻可以用来果腹和缝制叶恩斯、米基里及他们家人衣物所需毛皮的猎物。

米基里需要一条新的北极熊皮裤，因此也加入此次狩猎之旅。他已经整理好雪橇并且给狗套上了轭具。30 多岁的米基里身材矮小精悍，品性温和，面相温柔。他轻装上阵，只带了一名乘客，即摄影家克里斯·安德森。

富有极地风格[①]的雪橇长 12 到 14 英尺，前部的毛毯翻翘起来，床板则嵌在这个框架里。叶恩斯将粗帆布袋放置在防水布上，伊莱特苏克把驯鹿毛皮放在最上面。雪橇上的东西被紧紧绑住，步枪则被放置在鞭绳下面。和我们一同出发的丹尼尔森 5 岁的小孙子莫斯卡克躺在毛皮上，笑容满面。平时栓在长长的链绳上的猎狗们此时正急切地想要开始工作。叶恩斯弯腰解开缰绳——在我们的行程中他会做很多次的一件事。猎狗们一发现缰绳被系到雪橇上就兴奋地冲了出去——没有办法可以阻止他们——疯狂的狩猎之旅开始了。

我们沿着狭窄的小路横冲直撞地穿过村庄，旁观者、孩子们和狗都跳开让出路来。当我们驶近海岸线上崎岖不平的冰面时叶恩斯跳了下去，走在队伍前

---

① Thule-style 中 Thule 指"极北之地"，这里译为"富有极地风格的"。

面吹着口哨以便其他人能跟上他，伊莱特苏克在后面稳住雪橇，而我们在雪橇上被颠地前俯后仰，左摇右摆。猎狗不像在阿拉斯加时那样俩俩成行，而是沿长短不一的缰绳呈扇形散开，它们可以随意确定自己的位置，这样就能方便休息，或者跟同伴同步前行。伊莱特苏克和叶恩斯用力跑着跳上雪橇，我一直搂着那个小男孩。很快我们驶上了平滑的冰面，猎狗们快速地奔跑在冰冻的海面上，叶恩斯的鞭子在它们的头上"啪啪"地抽响。

我们向西驶去，接着转向正北方，驶过一长排搁浅的冰山，在夏季水流动时，这些冰山会由拉布拉多洋流①从巴芬湾②一直向南带到戴维斯海峡③，最终汇入北大西洋。冬季时这些冰山则会冻结在原地，像是拥有着银光闪闪的塔的小城市一样矗立着，形成了连接一个个敞开舷窗的天然的拱门，透过这些舷窗可以看见更多的冰山。

叶恩斯朝狗背上甩着鞭子，用假高音喊着"唉，唉，唉，唉……"催促着它们再跑快点。白雪皑皑的冰地在我们的雪橇下绵延起伏，远处的海岸线像城堡的围墙从身边轻轻掠过。雪橇上没有任何物理控制装置——没有方向舵，没有刹车，没有缰绳，只有命令和鞭子的声音。如果打猎顺利，就会有食物，这也许就是饿得半死几近疯狂的狗为什么会听从命令的原因。猎狗们漫步跑着——即我们向着格陵兰西北海岸行进的速度——大约为每小时四英里。狗的屁味不时飘过，它们的喘气声像一种节奏，似乎能防止我们走神。

向卡纳克北部行进半小时后，雪更厚了，狗也慢了下来，它们已经负载了700磅的重量。我们循着运送棺材的雪橇印迹行进。这周初，一位年轻的猎人死于一场冰上事故，地点在卡纳克前面的冰面上，那里是学校里孩子们玩耍的地方。现在他的尸体被运回了肖拉帕卢克④，从这儿沿着海岸向北可以到达一个小村庄，有几十个村民，全以打猎为生。有些人说那个猎人是自杀死的，"到处都有事，这儿也不例外。"叶恩斯说道。他坐在雪橇前部，把小孙子紧紧地搂在膝盖上，朝狗大声吼着，"Harru, harru!"（左转）。"Atsuk, atsuk!"（右转），小孙子学着发出命令，他转过身来，笑而不语。

中途我们两次停下来煮茶喝，把点燃的古老的普里默斯⑤火炉放到木盒子

---

① The Labrador Current，拉布拉多洋流，为一个在北大西洋的冰冻洋流由北冰洋南部沿着加拿大拉布拉多省（Labrador）岸边，经过纽芬兰岛，再向南流向新斯科舍。

② Baffin Bay，巴芬湾，北冰洋属海。位于北美洲东北部巴芬岛、埃尔斯米尔岛与格陵兰岛之间。

③ Davis Strait，戴维斯海峡，是巴芬岛和格陵兰岛之间的海峡，南接拉布拉多海，北连巴芬湾，南北全长约650公里，东西宽约325-450公里，平均水深2000米左右，是西北航道的一部分。

④ Siorapaluk，肖拉帕卢克，格陵兰最北部的村落。

⑤ Primus，普里默斯，专业户外炉具和汽灯的生产商。

里以防被风吹熄,从冰山上劈下大块的冰放到锅里煮化。每人都分到一些丹麦曲奇饼干,接着又把从家里带来的一整条比目鱼插在雪里。米基里、伊莱特苏克和叶恩斯劈开一边鱼肉,吃起了大块的"冰冻寿司"。狗在雪里打着滚使自己的体温冷却下来,而我们则站在一旁冻得簌簌发抖。

我们越靠近肖拉帕卢克天气越冷。叶恩斯从雪橇前部解开一只瘸脚的猎狗,让他回到大部队中间。外表确实重要:带着受伤的狗去往一个村庄看上去不大体面。我们转过弯,罗伯逊峡湾显露出来。3条冰河汇集在冰冻的海湾里,它们源自哪里又终于何处很难判断,隐没在白雪覆盖的山丘后面的冰冠依稀可见。在海湾朝东的远端,肖拉帕卢克村跃入眼帘,我们花了8个小时才到达那里。

我们在村庄前面的冰地上扎营,把两个雪橇并在一起搭起 *igliq*(睡觉的平台),并把布满血迹的粗帆布帐篷支在上面。抬头看时有个场景吸引了我的眼球:送葬队伍沿着房子上方的雪径蜿蜒行进,6个男人抬着猎人的棺材。我们听见隐约传来的歌声——赞美诗——之后哀悼者聚拢在一起,棺材被放置在雪地里接受祝福然后存放进小屋,直到冰雪融化后才能够下葬。

太阳悄悄隐入山后,气温骤然降至零下18度。我们6个人钻进帐篷,肩并肩,腿贴腿,都期冀能从他人身上汲取温暖。我们脚踏着冰地,品着茶,吃着饼干,没吃晚餐就睡觉了。在冰上生活得吃自己的猎物——在春季,这些猎物包括环斑海豹、海象或者北极熊。但是今天我们并没有狩猎。

30只狗的哼哼声和吠叫声唤醒了我。我的视线掠过蜷曲在睡袋里的一排身体,叶恩斯将孙子紧搂在宽阔的胸脯上。他们睁开眼睛,听着狗的合奏,两张圆脸笑咪咪的。有枪声传来,米基里把头伸出帐篷外看了一下,又躺了回去,嘴里嘟哝着,"他们射击了什么东西,但是没打中,"他说。"打中什么了?"我问道。"*Nanoq, immaqa*"(也许是北极熊),他说,调皮地笑笑。

灿烂的阳光,凛冽的微风,肯定是中午了。我们静默地坐着,眼巴巴地望着冰块融化为水以用来泡茶。"*Issi*,"伊莱特苏克又说道。冷。我的同伴不大会说英文,而我的格陵兰语,唉,只能算初级水平。有几天我们几乎不说些什么,其它时候我们摆出所有的字典享受词语大餐,我尽力记住一些有用的短语,比如"*nauk tupilaghuunnguaju*"的意思是:"你个笨蛋";"*taquliktooq*"指"眼睛上有白点的黑狗。"但是通常我记不住,不过这还是增添了更多的乐趣。

今天,我们的营帐悄无声息地就收拾好了。因纽特猎人干活的速度很迷惑人:因为他们看上去轻松自如,一点都不浪费精力,既不夸张也不闹腾。他们干活时悄无声息、从容不迫、快速敏捷。我还没缓过神来叶恩斯就把缰绳钩在雪橇上。我一把抓住那个小男孩,跳上了雪橇,与此同时伊莱特苏克和叶恩斯也跳上了快速移动的雪橇。叶恩斯嘲笑他的小孙子没有好好准备,小男孩哭了,叶恩斯笑得更厉害了。这就是爱斯基摩人教导孩子的方式——有幽默感、注意力要集中以及行事要精准。这些教训以后会保全他们的性命。

纷飞的大雪向我们袭来。"天气不是猎人的好朋友,"叶恩斯说道,"倘若猎人老指望着好天气,可能就会挨饿,是的,一定会挨饿。但是,如果天气状况很糟糕的时候出去打猎,又可能会掉入冰窟不见踪影。这里的生活就是这样。"

雪更大了,狗群也从慢跑改为缓步前行。我们右边灰褐色的悬崖此起彼伏,布满了雪崩造成的陡峭斜坡,上面交织着北极兔的踪迹。"*Ukaleq, Ukaleq*,"伊莱特苏克大声喊道。叶恩斯吹着口哨示意狗群停住,伊莱特苏克兴奋地指向那里。兔毛可以做成 *Kamiks*(靴子)的里衬,兔肉可以食用。我们顺着看去:白色的北极兔映衬着白色的山坡,然后便蹿到巨石后面。不够幸运,冰上没有海豹。今晚我们6个人再加30只狗吃什么呢?

我们拐过弯绕过一座圆形的岩石山,一个大型的海湾便呈现在眼前。我们慢慢地跨过宽阔的海湾口,向里望去,我看到一大片滑石粉,然后便是布满冰的悬崖:这是一条巨大的泛着青绿色、亮白色和岩石黑色的冰河的入口,河床上川流不息的岩屑就像屋顶的装饰。我的视线从冰冠上方移到下面冰冻的峡湾。带状色彩的变幻呈现出消融聚合的韵律的本质:时间的喧嚣与寂静——北极的时间——它没有小时和天的概念,只有极昼和极夜。当你坐上狗拉雪橇后,一天的24小时就变得有弹性了,而我们人类的习惯总是围绕着时钟来的;我们会发现自己在早餐时间吃晚餐,在极昼的亮光里睡觉,在亮堂堂的夜里行进。当我们继续向北行进到达最远的村庄时,放眼望去只有寒冷和积雪,饥饿感愈发强烈令我们痛苦不堪,这时我们所在意的就再也不是什么日程表,而是温暖、食物及好天气了。

我们改变了行进路线,行进已经变得异常缓慢了。我们不再沿着海岸线向正北走,而是转向了结冰的海面;我们沿着冰中的痕迹搜寻海豹。雪下得更大了。一场暴风雪接近了,穿过埃尔斯米尔岛,越过宽达数百英里的亨博尔特冰川[①]。风抽打着暴风雪的黑色边缘,卷起的碎雪就像乌鸦翅膀上的羽毛。风停驻时,内陆冰雪上那巨大的圆顶光芒黯淡了。

沿着裂缝到处都是透气孔,但是没有 *uuttuq*——那些费力爬上冰面的海豹,这在春季本来是很常见的。我们继续西行,远离内契[②]和伊塔[③]的历史上著名的

[①] Humboldt Glacier 亨博尔特冰川,北半球最大的入海冰川,同格陵兰西北部的凯恩盆地接壤,以德国博物学家亚历山大·冯·洪堡而命名。

[②] Neqi 内契,格陵兰北部的居住点。

[③] Etah 伊塔,北部格陵兰被遗弃的定居点,曾是北极探险之旅的起点。

野营地，晚上我们会再返回内契歇息。

整个下午和晚上我们都在暴风雪中行进。我记得一位猎人曾经告诉过我有关迷路的事情。"有时乘坐雪橇遇到浓雾或大雪时，我们会有迷失方向的感觉，分不清天和冰，感觉完全搞错了方向。"但是今天我们没有迷路。"我们可以靠风向来判断，"正是同一个猎人告诉我的，"如果一直与飘舞着的雪保持同样的角度就不会出错。"

到处都是白茫茫的。我们停下来喝茶，将两驾雪橇并在一起支起一块油布以防风。我们在粗帆布袋里找寻食物，克里斯找到一罐花生酱，看到标签上写着"低脂"我很是沮丧。不过不要紧，我们把花生酱涂在饼干上，喝着茶，共享了一块半苦半甜的巧克力。苦乐参半，正是我此时的感觉：同格陵兰的老朋友待在一起令我快乐，然而每吃一口巧克力，饥饿感就会更加强烈。

不难看出饥荒是如何频频席卷北极地区，狩猎如何迅速艰难起来，而饥饿又是怎样地肆虐着。商店和直升机出现之前，食人的习俗在北极很常见。人们吃完狗和煮熟的海豹皮后就会吃人肉——几乎总是死人的尸体，这虽然令人憎恶却是生存下去的唯一方法。丹麦探险家彼得·弗洛伊琴与库纳德·拉斯穆森一同旅行了14年，他如此描述了这个习俗："在品格卡林我见到一位令人惊叹的女性，她叫阿塔库塔卢克，在她成为复仇女神赫克拉海峡[①]第一女士之前我就听说过她——她之所以有名是因为她曾经吃掉了自己的丈夫和3个孩子。

弗洛伊琴继续描述这段苦难的经历，阿塔库塔卢克的部族在穿越巴芬岛时遇到温暖期，无法使用雪橇，并且那个地区没有动物可以捕杀，所以当食物耗尽时他们先吃了狗，接着吃了狩猎队伍中年老体衰的人。弗洛伊琴见到阿塔库塔卢克时，她说："看看，彼得，不要因为这个而有偏见。我现在有了新丈夫，和他生了3个孩子。这3个孩子都是以那3个为了支撑我活下来而死去的孩子的名字来命名的，这样，死去的孩子们就得到了重生。"

我们又向北行进，穿越了一大片辽阔的冰封洋面。我们前方兔子跑过的小径纵横交错但是却看不到它们的踪迹。暴风雪势头减弱，大片的光透了下来。雪、冰和空气闪烁着光芒。我和伊莱特苏克微微地抬起脸迎向阳光。太阳散发出的温暖是一种幸福，我们一时闭上双眼打起盹来。

突然传来一阵喊叫。伊莱特苏克挣扎着跪起身子看看四周，原来是将我们远远抛在后面的米基里，他跪在疾驰的雪橇上："*Nanoq! Nanoq!*"他大声叫着，指向远方，然后我们看见：一只北极熊正匆匆地走过辽阔峡湾的源头。

叶恩斯的狗向那边冲去，米基里已经放开了两只狗去追那头熊。他又放了

[①] Fury and Hecla Strait，位于福克斯湾北部，将其和布西亚海湾连接在一起。

两只。"*Pequoq*，*Pequoq*"叶恩斯大声叫喊着催促自己的狗再快点。正在那时我们看见一只幼熊在厚厚的积雪中挣扎着要站起来。母熊停住脚步转身跑了回来，米基里的狗群追了上去围住母熊。人们不会猎杀有了幼仔的母熊，因为失去母亲的幼熊会无法生存。

现在我们身处幼熊和母熊之间。母熊多次停住观望，转头想要回到幼仔身边，可是狗群逼近了，她扬起爪子，咆哮着，又跑开。这时情况突然恶化，其中一只狗看见了幼熊。我们没来得及赶到，狗就扑向幼熊，咬住它的脖子。我们冲过去想救幼熊，但是距离太远，行动太缓慢，等我们赶到幼熊那里时狗正咬着幼熊的脖子晃动着，其它的狗都凑了过去。米基里和叶恩斯跳下雪橇用鞭子驱赶狗群，但还是晚了，幼熊已经受到了重创。

米基里追赶母熊时我们一直和幼熊待在一起。幼熊还活着，但身体虚弱，一大片肉皮垂下来。虽然它有点晕乎乎的，状态也不稳定，但仍然精力充沛。我们一靠近它就冲着我们张牙舞爪。叶恩斯用一个软圈套住它的腿拖在雪橇后面，使它远离熊狗之间的打斗，让它休息。或许它会很快恢复，我们就能把他送回母熊那里。

远处，母熊开始逃跑，但狗群追上去阻止她逃离。在峡湾遥远的一边，母熊向西突围，藏在一座搁浅的破冰山后面。第一批狗开始累了，米基里于是放出更多的狗。熊站在冰山形成的围栏里，在狗群接近时便冲出来驱赶。她没有找寻自己的幼仔；她正在为自己的生命而战。

太阳出来了，熊热了，她掬起一大捧雪吃了。她依靠的坚冰变蓝了，形成了一个大大的"V"字，好像一本边缘融化在春天阳光下的敞开的书。狗群半包围着母熊，它们跳起来冲向她以挑战自己的勇气，但是当母熊冲向它们时又跳离开来。

我们在米基里身后 500 码开外注视着幼熊。我们靠近时它就猛地咬过来。有时能站起来但是很虚弱。它开始气喘吁吁，接着眼睛一翻，踉跄着倒地死去。

叶恩斯往幼熊的脖子上系上项圈，我们把它像玩具一样拖在雪橇后面。靠近米基里时他转过身来问道，"幼熊死了？"叶恩斯回答说是。我们做出决定：由米基里射杀母熊。我问是否有必要杀死母熊——毕竟她还年轻可以生养更多的幼仔——可惜我的格陵兰语讲得很难听懂。我用英语混杂着格陵兰语为她求情，叶恩斯说，"这由米基里决定。"

米基里的北极熊皮裤几乎破烂不堪，他听着我们说话，然后默默地给猎枪装上弹药。我们站得离母熊很近，近到她可以攻击到我们，但是她只关注着狗群，她踮着脚尖，肘部抵在山顶上，警觉地看着周围。

我在心底默默地为她打气：加油，加油！这是她生命的最后时刻，而我只能看着时间渐渐地逝去。她知道自己要死了吗？我再次为她求饶，看到的却是猎人们充满疑问的神情。我不忍目睹，瞥了一眼冰面，看见母熊心灰意冷地轰然倒下。她累了，孩子死了，也无处可逃。

米基里举起步枪，伊莱特苏克捂住莫斯卡克的耳朵，小男孩吓坏了，他已经看到幼熊死了，不想再看到别的什么了。

熊的鼻子、眼睛和爪子是白茫茫世界中小小的黑点，这个世界中人类的矛盾情绪对她来说是一无所知的。她盯着我的凌厉的眼神无异于盯着一只海豹——毕竟我也只是食物链中的一环。米基里现在向她投掷过去的也是同样的眼神，之所以凌厉不是由于缺乏感情，而是出于生存的需要。我明白，对于猎人而言捕获到一只北极熊是何等重要，熊肉可以食用，熊皮则会做成人们更需要的冬日的衣服。正是因为有北极熊皮做成的裤子和靴子我们才不会被冻死。尽管如此，我还是觉得目睹了一次死刑。

熊的毛皮是浅黄色的，冰墙是蓝色的。阳光炽热，时间消融，我所了解的生与死，寒冷与饥饿似乎无关紧要。三声枪响，一只熊爪在痛苦中竖了起来，抓着冰墙，母熊仰面倒地而亡。

我跪在熊旁边，它两爪之间的毛皮厚实。我听到汩汩的流水声，一年中这个时候流水潺潺稍嫌太早，接着我便看到血正从她致命的枪伤口涌出来。

米基里将狗牵回狗群里系住。刀子磨光了，茶水也烧开了。我们在傍晚的阳光下卷起袖子。伊莱特苏克通过望远镜搜寻冰上其它的动物；莫斯卡克待在雪地上的熊旁边，把小手放在它庞大的熊掌上。

熊被仰面推倒在地，叶恩斯用刀尖抵在熊的肚脐向脖颈方向剖开，锋利的刀尖向上推移直至下颌，然后切开黑色的嘴唇似乎想要阻止它开口说话。

很快熊皮被剥离下来在雪地里展开，擦尽血迹后被叠成四折小心地放置在雪橇上的粗麻袋里。然后熊的躯体被肢解开来放在防水布下面，因此当我们收起茶杯沿着西北方向赶往内契时，被切割成碎块的熊就在我们身子下面，我们坐在熊上面，根据因纽特传说，这只熊能听懂人类的语言，于是这天剩下的时间里我们都一言不发。

我们驶过宽阔的峡湾口继续前往几百年来因纽特猎人和欧洲探险者一直使用的营地内契。那里没有村庄，只有一个小屋，低矮而宽敞，坐落在两条冰河之间凸伸出的一长条陆地尖上，小屋俯瞰着冰冻的史密斯海峡[①]。内契的意思是"肉"，在这个地方前往格陵兰北部或北极的猎人和探险者可以储存肉类。

[①] Smith Sound，史密斯海峡，北冰洋海上通道，在加拿大埃尔斯米尔岛和格陵兰西北部之间，北为凯恩湾(Kane Basin)，南接巴芬湾，夏末通航。

我们把雪橇推到小丘上的小屋前,肉架上堆满了海象的鳍状肢体、死狗以及小块海豹肉,小屋看上去既像是庇护所又像是藏骸间。

我们站在小屋前结冰的台阶上,眺望着冰封的浩淼的海洋,迎接久违的阳光,温暖沁入我们体内,第一次有一种放松的感觉。叶恩斯从帆布包里拿出一瓶藏了很久的啤酒,给大家传着喝。

狐狸压抑的叫喊声飘荡在我们射杀熊的冰封的海湾上空。此刻那里升起一阵雾,遮掩住了拉班舞谱①——那是熊死亡之舞的脚本:在那里她停住脚,转过身发起攻击,又继续奔跑;那是血和足迹构成的难以辨认的象形文字;那是狗群在追猎之后休憩的雪洞。我很庆幸看不见这些。

点燃普里默斯油炉,将水放到上面烧开,接着把北极熊的背部——最软的部分——投入锅中。屋里很暖和,我们脱掉外套摘下帽子,叶恩斯分发了纸质盘子。"Nanoq,Nanoq"他低声说着。"北极熊是兽王,我们得以特殊的方式来吃。我们像煮海豹肉一样煮熟了她,但是对她致以特别的敬意,这样她的灵魂就不难找到回家的路。"

20分钟后,大块的肉被切成小块分给大家,盘子上冒着热气。"Qujanaq,"我说道,对米基里、叶恩斯、尤其是熊表示感谢。熊肉松软可口,就像水牛肉一样。

之后我们钻进睡袋躺在雪橇搭成的平台上,仍然很暖和,没人睡得着。叶恩斯和伊莱特苏克拥着小孙子,叶恩斯开始讲故事:"很早以前,巫师会潜入水下,动物能开口说话,有个名叫阿诺里托克的女人住在伊塔以北的陆地边上。Anoritoq 这个名字的意思是'被风席卷的人',这个女人没有丈夫,唯一的儿子没有父亲但是打猎很出色因而被嫉妒的猎人杀死。儿子死后,猎人给这个女人带来一只北极熊幼仔,她把他像儿子一样抚养大。熊学会了爱斯基摩语,和其他孩子一同玩耍,长大后猎取海豹非常成功,但是阿诺里托克为他担心,害怕猎人会杀死他,因为他毕竟是只熊,猎人需要他的毛皮来做衣服。她用煤灰把熊涂黑,然而有一天当熊露出一些白色毛皮时猎人杀死了它。阿诺里托克很伤心,不再吃饭,出去一直呆在那里,看着大海,最后变成一块岩石。现在我们到那个地区猎杀熊时都会把一块海豹油放在石头上祈祷狩猎会有好收获。"

早晨我们沿着海岸向北前往皮特拉维克②,这次旅行并不漫长,在那里我们将决定去往伊塔的路线——要么越过部分陆地冰川,要么沿着海岸在没有流

---

① labanotations,拉班舞谱,为"现代舞理论之父"——匈牙利人鲁道夫·拉班所创,以数学、力学、人体解剖学为基础,运用各种形象的符号,精确、灵便地分析并记录舞蹈及各种人体动作的姿态、空间运行路线、动作节奏和所用力量,被公认为是一种既科学又形象、并富有逻辑性的分析记录体系。

② Pitoravik,皮特拉维克,格陵兰的古迹遗址。

动的水或薄冰的地方行进。叶恩斯和米基里出发考察冰河上的小路，这时起风了，他们走了几个小时又折了回来，摇头示意不行。"漂浮物很厚，裂缝太宽，而且被雪都遮盖住了，"叶恩斯说，"下面的冰受到流水的猛烈冲击，太危险。等到明天早晨如果天气好的话我们就爬到冰山顶上去，如果天气不好的话就到冰的尽头去加拿大猎取海象和独角鲸。"

次日早上天气再好不过，雪不停地悄然落下。"我觉得去那边打猎更好，"叶恩斯一边说，一边居高临下地眺望史密斯海峡。远处，埃尔斯米尔岛成了一排映衬着白云的青山。我们下去沿着西南方向朝开阿塔克岛①驶去。

接下来的三四天里我们一直在乌云压顶的天气里前行。当我们停下让狗休息时，我、伊莱特苏克和莫斯卡克在冰上玩起捉人游戏取暖。那孩子从不抱怨，脚冷时他只是指着脚趾头，而伊莱特苏克则给他穿上及膝长靴，那是我们在内契的小屋休息时她连缀缝制的。之后他便坐在雪橇前面，任由风吹打着依然很快乐，模仿爷爷发出命令，用力甩着长鞭，俨然已经长大成人了。

耐心和坚定的意志是狩猎者的美德，当然灵活和幽默也是。叶恩斯向一只海豹射击却没打中，另一只海豹闻到他的气味潜入了透气孔。叶恩斯返回雪橇，自嘲着自己的失败，向米基里解释自己到底哪儿做错了。接着他又重新开始另一种冬日风格猎豹方法——这种方法被称为 *agluhiutuq*，即在 *agluq*（透气孔）边捕猎海豹。但是这种尝试也失败了。

我们继续前行。"*Hikup hinaa*，"叶恩斯喊着。冰的尽头，正是我们现在要寻找的地方，那里有着大量的海豹、海象和独角鲸。我饥肠辘辘，想起了大饥荒的传说，那时过了冬天还是冬天，期间没有春夏秋季。叶恩斯说去年冬天和春天是他记忆中最冷的季节。讽刺的是北极地区变冷可能是全球变暖带来的副作用。冰冠的碎片崩解融化汇入海洋，导致最北边地区的水温变冷，空气也随之降温。或许全球变暖的效果会自我抵消，我说。叶恩斯不明白我讲的"格陵兰英语"。"*Issi*，"他边说边搓着手臂，冷。"或许我们不得不像古时那样以彼此为食，"他说着，笑得很灿烂。

对爱斯基摩人而言，孤独纯粹是不快乐的标志，被认为是一种变态的行为，完全令人无法接受。我们紧紧地挤在雪橇上，裹着动物的皮毛，由于寒冷一动不动。挤在人体中间的感觉很好。我们扫视着冰面寻找猎物。大块的冰矗立着，投下的影子看上去像海豹一样。

接着我们真的看见一只海豹，一个躺在白茫茫雪地上的黑色小点。

叶恩斯和米基里让狗停住脚。叶恩斯把步枪放到可移动的遮挡物上——

---

① Kiatak，开阿塔克岛，无人居住的格陵兰小岛，位于卡纳克以西。

一个小架子，上面的白色帆布可以遮住他的脸。雪很薄，但风还好。他蹑手蹑脚地向前走了走，趴在地上瞄准。30条狗都警觉地坐在地上竖起耳朵。它们不再气喘吁吁时，整个世界都安静下来。它们一听到沉闷的枪声就冲了出去，像平时训练地那样跑向叶恩斯。

我们背着风围着血泊站成半圈。叶恩斯轻快地剥去海豹皮，掏出热腾腾的肝脏，插在刀尖上献给我们。这是因纽特的一道美味，热腾腾的海豹肝曾经救活过快要饿死的猎人。出于感激我们都咬了一口，嘴巴和下颌滴着血，温热的肉略带咸味。

伊莱特苏克叠好海豹皮和熊皮一起放在防水布下。叶恩斯用刀在海豹的鳍状肢上划开一道口以便手提，把看上去更小的粉红色的海豹身体拖上雪橇前部。我们拉紧缰绳，迎着飞舞的雪花起程了。

夜里10点半时我们仍在赶路，暴风雪突然来临。我们看着黑色的雪锋呼啸而过，比雪橇移动地更快。天空晴朗，气温却骤降至零下20度左右。

一只海豹对30只狗和6个人来说并不算多。我们停在一座冰山边上，砍下大块的冰，开始扎营。我和伊莱特苏克卸下雪橇，叶恩斯和米基里切开海豹肉，狗群排成队，急切地等着食物，它们上次吃新鲜肉已经是两天前了。大块肉被扔到空中，一块接着一块。叶恩斯和米基里的目标很明确，所有的狗都有份，吃得越快得到的份额就越大。

叶恩斯切开剩下的海豹肉作为晚餐。我们在帐篷里看着大块的肉在褐色的水中翻滚，冰屋变暖时脱去外衣。莫斯卡克的红色小T袖上用大写字母写着：我爱大象，尽管他从未见过也许永远也不会见到大象。

我们用小刀和手指吃着肉，一言不发。大块面包传了过来，每个人吃了一片，然后喝着茶共享了一捧饼干。之后伊莱特苏克往塑料桶里放了一块胶合板，把海豹皮撑在板上，开始用 *ulu*——一把有木柄的弯刀——用力向下刮脂肪，弄干净后她又用 *kiliutaq*——一把小型方刀——从皮毛中清理粉褐色的油。

伊莱特苏克让我试着刮刮，我害怕会割破并损坏毛皮，勉强刮了一下表面。

后来，我躺在睡袋里听着风的声音。叶恩斯一个接一个地讲着故事，有把熊抚养大的女人、同狐狸结婚的猎人、雾的起源等。他声音温柔，用词单调，使我们坠入甜美的梦里，这种感觉是如此的快乐，我不知道以后听不到这些故事自己是否还能入眠。

接下来的日子里我们在找寻冰的尽头，无论到什么地方，天一黑就在冰上扎营歇息。我们从开阿塔克岛的一端出发一直向西行进抵达位于格陵兰和埃尔斯米尔岛之间的冰封海域。一路上，叶恩斯教小孙子怎样对狗发号施令以及如何用鞭子才能不伤及动物的背部。"莫斯卡克也会成为猎人吗？"我问。叶恩斯答道，"我在教他需要知道的东西，然后由他自己作决定，他一定喜欢打猎超过其它任何事情。"

我们抵达一排冰山，叶恩斯和米基里登上山顶用望远镜观察整个辽阔的冰面，感觉我们似乎已经走过一半的史密斯海峡。叶恩斯回来时摇着头，"没有流水，"他怀疑地说道，"到加拿大一路都是冰。"记忆中的任何春天都没有发生过这种状况。今天是5月8号。

我们向南方行进，去往洋流滚滚冲击冰面的地区，或许那里会有冰的尽头。沿着海岸向南，在卡帕帕里①我们遇到两位来自相反方向的猎人。像往常一样，一阵沉默，然后随意提起有关流水的问题，他们摇着头，这边也没有冰的尽头。

那天晚上，我躺在睡袋里，紧紧地挤在米基里和伊莱特苏克之间。"我觉得我们困在了冬天。"米基里之前说过，看上去很沮丧，他有一大家子人要养。他同叶恩斯一样被认为是卡纳克最好的猎人之一，但是即便是他，春天不来的话也无法打到足够的猎物。我们醒着倾听风声。

中午时分我们登上形如悉尼歌剧院的冰山看是否能看见冰的尽头。叶恩斯摇头示意没有。下山时，米基里大叫着指向远处："Nanoq。"远处，一只北极熊舞动地穿过银色的地平线，幸亏它离得远，我们的子弹打不到它。一种由冰面升腾而起的反射光构成的幻境而非子弹吞没了它。这幻境吞没了它那舞动的双腿，将它们变成了仍在努力穿过最后严冬时分的春日热浪。

最后我们踏上归途，沿着开阿塔克的东边行驶。红色岩石构成一堵堵墙矗立着像古罗马的半圆形剧场一样；北极兔雀跃在白雪点点的草地上。一只乌鸦猝然飞过，一只狐狸沿着陡峭的山侧摆动着灰色的尾巴。接近悬崖底部，冰柱以奇特的角度从石床上垂下。我们经过由碎冰形成的地面，它们看上去似乎曾经像镜子一样竖立起来，然后倒地裂成碎片，使得雪橇颠簸起伏。有些冰块很是精致，我请求叶恩斯停下来以好好观看：精心蚀刻的冰面上铺满一层由星星状东西穿透的冰。

狗的动静使我回过神来，它们打闹、放屁、咆哮、气喘吁吁。其中一只叫帕皮的母狗正处于发情期，其它狗拼命想靠近它。帕皮溜到它们后面，夹住尾巴不再拉雪橇了。公狗们也向后退，相互打斗着，雪橇终于一动不动了。叶恩斯解开帕皮系到雪橇后面，但无济于事。帕皮跌倒在地被拖曳着站不起来。

最终叶恩斯松开帕皮，那一刻它如释重负，好像已经从一个冰天雪地、纪律严明的严苛的世界中解脱出来了。伊莱特苏克看着我笑了，她的脸在深夜的阳光下坚韧有力，小男孩戴着墨镜坐在爷爷的膝盖上。我们没有带回多少肉，

---

① Kap Parry，卡帕帕里，格陵兰的一个海角，海拔395米。

但叶恩斯对此不以为然，使我想起担忧在北极是没用的。他和之前的那些人已经一天天的如此生存了 4000 年，一次糟糕的狩猎不会使他感觉受挫。明天总会来到的。

现在帕皮快乐自由地奔跑着，叶恩斯催促她继续向前跑。雪夹杂着冰下得更大了，狗追逐着拉着雪橇疾驰。有时我们越过山坡时会腾空而起，小莫斯卡克就会趴在雪橇上高兴地尖叫。寒冷、饥饿、恶劣的狩猎境况全被抛到身后，在接近卡纳克时，狗群越发乐观，跑得更欢了。

（申彩红 译 温秀颖 校）

Lost in the Arctic

Lawrence Millman

【导读】你好，北极！四处游荡似乎是人类的一种天性，总是想去看一看山的那一边能否找到更适宜耕作的良田，河的另一头是否有更好的牧场。从古希腊雄伟的卫城到江南飘雨的小镇；从撒哈拉的新月沙丘到北极大陆绵延的冰壁，没有精神追求的生命是远离永恒的；缺乏探险远行的生活轨迹是没有宽度、缺乏空间的。作者便是这样不断追求、体味生命的人。作者只身一人探寻北极的奥秘，在两名因纽特伙伴的陪同下，展开了一系列新奇的体验。因纽特人的智慧、乐观、勇敢的精神跃然纸上。置身于一个具有挑战性的野外环境，完成某项既定的安排，在这过程中又遇到各种困难，作者深感自身的渺小懦弱，但通过克服这些困难又获得了自信和自尊，逐渐成为一个"完整"的人。在作者几乎陷入绝境之时："总而言之，我们不仅迷路，而且孤立无援"，是两位因纽特人的聪明才智力挽狂澜，真乃山穷水复疑无路，柳暗花明又一村。探险历程无比艰辛，却用智慧一一化解，这或许和爱斯基摩人的民族精神有着密切关联。从历史来讲，他们本身就是人类学奇迹：爱斯基摩人是黄种人。据说，他们的祖先是亚洲人，在3000多年前，沿着北极地区迁移到格陵兰。他们经受住了北极冰层的考验，恰如他们那自信满满、锋芒毕露的语言一样，引领作者比之前的任何时候、任何地点都走得更远。

The boat's motor had been making curious burbling noises all morning, as if there were a newborn trapped inside it. Then the engine died. My Inuit[①] guides Qungujuq and Zacharias bent over the outboard, trying to figure out what was wrong. Meanwhile, we started drifting southeast.

---

① The Inuit are a group of culturally similar indigenous peoples inhabiting the Arctic regions of Canada (Northwest Territories), Denmark (Greenland), Russia (Siberia) and the United States (Alaska). Inuit means "the people" in the Inuktitut language. An Inuk is an Inuit person. The Inuit language is grouped under Eskimo-Aleut languages.

"Motor very kaput①," Qungujuq announced, as if this weren't already obvious. "Must take it apart." It was also obvious that there wasn't any room on the overloaded boat to take apart a wristwatch, much less an eighty-five-horsepower Yamaha outboard.

I confess I wasn't in a particularly jovial frame of mind about our situation, since I knew how unforgiving the Arctic can be. The Inuit have many tales of people going off in boasts and disappearing; years later their bones turn up on some distant beach. We continued to drift southeast for the next few hours as Qungujuq examined various motor parts.

"Qikiqtaq!" Zacharias shouted. An island.

He pointed to a small patch of land about five miles away, then grabbed our lone oar and began paddling toward it. After a while, Qungujuq took over for him and then I took over for Qungujuq. I paddled until my arms were ready to fall off, then passed the oar to Zacharias, who was at least five years older than me but much stronger. He paddled the rest of the way, neatly parrying the ice floes that guarded the island. At last a wave thrust the boat onto the gravelly shore with a resounding crunch.

The Arctic had granted us a reprieve, of sorts.

In the Canadian North, ice is the final arbiter of human affairs. A few days before washing up on an unknown island, I was biding my time in Sanirajak, an Inuit community on the Melville Peninsula②. From there, I planned to travel across Foxe Basin③ to Prince Charles Island④, an uninhabited chunk of land almost as large as Connecticut. It wasn't officially documented until 1948, when a Royal Canadian Air Force pilot taking aerial photographs noticed an unknown landmass in one of his

---

① adj. (Informal) ruined, broken, or not functioning.

② Melville Peninsula is a large peninsula in the Canadian Arctic. Since 1999, it has been part of Nunavut. Before that, it was part of the District of Franklin. It's separated from Southampton Island by Frozen Strait.

③ Foxe Basin is a shallow oceanic basin north of Hudson Bay, in Nunavut, Canada, located between Baffin Island and the Melville Peninsula. For most of the year, it is blocked by ice floes.

④ Prince Charles Island is a large, low-lying island with an area of 9,521 km2 (3,676 sq mi), making it the world's 78th largest island and the 19th largest island in Canada. It is located in Foxe Basin, off the west coast of Baffin Island, in the Qikiqtaaluk Region of Nunavut, Canada. Despite the island's size, the first recording of it was in 1948 by Albert-Ernest Tomkinson navigating an RCAF Avro Lancaster, though it was likely known to the local Inuit long before that. The island was named for Prince Charles, who was born the same year. The island is uninhabited and its temperatures are extremely cold.

pictures. And even thought the low-lying, icebound island has now been charted, it has never been fully explored. But Foxe Basin turned out to be choked with sea ice, so I was stuck in Sanirajak, waiting for a gale to come along and whisk the ice away.

Sanirajak isn't the sort of place where most people would want to spend more than a few hours – maybe not even more than a few minutes. Imagine Appalachia crossbred with a Gypsy encampment, then struck by an earthquake. Imagine residential landscaping that consists of discarded snowmobile treads, fuel drums, cast-off Pampers, bottles, slops, and animal bones. The town's chief attraction, or, perhaps, its chief distraction, is a several-hundred-year-old whale carcass whose odor is still pungent enough to upset the nostrils. I couldn't wait to exchange Sanirajak for the wilds of Foxe Basin.

Each morning, Qungujuq would study the ice with the seriousness of a scholar gazing at a palimpsest①, then come to my tent and say, "Nagga." ("Not today.") Then he would join me for coffee. He got his caffeine fix by sticking the grounds② directly into his mouth like a wad of tobacco, thus avoiding the bland intercession of water.

Sometimes Qungujuq would bring along his father, a barrel-chested elder whose face resembled the contour lines on a topo map. Like a number of other people I'd met in Sanirajak, the old man, Sivulliq, knew only one expression in English: "You're a better man than I am, Gunga Din!" Some years ago, the town's Hudson's Bay Company trader would perform the occasional interment and, instead of reciting a proper burial service, would solemnly intone Rudyard Kipling's "Gunga Din."③ The poem's famous line had entered the local vernacular as a sort of vaguely reverential sentiment, although no one had the slightest idea what it meant.

---

① an ancient piece of writing material on which the original writing has been rubbed out, not always completely, so that it can be used again.

② small bits of solid matter which sink to the bottom of a liquid, esp. coffee.

③ "Gunga Din" (1892) is one of Rudyard Kipling's most famous poems, perhaps best known for its often-quoted last stanza, "Tho' I've belted you and flayed you, By the livin' Gawd that made you, You're a better man than I am, Gunga Din!" The poem is a rhyming narrative from the point of view of a British soldier, about a native water-bearer who saves the soldier's life but dies himself. Like several others among Kipling's poems, it celebrates the virtues of a non-European while revealing the racism of a colonial infantryman who views such people as being of a "lower order". But the last line in particular suggests a deep-down unease of conscience about these racial feelings, both in the depicted soldier and in Kipling himself. The poem was published as one of the set of martial poems called the Barrack-Room Ballads. "Din" is frequently pronounced to rhyme with "bin" although the rhymes within the poem make it clear that it should be pronounced to rhyme with "green".

Sivulliq said there were Tunit on Prince Charles Island, and he warned me to be very careful: They would attempt to unravel my intestines – a popular Tunit form of entertainment – if I gave them the opportunity.

According to archaeologists, the Tunit, or Dorset people, died out before A.D.1300. Yet if there was one place in the Arctic where a small band of them might have survived, I figured, that place would be Prince Charles Island. Another thing Sivulliq told me: The weather on Prince Charles Island is awful, and thus it's very easy to get marooned there.

Finally, one morning Qungujuq awakened me by shouting "Tuavi!['Hurry up!'] Ice blown away by big wind." Groggily, I lifted the tent flap and at once saw open water where the night before there had been only an uncompromising sheet of ice.

Within an hour, Qungujuq, his brother-in-law Zacharias, and I had piled our supplies into Qungujuq's twenty-four-foot motorized freighter canoe and were headed east across Foxe Basin. Rather, we tried to head east, but the wind kept shoving us in a more northerly direction. Finally we decided to wait it out, so we put ashore in a cove about twenty-five miles north of Sanirajak. Here we encountered some walrus hunters from Igloolik, a community farther north on the peninsula. One of the hunters had told me that the wind would die down during the night. I asked him how he knew this. Was he observing the flight patterns of certain birds or perhaps using some time-honored native technique to read the weather.

"No," he said. "I heard it on the radio."

The following day, the wind did in fact die down, but it left in its wake a strong lateral swell. Qungujuq and Zacharias took turns trying to keep the boat from being bashed by waves, but despite their expertise as helmsmen, we still got wet. At one point a wave rushed our gunwales and dumped a jellyfish into the boat. Zacharias found this vastly amusing, even though arctic jellyfish can deliver a nasty sting. But Zacharias seemed to find everything vastly amusing, even the albino walrus whoofling at us from an ice pan. An albino walrus, he informed me, means death.

"Death to whom?" I asked.

"Us," he said, grinning.

In spite of the swell①, we made good progress, motoring about fifty miles east to Rowley Island, which itself escaped detection until the mid-1930s. Earlier in the

---

① noun. a formation of long wavelength ocean surface waves.

day, Qungujuq had shot a ringed seal. After caching most of the meat on Rowley for our return trip, we cooked the flippers and liver. The meal reminded me of the first time I'd eaten seal liver, in Greenland. It was still steaming, having been plucked from a recently killed animal. Whatever hesitation I might have felt about eating it was quickly dispelled by the meat's tangy, iron-rich taste.

"Nattiup tingus mamarijara," I said. ("I like seal liver.")

"Uvanga ijingit mamarniqsaujakka," Qungujuq told me. ("Myself, I prefer the eyes.") Later, he dissected a seal eye and showed me how the clear inner spheroid could be used as a magnifying glass — useful information if you happen to have a seal eye handy.

The next day, the sea was as smooth as blue glass. By early afternoon, we were about twenty-five miles northwest of Prince Charles Island. I was, to put it mildly, excited to be within spitting distance of my goal. That's when the motor conked out[①].

The island on which we found ourselves stranded looked to be about two miles long and half a mile wide. It didn't appear on my Canadian Geological Survey map; more significantly, neither Qungujuq nor Zacharias knew about its existence. We were lost. Very lost.

"Maybe we've died and gone to heaven," quipped Zacharias.

If this really was heaven, then a lot of clean-living people were going to be very disappointed. There didn't seem to be any pearly gates, only scoured limestone intersected by the occasional quartzite dike. The closest thing I saw to an angel was an ivory gull hovering in the air above us, its stiff wings bright against a high overcast.

The only other winged entities were positively unangelic: mosquitoes. From the instant we landed, they attacked us so aggressively and in such biblical proportions that I figured they hadn't dined on any warm-blooded organisms for a very long time.

Soon Qungujuq had scattered pieces of the motor on the beach. It was ten P.M., but there was still enough light for him to work on our stricken motor. Enough light, too, for me to see a screw that had rolled away and retrieve it for him. But that's almost all I could do: I know less about machines than a dull three-year-old.

---

① conk out: to stop functioning; fail.

The Inuit, on the other hand, seem to have a knack for machines. I once saw an elderly Inuk take apart and repair a helicopter engine, much to the surprise of the Danish pilot, who hadn't been able to repair it himself. When I asked the old man where he had learned about such things, he pointed to his head and tapped it. He'd been born in a realm where you learn to improvise or you don't survive.

Qungujuq was still working on the motor at midnight when Zacharias and I turned in. When I awoke during the night to answer nature's call, there was Qungujuq beside me in the tent, snoring mightily. Zacharias was now on the beach, working in the semidarkness. In his hand was a tangle of wires that looked like a cat's cradle.

"Think you can fix it?" I said.

"*Immaqa*," Zacharias replied.

This is by far the most popular word in Inuktitut. It means "perhaps," with an intimation of "probably not." If you're someone who needs straight answers, the Inuit could easily immaqa you to a state of gibbering idiocy.

The next morning Qungujuq and Zacharias were alternately staring at pieces of the motor and swatting at mosquitoes. I tried to gauge from their expressions whether they'd made any headway, and I noticed that neither looked particularly pleased.

"We need a part for the gas line," Qungujuq told me.

"And it will be very hard to order it from here," added Zacharias.

We hadn't brought along a radio or a locator beacon (Stupid, yes: In our haste to leave Sanirajak, we'd also forgotten flotation jackets), so I had a hunch we'd be stuck on the island until someone rescued us. Already knowing what he would tell me, I asked Qungujuq whether he thought another boat might pass this way in the not too distant future. He didn't say "*immaqa*"; he said "*aakka*" ("no").

"Maybe an airplane?" I said.

Another "*aakka*": We were nowhere near a flight corridor. Also, our paddle had cracked when Zacharias beached the boat, and it now consisted of two useless pieces. (We'd somehow managed to leave the other one on Rowley Island.) So we were not only lost but marooned as well.

Maybe I was taking my cue from my companions, who weren't at all panicky, or maybe the true nature of our predicament hadn't sunk in yet, but I wasn't overly worried. I told myself: You're not dead until you're dead, and besides, you were the one who had the bright idea to go to a virtually unknown place. Now you've fetched up at just such a place — for God's sake, go out and explore it.

"You need me for anything?" I asked.

Both Qungujuq and Zacharias shook their heads vigorously, as if any attempt to help on my part would only make a sorry situation worse. So I wandered off, accompanied by a full escort of mosquitoes swarming around my bug hat. Qungujuq called me back and gave me his 30-06 rifle, uttering a single word: "*Nanuq*[①]." He was not suggesting that I shoot the hero of the silent movie but that I protect myself against a possible attack from the animal for which Robert Flaherty's hero was named, the polar bear.

Thus armed, I climbed the hogback behind our camp. Several minutes later, I was standing on another hogback — it was probably the highest point on the island — and staring out in every direction over the expanse of Foxe Basin. There was no other land in sight. Indeed, there was nothing at all in sight, since even the ice floes had disappeared during the night. If I'd been standing on the moon, I might have felt a greater sense of solitude, but I doubt it.

I then turned my attention to the island itself. In the sunlight, it was a lot more colorful than it had looked the previous evening. Here and there were delicate arctic wildflowers —purple saxifrage, Lapland rosebay, moss campion, arctic cinquefoil, and buttercups —rising bravely, it would appear, from solid rock. Gossamer tufts of arctic cotton swayed in an imperceptible breeze. A brilliant patch of yellow lichen exploded from its dour limestone host; an equally bright yellow butterfly flitted from flower to flower.

It was so quiet that my steps sounded downright raucous on the gravelly ground. I got the feeling that nothing had changed or even moved on the island since the end of the Ice Age. In every respect, it was a harsh place. Even so, its forlorn beauty took my breath away.

And then I came upon the cairns — half a dozen beehive-shaped structures piled along a gently sloping ridge. Peering through the chinks of one of them, I saw a human skull and several bone fragments; in another, there was a brownish skull fragment, a jawbone with worn teeth, and a scattering of vertebral arches; in a third,

---

[①] In Inuit mythology, Nanook or Nanuq, which is from the Inuit language for polar bear, was the master of bears, meaning he decided if hunters had followed all applicable taboos and if they deserved success in hunting bears.

a lone skull.

My first thought was: Here's what happened to the last group of people who washed up here when their motor conked out.

But then, in one of the cairns, I noticed a skeleton that had been interred with a large, circular soapstone lamp, which identified the site as dating from the Thule[①] period. The skeleton was curled in a fetal position. Was it possible that these people, who succeeded the Tunit, believed their journey to the afterlife would be less perilous if they left the world in the same posture in which they'd entered it? At any rate, I felt somewhat relieved: The Thule period ended approximately two hundred years before the invention of marine engines.

Still, the graves reminded me of my situation. There was the possibility that this bare speck of land might turn out to be my own final resting place. I imagined my last fragile thoughts drifting away, and then I imagined some archaeologist discovering my bones and wondering what a middle-aged Caucasian was doing so far from his native habitat. For almost the first time since I'd left Sanirajak, I found myself wondering the same thing.

Meanwhile, I was being sucked dry by the mosquitoes, whose persistent probing had helped them locate the holes in my bug net. Not relishing the prospect of death by acupuncture, I quickened my pace. Now only the most aerobically fit of the little bastards could keep up with me. But the island had not been set up as a racecourse, and I tripped over some glacial till and went flying through the air. Don't land on the rifle, I told myself. I didn't land on the rifle. Instead, I landed on my compass, which made a gouge in my chest — possibly the first compass-related injury in human medical history.

I also landed in a boneyard[②]. There were hundreds of ribs, scapulae, and vertebrae scattered around me. The skulls told me the bones were all from walruses, and they indicated why the occupants of the cairns had lived in such an apparently unbountiful place — the charnel pit was only a short distance from the floe edge, home to the paunchy, hulking *aivik*. For the Thule, bounty was determined not by soil but by the object at the end of a harpoon.

Back in camp, Qungujuq and Zacharias were hunched over a checkerboard.

---

① a region believed by ancient geographers to be the northernmost land in the inhabited world: sometimes thought to have been Iceland, Norway, or one of the Shetland Islands.

② A place where the bones of wild animals accumulate.

They were so intent on their game that neither one noticed me until I was standing beside them. Then Zacharias smiled and said, "We were hoping you would kill a big nanuq for our dinner."

In fact, I was a little concerned about our food supply. We hadn't expected this misadventure, so we had brought only enough for a few weeks. Likewise, we had planned to supplement our diet with meat from seals or a walrus, but we couldn't get within shooting distance without a functioning motor.

That food supply, which now seemed to me incredibly meager, included the following items: a box of expedition-standard oatmeal ("bloatmeal"), five boxes of rice, a bag of dried prunes, a pound of raisins, two bags of pilot biscuits (hardtack), two dozen Snickers bars, eleven packets of freeze-dried fettuccine Alfredo, six packets of freeze-dried chicken cacciatore, four packets of macaroni, a half-empty jar of Cheez Whiz[①], a small bag of flour, several slabs of *pipsik* (dried fish), a few rubbery pieces of *maktaaq* (narwhal skin), and one slightly moldy apple.

After my companions had finished their game, I asked Zacharias what would happen if we ran out of food.

"We eat each other," he said. He was grinning, but he was also studying me with, I thought, the appreciative gaze of a chef.

During the night the wind accelerated, first baying, then howling, and then shrieking, until it reached a higher decibel level than any wind I'd ever heard. Every hour or so, we would go outside and gather rocks to pile along the tent's guy lines. Were it not for them, I'm convinced, the wind would have picked up the tent — poles, occupants, and all — and deposited it somewhere in the middle of Foxe Basin.

The wind continued to blow the next day, and, except for the occasional rock-collecting mission, we stayed hunkered down inside the tent. Even so, the wind found us, pushing grit under the tent's fly and into our sleeping bags, our clothes, our food, our hair, our Primus stove — everything.

Being trapped in the tent made me even more aware of the degree to which we were imprisoned on the island. But Qungujuq and Zacharias were as composed as Zen Buddhist monks on a retreat, except when they were playing checkers, and then

---

① Cheez Whiz is a thick processed cheese sauce or spread sold by Kraft Foods. It was developed by a team led by food scientist Edwin Traisman (1915–2007) and was first marketed in 1953. The bright yellow, viscous paste usually comes in a glass jar and is used as a topping for corn chips, hot dogs, cheesesteaks, celery, and other foods. It is marketed in the United States, Canada, Venezuela, and the Philippines.

Zacharias —a less accomplished player than Qungujuq —would occasionally shout "*Tuqulirama! Tuqulirama!*" ("I'm dying! I'm dying!")

Ajurnarmat: This is doubtless the second most popular word in Inuktitut. It means something like "Why worry?" or "Hey, what can you do?" In our time together, I came to regard my companions as living, walking, checkers-playing embodiments of ajurnarmat. I envied them this attitude, not to mention their ability to remain unruffled in the face of what I felt was a pretty dire situation.

At one point, they burst into riotous laughter. They were talking about an Anglican minister, a member of the Bible Churchman's Missionary Society, who'd come to Sanirajak fifteen years ago. The man had learned just enough Inuktitut to mistake one word for another. One Sunday, he confused *ijjujut* (Bible) with *igjuuk* and ended up telling his congregation that they should pay more attention to their testicles.

Later, Zacharias recounted a story about a man who'd run out of food during a sledging trip on Baffin Island[①]. The starving man prayed for God's help. All at once he noticed a big slab of meat on the floor of his tent — God had provided! The man flensed the meat, chopped it up, and threw it into his pot. But he died before he could eat it: He had flensed and chopped his own thigh.

My companions thought this story was hilarious. I suspect Zacharias may have told it for my benefit, as a way of saying, "Come on, man, take it easy, or you might end up doing something rash, like eating yourself."

The wind, which I guessed was blowing at sixty-five or seventy knots, showed no sign of relenting. Once, when I ventured outside to pee, I was caught by a gust that was so strong it made my teeth ache. Back in the tent, I occupied myself with my journal: "If I ever get out of this mess, I'm going to adopt a more sedentary[②] lifestyle."

Three days later, with astonishing abruptness, the wind moderated to a mere breeze, as if it had suddenly grown tired after such a prolonged display of power. We could now go outside without being pummeled to jelly and, as it turned out, without being bitten by mosquitoes, which were nowhere in sight. It was early evening, and a sort of ethereal hush had fallen. There was a soft pink marbling in the clouds —

---

① An island of eastern Nunavut, Canada, west of Greenland. It is the fifth-largest island in the world.
② adj. tending to sit about without taking much exercise.

solar iridescence. The light had that tentative quality so typical of the Arctic, where every last sunbeam feels as if it's been snatched from the perpetually imminent winter.

Soon Qungujuq and Zacharias were disassembling and reassembling the motor for, it seemed, the hundredth time. I needed to stretch my legs, so I began wandering along the shore. The storm had washed up all kinds of oceanic booty — a golden plover's wing tangled in a matting of seaweed, a dismembered starfish, kelp, fish, and a dead seal. Initially, I thought the seal might be salvageable as food, but, upon closer inspection, I saw that it was scarcely more than a husk, its flesh and organs having already been consumed by crabs, isopods, and other creatures of the sea.

Now I began scavenging the beach in earnest for something that might bolster our rapidly diminishing larder. I wouldn't have turned up my nose at a newly dead fish or bird, but I found only very dead fish and a bundle of feathers so mangled that it was impossible to tell whether it was a bird or the stuffing from a mattress. Then I saw a patch of *Lycoperdon* puffballs on the mossy ground near the shore. I knew that neither Qungujuq nor Zacharias would eat them (the Inuit believe that mushrooms are the shit of shooting stars), but I certainly would.

My foraging was interrupted by the sound of a gunshot. I ran back along the beach. When I got closer, I noticed Zacharias had a bigger than usual grin on his face.

"All fix now," Qungujuq said. The motor was back on the boat and roaring with life.

At that lovely moment, all I could manage to tell him was this: "You're a better man than I am, Gunga Din."

Apparently, the motor's O-ring had been badly chewed up, which meant that the fuel line wasn't getting gas. Qungujuq had replaced the rubber gasket with some kelp, and that had done the trick.

So now the question was, Did I want to continue on to Prince Charles Island? We had enough fuel, Qungujuq told me. Well, maybe enough fuel. And we probably had enough food. If not, we could always shoot a seal or two. The gas might eat through our improvised O-ring, but if that happened, no problem, we'd just use more kelp.

I couldn't tell whether he was in ajurnarmat mode ("Whatever will be, will be") or trying to talk me out of a trip he considered risky. But it didn't matter. I had already decided that it was time to head back to the scuzzy[①] charms of Sanirajak. I had satisfied my desire to explore an island in the back of beyond, an island that had turned out to be even farther off the map than Prince Charles. Also, I didn't want to risk being marooned again. In the Arctic, fate doesn't like to be tempted, much less seduced.

And yet, as we pulled away from the stony beach, I felt a curious sadness. Maybe I'd left part of myself on these obdurate[②] shores, or maybe I just felt sad because I was surrendering a rare privilege — the privilege of solitude. As the island receded in the distance, I thought to myself, There are worse places to which you could bequeath your bones.

The trip back across Foxe Basin was uneventful. We spent another night on Rowley Island and gorged on the seal meat we had stored there. We didn't encounter another albino walrus, which seemed to disappoint Zacharias. Nor did we encounter any ice, except for a few vagrant floes. Most surprising, the only wind was a light breeze from the south, a compass point I hadn't thought about in a long, long time.

At last we came in sight of Sanirajak. Even at sea, I could detect the scent of the dead whale, and it seemed to me the sweetest smell in all the world.

---

① adj. Dirty; grimy.

② adj. Hardened against feeling; hardhearted.

极地野生

劳伦斯·米尔曼

都一上午了，小艇的发动机不停地发出古怪的打水的噪音，那噪音就好像有个新生的婴儿困在了里面。没过多久，发动机就彻底抛锚了。我的两位因纽特向导——库恩古雅各和扎卡赖亚斯赶忙把身子朝船外探去，想看看到底问题出在哪里。与此同时，我们开始向东南方向漂移。

"是发动机罢工啦，"库恩古雅各宣布，他的口气好像这不是明摆着的事。"得把它大卸八块才行。"在这艘严重超载的小艇上，明摆着的事就成了别说拆一个85马力的雅马哈舷外马达，就连拆一块手表的地方都没有。

我坦言，当时我的心情并不好，对我们的处境也不乐观，因为我早就知道北极的险恶。因纽特人有很多故事，讲的就是一些人乘船离开后便消失了；多年以后他们的骸骨出现在某片遥远的沙滩上。接下来的几个小时里，我们还是继续朝东南方向漂流着，库恩古雅各检查了马达的多处零部件。

"齐齐塔克！"扎卡赖亚斯大喊道。一座小岛。

他指了指大约五英里以外的一小块陆地，然后一把抓过了我们的单桨，开始向小岛划去。过了一会，库恩古雅各接替他继续划，然后我再接替库恩古雅各。我一直划一直划，直到胳膊快断了，把桨递给大我5岁却身壮如牛的扎卡赖亚斯。剩下的路他一直在划，巧妙地躲开小岛周围的浮冰。最后一个大浪将我们的小船冲到碎石滩上，发出响亮的吱嘎声。

北极给我们所有人判了缓刑，各种缓刑。

在加拿大北部，所有人类事务都要由冰雪做出最终裁定。在一座未知的小岛上度过了筋疲力尽的几天之前，我在萨尼然扎克（霍尔海滩）等待时机，这是一个位于梅尔维尔半岛上的因纽特人社区。我原本计划从那里穿越福克斯湾到达查尔斯王子岛，即一处无人驻扎的土地，面积几乎和康涅狄格州一样大。直到1948年，查尔斯王子岛才被官方记入档案，当时一位加拿大皇家空军飞行员正在进行航空拍摄，他在拍摄的一幅照片中发现了一片未被命名的陆地。时至今日，尽管这座低洼且被冰雪尘封的小岛已被纳入地图，但对它的探索还未完全展开。但由于福克斯湾被海上浮冰阻塞，所以我被困在萨尼然扎克（霍尔海滩）上，只待狂风大作，将冰块席卷而去。

大多数人来到萨尼然扎克（霍尔海滩）都不愿呆上几个小时——甚至几分钟都让人呆不下去。只需略微想象一下：这是阿巴拉契亚地区和吉普赛营地的结合，而后又经历了地震的摧残。只需略微想象一下：一片居民区，到处是雪车的车痕，丢弃的燃料桶，遗弃的帮宝适，瓶子，污水和动物的尸骨。这座小镇的主要景点，或者说，应该是它的主要败点，就是一具有着几百年历史的鲸鱼尸体，散发着刺鼻的气味。我已经迫不及待离开萨尼然扎克（霍尔海滩），到福克斯湾的荒郊野外去。

每天早晨，库恩古雅各都会认真地研究冰面，仿佛一位学究，严肃认真地凝视着一卷羊皮纸①，然后来到我的帐篷，说，"今天还是不行。"之后和我共饮咖啡。他的喝法，是直接将沉淀的咖啡渣一股脑吞下去，像对待一块鼻烟，以免掺水味淡了。

有几次，库恩古雅各带来了他的父亲，那是一位胸部宽阔的长者，面容沧桑，仿佛地形图上的等高线一般。这位叫斯乌里克的老人和我在萨尼然扎克（霍尔海滩）见过的其他人一样，只会说一句英语："Gunga Din，你这个人比我强！"几年以前，这座小镇的哈得孙湾公司的商人偶尔会举办葬礼。在葬礼上，并没有朗诵葬礼歌曲的服务，而是庄严地吟咏罗德亚德·吉普林②的《营房谣》。这首诗中的著名诗句已经进入了当地话，成为了一种淡淡的表达尊敬之情的语言，尽管没有一个人哪怕了解一丁点儿它的含义。

据斯乌里克说，查尔斯王子岛上有图尼特人，而且他警告过我要万事小心：他们有掏出我内脏的企图——这是一项图尼特人的娱乐项目——如果我给他们这个机会的话。

根据考古学家考证，图尼特人，也叫多塞特人，公元前1300年已经灭绝了。然而如果在北极有那么一个地方，这群人或许还能幸存下来，我想，这个地方就是查尔斯王子岛。斯乌里克还告诉我另外一个情况：由于查尔斯王子岛的天气条件恶劣，因此很容易让人陷入孤立无援的状况。

终于等到了一天早晨，库恩古雅各大叫把我喊醒"快点！大风把冰块吹散

---

① 古代一种可以擦去旧字另写新字的羊皮纸，书写材料。

② 罗德亚德·吉普林，英国作家、诺贝尔文学奖获得者。生卒年：1865年12月30日－1936年1月18日，又译吉普林或卢亚德·古卜龄），生于印度孟买，英国作家及诗人。主要著作有儿童故事《丛林之书》(The Jungle Book，1894年)、印度侦探小说《基姆》(Kim，1901年)、诗集《营房谣》(Gunga Din，1892年)、短诗《如果》(If—，1895年)以及许多脍炙人口的短篇小说。他是英国19世纪至20世纪中一位很受欢迎的散文作家，被誉为"短篇小说艺术创新之人"。吉卜林的作品在20世纪初的世界文坛产生了很大的影响，他本人也在1907年获得了诺贝尔文学奖。他是第一个英国诺贝尔文学奖获得者，也是至今诺贝尔文学奖最年轻的获得者。此外，他也曾被授予英国爵士爵位和英国桂冠诗人的头衔，但都被他放弃了。由于吉卜林所生活的年代正值欧洲殖民国家向其他国家疯狂地扩张，他的部分作品也被有些人指责为带有明显的帝国主义和种族主义色彩，长期以来人们对他的评价各持一端，极为矛盾，他笔下的文学形象往往既是忠心爱国和信守传统，又是野蛮和侵略的代表。然而近年来，随着殖民时代的远去，吉卜林也以其作品高超的文学性和复杂性，越来越受到人们的尊敬。

啦。"半梦半醒中，我掀起了帐篷，映入眼帘的就是一大片水面，前一天晚上还是结结实实的冰块。

1小时后，库恩古雅各、库恩古雅各的姐夫扎卡赖亚斯和我3个人把我们的装备装进了库恩古雅各的24英尺长的摩托小艇里，向着东面福克斯湾的方向出发。当然，我们试图向东面行进，但大风始终把我们推向北边。最后，我们决定等风停了再继续走，所以我们在距离萨尼然扎克（霍尔海滩）北部25英里的一个小浅湾上岸了。在这里我们遇到了一些来自依格鲁利克的海象狩猎人。依格鲁利克是半岛北部偏远的一个地区。一个狩猎人告诉我，夜间风会小些。我于是问他，他是怎么知道的。他大概是观察了某种鸟类飞行的模式，或者可能使用了某种历史悠久的当地技法来读懂天气的。

"不，"他说，"我从收音机听来的。"

第二天，风确实变小了，但却带来强烈的侧面涌浪。库恩古雅各和扎卡赖亚斯轮流保护小艇不被海浪卷走，尽管他们有作为舵手的专业经验，但我们还是浑身湿透了。甚至某一时刻，一阵浪朝我们的船舷打来，把一只水母甩到了船上。虽然北极的水母会带来糟糕的刺痛，但扎卡赖亚斯仍然觉得非常有趣。扎卡赖亚斯似乎觉得所有的东西都非常有趣，即使一头白化海象站在一块浮冰上面朝我们低声吼叫，他都觉得有趣。他告诉我，一头白化海象意味着死亡。

"对谁来说是死亡？"我问道。

"对我们，"他边说边笑。

尽管海浪汹涌，但我们前进了不少，向东行进了大约50英里到达了罗利岛。罗利岛本身是直到20世纪30年代中叶才被发现。当天的早些时候，库恩古雅各猎到了1头环斑海豹。在罗利岛上，我们为回城存了大部分的海豹肉，而后我们把脚蹼和肝煮好。这一餐让我想起在格陵兰第一次吃海豹的肝。那次吃的豹肝还冒着热气，是从一头刚刚宰杀的动物身上摘下来的。不管吃之前感觉多么犹豫，一尝到这肉扑鼻的富含铁质的味道，什么犹豫就都没了。

"我喜欢海豹肝，"我说道。

"我自己更喜欢海豹的眼睛。"库恩古雅各告诉我。过了一会，他切下了一只海豹的眼睛，给我演示这颗清澈的球体如何被用作放大镜——如果你恰好手边有一颗海豹的眼睛这是很有用的信息。

转天，海平面像蓝色的玻璃一样平滑。刚到下午，我们距离查尔斯王子岛西北部只有25英里了。委婉的说，我当时可兴奋了，看到距离目标近在咫尺。但就是在那时，发动机抛锚了。

我们发现自己搁浅的那个小岛，看上去大概2英里长，半英里宽。这座岛在我的加拿大地质调查图上面并没有出现；更为关键的是，就连库恩古雅各和扎卡赖亚斯也都不知道它的存在。我们迷路了,非常彻底的迷路了。

"或许我们就此离世,到达天堂了。"扎卡赖亚斯调侃道。

如果这就是天堂,那么许多严谨生活的人都会非常失望的。这里似乎并没有什么通往天国的珍珠门,只有被腐蚀了的石灰岩大门,被偶尔出现的石英岩墙阻隔着。如果非得和天堂扯上点关系,离天使的形象最近的就是一只象牙鸥。它在我们的头顶盘旋,那笔直的明亮的翅膀映衬着阴云密布的天空。

其他有翅膀的东西肯定就跟天国搭不上边了:蚊子。自从我们登岸的那一瞬间起,他们就开始对我们展开猛烈的袭击,而且袭击的范围之大,让我不禁猜测,它们已经很久没有以任何温血生物作为食物饱餐一顿了。

不一会儿功夫,库恩古雅各就在海滩上把马达拆开了。当时已经是晚上10点了,但光线仍然充足,足够他修理我们的命运多舛的马达。而且,也有足够的光线让我能够看清一颗滚跑的螺丝钉,我捡起来还给他。恐怕这是我所有能帮上的忙了:对于机械,我比一个3岁的孩子知道的还少。

反过来说,因纽特人似乎对机械有种天赋。有一次,我见过一位因纽特老人拆开并修理一副直升飞机的引擎,那位丹麦的飞行员对此惊讶不已,因为他自己都不能修。我当时问那位老人他从哪里学的这套,他指了指自己的脑袋,轻轻敲了一下。他出生在这样一个王国,要么你学会随时都能干活,要么你被淘汰。

到了午夜,库恩古雅各仍然在修理马达,我和扎卡赖亚斯便上床睡觉了。我夜里醒来如厕的时候,发现旁边躺着的却是库恩古雅各,鼾声大作。扎卡赖亚斯当时在帐篷外面的海滩上,工作着,伴着朦朦胧胧的光线。他的手里是一团交错缠绕的电线,好像翻线戏中缠绕的线条。

"你觉得能修好吗?"我说。

"Immaqa,"扎卡赖亚斯回答。

这个词是目前为止最流行的因纽特语了。它的意思是"可能吧,"暗含的意思是"可能不行。"如果你是个想要直接答案的人,因纽特人就用一句"immaqa",轻而易举地把你置于语无伦次的痴傻窘境。

第二天早晨,库恩古雅各和扎卡赖亚斯轮流盯着那一大堆马达零件,轮流拍打蚊子。我尝试从他们的表情中揣测是否有进展,但却发现他们两个都不特别高兴。

"我们需要一段输气管线,"库恩古雅各告诉我。

"但咱们在这很难订到,"扎卡赖亚斯补充道。

我们没带无线电设备,也没带定位信标(愚蠢之极,是呀:我们匆匆忙忙地离开了萨尼然扎克,连浮筏都忘带了),所以我有种不祥的预感,我们会被困在这个岛上，直到来人营救。既然已经知道库恩古雅各想要告诉我的话，我于是问他，短时间内是否会有船只经过我们的路线。这次他没说"immaqa"，而是"aakka"（不会）。

"或许会来飞机呢？"我说。

又是一句"aakka"（不会）：我们附近没有任何一条飞机通道。屋漏偏逢连夜雨，我们的划桨也断裂了，扎卡赖亚斯将船拖上岸的时候就坏了，现在划桨断成了没用的两段。（也不知怎么搞的，另外一支划桨被我们落在罗利岛上了。）总而言之，我们不仅迷路，而且孤立无援。

我的这两位伙伴似乎一点也不恐慌，或许我是从他们那里得到了某种暗示，又或者这种困境的真正本质还未被了解，我自己居然也不是太过担心。我告诉自己：没到死的那一刻，你就还算活着，而且，你曾经充满智慧，到达过一个不被世人知晓的地方。现在，你不过是刚刚到了这样的一个地方——看在上帝的份上，到外面去，探索一下吧。

"有需要我帮忙的吗？"我问道。

库恩古雅各和扎卡赖亚斯都使劲摇头，仿佛我的任何帮助都会使糟糕的情况变得更糟。于是我慢慢走开，一大群蚊子护送着我，在我的帽子周围嗡嗡地飞。库恩古雅各把我叫回去，把他的那把30-06来福枪交给了我，只说了一句："Nanuq（北极熊）"。他的意思并不是让我向无声电影的主角开枪，而是让我自卫，以防北极熊可能发起的攻击，罗伯特·弗拉哈迪[①]的主角正是以这种动物命名的。

既然身揣武器，我便斗胆攀爬我们帐篷后面的一处陡峭的山地。几分钟以后，我居然身处另一座陡峭的山地之上——这里恐怕是岛上的最高点——福克斯湾的一切尽收眼底。视线所及之处竟然没有一块陆地。的确，所见之处空空如也，因为即使是之前的浮冰也在夜间消失得无影无踪了。假使我站在月球上，或许才会有更强烈的孤独感，但我对此深表怀疑。

[①] 罗伯特·弗拉哈迪 Robert Flaherty（1884—1965），一位终其一生都在远离文明的世界里，以浪漫主义的眼光和探险家的品性追寻纪录片艺术和人生真实的导演，被尊为世界"纪录电影之父"和影视人类学鼻祖。罗伯特·弗雷哈迪生于美国密歇根州的铁山地区，是家里七个孩子中最年长的一个。19世纪中期弗雷哈迪的祖父从冰岛移民至此，在这里，弗雷哈迪同家人度过了一端快乐的童年时光，之后便随父亲到世界各地探险。父亲和他本人都是爱尔兰新教徒，母亲则是德国天主教徒。在这样的家庭氛围中，弗雷哈迪接受了各种文化的熏陶，美国人自由、民主的个性在他的血液里流淌。童年时期与父亲一起探险的经历让弗雷哈迪看到了美国以外的精彩世界，也逐渐培养了他热爱生活、崇尚自然的纯真个性。今天我们所看到的、听说的有关弗雷哈迪的一切故事，都是他作为纪录片导演的身份呈现。然而，弗雷哈迪在他第一部电影《北方的纳努克》放映时已经38岁。此前，他一直在世界各地进行探险，负责矿产的开采工作，与电影的第一次亲密接触也是由于探险的机缘。在他以后拍摄的所有电影中，探险精神始终贯彻其中，探索人类与自然的和谐、矛盾始终是他关注的主题。

而后我将视线转移到小岛本身。阳光的照耀下，小岛展现出更多的色彩，相比前一个夜晚绚丽得多。到处散落着星星点点的极地野花——紫色的虎耳草、拉普兰夹竹桃、苔藓剪秋罗、北极五指草，还有金凤花——从坚硬的岩石中勇敢顽强地生长、挺立着。北极棉的轻薄簇在微风中缓缓摇摆。一团绚烂的黄色青苔从坚硬的石灰岩宿主上爆发；一只同样绚烂的黄蝴蝶从花间掠过。

四下鸦雀无声，我的脚步走在碎石路上沙沙作响。我产生了一种幻觉，自从冰河时代以来，这座小岛上面的任何东西都没有改变甚至移动。无论从哪种角度说，这里都是一片严酷的地方。即便如此，它的凄美仍令我窒息。

之后我突然来到了一片石冢之上——五六个蜂窝状的结构，堆在微微倾斜的垄上。从缝隙中窥视其中一个，我看见一块人类的头盖骨和几片骨头碎片；窥视另一个，看到了一块褐色的头盖骨碎片，一个带牙齿的下颚骨，牙齿已经被磨损，以及散落的脊椎骨；从第三个中看到了单独的一个头盖骨。

我的第一反应是：上一次一组人来到此地，他们的马达出现故障，这大概就是他们的下场。

但是，在其中一个石冢里，我注意到一具骸骨，是被一盏巨大的圆形的皂石灯埋葬的，这也证明了这个地方的历史可以追溯到极北之地时期。骸骨的形态是以胎儿的姿势弯曲着。情况是否会是这样：这些人接替了图尼特人的脚步，他们相信，如果他们以来到这个世界的姿势离开的话那么他们通往来世的旅途会减少些许险恶。无论如何，我感到了一丝放松：极北之地时期在大约船用发动机发明两百年以前已经结束了。

仍然，这些坟墓在不断提醒我自己现在的处境。有可能这一片光秃秃的弹丸之地将最终成为我的安息之所。我想象着自己的最后一缕脆弱的思维随风飘逝，而后想象着某位考古学家发现了我的尸骨并纳闷，一个中年白人为什么来到如此远离他本土住所的地方。自从离开萨尼然扎克（霍尔海滩），我第一次发现自己为同一件事情寻思困惑。

陷入思考的同时，我正被大群的蚊子榨干，它们执着地寻寻觅觅终于帮助它们从我的蚊帐上找到一个个大洞小孔。我并非享受这种"针灸刺死"般的前景，因而加快了脚步。此刻，只有最适应有氧生存的小杂种们才能跟上我的步伐。然而毕竟这座岛并不是按照跑马场的场地建的，所以，我被某块冰碛物绊了一脚，"飞"到了空中。我下意识的对自己说，可别坠落在来福枪上面。终于我没有落在来福枪上。取而代之的是，我压在了指南针上，于是在我的胸口留下一个豁口——这恐怕是人类医学史上第一次由于指南针造成的伤病。

我也掉到了一个"万骨坑"里。成百上千条肋骨、肩胛骨、脊椎骨散落在我周围。头盖骨说明了这些都是海象的骸骨。这也解释了为什么石冢的占据者居住在这样一个明显贫瘠的地方——这处阴森恐怖的坑距离浮冰的边缘很近，这里也是笨重的艾维克驳船的家。对于极北之地来说，富饶与否并不是由土壤决定的，而是由鱼叉捕获的对象决定的。

说到帐篷里的库恩古雅各和扎卡赖亚斯，他俩正弯腰俯视着棋盘。他们专心致志地下棋，直到我站在旁边，没有一个人发现我。然后扎卡赖亚斯笑道："我们之前还指望着你打回来一只大北极熊作为晚餐呢。"

说实话，我有点担心我们的食物供应问题。之前我们可没预料到这种遭遇，所以只带了几周的食物。与此同时，我们当初还指望着靠海豹肉或海象肉补充膳食，但是我们的马达不工作，我们根本无法到达捕猎的距离。

所谓的食物供应，目前在我看来是极其匮乏的，所有的食物包括以下的东西：1 盒旅行装燕麦片（"膨胀餐"）、5 盒大米、1 包干西梅、1 磅葡萄干、2 包压缩饼干（硬饼干）、2 打士力架、11 包冷冻干燥的阿尔费雷多面条、6 包冷冻干燥的意大利罐焖鸡、4 包通心粉、半坛起士专家、1 小包面粉、几大片 pipsik（干鱼）、一些韧性十足的 maktaaq 片（独角鲸皮）和一个有点发霉的苹果。

他们俩结束游戏之后，我问扎卡赖亚斯如果我们断粮了怎么办。

"我们人吃人，互相吃好了，"他咧着嘴笑道。但他笑的同时上下打量着我，我想是从专业大厨的欣赏角度注视着我。

夜间狂风加速，开始如狗吠，进而若狼嚎，继而惊声尖叫，直至达到我从未听过的超高分贝。大约每过 1 小时，我们都到户外把捡来的石头沿着帐篷的绷索堆放好。假使没有这些石块，毫无疑问，帐篷早就被狂风拔起——雪杖、人和一切——无一例外都飞到福克斯湾的某个地方。

第二天依然狂风呼啸，并且，除了偶尔完成捡石头的任务，我们都老老实实地蹲在帐篷里。即便如此，狂风还是能觅到我们的行踪，推搡帐篷下面的粗砂飞入我们的睡袋、衣服、食物、我们的头发和普里默斯炉[①]——囊括一切，无孔不入。

困于帐篷的我更加意识到我们被囚禁在荒岛的程度之深。但库恩古雅各和扎卡赖亚斯仿佛隐居的禅宗佛教徒一般镇静自若，当然玩跳棋的时候除外。扎卡赖亚斯——和库恩古雅各相比稍逊一筹——偶尔会大喊"Tuqulirama! Tuqulirama！"（"我死定啦！我死定啦！"）

Ajurnarmat：这无疑是因纽特语中排名第二的流行语。意思大概是"有什

[①] 原文为"Primus"，词典中的解释是："普里默斯炉，一种便携式汽化煤油炉（名词）；第一的、首位的、资格最老的（形容词）。" PRIMUS 为注册商标，该企业作为专业户外炉具和汽灯的生产商，已拥有 116 年历史。其实 PRIMUS 这个名字来源于斯拉夫语，就是"炉子"的意思。通过对品牌名称的解译，即可推想来自瑞典的 PRIMUS 炉具曾经享有的名誉和辉煌。

么可担心的？"或者"喂，你又能做什么？"我们在一起的这段时间里，我逐渐将我的伙伴定义为鲜活的、能走路的、会玩跳棋的 ajurnarmat 化身。我非常羡慕他们的这种态度，更羡慕他们身处悲惨境遇仍能保持镇静的能力，当然这种悲惨境遇是我个人的感受。

某个时候，他们爆发出狂笑。他们正谈论一位英国首相，他是一名圣经传教会的成员，15 年前来到萨尼然扎克（霍尔海滩）。此人当时学习因纽特语刚好达到混淆用词的水平。某个星期天，他将 ijjujut（圣经）和 igjuuk 两个词弄混了，结果向会众宣传，告诫他们应当更加重视他们的睾丸。

过了一会，扎卡赖亚斯又讲述了以前的一个故事。有个人在巴芬岛雪橇旅行的时候食物都吃光了。这个饥肠辘辘的人祈祷上帝的帮助。突然，他在帐篷的地面上发现了一大块肉——是上帝施舍的！这个人将肉剥皮、剁碎，而后扔进了罐子里。但他在吃肉之前就死掉了——他刚刚是把自己的大腿剥皮剁碎了。

我的两位伙伴都觉得这个故事滑稽好笑。我怀疑扎卡赖亚斯讲这个故事是为了给我听，像是在说，"来吧，伙计，放松点，否则你鲁莽行事会自乱阵脚，比如把自己吃掉。"

据我的猜测，狂风以 65 至 70 节的航速[1]急刮，根本没有减缓的迹象。有一次我冒险到外面去撒尿，结果被一阵狂风吹得连牙齿都疼了。回到帐篷中，我只得靠写日志打发时间："如果能有幸从这次混乱中逃脱，我打算选择一种更为安稳的生活方式。"

3 天之后，令我们吃惊的事发生了，突然之间，疾风居然缓和下来，变成微风，仿佛在长时间力量展示之后忽然疲惫松懈了。现在我们出去，不会被冻成果冻，因为事实已经证明了这一点，我们也不会被蚊子叮咬，因为目光所到之处不见蚊子踪影。正值傍晚，一股无形的肃静笼罩四周。云中映现出一缕淡淡的粉红色纹彩——太阳的虹彩。光线显示出若隐若现的特质，这是北极地区的典型光线，即每一缕最后的阳光都使人感觉是从即将来临的永恒的冬季攫取而来。

很快库恩古雅各和扎卡赖亚斯便不断拆开又重新组装起马达来，这似乎是

---

[1] 航速即舰船在单位时间内所航行的里程。以海里/小时计算，简称节。是舰艇最重要的战术技术性能之一。通常用计程仪测定水面舰艇的航速分为最大航速、全速、巡航航速、经济航速和最小航速。"节"的代号是英文"Knot"，是指地球子午线上纬度 1 分的长度，由于地球略呈椭球体状，不同纬度处的 1 分弧度略有差异。在赤道上 1 海里约等于 1843 米；纬度 45°处约等于 1852.2 米，两极约等于 1861.6 米。1929 年国际水文地理学会议，通过以 1 分平均长度 1852 米作为 1 海里；1948 年国际人命安全会议承认，1852 米或 6076.115 英尺为 1 海里，故国际上采用 1852 米为标准海里长度。中国承认这一标准，用代号"M"表示。最快的超大型集装箱船舶可以达到 25-32 节的速度。一般散货船在 12-17 节之间，杂货船一般在 15-17 节之间。

第一百次的尝试了。我想伸展一下腿脚，于是开始沿着海岸散步。暴风雨似乎洗劫了各种海洋赃物——缠绕在海草垫上的一只金斑鸻[①]的翅膀、被肢解的海星、巨藻、鱼和一只死掉的海豹。一开始，我以为这只海豹可被用作食物，但是，近距离观察之后，我发现它仅仅剩下一副外壳了，它的肉和内脏已经被各种蟹类、各种等足类[②]动物以及其他海洋生物吃光了。

马上我开始一丝不苟的清理海滩，寻找能够支撑我们急剧减少的食物的代替品。我本不该对一条刚死的鱼或一只刚死的鸟嗤之以鼻，但我只找到了死了很久的鱼和一堆混乱的羽毛，乱到难以辨认是鸟的羽毛还是床垫的毛。而后我在岸边看见了一块长满苔藓的土地上长了一些马勃尘菌。我早就知道库恩古雅各和扎卡赖亚斯都不会吃这些（因纽特人认为蘑菇都是陨星的粪便），但我当然愿意吃了。

突然一声枪响，打断了我的觅食行动。我沿着海滩赶紧往回跑。走近了，我发现扎卡赖亚斯的脸上露出比平时更灿烂的笑容。

"现在一切搞定啦，"库恩古雅各说道。马达又回到了船上，轰然一声运转起来。

在那一可爱的时刻，所有我能对他说的就是："Gunga Din，你这个人比我强！"

显而易见，马达的密封圈磨损严重，意味着燃油管无法加油。库恩古雅各于是用一些巨藻代替了橡胶密封垫，这便是关键伎俩。

因而现在的问题是，我是否愿意继续去查尔斯王子岛？库恩古雅各告诉我，我们有足够的燃油。当然，只是可能足够。并且我们的食物也很可能足够。不够的话，我们总能猎到一两只海豹。燃油也可能腐蚀我们临时的"密封圈"，如果真的腐蚀了，也不要紧，我们只需用更多的巨藻代替就可以了。

[①] 鸻科。全长约24cm。雄鸟体上黑色，密布金黄色斑，体下黑色。一条白色带位于上下体之间极为醒目。雌鸟黑色部分较褐且具有许多细白斑。冬季上体灰褐色，羽缘淡金黄色，体下灰白色，有不明显黄褐斑，眉线黄白色。栖息于河岸附近农田、水塘、沼泽及空旷草原，以植物种子、嫩芽、软体动物、甲壳类昆虫为食。繁殖期5～7月，在沼泽地中干燥地面上营巢，每窝产卵4～5枚。雌雄共同孵卵，孵化期27～28天。迁徙时途经我国全境，在北纬25度以南越冬。种群数量较多。该物种已被列入国家林业局2000年8月1日发布的《国家保护的有益的或者有重要经济、科学研究价值的陆生野生动物名录》。

[②] 囊虾总目的一个较大的目。约有一万多种。它们的体形变化较大，多数身体背腹平扁，头部短小，盾形，与胸部第一节或前二节愈合。无头胸甲。腹部较胸部短，分节可能清楚或存不同程度愈合，最末腹节与尾节愈合。胸部附肢均无外肢，第一对为颚足，其他七对为步足，彼此形状相似。腹肢为双枝型，为游泳和呼吸器官，心脏很长，延伸到腹部。等足类一般是身体平扁，左右对称，少数种类如淡水产的扁虱虫类，身体为侧扁，也有呈圆筒形的（如背尾科）一些种，寄生亚目中雄雌性个体形状不同，雄性很小，附于雌性体上，左右不对称。等足类体长一般为5～15毫米，深海种如巨大深水虱，最大体长可达42厘米，宽15厘米，多数体色为土褐色，各种灰色或黄色，与其生活的环境相一致。

我不能确定他是否处于 ajurnarmat 的状态（"不管发生什么，就是什么"）或者说服我放弃他认为危险的旅行。但没关系。我已经决定了，是时候回到那个具有肮脏魅力的萨尼然扎克（霍尔海滩）了。我已然满足了自己探寻天涯海角之岛的欲望，更何况地图显示这座岛事实上比查尔斯王子岛远得多。与此同时，我并不想再次陷入孤立无援的境地，不想再冒险了。在北极，命运并不倾向引导，更不堪诱惑。

　　尽管如此，我们离开了多石的海滩之后，我有种莫名的伤感。或许我已将自己的一部分留在了这片冷酷无情的海滩上，又或许我的伤感出于对某种罕见特权的屈服——孤独的特权。随着小岛渐行渐远，我自思自忖，世上应有许多更可怕的地方，将你的骸骨深深掩埋。

　　返回福克斯湾的旅途可谓风平浪静。我们在罗利岛上又住了一晚，那里有我们之前储存的海豹肉，于是我们饱餐了一顿。我们并没再遇到白化海象，扎卡赖亚斯大失所望。我们也未碰到任何冰冻，仅有一些游移的浮冰。最令人吃惊的是，唯一一次刮风是来自南边的徐徐微风，也是许久以来我从未想到过的风向。

　　终于萨尼然扎克（霍尔海滩）映入我们的眼帘。甚至是在海上，我们都能嗅到鲸鱼尸体的味道，并且对我来说，这是世界上最甜美的气味。

（杨建 译　申彩红 校）

Winter Rules

Steve Rushin

【导读】你想过在冬日里燃烧一份激情,打一杆高尔夫吗?你想过豪爽地将酒吧的全部存货扫荡吗?你想过在北极的冰天雪地里将这两件事同时完成吗?如果你的答案是否定的,那么请塌下心来玩味这篇荡气回肠的《冬日独尊》吧!它能将你内心深处潜藏已久但又不敢付诸行动的天性解放,它能让你淋漓尽致地体味那份运动的畅快。

在寒冷的北极,有一个美丽的地方叫格陵兰,那里有古灵精怪的动物,有会漂浮的冰山,还有五彩斑斓的北极光……"没有阳光的冬天,没有月光的夏天"正是这冰雪仙境的真实写照。"什么都不能阻止你在地球上的任何地方、任何季节、任何一天去打高尔夫球。" 在冰川和冰山构成的场地上,挥杆一击,冰雪四溅,又是何等潇洒。或许正是这一份热爱,这一份执着,这一份坚定,才使作者与世界各地的朋友不远万里相聚在素裹银装的格陵兰。这里有因为睡过头而与世界冰上高尔夫球锦标赛擦肩而过的作者,有令人啼笑皆非的小丑艺人,有一群勇往直前的雪橇狗,还有一间世外桃源般的迪斯科舞厅和驻场乐队……冠军又如何?世界排名又何干?逃不过一曲赞歌对心灵的洗涤。相信读过本文,你会情不自禁的喜欢上格陵兰的一切和高尔夫的全部。

I

"I couldn't care less about Greenland[①]," William C. Starrett II said with disarming candor shortly after arriving in the northernmost country on Earth. "I'm here for the golf."

[①] Greenland is an autonomous country within the Kingdom of Denmark, located between the Arctic and Atlantic Oceans, east of the Canadian Arctic Archipelago. Though physiographically a part of the continent of North America, Greenland has been politically and culturally associated with Europe (specifically Norway and later Denmark) for more than a millennium. Greenland is, by area, the world's largest island. With a population of 56,615 (January 2011 estimate) it is the least densely populated dependency or country in the world.

Sixteen empty beer bottles were lined up in front of the retired California bankruptcy lawyer, so he looked like a contestant in a carnival midway game[1]. It was the last week of March, and Starrett, two photographers and I were passing a five-hour layover inside the modest air terminal in Ilulissat[2], a southern suburb of the North Pole, by systematically divesting the bar of its biennial beer supply. We began by drinking all the Carlsberg and then depleted the Tuborg[3] reserves, and we were grimly working our way through the supply of something called Faxe[4], evidently named for the fax-machine toner with which it is brewed, when Starrett began recounting his life's memorable rounds. Rounds of golf, rounds of beer — the distinction was scarcely worth making.

"Livingstone was an interesting course," he said. "It's in Zambia, near Victoria Falls. The greens fee is thirty-five cents, and the pro shop has one shirt. At Rotorua, in New Zealand, the hazards are geysers. Sun City, in South Africa, has an alligator pit, and you don't play your ball out of that." This summer, Starrett said, he would rent a house in County Cork ("Walking distance to the Jameson's distillery") and travel from Ireland to Iceland for the Arctic Open, played in twenty-four hours of sunlight. He was, on the other hand, unlikely ever to return to the Moscow Country Club. It has gone to seed, don't you think, after expanding hubristically from nine holes to eighteen?

I feigned a look that said *You're telling me* and shook my head world-wearily.

"It is said that once a traveler has seen the world, there is always Greenland," says the Lonely Planet guidebook *Iceland, Greenland and the Faroe Islands*[5], which only partly explains Starrett's presence here, 250 miles north of the Arctic Circle in

---

[1] A carnival game is a game of chance or skill that can be seen at a traveling carnival, charity fund raiser, amusement park, or on a state and county fair midway.

[2] Ilulissat is a town in the Qaasuitsup municipality in western Greenland, located approximately 200 km (120 mi) north of the Arctic Circle. With the population of 4,546 as of 2010, it is the third-largest settlement in Greenland, after Nuuk and Sisimiut.

[3] Tuborg is a Danish brewing company founded in 1873 by Carl Frederik Tietgen. Since 1970 it has been part of Carlsberg. The brewery was founded in Hellerup, a northern suburb of Copenhagen.

[4] Faxe Bryggeri A/S is a Danish Brewery located in the town of Fakse. The Brewery was founded in 1901 by Nikoline and Conrad Nielsen and it is best known for its strong export beers. In 1989 Faxe Brygeri merged with Bryggerigruppen which later developed into Royal Unibrew. It is well known around Germany for its 10% 1 litre cans.

[5] A book series of travel guides exploring countries, regions and cities in depth and for every budget, with maps, first-hand recommendations, background information and coverage of all the sights. There are more than 230 titles in the book series covering nearly every country in the world.

Ilulissat, at the exact point at which mankind's appetite for golf exceeds the capabilities of fixed-wing aircraft.

Our profane party of golfers and journalists had flown five hours to Greenland on its national airline, Grønlandsfly, after first laying waste to the duty-free liquor shop in the Copenhagen airport so that its ravaged shelves resembled those of a 7-Eleven in the hours immediately following a hurricane warning. After alighting on Greenland, the world's largest island, we required two more northbound flights of an hour each to reach Ilulissat. This was the end of the line for the four- prop de Havilland DHC-7, and we now awaited the arrival of a Vietnam-vintage Sikorsky military transport helicopter to take us the last hour-and-twenty-minute leg north, to the frozen coastal island of Uummannaq①, for the first — and possibly last — World Ice Golf Championship (hereafter known as the WIG).

The WIG was open to anyone with two thousand dollars, a titanium② liver and a willingness to spend a week 310 miles north of the Arctic Circle, in one of the northernmost communities in the world. Who could resist such a powerful come-on? Every citizen of planet Earth save twenty, it turns out.

Still, though the tournament was a sponsored contrivance designed to promote Greenland tourism — and a Scottish liqueur company, Drambuie③ — winter golf on Greenland promised to have singular benefits for the high handicapper. For starters, the island's 840,000 square miles are virtually unblighted (from a strictly golf-centric view of the ecosystem) by trees. Nor would water come into play, as 85 percent of Greenland is covered by a permanent icecap, which in places is two miles thick. Most significant, the Greenlandic counting system goes only to *arqaneq marluk*, or 12, after which there is simply *passuit*, or "many" — an idiosyncrasy surely to be exploited to my advantage on a scorecard.

The incoming Sikorsky at last set down in Ilulissat like a great mosquito of

---

① Uummannaq is a town in the Qaasuitsup municipality, in northwestern Greenland. With 1,299 inhabitants as of 2010, it is the eleventh-largest town in Greenland, and is home to the country's most northerly ferry terminal. Founded in 1763, the town is a hunting and fishing base, with a canning factory and a marble quarry.

② Titanium is a strong, low-density, highly corrosion-resistant, lustrous white metallic element that occurs widely in igneous rocks and is used to alloy aircraft metals for low weight, strength, and high-temperature stability. Here it is used to describe the "strong" liver that a person has to have because he has to drink a lot to survive in the freezing Arctic.

③ Drambuie is a honey-and herb-flavoured golden liqueur made from aged malt whisky, heather honey and a secret blend of herbs and spices. The flavour suggests saffron, honey, anise, nutmeg and herbs.

death. The vehicle was so old, a Dane living in Greenland told me with perverse pride, that its manufacturer wants the relic returned for display in a museum when Grønlandsfly retires it. At this news I signaled the bartendress for a final round of Faxes, but she gestured to her glass-fronted refrigerator, now empty, and said accusingly, "No more beer."

With growing dread, I returned to my companions in the waiting area. In the lounge chair facing me was a London-based sports photographer named Gary Prior. A janitor who moments earlier had been cleaning the men's room approached Prior from behind and began massaging his scalp, and a look of supreme serenity spread across his — the janitor's — face. Prior prudently avoided any sudden movement as he mouthed, "This bloke[①]'s gone mad."

So it was with a profound sense of foreboding that we boarded the Sikorsky, its belly filled with golf clubs, and set out to defy Robert Louis Stevenson[②], who wrote, "Ice and iron cannot be welded." Would this prove to be a prophecy? With a terrible shudder, the rotored beast rose above the icebergs, carrying us, its human prey, deeper, ever deeper, into a golfing Heart of Darkness[③].

II

I had first heard of ice golf two summers earlier, while traveling under the midnight sun in northern Scandinavia. "You must return in the winter," implored the deskman at the Strand Hotel in Helsinki, "when we play ice golf on frozen lakes and snow, in freezing temperatures, with balls that are purple."

"Yes, well, I imagine they would be," I stammered, but truth be told, the idea

---

① Bloke is a British slang term for a man, which is commonly used in the UK, Ireland, South Africa, Australia and New Zealand.

② Robert Louis Balfour Stevenson (13 November 1850 – 3 December 1894) was a Scottish novelist, poet, essayist, and travel writer. His best-known books include *Treasure Island, Kidnapped,* and *Strange Case of Dr Jekyll and Mr Hyde.*

③ *Heart of Darkness* is a novella written by Joseph Conrad. Before its 1902 publication, it appeared as a three-part series (1899) in Blackwood's Magazine. It is widely regarded as a significant work of English literature and part of the Western canon. The story tells of Charles Marlow, an Englishman who took a foreign assignment from a Belgian trading company as a ferry-boat captain in Africa. *Heart of Darkness* exposes the dark side of European colonization while exploring the three levels of darkness that the protagonist, Marlow, encounters: the darkness of the Congo wilderness, the darkness of the Europeans' cruel treatment of the natives, and the unfathomable darkness within every human being for committing heinous acts of evil.

intrigued me. Greenland was among the last outposts — on Earth or in its orbit — to resist golf's colonial overtures. Man first walked on the moon in 1969, and within two years he was golfing there. Greenland was first inhabited five thousand years ago, yet it had only a nine-hole track near the main airport, in Kangerlussuaq[①], to show for it. Until two months before our arrival, the game had never been seen in Uummannaq, and when the Sikorsky touched down outside the village, I had an irresistible impulse to plant a numbered flagstick, as if landing at Iwo Jima[②].

A week before our visit, 200 of Uummannaq's 1,400 residents had turned out for a golf clinic[③] conducted on a makeshift[④] driving range[⑤]: the frozen fjord waters that surround the island. "I think it is very difficult to hit this ball," said Jonas Nielsen, a fifty-eight-year-old resident, after taking his hacks off a rubber tee. "But the young kids, they are very interested and would like to learn more about this game."

As well they should. Greenland's 56,000 residents, 80 percent of whom are Inuits (the word "Eskimo" is best avoided), are said to be temperamentally suited to golf. "One thing about Greenlanders," wrote Lawrence Millman[⑥] in his Arctic travelogue *Last Places*, "they tend to find misfortune amusing."

You have to, on Greenland or in golf. "When they contacted me many months ago to attend this event," said Ronan Rafferty, referring to the tournament's

---

① Kangerlussuaq is a settlement in western Greenland in the Qeqqata municipality, located at the head of a fjord of the same name. It is Greenland's main air transport hub, being the site of Greenland's largest commercial airport.

② Iwo Jima is famous as the setting of the February–March 1945 Battle of Iwo Jima between the United States and the Empire of Japan during World War II. The island grew in recognition in the west when the iconic photograph *Raising the Flag on Iwo Jima* was taken during the battle. The U.S. occupied Iwo Jima until 1968, when it was returned to Japan.

③ A clinic is a group session offering counsel or instruction in a particular field or activity.

④ adj. Suitable as a temporary or expedient substitute: e.g. used a rock as a makeshift hammer.

⑤ A driving range is an area where golfers can practice their golf swing. It can also be a recreational activity itself for amateur golfers or when enough time for a full game is not available. Many golf courses have a driving range attached and they are also found as stand-alone facilities, especially in urban areas.

⑥ Lawrence Millman (born January 13, 1948 in Kansas City, Missouri) in is an adventure travel writer from Cambridge, Massachusetts. He is the author of eleven books, including *Our Like Will Not Be There Again, Northern Latitudes, Last Places, An Evening Among Headhunters, A Kayak Full of Ghosts,* and *Lost in the Arctic*. His work has also appeared in *Smithsonian, National Geographic Adventure, the Atlantic Monthly, Sports Illustrated,* and *Islands*. He has won numerous awards, including a Northern Lights Award, a Lowell Thomas Award, an award for the best article on Canada in a U.K. publication (1996), and a Pacific-Asia Gold Travel Award; he has been anthologized in the Best American Travel Writing (Houghton Mifflin) three years in a row.

sponsors, "I thought it was a joke." Rafferty, a thirty-five-year-old native of Northern Ireland, was the leading money winner on the European tour in 1989 and a member of that year's Ryder Cup team. He was paid by sponsors to attend the WIG, but a wrist injury would prevent him from actually playing. Mercifully he had his own wines shipped to Greenland, and he was toasted at dinner by the mayor of Uummannaq as "Ronan Rafferty, the famous golfer which I never heard of."

Rafferty arrived the night before I did with another party of golfers and journalists. All told, twenty competitors and twenty noncompetitors, representing six nations, attended the WIG. From Holland came Lex Hiemstra, who won the trip in a contest and was often asked if second prize was *two* tickets. Joining me from the United States were Starrett and Mark Cannizzaro, a *New York Post*[1] golf columnist who turned up some instructive literature on local customs. "The stomach of a reindeer is like a large balloon, and the green substance in the stomach has a very particular smell," read the section headed *Food and How We Eat It* in a Greenland publication. "It is neither delicious nor revolting, but somewhere in between." This would prove useful, as our menus for the tournament would include whale jerky, blackened musk ox and battered auk.

Jane Westerman joined my table at the welcoming dinner in the Hotel Uummannaq. Westerman, a widow from England with a newfound love of golf ("I'm quite keen, really"), is a member of the Roehampton Club in southwest London. "We have bridge, croquet and golf," she said. "But hardly any ice golf a-tall."

Peter Masters, also English, asked Westerman where exactly the club was located. "It's near The Priory," she replied. "Do you know The Priory? The upmarket psychiatric hospital?"

Masters did not know The Priory, but soon enough, surely, we all would. Outside the hotel, hundreds of Greenlandic sled dogs — frightening creatures resembling wolves — wailed all night at the moon. A message posted in the hotel said that alcohol was forbidden in guest rooms. A man explained that a drunk once

---

[1] The *New York Post* is the 13th-oldest newspaper published in the United States and is generally acknowledged as the oldest to have been published continuously as a daily, although – as is the case with most other papers – its publication has been periodically interrupted by labor actions.Since 1993, it has been owned by media mogul Rupert Murdoch's News Corporation, which had owned it previously from 1976 to 1988. It is the seventh-largest newspaper in the U.S. by circulation.Its editorial offices are located at 1211 Avenue of the Americas, in New York City, New York.

wandered out and lay down among the dogs. In the morning all that was found of him was a button. A single button.

"What's the saying?" Masters asked, with more portent than he could possibly know. "Mad dogs and Englishmen ...?"

III

It was fifteen degrees below zero when I rose to play a practice round with Starrett. On the course he stood up his stand-up bag, and its plastic legs snapped in half. The bag collapsed to the ice, legs dangling at odd angles, like Joe Theismann[①]'s.

My own legs buckled at the beauty of the layout. The course was constructed entirely of ice and snow, nine holes laid out like a bracelet of cubic zirconiums on the frozen fjord waters surrounding Uummannaq. Fairways doglegged around icebergs ten stories tall. This is what Krypton Country Club must look like. My disbelieving eyes popped cartoonishly, and I had half a mind to pluck them from my face, plop them in a ball washer, and screw them back into their sockets to see if the scene was real.

The fairways were snow-packed and groomed and set off by stakes from the icy rough[②]. The greens, called whites, were smooth ice, like the surface of a skating rink. No amount of Tour Sauce could get a ball to bite on these whites; bump-and-run, I could see, was the only way to play.

The hole itself was twice the diameter of a standard golf hole, and players were allowed to sweep their putting lines clean with a broom. Other winter rules were in effect: all balls in the fairway could be played off a rubber tee, while balls in the rough could be lifted and placed within four inches of where they landed, on a line no closer to the hole. My own balls, alas, were not purple, but rather optic yellow

---

① Joseph Robert "Joe" Theismann (born September 9, 1949 in New Brunswick, New Jersey) is a former quarterback in the National Football League (NFL) and Canadian Football League (CFL). He was inducted into the College Football Hall of Fame in 2003.

② Rough is the area outside the fairway in golf. The area between the tee box and the putting green where the grass is cut even and short is called the fairway and is generally the most advantageous area from which to hit. The area between the fairway and the out-of-bounds markers and also between the fairway and green is the rough, the grass of which is cut higher than that of the fairway and is generally a disadvantageous area from which to hit.

low-compression Titleists[①], replete with the WIG logo.

I discovered many things during my practice round of ice golf: I discovered that any given golf shot is 30 percent shorter in sub-zero temperatures than it is at seventy-two degrees. (The course was appropriately abbreviated, at 4,247 yards for eighteen holes.) I discovered that it's difficult to make a Vardon grip in ski gloves, to take a proper stance without crampons, and to find a ball that has landed in fresh powder. But mainly I discovered this: that with suitable clothes, no spouse and no desire for country club indulgences — caddies, shoeshines, combs adrift in a sea of blue Barbicide — there is nothing to prevent you from playing golf anywhere on Earth, in any season, any day of the year.

That alone seemed a more worthwhile discovery than anything Admiral Peary[②] stumbled on in the Arctic.

IV

The WIG had a shotgun[③] start. Except that a cannon was used instead of a shotgun, and the cannoneer reportedly suffered powder burns on his face and had to be treated in the village hospital. The next shotgun start employed an actual shotgun.

I was playing with Masters, an editor at the British magazine *Golf World* and a seven handicapper. On the second hole, a 284-yard par-4 with an iceberg dominating the right rough, Masters uncoiled a majestic drive. As he did so, a team of speeding dogs pulling a sled abruptly appeared to our left, two hundred yards from the tee box. The ball was hurtling up the fairway at speed x, the dogs were sprinting toward the fairway at speed y, and suddenly, as the two vectors approached each other, we

---

① Titleist is a brand name owned by Fortune Brands for golf equipment and apparel products produced by its subsidiary called the Acushnet Company, which is headquartered in Fairhaven, Massachusetts.

② Rear Admiral Robert Peary, full name Robert Edwin Peary, Sr. (May 6, 1856 – February 20, 1920) was an American explorer who claimed to have led the first expedition, on April 6, 1909, to reach the geographic North Pole. Peary's claim was widely credited for most of the 20th century, though it was criticized even in its own day.

③ 业余高尔夫比赛中，shotgun 比赛就是参赛的选手同一时间在不同的球洞开始比赛。比如第一组 4 名球员 10 点钟从第一洞开始，到 18 洞结束，而第 5 组 4 名球员也是在 10 点中开始，但是是从第 5 洞开始，然后到第 4 洞结束。该比赛的优势在于大家在同一时间段比赛，赛后可以立刻统计成绩，然后进行一些餐饮，社交活动，而不是先比赛的要花几个小时等其他人结束。有些人抱怨这种比赛形式可能不公平，有人从比较容易的洞开始，有人从比较难的洞开始，会影响成绩。不过，对业余选手来说，这个可以忽略。这种比赛，每一个人付费可能要高一些。因为球场在比赛开始前需要清场，不能安排其他人打球。一般来说，至少要有 30-40 个人的比赛，球场才愿意安排这种比赛。

were witnesses to a complicated math problem sprung horribly to life.

With what can only be described as a plaintive wail, one of the dogs collapsed. The rest of the team kept sprinting, dragging their fallen comrade behind the sled so that he resembled a tin can tied to the bumper of a newlywed couple's car. The driver glanced back at the dog and, with barely a shrug, continued to mush. Greenlandic sled drivers, in sealskin jackets and pants made of polar-bear pelt, are not given to great displays of emotion, and the entire hallucinatory vision quickly disappeared into the white glare of an Arctic horizon.

Masters couldn't have anticipated this ludicrously improbable event, but a Danish woman following our foursome — she composed our entire gallery — repeatedly accused him of huskycide. "How could you?" she kept saying. "We are guests here." What the sled driver made of this act of God[①] — a single optic-yellow hailstone falling from the sky and smiting his dog — is lost to history.

The very next hole was a righthand dogleg — a word our foursome now studiously avoided using in Masters's presence — around an iceberg. I sliced consecutive tee shots on top of the berg and never recovered, especially as I had exhausted my one sleeve of optic-yellow Titleists and was now playing with the most garish range balls in my bag. Masters, shaken, carded a 40 on the front nine but recovered his composure to post a three-over-par 75 for the round.

At day's end Englishman Robert Bevan-Jones, whose record 31 on the back nine gave him a first-round 70, held a one-stroke lead over Scotsman Graeme Biases. My first-round 99 left me in eighteenth place and in a powerful melancholia, especially considering that the tournament lasted but two days. We had come all this way, and it was already half over. Long after the mood ended, I remained on the fjord, seasonal affective disorder[②] setting in, and lost myself in the endless white.

I was wallowing in a profound silence, two miles from Uummannaq on the frozen fjord, when my driver, a Dane raised in Greenland, broke the spell. "Uummannaq means 'heart,' " said Christian Dyrlov while tracing a valentine in the

---

① Act of God, a manifestation especially of a violent or destructive natural force, such as a lightning strike or earthquake, that is beyond human power to cause, prevent, or control.

② Seasonal affective disorder (SAD), also known as winter depression or winter blues, is a mood disorder in which people who have normal mental health throughout most of the year, experience depressive symptoms in the winter or, less frequently, in the summer,[1] spring or autumn, repeatedly, year after year. In the Diagnostic and Statistical Manual of Mental Disorders (DSM-IV), SAD is not a unique mood disorder, but is "a specifier of major depression".

air with his index finger. "Because the island is shaped like a heart, or like the back of a woman."

Hours later, back in my room, I unfolded a map and concluded that it would take the entire imaginative arsenal of a powerfully lonely man, in a frigid climate, at a far remove from the rest of the world, to see Uummannaq as even vaguely resembling a valentine. Or the tapering back of a beautiful woman.

It was beginning to look like both to me.

V

Saturday night in Uummannaq began uneventfully enough: The dinner was verbally hijacked, as usual, by the speechifying representative of Drambuie, who kept urging us, somewhat salaciously, to *nose* his product. Two clowns performed. Then a few of us walked through the restaurant's kitchen. Which is to say, through the looking glass.

Behind the kitchen in the Hotel Uummannaq, should you ever find yourself there, is a disco. Greenland, I kid you not, is a hotbed of something called Arctic Reggae. Alas, the headliners on this night were not Bob Marley & the Whalers. Rather, two aspiring rock stars from Moldavia took the stage, and they introduced themselves as Andy and Andreas. One played keyboards, the other guitar. "Our band is called Tandem[1]," said Andy, or possibly Andreas. "You know, the bicycle with two seats?"

Andy and Andreas, singing from a notebook filled with handwritten lyrics to Western pop songs, performed phonetic covers of such unforgettable standards as "Unforgettable" ("Like a song of love that clins to me/How a follow you that stins to me") and "Country Roads" ("Almost heaven, West Virginia/Blue Ridge Mountain, Shenandoah River"). A toothless woman forced me, at beer-point, to dance with her, while leathery Inuit fishermen watched our group of golfing toffs[2] and scrawny scribes pogo to the music and decided — for reasons known only to them — not to kill us with their bare hands.

"Why do you laugh during 'Mustang's Alley'?" Andreas (or maybe it was

---

[1] a bicycle with two sets of pedals and two saddles, arranged one behind the other for two riders.
[2] British slang, a rich, well-dressed, or upper-class person, especially a man.

Andy) asked as I flipped through his notebook at a set break.

"It's 'Mustang Sally,'" I replied, and a light bulb buzzed to life above his head.

"Ahh," he said, as if his world had finally begun to make sense. "Thank you."

Forget love and Esperanto: The only two international languages are music and sports. While Greenland has a home-rule government, it remains a province of Denmark, and just fourteen hours had elapsed since Denmark played Italy in a qualifying match for soccer's European Championships. The match had been broadcast live on Greenland's lone television network. This qualified as event programming; the fare on another day consisted principally of a travel agent riffling through brochures for tropical resorts.

I now understood why our gallery had been infinitesimal earlier in the day: oblivious to golf, Greenlanders are soccer obsessives. The only permanent athletic facility visible in Uummannaq is a soccer pitch. Every fifth child wore a Manchester United ski cap. Man United's goalkeeper is Peter Schmeichel①, who is also captain of the Danish national team. Additionally, England had played Poland that afternoon, and Man United star Paul Scholes② scored all three goals for England.

So wired Uummannaqana were not ready to retire when the disco closed at 3 A.M., and we all repaired to a house party, which is when things began to get surreal. Just inside the door was a pair of size 20 clown shoes. Fair enough. On a shelf were several impressive ivory souvenirs — swords, perhaps, or walking sticks — that are difficult to describe. An English photographer was twirling one like Mary Poppins③'s umbrella when the Faroese hostess materialized to say, "I see you found my collection of walrus penis bones."

The clown shoes belonged to a thirty-one-year-old American named Joel Cole,

---

① Peter Bolesław Schmeichel MBE (born 18 November 1963) is a retired Danish professional footballer who played as a goalkeeper, and was voted the "World's Best Goalkeeper" in 1992 and 1993. He is best remembered for his most successful years at English club Manchester United, whom he captained to the 1999 UEFA Champions League to complete The Treble. He was a key member of the Danish national team that won Euro 92.

② Paul Scholes, born 16 November 1974, is an English footballer who plays for Manchester United as a midfielder. He is a one-club man, having spent his entire professional career with the Red Devils. Scholes has been described by Sir Bobby Charlton as "the embodiment of all that I think is best about football."

③ Mary Poppins is the main character of the books of the same name, a magical nanny who sweeps into the Banks home of Cherry Tree Lane and takes charge of the Banks children. She never openly acknowledges her strange and magical powers, and feigns insult when one of the children refers to her previous adventures. She flies in on an umbrella, and departs when the children have learned enough lessons that they need her no longer.

who was visiting Uummannaq from his native Shakopee, Minnesota — a town nearly adjacent to the one I grew up in. The odds against our meeting near the North Pole were roughly six billion to one, but by this time I had come to expect anything in Uummannaq. Cole was once the national track and field coach for the Faroe Islands and led them to a respectable showing at the 1989 World Island Games, a kind of Olympics among Greenland, Iceland, the Isle of Wight, the Isle of Man, the Faroes, Shetlands, Gilligan's and so forth. Cole now clowns — he used the word as a verb — in the world's underprivileged places for the real-life Patch Adams[1], whom Robin Williams portrayed in the film of that name. Indeed, Cole was the man who had clowned us at dinner just before we nosed our Drambuie. Said Cole, memorably, "I've clowned in Bosnia."

By 6:30 A.M. the evening was running out of steam, and I made my way back to the hotel with four journalists turned English soccer hooligans. As all 29,000 of northeastern Greenland's sled dogs howled in unison, we strolled the streets — or, rather, street — of Uummannaq and sang (to the tune of "Kumbaya, My Lord"):

"He scores goals galore, he scores goals.
He scores goals galore, he scores goals.
He scores goals galore, he scores goals.
Paul Soho-oles, he scores goals."

I was due to tee off in two hours.

VI

I neglected to answer my wake-up call. I neglected to request a wake-up call. And I certainly neglected to "spring ahead" one hour in observance of Daylight Saving Time. So I missed my tee time. Which is why in the final WIG results, listed in several international newspapers the next day — from the *New York Post* to *The Times* of London — my name would be followed by the ignominious notation WD.

---

[1] *Patch Adams* is a 1998 comedy-drama film starring Robin Williams. Directed by Tom Shadyac, it is based on the life story of Dr. Hunter "Patch" Adams and the book Gesundheit: Good Health is a Laughing Matter by Adams and Maureen Mylander. The film was a box-office success, grossing over twice its budget in the United States alone; however, it was poorly received by most critics.

Which stands, I gather, for "Was Drinking."

Having officially withdrawn from the WIG, I was free to follow the leaders. The gallery pursuing the final foursome on this soccer-free Sunday numbered several hundred townsfolk, whose mittened applause sounded like a million moth wings flapping.

Ronan Rafferty emerged from the hotel to watch the tournament play out. "You can cut the tension with a knife," someone said to him when three strokes separated the top three players with three holes to play. "Not really," said Rafferty. "You could maybe chip away at① it a bit..."

The improbable leader, by a single stroke, was Peter Masters, who had put his game and life back together after dropping a dog in the first round. When he finally holed a short putt to win the first WIG with a final round of 67, two under on the tournament, he was rushed by a jubilant gallery. An old woman thrust a napkin at him, and Masters, brand-new to Greenlandic fame, didn't know whether to blow his nose or sign his name. He signed with a felt-tip pen②. "Being on the other side of that," said the journalist, more accustomed to interviewing golf champions than being one, "was surreal." There was that word again.

"What does Peter win?" asked Graeme Bissett, the Scotsman, who finished third, two strokes behind Masters.

"A ten-year exemption," I speculated.

Bissett chewed on this and said, "From coming back?"

On the contrary, returning is almost compulsory. Masters won an all-expenses-paid trip to defend his WIG title next year. Organizers were quite keen, really, to make this an annual event. Said a representative from Royal Greenland, the prawn-and-halibut concern that cosponsored the affair: "Bringing golf here shows we are not a static society." Imagine that. For the first time in recorded history, golf was a symbol of unstodginess: of forward-thinking, bridge-building multiculturalism.

Life is too often like the stomach of the reindeer, I reflected at dinner: neither delicious nor revolting, but somewhere in between. We had all come to the end of the earth to be delighted or revolted — be anywhere but in the everlasting

---

① Chip away at: remove or withdraw gradually.

② Felt-tip pen, a pen having a writing point made from pressed fibres Also called fibre-tip pen.

in-between of daily life. In that regard Greenland — without sunlight in winter, without moonlight in summer — succeeded on a grand scale.

"There are many difficulties here," said the mayor of Uummannaq. "The difficulties are darkness and harsh weather." He paused and added, "But there are also many beautiful times. The beautiful times are days like this."

The men, women and children of the Uummannaq village choir appeared from nowhere and began to sing a cappella in their native tongue. One didn't have to speak Greenlandic to recognize the hymn. It was "Amazing Grace[①]."

In that instant it occurred to me: Uummannaq is a Rorschach test[②]. It really does resemble a human heart, for those willing to look long enough.

---

① "Amazing Grace" is a Christian hymn written by English poet and clergyman John Newton (1725–1807), published in 1779. With a message that forgiveness and redemption are possible regardless of the sins people commit and that the soul can be delivered from despair through the mercy of God, "Amazing Grace" is one of the most recognizable songs in the English-speaking world.

② The Rorschach inkblot test is a method of psychological evaluation. Psychologists use this test to try to examine the personality characteristics and emotional functioning of their patients. The Rorschach is currently the second most commonly used test in forensic assessment, after the MMPI, and is the second most widely used test by members of the Society for Personality Assessment. It has been employed in diagnosing underlying thought disorder and differentiating psychotic from nonpsychotic thinking in cases where the patient is reluctant to openly admit to psychotic thinking.

冬日独尊

史蒂夫·如森

一

"我对格陵兰[①]可是情有独钟啊，"威廉·C·斯塔瑞特二世刚一踏上地球最北端的国土，就长舒了一口气，直率地说道，"我是来打高尔夫的。"

斯塔瑞德原本是加州处理破产诉讼的律师，现在已退休。此时，他面前齐刷刷地排列着整整16个空空的啤酒瓶，无怪乎他看上去像是在嘉年华游戏场，兴头正酣。正值3月的最后一周。伊卢利萨特位于北极南部的城郊，拥有一个不算大的航空集散站。斯塔瑞特、两名摄影师和我一行四人在这个集散站已经逗留了5个小时。我们有组织按步骤地喝光了酒吧里2年的啤酒供给，以此打发那5个小时。我们先是喝光了嘉士伯啤酒，接着耗尽了图堡的储备，之后，我们又冷酷地朝法克瑟牌啤酒挺进。法克瑟本是一种传真机增色剂的牌子，显然，在啤酒酿造中使用了同样颜色的增色剂，啤酒因而得名为法克瑟。我们边喝啤酒，斯塔瑞特边讲述他生命中那些值得回忆的各种回合。打高尔夫的回合，畅饮啤酒的回合——几乎没什么分别。

"利文斯顿是个很有趣的球场，"他说到。"它位于赞比亚，临近维多利亚瀑布。果岭费是35美分，专业店里只有一件衬衫。在新西兰的罗托鲁瓦，间歇喷泉便是水障碍。在南非的太阳城则有一处鳄鱼坑，在那里你可没法把球打出去。"今年夏天，据斯塔瑞特之前所说，他将在科克郡（走路就能到詹姆士的酿酒厂）租下一间房子，从爱尔兰出发去冰岛，参加北极公开赛，也就是一场24小时都有日照的比赛。另一方面，他不可能回到莫斯科乡村俱乐部了。不可一世地从9洞扩张到18洞，接下来岂不是该修生养息了？

我佯装一副"你告诉我吧"的表情，愤世嫉俗的摇着头。

"有个说法是，对一个旅者而言，不到格陵兰，就不算看过全世界，"《寂寞星球》旅游指南中的一篇《冰岛、格陵兰岛和法罗群岛》如此写道。这篇文章仅仅部分地解释了为何斯塔瑞特为何会出现在这里。这里属于北极圈以北

[①] 格陵兰（岛），世界最大岛，面积2,166,086平方公里，在北美洲东北，北冰洋和大西洋之间。从北部的皮里地到南端的法韦尔角相距2574公里，最宽处约有1290公里。海岸线全长三万五千多公里。丹麦属地。首府努克，又名戈特霍布。

250 英里处的伊卢利萨特。这个位置恰好位于一个临界点：装有翅膀的飞机飞不到的地方，而人类要打高尔夫球的欲望却已膨胀到此。

我们这一伙打高尔夫的凡夫俗子和各色记者飞了 5 个小时，终于来到了格陵兰。我们乘坐的飞机属于格陵兰国内航班，名曰 Grønlandsfly。上飞机之前我们就首先扫荡了哥本哈根机场的免税酒水商店，那里的货架被我们洗劫一空，如同飓风警报过后数小时内 7-11 便利店①的场景。飞机降落在格陵兰这个世界上最大的岛屿之后，我们还得再接连向北飞行 2 次，每次飞行要 1 个小时，最后才能抵达伊卢利萨特。这里是装有 4 组螺旋桨的哈维蓝特 DHC-7 型飞机所能飞行的最终端。此刻我们正在等待一架军用运输直升机的到来。该直升机由西科斯基公司制造，曾在越战时期服役。它将搭载我们向北飞行 1 小时 20 分钟，最终到达冰天雪地的乌马纳克岛屿②，为的就是参加第一次——恐怕也是最后一次——世界冰上高尔夫球锦标赛（以下简称为 WIG）。

该锦标赛向所有人敞开大门，只要你愿意花费 2000 美元，而且你还长有一副耐酒精的肝③，又情愿在北极圈以北 310 英里的地方呆上一个星期。这个地方可是世界最北端的社区之一。谁又能抵御得了如此强烈的诱惑？结果显示，每个地球公民都攒够了钱。

当然，尽管这次锦标赛是赞助商的发明，旨在推动格陵兰地区的旅游业——赞助商是一家苏格兰酒品公司，生产杜林标利口酒④——在格陵兰地区的冬日，高尔夫的确会给高级裁判人员带来独一无二的益处。对高尔夫初级水平者来说，岛上方圆 840,000 平方英里因树木稀少而空旷开阔（严格遵照高尔夫生态标准界定）。而且，水也不会成为障碍，因为格陵兰 85%的面积都被永久冰盖所覆盖，而且有些地方冰的厚度达到 2 英里。最重要的是，格陵兰的计数系统，只能到 12，超过 12 就是"很多"——这一特质肯定对我极其有利，能够在记分卡上被发挥到极致。

---

① 7-11 便利店（Seven-eleven），品牌原属美国南方公司，2005 年成为日本公司。1927 年在美国德克萨斯州创立，Seven-eleven 的名称则源于 1946 年，藉以标榜该商店营业时间由上午 7 时至晚上 11 时，后由日本零售业经营者伊藤洋华堂于 1974 年引入日本，从 1975 年开始变更为 24 小时全天候营业。发展至今，店铺遍布美国、日本、中国、新加坡、马来西亚、菲律宾等国家和地区。

② 格陵兰西部巴芬湾的一个海湾和城镇。长约 160 公里（100 哩），分为数个小峡湾，均向东延伸至内陆冰盖。乌马纳克镇建于 1763 年，位于努苏阿克（Nuussuaq）半岛北面的小岛上。为渔猎基地，有医院、气象站和电台。乌马纳克镇人口约 1,395（1994）。

③ 北极冰天雪地，十分寒冷，人们要大量饮酒来御寒。所以要想来这里，就得有一副耐酒精的心肝，原文字面意思为"钛肝"。

④ 杜林标利口酒，产于英国爱丁堡，是一种以威士忌酒为基酒、用蜂蜜增甜的利口酒，其主体风味为苏格兰威士忌酒的烟熏味。据说，杜林标利口酒可追溯到酿造蜂蜜酒的盖尔特人和掌握蒸馏技艺的北爱尔兰僧侣。

那架继任的西科斯基直升机如同一只巨大的死神之蚊般最终降落在了伊卢利萨特。这个庞然大物太过陈旧，一位居住在格陵兰的丹麦人乖张又自豪地告诉我，这一直升机的制造商希望格陵兰航空将它淘汰之后能把其残遗之体接收过来放在博物馆展览。听到这一新闻，我示意酒吧女服务员再上最后一轮法克瑟酒，但她指了指冰箱的玻璃门，里面空无一物，而后不无指责地说道，"再也没有啤酒了。"

心中恐惧之感越来越强。我回到等待区的同伴那里。坐在我对面长沙发上的是一位来自伦敦的体育摄影师，名叫盖里·普埃尔。刚还在打扫男卫生间的看门人，这会儿正从普埃尔后面走过来，接着就为他按摩起头皮来。一种至高无上的平静掠过他的——看门人的——脸庞。普埃尔怒骂道："这家伙疯了吧"，话虽出口，但他还是谨慎地避免发出任何突然的动作。

因此，我们带着某种意味深远的预感登上了西科斯基。它的内仓装满了高尔夫球杆。我们升空而行，公然藐视罗伯特·路易斯·史蒂文森[1]。史蒂文森曾经写道："冰和铁难熔。"难道这将成为预言？瑟瑟战栗中，这个旋转的野兽超然越过冰山，载着我们——它的人类猎物，深入、再深入，到达高尔夫球赛的黑暗之心[2]。

二

两年前的夏日时分，我第一次听说冰上高尔夫。当时我正在斯堪的纳维亚半岛北部午夜的阳光下旅行。"你冬天一定要回来啊，"赫尔辛基海滨酒店的办公人员用几乎恳求的语气说，"那时我们会在冰冻的湖面和雪地上打高尔夫球，气温到了冰点，击打着紫色的球。"

"是呀，哎，我想会的。"我结结巴巴的说，但说心里话，这个主意使得我五迷三道。格陵兰属于最后一批用来抵抗高尔夫场地扩张的前哨基地——在地球上或在地球飞行轨道上都是如此。人类第一次探月是在1969年，并且在2年之内就在那里打高尔夫了。格陵兰5000年以前迎来第一批居民。这座岛屿

---

[1] 罗伯特·路易斯·史蒂文森是英国浪漫主义代表作家之一。代表作品有《沃尔特·斯科特爵士》、《金银岛》等。早请他到处游历，为其创作积累了资源。到了20世纪中期，评论家对其作品进行了新的评价，开始审视史蒂文森而且把他的作品放入西方经典中，并将他列为20世纪最伟大的作家之一。

[2] 《黑暗之心》是英国著名作家约瑟夫·康拉德的作品，描写一家英国贸易公司委托小说中的"我"到非洲丛林寻找该公司失踪的贸易代表库尔茨，当找到时，发现其已经变疯并很快死去。作者借寻找的经历描写了殖民者在非洲大陆的感受。黑暗之心表面上指非洲大陆的腹地，同时也比喻了在这片土地上受到腐蚀的人心的黑暗。

上曾有一个只有 9 洞的高尔夫球道,位于在康克鲁斯瓦格①主机场附近,仅仅是做个样子而已。我们抵达此地的 2 个月前,还从来没有见过高尔夫球赛在乌马纳克举行。西科斯基在村子外面着陆之时,我有种不可抵抗的冲动,想要插下一个有编号的标指旗,就像在硫磺岛②时竖起了旗帜一般。

乌马纳克共有 1400 名居民。我们来访的前一周,有 200 名岛民参加了高尔夫技术诊疗所,在临时搭建的练习场练习挥杆击球技术。这一练习场其实就是围绕小岛的冰冻峡湾水域。"我觉得很难把球打出去,"乔纳斯·尼尔森说道。他是其中的一位岛民,现年 58 岁,刚刚打完一杆。"但是那些孩子们很感兴趣,想多了解这项赛事。"

他们也应该了解。格陵兰岛上共有居民 56000 人,80%是因纽特人(最好避免使用"爱斯基摩人"这个词),据说他们具有适合打高尔夫球的潜质。"格陵兰人的一个特点是",劳伦斯·米尔曼在他的北极旅行指南《最后的地方》中说,"他们往往会在不幸中发现乐趣。"

你只得如此,不管是在格陵兰岛上,还是在高尔夫球场上。"几个月前他们联系我参加这个赛事",罗南·拉菲尔蒂说道,他指的是锦标赛赞助商,"我原以为只是个玩笑。"拉菲尔蒂是北爱尔兰籍,35 岁,是 1989 年欧洲巡回赛的主要奖金得主,并且是那一年的莱德杯③队的一员。赞助商为他出资参加 WIG,但由于腕关节受伤,他并不能真正参赛。好在他请人将自己的葡萄酒运到格陵兰,乌马纳克镇镇长宴会上,镇长向他敬酒:"罗南·拉菲尔蒂是一位我从来没听说过的著名高尔夫球员。"

拉菲尔蒂和另一队高尔夫球手并记者比我早到了一个晚上。总共 20 名参赛

---

① 康克鲁斯瓦格机场是格陵兰中西部的机场,是格陵兰唯一能够处理大型客机的民用机场,由于远离海岸,天气状况稳定,因此机场不会受雾气暴风影响。康克鲁斯瓦格机场是格陵兰航空公司的总部枢纽。提供航班服务的航空公司有格陵兰航空公司和北欧航空公司。

② 硫磺岛是一座位于西太平洋小笠原群岛的火山岛,为日本的领土,行政区划隶属于东京都(小笠原支厅)小笠原村,因为岛上覆盖着一层由于火山喷发造成的硫磺而得名。1945 年 2 月 16 日至 3 月 26 日,日军和美军在岛上爆发硫磺岛战役,双方均死伤惨重。硫磺岛战役是太平洋战争中唯一一场美军登陆部队阵亡人数大于日军守军阵亡的一场战役,该战役也被称为"太平洋的绞肉机"。二次大战后硫磺岛由美国接管,传闻美军在硫磺岛上储有核弹装备,但将引发装置存放于邻近的美军船只上,以回避美军不得于日本领土储放核子武器的协议。1968 年 6 月 26 日,硫磺岛归还日本,岛上超过一万枚的未爆弹使得岛上原住民居民几乎无法重返。只有在举行纪念活动时才有较多人回到岛上。

③ 莱德杯(Ryder Cup,全名是莱德杯高尔夫球对抗赛)是一项高尔夫球顶级赛事,以森姆莱德命名,每两年举行一次,由美国队与欧洲队对赛。赛于 1926 年由美国队对英国队一场表演赛揭开序幕,1927 年正式举行第一届赛事,曾因第二次世界大战而中断十年,1973 年至 1977 年期间改为美国队对英国爱尔兰联队,1979 年再加入其他欧洲优秀的高尔夫球选手,变成美国队对欧洲队,并沿袭至今。原定于 2001 年举行的赛事,因美国发生 911 事件而推迟到 2002 年举行。

选手、20 名非参赛选手，分别代表六个国家参加了 WIG。莱克斯·哈姆斯特拉来自荷兰，他赢得了一次比赛，奖品就是此次旅行，因而经常有人问他，二等奖的奖品是否就是两张票。和我一样来自美国的是斯塔瑞特和马克·卡尼扎罗。马克·卡尼扎罗是《纽约邮报》[①]的专栏作家，曾发掘过一批有启发性的地方风俗文献。"驯鹿的胃就像一个巨大的气球，胃里的绿色物质味道很特别，"一本格陵兰出版物上有篇冠名为《食物及其吃法》的文章如此写道。"既算不上美味也不令人作呕，是一种介于二者之间的一种味道。"这种描述会很有用的，因为锦标赛的菜单上包括了鲸鱼肉干，熏麝牛和面糊海雀。

在乌马纳克宾馆举行的欢迎晚宴上，简·韦斯特曼和我坐到一桌。韦斯特曼来自英国，是某人之遗孀，新近发现自己喜欢高尔夫球（"我非常热衷，真的"），她是伦敦西南部罗汉普顿俱乐部的会员。"我们有桥牌、槌球和高尔夫，"她说。"但压根没有冰上高尔夫。"

彼得·马斯特斯，也是英国人，问韦斯特曼俱乐部的确切位置。"在普埃尔瑞附近，"她回答。"你知道普埃尔瑞吗，一家高级精神病院？"

马斯特斯之前不知道普埃尔瑞，但很快，当然，我们就都知道了。在宾馆外面，成百上千的格陵兰雪橇狗———一种外形酷似狼的可怕动物——整夜向着月亮嚎叫。宾馆里面张贴了一条信息：客房里面禁止饮酒。一位男士解释道，曾经有一个醉汉晃晃悠悠出去，躺在了狗群中间。转天早晨，只找到了他的一个纽扣。只有一个纽扣。

"常言道什么来着？"马斯特斯问，语气中带着更多的不确定。"疯狗和英国人……？"

三

零下 15 度的时候，我起了床，和斯塔瑞特打了一场练习赛。在球场上，他依靠在他的立式背包上，包的塑料支架噼啪一声断为两截。包坍塌到了冰上，支架怪异地晃来晃去，像乔·赛斯曼的一样。

球场布置得如此精美，我自己的双腿也不由得发软。球场完全由冰和雪建成，9 个洞分置在乌马纳克周围的冰冻峡湾水域，就好像一个锆立方体手镯。球道围绕着有 10 层楼高的冰山，曲折蜿蜒。这想必就是克雷普顿乡村俱乐部的样子了。我的双眼对此美景难以置信，眼球像卡通人物一样突然爆开。我当时

[①] 纽约邮报是美国历史最悠久的报纸之一。创办于 1801 年，现属媒体大亨默多克的新闻集团。其报道风格以煽情、八卦而闻名。在 1960 年代后半期，日发行量曾达 70 万份，现虽下降到 41.8 万份，但仍然是纽约最重要的报纸之一。

真有点想把它们从脸上拔下来,扑通一声放到洗球机里,洗净后重新拧回托座,再看一看眼前的景色是不是真的。

球道被厚厚的积雪覆盖,整饰一新,用木桩和结冰的长草区分开。果岭区,也叫白色区,都是光滑的冰,好像滑冰场的表面一样。即使再多的果酱也难以使得球粘在这些白色冰面上;据我看,切滚球,是唯一比赛的方法。

这里的球洞直径就比标准高尔夫球洞多出两倍。还允许选手用扫帚扫净推杆线。其他的冬季规则依然生效:所有球道上的球可以由橡胶球座上击落,而长草区的球可以抬高,可以放置在落地的四英寸之内,不接近球洞的线上。我自己的球,天啊,不是紫色的,其视觉效果却是黄色的,低压缩的特尔怡斯特,布满 WIG 的标志。

冰上高尔夫练习的时候,我发现了很多情况。我发现任何给定的零度以下击球都比在 72 度的时候短 30%。(球场已经适当缩短,18 个球洞,4247 码。)我发现戴着滑雪手套很难以瓦登握杆法握住球杆,很难不穿钉鞋找到适当的击球姿势,很难找到落进雪窝中的球。但更重要的发现却是这一个:衣着得体,没有配偶,不想沉迷于乡村俱乐部——球童,擦鞋,梳子漂浮在一片蓝色的巴柏塞得①消毒剂水上——那也就没有什么能阻止你在地球上的任何地方、任何季节、任何一天去打高尔夫球。

相比任何海军上将皮里②在北极误打误撞发现的情况而言,这点本身看上去就是一项更有价值的发现。

四

WIG 一开始是以猎枪射击开始比赛的。尽管用大炮代替了猎枪。并且据传闻,炮手的脸部由于遭受火药灼伤,所以正在乡村医院接受治疗。因此后面一次比赛真的就雇佣了猎枪手。

我正在与马斯特斯打球,马斯特斯是一家英国杂志《高尔夫世界》的编辑,是差点③为四的选手。在第二个球洞,284 码,10 个四杆洞,冰山主宰右面的

---

① 字面意思为:理发杀手(Barbicide),是一美国理发店消毒水品牌,为梳子和刀剪消毒。
② 罗伯特·埃德温·皮里(1856 年 5 月 6 日—1920 年 2 月 20 日),美国极地探险家,曾多次探险格陵兰,并证明其为第一大岛。皮里出生于宾夕法尼亚州,1877 年毕业于鲍德温学院,1886 年开始北极探险。1909 年 4 月,他率队从埃尔斯米尔岛北岸的哥伦比亚角(C.Columbia)出发,乘雪橇向北极点发起冲击,4 月 6 日,皮里到达北极点,成为世界上有史以来首位徒步抵达北极点的人。
③ "差点"为调节一名选手与差点球员之间的得分能力,可从他的实际分数中扣除一定的杆数。这样做的目的是允许不同能力的高尔夫球选手在同一水准上比赛。

长草区，马斯特斯展开了一次雄壮的击球。他击球的时候，一队高速行驶的狗拉雪橇突然出现在我们的左面，距离发球台只有 200 码。球以 x 的速度在球道上飞驰起来，那群狗以 y 的速度冲向球道，突然之间，两股向量向对方靠近，越来越近，我们目击了一道复杂的数学难题，恐怖地变成现实。

只能用一声哀嚎来描述，随着这声哀嚎，队伍中的一只狗倒下了。剩下的狗继续向前冲，在雪橇后面拖着它们倒下的同志，样子酷似一个罐头系在婚车的保险杠上。司机回头看了一下那只狗，稍稍耸了一下肩，继续驾狗前行。格陵兰的雪橇司机，穿着海豹皮夹克、北极熊毛皮裤子，他们不善于过于外露地表达感情，而整个情景像是一场幻觉，一下子就消失在白得刺眼的北极地平线上了。

马斯特斯不曾预料到有这样一场滑稽荒唐的突发事件。然而，一位跟随我们四人小组的丹麦女士——她便是全部观众——几次三番指控他杀害哈士奇。"你怎么能这样？"她不断的说。"我们是这里的客人。"雪橇司机使得这一事件化作了天灾——一块黄色的冰雹从天而降，重重砸在了他的狗身上——这一切悠然而逝。

接下来的球洞正是右侧的狗腿洞——这个词我们四人小组目前在马斯特斯面前尽量故意避免使用——正在冰山脚下。我连续不断的击右曲球，球座就放在冰山顶上，击出去的球再也找不回来了。我带了一筒特尔怡斯特球，看上去都是黄色的，尤其，当我把这一筒都用完的时候，不得不使用包里颜色最鲜艳的球了。马斯特斯，颤栗着，前 9 杆计分 40，而后恢复了镇定，这一回合最终，超过标准杆 3，得分 75。

晚上，英国人罗伯特·贝文琼斯，第一回合得了 70，纪录是后九洞 31，以 1 杆超过苏格兰人格雷姆·拜厄瑟斯。我第一回合 99，排名第 18。这使我极为抑郁，尤其想到到锦标赛赛程只有 2 天。我们不远万里来到这里，而且已逗留时间已经过半。这种情绪结束后的很长一段时间，我一直呆在峡湾，开始出现季节性情绪失调，在无限的一片白茫茫中迷失自我了。

我沉湎于极端僻静之中，距离乌马纳克 2 英里，在冰冻峡湾上，当时我的司机，一位在格陵兰长大的丹麦人，打破了这个咒语。"乌马纳克意思是'心脏'，"克里斯蒂安·多利洛夫一边说，一边用食指在空中划了个情人的心。"因为这个小岛形状像心脏，或像女人的屁股。"

几个小时以后，我回到房间，打开一张地图，得出一个结论：需要耗费一个极为孤独的人的全套想象力，在如此严寒的气候环境下，处在一个被世界的其他地方抛弃的位置，却怎么看乌马纳克也还是不像个情人的心形。也不像减了分量的美人的臀。

渐渐的，在我看来，两个又都像了。

五

周六晚上，乌马纳克太平无事：晚餐一如既往地被言辞所劫持，劫持者正是喋喋不休的杜林标利口酒的酒商代表，他不停的，甚至是有点儿淫荡地，敦促我们嗅一嗅他的产品。期间两位小丑献艺。而后，我们几个人穿过了酒店的厨房，也就是说，穿过了窥视镜。

在乌马纳克宾馆厨房的后面，你会发现自己身在其中的是一间迪斯科舞厅。我可不骗你，格陵兰是一种叫做北极瑞歌舞的发源地。啊，今晚的头牌人物不是鲍勃·马利和捕鲸船。然而，两位志存高远的摇滚歌星登台亮相，他们来自摩尔达维亚，并自我介绍为安迪和安德里亚斯。一位主攻键盘乐器，一位主奏吉他。"我们的乐队叫做串座双人自行车，"安迪说道，或者是安德里亚斯说的。"你知道吗？是那种两个座的自行车。"

安迪和安德里亚斯照着笔记本里的歌词演唱，歌词都是手写的，歌曲大多是西方的流行歌曲。他们演唱了一些令人难忘的经典好歌的主题唱段，比如《难以忘怀》（"好比一首爱之恋歌依附着我，你与我如影随形"），还有《乡村路》（"天堂般的西弗吉尼亚州，高高的蓝岭山脉，滚滚流淌的谢南多亚河"）。我酒喝得正尽兴的时候，一个没了牙的女人强拉着我和她跳舞，与此同时，那些身裹皮毛的因纽特渔夫们，紧盯着我们这群打高尔夫的花花公子和瘦骨嶙峋的新闻记者，随着音乐原地舞动，最后决定还是不要赤手空拳地要我们的命——个中因由恐怕只有他们自己才懂。

"演唱《野马艾莉》时你们为什么大笑？"安德里亚斯（或许是安迪）问我们，此时是演出间歇，我们正在翻阅他的笔记本。

"应该是《野马莎莉》"我回答，弄得他云里雾里地摸不着头脑。

"啊，"他说，仿佛恍然大悟的样子，"谢谢你。"

忘了爱和世界语吧：唯一两种世界共同语就是音乐和运动。尽管格陵兰有自治政府，它仍然是丹麦的一个省。而且，在一场晋级欧洲足球锦标赛的资格赛中，丹麦对意大利，这项赛事才刚刚过去 14 个小时。这场比赛自开赛就在格陵兰唯一的广播电视网络进行实况直播。这可称得上是事件驱动编写程序，事情一桩接一桩；还有一天的晚饭时间，一名旅行代理人在大肆宣扬热带度假名胜。

我此刻终于明白为什么一天的较早时候我们极少有观众的缘故：格陵兰人对足球非常痴迷，当然容易忽视高尔夫球。在乌马纳克，唯一看得见的永久性运动设施就是一个足球场。每 5 个孩子中就有 1 个孩子戴着曼彻斯特联队的滑雪帽。曼彻斯特联队的守门员是彼得·舒梅切尔[①]，他也是丹麦国家队的队长。此外，那天下午，英国和波兰的比赛中，曼彻斯特联队的球星保罗·史高斯[②]为英国进了 3 个球。

因此，接通有线电视的乌马纳克居民们直到凌晨 3 点迪斯科舞厅打烊的时候才离去。接着我们所有人又补办了一个盛大派对。就是开这种派对的时候，情况开始变得离奇。屋里有一双 20 号的小丑鞋，很是漂亮。架子上有几件很不错的象牙纪念品——或许是剑，或许是拐杖——难以名状。一位英国摄影师拿着它不停旋转，好像玛丽·波平斯的伞一样，这时，一位法罗群岛的女主人突然发话，"我明白了，你们发现了我收藏的海象阴茎骨。"

小丑鞋的主人是一名 31 岁的美国人，叫约珥·科尔，从老家明尼苏达州的沙科皮来到乌马纳克。沙科皮是一座小镇，毗邻我的故乡。我俩在北极附近相遇的几率大概为 60 亿分之一，但至此，我情愿接受在乌马纳克能发生任何事。科尔曾经是法罗群岛国家田径队的教练，并带领国家队征战 1989 年世界岛国比赛，他们在该赛事上表现不俗。这是一项在格陵兰、爱尔兰、怀特岛、曼岛、法罗群岛、设得兰、吉利根等一些岛屿国家间举办的类似奥林匹克的运动会。科尔现在小丑着——他用小丑这个词做动词——在世界极为落后的地方扮演着现实生活里的"亚当医生[③]"，这是由罗宾·威廉姆斯扮演的同名电影的一个角色。的确，科尔正是在晚宴上扮作小丑的人，就在我们嗅过杜林标利口酒之前。科尔不无怀念的说，"我已经在波斯尼亚当过小丑啦。"

直到早上 6 点半，夜晚的兴头才逐渐褪去。我终于摸索着回到了酒店，与我一起回去的还有四个记者，他们俨然已经成了英国足球流氓。就像 29000 只格陵兰东北部的雪橇狗集体嚎叫一样，我们漫步在大街上——或者干脆说，就在这乌马纳克唯一的大街上——并高声歌唱（按照《空巴亚，我的主》[④]的曲

[①] 彼得·舒梅切尔是丹麦前足球运动员，舒梅切尔是丹麦夺得 1992 年在瑞典举行的欧洲国家杯冠军的主力成员。司职守门员，舒梅切尔获选为 1992 及 1993 年的"世界最佳门将"。1991 年彼得·舒梅切尔以 75 万英镑的低价加盟红魔曼联，这位高大、身手敏捷的门将在老特拉福德为曼联赢得了无数的荣誉，包括 1998/99 赛季的三冠王，成为了世界顶级守门员。

[②] 保罗·史高斯（1974 年 11 月 16 日—），英格兰足球运动员，出任中场，精于长传及后上射门。在他职业生涯中，一直都效力曼彻斯特联队，球衣号码为 18 号。他初出道时，亦曾先后穿上曼联的 24 号及 22 号球衣。2011 年 5 月，曼联官方宣布史高斯退役。半年多后，他于 2012 年 1 月初的曼市复出，暂时解决曼联中场荒。

[③] 《亚当医生》，又译《妙手情真》，是由汤姆·沙迪亚克导演，罗宾·威廉斯，莫妮卡·波特，菲利普·西摩尔·霍夫曼，艾尔玛·霍尔，哈威·普尔斯内尔，弗兰西斯·李·迈克凯恩主演的一部美国喜剧电影。

[④] 非洲福音歌曲，呼唤上帝来到自己这里。

调）：

"他的得分比比皆是，他进球了。
他的得分比比皆是，他进球了。
他的得分比比皆是，他进球了。
保罗·史—高—斯，他进球了。"
2个小时后，就该我发球了。

六

我忽略了接听电话叫醒服务。我忘了请求电话叫醒服务。所以我当然忽略了，按照夏令时的规定，提前一个小时"从床上跳起"。所以我错过了开球时间。事情的结果就包含在 WIG 决赛结果之中。比赛结果在转天的各大国际报纸上刊登——从《纽约邮报》到伦敦的《泰晤士报》——我的名字后面紧跟一个不光彩的 WD 符号。我猜测，WD 代表"醉酒"。

既然已经正式退出 WIG，我可以自由地追捧分数领先的球手。在这个无足球的星期天，看台上追随四人组决赛的观众已多达几百名镇民。他们戴着连指手套鼓掌，掌声好像 100 万只飞蛾拍打着翅膀。

罗南·拉菲尔蒂突然从宾馆里冒出来观看锦标赛的大结局。"你可以用刀子缓解紧张，"某人跟他如是说。当时，3 次击球拉开了排名前三的选手，况且再比 3 个球洞就结束了。"那可不行，"拉菲尔蒂说道，"你或许可以近击，使之离开一点……"

通过简单的一击，最不可能的名人就成了彼得·马斯特斯。通过在第一回合抛球进了狗腿洞，他总算挽救了自己的比赛和自己的命运。他最终轻轻一记短球，以最后一回合 67 的成绩赢得了首届 WIG 比赛，另 2 名球手位居其后。他随即被欢呼雀跃的观众簇拥。一名老妇使劲将餐巾纸扔向他，此刻的马斯特斯，完全不了解格陵兰人的出名方式，不知道该用餐巾纸擤鼻涕还是在上面签名。他用毡头笔签了名。"餐巾纸的另一面，"记者说道，相比成为一名高尔夫球赛冠军而言，记者更习惯于采访冠军，"是离奇的。"又是这个词。

"彼得得了什么奖品？"格雷姆·比塞特问道，他是苏格兰人，打了第三名，在马斯特斯后面差两杆。

"10 年的豁免权，"我推测。

比塞特仔细考虑了一下，而后说，"豁免不用再来这里了？"

与此相反，返回几乎是强制性的。马斯特斯赢得一次费用全包的旅行，明年他还会回来捍卫自己的 WIG 头衔。组织者们非常热衷，真的，想把这项赛事办成每年一次。皇家格陵兰岛的一名代表说，正是为了对虾和比目鱼的担忧协办了这项赛事："把高尔夫运动带进来，体现出我们的社会不是静止的。"想象一下。有记录可循的历史中，高尔夫球第一次成为了不平凡的象征：成了高瞻远瞩的、增进关系的多元文化的代名词。

人生经常就像驯鹿的胃口，晚饭的时候我思忖着：既不美味也不恶心，而处于中间的某个位置。我们都来到了地球的边缘，欢乐或厌恶——不过是处于永恒的日常生活的中间。在这方面，格陵兰——没有阳光的冬天，没有月光的夏天——在很大程度上成功了。

"这里有很多困难，"乌马纳克镇镇长说道。"困难在于黑暗和恶劣的天气。"他停顿了一下，补充道，"然而，这里也有很多美妙的时刻。美妙的时刻就是像今天这样的日子。"

乌马纳克的乡村唱诗班里有男人、女人和孩子。他们不知从什么地方一下子全出来了，开始用他们的母语清唱起来。无须懂格陵兰语就能辨别出他们唱的是赞美歌。是《奇异恩典》[①]。

在那一瞬间，我脑海中出现：乌马纳克是一次罗尔沙赫氏试验[②]。它确实类似一颗人类的心脏，这一点是对于那些愿意花足够长时间去观看的人来说的。

（杨建 译　张慧芳 校）

[①] 《奇异恩典》创作于18世纪的赞美歌，歌词作者是由1725年出生于伦敦的美国白人约翰·牛顿，歌词简洁充满敬虔、感恩的告白，也是他的生命见证，约翰·牛顿本是一名黑奴船长，无恶不作，后来反而沦落非洲。在一次暴风雨的海上，他蒙上帝的拯救，于是决心痛改前非，奉献一生，宣扬上帝的福音，成为19世纪伟大的传道人。去世之前，他为自己写了墓志铭："约翰·牛顿牧师，从前是个犯罪作恶不信上帝的人，曾在非洲作奴隶之仆。但借着主耶稣基督的丰盛怜悯，得蒙保守，与神和好，罪得赦免，并蒙指派宣传福音事工。"这首诗歌就是他一生得拯救的见证。在歌中充满了他对自己过去贩卖奴隶的悔恨，和对不计较这些仍赐福于他的真主的感激之情。

[②] 罗尔沙赫氏测验是指把被测试者对10种标准墨迹的解释作为情感、智力机能和综合结构的检测方法来分析的投射测验方法。

The Very, very, very Big Chill

Marcel Theroux[①]

【导读】位于俄罗斯北亚境内的西伯利亚是一片富饶而尚未得到开发的辽阔地带，那里有令人叹为观止的丰富的自然资源，从而为今日的快速发展带来了契机，同时也吸引着数以万计的游客前去观光。这片被称为"沉睡的土地"的区域以气候寒冷而著称，尤为出名的是拥有北半球的两大"寒极"，其中之一便是《极寒》中马赛尔·泰鲁所描述的上扬斯克———一座位于萨哈共和国境内的城镇，年平均气温在-15℃左右，1月份平均气温低至-50℃，被认为是有人居住的最寒冷的地方之一。本文中马赛尔·泰鲁这位集编剧、播音主持人和小说新秀于一身的才子以其一贯的简朴文风引领我们进行了一场难忘的极具异域色彩的上扬斯克之旅：冷到极致的天气状况、独特的饮食习惯、冰雕玉砌的美丽风景以及文人发自内心的对传统文化的自豪感。整篇文章行文语言简洁利落，描写形象生动，层次清晰分明，视角新颖而又不乏客观，笔法活泼而又不失诙谐，读来令人身临其境又忍俊不禁，实为一篇风格自然亲切的游记佳作。

WHEN I FINALLY got to the coldest town on earth, the first person I met had a frozen fish tucked into one of his felt boots. He was swaying slightly in the headlights of our truck, which had broken down two hundred yards short of our final destination.

"Hey," he said, "have you got a bottle for me?" His vodka breath rose up in clouds of ice crystals. It was then that I noticed the fish. He pulled it out of his boot and gave me a welcoming wave with it. *"Pokushaite!" h*e cried — "Have something to eat!" The fish was a foot and a half long and as solid as an iron bar.

It was past midnight. By local standards, we were enjoying balmy February weather — just a few degrees shy of forty below, Fahrenheit.

---

① Marcel Theroux, a British novelist and broadcaster, won the Somerset Maugham Award in 2002 for his novel *The Confessions of Mycroft Holmes*: a paper chase. He is also a contributing editor of the Travel & Leisure magazine.

Verkhoyansk①, in the republic of Sakha②, northeastern Siberia, has the dubious distinction of being the coldest inhabited place on the planet. It's not considered chilly here until the thermometer has dipped to about sixty below. And the record set in 1892 and celebrated on the town's most famous landmark — a monument called the Pole of Cold — is minus-ninety degrees.

I'd come to Russia with a cameraman, a soundman, and a television director to make a program for the Discovery Channel③ about traveling through Siberia in winter. Three weeks earlier we had flown from Moscow to the Siberian city of Irkutsk④. We'd filmed on Lake Baikal⑤ and in the Buddhist republic of Buryatia⑥ before flying north to Yakutsk⑦, where we began our journey to Verkhoyansk. For ten days we would travel by truck and reindeer sleigh through unmarked snowfields and along frozen rivers, spending nights with reindeer herders in isolated winter cabins.

Siberians are fond of telling you that there's no road, just a direction, and on the way to Verkhoyansk this was often literally true. The truck drivers had to read the pattern of the snowdrifts to see where we could safely drive. We often got stuck — hence the need for two vehicles. One night both of them sank and froze fast in the thin ice of the river Nyura. Eight of us spent a sleepless night in the back of one truck, jostling for positions farthest from the wood-burning stove that was welded to the floor. Inside we were sweating and restless. Outside it was fifty below.

As we made our way into Russia's northern regions, the temperature dropped further and the fur hats grew bigger and bigger. When I'd arrived in Moscow, the local men were wearing small hats perched on top of their heads; the earflaps seemed purely decorative — throughout Russia it's considered effeminate for a man

---

① A town of the Sakha Republic, Russia, situated on the Yana River, near the Arctic Circle, Verkhoyansk is one of the places considered the northern Pole of Cold.

② The Sakha Republic is a federal subject of Russia and the largest subnational governing body by area in the world. Its capital is the city of Yakutsk.

③ An American satellite and cable specialty channel founded by John Hendricks and distributed by Discovery Communications, it provides documentary television programming focused primarily on popular science, technology, and history and has covered more than 160 countries in the world.

④ a city and the administrative center of Irkutsk Oblast, Russia, one of the largest cities in Siberia.

⑤ the world's oldest and deepest lake and the most voluminous freshwater lake in the world, which is located in the south of the Russian region of Siberia.

⑥ a federal subject of Russia (a republic) with the capital city Ulan-Ude.

⑦ the capital city of the Sakha Republic, Russia, located about 450 kilometers south of the Arctic Circle.

to put his flaps down if the temperature is above minus-twenty. By the time I reached Yakutsk, a city built entirely on permafrost, women and men alike wore giant fox-fur bonnets that reminded me of the most outlandish 1970s Afros[1]. Finally, in the villages around Verkhoyansk, I saw people whose faces bore the physical scars —burns around the mouth and cheeks — of a lifetime of intense cold.

The man with the fish had ruby cheeks and the genial glow of a benign drunk. Seeing him made me think of the taxi driver in Moscow who had advised me to drink a glass of vodka every hour or so when I reached Sakha, "whenever you start feeling ill." When I tried to explain that alcohol gives an illusory feeling of warmth and actually speeds up heat loss, he looked at me as though I'd suggested we lower our earflaps.

I politely refused the man's offer of food. Thin slices of raw frozen fish — *stroganina* — are tasty dipped in salt, but I wasn't sure how long this one had been tucked into his boot. The last thing I wanted was extra visits to a dark and drafty Siberian outhouse.

But the fish-man didn't give up easily. Our guide, Anatoly, had mischievously told him we were carrying cases of neat alcohol in the truck: *spirt*, the tipple of Russia's poorest. The fish-man offered to put two of us up in his house. I told him we already had a place to slay. He shook my hand several times and disappeared into the darkness.

Imagine the set of a spaghetti western[2] erected in the Arctic Circle, and you have some idea of what Verkhoyansk looks like. Cossacks[3] founded the village in 1638 as they moved east in search of fur pelts; parts of it retain the ramshackle charm of a frontier town. Low wooden buildings line the streets, which seem all the wider because there are no cars: some two thousand people live here, but the only vehicles I saw were ours. Most of our time in Verkhoyansk was spent trying to scrape together enough petrol to get us to the airport.

Until the 1980s, Verkhoyansk was a tin- and gold-mining center, but today its

---

[1] a hairstyle worn naturally by people with lengthy kinky hair texture or specifically styled in such a fashion by individuals with naturally curly or straight hair, which is particularly popular in the African-American community of the mid-to-late 1960s.

[2] a nickname for a broad sub-genre of Western films that emerged in the mid-1960s and, usually produced and directed by Italians, were of unique and much copied film-making style and international box-office success.

[3] a group of predominantly East Slavic people who originally were members of democratic, semi-military communities in what is today Ukraine and Southern Russia.

residents survive through their own resourcefulness. Our hosts, for one, kept cows, and a frozen haunch of moose was stashed beneath their porch.

People in Sakha eat a lot of frozen food. Frozen raw fish, frozen raw reindeer meat, frozen patties of whipped cream and blueberries, and frozen patties of raw pony liver are all regional specialties. Milk is sold at the market in frozen chunks, and in smaller villages the winter water supply is stacked by each house in huge frozen blocks like outsized pieces of pale blue Turkish delight[①].

Frozen pony-liver patties turned up on our breakfast table the first morning. Curious, but too squeamish to try it myself. I told Nigel the cameraman that it was whipped cream and strawberries. As soon as he bit into one, he spat it out like a hot coal and swore at me. I asked what it tasted like. "Blood," he said, with a murderous look in his eye.

Local people told me that at minus-sixty and below, a dense fog settles in the streets, and pedestrians leave recognizable outlines bored into the mist behind them. A drunkard's tunnel will meander and then end abruptly over a prone body. At minus-seventy-two, the vapor in your breath freezes instantly and makes a tinkling sound called "the whisper of angels."

In fact, the temperature never fell past sixty below during the month I was in Siberia. People here agree with experts on climate change: Every year the winters are getting warmer. School is canceled whenever the temperature slips into the negative sixties; this used to happen for weeks at a time, but now only a few school days are missed each year. Even so, I learned to distinguish different levels of extreme cold as we traveled northward.

My nose was one reliable gauge: at zero degrees, it crackled when I breathed as the hair in my nostrils froze; twenty degrees colder, and it would stream and then freeze. At minus-forty, an apple froze solid in my hand when I paused too long between bites. Plastic becomes rock-hard within seconds. The soundman's wire cables froze into absurd shapes. The resin grips on my Extremities mittens became sharp and rigid like plastic hatchets. When I retreated indoors, Edward

---

① a family of confections based on a gel of starch and sugar, consisting largely of chopped dates, pistachios and hazelnuts or walnuts bound by the gel, the cheapest being mostly gel, generally flavored with rosewater, mastic, or lemon.

Scissorhands[①] turned into Mr. Magoo[②] as a thick layer of ice formed on my glasses. I would stumble around blindly in the dim lamplight, trying not to trip over discarded footwear or collide with the woodstove. It took me a week to realize that the sore on the bridge of my nose was a frost burn caused by the metal frame of my spectacles.

One compensation for the intense cold is a landscape as beautiful as any I've ever seen. The countryside around Verkhoyansk is wooded, not at all bleak. During the day, the low sun painted every-thing with golden light and long blue shadows. The trees, trimmed with ice, became elaborate glass sculptures. When the wind blew, the air sparkled with snow crystals. It was too cold for anything to smell of much —even the outhouses. And the snow itself acted as an acoustic blanket, throwing every sound into sharp relief: the squeaking of boots or hooves, the bells on a reindeer's harness, the soft crump of snow thrown aside by a shovel. Just below the Arctic Circle, I saw the northern lights for the first lime: luminous green gauze curtains blowing around in outer space.

The Russian word for Siberia, Sibir, comes from Mongolian Altai and means "sleeping land." The woods and rivers and mountains did seem to be in suspended animation. I was reminded of the impenetrable forest around Sleeping Beauty's castle, where everything is frozen at the moment she pricks her finger: the waves sculpted into the rivers, the autumn berries iced onto the bushes, a skinned wolf carcass frozen into an unspeakable shape outside a reindeer herder's hut.

Anatoly, our anthropologist guide, was himself born into a family of Even[③] reindeer herders. The Even were nomads until they were collectivized by the Soviets in the 1920s and 1930s and moved into villages. They live hard lives, ignored by the regional and national governments, which are far more interested in the land beneath them (Sakha holds diamond reserves as vast as South Africa's).

Anatoly bears an open grudge against the European civilization that has so

---

① a 1990 American romantic fantasy film directed by Tim Burton and starring Johnny Depp about the story of an artificial man named Edward, an unfinished creation, who has scissors for hands. 这里作者生动形象地将手套冻得僵硬的自己比作拥有剪刀手的爱德华。

② A cartoon character created at the UPA animation studio in 1949, Mr Magoo is a wealthy, short-statured retiree who gets into a series of sticky situations as a result of his nearsightedness. 这里指作者自己在极度寒冷的状况下从屋外进入屋内眼镜上结了一层厚厚的冰，就像高度近视的脱险先生一样跌跌撞撞，显得异常笨拙。这个比喻表现出作者幽默的写作风格。

③ an ethnic group from Siberia and Russian Far East.

disrupted the Even's traditional life. He enjoyed subjecting me to funny and unsettling lectures about my personal responsibility for the destruction of Even culture. He also liked to point out the shortcomings of our high-tech apparel. He laughed at our bulky Canadian boots. "Pure European approach!" he snorted. "Below minus-forty, you will freeze. We should just take a match and set fire to them now." He warned me that if I insisted on wearing my North Face[①] hat instead of a fur one, an archaeologist would be digging me out of the permafrost in a thousand years' time like a woolly mammoth[②].

On his own feet, Anatoly wore *unty*, made from reindeer leg fur, and hardly larger than a regular shoe. When we traveled by reindeer sleigh, I borrowed fur clothes from the herders: *unty*, trousers made from wolverine, snow-sheep mittens, a reindeer jacket. These were not only warmer than my other clothes but stayed quiet and flexible, and the smell of the fur seemed to put the reindeer at ease.(Nigel the cameraman, rustling around in artificial fibers and big boots, kept startling the animals, who would get all tangled up in their harnesses as they leaped to avoid him.) At the end of the day, the fur clothes were placed in a sack and left outside. Warmth and damp destroy them. Yet after a night at forty below, they were never cold to the touch when I put them on in the morning.

While few in the West have heard of the Even, everyone knows one word of their language. *Shaman* is the Even term for a traditional spirit healer. Its etymology is uncertain — it may mean "one who knows" — but the word has been internationalized, passing into various languages from Russian ethnography. During long hours in our overheated truck, Anatoly told me stories about the Even shamans, celebrated by his people as the most powerful shamans of all. According to Anatoly, not only were most Western scientific discoveries preempted by the shamans, but it was also commonplace for Even shamans to visit the moon.

Anatoly told me all this with a smile on his face, but his stories correspond to a

---

① an American outdoor product company specializing in outerwear, fleece, shirts, footwear, and equipment such as backpacks, tents, and sleeping bags.

② a species of mammoth living in the Pleistocene (10,000 years ago) and becoming extinct in roughly 2,000 BC 这里以自己文明为傲的安纳托利讽刺了现代文明中所研制的防寒衣物远远不如最原始的皮毛保暖，因而笑称坚持穿这些衣物的作者千年后会像已经灭绝的长毛象一样被发掘出来。

belief in Siberia that when Neil Armstrong[①] landed on the moon, he was met by an old Russian wise man called Ivanov. It would be interesting to ask Armstrong about this. In particular, I'd like to know whether Ivanov had a frozen fish in his boot.

---

① an American former astronaut, test pilot, aerospace engineer, university professor, United States Naval Aviator, and the first person to set foot upon the Moon.

顶极酷寒

马赛尔·泰鲁[①]

  我终于抵达了地球上最寒冷的城市，在那里见到的第一个人在自己的毛毡靴筒里掖着一条冻鱼。我们的卡车在离目的地 200 码远的地方抛锚了，这个人在卡车车灯的照射下微微地晃动着身体。

  "嗨，"他说，"你给我带了瓶酒吗？"他嘴里呼出的伏特加酒气成团团冰晶上升，就在那时我看到了鱼，他从靴子里掏出鱼来挥舞着对我表示欢迎。"Pokushaite！"他大叫——"吃点东西吧！"那条鱼长 1 英尺半，硬如铁棒。

  已过午夜时分，按当地的标准我们正享受着 2 月里温暖的天气——还差几度到华氏零下 40 度。

  上扬斯克[②]属于西伯利亚东北部的萨哈共和国[③]，据说是这个星球上最冷的有人类居住的地方，当然这一点尚未得到证实。这里的气温降至约零下 60 度时才会被认为寒冷，而 1892 年所创下的记录为零下 90 度，这个城市里最著名的标志性建筑——被称为"冷极"的纪念碑正是对这一记录的纪念。

  我和摄影师、收音师以及电视导演一同来到俄罗斯为探索频道[④]制作一期冬天穿越西伯利亚的节目。3 周前我们从莫斯科飞往西伯利亚的伊尔库茨克市[⑤]，然后在贝加尔湖[⑥]和布里亚特共和国[⑦]取景拍摄，之后北飞到雅库茨克[②]，

  [①] Marcel Theroux 马赛尔·泰鲁，英国小说家、节目主持人。1968 年在乌干达首都坎帕拉出生，在剑桥大学学习英国文学，后获得耶鲁大学的研究生奖学金，并在耶鲁取得了苏维埃和东欧国际关系专业的文学硕士学位。曾为美国和英国的多家电视公司工作，同时从事小说的写作，其小说曾获毛姆文学奖，是美国杂志《旅游与休闲》的特约编辑。

  [②] Verkhoyansk 上扬斯克，俄罗斯萨哈共和国的一个城镇，位于亚纳河畔，接近北极圈，距雅库茨克约 675 千米。上扬斯克有河港、机场以及一间储存动物软毛的仓库；当地也是驯鹿饲养业的地区中心。上扬斯克冬季十分寒冷，1 月平均气温低至零下 50 摄氏度。

  [③] The Republic of Sakha 萨哈（雅库特）共和国，是俄罗斯远东地区的一个自治共和国，依面积计是世界第七大共和国，北临北冰洋。

  [④] The Discovery Channel 探索频道，由探索传播公司（Discovery Communications）于 1985 年创立,主要播放流行科学、崭新科技和历史考古的纪录片，覆盖全球超过 160 个国家。

  [⑤] Irkutsk 伊尔库茨克市，伊尔库茨克州首府，1661 年建城。位于贝加尔湖西 66 公里伊尔库特河入安加拉河河口处，被称为"西伯利亚的心脏"、"东方巴黎"、"西伯利亚的明珠"，该市人口 75 万，是东西伯利亚仅次于克拉斯诺亚尔斯克的第二大城市和最大的经济中心之一。

  [⑥] Lake Baikal 贝加尔湖，位于俄罗斯西伯利亚的南部伊尔库茨克州及布里亚特共和国境内，呈新月形，是亚洲第一大淡水湖，也是世界第七大湖，是世界最深的湖泊。

从那里开始前往上扬斯克。10 天来我们乘着卡车和驯鹿雪橇穿越尚未设置路标的雪原，沿着冰冻的河流前行，晚上则同牧鹿者在与世隔绝的冬日小屋中渡过。

西伯利亚人喜欢告诉你：没有路，只有方向。在去往上扬斯克的路上确实如此。卡车司机得看着雪堆的形状判断哪里才能安全行驶，我们经常被冰困住——因而需要准备 2 辆车。有天晚上 2 辆车都陷入纽拉河的薄冰中，很快被冻住。我们一行 8 个人在其中一辆卡车的车斗里度过了一个不眠之夜，争抢离烧柴炉最远的位置，炉子是焊接在车斗的底部。车里我们汗流浃背、焦躁不安，车外零下 50 度。

我们进入俄罗斯北部地区时，气温降得更低了，人们戴着的皮帽越来越大。我到莫斯科时，当地人头上都顶着小帽子；护耳似乎纯粹只是装饰——在俄罗斯，人们都认为气温高于零下 20 度就放下护耳太没男子汉气概了。等我到达完全建在永冻土上的城市雅库茨克时，男女都戴着硕大的狐皮软帽，使我想起了 20 世纪 70 年代最奇特的非洲人发型[③]。最后在上扬斯克附近的村庄里，我看见人们脸上都有伤疤——嘴和脸颊上的冻伤——这是终生处于极寒之地造成的。

拿鱼的男子双颊通红，流露出怡然自得的神情，这是态度和善的醉汉特有的。看见他使我想起莫斯科那位建议我到萨哈后大约每小时就喝一杯伏特加的出租车司机。那时我尽力向司机解释酒精给人一种暖和的错觉，实际上加速了热量的散失，他看着我的表情好像我建议他放下护耳。

我婉拒了那位男子吃鱼的邀请，冰冻的生鱼薄片（*stroganina*）浸在盐中很是可口，但是我不确定这条鱼在他的靴子里塞了多久了。我可不想老去拜访西伯利亚昏暗漏风的户外厕所。

然而拿鱼男子并没有轻易放弃。我们的向导安纳托利骗他说我们车里带了好几箱烈酒：spirt，俄罗斯穷人常喝的烈酒。拿鱼男子主动邀请我们两人去他家里过夜，我告诉他我们已经有住宿的地方了，他握住我的手摇了几下便消失在黑暗中。

想象一下在北极圈搭建意大利式西部片[④]的场景，你就知道上扬斯克看起来

---

① The Buddhist republic of Buryatia 布里亚特共和国，是俄罗斯联邦成员国。南邻蒙古国，西邻图瓦共和国，而北部与西北部与伊尔库茨克州接壤，东邻赤塔州。

② Yakutsk 雅库茨克，俄罗斯萨哈共和国的首府及科学、文化和经济中心，距北冰洋极近，有"冰城"之称。

③ Afros 非洲人发型，一种类似非洲黑人蓬松鬈发的埃弗罗发式；爆炸式。

④ spaghetti western 意大利式西部片，西部片的其中一种类型，泛指一些出现在 1960 年代、由意大利人导演及监制（多与西班牙或德国联合制片）的西部片。

怎么样了。1638 年哥萨克人①向东搜寻毛皮时建立了这个村庄；村庄的部分区域仍保持着边疆小镇破破烂烂的特点。街道两旁林立着低矮的木屋，由于没有车辆而显得更为宽阔：大约 2000 人住在这里，但是我看见的唯一的车辆还是我们自己的。我们在上扬斯克花的大部分时间就是设法弄到足够的汽油到飞机场。

20 世纪 80 年代之前上扬斯克是锡矿和金矿中心，但今天这里的居民靠自己灵活应变的能力存活下来。我们的房东就是这样的人，他们养牛并在门廊地下储存冰冻的驯鹿肉。

萨哈人吃很多冰冻食物，冰冻的生鱼、生鹿肉、搅打奶油和蓝莓混和制成的小馅饼以及生驹肝肉饼都是当地的特色食物。市场上牛奶都以冻块出售，小些的村庄里每个房子旁都堆放着巨大的冰块作为冬天的水源，好像特大号的淡蓝色的土耳其软糖②。

冰冻驹肝肉饼出现在我们的早餐桌上。虽然好奇，但是我觉得太恶心没敢亲自尝试，于是告诉摄影师奈杰尔这是搅打奶油和草莓，他咬了一口就像吃了热炭一样吐了出来，还骂了我。我问他味道如何，"血腥味，"他说着，眼神里透着杀气。

当地人告诉我，已到零下 60 度或更冷时，浓雾笼罩着街道，行人隐约的轮廓隐入身后的雾霭里。在雾中，醉汉走得歪歪扭扭，最终会突然栽倒在倾斜的物体上。零下 72 度时呼出的气息会立刻结冰并发出叮当的响声，被称之为"天使的低语"。

事实上我待在西伯利亚的这段时间气温从未低于零下 60 度。这里的人赞同专家有关气候变化的观点：每年冬天天气都在变暖。气温一旦降到零下 60 几度时学校就会放假；这种情况在过去经常持续数周，但现在每年学校只放几天。即便如此我在向北行进的过程中还是学会了区分不同程度的极寒状况。

我的鼻子是一个可靠的计量器：在零度我呼吸时由于鼻毛结冰鼻子会发出轻微的崩裂声；零下 20 几度时会流鼻涕并冻住。零下 40 度时手中的苹果如果咬的间隔时间过长会立时冻僵，塑料制品数秒内冻得硬如石头，收音师的线缆被冻成了奇怪的形状，我的厚手套虎口部分的树脂材料会变得像塑料斧头那么

---

① Cossacks 哥萨克人，俄罗斯和乌克兰民族内部具有独特历史和文化的一个地方性集团。现多分布在苏联顿河、捷列克河和库班河流域等地。属欧罗巴人种东欧类型，使用俄罗斯语南部方言。

② Turkish delight 土耳其软糖，以淀粉与砂糖制成的土耳其甜点，通常以玫瑰香水、乳香树脂与柠檬调味。土耳其软糖呈胶状，质地柔软有弹性、类似果冻，有的还会添入微量坚果，如开心果、榛果或核桃。

锐利僵硬。回到屋里，由于眼镜上结了一层厚冰我从剪刀手爱德华①变成了脱线先生②，在昏暗的灯光下跌跌撞撞，尽力不要让废弃的鞋子绊倒或撞上火炉。过了1周我才意识到鼻梁上的冻疮是眼睛的金属框造成的。

这里的风景就像我所见过的其它景色一样美丽，弥补了严寒的不足。上扬斯克周围的乡村有着茂密的树林，一点也不荒凉。白天，太阳靠近地平线，给所有的一切披上了金黄色的光，投下长长的蓝色的影子，冰将树木妆点成精致的玻璃雕塑。风吹过时，空气中闪烁着亮晶晶的雪晶体。天气太冷了，所有东西都散发不出什么气味——甚至连户外厕所都一样。雪本身就是一张吸音毯，极大地削弱了各种声响：靴子或蹄子的吱吱声，驯鹿轭具上的铃铛声，以及铲雪时发出的轻微的嘎吱声。正是在北极圈，我生平第一次看见北极光：恍若翠绿色的纱帘飘浮在空中。

西伯利亚在俄语中用 Sibir 表示，来自蒙古族的阿尔泰语，意思是"沉睡的土地"。树林、河流和山脉似乎真的进入了休眠状态，这使我想起睡美人城堡附近无法穿越的森林，在那里只要她用手指一指，任何东西都会冻结：浪花凝固在河流上，秋天的草莓冻结在灌木丛中，被剥了皮的狼的残骸在牧鹿者的小屋外冻成了无以言说的形状。

我们的人类学向导安纳托利来自一个伊文③牧鹿者家庭。伊文人一直过着游牧生活，直到20世纪二三十年代被吸纳入苏联并迁进村庄居住。他们生活艰难，地方政府和国家政府更感兴趣的是他们脚下的土地（萨哈拥有和南非同样巨大的钻石资源），对他们却置之不理。

安纳托利因欧洲文明扰乱了伊文的传统生活而对其怀有公开的敌意。他乐于就我个人在毁灭伊文文化中所应承担的责任给我进行有趣且令我忐忑不安的教育，他喜欢指出我们高科技装束的缺点，他还嘲笑我们笨重的加拿大靴子。"纯欧式风格！"他轻蔑地说道，"气温低于零下40度时，你们会冻僵的。我们现在就该拿根火柴生火烧掉它们。"他警告我如果我还坚持戴乐斯菲斯④帽

---

① Edward Scissorhands 剪刀手爱德华，电影《剪刀手爱德华》中的主角，是由一个类似科学怪人的发明家制造的机器人，他具备人类的一切肉体和精神的功能，但是却没有双手只有一双剪刀手。这里形容"我"冻得僵硬的手套。

② Mr.Magoo 脱线先生，美国联合制片动画工作室于1949年创造的卡通人物，后被拍摄成同名电影。他高度近视并因此有了很多滑稽的遭遇。这里指我从屋外到屋内眼镜由于结冰而变得朦胧不清。

③ Even 伊文，西伯利亚和俄罗斯远东地区的一个民族。

④ North Face 乐斯菲斯，全美国唯一一家生产范围涵盖外套、滑雪服、背包、帐篷等一系列户外用品的生产商。

而不是裘皮帽的话，千年后考古学家就会像挖长毛象①一样把我从永冻土里挖出来。

安纳托利脚上穿着由驯鹿腿部皮毛制成的 *unty*，一种同普通鞋子大小差不多的鞋。我们乘坐驯鹿雪橇行进时，我从牧鹿者那里借了毛皮做成的衣服：*unty*、狼獾皮裤子、雪羊皮连指手套和鹿皮茄克。这些衣服不仅比我的其它衣服暖和轻便，而且毛皮的味道似乎使驯鹿感觉轻松自在。（摄影师奈杰尔穿着人工纤维做成的衣服和大号靴子，走动时沙沙作响，吓得套上轭具的动物们跳起来躲避他，结果却绞缠在一起）。温暖和湿气会毁掉这些衣服，所以晚上要把皮衣装进麻袋放到屋外，然而经过零下40度的夜晚，我次日早晨再穿时丝毫不会感到冰冷。

西方很少有人听说过伊文族，但是所有人都知道他们语言中的一个词 *Shaman*，这个词在伊文语中指传统的精神治疗师，其词源不太确定——可能表示"知者"——但这个词已经从俄罗斯民族语言传到各种各样的语言中因而国际化了。待在过度加热的卡车中的漫长时间里，安纳托利给我讲述了很多被他的族人称颂为伊文最强大的精神治疗师的故事。在安纳托利看来，伊文的这些精神治疗师不仅预见了西方的大多数科学发现，而且登上月球对他们来说也是司空见惯的事情。

安纳托利面带笑容给我讲述了这一切，他的故事符合西伯利亚的一种观点，那就是尼尔·阿姆斯特朗②登上月球时受到一位名叫伊凡诺夫的俄罗斯年长智者的接见。问问阿姆斯特朗这件事会很有意思，尤其我想知道伊凡诺夫是否在靴子里掖着一条冻鱼。

（申彩红 译　温秀颖 校）

---

① A woolly mammoth 长毛象，又称猛犸，古脊椎动物，哺乳纲，长鼻目，生活在约1万1千年前，源于非洲，后分布于欧洲、亚洲、北美洲的北部地区，可以适应草原，森林，冻原雪原等环境，最后一批猛犸象大约于公元前2000年灭绝。

② Neil Armstrong 尼尔·阿姆斯特朗，是第一个登上月球的宇航员。1930年8月5日生于俄亥俄州瓦帕科内塔。1955年获珀杜大学航空工程专业理学硕士学位。1949－1952年在美国海军服役（飞行员）。

尾 声

　　合书掩面，意犹未尽之时，仍有几篇美文翘首以待来慰藉我们对自然美景自在自为之态的渴望……

A Girl's Guide to Saudi Arabia

Maureen Dowd

【导读】在21世纪的今天，地球上依然有这样一个王国：这里《古兰经》和穆罕默德的圣训是国家的宪法；这里依然保留鞭刑及截肢刑罚，贩毒是死罪，偷窃要砍手；这里是世界上唯一禁止女性驾车的国家；这里男性和女性的活动区域严格区分；这里严禁女士在公共场合裸露皮肤，外国人也不例外。这里就是古老的沙特阿拉伯王国。虽然国际舆论对王国人权问题尤其是女性地位问题颇有微词，但是对于大多数人来说，王国中女性的真实生活状况正如同她们的头巾和面纱所遮掩的容颜一样神秘难测。沙特女人给世界留下的形象大概仅限于一身包裹严密的黑色长袍和头巾，唯有那一双深邃的眼睛暴露在外。"沙特"取自于沙特阿拉伯王国的创始人伊本·沙特之名，在阿拉伯语中，为"幸福"之意；"阿拉伯"一词，为"沙漠"之意。"沙特阿拉伯"即为"幸福的沙漠"。那么沙特女人在这片沙漠王国里究竟幸福与否？沙特王国真的是如此保守原始吗？沙特女性究竟有多少禁忌与约束？《纽约时报》的专栏女作家莫琳·多德对沙特王国进行了为期10天的游览访问，并从一位时尚现代的纽约女性的角度，用犀利幽默的语言记录了自己的沙特之行，同时将沙特的历史和文化点缀其中，任何不同的文化都会为我们开辟全新的视角，就让我们跟随莫琳进行一场饶有生趣的异域文化之旅吧！

I WANTED TO KNOW ALL ABOUT EVE. "Our grandmother Eve?" asked Abdullah Hejazi, my boyish-looking guide in Old Jidda[①]. Under a glowing Arab moon on a hot winter night, Abdullah was showing off the jewels of his city — charming green, blue, and brown houses built on the Red Sea more than a hundred years ago. The houses, empty now, are stretched tall to capture the sea breeze on streets squeezed narrow to capture the shade. The latticed screens on cantilevered

---

[①] Jidda is a port city in western Saudi Arabia on the Red Sea and is known as "the bride of the red Sea"; near Mecca. （编者注）

verandas were intended to ensure "the privacy and seclusion of the harem," as the Lebanese writer Ameen Rihani[①] noted in 1930. The preservation of these five hundred houses surrounding a souk marks an attempt by the Saudis, whose oil profits turned them into bling addicts, to appreciate the beauty of what they dismissively call "old stuff."

Jidda means "grandmother" in Arabic, and the city may have gotten its name because tradition holds that the grandmother of all temptresses, the biblical Eve, is buried here—an apt symbol for a country that legally, sexually, and sartorially buries its women alive. (A hard-line Muslim cleric in Iran recently blamed provocatively dressed women for earthquakes, inspiring the *New York Post* headline SHEIK IT![②]) According to legend, when Adam and Eve were evicted from the Garden of Eden they went their separate ways, Adam ending up in Mecca and Eve in Jidda, with a single reunion. (Original sin reduced to friends with benefits?) Eve's cemetery lies behind a weathered green door in Old Jidda.

When I suggested we visit, Abdullah smiled with sweet exasperation. It was a smile I would grow all too accustomed to from Saudi men in the coming days. It translated into "No f - ing way, lady."

"Women are not allowed to go into cemeteries," he told me.

I had visited Saudi Arabia twice before, and knew it was the hardest place on earth for a woman to negotiate. Women traveling on their own have generally needed government minders or permission slips. A Saudi woman can't even report harassment by a man without having a *mahram,* or male guardian, by her side. A group of traditional Saudi women, skeptical of any sort of liberalization, recently started an organization called My Guardian Knows What's Best for Me. I thought I understood the regime of gender apartheid pretty well. But this cemetery bit took me aback.

"Can they go in if they're dead?," I asked.

"Women can be buried there," he conceded, "but you are not allowed to go in

---

① Ameen Rihani, (1876-1940), Lebanese Arab-American writer, intellectual and political activist. He was also a major figure in the Al-Mahjar（移民诗人）literary movement developed by Arab emigrants in North America, and an early theorist of Arab nationalism. He became an American citizen in 1901.

② "SHEIK IT" is the New York Post headline for the "boobquake"（乳震） movement on Apirl, 26th, 2010 . After an Iranian cleric claimed that women's "immodest" dressing caused earthquakes, Purdue University senior Jennifer McCreight responded by asking women nationwide to show a little skin on the same day, hoping to prove to the sheik that "immodest" dressing won't cause shake.

and look into it."

So I can only see a dead woman if I'm a dead woman?

No wonder they call this the Forbidden Country. It's the most bewitching, bewildering, beheading vacation spot you'll never vacation in.

Hello—and Good-Bye!

Saudi Arabia is one of the premier pilgrimage sites in the world, outstripping Jerusalem, the Vatican, Angkor Wat, and every other religious destination, except for India's Kumbh Mela① (which attracts as many as 50 million pilgrims every three years). Millions of Muslims flock to Mecca and Medina annually. But, for non-Muslims, it's another story. Saudi Arabia has long kept not just its women but its very self behind a veil. Robert Lacey②, the Jidda-based author of *The Kingdom* and *Inside the Kingdom,* explains that only when revenues from the hajj pilgrims fell drastically, during the Depression, did the Saudis allow infidel American engineers to enter the country and start exploring for oil.

Before 9/11, Saudi Arabia was in fact gearing up to welcome, or at least accept, a trickle of non-Muslim visitors, dropping a handkerchief to the world. Crown Prince Abdullah—now the king—was a radical modernizer by Saudi standards. He wanted to encourage more outside contact and to project an image other than one of religious austerity (with bursts of terrorism). The Saudis had already cracked open the door slightly for some degree of cultural tourism. Leslie McLoughlin, a fellow at the University of Exeter's Institute of Arab and Islamic Studies, led tours to the Kingdom in 2000 and 2001, and both groups included affluent and curious Jewish men and women from New York. But on 9/11 the passageway narrowed again as Saudi Arabia and the United States confronted the reality that Osama bin Laden and fifteen of the nineteen terrorist hijackers were Saudi nationals.

The news cut to the very character of the Saudi state. Back in 1744, the oasis-dwelling al-Saud clan had made a pact with Muhammad bin Abdul Wahhab, founder of the Wahhabi sect, which took an especially strict approach to religious

---

① Kumbh Mela is a mass Hindu pilgrimage in which Hindus gather at the Ganges river, which takes place at four places (Allahabad, Haridwar, Ujjain, and Nashik) in India in turn every three years.

② Robert Lacey (1944-) is a British historian and biographer. His 1981 work *The Kingdom* and its 2009 follow-up *Inside the Kingdom* have now both been cited as standard study texts for the diplomatic community working inside the Kingdom of Saudi Arabia.

observance. The warrior al-Sauds got religious legitimacy; the anhedonic Wahhabis got protection. To this day the Koran is the constitution of Saudi Arabia, and Wahhabism its dominant faith. The royals doubled down on the deal when Islamic fundamentalists took over the Grand Mosque, in Mecca, in 1979. Now, with bin Laden's attacks, the bargain the royals struck with the fundamentalists — allowing anti-Western clerics and madrassas to flourish and not cracking down on those who bankroll al-Qaeda[①] and terrorism — had borne its poison fruit.

Three years after 9/11, in 2004, the Kingdom decided to give the tourism business another try, this time hiring a public relations firm to get things rolling. The website of the resulting Supreme Commission for Tourism was "a disaster," one Saudi official abashedly recalls, shaking his head. The site noted that visas would not be issued to an Israeli passport holder, to anyone with an Israeli stamp on a passport, or, just in case things weren't perfectly clear, to "Jewish people." There were also "important instructions" for any woman coming to the kingdom on her own, advising that she would need a husband or a male sponsor to pick her up at the airport, and that she would not be allowed to drive a car unless "accompanied by her husband, a male relative, or a driver." Needless to say, there would be no drinking allowed—Saudi officials even try to enforce no-drinking rules on private jets in Saudi airspace, sometimes sealing the liquor cabinets. Finally, belying the fact that Arabs consider hospitality a sacred duty, there was the no-loitering kicker: "All visitors to the Kingdom must have a return ticket." After New York congressman Anthony Weiner kicked up a fuss, the anti-Semitic language on the website was removed.

Now, six years later, the Saudis are trying yet again. But they aren't opening their arms unless (with a few exceptions) you are part of a special tourist group. "No backpacking stuff," says Prince Sultan bin Salman, the tall and chatty former astronaut who is the president and chairman of the Saudi Commission for Tourism and Antiquities. "You know, high level," he goes on, and involving only "fully educated" groups.

You still have to accept all the restrictive rules. And it won't be easy getting in. Visas these days for Westerners are so scarce that even top American diplomats have

---

① A terrorist network intensely opposed to the United States that dispenses money and logistical support and training to a wide variety of radical Islamic terrorist groups. 基地组织。

a hard time obtaining them for family members. The Kingdom recoils at the thought of the culture clash that could be caused by an invasion of French girls in shorts and American boys with joints. A sign at the airport warns: DRUG TRAFFICKERS WILL BE PUT TO DEATH.

Saudis fret that the rest of the world sees them as aliens, even though many are exceptionally charming and welcoming once you actually breach the wall. They are sensitive about being judged for their Flintstones[①] ways, and are quick to remind you of what happened to the Shah of Iran when he tried to modernize too fast. Not to mention their own King Faisal[②], who was assassinated in 1975 (regicide by nephew) after he introduced television and public education for girls. This prince-and-pauper society has always had a Janus[③] face. Royals fly to the South of France to drink, gamble, and sleep with Russian hookers, while reactionary clerics at home delegitimize women and demonize Westerners. Last winter, a Saudi prince found himself under arrest for allegedly strangling his servant in a London hotel. (He has pleaded not guilty.) The Kingdom didn't have widespread electricity until the 1950s. It didn't abolish slavery until the 1960s. Restrictions on mingling between unrelated members of the opposite sex remain severe. (Recently, a Saudi cleric advised men who come in regular contact with unrelated women to consider drinking their breast milk, thereby making them in a sense "relatives," and allowing everyone to breathe a sigh of relief.) Today, Saudi Arabia is trying to take a few more steps ahead — starting a coed university, letting women sell lingerie to women, even toning down the public beheadings. If you're living on Saudi time, akin to a snail on Ambien[④], the popular eighty-six-year-old King Abdullah is making bold advances. To the rest of the world, the changes are almost imperceptible.

---

① The Flintstones is an animated American television sitcom, which was about a working class Stone Age man's life with his family and his next-door neighbor and best friend.

② King Faisal (1906 – 1975), was King of Saudi Arabia from 1964 to 1975. As king, he is credited with rescuing the country's finances and implementing a policy of modernization and reform. In 1975, he was assassinated by his nephew.

③ In Roman mythology, Janus is the Roman god of doorways and passages, who is depicted with two faces on opposite sides of his head.

④ A kind of prescription medication used for the short-term treatment of insomnia.

"Lots of Attentions"

The idea of seeing Saudi Arabia with the welcome mat[①] out was irresistible — even when the wary Saudis kept resisting. I made plans for a Saudi vacation, knowing that the only thing more invigorating than ten days in Saudi Arabia would be ten days there as a woman. Actually, it would be two women: joining me was my intrepid colleague and trip photographer Ashley Parker. I was a little squeamish about boarding a Saudi Arabian Airlines flight with a cross on my forehead. (It was Ash Wednesday[②].) Some Saudi flights embark with an Arabic supplication, in the words of the Prophet Muhammad. The flight attendants—who are not Saudi, because it would be dishonorable for the airline to employ Saudi women—bring around baskets of Saudi newspapers. A glance at the headlines underscored the fact that we were in a time machine hurtling backward. One article in the English-language *Arab News* was titled "Carrying Dagger a Mark of Manliness." Another warned, "Women lawyers are not welcome in the Kingdom's courts." It was startling to see a thumbnail portrait of a female columnist — my counterpart — in which only her eyes were not concealed by a veil. Reading the airline magazine is like the moment in *The Twilight Zone*[③] when you sense there's something slightly off about that picture-book town. The magazine is called *Ahlah Wasahldn,* meaning "Hello and Welcome," but the welcome seems to be to Versailles, Provence, and Belize. There's no hint that Saudi Arabia itself might be a destination.

The in-flight movies offer a taste of things to come. If you order *The Proposal*[④], you get a blurry blob over Sandra Bullock's modest décolletage, and even her clavicles, and the male stripper scene and the erection joke have vanished altogether. A curtained partition goes up so that Saudi women can nap without their abayas. There's no alcohol on board, although some veteran business travelers en route to the Kingdom order vodkas at the airport bar and pour them into a water bottle for

---

① Welcome mat is a mat placed outside an exterior door for wiping the shoes before entering, the figurative meaning of which is warm welcome.

② Ash Wednesday is the 7th Wednesday before Easter; the first day of Lent; the day following Mardi Gras ('fat Tuesday'); a day of fasting and repentance.

③ *The Twilight Zone* is an American anthology television series, which depicts paranormal, futuristic, dystopian, or simply disturbing events.

④ *The Proposa*l is a 2009 American romantic comedy film, which features Sandra Bullock and Ryan Reynolds as the leading roles.

sustenance along the way. At the airport in Riyadh①, the gender segregation ratchets up. There's a Ladies' Waiting Room and a Ladies' Prayer Room. If there hadn't been a Saudi majordomo to come and collect us, we would have been in limbo — a pair of single women wandering the airport with no man to get them out, trapped forever like Tom Hanks in *The Terminal*②.

In America, you get chocolates in your hotel room. In Riyadh, you might get a gift bag from your hosts in the Kingdom with something to slip into for dinner—a long black abaya and a black headscarf that make you look like a mummy and feel like a pizza oven. And even then they'll stick you behind a screen or curtain in the "family" section of the restaurant. The big Gloria Steinem③ advance in recent years is that women now wear abayas with dazzling designs on the back (sometimes with thousands of dollars' worth of Swarovski crystals) or Burberry④ or zebra-patterned trim on the sleeves.

I respect Islam's mandate for modest clothing. But I don't see why I have to adopt a dress code, as Aaron Sorkin put it on *The West Wing*⑤, that makes "a Maryknoll nun look like Malibu Barbie." Needless to say, Barbie herself was banned in Saudi Arabia, though I did see Barbie paraphernalia for sale in a Riyadh supermarket and a Barbie-like doll, accessorized with headscarf and abaya (and of course not in a box with Ken⑥), in the National Museum gift shop. As for *Hello!* ⑦magazine, a recent import to the Kingdom, Saudi censors paste small white squares of paper on the models' glossy thighs.

---

① Riyadh is the capital of Saudi Arabia, which is located in the central oasis; the largest city in Saudi Arabia.

② *The Terminal* is a 2004 American comedy-drama film directed by Steven Spielberg and starring Tom Hanks and Catherine Zeta-Jones. It is about a man trapped in a terminal at New York's John F. Kennedy International Airport when he is denied entry into the United States and at the same time cannot return to his native country.

③ Gloria Steinem (1934-) is an American feminist, and social and political activist, who helped to strike down many long-standing sex discriminatory laws.

④ A British luxury fashion house, manufacturing clothing, fragrance, and fashion accessories.

⑤ *The West Wing* is an American television serial drama created by Aaron Sorkin that was originally broadcast on NBC from September 22, 1999 to May 14, 2006. The series is set in the West Wing of the White House — where the Oval Office and offices of presidential senior staff are located—during the fictional Democratic administration of Josiah Bartlet.

⑥ Ken (Ken Sean Carson) is a Mattel toy doll introduced by Mattel in 1961 as the fictional boyfriend of toy doll Barbie introduced in 1959.

⑦ *Hello* (stylized as HELLO!) is a weekly magazine specializing in celebrity news and human-interest stories, published in the United Kingdom since 1988.

Soon after our arrival I asked Prince Sultan bin Salman, the tourism minister, about the dress code for foreigners. "Well, the abaya is part of the uniform," he said. "It's part of enjoying the culture. I've seen people who go to India dress up in the Indian sari." Najla Al-Khalifah, a member of the prince's staff in the female section of the tourist bureau, offered another analogy: "You can't wear shorts for the opera. You must dress for the occasion. If you don't like it, don't go." Fair enough, but if you do wear shorts to the opera, you won't get arrested by the roving outriders of the Commission for the Promotion of Virtue and Prevention of Vice — that is, the *mutawa*, or religious police.

Being in purdah pricks more deeply when you're dealing with American-owned enterprises — it's as if your own people are in sexist cahoots with your captors. In 2008, covering President Bush's trip to the Middle East, I was standing next to ABC's① Martha Raddatz at the desk at the Riyadh Marriott when she angrily pressed the clerk about getting into the gym. He gave her The Smile. How about never, lady? On this trip, at Budget Rent a Car, the man at the counter explained to me that women could rent cars only if they paid extra for a driver. (And, to boot, it would be dishonorable for a woman to sit in the passenger seat unless a male relative were driving.) When I said I could drive myself, the man's head fell back in helpless laughter. I enlisted Nicolla Hewitt, a gorgeous, statuesque blonde New Yorker on business in Saudi Arabia, to join me in a brief sit-in at the men's section of Starbucks in the upscale Kingdom Centre mall. Her head was swirling with lurid news accounts of a Western woman who had been dragged from a Starbucks for committing the crime of attempted equality. "If I see the bloody *mutawa*," she said, gripping her latte nervously, "I'm hoofing it."

At various establishments I began amusing myself by seeing how long it took for male Cerberuses② to dart forward and block the way to the front sections reserved for men. At McDonald's, dourly observing my arrival, a janitor barred the door with a broom in two seconds flat. At the posh Al Faisaliah Hotel, in Riyadh, I was asking the maître d'③ why I couldn't sit with the businessmen when he

---

① American Broadcasting Company（美国广播公司）。

② In Greek and Roman mythology, Cerberuses is a multi-headed hound (usually three-headed) which guards the gates of the Underworld, to prevent those who have crossed the river Styx from ever escaping.

③ Maître d 'hôtel or maître d' manages the public part or "front of the house" of a formal restaurant.

suddenly caught sight of an elegant woman sashaying through the men's section. He made a Reggie Bush[①] run to knock her out of bounds before turning back to thwart my own entrance with a Baryshnikov[②] leap. I did manage a moment of Pyrrhic triumph in the deserted men's section in the lobby café of the Jidda Hilton, ordering a cappuccino, but then the waiter informed me that he couldn't serve it until I moved five feet back to the women's section.

Hotel desk clerks would warn me to put on my abaya merely to walk across the lobby, even when I was wearing my most modest floor-length navy dress, the one reserved for family funerals. "You will get lots of attentions—not good attentions," one clerk said. Not wearing an abaya can be hazardous — but so can wearing one. Signs on the mall escalators caution women to be careful not to get their cloaks caught in the moving stairs. (A Muslim woman was recently choked to death by her hijab while on holiday in Australia; it had gotten caught in a go-cart at high speed.) You soon become paranoid, worrying that if you open the door for room service wearing a terry-cloth robe, you'll end up in the stocks[③]. But the top hotels are staffed by foreign men—something I realized must be the case when my butler at the Al Faisaliah folded my underwear unprompted. If I were buttled by a Saudi, we'd probably be shuttled to Deera Square[④] — or Chop Chop Square, as it's better known — where the public beheadings occur. It's the one with the big drain, which the Saudis claim is for rain.

Sunny Side of Repression

The first time I traveled to Saudi Arabia was in the aftermath of the 9/11 attacks: Prince Saud al-Faisal, the foreign minister, had invited me to come over and see for myself that not all Saudis are terrorists. On that trip, I was more heedless and cavalier. I wore a hot-pink skirt, with fringe, to go to an interview with the Saudi education minister. When I came down from my hotel room, the men in the lobby glared with such hostility that I thought they'd pelt me to death with their dates. My

---

① Reggie Bush (1985-) is an American football running back for the Miami Dolphins of the National Football League.

② Baryshnikov (1948-), is a Soviet and American dancer, choreographer, and actor, one of the greatest ballet dancers of the 20th century.

③ Stock: (ancient) hobbles, here referring to the prison.

④ Deera Square is a public space in Riyadh, Saudi Arabia, where public executions take place. It is sometimes known as Justice Square or Chop Chop Square.

minder turned me back to the elevator. "Go get your abaya!" he yelled. "They'll kill you!" (My Guardian Knew What Was Best for Me.) This was right around the time when fifteen Saudi schoolgirls had died in a fire because the *mutawa* wouldn't let them escape without their headscarves and abayas, a horrifying episode that shook the Kingdom. Confronted by carloads of screaming men whenever I wore my own clothes, I added more layers but still got into trouble. I was swathed in black with a headscarf at a mall next to the Al Faisaliah Hotel when four members of the *mutawa* bore down. They barked in Arabic that they could see my neck and the outline of my body, and they confiscated my passport. All this was happening against the backdrop of a storefront underwear display featuring a lacy red teddy. My companion, the suave Adel al-Jubeir[①], an adviser to King Abdullah and now the Saudi ambassador to Washington, managed to retrieve the passport and obtain permission for me to leave the mall (and the country), but it took a disconcertingly long time.

With each incident, you feel more cowed and less eager to defy the dress-to-repress rules. For this trip, I had an abaya made so I wouldn't have to swelter inside the standard polyester ones in the baking heat. I didn't go for anything as gauzy as Dorothy Lamour's in *The Road to Morocco*[②]. I wanted simple black linen. But the tailor tried too hard to give it a flattering shape, adding slits so high they could get my throat slit. When I wore it, my minders pestered me to put an abaya over my abaya. It reminded me of Martin Short[③]'s mischievous question about Hillary Clinton's nightwear: "Does she have a pantsuit on under her pantsuit?"

Still, this time around, I decided to look on the sunny side of repression. Feel guilty about not jogging? Don't even try! Tired of running off to every new exhibition? Lucky you — there aren't any art museums! Can't decide which sybaritic treatment to select at the hotel spa? Relax—the spa's just for men. And you never have to stress about a bad-hair day.

The two words you'll quickly learn are *haled* (permissible) and *haram* (forbidden) — the kosher and nonkosher of the Arab world. Since your old pastimes

---

① Adel A. Al-Jubeir (1962-) is the Saudi Arabian Ambassador to the United States, and a former foreign policy advisor to King Abdullah bin Abdulaziz of Saudi Arabia. He is a well-known representative of the Saudi kingdom in the West, particularly the United States.

② *Road to Morocco* is an 1942 American comedy film about two fast-talking guys tossed up on a desert shore and sold into slavery to a beautiful princess. Dorothy Lamour played the part of the princess.

③ Martin Hayter Short (1950-) is a Canadian actor, comedian, writer, singer and producer. He is best known for his comedy work, particularly on the TV programs *SCTV* and *Saturday Night Live*.

are now mostly *haram*, you'll have to pick up some new vices. Gorge on gamy camel bacon at Friday brunch. (Friday is the Muslim Sunday.) Develop a new obsession with tweezing and threading your eyebrows and blackening your Bedouin bedroom eyes[1]—now literally the windows to the soul. Enjoy a country that is the last refuge of indoor smoking. I went to the cigar bar at the fancy Globe restaurant in Riyadh and enjoyed a "Churchill's Cabinet" stogie for 180 riyals[2] ($50), with its "lovely notes of leather and cream, hints of coffee, citrus, and spice." To go along with beluga caviar and Maine-lobster snacks there was an elaborate wine presentation, with the waiter showing off the label of a nonalcoholic Zinfandel[3] before nestling it in a silver ice bucket. "It's from California," he said proudly. I fell into tippling in the morning, starting the day with Saudi champagne, a saccharine apple juice concoction.

You might also want to emulate the spoiled Saudi set and just loll about until the sun sets, watching *The Bold and the Beautiful*[4] or Glenn Beck[5] on satellite TV. (There are no public movie theaters.) The Saudis have a homegrown version of the *Today*[6] show in English, with their own Meredith Vieira[7] in headscarf, promoting buttocks exercises and colon cleansing, and a hefty Martha Stewart[8] doppelgänger in a babushka, baking dried-apricot sandwiches in flower shapes. It's all very cozy, even if the crawl underneath is crawling with less-than-flattering stories about Israel's treatment of the Palestinians. One night, deciding to take a risk, I smuggled a young Saudi man up to my hotel room to translate some of the scary-looking rants on TV by guys in *thobes* and kaffiyehs. Were they trashing the Great Satan? He told

---

[1] Bedroom eyes mean provocative eyes of women, which also refers to the sexy image of women. Since women in Saudi can only show their eyes, so if they want to be sexy, they can only concentrate on their eyebrows and eyes.

[2] The Riyal is the currency of Saudi Arabia.

[3] Zinfandel is a variety of red grape planted in over 10 percent of California vineyards.

[4] *The Bold and the Beautiful* is an American television soap opera, which premiered on March 23, 1987.

[5] Glenn Beck (1964-) is an American radio host, author, entrepreneur, political commentator and former television host. He hosts the" Glenn Beck Program", a nationally syndicated talk-radio show.

[6] *Today* is an American breakfast television show that airs every morning on NBC. Meredith Vieira is one of the hosts.

[7] Meredith Vieira (1953-) is an American journalist, television personality, and game show host.

[8] Martha Stewart (1941-) is an American business magnate, author, magazine publisher, and television personality. As founder of Martha Stewart Living Omnimedia, she has gained success through a variety of business ventures, encompassing publishing, broadcasting, and merchandising.

me that the serious-looking bearded guy talking a mile a minute[①] was merely chatting about soccer, and another scowling fellow with intense brown eyes was just praying. Likely story.

Once out of your room, you can stroll through the malls with your girlfriends for some Bluetooth flirting, where Rashid and Khalid detect your cell phone network as you walk by and send text messages that range from chatty to creepy. One of my young married minders said he regularly gets hassled by the *mutawa* when he's out flirting with female friends: "They say, 'Can I ask who you are with?,' and I tell them, 'Oh, she's my sister.' And they say, 'Your sister? Do you laugh like that with your sister?'" There's no date night in Saudi Arabia. The romance strictures here—a few virginal meetings, a peek under the veil, a marriage contract, an all-female wedding reception, and a check of the bloody sheets — make *The Rules*[②] look like the Kama Sutra[③]. In Jidda, there's a Chinese restaurant called Toki, where unmarried girls can show themselves off in front of likely prospects on a fifty-eight-meter catwalk. The prospects are not young men, however, but their mothers, who traditionally made the match with help from the *khatabah,* or yenta, who was sometimes sent over to surreptitiously look under the hood and kick the tires of the bride-to-be. She would give the girl a hug to check the firmness of her breasts and then drop something on the floor to watch the girl pick it up. When the young lady would bend over and her abaya lifted ever so slightly, the *khatabah* could see her ankles and infer the shape of the legs and derrière.

"The Time of Ignorance"

Back in the 1940s, when the oil began gushing, Saudi Arabia was the sort of place where the country's first king, Abdul Aziz ibn Saud, traveled in a Ford convertible with his falcons and shot gazelles from the car. The king knew the name of every visitor to Riyadh. Travelers could not move around the Kingdom without

---

① Talk a mile a minute : (idiomatic) to speak quickly or excessively.

② *The Rules: Time-Tested Secrets for Capturing the Heart of Mr. Right* is a controversial self-help book which suggests rules that a woman should follow in order to attract and marry the man of her dreams.

③ Kama Sutra: (Hinduism) an ancient Sanskrit text giving rules for sensuous and sensual pleasure and love and marriage in accordance with Hindu law.

the king's express consent, and he personally tracked each one's odyssey[①]. Some Saudis, who had rarely seen airplanes, assumed they were cars that simply drove off into the sky. Prince Sultan bin Salman is a natural choice for tourism czar[②], given that he was the first Muslim in space. In 1985 he went up as part of an international crew on the *Discovery*[③] shuttle. Trying to find Mecca from space — imagine gravity-free kneeling — was nothing compared with persuading other royals (thanks to polygamy, there are now thousands of them) to consider the desirability of making Saudi Arabia tourist-ready. For one thing, Saudis don't have that fondness for their own history that the British and Italians do. Many pious Muslims look askance at civilizations that predate Islam ("the time of ignorance," as they call it), and they have reservations about archaeological digs that may turn up Christian sites. Archaeology was not fully recognized until the last few years as a field of study in Saudi universities. In other countries, many of the famed tourist sites are what you might call "big broken things" — Machu Picchu[④], the Colosseum. Saudis don't go for broken, or even slightly worn. You will never see a Melrose Avenue[⑤] — style vintage store; it would be considered shameful to buy or sell old clothes. It's all about the new and shiny.

Prince Sultan was traveling through Tuscany a few years back, snapping pictures of big broken things and talking to preservation experts, when it hit him: maybe there was a way to get Saudis to appreciate their own ancient heritage. He gathered forty or so mayors and governors who liked nothing better than to tear down their cultural heritage, and showed them that they could develop historic sites where local crafts and fresh produce are sold in a "joyous" setting. The cultural

---

① The Odyssey is one of two major ancient Greek epic poems attributed to Homer. The poem mainly centers on the Greek hero Odysseus and his ten-year journey home after the fall of Troy. Odyssey here refers to journey.

② Czar is a male monarch or emperor (especially of Russia prior to 1917), which means a person having great power here.

③ Discovery shuttle is one of the retired orbiters of the Space Shuttle program of NASA, the space agency of the United States, and was operational from its maiden flight, STS-41-D on August 30, 1984, until its final landing during STS-133 on March 9, 2011.

④ Machu Picchu Inca fortress city in the Andes in Peru discovered in 1911; it may have been built in the 15th century. 马丘比丘（古城，位于秘鲁中部偏南）。

⑤ Melrose Avenue is an internationally renowned shopping, dining and entertainment destination in Los Angeles that starts from Santa Monica Boulevard at the border between Beverly Hills and West Hollywood and ends at Lucille Avenue in Silver Lake.

education did not begin well. The prince had wanted the officials to see Siena①. "And I get a phone call at four A.M. that woke me, and the pilot was calling. He said, 'I'm in Vienna.' " Eventually, the Saudi mayors and governors began to acquire a taste for old stuff. They've done five more trips, and one to Seville was coming up, though maybe they'd end up in Savile Row②. (Saudis certainly know the way.)

Prince Sultan is now training native Saudis — who have always left the heavy lifting as waiters, maids, and drivers to a servant class of Filipinos, Bangladeshis, Indonesians, Pakistanis, and Indians — to work as tour guides, tour operators, and hotel operators. He hopes that Saudis will get better at sightseeing as they travel elsewhere. "Saudis are not trained as good tourists," he told me over tea one night. "They didn't know how to respect the sites, not throw Kleenex③ at places."

With Prince Sultan's assistance we flew to an attraction we'd never heard of before: the spectacular Madain Saleh, sister city to Jordan's renowned Petra④, three hundred miles to the northwest. After flying across the desert for hours, you suddenly come upon strange and wonderful classical structures. Today they're in the middle of nowhere. Eons ago, at the time of ancient Rome, they stood athwart the Incense Route, controlled by the Nabataean kingdom. An airport is only just being built, so we bumped down in our puddle jumper on what was essentially a cleared track. Our guide barely spoke English, but he was giddy with pleasure at finally having someone to show around. There are more than a hundred sumptuous sandstone tombs here, many of them cavernous, sculpted into solid rock between the first century B.C. and the first century A.D. Only in recent years have the Saudis come to appreciate Madain Saleh's value, registering it as a UNESCO World Heritage Site in 2008.

They're also restoring the old train station in Madain Saleh to its former glory,

---

① Siena (in English also spelled Sienna) is a city in Tuscany, Italy. It is the capital of the province of Siena.

② Savile Row is a shopping street in Mayfair, central London, famous for its traditional men's bespoke tailoring.

③ Kleenex is a brand name for a variety of toiletry paper-based products such as facial tissue, bathroom tissue, paper towels, and diapers, which also represents a piece of soft absorbent paper (usually two or more thin layers) used as a disposable handkerchief.

④ Petra is a historical and archaeological city in the Jordanian governorate of Ma'an that is famous for its rock cut architecture and water conduits system. It is established sometime around the 6th century BC as the capital city of the Nabataeans.

with a shiny black engine from the Hejaz railway[1], like the one Peter O'Toole blew up in *Lawrence of Arabia*[2]. Don't bother asking about T. E. Lawrence here — he's remembered for selling the Saudis out. (Saudis love the movie, though, and spout lines from it like "Thy mother mated with a scorpion.") The guides in Saudi Arabia have a hard time staying on message, veering wistfully toward memories of time spent in the United States, studying in Palo Alto, San Diego, or Boulder. They still obsess about their college sports teams — staying up until all hours to watch games via satellite. At the Masmak Fortress, in Riyadh — the scene of a critical battle for Abdul Aziz ibn Saud — the guide soon lost interest in leading us among displays labeled "Some Old Guns" and "Cover for the Udder of the She-Camel" and began to wax nostalgic about a married woman named Liz in Grand Rapids[3].

In Abha[4], a cool, green, mountainous area to the south, near Yemen, we had our sole encounter with an actual Saudi tourist. He was checking out the Hanging Village[5], where some people of yore had settled on the side of a sheer cliff to get away from the Ottomans. Supplies were lowered down by rope. The Saudi was a paunchy man from Riyadh named Fahad, who liked to be called Jack. Jack, wearing a stained tracksuit, volunteered that he had once lived in Fort Worth[6]. "I enjoy it," he said, taking a drag on his cigarette and giving Ashley and me an appreciative look, "when I see these girls with the smell of the United States."

---

[1] The Hejaz Railway was a narrow gauge railway (1,050 mm track gauge) that ran from Damascus to Medina, through the Hejaz region of Saudi Arabia, with a branch line to Haifa, on the Mediterranean Sea. The line was repeatedly damaged in fighting during World War I, particularly at the hands of the guerrilla force led by T. E. Lawrence during the Arab Revolt.

[2] *Lawrence of Arabia* is a 1962 British film based on the life of T. E. Lawrence. O'Toole achieved stardom in 1962 by playing T. E. Lawrence in this movie.

[3] Grand Rapids is a city in the U.S. state of Michigan. The city is located on the Grand River about 40 miles east of Lake Michigan.

[4] Abha is the capital of Asir province in Saudi Arabia. It is situated at 2,200 meters above sea level in the fertile mountains of south-western Saudi Arabia near the National Park of Asir.

[5] This is a once inhabited village and is located about 40 miles from Abha and 2000 meters above sea level. It is seems to hang from a 300 meter cliff face, above terraced fields and a wide valley.

[6] Fort Worth is a city in northeastern Texas (just west of Dallas); a major industrial center.

Peeping Abdul[①]

The charm of Riyadh is that it has no charm. The only visual icon, the one captured in snow globes at souvenir shops, is the city's tallest building, Kingdom Centre, the home of the Four Seasons Hotel and the Kingdom Centre mall. It is owned by Prince al-Waleed bin Talal, the billionaire nephew of King Abdullah who has been called "the Arabian Warren Buffett[②]" by *Time* magazine. (Rudy Giuliani[③] turned down a $10 million donation to New York from al-Waleed after 9/11 when al-Waleed suggested that U.S. policies contributed to the attacks.) The skyscraper features a V-shaped hole at the top, and Saudis tastelessly joke that it's "the Hijacker Training Academy."

A Jordanian staffer at the Riyadh Four Seasons complained to me that the only things Saudis do are "shop and eat, shop and eat." Or subject you to "ordeal by tea," as I've heard it called. At the ubiquitous malls, women covered in black robes and gloves, with only their eyes showing, shop for La Perla lingerie, Versace gowns, Dior handbags, and Bulgari jewelry[④]. Beauty is a drug for Saudi women, even though they're stuck at home most of the time—or maybe because of that. Saudi Arabia is more than three times the size of Texas and glitters with three times as many Swarovski[⑤] crystals. "Bling H_2O"[⑥] water is imported from Tennessee. The shopaholism pauses only at prayer time, when metal grates come down over the stores. Men, who carry more of the burden of the five-times-a-day obligation, head off to the prayer rooms. The women wander zombie-like among the shuttered shop

---

① Abdul is the primary transliteration of the Arabic compound words: Abd (عبـ: meaning servant) and al (ال: meaning the). Abdul's most common use by far, is as part of a male given name, written in English. It appears as a component of many Arabic and specifically Muslim names, where it is the opening of a religiously based name, meaning: Servant of God. Here, Abdul refers to the male Muslims.

② Warren Buffett (1930-) is an American business magnate, investor, and philanthropist. He is consistently ranked among the world's wealthiest people. He was ranked as the world's wealthiest person in 2008 and is the third wealthiest person in the world as of 2011.

③ Rudy Giuliani (1944-) is an American lawyer, businessman, and politician from New York. He served as Mayor of New York City from 1994 to 2001.

④ La Perla, the leading Italian creator of luxurious and fashionable lingerie, nightwear, swimwear, and loungewear since 1954; Versace, Italian fashion label founded by Gianni Versace in 1978; French luxury brand; Bulgari , an Italian jeweler and luxury goods retailer.

⑤ Swarovski is the brand name for a range of precisely-cut crystal and related luxury products.

⑥ Bling H_2O is sold as high-end, fashionable, bottled water. The brand features frosted bottles decorated with Swarovski crystals. The water contained in the bottle comes from a Tennessee (United States) spring and is purified in a nine-step process.

fronts. The atmosphere is watchful. Once, when Ashley tried to snap some pictures of Saudi women shopping at a lingerie store, a female security guard came running up to confiscate the camera. "Just walk away," a Western woman advised us. "She's a woman — she has no power over you." At last: a fringe benefit of misogyny.

The Kingdom Centre mall has a ladies' floor on top shielded by high, wavy frosted glass, so that men—with all the maturity of Catholic schoolboys in stairwells — can't peer up from below. Signs on the ladies' floor tell women, once inside, to take off their head coverings: that way, a Peeping Abdul can't disguise himself in female garb and wander lustfully among them. On the ladies' floor, you're actually allowed to try on clothes. On floors where the sexes mingle, you often have to buy whatever you want in different sizes and take it all home to try on. The mere thought of a disrobed woman behind a dressing room door is apparently too much for men to handle. There's something profoundly poignant about seeing little girls running around the malls in normal clothes, playing with little boys in normal ways — you know what's in store for them in just a few years. When I reached puberty, my mother gave me a book called *On Becoming a Woman*. When these girls reach puberty, they'll have a black tarp thrown over their heads.

In recent years, Riyadh has gotten a dash of[①] sophistication. "Oh my!" says Princess Reema bint Bandar al-Saud, the lovely Riyadh businesswoman who is a daughter of Prince Bandar bin Sultan, the former longtime Saudi ambassador to the U.S. "There's a new restaurant almost every week, and I assure you, the way they look, the way the food is, is on a par with — I wouldn't say the top 10 restaurants in New York or London, but definitely 11 to 50." There's a two-week wait to get a table at B & F Burger Boutique, even though it's just high-end fast food served in a hip decor. The concrete walls and dim lights evoke SoHo[②], and gender segregation is more subtle. The women wear abayas with fashionable trim, and the guys trade their white *thobes* for blue jeans. The religious police showed up on opening night; they wanted the music eliminated and the women screened off by bigger partitions. The restaurant obliged only on the music.

Going from Riyadh to the Red Sea is like going from black-and-white Kansas

---

① a dash of: a little.
② SoHo is a neighborhood in Lower Manhattan, New York City, notable for being the location of many artists' lofts and art galleries.

to Technicolor Oz. The main port of entry for hajj pilgrims, Jidda is Saudi Arabia's business capital. "The bride of the Red Sea" is home to many female entrepreneurs, and residents say they are trying to tell the rest of the country to relax. Women leave their abayas open in front, or wear nighties or tight jeans underneath. But the enticing blue mosaic pool at the Jidda Hilton is still only for men. I watched a Saudi man swim while a woman in "full ninja[①]," as American businessmen here call it, tiptoed around the edge, chatting with him.

When I asked the concierge about the hotel mosque, he said I couldn't go in unless I was a Muslim. Later, Prince Saud told me that I could simply have asked the emir[②] of the region for permission. (Like the emir's listed?) Men in the Kingdom often reflexively say "No, no, no" — "La, la, la!" — to women because it's the safer answer. But an essential point about Saudi Arabia is that everything operates on a sliding scale, depending on who you are, whom you know, whom you ask, whom you're with, and where you are. Drinking is not allowed, but many affluent Saudis keep fully stocked bars. "Take off your abaya when you drink your whiskey," instructed one Saudi mogul as his bartender handed us cocktails in his home. Some Saudi men glean the future from coffee grounds, and many Saudi women love horoscopes, but police here snatched a Lebanese TV host and clairvoyant from a pilgrimage and sentenced him to death by beheading for sorcery. (After international media pressure, the execution has for now been postponed.) Non-Muslims are not allowed to enter the holy cities of Mecca and Medina. But Leslie McLoughlin[③] led a tour near Medina prior to 9/11, where he could view the city and the Prophet's Mosque[④] from his hotel.

Saudi Arabia may now be in semi—Open Sesame[⑤] mode (and it's funny to see

---

① A ninja is trained in martial arts and hired for espionage or sabotage or assassinations, who dresses all in black.

② Emir is an independent ruler or chieftain (especially in Africa or Arabia).

③ Leslie McLoughlin was Director of Studies at the Middle East Centre for Arab Studies in Lebanon, between 1965-68 and 1970-75. He lectured in Arabic and Islamic studies at many universities and has published numerous text books for modern Arabic.

④ Prophet's Mosque is a mosque situated in the city of Medina. As the final resting place of the Islamic prophet Muhammad, it is considered the second holiest site in Islam by Muslims (the first being the Masjid al-Haram in Mecca) and is one of the largest mosques in the world.

⑤ In adventure tale of *Ali Baba and the Forty Thieves* from Arabic literature, there is a mysterious door which opens on the words "Open Sesame" and closes on the words "Close Sesame".

how many people have named their camels "Barack[1]"), but the holy sites won't be officially open to non-Muslims anytime soon. On the highway to Mecca, a "Christian bypass" tells the rest of us when to turn off the road: heathens exit here. Perhaps from a distance you'll one day be able to glimpse what is expected to be the second-tallest building in the world, now being constructed by the bin Laden family real estate company. It is a hotel complex that will be topped by a clock six times larger than London's Big Ben. (The Saudis harbor a hope that Mecca Time will dislodge Greenwich Mean Time from its current prominence.) For now, even planes must avoid violating the holy cities, keeping safely away from sacred airspace lest infidels spy from above. There has been talk of building an Islamic, Disneyland-style park on the road between Mecca and Jidda. The Saudis find monkeys and parrots far funnier than mice and ducks, so watch out, Mickey and Daffy[2]. And Qatar[3] recently pushed the Gulf states[4] to create a common Gulf Cooperation Council tourist visa, in order to make the region more attractive to cruise ships.

Jidda has many charms. The median strip on the corniche has a magical open-air museum, with huge, whimsical sculptures by Miró, Henry Moore[5], and other artists who created works consistent with Islamic values — that is, no representations of the human form. The neon-lit boardwalk is lined with snack shacks, toy shops, and mini amusement parks. But it's missing the sexy, seedy elements that make shore vacations fun. Instead of teenagers necking or kids splashing in the water, there are men spreading out prayer rugs on the seawall.

Libertarian Zone

I had bought a Burqini on-line from an Australian company, figuring I'd need one to go swimming. A Burqini — a burka bikini — is a full-body suit that resembles Apolo Ohno[6]'s Olympic outfit or the getup Woody Allen wore to play a

---

[1] The full name of the current American president is Barack Huseein Obama.
[2] Mickey is the name for the cartoon mice and Daffy is the name for the cartoon duck.
[3] An Arab country on the peninsula of Qatar, achieved independence from the United Kingdom in 1971.
[4] Gulf states refer to the countries in southwestern Asia that border the Persian Gulf.
[5] Joan Miró i Ferrà (1893-1983) was a Spanish painter, sculptor, and ceramicist; Henry Moore (1898-1986) was an English sculptor and artist.
[6] Apolo Ohno (1982-) is an American short track speed skating competitor and an eight-time medalist (two gold, two silver, four bronze) in the Winter Olympics.

sperm in *Everything You Always Wanted to Know About Sex*①... But as it turned out I didn't have to swaddle myself in one, because I discovered a place called Durat al-Arus.

Sarah Bennett, a stunning thirty-two-year-old, blue-eyed California Mormon who converted to Islam and blackened her blond hair, now works in Jidda for a conglomerate. She wears Chanel abayas. Bennett took us to Durat al-Arus, a marina and tourist village where wealthy Saudis and royals have homes and boats. The architecture is 1970s, the colors are *Miami Vice*②, and the mood is downright hedonistic compared with that of the rest of the country. It's a rare libertarian zone. Women can drive and wear what they want, and men and women can mingle without fear. I quickly commandeered a BMW from a cute sheikh so I could tool around for a few minutes in a meaningless spurt of emancipation. Then the sheikh, who wore a Jack Sparrow③ bandanna and called himself "the Pirate," took Sarah, Ashley, and me out on his yacht, with a motorboat trailing behind, for some snorkeling in the turquoise Red Sea. He was a Muslim and served us only soft drinks as we made our way to a desolate desert island. But other than that you could wear a real bikini and live the high life: listening to club music booming from an iPod, eating melting butter-pecan ice cream and fresh berries, sipping flutes of sparkling pomegranate juice. With a small shock, I was struck by the sensuality of the scene — it was hard to believe this was Saudi Arabia. My thoughts drifted to the silent movie *The Sheik*④, and the moment when Rudolph Valentino drags Agnes Ayres onto his horse in the desert and says, "Lie still, you little fool."

And that, I guess, is why they have the *mutawa*.

---

① *Everything You Always Wanted to Know about Sex* is an American comedy movie, which was produced in 1972 and Woody Allen acted the leading role.

② *Miami Vice* is an American television series produced for NBC and ran for five seasons on NBC from 1984–1989. The show became noted for its heavy integration of music and visual effects to tell a story. *People* magazine stated that Miami Vice "was the first show to look really new and different since color TV was invented."

③ Captain Jack Sparrow is a fictional character and the central protagonist of the *Pirates of the Caribbean* film series, who wears a red bandanna on his hair.

④ *The Sheik* is a 1921 silent film, with Rudolph Valentino playing the part of Sheik and Agnes Ayres playing the part of Lady Diana Mayo, who finally fell in love with the Sheik.

一个女孩的沙特阿拉伯旅行指南

莫琳·多德

"我想知道关于夏娃的一切"。

"我们的祖先夏娃?"阿布杜拉·赫贾齐问道。阿布杜拉是我在老吉达市①的向导,看上去很孩子气。这里冬季的夜晚依旧炎热。在皎洁的月光下,阿布杜拉向我炫耀这座城市的珍宝——红海边上百年之久的房屋,绿色,蓝色,褐色,优雅迷人。这些房屋现在已空空如也,但依然鳞次栉比地耸立在街道两旁,沐浴着海风,享受着阴凉。悬臂式的阳台上镶嵌着网格状屏风,为的是确保"闺房的私密和隐蔽",黎巴嫩作家阿明·雷哈尼②在1930年如是写道。阿拉伯人把这五百所围绕着露天剧场的房屋保留了下来,因为石油带来的巨额利润曾使他们一度沉溺于锦衣珠宝,现在他们开始试着去欣赏古旧之美,而他们曾轻蔑称这些古旧之物为"老东西"。

在阿拉伯语中,"吉达"的意思是"女祖先"。而这座城市名字的由来或许是因为《圣经》中的夏娃埋葬于此,而在《圣经》以外的传说中,夏娃被看做引诱人之妖妇的始祖。对于一个在法律上、两性关系上和服装上都足以将女性禁锢得近似活葬的国家而言,这倒是一个很贴切的象征。(最近,伊朗一位态度强硬的神职人员居然将地震归咎于穿着挑逗的女性,这一言论引发了《纽约邮报》以"乳震!"③为题的新闻头条。)传说,从伊甸园被驱逐出来之后,亚当和夏娃各奔东西;亚当流落到了麦加,而夏娃则停留在了吉达;两人后来只重聚过一次。(曾不惜背负原罪恶名的爱侣,最后竟沦为萍水之交?)夏娃之墓就躺在老吉达市内一扇久经风霜的绿门之后。

我提议前往参观,阿布杜拉笑了笑,却面带愠色。在接下来的日子里,我对这种笑容已经习以为常,它的言下之意就是"不可以,女士"。阿布杜拉告诉我:"女士不能去墓地。"

这之前,我曾两次到访沙特阿拉伯,知道这里是地球上女性最没有话语权

---

① 吉达市位于沙特阿拉伯王国西部,红海之滨,被誉为"红海新娘",行政上属麦加地区。

② 阿明·雷哈尼(1876-1940),黎巴嫩裔美国阿拉伯作家,知识分子和政治活动家。他也是北美阿拉伯移民作家组织的"移民诗人"文学运动的重要人物。他在1901年成为美国公民。

③ 这是《纽约邮报》描述2010年10月26日的"乳震运动"的标题。伊朗一名教士称,妇女衣着暴露造成地震,引发抗议浪潮,普度大学四年级女生珍妮佛·麦克瑞特号召女性26日一起露出乳沟,证明教士言论的荒谬。

的地方。只身到这里旅行的女性一般都需要有政府委派的看管人或者政府颁发的许可证。对一名沙特女性而言，如果没有看管人或者男性监护人在其身边，即便是受到男人的骚扰，她也不能告发。最近，一群对任何形式的自由化都持怀疑态度的传统沙特妇女发起了一个组织，名为"我的监护人知道什么最适合我"。我原以为已经算是相当了解这个充斥着性别隔离制度的国家了，但是这个关于墓地的规定还是让我有点大跌眼镜。

"那她们在去世之后能进去吗？"我问道。

"女人可以埋在那里，"阿布杜拉勉强承认，"但是你们不能进去观看。"

如此说来，如果我要凭吊一位已逝的女性，那我就得先去死？

难怪人们称沙特为"禁忌之国"。如此之度假胜地，充满蛊惑而妖媚，让人迷惑而无措，稍有不慎就会引来杀身之祸，一个让你来一次不想来第二次的地方。

你好——再见了！

沙特阿拉伯是世界上首要的朝圣地之一，胜过了耶路撒冷、梵蒂冈、吴哥窟和其他宗教游览地。除了印度的大壶节①之外（大壶节每三年吸引多达 5000 万的朝圣者），每年数以百万计的穆斯林涌向麦加和麦地那市。但是，对于非穆斯林来说，那就另当别论了。长久以来，不管是沙特阿拉伯的妇女还是这个国家本身，都将自己隐藏在面纱之后。《王国》和《王国之内》的作者罗伯特·莱西②曾经在吉达生活过。他解释说，只有在大萧条时期，出自麦加朝圣者的税收锐减，沙特阿拉伯人才允许身为异教徒的美国工程师进入国境探索石油。

事实上，在 9.11 之前，沙特阿拉伯对外界的欢迎就不断持续升温，至少接受了少量的非穆斯林参观者，算是向世界丢出了欢迎的手帕。按照沙特的标准来衡量，当时的阿布杜拉王储——现在已经是国王——是一位激进的现代化推进者。他希望鼓励更多的外界交流，也想树立新的国家形象，以区别以往的宗教严苛（恐怖主义的盛行）。当时沙特已经为某种程度的文化之旅稍稍敞开了些门缝。莱斯利·麦克洛林是埃克塞特大学的阿拉伯国家暨伊斯兰教研究所的研究员，他分别在 2000 年和 2001 年带队前往沙特王国参观。两个参观团队中都有来自纽约的、富有而又好奇的犹太人。但在 9.11 之后，这条开放通道再次关闭，因为沙特阿拉伯和美国都面临同样的现实：奥萨马·本·拉登和 19 名劫

---

① 大壶节是印度教大型朝圣活动，大量印度教徒聚集恒河沐浴，每三年轮流在印度的阿拉哈巴德、哈里瓦、乌疆和纳锡四个地方举行。

② 罗伯特·莱西（1944-），英国历史学家和传记作家。他的《王国》（2008）和《王国之内》（2009）两部作品成为沙特王国外交工作的标准学习文本。

持恐怖分子中的 15 名都是沙特国籍。

这要追本溯源到沙特王国的国家性质。早在 1744 年，居住在绿洲地区的阿尔沙特家族曾经与穆罕默德·阿卜杜勒－瓦哈卜达成过一项协议。阿卜杜勒-瓦哈卜达是瓦哈比教派的创建人，该教派要求严格遵守宗教仪式。协议内容是沙特军队拥有宗教合法性，苦行僧般的瓦哈比教徒则得到保护。迄今为止，《古兰经》始终是沙特阿拉伯的宪法，而瓦哈比教派的教义是沙特的主要信仰。当伊斯兰教原教旨主义分子 1979 年在麦加接管大清真寺时，皇室与其同样达成协议，并增加条款：允许反西方的神职人员和宗教学校繁荣发展，不镇压为基地组织和恐怖主义提供经济援助的人。而本·拉登恐怖袭击事件的发生可谓是沙特皇室自食苦果。

在 2004 年，也就是 9.11 事件的 3 年之后，王国决定再次尝试开放旅游业。这一次沙特雇佣了一个公共关系公司来启动这项活动。但是一位沙特官员摇头长叹，追悔不已：随后成立的旅游业最高委员会的网站简直就是个"大灾难"。网站强调，签证不能够发放给以色列护照持有者，甚至也不发给护照上有以色列戳记的任何人，或者是"犹太人"——就好像为了防止表述的还不完全明了，特意清楚地写上了这 3 个字。同时也有关于所有独自前来沙特王国的女性游客的"重要说明"，建议女性在机场要有丈夫或者男性担保人来接机；只有在丈夫、男性亲属或者司机"陪伴"下才能开车；毋庸置疑，当然也不会允许饮酒了——沙特官方还曾尝试过在沙特领空的私人喷气式飞机上也强制实施禁酒令，有时候甚至会将酒柜都封起。最后，还有一则不得滞留的要点：所有游客都必须持有返程机票，这一点与阿拉伯人所标榜的热情好客是神圣职责的事实可不大相符。在纽约国会议员安东尼·韦纳借此大做文章之后，网站上反犹太的语言才被清除。

现在，在六年之后，沙特人又开始再次尝试。但是除非你是特殊旅行团的成员，否则他们是不会欢迎的（除了一些特例）。"不欢迎背包客"，苏丹·本·萨尔曼王子说。这位王子身材修长，善于言谈，曾经是一位宇航员，现在是沙特旅游文物部委员会的会长兼主席。"你们要知道，（受欢迎的只有）高层次的，"他继续说道，只包括"受过系统教育"的团队。

你仍然要接受所有严格的规定。就算这样，你依然不能轻易进入沙特王国。近来，发放给西方人的签证非常稀少，即使是美国高级外交官给家庭成员取得签证都很困难。穿着短裤的法国女孩和吸着大麻烟卷的美国男孩进来以后势必侵犯当地文化而导致文化冲突，沙特王国一想起这点，就马上退缩了。机场还有一个警用告示牌：贩卖毒品者将被判处死刑！

沙特人并不喜欢被世界上的其他人视作异类。其实只要你能够真正地打破隔阂，很多沙特人还是非常有魅力而又热情好客的。有人评价沙特人的生活方式就像"摩登原始人"①。沙特对此评价非常敏感，会马上提醒你伊朗国王试图过快地推进现代化时的遭遇。更不用说他们自己的费萨尔国王②了。费萨尔国王在引入电视和女孩公共教育之后于 1975 年被暗杀(弑君者是国王的侄子)。这个由王子和乞丐构成的两极分化的社会总是有着雅努斯③一般的双重面孔。皇室成员飞到法国南部去饮酒、赌博，与俄国妓女鬼混，而反动的教士却在国内进行着女性非合法化、西方人妖魔化的活动。去年冬天，一位沙特王子被指控在伦敦酒店勒死一名仆人而被逮捕(他已经辩称无罪)。直到 20 世纪 50 年代，电才在沙特普及开来；直到 20 世纪 60 年代，奴隶制才得以废除。对非亲属异性交往仍然有着严格的限制。(最近，一位沙特教士建议说，与非亲属女性来往的男性应该考虑喝这些女性的母乳，从而成为某种意义上的"亲属"。)今天，沙特阿拉伯正试图多朝前走几步——开办了一所男女同校的大学；允许女性向女性售卖女式内衣；甚至减少了斩首示众的刑罚次数。如果你按照沙特的时间生活，就好像是服用了安必恩④的蜗牛。广受拥戴的 86 岁国王阿布杜拉正在进行大胆的革新，但是对于世界其他地方而言，这些改变几乎是微乎其微。

"很多的关注"

想要看到沙特阿拉伯人热情好客的念头不可抗拒——即使警觉的沙特人不断地抗拒。在为沙特之旅做计划时，我就知道，唯一比在沙特阿拉伯呆 10 天更振奋人心的事情就是作为一名女性在沙特呆 10 天。事实上，是两名女性：与我同行的是勇敢的同事阿什利·帕克，也是我的旅行摄影师。在登上沙特阿拉伯的航班时，我有一点紧张，在额头上划了一个十字架。(那天是圣灰星期三⑤)一些沙特航班在出发时会用阿拉伯语进行祈祷，祈祷内容主要是先知穆罕默德所说过的话。飞机乘务员拿来篮装沙特报纸。这些乘务员并不是沙特人，因为雇佣沙特女性对于航空公司来说是不光彩的。只要瞥一眼报纸的标题就会强烈感受到：我们仿佛正乘坐着驶向过去的时光机。《阿拉伯新闻报》上一篇英语文

---

① 《摩登原始人》是一部有趣的美国情景喜剧，讲述了一个工人阶层石器时代的人和他家人的生活以及好友邻居的家庭生活。
② 费萨尔国王（1906-1975），1964-1975 年期间在位。作为国王，他因为发展国家经济和实行改革受到赞誉。1975 年，费萨尔国王被其侄子暗杀。
③ 雅努斯 (Janus) 是罗马神，来自古意大利，兼司开端与终结，所以他有两张面孔，象征着种种矛盾的两面性。
④ 美国产的一种安眠药。
⑤ 圣灰星期三，大斋首日(大斋节或称四旬斋的第一日，复活节前 40 天即星期三，是日有用灰抹额表示忏悔之俗)。

章的标题是"携带匕首是男子气概的标志"。另一篇文章警告说:"王国法庭不欢迎女性律师"。报纸上,一位专栏女作家(和我是同行)的肖像小照令人触目惊心,照片上只有一双眼睛,其余的全被面纱遮盖。阅读这家航空公司提供的杂志就好像在魔幻剧集《阴阳魔界》①中的某一时刻,让人感觉图画书中才有的小镇好像在现实中复活了。杂志名字是《AhlanWasahlan》,意思是"你好,欢迎",但欢迎的字样似乎更容易让人想到凡尔赛、普罗旺斯和伯利兹城。没有任何迹象能令人感觉沙特阿拉伯也会是人们的旅游目的地。

飞机上的电影倒是有点意思。如果你点播《假结婚》②,你在桑德拉·布洛克端庄的露肩衣上看到的只是模糊一片,而她的锁骨、男脱衣舞郎和关于勃起的笑话都已经消失得无影无踪了。挂有帘子的分隔区可以让沙特的女士不穿长袍小睡一会。飞机上没有酒,但是一些前往沙特的资深商务旅行者会在机场酒吧买点伏特加,倒到水瓶里以备旅途之需。在利雅得③机场,性别隔离尤为严重,分别有女士等候室和女士祈祷室。如果不是有位沙特男管家来接应我们,我们就会在监狱里呆着了——一对单身女性因为没有男士来接机而在机场游荡,像《幸福终点站》④里的汤姆·汉克斯一样永远地被困在机场里。

在美国,你在酒店房间会得到巧克力。在利雅得,你可能会从你在沙特王国的东道主那里得到一个礼包,里面是你可以钻进去以便参加晚宴的东西——一件又黑又长的阿拉伯长袍和一块黑色头巾,这身行头让你看起来简直就像是个木乃伊,感觉自己好像是个披萨炉。即使这样,他们也还会让你一直呆在餐厅里的家庭区域,隐藏在屏风或者帷幔之后。近年有了很了不起的进步,一如当年格洛丽亚·斯泰纳姆⑤的倡导,也就是说,女式长袍的后背上有了亮闪闪的装饰(有时候是价值几千美元的施华洛世奇水晶),或者可以佩戴巴宝莉⑥饰品,或者袖口可以设计成斑马纹。

我尊重伊斯兰对得体着装的管制,但不明白我为什么也要遵守这套着装规范。如同阿伦·索尔金在《白宫风云》⑦中所说,这使得"一个玛利诺修女看上去像个马利布芭比。"不用说,芭比娃娃在沙特阿拉伯也是禁止的,尽管我的

---

① 一部多元的美国科幻电视连续剧,亦有同名电影。
② 2009年出品的美国爱情喜剧,桑德拉·布洛克和瑞安·雷诺兹主演。
③ 利雅得为沙特阿拉伯首都,沙特最大的城市。
④ 2004年斯皮尔伯格执导的剧情片,汤姆·汉克斯和凯瑟琳·泽塔-琼斯主演,讲述了主人公因为签证无效而被困在美国肯尼迪机场长达9个月的故事。
⑤ 格洛丽亚·斯泰纳姆(1934—),美国女性主义者和社会政治活动家,对消除很多性别歧视性法律做出贡献。
⑥ 英国女装,香水和装饰品的奢侈品品牌。
⑦ 《白宫风云》是阿伦·索尔金出品的美国电视连续剧,从1999年到2006年在NBC电视台播出。

确在一家利雅得超市看到有芭比和全套装饰品出售，也在国家博物馆的礼品店看到装饰着头巾和长袍的类似芭比的娃娃（当然不会和肯[①]一起放在包装盒里）。最近，《你好》杂志[②]被引进到了沙特王国，沙特的报刊审查官员悉心地在模特光润的大腿上贴满了白色小方格纸。

　　抵达沙特不久，我就外国人的着装规范问题咨询了旅游部长苏丹·本·萨尔曼王子。"长袍是统一标准的一部分，"他回应道，"这是感受我们文化的一种方式。我曾见过到印度去旅行的人都穿印度莎丽。"纳伊拉·阿勒哈利法是王子的一名副手，负责旅游局有关女性问题的工作。阿勒哈利法用另一种方式做了解释："你不能穿着短裤去聆听歌剧。你必须为这种场合慎重打扮。如果你不喜欢这样，你可以不去。"听起来相当合理，但是如果你穿着短裤去观赏歌剧，你可不会被"道德促进和恶习预防委员会"四处逡巡的外勤逮捕——这些外勤人员叫做 mutawa，也就是宗教警察。

　　戴着面纱与美国独资企业打交道，我更觉得受了很大伤害——仿佛是自己的同胞与抓获你的人合起伙来搞性别歧视。2008 年，为报导布什总统对中东的访问，我来过沙特。当时，我就站在美国广播公司玛莎·拉达茨的身边。她在利雅得万豪酒店的接待处与工作人员起了争执，非要进入体育馆。这位工作人员也是脸上带着那种特有的笑容：要进去？想都不要想，女士！在这次旅行中，巴基特汽车租赁公司的接待人员向我解释，女士只要支付司机额外费用，就可以租车。（而且，除此之外，除非是一位男性亲属开车，不然一个女人坐在副驾驶就有伤风化。）我说我要自己开车，这位接待人员一点不帮忙，反而仰头大笑。尼古拉·翰威特来自纽约，是位端庄优雅的金发美女，正在沙特阿拉伯出差。我争取到了她的支持，答应和我一起进行一次简短的静坐抗议。我们两个就坐在王国的高档中心商场的星巴克男人区。她胡思乱想，脑子里全都是关于我的可怕的新闻报道：某位西方女性因为企图争取平等而犯罪，因而从星巴克里被强行拖走。"要是我看到那些讨厌的宗教警察，"翰威特说，紧张地攥着她的拿铁咖啡，"我要踢它几脚。"

　　在各种不同的场所，我开始自娱自乐，我倒要看看那些男刻耳柏洛斯[③]们多会儿能冲过来拦住我的去路，把我挡在男性专享区之外。在麦当劳，严厉的守卫一看到我的出现，两秒钟内就用扫帚堵上了门。在利雅得豪华的阿法沙利亚酒店，我询问大堂经理为什么我不能和男性生意人坐在一起。就在这时，他

[①] 肯是美泰公司 1961 年推出的男孩娃娃，是 1959 年推出的芭比娃娃的虚拟男友。
[②] 《你好》是一家英国杂志，每周出版一期；主要内容是名流新闻、趣闻。
[③] 刻耳柏洛斯是希腊和罗马神话中守卫冥府的有三个头的狗。

突然发现了一位高雅的女士在男士区域大摇大摆地走动。大堂经理像雷吉·布什①一样飞速地跑了过去,将这位女士赶出了禁区,然后又像巴瑞辛尼可夫②一样灵巧地跳回我的面前,打消了我企图进入的念头。我在吉达希尔顿大堂的咖啡厅确实取得了来之不易的片刻胜利。当时,咖啡厅的男人区没有顾客,我点了杯卡普契诺,但服务生却告诉我,我要是不后退五英尺回到女士区,他就无法为我提供咖啡。

酒店前台的工作人员会警告我穿上长袍,哪怕我只不过是经过大堂,而且还穿着最保守的垂地海军蓝长裙,这是我参加家庭葬礼的保留服装。"你会得到很多关注——但不是什么善意的关注,"一位工作人员说。不穿长袍是危险的,但穿了也同样危险。购物中心的电梯指示牌警示女性小心谨慎,不要让自动楼梯夹到她们宽大的外衣。(前不久,一位在澳大利亚度假的穆斯林女士被自己的面纱给闷死了,因为她的头纱缠在一辆快速滑行的轻便手推车里。)你很快会变得偏执而焦虑,害怕自己穿着毛巾浴袍给房间服务生开门,结果却进了监狱。但顶级酒店的工作人员都是外国男士——我在阿法沙利亚酒店的男管家主动为我叠内衣时,我才明白这一点。如果是一位沙特男人来服侍我,我们很可能会被运送到迪拉广场③——或叫作砍砍广场,这是广场更有名的叫法——那里是进行公示斩首的地方。这个广场有着庞大的排水管,沙特人说是用来排雨水的。

约束的阳面

我的首次沙特阿拉伯之旅是在9.11袭击余波未了之时:外交大臣费萨尔亲王邀我前往,为的是让我看看并不是所有沙特人都是恐怖分子。那次旅行,我比较随意,也比较大胆,穿着一件艳粉色带流苏的裙子去采访沙特教育部长。当我从酒店房间下来的时候,大堂里的男人们充满敌意地怒视着我,那架势好像是他们要合起伙来活剥了我。我的看护人马上让我回到电梯里。"去穿上你的长袍!"他大声喊道,"他们会杀了你的!"(我的监护人可知道什么对我才是最好的。)同样的情形也发生在15名女学生的身上。这15名女生在一次火灾中丧生,因为她们没穿长袍、没带面纱,所以宗教警察不允许她们逃离火海。这件骇人听闻的事件震惊了整个王国。不管什么时候,只要我穿我自己的衣服,就会招来好几车尖声怪气叫喊的男人。面对如此境况,我多加了好几层的衣服,

---

① 美国职业橄榄球联盟(NFL)新奥尔良圣徒队的跑锋。
② 巴瑞辛尼可夫(1948-),苏联舞蹈家,编舞家,和演员,后加入美国国籍,是20世纪最伟大的芭蕾舞舞蹈家之一。
③ 迪拉广场是利雅得进行公示斩首的地方,有时也被称作正义广场或砍砍广场。

可是依然麻烦不断。在阿法沙利亚酒店附近的一家购物中心里，我头上裹着头巾，身上裹着一袭黑衣，可四个宗教警察仍然逼了过来，用阿拉伯语叫嚣着，说他们能够看到我的脖子和身体的轮廓，还没收了我的护照。这一幕所发生的背景恰好是内衣专卖展示秀，主打商品是一件带蕾丝边的红色连衫衬裤。伴我同行的是温文尔雅的德尔·朱贝尔[①]。他是国王阿布杜拉的顾问，现在是沙特驻华盛顿的大使。当时，他设法帮我要回了护照，也获得准许让离开购物中心（和这个国家），但却花了很长时间，等得我心烦意乱。

　　随着一件又一件事的发生，你会感到越来越胆怯，越来越不愿意反抗衣着约束的条条框框。此次旅行，我专门定制了一件长袍，省得在炎热的天气里还得裹着标准式聚酯纤维长袍，也就不会中暑了。我并没有用像萝西·拉莫尔在《摩洛哥之路》[②]里所穿的那种罗纱面料。我想要的是素朴的黑色亚麻。"但裁缝费了九牛二虎之力也没能做出讨沙特人喜欢的样式。长袍的开叉开得太高了，高得足可以让沙特宗教警察割开我的喉咙。看到我穿上这件长袍，我的看管人不厌其烦地催我在我的长袍外面再套一件长袍。这让我想起马丁·肖特[③]就希拉里·克林顿的睡衣所提的刁钻问题："她的衫裤里面是不是还套着衫裤？"

　　不过，这次我打定主意要看看衣着约束阳光的一面。对不进行慢跑锻炼感到内疚？在沙特，你根本用不着跑！赶场似的展览品参观让你不厌其烦？你幸运极了——这里根本没有艺术博物馆！在酒店温泉中心该选哪种享受方式？大可不必费心了——水疗只为男士服务。而且，你永远也不用为糟糕的发型而备受折磨。

　　你很快就能学会的两个阿拉伯语词汇是halal（允许的）和haram（严禁的）——在阿拉伯世界里，这两个词就代表着"正确的"与"不正确的"。既然你原有的娱乐休闲方式都是"被严禁的"，你就会添些新毛病。周五上午不当不正的时候，大吃大嚼野骆驼腌肉（星期五是穆斯林教的礼拜日）。又添了一项新嗜好：因为阿拉伯女人只能露出双眼，想表现性感，只能花功夫拔眉毛，勾眼线，涂上黑眼影——眼睛现在的的确确成了心灵之窗了。尽情感受这个国度吧，这可是最后一个可以在室内吸烟的庇护所了。利雅得有一家别出心裁的"环

---

　　① 阿德尔·朱贝尔（1962-），沙特阿拉伯驻美国大使，前国王阿布杜拉的顾问，是沙特在西方特别是美国的著名代表。

　　② 《摩洛哥之路》一部1942年的美国喜剧电影，讲述了两个花言巧语的家伙被困在沙漠海岸，被卖给了一位美丽的公主的故事。萝西•拉莫尔饰演公主。

　　③ 马丁•肖特（1950-）加拿大喜剧演员，作家，歌手，和制片人。因为主持喜剧节目《第二城市电视台》和《周六夜现场》而著名。

球"餐厅,我在这家餐厅的香烟吧享用了价值 180 里亚尔[①](50 美金)的"丘吉尔内阁"牌雪茄烟,这种雪茄"有皮革和奶油的味道,以及少许咖啡、柑橘和香料的气味"。与鲟鱼鱼子酱和缅因州龙虾这些吃食搭配的是经过精心准备的献酒仪式:服务生首先向客人展示仙粉黛[②]商标,证明这酒不含酒精,然后再把酒小心地放进银质冰桶里。"这酒来自加利福尼亚,"服务生骄傲地说。我沾染上了早晨啜酒的习惯,一天的生活从沙特香槟开始,不过这香槟是加糖的苹果汁调和物。

或许你还想学着沙特人那唯我独尊的架势,懒懒散散地逛游到日落西山,看看卫星电视节目,什么肥皂剧《大胆而美丽》[③]了,什么格伦·贝克[④]了。(这里没有公共电影院。)沙特有一档国产的英文版"今日秀"[⑤]节目,节目中他们自己的梅瑞迪丝·薇拉[⑥]带着头巾,推广臀部运动和结肠清洗;还有一位带着头巾的肌肉发达的玛莎·斯图尔特[⑦]烘焙出花儿状的杏干三明治。一切都是如此的舒适温馨,尽管电视节目下方的滚动字幕正在报道着有关以色列如何对待巴勒斯坦人之类不那么令人愉悦的事情。一天晚上,我决定冒一次险,就偷偷把一个沙特年轻男子带到我在酒店的房间里,让他给我翻译电视上的那些人究竟在说什么。这些人看上去很恐怖,穿着大袍戴着头巾,一直大嚷大叫。他们是在攻击魔鬼撒旦吗?年轻人告诉我,那个一本正经、滔滔不绝、留有胡子的家伙只不过是在谈论足球,而另一个闷闷不乐、眉头紧锁的家伙是在祷告。诸如此类。

一旦出了房间,你可能会与女友们在购物中心闲逛,用手机蓝牙谈情说爱。而沙特人看见你经过,还发手机短信,他们就会监控你的手机网络,不管你发的短信是亲切的还是吓人的。我有位年轻的看管人,已经结婚了,要是他在外面和一些女性朋友说笑,就总会受到宗教警察的干涉:"他们说'我能问问和你在一起的是谁吗?'我告诉他们说,'哦,她是我妹妹。'他们就说,'你的妹

---

① 里亚尔是沙特阿拉伯的货币单位。
② 仙粉黛 19 世纪由意大利传入加州,目前为当地种植面积最大的品种,主要用来生产一般餐酒和半甜型白酒或甚至气泡酒。
③ 《大胆而美丽》是美国 CBS 电视台播出的肥皂剧,1987 年首播。
④ 格伦·贝克(1964-)美国电台主持人,作家,企业家,政治评论员和前电视主持人。他主持的一档"格伦·贝克节目",在全美网络电视播出。
⑤ 今日秀节目是美国 NBC 电台的早餐时间电视节目,梅瑞迪丝·薇拉是节目主持人之一。
⑥ 梅瑞迪丝·薇拉(1953-)美国记者,电视名人和节目主持人。
⑦ 玛莎·斯图尔特(1941-),美国著名商业巨头,作家,杂志出版商,节目主持人。她通过电视、广播、杂志以及数十本著作,对全球超过千万户的家庭兜售烹饪、持家、装潢、育子的秘诀,缔造了一代美国妇女的生活观念。

妹？你和你妹妹在一起，会那样笑吗？'"沙特阿拉伯没有约会之夜。在这里，从恋爱到结婚有着严格的规定——处男处女见几次面，面纱下瞥上一眼，定婚约，举办一场只有女性参加的婚礼宴会，检查染血的床单——这些规定使得《法则》①这本书看起来就像《印度爱经》一样色情②。在吉达，有一家名叫"托吉"的中国餐馆，这家餐馆有一张58米长的走秀台。未婚女孩儿可以在这台子上向有意的求婚对象展示自己。可是，这些对象并不是年轻小伙儿，而是他们的母亲。按照传统，男方的母亲为自己的儿子进行婚配，她们会从 khatabah，也就是媒婆那里寻求帮助，会派媒婆偷偷地去窥看准新娘的相貌和体型。媒婆会拥抱女孩以检测其胸部的坚挺度，然后在地上丢些东西，看着女孩捡起来。当年轻女孩弯下腰时，她的长袍会微微抬起，媒婆就可以看到她的脚踝，据此推测女孩儿大腿的粗细和臀部的大小。

"蒙昧时代"

退回到20世纪40年代，正是石油喷涌的时候。在那时候的沙特阿拉伯，第一任国王阿布杜勒·阿齐兹·伊本·沙特会乘坐福特折篷车，手臂上架着猎鹰，从车里射杀小羚羊。国王能叫出每个到访利雅得的人的名字。未经国王的特别许可，旅行者不得在王国内随意走动。国王本人对每个旅者的行踪了如指掌。有些沙特人，因为几乎从未见过飞机，以为飞机就是开到天上去的汽车。苏丹·本·萨尔曼王子是第一位进入太空的穆斯林，所以他自然是旅游负责人的最佳人选。1985年，他以国际工作人员的身份搭乘"发现号"③航天飞机进入太空。比起说服其他皇室成员（多亏了一夫多妻制，现在已经有几千名皇室成员了）考虑开放沙特阿拉伯旅游业的可行性，从太空找到麦加简直是小事一桩——想象一下，失重状态下下跪祈祷是什么情形。一方面，沙特人不像英国人和意大利人那样热爱自己的历史。很多虔诚的穆斯林对伊斯兰之前的文明（用他们的话说，就是"蒙昧时代"）嗤之以鼻。他们对考古发掘持保留态度，因为那样可能会发现基督教遗址。前些年，在沙特的大学内，考古学的学科地位并没有得到充分的认可。其他国家很多著名的观光地点都被沙特人称之为

---

① 《法则：经过时间检验的捕获白马王子的的秘诀》是一本有争议的自助读物，为女性如何追求心仪男性提供建议。

② 《印度爱经》是一部古老印度关于性爱和婚姻的典籍。

③ 发现号航天飞机是美国国家航空暨太空总署（NASA）肯尼迪航天中心（KSC）旗下，第三架实际执行太空飞行任务的太空梭。首次飞行是在1984年8月30日，负责进行各种科学研究与作为国际太空站计划的支援。2011年3月7日，"发现"号航天飞机脱离国际空间站，9日在肯尼迪航天中心安全着陆，结束了近27年的飞行。

"又大又破"，比如马丘比丘①和罗马竞技场。沙特人不会去看破碎的东西，或者仅仅是有点破旧。你永远不会看到像梅尔罗斯大道②上的那种古董风格商店；买卖旧衣服会被认为是丢人现眼。所有的东西都是崭新的，闪耀的。

几年前，苏丹王子在意大利托斯卡纳区旅行时拍摄了很多又大又破的东西。在与保护专家商谈时，王子突然有个想法：也许会有个法子能够让沙特人开始喜欢他们自己的历史遗产。他召集了大约 40 位最喜欢拆除文化遗产的市长和地方长官，向他们展示可以如何发展历史遗址：他们可以以历史遗迹作为"令人愉悦"的背景来出售当地手工品和新鲜产品。这种文化教育的开端不算良好。王子还希望这些官员能看看意大利的锡耶纳市③。"然后凌晨 4 点有电话吵醒了我，是飞行员打来的电话。他说，'我现在在维也纳。'"最终，沙特的市长和地方长官开始对老古董有了点品味。他们已经去旅行了 5 次，还有一次塞维利亚之旅即将成行，虽然也许最后他们去的还是萨维尔街④（沙特人无疑是知道路的）。

苏丹王子正在培训本土的沙特人来担任导游、旅游组织者和酒店运营者的工作——沙特人总是把侍者、女仆和司机这些重活留给一些外籍务工者所构成的服务阶层来做，比如菲律宾人、孟加拉国人、印度尼西亚人、巴基斯坦人和印度人。王子希望沙特人随着多去其它地方旅行，能够学会更好地观光。"沙特人没有被培养成好的旅行者，"王子一天晚上在喝茶时告诉我，"他们不知道如何尊重景点，不乱扔面巾纸。"

在苏丹王子的帮助下，我们飞往一处前所未闻的魅力之地，壮观的迈达·萨利赫，这是约旦久负盛名的佩特拉古城⑤的姐妹城，位于佩特拉古城西北方向的 300 公里处。在穿越沙漠飞行数个小时之后，在你面前突然出现一片怪异奇妙的古典建筑群。虽然今天他们身处不毛之地，但在很久以前的古罗马时期，它们横越朝圣之路，由纳巴泰王国⑥统治。这里的机场刚刚建成，因此我们的

---

① 马丘比丘是古代印加城遗址，位于今秘鲁中部偏南。

② 梅尔罗斯大道约一英里长，介于 Fairfax 和 LaBrea 大道之间，大都是高级画廊和家具店和古怪抽象的服饰商店，充斥年轻人的文化色彩。商店里从二手鞋店到几百元的紧身裤都有，古董精品、个性饰品、漫画店、还有每个年代的流行音乐唱片。

③ 锡耶纳位于南托斯卡纳地区，佛罗伦萨南部大约 50 公里，建在阿尔西亚和阿尔瑟河河谷之间基安蒂山三座小山的交汇处。锡耶纳建立于公元前 29 年，历史上是贸易、金融和艺术中心，现为锡耶纳省的首府。

④ 英国伦敦萨维尔街位于伦敦市中心的梅菲尔区，这里聚集了英国甚至是全世界最顶尖的裁缝，是高级定制男装的圣地。

⑤ 佩特拉古城是位于约旦马安省，因此石刻建筑和水管道系统而著名，创建于公元前 6 世纪，是纳巴泰王国的首都。

⑥ 纳巴泰王国是在古典时期统治中东地区的一个政治国家，公元 106 年附属于罗马帝国。

小飞机跌跌撞撞地降落在基本空荡荡的跑道上。我们的导游几乎不会说英语，但是他极为高兴，因为终于有人可以让他带领参观了。这里有100多个奢华的砂岩坟墓，其中很多是洞穴状的，都是在公元前1世纪和公元1世纪期间雕刻成坚固的岩石。沙特人只是在最近几年才开始欣赏迈达·萨利赫的价值，于2008年将其注册为联合国教科文组织的世界遗产。

　　他们也在恢复迈达·萨利赫的古老火车站昔日的光辉，从汉志铁路①运来一个闪耀的黑色引擎，就好像电影《阿拉伯的劳伦斯》②里彼得·奥图尔所炸掉的那个。不用费心在这里询问关于T.E.劳伦斯的事情——他是因为出卖沙特人而被记住的。（但是沙特人喜爱这部电影，滔滔不绝地说里面的台词，像什么"你妈妈和蝎子是一对。"）沙特阿拉伯的向导们总是跑题，偏离要点，会突然忧伤地回忆起他们在美国的日子，那时他们在帕洛阿尔托、圣地亚哥、或博尔德读书。他们现在对大学运动队依然痴迷，因此经常熬到深夜通过卫星看比赛。在利雅得马斯马克（Masmak）要塞——这里曾经是国王阿齐兹·伊本·沙特一个至关重要的战场——向导很快就没兴趣带领我们了，而是自己沉浸到一些展览品中，其中有的标着"一些老式枪支"，有的标着"雌骆驼乳房的保护物"。导游甚至开始怀念起在密歇根州大湍城的一个叫莉斯的已婚女人。

　　艾卜哈③是南方一片凉爽宜人、绿荫环抱的多山地区，靠近也门。在这里我们唯一一次邂逅了一位真正的沙特旅行者。他正在考查挂村，在这里，昔日的村民为了摆脱土耳其人而在一片陡峭的悬崖上定居。日用品则是通过绳子递送下去。这位肚子挺大的沙特旅行者来自利雅得，叫法赫德，不过他喜欢别人叫他杰克。杰克穿着一件彩色运动服，主动说起他曾经在沃思堡市④居住过。"我喜欢那里，"他吸了口烟说道，赞赏地看了我和艾希莉一眼，"当我看到那些带着美国气息的女孩们。"

偷窥的男性穆斯林

　　利雅得的魅力就是它没有魅力。城市唯一的视觉标识就是市里最高的建筑，王国中心大厦，四季酒店和王国购物中心都坐落于此，纪念品商店里有大厦的

---

① 汉志铁路，奥斯曼帝国苏丹兼哈里发阿卜杜勒·哈米德二世下令修建的一条铁路，起自大马士革，终点至汉志首府麦地那，总长1300公里。汉志铁路的轨距为1050毫米，属于单线窄轨铁路。1916年阿拉伯大起义爆发后，英国军官劳伦斯率领阿拉伯部队对汉志铁路展开了破坏性的游击战。

② 《阿拉伯的劳伦斯》是英国1962年以军官劳伦斯的真实经历为基础的电影，彼得·奥图尔因为扮演劳伦斯而成名。

③ 沙特阿拉伯西南部的一座城市，阿西尔省首府。该城位于肥沃的山区之上，邻近阿尔国家公园，平均海拔高度为2,200米，温和的气候使艾卜哈成为沙特阿拉伯人热门的旅游目的地。

④ 美国得克萨斯州北部城市，主要的工业中心。

微型纪念品，就是把大厦的模型放到雪花玻璃瓶里的那种。大厦的所有人是个亿万富翁，他是国王阿布杜拉的侄子——瓦利德·本·塔拉勒王子，《时代》杂志称他为"阿拉伯·沃伦·巴菲特①"。（在9.11事件后，因为瓦利德认为是美国的政策造成了此次袭击，鲁迪·朱利安尼②拒绝了他提供给纽约市的一千万美金捐助。）摩天大厦的顶部有一个字母 V 形状的镂空造型，沙特人大煞风景地开玩笑说那是"劫机者训练学院。"

一位在利雅得四季酒店工作的约旦人向我抱怨说，沙特人所做的唯一事情就是"购物和吃饭，吃饭和购物"，或者是"通过茶让你遭受折磨"，至少我听到的是这么说的。在无处不在的购物中心里，女人们都包裹在黑色长袍和手套里，只露出双眼，她们采购拉佩尔拉内衣，范思哲礼服，迪奥手提包和宝格丽珠宝③。美貌是沙特女人的麻醉品，虽然他们绝大部分时间都呆在家里——也许这正是她们如此重视美貌的原因。沙特阿拉伯比德克萨斯州大3倍多，但是其拥有的施华洛世奇水晶也要多上3倍之多，整座城市也因此而灿烂夺目。"亮闪闪"瓶装水④是从田纳西州进口来的。购物狂症只有在祈祷时间才会暂停，此时商店的金属格栅门全部关闭。每天必须要祷告五次的男人们径直走向祈祷室。女人们则像行尸走肉一样在百叶门关闭的店铺门口游荡。这种环境是要警惕的。有一次，艾希莉想给在一家内衣店购物的沙特女人拍几张照片，一位女保安马上跑过来没收了照相机。"走吧，走吧，"一位西方女性建议我们，"她也只是一个女人——她对你没什么权力。"终于，女性歧视也算有点小便利。

王国购物中心在顶层有一个女士专用层，由高高的、波纹状的毛玻璃围护起来。这样，男人就无法从下面偷窥，而所有成年的天主教男学生都在楼梯间里。女士专用层的标识告诉女人们：一进入该楼层，就摘下头巾。这样，偷窥的男性穆斯林就不会用女性的长袍伪装自己，然后色迷迷地在女性中走动。在女士专用层，你是可以试衣服的。但是在男女共用的楼层，你通常只能把中意的衣服的各个尺寸都买下，然后带回家再一一尝试。仅仅是想到更衣室门后有个没穿长袍的女人就显然已经令沙特男人不知所措了。购物中心里穿着正常的

---

① 沃伦·巴菲特（1930 -），美国投资家、企业家、及慈善家，被称为股神。根据《福布斯》杂志公布的2008年度全球富豪榜，巴菲特为全球首富。2010年，巴菲特，以净资产470亿美元位列福布斯榜第三名。

② 鲁迪·朱利安尼(1944 -)美国律师，商人和政治家。1994年- 2001年间任纽约市长，在世界贸易中心遭受恐怖攻击的九一一事件期间，他以突出的坐镇领导能力而闻名全国。

③ 拉佩尔拉，意大利奢华时尚内衣，睡衣和泳衣的顶级制造商；范思哲，意大利高级时装品牌；迪奥，法国奢侈品牌；宝格丽，意大利时尚珠宝和奢侈品牌。

④ "亮闪闪"瓶装水是美国高端时尚瓶装水品牌，其特点是玻璃瓶有施华洛世奇水晶装饰，瓶中水来自田纳西州的泉水，并经过九道净化程序。

小女孩在跑来跑去，以正常的方式和小男孩玩耍，看到这种场景会有一种深深的辛酸感——因为你知道仅仅几年之后等待他们的会是什么。当我到青春期的时候，我的母亲给了我一本《关于成为一名女人》。当这些女孩到达青春期时，她们能得到的只是一块裹头的黑油布。

最近几年，利雅得有点向高端城市发展的势头。"天哪！"列玛·宾特·班达尔·阿勒沙特公主惊叹，她是一位可爱的利雅得生意女性，班达尔·本·苏丹王子的女儿，苏丹王子是以前沙特的美国常驻大使。"几乎每周都有一家新餐厅开张，而且我向你们保证，他们的店面和食物，我不敢说能跟纽约或者伦敦的前10位餐厅相提并论，但绝对能跻身前11位到50位。"在B&F汉堡专卖订到桌子要等上2个星期，虽然那不过是在时髦装饰的环境里提供的高端快餐食物罢了。水泥墙面和微弱的灯光令人联想到索霍区①的氛围，性别隔离也更微妙。女人穿着镶有时尚装饰的长袍，男士则将白色长袍换成了蓝色牛仔。宗教警察在餐厅开业首夜就大驾光临；他们希望取消音乐，用更大的隔墙将女性分离。但餐厅只是在音乐方面予以让步。

从利雅得来到红海就好像在《绿野仙踪》电影中从黑白单调的堪萨斯州来到了色彩鲜明的奥兹王国②。吉达是朝觐者的主要入境港，也是沙特的商业之都。这座被称为"红海新娘"的城市是很多女性企业家的故乡，当地居民说他们正在努力告诉这个国家的其他同胞放轻松。因为虽然这里会有女性前胸的长袍敞开，或者在长袍下穿着睡衣或是紧身牛仔，但是吉达希尔顿酒店里诱人的蓝色马赛克泳池仍然是男性专享的。我曾看到一位沙特男人在泳池里游泳的同时，一位妇女一边踮着脚尖沿着泳池边行走一边和他说话，按照当地美国生意人的描述，她的打扮活像个"全副武装的忍者③"。

当我向管理人员询问酒店中的清真寺时，他说，除非我是一名穆斯林，否则不允许进入。后来，沙特亲王告诉我，我其实可以向当地的埃米尔④请求批准。（装作是埃米尔的嘉宾？）王国里的男人经常条件反射一般对女人说"不，不，不！"——"啦，啦，啦！"因为这是更安全的答案。但是沙特阿拉伯的一个重要特点是一切事物都是具体情况具体对待，取决于你是谁，你认识谁，

---

① 索霍区是美国纽约曼哈顿南部一地区，以先锋派艺术、电影、音乐与时装款式等著称。
② 《绿野仙踪》是一部美国歌舞童话片，由米高梅电影公司于1939年发行。该影片根据同名系列童话改编，讲述了女孩桃乐丝在离开她德克萨斯的家后前往奥兹王国的冒险故事，该片是用三色带摄影技术拍摄，然后染成棕褐色调，但是关于德克萨斯州的部分采用了单色调，为了表现德克萨斯乡村的枯燥和灰白。
③ 忍者指受过专门训练被雇作间谍或刺客的日本武士，通常穿一身包裹严密的黑衣。
④ 埃米尔是某些阿拉伯穆斯林国家的酋长、王公或统帅的称号。

你请求的是谁，你和谁在一起，以及你在哪里。饮酒是不允许的，但是很多富有的沙特人自己拥有储备充足的酒吧。"喝威士忌的时候脱下长袍，"我曾在当地一位沙特的权贵人物家里做客，当他家中的酒保递给我们鸡尾酒时，他如是吩咐我。一些沙特男人会从咖啡产地观测未来，而一些沙特女人热爱占星术，但是当地警察却在朝圣之路上逮捕了一位能预测未来的黎巴嫩电视主持人，并因为巫术而判决他斩首。（在国际舆论压力之下，死刑处决现在已经被推迟。）非穆斯林不允许进入麦加和麦地那的神圣地点。但是莱斯利·梅洛芙琳[1]在9.11之前在麦地那附近进行了一次旅行，在那里他能够从酒店里看到这座城市和先知清真寺[2]。

沙特阿拉伯现在可能正处于半开放状态（看到很多人给他们的骆驼起名叫"巴拉克[3]"非常有趣），但是神圣的地方不会很快向非穆斯林正式开放。在去麦加的高速公路上，一条"基督徒通道"告诉我们什么时候该转方向：异教徒出口在此。也许有一天你能够从远方就眺望到世界第二大高楼，这座大厦正在由本·拉登家族房地产公司建造。这将是一个综合性酒店，顶部将装有比伦敦大本钟大六倍的钟。（沙特人希望麦加时间将取代现今格林威治标准时间的重要地位。）现在，即使是飞机也必须避免冒犯圣城，与神圣的空域保持安全距离以防止从天而降的异教徒间谍。一直有传闻说要在麦加和麦地那之间建一所迪士尼风格的伊斯兰公园。但沙特人认为猴子和鹦鹉远比老鼠和鸭子有趣的多，因此米奇和达菲[4]要小心了。为了让该区域对游轮更有吸引力，卡塔尔[5]最近敦促海湾国家[6]创建了共同的海湾合作委员会的旅游签证。

吉达其实有很多魅力之处。在海边悬崖大道的中间地带，有一个神奇的露天博物馆，里面有很多硕大无比、异想天开的雕塑，都是米罗、亨利·摩尔[7]和其他艺术家们创作的。这些作品都与伊斯兰价值观相符合——也就是，不是人类体态的表现。亮着霓虹灯的木栈道两旁排列着小吃摊、玩具店和迷你乐园。

---

[1] 莱斯利·梅洛芙琳曾两次担任中东阿拉伯研究中心主任，在很多大学开设阿拉伯和伊斯兰研究课程，并出版过很多关于现代阿拉伯的书。

[2] 先知清真寺，又称麦地那清真寺，坐落在沙特阿拉伯麦地那的白尼·纳加尔区，是先知穆罕默德去世的地方，伊斯兰教第二大圣寺（伊斯兰教第一大圣寺是麦加大清真寺）。

[3] 现任美国总统的全称为巴拉克·侯赛因·奥巴马。

[4] 迪士尼动画中老鼠和鸭子的名字分别叫米奇和达菲。

[5] 卡塔尔，阿拉伯半岛东部国家，1971年9月独立。

[6] 海湾国家，波斯湾各国，指伊朗、伊拉克、沙特阿拉伯、科威特、巴林、阿拉伯联合酋长国、卡塔尔、阿曼等海湾沿岸盛产石油诸国。

[7] 米罗（1893-1983），西班牙画家，雕塑家，和陶艺专家。亨利·摩尔（1898-1986），英国雕塑家和艺术家。

但是缺少了一点性感、色情的元素，正是这两者才让海滨度假地变得趣味盎然。没有青少年的搂搂抱抱或者孩子们的戏水打闹，只有男人们在海堤上铺开祷告毯。

自由区

我在网上买了一套由澳大利亚公司生产的布基尼，估摸在游泳时需要一个。布基尼——布尔卡比基尼——是一种全身的套装，很像阿波罗·奥诺①的奥林匹克服装或者是《性爱宝典》②中伍迪·艾伦扮演一个精子时所穿的衣服……但是结果我不用把自己包到这个襁褓里，因为我发现了一个叫杜阿特·艾尔阿鲁的地方。

32岁的莎拉·班纳特是一个了不起的加利福尼亚摩门教徒，有着一双蓝色的眼睛。她后来皈依了伊斯兰教，将金发染成黑色，现在在吉达为一家企业集团工作，平时穿着香奈儿长袍。班纳特将我们带到杜阿特·艾尔阿鲁，一个小艇停靠区和旅游村。富有的沙特人和皇室成员在这里都有房子和游艇。建筑物是20世纪70年代的，色彩丰富，就像《迈阿密风云》③一样令人印象深刻。比起沙特的其他地方，这里的氛围是完全的享乐主义。这是少有的一片自由区。女性可以开车，可以随心所欲地穿戴，男人和女人也可以呆在一起，再不用提心吊胆。我立刻从一位可爱的酋长那里征用了一辆宝马，以便随意开上几分钟来释放突然解放的欣喜。然后，这位酋长带着莎拉、艾希莉和我到他的游艇上，一辆摩托艇尾随其后，在蓝绿色的红海里进行一些浮潜活动。酋长戴着杰克·斯派洛那种扎染印花大手帕头巾，自称为"海盗"。因为他是穆斯林，所以在去一个荒岛的路上，只为我们提供了软饮料。但是除此之外，你可以穿着真正的比基尼，过着养尊处优的生活：用苹果播放器听酒吧音乐，吃着融化了的胡桃奶油冰淇淋和新鲜浆果，用吸管唑着闪闪发光的石榴汁。这样活色生香的场景确实让我有些惊讶——很难相信这是在沙特阿拉伯。此时，我联想到无声电影《酋长》④，电影中有这样的场景：当鲁道夫·瓦伦蒂诺在沙漠里把艾尔斯·艾格尼丝拖到自己的马背上时说，"躺着别动，你这个傻瓜。"

---

① 阿波罗·奥诺（1982-），美国最优秀的的短道速滑选手。阿波罗在冬奥会中曾获得过八枚奖牌（两金，两银，四铜），他是短道速滑项目上唯一能与韩国、加拿大抗衡的美国选手。

② 《性爱宝典》是1972年出品的美国喜剧电影，伍迪·艾伦主演。

③ 《迈阿密风云》是一部美国电视连续剧，从1984年到1989年在NBC电台公播放了5季。这部电视因其大量借助音乐和视觉效果的混合来讲述故事而著名。《人物》杂志评价称这部电视是"自有彩色电视以来，首部崭新而与众不同的电视作品。"

④ 《酋长》是1921年出品的无声片，鲁道夫·瓦伦蒂诺饰演酋长，艾尔斯·艾格尼丝饰演戴安娜·梅奥，梅奥最终爱上了酋长。

我想，那大概就是为什么他们需要宗教警察的原因。

（张小薪 译　张慧芳 校）

The Vanishing Point[1]

Verlyn Klinkenborg

【导读】"旅行"和"旅游"有什么不同?"旅行"偏重一个"行"字,而"旅游"不仅有"行"还有"游"。"行"是所走之路,"游"是所思所感之情。古代圣贤大都推崇一个"游"字,如庄子的《逍遥游》。在庄子所处的时代,旅游受到种种条件的限制,因而也就有了脱离物质限制的"心游"和"神游"。当然,我们或许很难达到庄子的这种境界。但庄子给我们的启示在于,突破物质表象对我们的束缚,自由地思想,尽情地感受,充分挖掘景观表象之下的无限可能。这点在澳大利亚的旅游中尤为重要。澳大利亚因其独特的地理位置,保留着很多珍稀的动植物种类和自然景观,被誉为"世界活化石博物馆"。在这样一片现代文明与远古文明并存的土地上,只有独立的思想与感受才能赋予我们追寻远古文明的力量。本文讲述了作者在澳大利亚大北角的经历。作者通过对景观的描述,追寻远古的文明,思索文明保护的重任。这种思虑体现了一个真正的旅游者所应有的对景观的人文关怀。让我们一起随作者去找寻、去思考、去感受那些看得到的以及看不到的、存在的、灭亡的以及正在灭亡的。

Australians call the northernmost chunk of their continent the "Top End"[2], a breezy moniker, as though Australia were a boiled egg sitting upright in an eggcup waiting to be cracked open with a silver spoon. Just how much Top End there is is open to debate, the kind that gets worried out with maps drawn in the dust. While I was there last September, I saw dust maps that gave the Top End most of Australia north of the Tropic of Capricorn — about a third of the continent. Others included only Cape York and the rather windswept-looking peninsula that includes the

---

[1] As a painting term, a vanishing point is a point in the distance at which parallel lines appear to converge. Here is a pun and its figurative meaning is that the concerned "Top End" is losing its original native landscape.

[2] Top end 一般指物体两端中较细或者较窄的一头儿;下句把澳大利亚地理形状比作鸡蛋,top end 的意思就是鸡蛋尖儿。

roistering town of Darwin, the capital city of the Northern Territory[①].

The Top End I visited was vastly narrower — the river flats and hill country just inland from Van Diemen Gulf. But it was still an imponderable slice of terrain, long ridges of sandstone giving way to the floodplains that edge Kakadu National Park[②], a UNESCO World Heritage site[③] and the largest park in Australia — bigger than Connecticut and Delaware combined. To Australians, Kakadu and the country around it feels like an ancestral reservoir, a cultural repository with Aboriginal roots and an oasis of native biodiversity. Here, the sandstone endures, the monsoon floods come and go, and then the fires follow — erratic and regenerative in the early part of the dry season, unforgiving in the later part. But this oasis is going dry almost unnoticed.

This is a landscape that seems to ask, "Why have you come here?" There's no hostility in the question, only the indifference native to a continent of punitive, natural harshness. Every traveler will have a different answer. Mine was mud, and also, more broadly, the difference between nature as a norm and nature as merely what is, whether it should be or not. Here, the grandeur of nature is well disguised by the impenetrable thicket of life itself.

For weeks after visiting Australia, I found myself thinking about mud: the living mud on the banks of Sampan Creek, which insinuates itself into Van Diemen Gulf, not far from Bamurru Plains, a safari-style eco-lodge that opened here a few years ago. When the wicked tide falls on the creek's lower reaches, it leaves behind long, sloping shelves of ooze. In December, the monsoon comes, and when it does, Sampan Creek and all its fellow creeks and rivers break their bounds and spread their mud — an originating mud — out over the coastal plains. It daubs the fur of Agile wallabies grazing on the floodplains. The water buffalo seem compounded of it. The magpie geese glory in it by the tens of thousands. I saw a similar mud in the

---

① The Northern Territory is a federal territory of Australia, with Darwin as its capital city. It consists of much of the centre of the mainland continent and the central northern regions, sharing borders with Western Australia to the west, South Australia to the south, and Queensland to the east. In spite of its large area, it is sparsely populated.

② Kakadu National Park is in the Northern Territory of Australia, 171 km southeast of Darwin. It covers an area of 19,804 km2, nearly half the size of Switzerland. Kakadu National Park was listed on the UNESCO World Heritage List in 1981 for its natural and cultural value, which lies in the natural richness and Aboriginal culture with a history of over 40,000 years.

③ A UNESCO World Heritage Site is a place that is listed by the UNESO (United Nations Educational, Scientific and Cultural Organization) as of special cultural or physical significance and value.

billabongs at Kakadu and beneath the freshwater mangroves at Wongalara, a former cattle station southeast of Kakadu that has been converted into a nature sanctuary by the Australian Wildlife Conservancy[①].

On Sampan Creek, canoe-length saltwater crocodiles come creasing down the banks, slicking their tiled bellies across the mud. They slip into the silted current, eyes like dark and watchful bubbles. You may be on dry ground, termite plinths all around you, the astringent scent of crushed tea tree leaves in the air, but a part of your mind will still be thinking of those estuarine eyes not quite looking at you, yet not quite minding their own business either.

One afternoon, I saw four young Australian men fishing in a Kakadu billabong. They were standing in a small pram with plenty of beer. Meanwhile, around the corner, a line of crocodiles waited their turn at the carcass of a water buffalo, which lay half in the water, its central cavity opened, its wet, white ribs showing. The crocodile at work seemed almost drugged by the turbid scent of decomposition. At long intervals, it drove itself up onto the ribcage, rolling sideways, then using its weight to tear free a mass of rotting flesh. It showed a white stump where its left foot had been, lost in some recent crocodilian controversy — the very antithesis of Captain Hook[②].

Throughout the Top End, I sensed an incoherence, an unresolved moral burden in the landscape. Take Kakadu National Park. It is a very recent creation, first proposed in the mid-1960s but not confirmed until more than a decade later. It is mostly escarpment country, gouged wilderness, a landscape of rock and time. And yet in some sense Australia has not yet decided what Kakadu should be — a reminder of just how new the conservation ethic is here and how hard it is to create coherent preservation schemes in a place where time collides the way it does down under. In some ways, Kakadu is an experiment in trying to resolve historical tensions rather than a place of natural conservation.

---

① Australian Wildlife Conservancy (AWC) is an independent, non-profit organisation. It works to conserve endangered wildlife and ecosystems in Australia by establishing conservation reserves, which are known as sanctuaries. Now AWC owns and manages 21 sanctuaries. Wongalara Sanctuary, covering an area of 1,910 km², was established by WAC in 2007.

② Captain Hook is the main antagonist of *Peter Pan: The Boy Who Wouldn't Grow Up* (1904) written by J. M. Barrie, a Scottish author and dramatist. The character is a pirate captain, a villain. His right hand was cut off by Peter Pan and eaten by a saltwater crocodile. Therefore he wears a big iron hook in place of his missing hand.

For one thing, Kakadu is one of the few truly national parks in the country — administered by federal, not state authority, for the simple reason that it sits on Aboriginal land. One of the great sticking points in the park's recent history is whether Australians should pay an entrance fee. At present, the answer is best summed up by the empty site of the former east entrance station, expensively built and expensively bulldozed when fees were rescinded in 2004. The fees have just been reinstated.

Then, too, there is the critical shared management of Kakadu with its traditional owners, many of whom, mostly Aboriginal Bininj/Mungguy, still live within the park. They're conservators of the land and their traditions within it, visible in its rock art and its sacred sites, but the Aborigines hunt and fish throughout the park practically at will. They also harbor nonnative animals like buffalo and, notoriously, a herd of shorthorn cattle visible in the grasslands around Yellow Water, for reasons that are both spiritual and carnivorous.

The park's Aboriginal heritage is also overlaid with the more recent history of white holdings within its boundaries. The strangest and most significant is the Ranger uranium mine[①], which is still being worked within the park's borders. And then there is Jabiru — a town established to service the Ranger mine. The streets are quiet, utterly domestic in feel. Apart from the vegetation, and the flying foxes hanging dormant in a tree at midday above the elementary school, Jabiru could be a suburb of Dallas[②].

Like much of Australia, the Top End demonstrates that nature favors invasive species over native ones, at least in the short term. They proliferate. They burgeon. But what matters isn't only what invasive species do to the balance of life in the wild. What matters too is what they do to our minds, since that's where the difference between native and invasive is finally assessed.

In their proper element, for instance, cane toads are no more loathsome than any other toad, though they are poisonous. On the floodplains east of Darwin, they will be clustering near the oil lamps by night, bobbing for insects and getting underfoot. Or they'll be lying tire-flattened on the Arnhem Highway (the east-west

---

① Ranger uranium mine is surrounded by Kakadu National Park. The orebody was first discovered in 1969, and in 1980 the mine came into operation.

② Dallas is the third-largest city in the state of Texas and the ninth-largest in the United States.

road between Darwin and Kakadu) or splayed out, on their backs in a dusty paddock somewhere, their digestible meaty bits eaten away by the few birds that have already somehow learned how to eat them without fatality. For cane toads are relatively new to Australia, which is not their proper element.

Cane toads explain the wistfulness you hear among some Australians when they talk about their roadkill. "You used to see a lot of pythons dead on the highway," said Sab Lord, a legendary bush guide, as we drove one day across the Top End toward Darwin. The toads have spread outward across the country from Queensland cane fields, where they were introduced to help control beetles, and they have decimated the reptiles and birds that have eaten them. As a result, the roadkill census — which is how most people see most wildlife — reveals fewer and fewer native reptiles and more and more cane toads, which hark back to the Americas. The first cane toad arrived in Darwin only recently, and believe me, it was not welcomed.

I didn't fly halfway round the world from New York to see cane toads. But then that's the point of flying halfway round the world — to see what you didn't expect to see.

I didn't expect to see swamp buffalo in the Top End, either, and yet there they were, some domesticated and bucolic, some feral and simply rancid with anger, but all descended from the few Indonesian buffalo brought by the British to the Cobourg Peninsula in the 1820s. In the 1980s and 1990s, the government tried to shoot out the buffalo, to control disease. But the buffalo are making their way back, crossing out of the Aboriginal reserves, where they were never shot out, into Kakadu and the floodplains north of it. There, on places like Swim Creek Station, where Bamurru Plains is sited, the buffalo are a cash crop, gathered by airboats and helicopters in February during the monsoon and shipped back to Southeast Asia for human consumption.

One night, I walked back to my tent-cabin from the lodge at Bamurru Plains through the corkscrew pandanus palms. The full moon was high, cane toads were clustering in the dim glow, and the wallabies were moving through camp nearly silently. The water buffalo out on the floodplain had receded from view — drifting at sunset for the night into the woods, just up the trail from me. From outside, the inward-sloping walls of the tent-cabin looked opaque. But when I stepped inside and doused the lights, the sheer canvas seemed to vanish, and I was left with only the faintest scrim between me and the outer world, which lay in silhouette under the moon.

Out there was a realm of exceeding flatness, where salt water and fresh water are fighting over the land. Each has its season. Fresh water has the monsoon, when rain drowns the country. Across the Top End, Aussies lead visitors to high spots, extend their arms, and say, like so many Noahs[1], "All this will be under water during the wet" — the local name for the monsoon. Salt water owns the rest of the year, and it's always seeking to work its way inland, always trying to claim another portion of solid earth. As the planet warms and the oceans rise, this coastal fringe will be one of the drowned lands.

But for now there's still a temporary truce between salt water and fresh. One sign of it is the chenier just beyond the lodge at Bamurru Plains. A chenier — the name is Louisiana French — is a historic, hard-packed ridge of sand and shell rubble laid down by the sea. At Bamurru, it looks like a slightly raised roadbed, a foot-high levee. During the wet, water fills the floodplains and advances right up to the chenier, where the guides park their airboats. You'd be tempted to say that the coastline, some three miles to the north, had wandered inland. But the floodwater is fresh — runoff from the rugged sandstone escarpment farther inland, which sheds water like oilskin. And in this harsh but delicate landscape, where the overriding ecological concern is the balance between salt water and fresh water, the buffalo trails act as unwanted capillaries, breaking through the all but indiscernible high ground and allowing salt water to infiltrate the swamps.

I'd spent the morning on an airboat with a Scottish guide named Kat, flat-bottoming our way into the paperbark[2] swamps. It wasn't merely the mud that seemed primeval. It was also the abundance of life — the jabirus stalking the open shallows and the endless chatter of magpie geese. Ducks rose in whistling clouds, and from the tops of the paperbarks, sea eagles watched us, drifting among the shadows. So did the crocodiles disguised as floating swamp scum.

This was nearly the end of the dry season, and the shrinking floodwaters had

---

[1] The story of Noah is included in the book of *Genesis*. God sees the wickedness of mankind and resolves to send a great flood to cleanse the Earth. However he finds that Noah is a righteous man and therefore instructs Noah to build an ark to save himself, his family and the representatives of all animals. When the flood comes, it rises until all the mountains are covered and the ark rests on mountaintops, while all life on earth is destroyed. When the flood recedes, Noah, his family, and the animals leave the ark to repopulate the Earth.

[2] Paperbark is one of the main species of melaleuca. Its bark is shed in flat, flexible sheets.

concentrated the flocks and extended the grassland, where buffalo and horses grazed in the distance. And because large mammals are endemic in the American imagination of nature — in my imagination, that is — it was hard to perceive them as historically "unnatural." There they were, after all, their presence as undeniable as that of the wallabies and striated herons.

But the horses are wild, the feral relics of white men who came to this district for the buffalo shooting in the late nineteenth century. The horses — "brumbies," in Australian — stand hock-deep in water and develop swamp cancer: tumorlike, pustulant growths on their legs and bellies and noses. This is the northern edge of a continent-wide herd of feral horses and donkeys — about 300,000 horses and more than 5 million donkeys nationwide.

At Wongalara we flew low over the brush, stirring a small herd of horses and donkeys. They loped ahead of our helicopter, casting scornful glances in our direction. The true work of restoration can't begin until these animals are gone.

At Wongalara, too, I watched a pitfall trap[①] being set for small, nocturnal marsupials — which is mostly what the Top End has for native mammals. The trap is a long wall of toughened rubber belting. Mammals run into the wall and scurry down its length, only to fall into a plastic bucket set into the ground. In the morning, they're weighed, counted and released. But scientists are finding almost nothing in the traps anymore. The marsupials are ideal prey for feral cats, millions of them, which are also devastating small reptiles and ground-nesting birds. There are now indications of a full-blown population crash.

Wherever I went, I felt I was looking at a hidden landscape. What I needed most were guides to what could not be seen, to what was invisible. I don't mean the Aboriginal spirits inscribed in the rock of Kakadu itself. I mean the species that had gone or were going missing. As the days passed, I found myself becoming more and more a tourist of the vanished and the vanishing.

Saltwater crocodiles have rebounded since hunting was banned in 1971, and they now pervade nearly every body of water in the Top End. But for many other species, time in the Top End is now over. What makes it all the harder is this: the species becoming invisible through extinction were largely invisible to begin with.

---

① A pitfall trap is a trapping pit for small animals, such as insects and reptiles. It is mainly used for ecology studies and ecologic pest control.

Perhaps it would be easier just to take the Top End at face value: the uranium mine, the cankered horses, the missing mammals, the plague of toads. Perhaps it would be easier just to give in to the "naturalness" — to stand, as I did, one day, on a sandstone ridge with Sab Lord and look out over a beautiful grassland enclosed by rugged hills. Out on the plain, a herd of horses grazed beside a copse that might almost have been aspen. It looked more than natural. It looked like a pictorial vision of natural completeness, or would have if we'd been in New Mexico. But as we walked down the hill, Sab and I saw a small monitor — a type of native lizard — peering out of the stony shade. "That's the first one of those I've seen this year," Sab said, and there we were, back in the extinction we had never left.

正在消逝的端点[①]

韦尔兰·克林肯博格

澳大利亚人通常将澳洲最北部的一大片区域称作"尖顶"[②]。这是一种很风趣的称呼，仿佛整个澳洲大陆就是一枚立在蛋杯中的熟鸡蛋，等着被银汤匙敲开。然而"尖顶"地区到底有多大，目前仍没有定论。人们绞尽脑汁，绘制了各种地图来描绘这一区域，却没有一张权威的地图可依。去年9月份，我在澳大利亚就看到过一些地图，它们将绝大部分南回归线以北的澳洲地区都归入了"尖顶"的版图，占据了澳洲大陆约三分之一的面积。而其它的一些地图则只囊括了约克角和那形如被风吹散的群岛地带，其中就有北领地[③]的首府——繁华的达尔文市。

但我这次要去的"尖顶"范围要小得多——位于范迪门湾内陆地区的河流冲积平原和丘陵地带。但那仍然是一片广袤得无法估量的地区。长长的脊状沙石岩通往广阔的冲积平原，与之接壤的是被联合国教科文组织确定为世界遗产[④]的卡卡杜国家公园[⑤]，其面积超过美国康乃迪克州和特拉华州的总和。对澳大利亚人而言，卡卡杜国家公园及其周属地区就像一座古文明的宝库，一片蕴藏着澳洲土著文化和丰富的本土生物的"绿洲"。在这片土地上，沙石岩经年不变，季风性洪水潮起潮落，还有那林火，在旱季刚刚开始时反反复复，随着旱季的推进，便汹涌猛烈起来。然而，这片"绿洲"日渐干涸，却几乎没有人意识到这一点。

周围的一切仿佛在问："你为什么要来这里呢？"这话并没有任何敌意，只是流露出一个自然环境恶劣严酷的大陆所固有的冷漠。每一个到此的游客都

[①] 原文应直译作"消失点"，绘图用语，指透视图中平行线条的汇聚点。原文使用了双关语，其含义是"正在消失的顶端"，因为 point 有"尖端，顶端"的意思，与文中的 Top End 对应，而 top end 指物体两端中较细的一段。

[②] "尖顶"是对这一地区的一种形象的说法，下句把澳大利亚地理形状比作鸡蛋，"尖顶"地区就相当于鸡蛋尖儿。

[③] 北领地是澳大利亚的一个自治区，首府达尔文。该领地占据澳大利亚中北部地区，西、南、东三面分别和西澳大利亚州，南澳大利亚州，昆士兰州接壤。尽管占地面积大，人口稀少。

[④] 世界遗产，是指被联合国教科文组织确认的，具有突出意义和价值的文化或自然景观。

[⑤] 卡卡杜国家公园位于澳大利亚的北领地内，达尔文市以东171千米。占地面积约19,804平方公里，相当于瑞士国土的一半。卡卡杜国家公园因其文化和自然的双重价值于1981年被联合国教科文组列为世界遗产。其价值主要体现为复杂而独特的自然景观以及4万多年的土著文明。

会给出自己的答案。而我的答案则是泥土，或者更宽泛地说，是为了看看标准规范的自然是什么样子，而自在自为的、不受人为规则干涉的自然是什么样子。在这里，不可测知的、盘根错节的生命活动结结实实地把大自然的宏伟壮丽掩盖了起来。

在澳大利亚呆上几个星期后，我发现自己一直在思考着有关泥浆的事情，那些舢板溪两岸富有生命力的泥浆。舢板溪缓缓注入范迪门海湾。范迪门海湾不远处就是巴姆卢园。巴姆卢园是当地一家游猎风格的生态型小旅馆，几年前才开始营业。当湍急的潮水退回溪流的下游时，拖下长长的层层叠叠的淤泥。12月份季风到来时，舢板溪和其它的溪水河流开始漫过两边的堤岸，将河里的淤泥——那充满了生机的泥浆，推拥而上覆盖了岸边的平原地带。泥浆涂花了平原上大沙袋鼠的毛皮外衣。水牛也仿佛和泥浆融在一起。而成千上万的鹊雁在泥泞中享受着快活。像这样的淤泥，我在卡卡杜公园里的死水潭以及湾格勒拉的淡水红树林下也曾看到过。湾格勒拉曾经是卡卡杜公园东南部的一座牧牛场，后来被澳大利亚野生生物管理局①改建成了自然保护区。

在舢板溪，独木舟大小的咸水鳄皱皱巴巴地爬下河岸，盖满鳞片的腹部滑过岸边的淤泥。它们滑入满是泥浆的水流中，一双双眼睛像暗黑色的水泡，机警而阴郁。或许你已经回到了干燥的陆地上，周围到处都是带有基座的柱状白蚁巢穴，空气中弥漫着茶树叶磨碎后散发出的苦涩且清新的气味，然而此时此刻，你仍然放不下河湾中那些对你似看非看、走神发呆的眼睛。

一天下午，我在卡卡杜公园里看到四个澳大利亚年轻人在死水潭捕鱼。他们站在河中的一条平底小船上，船里满是啤酒。与此同时，不远处，一排鳄鱼围着一具水牛的尸体等待机会饱餐一顿。水牛的尸体一半浸在水中，体腔敞开着，里面湿漉漉、白森森的肋骨暴露着。正在用餐的那只鳄鱼好像已经被尸体散发出的腐败恶浊的气味迷醉了。过了好长一段时间，它爬到了水牛的胸腔上，只一个侧翻，就利用自己的体重撕扯下了一块腐肉。水牛尸体上的一段白晃晃的残肢露了出来，很明显那是曾经的左腿，大概是在刚刚鳄鱼们争抢食物时咬掉的——这残肢和铁钩船长②的残臂可真是鲜明的对比。

---

① 澳大利亚野生生物管理局(AWC)是一所独立的非盈利性机构。致力于保护澳大利亚濒临灭绝的野生动植物和生态系统。AWC通过建立自然保护区（英文 sanctuary）的方式运作。目前AWC拥有21座自然保护区。湾格勒拉自然保护区建立于2007年，占地面积1,910平方公里。

② 铁钩船长是苏格兰小说家及剧作家詹姆斯·马修·巴利的著作《彼得·潘：不会长大的男孩》里面的反面角色。该角色是一个海盗船长，一个恶棍。他的右手被彼得潘砍下，让咸水鳄吃了。因而他在右手的位置上装了一个大大的铁钩子。

在整个"尖顶",我感觉到一种不协调的、无法排解的道德负重感。以卡卡杜公园为例。卡卡杜最近几年才修建起来。修建草案早在20世纪60年代中期就提了出来,可直到十几年后才获得批准。这是块到处耸立着悬崖峭壁的土地,杂草丛生,岩石磊磊,满目苍凉。在某种程度上,澳大利亚政府也并不确定应该将卡卡杜建造成何种模样——这一事实提醒着我们,在这块土地上,自然保护的观念不过是刚刚兴起;同时,这里同澳大利亚其它地方一样,多种时代风貌并存却又互不协调,想要建立起一个统一的保护体制实在是困难重重。某种程度上,卡卡杜仅仅是一种尝试,它的出现是为了解决该地区的历史遗留问题,而并非出于对自然环境保护的考虑。

一方面,卡卡杜是澳大利亚境内仅有的几座真正意义上的国家公园之一。卡卡杜由联邦政府、而不是州政府管理。原因很简单,卡卡杜的园址就坐落在澳洲土著居民的领地上。在卡卡杜近期的历史事件中,一个颇受争议的焦点问题就是:澳大利亚游客是否应该买门票。如今,从那空荡荡的东门收费站的旧址上我们就能找到答案,那里曾经斥巨资修建。2004年门票取消,该收费站又被拆除,同样耗资巨大。最近又刚刚恢复收取门票。

另一方面,在卡卡杜公园的管理上,澳洲原住民占有很大比重——大部分来自比宁基/蒙盖伊族。他们如今仍旧居住在这一地区,守护着这片土地,守护着在岩石的壁画中、在原住民的圣地中随处可见的土著传统。然而,实际上,这些原住民也在卡卡杜的领土上肆意地狩猎和捕鱼。他们还会豢养水牛一类的非本土动物,其中,造成很坏的影响的是,因为信仰,也为了获取食物,他们在黄水河湿地旁的草场上饲养大群大群的短角牛。

而且,在卡卡杜园内,这片原住遗产的土地却几乎被近代白人的活动所覆盖。其中最古怪也最著名的是朗奇铀矿[①],直到今天它还在卡卡杜园内运营。然后就是鹳城,为了服务朗奇铀矿而修建的一座小镇。小镇的街道十分安静,环境很适宜居住。除了小镇周围的植被,以及正午时分,小学校园里一棵高高的树上倒挂着正在休息的狐蝠以外,鹳城甚至可以称得上是达拉斯[②]近郊的小镇了。

像澳大利亚的大部分地区一样,"尖顶"也向我们证明了大自然实际上更加偏好入侵物种而不是本地物种,至少在短期内是这样的。入侵物种在这里不断繁殖,数量激增。但是,入侵物种不仅仅影响了野生动植物的生态平衡,更重要的是,它们影响了我们的观念,因为正是我们的观念决定了本土物种与入

---

① 朗奇铀矿位于卡卡杜国家公园内。1969年勘探出矿体,矿场于1980年投入运营。
② 达拉斯是美国得克萨斯州第三大城市,美国第九大城市。

侵物种之间的不同。

举例来说，如果生活环境适当，甘蔗蟾蜍并不比其它种类的蟾蜍更令人厌恶，尽管它们的毒性极大。甘蔗蟾蜍生活在达尔文市东部的冲积平原地带。夜晚时分，它们会聚集在油灯附近，上跳下窜地捕捉昆虫；它们也时常会被行人踩在脚下；或是出现在阿纳姆高速公路上（连接达尔文市与卡卡杜公园的东西向公路），被来往的车辆轧得瘪烂；有时它们也会四脚朝天地躺在某个脏兮兮的小牧场里，能够食用的部分已经被为数极少的几种鸟类吃掉了，这些鸟已经通过某种方式学会如何吃下它们而不被毒死。对澳大利亚而言，甘蔗蟾蜍是较新的物种，而这里并不适宜它们生存。

了解了甘蔗蟾蜍，我们就能理解为什么有些澳大利亚人谈起公路上被轧死的动物时会流露出不忍的神情。"过去你经常会在高速公路上看到被轧死的蟒蛇。"当我驾车穿过"尖顶"地区向达尔文市驶去的时候，一位著名的丛林向导萨布·罗德这样说道。甘蔗蟾蜍最早被引进到昆士兰地区，为的是控制甘蔗地里的甲虫。但是甘蔗蟾蜍迅速蔓延开来，大量的爬行动物和鸟类因吞食它们而被毒害。结果，根据一项对公路上轧死动物的调查——绝大多数人都是在这种情况下见到野生动物的，澳大利亚本土爬行动物的数量日趋减少，而甘蔗蟾蜍的数量却日益增加。这让我想到了美洲大陆发生的类似事件。就在不久前，达尔文市也首次发现了甘蔗蟾蜍的踪迹。相信我，它们是不速之客。

我从纽约飞越半个地球来到这里，并不是来看甘蔗蟾蜍的。但问题的关键是，我跨越了半个地球来到这个地方却只看到了我并不想看到的事情。

在"尖顶"，我同样不希望看到沼泽水牛，但它们确实存在。它们有些是家养水牛，生活在牧场中；有些则是野生水牛，性情暴躁。但它们都是同一批印尼水牛繁育的后代。这批水牛在19世纪20年代被英国人引进了科堡半岛。1980年至1990年，澳大利亚政府极力捕杀这些水牛来控制疫情的传播。实际上水牛根本没有被捕杀光。一些水牛还越过了保护区的边界进入卡卡杜公园及其以北的冲积平原地带，在那里繁殖开来。在有些地方，比如坐落在巴姆卢园上的游水溪牧场，水牛已经成为了一种"经济作物"。每年2月份，雨季来临，当地人用汽船和直升机将水牛驱赶到一起，然后将这些水牛用船运回到东南亚，作为肉食牛出售。

一天夜里，我从巴姆卢园出来，徒步穿过一片螺旋棕榈林，回我的帐篷去。空中满月高悬，甘蔗蟾蜍在苍白的月光下聚集成团，小沙袋鼠们在营地附近潜行。冲积平原上的水牛已经淡出了我的视线——日落时分它们溜达着往不远处的树林里去过夜。从外面看，向内凹陷的帐篷黯淡无光。可是，等我进到里面，熄了灯，那层稀薄的帆布了无踪影，只剩下一层薄棉纱把我与外面的世界隔离开来，而月光下的世界轮廓分明，如同剪影一般。

　　帐蓬外面是一片绵延的洼地，在那里，咸水与淡水争夺着各自的领地。它们有着属于自己的季节。淡水掌管着雨季。在雨季，丰沛的降水会淹没整个地区。穿越整个"尖顶"，澳大利亚人总会把游客带到高地上，伸出他们的双臂，仿佛无数个诺亚①在说："所有这一切都会在雨季到来时被洪水淹没。"雨季是当地人对季风季节的称呼。咸水则掌管着一年里剩下的季节，它们总是试图侵入内陆，抢占更多的领地。随着全球气温的升高和海平面的上升，这一海岸地区终将会被海水淹没。

　　但目前，淡水与咸水仍势均力敌。巴姆卢园附近的那片沼泽沙丘就证实了这一点。"沼泽沙丘"一词是路易斯安那法语，指的是一种历史悠久的，堆积在海边的由砂石和碎贝壳组成的紧密而结实的山脊状丘陵。在巴姆卢园里，这片沼泽沙丘看起来像是微微隆起的路基，一英尺高的防洪堤。雨季到来的时候，雨水灌满了冲积平原，水位持续上升至这片沼泽沙丘。向导们常把他们的汽船停靠在这里。你可能会说，北面大约3英里处的海岸线已经向内陆逼近了。但洪水，即淡水，会经内陆崎岖的砂石峭壁流下，如同滑过油布一般。这里，自然环境恶劣且脆弱。最重要、最令人担忧的环境问题就是维持淡水与咸水之间的平衡。水牛是这里的不速之客，它们穿过那微微隆起的沼泽沙丘，留下的足迹如毛细管般遍布在沙丘上，咸水就借着这些足迹缓缓地渗入到沼泽里去。

　　整整一个早上，我都和一位名叫凯特的苏格兰向导在一起。我们乘着汽船驶入一片长满白千层②的沼泽地。在这里，不仅仅是泥浆散发着原始的气息，还有大群的本土野生动物：大鹳们在开阔的浅滩上昂首阔步，周围到处是鹊雁喋喋不休的吵闹声，成群的野鸭鸣叫着跃入空中，海雕透过千层白的层层树冠注视着我们，它们的身形仿佛在树影中浮动。同样注视着我们的还有沼泽中伪装成浮萍的鳄鱼。

　　旱季快结束了，洪水泛滥区不断缩减，草地增多，兽群聚拢。水牛和马群正在远处的草地上吃草。因为在美国人的印象中——至少在我的印象当中是这样的，大型哺乳动物大都是属于本土物种。所以，很难想象水牛和马这样的大型哺乳动物其实是外来物种。的确，它们就在那里，沙袋鼠和绿鹭一样不可否认地存在着。

---

　　① 诺亚的故事记载在《创世纪》一书中。上帝眼见人类的罪恶，决定借洪水来毁灭一切，净化大地。然而上帝见诺亚是一个正直的人，故命令他修建一方舟，让他同家人以及每种动物的代表都得以保命。洪水来袭，水位不断上涨，直到淹没所有的山，方舟就停靠在山顶，而地面上的一切都被洪水吞噬了。直到洪水退去，诺亚同他的家人和那些动物才离开方舟，继续繁衍生息。

　　② 白千层树是白千层属灌木的一种，因其树皮脱落时呈层层的白色片状而得名。

但这些马确实是外来物种。它们是19世纪后期来此猎捕水牛的白人遗留下来的。这些马——在澳大利亚被称作野马——由于常年生活在水深及跗关节的沼泽地中，患上了一种瘤症——它们的四肢、腹部和鼻部生着肿瘤状的脓包。野马及野驴种群遍及整个大陆，这里不过是北部一隅。全国总共有大约30万匹野马和500多万头野驴。

在湾格勒拉，我们的直升机低空飞过灌木丛，惊扰了一小群野马和野驴。它们在直升机前撒蹄狂奔，一边还朝我们投来轻蔑的目光。这些动物不离开，这片土地的原貌都难以切实复原。

在湾格勒拉，我还看到一个陷坑捕捉器[①]，是专为夜间出没的小型有袋动物设置的。"尖顶"主要的本土哺乳动物就是这些小型有袋动物。陷阱的墙壁由一段很长的强韧的橡胶皮带围建而成。当哺乳动物闯入陷阱，一路小跑到尽头时，就会落入一只埋入地面下的塑料桶中。第二天清晨，它们会被拿来称重、计数，然后释放回去。可现在，科学家们几乎在陷阱中再没发现过任何动物。有袋动物是野猫们最理想的猎物。这里有数以百万计的野猫。有迹象表明，有袋动物的数量正在锐减。与此同时，野猫甚至还猎杀了大批的小型爬行动物以及在陆地上筑巢的鸟类。

所到之处，我时刻感觉自己看着一幅隐而不见的风景。我最需要的是把我引见给那些看不到的隐形的东西。我不是说那些刻在卡卡杜岩石上的土著精灵鬼怪，而是那些已经消失或正在消失的物种。在这里度过了一天又一天，我越来越觉得自己也变成了一位已经消失或者正在消失的游客。

自从1971年禁捕令颁布后，咸水鳄的数量已经回升。如今它们几乎遍布"尖顶"的所有水域。但是对于很多其他物种来说，它们在"尖顶"的时代已经结束了。而导致本土化复原越来越困难的问题是：由于再也无法看到那些因灭绝而找寻不到的物种，我们也无从对它们进行保护。

或许，仅仅从表面看待"尖顶"会容易得多：铀矿，脓疮腐烂的野马，濒临灭绝的哺乳动物，以及泛滥成灾的甘蔗蟾蜍。又或许，仅仅顺从于所谓的自然也会容易得多。比如，有一天，我和萨布·罗德站在一段砂岩脊上，向着一片被群山环绕的美丽的草原眺望。平原上，一群野马在一片好像是山杨树的树丛边吃草。一切看上去有些过于真实，仿佛是一幅描绘完美自然的画作。至少在新墨西哥州可以称得上是完美了。可是，当萨布和我漫步下山，我们看到了一只当地的小巨蜥，它正从阴暗的石缝向外张望。"这种蜥蜴今年还是第一次看到。"萨布说道。于是，我们就这样被再次拉回到那从未远离的、物种灭绝

[①] 陷坑捕捉器是一种捕捉小型动物（如昆虫，爬行动物等）的陷阱，主要用于生态研究和害虫防控。

的现实当中。

(曲美茹 译　张慧芳 校)

A Year of Birds

Annie Proulx

【导读】唐朝诗人常建有一句诗："山光悦鸟性，潭影空人心。"仅仅10个字就构筑起了一个天地：鸟因山的明净而欢快不已，人也因潭水的清澈而获得内心的宁和。山、潭、鸟、人一切都恰到好处，相映成辉。这就是天人合一吧！但对于大多数人来说，这一切都美好得不够真实。山、潭且不提，忙忙碌碌的我们在熙熙攘攘的街道上形单影只。抬头望去，还有多少只鸟守在这里不肯离去呢？或许冬日的阳光也会给零零落落的鸟巢徒添几分孤单吧。可即便就只有这为数不多的几个巢，你能不能叫出它们主人的名字呢？你又知不知道这些鸟何时离巢觅食？何时归巢？如何哺育幼鸟？又是否长驻此地呢？我想多数人的答案都是否定的。可见，一定程度而言，不在于环境给了我们什么，而在于我们以什么样的心态去对待周围的一切。鸟会因山而欢快；山也会因鸟更为悦目。人会因潭而宁和；潭在宁静的心中会更显其碧绿。心态是一种力量，助我们跨越现实的藩篱，观鸟也更是如此，只有用心的人才会看到鸟，读懂鸟。本文的作者正是一个用心读鸟的人，她怀着一颗尊重、热爱的心去观察自己农场上的每一只鸟，让我们跟随她一起去体会鸟儿们生活中的酸甜苦辣吧。

On my first day alone at Bird Cloud, my ranch near the Medicine Bow range in southern Wyoming, a bald eagle sat in a favorite perch tree across the river. It was December 30, 2006. The day before, two of them had sat side by side for hours, gazing down through the pale water sliding over the rocks, waiting for incautious fish. This was eagle-style fishing. Sometimes they stood in the shallows, cold water soaking their fancy leggings. Bald eagles are skillful at their trade, and I have seen them haul fish out of the freezing water onto the ice, or swoop down, sink their talons into a big trout, and rise up with the heavy fish twisting futilely. Bird Cloud's construction crew was lucky enough to see one of them dive onto a large fish, lock its talons, then struggle to get into the air with the heavy load, meanwhile riding the fish like a surfboard down the rushing river.

The house at Bird Cloud took two years to build. During that period I tried to identify the habits of the birds in the area and gradually recognized seasonal waves of avian inhabitants. Watching a large number of birds took concentration and time — there was nothing casual about it. The bald eagles were permanent residents. Some hawks stayed and some hawks went south. The great horned owls stayed. The ravens raised families every year and then went somewhere else for the summer to hunt once the young began flying. They came back in autumn to tidy up the nest and poke around, then departed again before the winter storms came. In early spring hundreds of red-winged blackbirds hit the copper-stemmed willows on the island and the cliff echoed their yodeling *aujourd'hui! aujourd'hui*[①]! I put out feeders to attract the smaller birds, but days, weeks, and months went by with no visitors. These wild birds were too naive to recognize feeders as a source of food.

I was impressed that the bald eagles stuck around. The *Stokes Field Guide*[②] stated: "Once a pair is established on a territory, they are very reluctant to move elsewhere to breed." That fit the case. Stokes also warned readers to stay at least a quarter of a mile away from the nest during the "egg-laying to early nesting" period, as alarmed parents might abandon their young. But these eagles hadn't read *Stokes* and tolerated all of us. The house itself was roughly a quarter of a mile from them and they warned us away only if we stood on the riverbank directly across from the nest or got over to the other side of the water and walked near their tree. The bald eagles have raised two chicks every year except one, when only a single chick survived. The books say one surviving chick is the norm, but these eagles have been calm and laid-back — wonderful parents with a high success rate. Whenever a stranger came to the house the bald eagles took turns flying over and scrutinizing them. Anything new—lawn chair, garden hose, shrubs — piqued their curiosity, and they flew over low and slow, examining the object. In fact, they were nosy. It was quite fair. I peered at them through binoculars, they peered back.

The North Platte River runs through the property, taking an east-west turn for a few miles in its course. Bird Cloud is 640 acres, a square mile of riparian shrubs and

---

① (French) today.

② There are a series of *Stokes Field Guide*, such as *Stokes Field Guide to Birds*, *The Stokes Field Guide to the Birds of North America*, *Stokes Field Guide to Birds: Eastern Region* and *The Stokes Field Guide to Bird Songs: Western Region* written by Donald & Lillian Stokes.

cottonwood, some wetland areas during June high water, sage flats, and a lot of weedy overgrazed pasture. On the lower portion, about 120 acres, Jack Creek, an important spawning site for trout, comes down from the Sierra Madre, thirty miles distant, and angles through the property to enter the North Platte. Jack Creek is big enough to need a bridge, and it has one, a sturdy structure made from the floor of a railroad freight car. Just below Jack Creek there is a handsome little island, a shady cottonwood bosque, in the North Platte. The bulk of the property, more than five hundred acres, lies at the top of a sandstone cliff, a sloping expanse of sedge and sage. The cliff is four hundred feet tall, the creamy cap rock a crust of ancient coral. This monolith has been tempered by thousands of years of polishing wind, blowtorch sun, flood and rattling hail, sluice of rain. After rain the cliff looks bruised, with dark splotches and vertical channels like old scars. Two miles west the cliff shrinks into ziggurat[①] stairs of iron-colored stone. At the east end of the property the cliff shows a fault, a diagonal scar that a geologist friend says is likely related to the Rio Grande Rift, which is slowly tearing the North American continent apart.

  On that first solitary day at Bird Cloud, I walked east to the Jack Creek bridge and looked up at a big empty nest high on the cliff across the river. It was clearly an eagle nest. Had the bald eagles used it before moving half a mile west to the cottonwoods? Had it belonged to another pair of eagles? The huge structure was heaped with snow. Somehow it had a fierce look, black and bristling with stick ends. At 4:30 the sun still plated the cliff with gold light. Ten minutes later it had faded to cardboard gray. I looked again at the distant big empty nest, then noticed that on the colluvium below and a little to the west of the nest there were two elk, likely refugees from a big herd that had moved through the property several weeks earlier when hunting season opened. Twenty or thirty geese flew upriver high enough to be out of gun range. Dusk thickened, and then, in the gloaming, I saw a large bird fly into a cranny directly above the elk. Roosting time for someone, but who?

  The next day—the last day of the year — the sun cleared the Medicine Bows at

---

[①] Ziggurats (Akkadian ziqqurat "to build on a raised area") were grand structures built in the ancient times for local religions, having the form of a step pyramid of successively receding levels. Ziggurats were mainly built by the Sumerians, Babylonians, Elamites, Akkadians, and Assyrians. Each ziggurat was part of a temple complex which also included other buildings.

7:45. It was a beautiful, clear winter morning, the sun sparkling on the snow, no wind, two degrees below zero, and a setting moon that was almost full. As Richard Lassels, a seventeenth-century guide for the Grand Tour①, said of fireflies, "Huge pretty, methought." By noon both bald eagles were in the trees above the river, watching for fish below. After half an hour they flew upriver to try their luck in another stretch of water.

In mid-morning out of the corner of my eye I saw a large bird flying upriver with steady, brisk flaps, and remembered the one I had seen the previous evening taking shelter near the big, empty nest. Was it the same bird? What was it? It was too large to be a hawk.

New Year's Day was warm and sunny, thirty-two degrees, encouraging a few foolish blades of grass to emerge from the snow. A flock of goldeneyes, diving underwater to forage, dominated a part of the river that stayed open all winter. I thought there might be a hot spring there that kept it clear of ice.

At the end of the daylight the bald eagles sat in trees three hundred yards apart, merging into the dusk but still staring into the river. Their low-light vision must be good. At 4:40 a dozen Canada geese flew upstream. An orange ribbon lay on the western horizon. I waited, binoculars in hand. Two minutes later the last sunlight licked the top of the cliff, then was gone. They sky turned purple to display a moon high and full. I did not see the large mystery bird. Perhaps it was an owl and had no problem flying after dark. But I doubted it. I had a strong suspicion that it was an eagle, the owner of the big, sinister nest.

For me the keeping of a list of birds sighted has neither value nor interest. I am more interested in birds of particular places, how they behave over longer periods and how they use their chosen habitats. What the birds did, ate, and raised attracted me. I suppose I could say I was drawn to their stories. But in thinking about all this the next morning I once again missed seeing the big mystery bird. In the fleeting seconds it was in view I saw that its coloring was uniformly dark. The rhythm of its

---

① The Grand Tour was the traditional trip of Europe undertaken by mainly nobility and upper-class wealthy young men. The tradition was extended to include more of the middle class. Grand Tour served as an educational rite of passage. The term was first used in the book *The Voyage of Italy* written by Richard Lassels, who was a Roman Catholic priest, a travel writer and a tutor to several of the English nobility. In this book, he presents the importance of Grand Tour.

wingbeats was similar to that of an eagle. Could it be a juvenile bald eagle from last year's hatch? Or was it a golden? Maybe.

Days of flailing west wind, strong enough to push its snout under the crust of the fallen snow wherever the hares or I had left footprints, strong enough to then flip up big pancakes of crust and send them cartwheeling east until they disintegrated in puffs. Eagles love strong wind. It is impossible to miss the joy they take in exhibition flying. The bald pair were out playing in the gusts, mounting higher and higher until they were specks, then splitting apart. After a few minutes of empty sky the unknown big dark bird flapped briefly into view before disappearing in a snow squall.

Late in the afternoon, as dusk crept up the eastern rim of the world, one of the bald eagles showed up with talons full of branches and dropped out of sight at the nest tree. Were they redecorating the nest on a cold winter day? The wind swelled and blustered. A solitary duck appeared, blown all over the place. White underside and black head and wings and was that a round white spot on its face? — probably a goldeneye, but for second it resembled a penguin shot out of a cannon. Half an hour later two more eastbound ducks appeared, clocking along with the wind at about eighty miles per hour. The second bald eagle came into sight fighting the headwind, just hanging in the air and flapping vainly, until finally it turned and in seconds was miles away. The nest eagle rose up and followed.

The next morning the wind had calmed to thirty miles an hour with gusts hitting fifty. It was a cold and sunny day, and the bald eagle team was out flying at 8:00. As I made coffee I saw the big mystery bird flapping out of sight toward the neighboring ranch. Why was it so elusive? I wanted badly to get a good look at it, but it seemed to fly past only when my head was turned. The two isolated elk stood on a knoll at the west end of the cliff, antlerless, dark brown necks, yellow rumps, and red-brown body color. At first sight I could imagine they were the mountain sheep that used to live on the cliff in Indian times. Their faces seemed rather dished, like sheep faces. Magpies were busy across the river, and one raven sat in a tree slightly to the west of its nest site in the cliff. Could the raven, like the eagle, be interested in fixing up its nest so early in the year?

By afternoon the wind was up again, and at the top of the sky were three eagle-shaped specks. Three eagles playing in the wind. Three? Was one of them a juvenile bald planning to nest here, or was it the big mystery bird? And just how many eagles called this cliff home?

That night the wind went berserk, terrific shrieking and battering. In the morning it was still intense and I could see the windows moving slightly in and out. The worst wind yet. I went out into the driveway to see how badly it was drifted. Huge impassable drifts. The wind almost knocked me over. A small bird shot past the kitchen window, but on the far side of the river the two bald eagles sat calmly in the trees near their nest.

During the nights of high-velocity wind I lay tense and awake in the dark listening to the bellowing and roar. In the daytime it was easier to ignore. The television would not work because the wind had wrenched the satellite dish out of alignment. After four or five days of relentless howling the wind fell into a temporary coma, turning everything over to a warm, sunny, and calm day. Temperatures climbed into the forties. But the weather report warned that another storm was approaching. A friend in town smashed a narrow alley through the drifts on the county road and cleared out the driveway. I was no longer snowbound. The power company made it out and realigned the dish.

The daylight hours were lengthening by a few minutes each day. While it was calm I walked down to the east end of the property, and glancing up at the cliff I saw not one but two big dark birds. They were playing in the air, obviously delighted with the calm, with each other, with life in general. Then they both dove into their bedroom niche in the chimney west of the big, empty nest. I could not hear their voices, because a large flock of ducks, more than a hundred, flew over, twittering and whistling. The birds looked like eagles, they flew like eagles, but they were completely dark. They did not have the golden napes pictured in the bird books. Goldens soar with a slight dihedral; bald eagles soar with their wings almost flat. But I was now almost sure that a pair of golden eagles owned the big nest and were preparing to use it.

The next day started sunny but another three-day storm was on the way, and by late morning low, malignant clouds smothered the ranges in all directions. The weather people said it was going to turn very cold. I took advantage of the lull before the storm to get outdoors with the binoculars. A raven was fooling around the cliff face, trying out several niches. Then the big dark birds appeared above the cliff in a tumbling display. The binoculars showed that they did have lighter necks and heads. I had no doubt now. They were a pair of golden eagles and they were courting, planning to fix up the empty nest and raise a family only half a mile from the bald eagles. I felt fabulously wealthy with a bald eagle nest and a golden eagle nest both visible from my dining room window. I wanted to spend the day watching them, but the storm was due to hit during the night so I headed out to get supplies while the road was still open.

 January wore on. It was cold, and day after day the snow fell as in Conrad Aiken's story "Silent Snow, Secret Snow," ① which I read when I was eight years old, thinking it was a story about a profound snowfall. Later, when I learned it was an oblique study of intensifying juvenile madness, I was disappointed. On the frozen river four coyotes nosed around the north shore margins. Upstream the goldeneyes' strip of water was still open but shrinking daily.

 On a Sunday morning of flat calm it was twenty-one degrees below zero. The air was stiff. Freezing mist had coated every tree and shrub. The river pinched in, making waists of black water in the ice. There were no birds in sight. The sun struggled up and the mist rose in great humps over the remaining ribbons of open water. The tops of the cottonwoods glittered like icy nosegays, stems wrapped in gauze. Spring seemed very far away, but the bald eagle pair sat side by side catching the first rays. They often sat this way, one great eagle-beast with two heads. As the sun gained height the eagles fluffed themselves out and began to preen. A lone magpie flew over the mist. In the afternoon I skied down to the east end and into the cottonwood bosque. A golden eagle and four magpies were eating the scanty remains of a snowshoe hare. The eagle fled as I came in sight, and the magpies followed reluctantly, sure I was after their feast. It was easy to see what had happened. The hare's tracks zigged and zagged through the brush, but one foot east of the corpse I saw the snow-angel wing prints of the attacking eagle.

Wyoming was once a haven for eagle killers. In the bad old days of the 1960s and 1970s in this valley many men who are now cattle ranchers raised sheep and firmly believed that bald and golden eagles carried off young lambs. If you raised sheep you killed eagles — bald or golden, but especially goldens, though both birds were protected by law — by poison (thallium sulfate was popular), or by shotgun

---

① "Silent Snow, Secret Snow" (1934) is Conrad Aiken's best-known short story. The story tells of a boy, who progressively withdrew from reality and social relationships and instead became more and more entranced by daydreaming about snow.

from rented helicopters and small planes, or by rifle from an open pickup window. Eagles were killed in other states, especially in the West, but Wyoming became notorious to the U.S. Fish and Wildlife Service[①], to the Audubon Society[②], and to newspaper readers across the country as the home ground of the most ignorant and vicious eagle-killing ranchers. Chief among them was the wealthy and powerful sheep rancher Herman Werner, ex-president of the Wyoming Stock Growers Association[③]. He and his son-in-law were called "the Wyoming helicopter monsters" after they used a hired helicopter to "sluice" eagles.

Nathaniel P. Reed, an assistant secretary of the interior under Richard Nixon, made stopping the killings a primary goal. In 1971 the FBI[④] set up a sting. An agent who had been raised in the West posed as a ranch hand and got a job on Werner's spread, where, in the bunkhouse, he heard about dozens of dead eagles. Because this was hearsay, a federal judge would not issue a search warrant. But two Audubon Society members who had been monitoring the eagle killings were out at the airfield one day and happened to notice someone working on a nearby helicopter. They could see a shotgun and empty shells in the craft. They had a camera with them and they used it. The man working on the helicopter realized he had been photographed. Weeks later the anxiety-ridden helicopter pilot showed up at the Department of the Interior in Washington. He said that if he were granted immunity he'd tell about the eagle killings, and so he did, telling a Senate subcommittee that he had carried eagle-hunting shooters into the Wyoming skies, that Werner was one of the air service's best customers, and that the gunners had shot more than five hundred bald

---

① The United States Fish and Wildlife Service (FWS) is a federal government agency within the United States Department of the Interior. FWS is dedicated to the management of fish, wildlife, and natural habitats.

② The National Audubon Society is an American non-profit environmental organization dedicated to conservation. It is named in honor of John James Audubon, an ornithologist and naturalist who painted and described the birds of North America in his well-known book *Birds of American*. The society's journal is named *Audubon*, a profusely illustrated magazine on subjects related to nature, with an emphasis on birds.

③ The Wyoming Stock Growers Association (WSGA) is a historic American cattle organization established in 1873. It was started among Wyoming cattle ranchers to standardize and organize the cattle industry, but later grew into a political force.

④ The Federal Bureau of Investigation (FBI) is an agency of the United States Department of Justice, established in 1908 as the Bureau of Investigation (BOI). Its name was changed to FBI in 1935. FBI serves as both a federal criminal investigative body and an internal intelligence agency.

and golden eagles. *Time*[①] reported that the Wyoming dead-eagle count was 770 birds. Despite "national outrage" the department was still not able to get a search warrant for Werner's land. But the U.S Air Force flew a surveillance plane over the ranch, and an infrared camera picked up a pile of decomposing flesh. That finally got the search warrant and led to the discovery of a great number of eagle carcasses. As Dennis Drabelle reported in *Audubon* magazine:

There was still a hitch. The U.S. attorney for Wyoming balked at bringing a case against the rancher because he was sure that Herman Werner would never be convicted by a Wyoming jury. Werner... made a surprise visit to [Nathaniel] Reed's office. "He simply bolted in," Reed remembers, "a wiry man wearing a Stetson hat. He said he was going to get me. I said quietly, 'Before you get me, please tell me who you are.' He said, 'I am Herman Werner, the man who protects his sheep by killing eagles. And you don't know anything about eagles.'"

The tough alternative newspaper *High Country News*[②] took up the cause and public opinion began to quiver and shift. The U.S. attorney general pressed for prosecution. But Werner never came to trial. A few months before the court date, he was killed in a car wreck. In Wyoming, as the wool market declined and sheep men turned to cattle, as the fine for killing eagles greatly increased, as ranchers began to learn that the Department of the Interior had sharp teeth and that bald eagles were interested in carrion and fish, not lambs, the killings mostly stopped.

A very Wyoming touch to the whole affair is in the Werner Wildlife Museum at Casper College. The museum includes "an extensive bird collection."

Finally, after weeks of swinging in the wind, the bird feeder attracted a clientele—around fifty gray-crowned rosy finches. Rosies started coming in from everywhere. Chris Fisher in *Birds of the Rocky Mountains* put it well: "During the winter, Gray-crowned Rosy Finches spill out of the attics of the Rockies to flock

---

① *Time* is an American weekly news magazine published in New York City. It was created in 1923 as the first weekly news magazine in the United States.

② *High Country News* is a magazine that primarily focuses on public policy, environmental issues, and culture in the Western United States. It was founded in 1970 in Wyoming by rancher and environmentalist. "High Country" is a nickname for the Colorado Plateau.

together at lower elevations." So they were likely coming into this valley from both the Sierra Madre and the Medicine Bows. They rose into the sky for no reason I could ascertain, paused, and then returned to the feeder. There were no birds of prey in sight, no humans, no dogs or cows or snares, the wind was calm and the day sunny. Did they all fly up to spy out the land for distant threats? Or to reassert a (to me, invisible) hierarchy? Sometimes they flew to the trees near the river for a few minutes, then back to the feeder, I had to refill the thing several times a day.

The beautiful days had grown longer. One morning I watched one of the bald eagles dive toward an open stretch of water off the island, and I ran madly upstairs with the binoculars just in time to see it heave a fish onto the ice. It ate part of the fish and then flew to the nest. At ten past five the sun still gilded the top fifty feet of the cliff. One bald eagle was in the nest tree, the other flying downriver. The cliff turned the color of a russet apple, and I enjoyed the rare deep orange sunset smoldering under the edge of a dark dirty-sock cloud.

I bought a telescope and set it up in my bedroom, which has a grand view of the river and the cliff. The eagles weren't in sight but one of the elk was. Oddly, it seemed to be wearing a canvas jacket, different and lighter in color than its neck and haunches. Was it a trick of the light? It looked like a boulder in the middle. After an hour the elk stood up and disclosed the second elk lying close behind it. With the telescope, details leaped into prominence. The first elk pulled some tufts of hair from its back, then nibbled on sage or rabbit brush. The second elk became invisible again. There looked to be well over a hundred rosy finches at the feeder. I tried to walk along the river but the golden eagles became so agitated that I turned back. One golden angrily escorted me all the way to the house. I had once thought of inviting bird-watchers onto the property but I knew then that was impossible. The goldens had to have privacy.

A few days later I went for an evening walk on the old property-line road, keeping a quarter-mile distance between myself and the goldens. They came out but did not call, just flew along the cliff, watching me. Near the end of the property another pair of goldens appeared, silent and flying rather low as though also checking me out. Suddenly the nest pair came roaring east along the cliff and drove the strange pair away. I could see the new goldens settling in a tree to the east. Perhaps they were nesting there. Six eagles in three pairs in the space of a mile.

The next morning one of the bald eagles and a prairie falcon had a sky-filling quarrel, the falcon darting, the eagle swooping. The falcon disappeared suddenly. At noon the wind began to rise and in an hour it was lashing the cottonwoods. One of the bald eagles sat on a branch above the river watching for fish. The branch moved vigorously to and fro. With each lurch the eagle braced its tail against the branch like a woodpecker, and for some reason I found this endearing. Sometimes I thought of these birds as Evan Connell's Mr. and Mrs. Bridge[1]. The falcon flew around near the goldens' part of the cliff. The big birds were not in sight. Something about the falcon's busybody day bothered me. Was it looking for a nest site? In previous years they had nested at the far eastern end of the cliff near another pair of prairie falcons. Every bird the falcon came near seemed agitated.

  Chickadees were rare at Bird Cloud. At my first Wyoming home, in Centennial, dozens of mountain chickadees came to the feeder on the lee side of the house every day, but I almost never saw them at Bird Cloud. Of course, Centennial was close to the forest and Bird Cloud was surrounded by open grazing land. The prevailing weather at Bird Cloud had, as its basic ingredient, a "whistling mane" of wind from the northwest. It built concrete snowdrifts in winter. In summer it desiccated plants, hurled sand and gravel, and dried clothes in ten minutes. The eagles, falcons, and pelicans loved windy days and threw themselves into the sky, catching updrafts that took them to mad, tilting heights. Why was it so windy at Bird Cloud? With the top of the cliff checking in at a little more than seven thousand feet above sea level the wind was almost never flat calm, and often like a collapsing mountain of air. The cliff directed the wind along its stony plane face as boaters coming down the river knew only too well. And because vast tracts of land to the west were heavily grazed cow pastures unbroken by trees or shrubs, the wind could rush east unimpeded. And this, I found, rereading Aldo Leopold's *Sand County Almanac*[2], was deadly for chickadees.

  I know several wind-swept woodlots that are chickless all winter, but are freely

---

 [1] Evan Connell is an American novelist, poet, and short story-writer. His novels *Mrs. Bridge* (1959) and *Mr. Bridge* (1969) are bittersweet portraits of a traditional upper middle-class couple living in Kansas City from the 1920s to the 1940s. The couple struggles to live up to societal expectations and to be good parents. The novels were adapted as a motion picture, *Mr. and Mrs. Bridge*.

 [2] Aldo Leopold was an American author, scientist, ecologist, forester, and environmentalist, best known for his book *A Sand County Almanac* (1949). He was an influential figure in the development of modern environmental ethics and in the movement for wilderness conservation.

used at all other seasons. They are wind-swept because cows have browsed out the undergrowth. To the steam-heated banker who mortgages the farmer who needs more cows who need more pasture, wind is a minor nuisance ... To the chickadee, winter wind is the boundary of the habitable world.

He adds "books on nature seldom mention wind; they are written behind stoves."

Fresh snow fell overnight and the rosy finches were fighting over the woodpecker picnic mix as rich suet held the seeds together. I wondered if something was dead at the top of the cliff. The goldens were up there, rising and falling, and the balds were there as well. I remembered several years earlier in Centennial when a deer got into our small herb garden, got panicked by something, tried to squeeze through a six-inch space between fence slats and got its broad chest wedged in, and was unable to escape. Whatever had frightened it tore out its heart, leaving the body still jammed in the fence. We dragged the carcass down into the willows. A pair of goldens found it within hours and in three days had eaten the entire deer. Now I hoped that whatever attracted the eagles was not one of the elk. I had not seen either for about a week. A little later one of the balds was back in its fishing tree and half a dozen whistler ducks flew over the house with one of the goldens right above them, maybe trying for a feathered jackpot.

As March came in the river deepened and widened. I could hear the water gurgling under the ice from the house. As I knew they would, red-winged blackbirds took over the bird feeder. Their main meeting place was the willow thicket on the west end of the island where hundreds jammed into the same clump of trees, sang and sang, flashed their epaulets[①], then all flew away only to return and sing and flash again. The prairie falcon cruised back and forth in front of the cliff, its color so like that of the pale rock it was virtually invisible. A marmot showed up from somewhere — a leftover pile of lumber — and took up a station beneath the bird feeder, happy with the seed that the redwings dropped. Walking down at the east end of the property in a light rain I saw a large marmot on the top of the cliff, peering down. A

---

① Epaulet is a type of ornamental shoulder piece or decoration. Here it refers to the distinctive red shoulder patches of the male Red-winged Blackbird, which are visible when the birds are flying or displaying.

few hundred yards east I caught a glimpse of a large coyote as it ducked out of view. Both were oversized. With hindsight I later thought the marmot was really a mountain lion cub and the large coyote probably its mother, as I saw both cats at close range later in the spring.

One lovely warm afternoon the goldens were sunning themselves on the cliff top above their nest site. They flew outward, wheeled, and returned to a projecting rock they favored. When they flew, their shadows also flew along the cliff and it was not easy to sort out the birds from their shadows. The larger golden sat on the rock while the smaller darker eagle did some fancy wingwork, glided down to his lover, presented her with something to eat, then mounted her. I had never seen a pair of eagles mate before.

Every day Bird Cloud showed remarkable changes. The dull mud was inescapable. A few pale green rushes sprouted at the end of the island. The river grew larger and faster. One of the elk reappeared after a two-week absence. It, or they, may have been feeding on the back slope, which could not be seen from the house. In mid-month a little burst of warm days cleared most of the ice out of the river. Falcons, ducks, geese, hawks, and eagles sped in all directions, coming and going. I counted twenty mountain bluebirds and knew there was a housing shortage. But the ravens, harassed mercilessly by the prairie falcons, abandoned their old nest site. I was left with only the memory of the previous year when four young ravens teetered, flapped, and finally pushed off from the home nest late one afternoon to try their wings. It had been Memorial Day① weekend and one of the season's first thunderstorms was moving in. The young ravens fluttered and hopped, clung and dropped, flew short distances, always close to the cliff face with its thousand crannies. We watched them with pleasure, but their hopping and unpracticed flying also attracted the attention of every other bird in the vicinity. The bald eagles, red-tailed hawks, and falcons circled or chose high perches suitable for diving attacks. The great horned owls hooted from the island. The storm arrived, dropping first a few splattering drops, then sheets of cold rain that drowned our campfire. I

---

① Memorial Day is a United States federal holiday observed annually on the last Monday of May. It originated from the Civil War. Later it had been extended to honor all Americans who have died in all wars and was even considered as an occasion for more general expressions of memory, as people visited the graves of their deceased relatives. It also became a long weekend increasingly devoted to shopping, family gatherings, or trips to the beach. As a marker Memorial Day typically marks the start of the summer season.

was sure the young ravens were done for. They could not seem to get back to the nest ledge and huddled on narrow shelves or exposed knobs of rock. With sadness we went inside, dreading what the morning would bring. Would any of them survive the waiting predators? Would the storm batter them?

The dawn showed off one of those fragrant, polished days so rare in Wyoming, windless and fresh-washed. We all rushed to the cliff with binoculars wondering whether any of the young birds had survived. "I see one!" someone called and then another came into the sunlight form its hiding hole, rather damp and bedraggled. The last two joined them from some cranny, and there they all were, preening in the sun, smart and sassy and very much alive. They spent the day practicing evasive flying and I didn't worry about them any longer.

An early-morning walk on the island brought me face to face with a great horned owl in a willow thicket. So strange. The left eye was brilliant yellow, the right one a rusty brown, very likely from an injury. It fled into a cottonwood and stayed there all day. Now migrating birds flew over constantly, following the river. One afternoon there were six golden eagles on their way somewhere else but unable to resist playing in the air currents above the cliff. Mallards, mergansers, and dippers arrived, then black scoters, a pair of northern flickers, a northern harrier, and a single western meadowlark. The river, fed by rapid snowmelt, continued to rise, and on March 19 it was high enough to lift the bridge and swing it onto the island shore, cutting it off from the mainland. The warm days continued, worrisome because everything was drought dry. A forecast for rain brought nothing. When it finally did fall it made the roads into an icy, slippery mush.

One of the Canada geese, no doubt thinking itself clever, built a nest high up on the east end of the cliff, not far from a peregrine falcon nest. I wondered if this was the same foolish goose that had built a nest the year before in the top of a tall tree and open to the sky between the golden eagle nest and the prairie falcons. She and her mate lost all their chicks to predators and had to try again, this time with a nest on the ground beneath the tree and the male standing guard.

In late March a winter storm moved in for a day and a night. Despite the snow and wind a flock of horned larks gleaned seed among the sage and rabbit brush. The prairie falcon roared down out of nowhere and the larks exploded into fleeing rockets. Other carnivorous birds, especially the bluebirds, sat dejectedly on the fences waiting for spring. When the storm sailed away it left a foot of fresh snow. At the cold sunrise there was a heavy fog over the river that expanded and blotted out the sun. Beneath the snow the ground was wet, half-frozen mud. Just to have somewhere to walk I drove the truck back and forth in the driveway, flattening the snow. The snow turned the black metal ravens on the gateposts into magpies.

April came in windy and warm. On a walk to the east end I found a dead osprey on the ground, its gray feet curled in an empty grasp. There was no way to tell what had brought it to its death. There were so many jealous and territorial birds around that any one of them might have seen the osprey as an interloper — within half a mile two pairs of goldens, red-tailed hawks, and a pair of peregrine falcons, and a little farther west the raven family and the prairie falcons. Spring is the time for death. A calf carcass washed up on the island to the delight of the magpies and perhaps the eagles.

I was not sure of the timing of the bald eagles' family life. They had started fixing up their huge nest in December, a task that can go on for several months. It looked to be more than six feet across. But I suspected there were young in the nest the first week in April, mostly because I saw one of the bald eagles determinedly chasing a red-tailed hawk near the nest. The hawk had been patrolling the western section of the cliff for several days. That would put the eagles' egg-laying in the last week of February or the first week of March. The female lays two or three eggs over a period of about a week. Both eagles take turns brooding the eggs. Though the females do more of this duty than the males, both have a brood patch[①] on their bellies: bare, hot skin that rests directly on the eggs. Whoever is not on the eggs rustles food. On a warm, sunny day both parents can have a little break. Incubation takes thirty-five days, more or less. Once the eaglets have hatched, exhausting work begins. If the weather is still cold one of the parents stays with the babies and keeps them warm. When the spring sun beats down hot and fierce the parent eagles transform themselves into wide-wing umbrella shades. In the early days the male was kept busy finding and bringing food to the nest, four to eight times a day. After the first few weeks the female hunted as well, and in the late stages of rearing a nestling the mother did most of the hunting.

---

① A brood patch is an area of featherless skin that is visible on the underside of birds during the nesting season. It is well supplied with blood vessels at the surface for the birds to transfer heat to their eggs.

By the third week in April the American pelicans had arrived, big knobs on their beaks showing it was breeding time in their world. The pelicans were fabulous fliers and on windy days put on astonishing exhibitions of soaring and diving. Fishermen in Wyoming shoot pelicans because they believe the birds eat all the fish, leaving nothing for them. That first spring at Bird Cloud I was appalled by all the big, fluffy white carcasses that floated down the river.

In May the weeds came and I spent hours pulling evil hoary cress and trying to claw out the prolific white roots. The air was stitched with hundreds and hundreds of swallows. Several persistent rough-winged swallows tried to build nests in the house eaves. To reduce the number of possible spots for porcupine dens I started piling up dead wood and fallen branches on the island, planning to have a bonfire on a rainy day. There was plenty of undisturbed room for them on the other side of the river. A tiny, dark house wren had found the wren-sized birdhouse on the island and was moving in, carrying wisps of dead grass and minuscule twigs not much larger than toothpicks.

It was a big thrill when I saw a white-faced ibis near the front gate where there was irrigation overflow. The ibis stayed around for weeks. A few days after this sighting I was sitting near the river and saw two herons fly to the bald eagles' fishing tree. They were too small to be great blue herons and did not really look like little blues. A few minutes with the heron book cleared up the mystery; they were tricolor herons, the first I had ever seen. By the end of the month American canaries were shooting around like tossed gold pieces despite another cold spell.

Suddenly it was mid-June and noxious weeds grew everywhere — leafy spurge, cheatgrass, Canada thistle, and more hoary cress. Nests were full of young birds, and the predator birds, who had hatched their young earlier, had rich pickings. Even a raiding great blue heron flew over pursued by smaller birds. I hadn't dared go near the fence across from the big nest for fear of forcing the goldens to abandon, but I could see now that they had two big chicks in the nest. And June marked the appearance of an insect I had never seen before — *Eremobates pallipes*, a.k.a. wind scorpion, a resident of deserts and the Great Basin. It is straw-colored, about three quarters of an inch long, and very much resembles a scorpion although it is not poisonous. It will bite if disturbed. It feeds on smaller insects, so I caught it and put it outside, hoping it could catch mosquitoes. More likely it made a snack for the myriad hungry birds rushing around outside.

On a hot, dusty Fourth of July, I walked down the road to the east end, pleased not to be cursed by the parent goldens. One of their chicks had found a narrow shelf with an overhanging ceiling not far from the nest, and there it sat, harassed by — who else? — the prairie falcon. But even young goldens are tough, and the falcon departed. When I got back from my walk I found some bird had dropped the corpse of a large nestling on the deck, white downy feathers, wings not fully fledged, the head gone. I thought it might have been the chick of a great blue heron or sandhill crane. The drought was bad, very hot and dry day after day and no rain for a long time. The grass cracked and broke when stepped on and it was too hot to sleep at night. Wind scorpion weather.

A hard, hot wind blew incessantly, drying out the lettuces in the garden, tearing petals off any flowers not made of steel. But the young eagles, both bald and golden, loved this hot wind. They and their parents were all soaring and zooming, trick flying, mounting high and then rolling down the air currents. At one point I could see seven eagles flying above the cliff at various altitudes, some so high they resembled broken paperclips.

A few mornings later a bird with an ineffably beautiful song woke me. I had no idea what it was and it was not visible from the high bedroom windows. I tried to identify it from birdsong CDs without success. It was the harbinger of a nasty little frost, a complete surprise that killed the tops of my tomato plants and beans, scorched the zucchini and cucumbers. I didn't realize it but the surprise mid-August frost would be an annual event at Bird Cloud, striking just when the garden was approaching high ripeness.

On the first of September, making coffee in the kitchen, I glanced up at the cliff and saw the big tawny-red mountain lion walking along the top. It descended to an area of outcrop above and to the right of two huge square stones balanced almost on the edge. Three weeks later, just before dark, I glassed the cliff and the colluvia below and noticed a large round rock on the debris pile that I couldn't remember having seen before. The telescope revealed it as a dead deer that had apparently fallen from the top of the cliff. Falling off a cliff was not something even the most addlepated deer would do. I surmised the lion had chased the panicked deer over the edge, and until dark I kept peering through the telescope, looking for the lion come to claim its kill. But the lion did not come. The next morning two ravens were on the carcass. As I made coffee I noticed that the ravens were gone, replaced by thirty magpies and two coyotes. It took the coyotes half an hour to break through the hide. The bald eagles perched nearby, waiting for their chance, and several ravens also waited. One of the coyotes departed. There was no sigh of the lion. By mid-morning the remaining coyote, bloody-muzzled and gorged, waddled away. The magpies move in. The most cautious diners were the eagles and ravens, who waited until after eleven for a turn at the deer. The first coyote returned with two friends and all three began to tug the carcass toward the edge of the colluvium, a drop-off of about ten feet. By afternoon the carcass was no longer in sight, now fallen into the brush below where perhaps the lion would claim it. The renegade thought occurred to me that perhaps the neighbor's cow that had fallen off the cliff the year before had been chased to its death by the lion.

The prairie falcons left, and the next week the ravens were back. A lesser goldfinch flew into a window. I left it on the deck and in the morning it was gone — I hope because it revived. Many birds knock themselves out and then come back from apparent death rather groggy and confused, but alive. The big, handsome northern flicker is an aggressive bird that often hurls itself at its reflection, falls like a stone, lies on its back with its feet curled up for a while, opens one eye, gets shakily up, and staggers through the air to a nearby branch, where it spends an hour or two thinking black thoughts — and then flies into the window again.

By the end of the month most of the migratory birds were gone. I remembered an earlier September when some friends and I had camped at the top of Green Mountain where we could look down at the Red Desert and make out the old stagecoach road and a few bunches of wild horses. We hiked around, noticed quite a few hawks, and by mid-morning realized that the hawk migration was in full spate. Hundreds of hawks flew over us that day, swiftly, seriously intent on getting away. Also intent, not on getting away but on filling up great pantries with pine seeds, were gray jays. They would cram seed after seed into their pouches and then take them to their secret caches. One smart gray jay, trying to pack in more than his crop could hold, hopped (heavily) to a little pool of water in the top of a boulder, took a few sips to wet down the seeds, and resumed gathering.

By mid-October most of the birds had gone south. The meadowlarks were the last to leave. The golden eagles were somewhere else, though probably in the area.

The bald eagles were involved in a major undertaking — the building of a new nest in a cottonwood closer to the river and closer to our house. One eagle flew in with a double-talon bunch of cut hay, likely swiped from a cattle ranch's bales. This new nest, unlike the old one, was highly visible. I worried about people who floated the river in summer. Of course, this eagle pair had shown that they were more interested in river traffic and what we are doing around the house than in privacy and isolation. As with humans, in the bird world it takes all kinds. For weeks they hauled materials in, mostly sticks and a dangerous length of orange binder twine that could tangle young birds tramping around in the nest. They took breaks from the construction and went fishing at the east end of the cliff, something they would not do when the goldens were in residence. But were the goldens really gone? There were a few days of rain and wet snow that made the county road a slithery mass of greasy mud.

On the first of November I walked along the river fence line in the evening, and as I came abreast of the big nest, the scolding "GET AWAY, FOOL!" call came from the cliff. The goldens were in their bedroom niche.

Colder and colder the days, clear and windless, the kind of days I have loved since my New England childhood. A rough-legged hawk, a stranger in these parts, came hunting over the fields. The bald eagles did something unusual—they chased it furiously, asserting their territorial rights. The hawk fled. The new nest looked large and commodious. The day after Thanksgiving a Clark's nutcracker appeared briefly. It looked a little like a gray jay but had dark markings on its face like a small black mask, and the body and wings were utterly Clark's. I saw it for only a few seconds before it sprang away, but it seemed that very often I saw birds that were subtly at variance with Sibley's illustrations[①].

Near the end of the month a little warm wind pushed in a bank of cloud. A northern harrier coursed over the bull pasture, just barely skimming the grass, floating on and on in lowest gear, then landing in the distance, hidden from me. It rose again, higher, using the wind. One morning one of the bald eagles brought a hefty stick to the new nest. It was long and awkward, and to get it in place the bird had to circle behind the nest and trample it in from the back with the help of its mate. It was a really big nest. A few hours later a bold raven came and sat on the west

---

① David Sibley is an American ornithologist and author. His well illustrated book The Sibley Guide to Birds is considered to be the most comprehensive guide for North American field identification.

branch of the bald eagle's fishing tree, about twenty feet away from the male eagle. They both seemed uneasy. The raven pretended unconcern and stretched his wings. The eagle shifted from one foot to another as if muttering, "What is this clown doing in my tree?" The big female eagle came in for a landing and sat beside her mate, and as she put down her landing gear the raven took off.

In the afternoon the wind strengthened after four days of calm and the goldens enjoyed it, rising into the empyrean until they seemed to dissolve in blue. It was like one of the *Arabian Nights* tales in reverse, the tale in which someone fleeing looked back and saw something the size of a grain of sand pursuing, and a little later looked again and saw something the size of a lentil. Later still the pursuer resembled a beetle, then a rabbit, and finally a slavering, demonic form on a maddened camel. But to my eyes the goldens shrank first to robins, then to wrens, then hummingbirds, and finally gnats or motes of dust high in the tremulous ether. Just before gray twilight the northern harrier returned but strayed into enemy airspace above the cliff, and suddenly there were four ravens chasing and nipping. The extra pair of ravens came from nowhere, like black origami conjured from expert fingers. As darkness swelled up from the east a full moon rose and illuminated great sheets of thin cloud like wadded fabric drawn across its pockmarked white face.

November fell through the floor and December began with the tingling, fresh scent of snow. Seven or eight inches fell. I had hoped this month would be snow-free, but that hope was dashed. Getting the mail or supplies was chancy. Usually I could put the old Land Cruiser[①] in low and smash through the snow, but in places the wind had packed the snow into unsmashable drifts and I got well and truly stuck on the county road. I tried to barrel through a five-foot drift that looked fluffy, small in comparison with the big piles that would come later in the winter, and ended up high-centered on a solid pedestal of snow, all four wheels off the ground. It snowed again just before Christmas, deep and beautiful snow that lay quiet in a rare calm. The hero sun came out for a quarter hour, then fell as though wounded. Eagles and goldeneyes were the only birds around. At dusk I skied down to the Jack Creek bridge. Mist rose from the river and the cliff seemed to be melting, the top floating on quivering froth.

---

① The Toyota Land Cruiser is a series of four-wheel drive vehicles produced by the Toyota Motor Corporation. Its reliability and longevity has led to huge popularity.

I made it down to the last days of December. It was fifteen below zero and the snow squealed when I walked on it. Later in the morning I saw the pair of golden eagles flying high over the cliff, playing in the frigid air. It began snowing again and I decided I would try to get out the next day. The lane was half choked with snow. If I didn't go the next day I knew I could be isolated for a long time, jailed at the end of the impassable road. I packed the old Land Cruiser and fled to New Mexico.

鸟之年鉴

安妮·普露

记得那是我独自留守"飞鸟云海"的第一天。"飞鸟云海"是我的农场,坐落于怀俄明州南部,离梅迪辛博山脉不远。河对岸的一棵树上,一只白头鹰正栖落枝头。那天是 2006 年 12 月 30 日。而在之前的一天,曾有 2 只白头鹰肩并肩地在那里呆了几个小时,静静地凝望着树下,目光透过岩石间流淌的幽幽河水,搜寻那些不甚警惕的鱼儿的身影。这就是白头鹰的捕鱼方式。有的时候,白头鹰也会矗立在浅滩处,任由冰冷的河水浸湿它们华丽的绑腿。白头鹰都是技术精湛的捕鱼高手。我曾见识过它们从结冰的河水中将鱼拖拽到冰面上,或是通过一个疾速的俯冲,将两只尖爪刺进一条大鲑鱼的身体,然后腾空而起,任凭那沉重的大鱼徒劳地扭曲挣扎。负责修建"飞鸟云海"的施工人员,就曾有幸亲眼目睹过,一只白头鹰刺向一条大鱼,锁紧双爪,骑在大鱼身上,负重奋力上冲。那场景就好像一条冲浪滑板正沿着湍急的河水疾驰而下。

我在"飞鸟云海"的居屋用了 2 年时间才建造完成。在那段时间里,我尝试着去了解这里各种鸟类的生活习性,渐渐地我能够辨认出栖息在这里的鸟群的季节性迁徙。观察这样一支数量庞大的鸟群既耗费精力又耗费时间——这项工作一点都不轻松。白头鹰是这里的永久居民。有些其它种类的鹰也会留在这里,还有一些则会迁移至南方。大雕鸮也会选择留下来。乌鸦们每年都会到这里来繁育后代。夏季到来,幼鸟学会了飞行,就飞到其它地方去觅食。秋天,它们会回到这里重新整理巢穴,四处翻查。最后,它们又会赶在冬季暴风雪来临前再次离开这里。初春时节,数以百计的红翅黑鹂飞到海岛上,聚集在长着铜色树干的柳树丛里,峭壁上回荡着它们高低起伏的歌声 aujourd'hui! aujourd'hui![1]。我放置了一些饲喂器,希望可以吸引一些小鸟儿。可是几日、几周、甚至几个月过去了,仍然没有任何鸟类光顾的迹象。这些野生的鸟儿太过于天真纯朴,根本就没想到从饲喂器里找寻食物。

使我印象深刻的是,白头鹰在这里安了家。《斯托克斯野外手册》[2]里有这样一段叙述:"当一对白头鹰在某处安家落户后,它们就极不情愿再到其它地方去繁殖后代。"事实确实如此。斯托克斯还告诫读者,在这些鸟"产卵到伏

---

[1] (法语) 今天。

[2] 唐纳德·斯托克斯和莉莲·斯托克斯著有一系列《斯托克斯野外手册》,如《斯托克斯野外手册之鸟类》,《斯托克斯野外手册北美鸟类》,《斯托克斯野外手册东部鸟类》,《斯托克斯野外手册西部鸟鸣》。

窝初期"的这段时间里,人们要远离它们的巢穴——至少保持四分之一英里的距离,因为受惊的父母可能会因此抛弃它们的幼鸟。但是,这对白头鹰并没有读过该手册,并且表现出对我们极大的容忍。我的居屋距离白头鹰的巢穴大约就是四分之一英里远的样子。然而,只有当我们站在河岸边正对着它们的巢,又或是到对岸去,在它们筑巢的树下散步的时候,它们才会警告我们要保持距离。每年,这对白头鹰都会繁育两只幼鸟,有一年除外。那年,仅有一只幼鸟存活了下来。书上说通常就仅有一只幼鸟能存活下来,但这对白头鹰却表现得如此轻松淡定——能有这样高的存活率,真是了不起的父母。每当有陌生人来到我的居屋,这对白头鹰就会轮流飞过来仔细地审查一番。一切新鲜的事物——比如草坪的躺椅、花园里用来浇水的橡胶管、新移栽的灌木,都会激发起它们的好奇心,它们会一边缓慢地低空飞过来,一边细细观察这些陌生的东西。实际上,它们都是好事的家伙。这很公平。我用双筒望远镜观察它们,它们也同样观察着我。

北普拉特河穿过我的农场,河道转为东西向绵延数英里。"飞鸟云海"总面积为 640 英亩,包括一平方英里的河岸灌木林和棉白杨树林、一些在每年 6 月份河水暴涨时会变成湿地的区域、一片鼠尾草草场,以及大片大片的过度放牧、杂草丛生的牧场。而在地势较低的地方,大约有 120 英亩的区域,那里被称作杰克溪,是鲑鱼们重要的产卵地。杰克溪沿马德雷山脉顺势向下,纵贯 30 英里,斜向穿过农场所在地,汇入北普拉特河。杰克溪河面宽阔,建一座桥非常有必要。也确实有一座,就建在一条货运列车轨道的地基之上,十分坚固耐用。在杰克溪的下游,北普拉特河地区,有一座美丽的小岛,生长着一片茂密的棉白杨林。农场的主体部分,大约 500 多英亩,坐落于砂岩峭壁之上,形成了一片倾斜广袤的草场,长满了莎草和鼠尾草。峭壁约有 400 英尺高,淡黄色的覆盖岩层由古代珊瑚构成。这块巨大的峭壁岩,在历经数千年烈风的打磨、酷日的灼烧、洪水的冲刷、冰雹的敲打、暴雨的洗礼之后,早已消蚀了锋芒。雨后的峭壁岩,如同受了重创,布满了暗色的斑点,以及纵深的裂痕,像极了旧日的伤疤。峭壁西面 2 英里处的地方,岩石逐渐收缩成一级级的铁褐色石阶,如金字形神塔①的台阶一般。在农场东端,峭壁出现了断层,犹如一条斜向的伤痕。据我的一位地质学家朋友讲,这个断层很可能与里奥格兰德裂谷有关,这道裂谷正缓慢地撕裂着美洲大陆。

---

① 金字形神塔(苏美尔语: ziqqurrat,意思是"建造在一块高地上")是古代建造的宏伟宗教建筑,层层叠叠,形似阶梯金字塔。金字形神塔的建造者主要包括苏美尔人、巴比伦人、埃兰人、阿卡德人和亚述人。每一个神塔都是某一神庙建筑群的组成部分。

在"飞鸟云海"独自度过的第一天，我向东走到了杰克溪桥，看到河对岸高高的峭壁上有一个空荡荡的鸟巢。那显然是鹰的巢穴。它是否曾经属于我见过的那对白头鹰？它们如今已迁徙到西边半英里外的棉白杨林中。抑或是另一对鹰曾经的住所？巨大的巢穴被积雪覆盖，黑黑的且布满了交错的尖刺，样子有些可怕。下午4点30分，峭壁上依然洒满了金色的阳光。而10分钟后，这种金色渐渐消褪为硬纸板一样的灰色。我再次仰望远处峭壁上巨大而空洞的巢穴，发现在峭壁下方，巢穴偏西的崩积岩石上有两只驼鹿，它们很可能属于一支庞大的避难队伍，那支队伍在数周前狩猎季节到来时途径这片农场。二三十只鹅向河的上游飞去，远离了猎枪伏击的范围。暮色渐浓，在一片朦胧的暮色中，一只巨大的鸟飞入峭壁的深穴中，就在驼鹿的正上方。该是鸟儿归巢的时间了。可，那是什么鸟呢？

第二天——也是一年的最后一天，在7点45分，太阳照亮了整个梅迪辛博山脉。这是一个美丽而晴朗的冬日清晨，阳光照耀在雪地上，没有风，温度在华氏零下2度，只有一轮近乎完美的落月。就如同理查德·拉塞尔斯——17世纪"壮游"①的倡导者——形容萤火虫时所说的："我想，那美极了。"到了中午时分，2只白头鹰在河边的树上凝视着树下的鱼。半个小时后，它们沿河向上游飞去，希望在另一段水域碰碰运气。

上午过半，我偶然瞥见一只体型巨大的鸟正向河流上游飞去，双翼有力而轻快地拍动着。我记起了前一天傍晚看见的那只栖息在峭壁空巢边深穴中的巨鸟。会是同一只鸟吗？那又是什么鸟呢？它的体型太大了，不可能是鹰。

新年的第一天，阳光明媚而温暖，华氏32度，鼓动着一些青草叶片冒冒失失地钻出雪地。一群鹊鸭正钻入水面下觅食，占据了河中一片整个冬季都未曾结冰的水面。我想，那可能有一眼温泉，所以河水即便在冬季也不会结冰。

傍晚时分，那对白头鹰正站立在树上，彼此相距300码。它们的身影渐渐融入暮色之中，但它们仍静静注视着河面。白头鹰在昏暗环境中的视力一定非常好。下午4点40分，十几只加拿大雁沿河逆流而上。一抹橘红色丝绸般的晚霞铺满了西方的地平线。我手里拿着双筒望远镜，静静地等待着。2分钟以后，最后一道阳光亲吻过峭壁的顶端，消失了。天空换上了紫色，映出了空中高高的圆月。我没有再看到那只神秘的巨鸟。我猜想，或许它是一只猫头鹰，那样它就可以轻松地在黑暗中飞翔。但我又心存怀疑，我强烈地感到那是一只鹰，

---

① 壮游是欧洲的贵族和上流社会年轻人进行的一种欧洲传统的旅行，后来也扩展到中产阶层，是一种有教育意义的成年礼。壮游一词，最早出现于《一次意大利之旅》一书。作者是罗马天主教神甫兼旅行作家理查德·拉塞尔斯，他同时还是几位英国贵族的导师。在该书中，拉塞尔斯阐述了壮游的重要性。

那个峭壁上巨大的、可怕的巢穴的主人。

  对我而言，将所有见过的鸟的种类罗列出来，既毫无价值，也缺乏乐趣。我倒是对生活在特定地区的鸟类有更大的兴趣，我还想知道它们在很长一段时间里都做些什么，以及它们如何善加利用自己精心挑选的栖息地。这些鸟儿在做什么，以什么为食，怎样繁育幼鸟等等，这些问题深深吸引着我。我想我完全被这些鸟儿的故事给迷住了。第二天早上，当我还在思考着上面那些问题的时候，我再一次错过了那只神秘的巨鸟。在那一闪而过的瞬间，我仅捕捉到了那只巨鸟身上的颜色，全身都是黯黑色。它拍打双翼的节奏，和鹰十分相似。那会是一只去年才孵化尚未完全成熟的白头鹰吗？抑或是一只金雕？或许吧。

  几天以来，西风不断肆虐着。风很猛烈，无论野兔还是我把脚印留在哪片雪地上，风都可以轻易钻进脚印周围硬质的雪壳里，然后掀起像大号薄煎饼一样的一块雪壳，吹着它一路向东滚去，直到雪壳最终碎成粉末。鹰都喜欢强风，绝不会错过在强风中展翅翱翔的乐趣。那对白头鹰正在强风中嬉戏玩耍，越飞越高，直到它们小得变成了空中的一对小圆点，然后分开。此时天空中空无一物，几分钟后，那只不知名的黯黑色巨鸟拍动着羽翼迅速闯入了我的视野，又很快消失在风暴中。

  傍晚，暮色爬上东边的天空，一只白头鹰出现了，两只尖爪抓满了树枝，然后落入巢中，不见了。难道这对白头鹰要在这样一个寒冷的冬日里重新修整巢穴吗？风，汹涌且咆哮着。一只孤零零的鸭子出现了，被风吹得四处乱撞。它的腹部是白色的，头部和翅膀则是黑色的，脸颊上是不是还有一块圆形的白斑？那可能是只鹊鸭。但一时间它又像一只从大炮里发射出来的企鹅。半个小时以后，又有两只向东行进的鸭子出现了，它们和风一起全速前进，速度大概有每小时 80 英里。这时另一只白头鹰也出现了，在空中逆风而行，那样子像是悬挂在空中，徒劳地拍打着翅膀，直到最后它调转方向，一转眼就飞出了几英里远。而在巢穴里的另一只白头鹰也飞了起来，紧随其后。

  第二天清晨，风力减弱到每小时 30 英里，阵风达到每小时 50 英里。天气寒冷，阳光却很充足。那对白头鹰从早上 8 点就在外面飞来飞去了。在煮咖啡的时候，我又一次看到那只神秘的巨鸟，它挥动着羽翼朝着邻家农场的方向飞去，从我的视线中消失了。为什么它总是这样难以捉摸呢？我很想好好看看它的样子，但它总是在我刚转过头时就飞走了。那 2 只孤单的驼鹿站在峭壁西端的小山上，头上还没长茸角，深棕色的脖颈，黄色的尾巴，红棕色的身体。第一眼看到它们的时候，我还以为是山区野羊——在印第安人居住在这里的时候，峭壁上曾生活着这种羊。这 2 只驼鹿的脸向内凹下去，看上去很像羊。喜鹊们忙着飞过河去，一只乌鸦在峭壁的巢穴西侧不远处的一棵树上落了下来。难道这只乌鸦也像白头鹰一样，想要早早地修整巢穴？

到了下午，风又猛烈起来，天空中有3个像鹰一样的小斑点。3只鹰在风中嬉戏。怎么会是3只？难道有一只幼年的白头鹰打算在这里筑巢？又或是那只神秘的巨鸟？到底有多少只鹰要在这里安家呢？

那天夜里，风势猛烈，尖叫着，拍打着。第二日，风势依然不减。我看到居屋的窗户在轻微地颤抖着。这是迄今为止最大的一场风了。我走出居屋来到车道上，想看看它被大风吹成了什么样子。车道上堆满了积雪，根本无法通行。大风险些把我吹倒在地。一只小鸟极速飞过厨房的窗户，而在河的另一端，那对白头鹰仍然稳稳地落在巢穴旁的树上。

狂风肆虐了一整夜，黑暗中，我躺在床上，焦躁的神经令我难以入睡，只能听着窗外风的呼啸与怒吼。白天让我感觉好一些，强风不像夜晚那样让人难以忍受。电视机不能正常工作了，因为卫星信号接收装置已经完全被风吹弯了。一连四五天都充斥着狂风的嘶吼声，之后风终于停了，一切又回复了温暖、晴朗与平静。气温攀升到华氏40度。但天气预报仍然提醒我们注意，另一场风暴正在临近。我镇里的一位朋友，在雪封的公路上强行开辟了一条小道，同时清理出自家的车道。而我也摆脱了雪的围困，电力公司清理了道路，为我修好了卫星信号接收器。

现在，每天日照的时间都会比前一天多上几分钟。趁着无风，我来到户外，一直走到农场的东面。我仰首翘望峭壁，看到了两只、而不是一只黯黑色的巨鸟。它们正在空中玩耍嬉戏，显然，它们很快乐，因为好天气而快乐，因为彼此而快乐，总之，为了生活而快乐。然后它们一同飞回了自己的寝巢，就在峭壁上那座巨大空置的巢穴西侧的裂缝中。我无法听清它们的叫声，因为这个时候刚好有一大群野鸭——有100多只，一边飞过来，一边大声鸣叫。那两只黯黑色的鸟看起来像是金雕，它们飞翔时的样子也像金雕。但它们全身都是黯黑色的，没有鸟类图册中描绘的金色颈背。金雕翱翔时，双翼会稍稍地翘起；白头鹰则会将双翼平展开来。但是我几乎可以肯定那是一对金雕，它们占据了这座巨大的空巢，正准备在此栖息。

第二天早上阳光露了出来，但是一场持续3天的暴风雪即将来临。将近中午的时候，低沉且不祥的乌云从四面八方压了过来。天气预报员提醒说，天气即将转寒。我趁着暴风雪来临前的宁静，带着双筒望远镜出发了。一只乌鸦在悬崖的石壁周围游荡，尝试着钻进石壁上壁龛一样的裂缝中。然后那对黯黑色的巨鸟出现在悬崖上空，表演着翻滚俯冲。我从望远镜中观察到，它们的头部和颈部的颜色确实比身体上的颜色浅一些。我现在可以肯定了，它们是一对金雕，一对正在求爱的金雕，正打算重建那座空巢，在那里繁育后代。而在离此半英里外的地方则住着那对白头鹰。我感到万分的欣喜和满足，我可以透过餐厅的窗户同时看到这对金雕和那对白头鹰的巢穴。我真想花上一整天观察它们，但是晚上暴风雪就来了，我必须趁着道路还未被大雪封死前出去买一些生活用品回来。

1 月慢慢地流逝着。天气很冷，日复一日的落雪正如康拉德·艾肯在故事《沉默的雪，神秘的雪》①中描述的一样。我在 8 岁的时候曾读过那本书，当时我以为那是一个关于厚厚的雪的故事。后来我才知道，那个故事其实是在间接地探讨一个男孩子日益严重的疯狂举动，对此我感到非常失望。在结了冰的河面上，4 只草原狼正在河的北岸寻找食物。而在河的上游，鹊鸭们畅游的水域还没有完全冻结，但是未结冰的水面每天都在缩减。

星期天的早晨，平静而单调，气温降到了华氏零下 21 度，空气阴冷凛冽。凝结的晨雾包裹着树木与灌木丛。河水因结冰而缩紧，及腰深的黑色河水被冰层牢牢封住。视野内见不到任何鸟的踪迹。太阳挣扎着露了出来，水汽在仅存的几条狭长的、尚未冰封的水面上蒸腾，形成巨大的隆起。棉白杨的顶端闪烁着微光，仿佛结冰的花束，树干则被薄纱般的雾气包裹着。春天似乎遥不可及。那对白头鹰正并肩站着，捕捉着第一缕阳光。它们常常这样肩并肩在一起，像一只长着两只头的鹰一样的野兽。当太阳升起时，白头鹰抖抖身上的羽毛，开始用喙梳理起来。一只喜鹊独自在薄雾中飞过。下午的时候我滑雪到农场的东面，进了一片棉白杨林。一只金雕和 4 只喜鹊正在啄食一只白靴兔少得可怜的遗骸。当我靠近它们的时候，金雕发现了我，便挥翅离开了。那 4 只喜鹊也跟着飞走了，很是不情愿。它们认定我是来和它们抢食物的。我可以轻易地推测出当时的情景：雪地上，野兔的足迹不断地急转，呈"之"字形穿过灌木丛。而在距离尸体东边 1 英尺远的雪地上，残留着雪天使一般的羽翼形的印迹，肯定是金雕袭击野兔时留下的。

怀俄明州曾经是屠鹰者聚集的天堂。那是在 20 世纪 60 年代至 70 年代，一段充满苦难的旧日时光。现如今居住在这座山谷里的很多牧牛场场主，那个时候都养羊，他们固执地认为白头鹰和金雕会捕掠羊羔。尽管白头鹰和金雕都受法律保护，但如果当时有谁养羊，那么他就一定会去猎杀这两种鸟类，特别是金雕。猎杀的手段包括：毒杀（大多使用硫酸铊）；使用租赁的直升机或是小型

---

① 《沉默的雪，神秘的雪》(1934) 是康拉德·艾肯最著名的短篇小说。书中讲述的是一个男孩渐渐地把自己和现实世界隔离开来，拒绝和他人接触，而是将自己沉浸在对雪的幻梦之中。

飞机,从空中使用猎枪射杀;或是透过敞篷卡车的车窗用步枪射杀。虽然在其它几个州也有屠鹰的事件发生,特别是在西部,但怀俄明州却格外地声名狼藉。在美国渔业及野生生物局①、国家奥杜邦学会②以及媒体大众眼中,怀俄明州早已成为最愚昧无知、最恶名昭彰的屠鹰者的主要阵地。这些人当中的首脑人物,是集财富与权力于一身的赫尔曼·沃纳,他曾是怀俄明家畜饲养者协会③的会长。他和他的女婿租用直升机对鹰进行血洗后,这对翁婿便被人们称作"怀俄明州的直升机怪兽"。

纳撒尼尔·P.里德是理查德·尼克松手下的内政部助理部长,他致力于制止这种屠鹰行为。1971年FBI④为此设计了一个圈套。一名在西部长大的探员假扮成牧场工人进入沃纳的牧场工作。在牧场的工人宿舍中,该探员听说了许多有关屠鹰的事情。由于这些证据仅仅是道听途说,联邦法官无法为此签署搜查令。但有2名长期监视屠鹰行为的奥杜邦学会会员,有一天在机场上偶然发现了一架直升机及其驾驶员。他们在直升机的机舱中看到了猎枪及空弹壳,于是用随身携带的照相机拍下了当时的情景。驾驶员意识到被拍了照,几星期后,忧心忡忡地来到位于华盛顿的内政部,声称只要能免于起诉,他将提供有关屠鹰的证据。后来,该驾驶员向参议院小组委员会供认,他曾开着直升机把那些屠鹰者运送到俄怀明上空去射杀鹰隼。他们至少枪杀过500只白头鹰和金雕,而其中沃纳是他最重要的客户。《时代周刊》⑤则将怀俄明州遭屠杀的鹰类总数确定为770只。尽管这种行为激起了全国性的愤怒,但仍然无法获得对沃纳领地的搜查令。美国空军为此出动了侦察机,在沃纳的牧场中用红外线照相机捕捉到一堆腐烂的肉。搜查令最终获得签署,搜查结果发现了牧场中藏匿的大量鹰类尸体。丹尼斯·德拉贝尔勒在《奥杜邦》画报中写到:

我们仍遇到了一些麻烦。怀俄明州的联邦检察官不肯对牧场经营者提起诉讼,因为他确信,怀俄明州的陪审团是绝不会判赫尔曼·沃纳有罪的。沃纳本

---

① 美国渔业及野生生物局(FWS)是联邦政府机构,归美国内政部管辖,致力于渔业、野生生物和自然栖息地的管理。

② 奥杜邦学会是美国的一个非赢利性环保组织,致力于自然保护。取名为奥杜邦学会旨在纪念鸟类学家、博物学家约翰·詹姆斯·奥杜邦。奥杜邦在他的著作《美国鸟类》一书中绘制并详细描述了北美的各种鸟类。该学会出版一本名叫《奥杜邦》的杂志,配以大量插图,是一本以自然为主题的画报,重点关注鸟类。

③ 怀俄明家畜饲养者协会(WSGA)是历史上著名的美国牧牛业组织,建立于1873年。该协会由怀俄明州牧牛场主发起建立,目的是制定牧牛业标准化管理,之后具备一定的政治影响力。

④ 联邦调查局(简称FBI)是美国司法部的主要调查机关,成立于1908年,一开始叫做调查局(简称BOI),1935年改名称为联邦调查局。主要任务是调查违反联邦犯罪法,支持法律,保护美国调查来自于外国的情报和恐怖活动。

⑤ 《时代周刊》是美国出版的新闻杂志,在纽约出版。创刊于1923年,是美国的第一份周刊。

人突然造访了纳撒尼尔·里德的办公室。"他简直是闯进了我的办公室，"里德回忆道："那是个瘦高而健壮的男人，戴着斯泰森毡帽。他说他要和我谈一谈。我很平静，问他说：'在那之前，你得先告诉我你是谁？'他说：'我就是赫尔曼·沃纳。我杀鹰是为了保护我的羊。你对这些鹰一点都不了解。'"

而另一本杂志《高地新闻》[①]则更明确地报道了该事件发生的始末，使得公众的态度开始动摇甚至是倒向。美国总检察长强烈要求起诉当事人。但是沃纳却从未接收审讯。就在开庭前的几个月，沃纳在一场交通事故中丧生。而在怀俄明州，羊毛市场开始萎缩，牧场主们开始纷纷转向养牛；政府对于猎鹰行为的罚金也大大增加；牧场主们一方面领教了内政部处理该事件的强有力的手段，另一方面也认识到白头鹰的主要食物来源是腐尸和鱼类，而非羊羔。在这种情况下，对鹰类的捕杀几乎全部停止了。

而怀俄明州对此事的态度则在卡斯帕尔学院的沃纳野生动物博物馆中有所体现。该馆收藏着丰富的鸟类标本。

终于，我的饲喂器在风中摇荡了几周以后，迎来了它的第一批访客——大约 50 只灰头岭雀。它们开始从四面八方向这里涌来。克里斯·费舍尔的《洛基山脉的鸟类》一书这样说道："冬季，灰头岭雀从洛基山脉的巢穴蜂拥而出，纷纷聚集到地势较低的地方。"因此这些灰头岭雀很可能是从马德雷山脉和梅迪辛博山脉聚集到这个山谷来的。不清楚是什么原因，它们飞上天空，逗留一阵后又返回到饲喂器旁。这里看不到其它的鸟类掠食者，没有人，也没有狗、牛或是陷阱，只有安静的风和灿烂的阳光。它们全都飞起来是不是要监视那些存在于远处的危险？或是为了重申它们中的等级划分（这对我来说完全不可见）？有时候它们飞到河边树丛中停留数分钟，然后再次返回饲喂器。每天我都要给饲喂器里添几次饲料。

美丽的日照时光渐渐变长。一天早晨，我看到一只白头鹰俯冲向小岛附近一段未结冰的水域，我拿起双筒望远镜往楼上冲去，刚好看到它将一条鱼拖到了冰面上。它吃掉了一部分鱼，然后飞回了巢穴。下午 5 点 10 分，峭壁顶端 50 英尺的区域被阳光镀成了金色。一只白头鹰驻留在巢穴中，而另一只则朝河的下游方向飞去。峭壁披上了像赤褐色粗皮苹果一样的颜色，我很喜欢这种难得一见的橙红色晚霞，紧挨在深色的如同旧袜子一般的云层下面，无声地燃烧着。

[①]《高地新闻》杂志主要关注美国西部的公共政策，环保和文化。该杂志于 1970 年由怀俄明州的牧场主和环保人士组织创办。"高地"是对科罗拉多高原的昵称。

我买了一架单筒望远镜，把它安装在我的卧室里，用它可以更好地观察河流和哨壁。我看不到那些鹰，却发现了一只驼鹿。奇怪的是，它身上的颜色与脖颈及腰腿处的颜色不同，要浅一些，就像穿了一件帆布夹克。我怀疑这是否是光线造成的错觉？它体的中间部分看起来像一块硕大的圆石。1个小时后，这头驼鹿站了起来，露出了一直躺在它身后的另一头驼鹿。透过单筒望远镜，驼鹿们的各种细节完完全全地展现在我面前。前一只驼鹿从后背上拉下几缕毛，然后开始啃食地上的鼠尾草和一枝黄。第二只驼鹿却又看不到了。饲喂器周围已经聚集了100多只灰头岭雀。我想要沿河散步，但是那对金雕变得十分的狂躁不安，我只得返回。其中一只金雕怒气冲冲地一路尾随着我，直到我返回家中。我曾打算邀请一些观鸟者到我这里来参观，但我知道那是不可能的。金雕们有权利不受到打扰。

　　几天后的一个晚上，我沿着农场边界的旧公路散步，与金雕之间时刻保持着四分之一英里的距离。它们飞出了巢穴，却没有发出任何叫声，只是沿着哨壁滑翔，密切注视着我。这时，在农场的尽头，另一对金雕出现了，它们沉寂无声，飞得很低很低，好像也在打量着我。原先的那对金雕突然沿哨壁向东面飞去，嘶吼着要把这对初来乍到的金雕赶走。我看到那对新来的金雕栖息在东边的一棵树上，可能它们已经在那里筑了巢。这样一来，在这1英里的范围内已经有6只又或者是3对鹰落户了。

　　第二天清晨的时候，一只白头鹰与一只草原隼发生了冲突，在天空中打成一片，草原隼在空中猛烈地冲刺，白头鹰则俯冲着发动攻击。突然间草原隼就消失了踪迹。中午的时候，风势渐渐猛烈，整整1个小时，烈风鞭打着整片棉白杨林。在河面上方，一只白头鹰站在树枝上，在河水里搜寻着鱼的身影。树枝被风吹得剧烈地摇摆，而白头鹰则像啄木鸟一样不停地用尾巴抵住树枝，才不至于从树上掉下去。我觉得这一切都太可爱了，虽然我也说不出个缘由来。有时候我觉得这些鸟就像埃文·康奈尔笔下的布瑞吉夫妇①。那只草原隼又开始在金雕盘踞的哨壁上空盘旋，却不见金雕的踪迹。整整一天，草原隼都在四处惹是生非，这让我有些不安。它是不是在找地方筑巢？几年前，草原隼曾在哨壁的最东端筑巢，不远处就住着另一对草原隼。草原隼总是会让它周围的鸟感到烦躁。

　　在"飞鸟云海"很少见到山雀。我在怀俄明的第一个住所位于森提尼尔。那时，每天都会有几十只山雀聚集到我居屋避风处的饲喂器旁。但我几乎从没

---

① 埃文·康奈尔，美国小说家，诗人，短篇小说作家。其作品《布瑞吉太太》(1959)和《布瑞吉先生》(1969)以苦涩却温馨的笔触描绘了20世纪20年代至40年代美国堪萨斯城的一对传统的中上层阶级老夫妻的生活。他们努力生活，并希望成为成功的父母。两部小说后来被改编成电影《末路英雄半世情》。

有在"飞鸟云海"见过山雀。当然，森提尼尔靠近森林，而"飞鸟云海"的四周则都是开阔的牧场。"飞鸟云海"的一大特色，就是长年盛行来自西北方向的如骏马般咆哮奔腾的烈风。冬季，烈风筑起坚固的"雪墙"。夏日，它又风干植被，卷起沙粒和碎石，并在10分钟内吹干衣物。鹰、隼和鹈鹕钟爱多风的日子，它们将自己放逐于空中，乘风倾斜而上，到达惊人的高度。"飞鸟云海"为什么总是如此多风呢？悬崖顶端海拔高达7000多英尺，狂风在这里几乎从未停止过，风势总是猛烈得如山之石。强风沿着嶙峋的峭壁表面前行，如同河面上顺流而下的小船。我想乘船者会很容易体会。西边广袤的土地尽是牧牛的草场，没有那些高树和矮灌木的阻挡，风可以毫无阻碍地向东穿行。而在重读了奥尔多·利奥波德的《沙乡年鉴》[①]后，我发现这种天气对山雀来说是致命的。书中写道：

我知道有几处受强风吹袭的林地，在那里，整个冬天都见不到山雀的踪影，但在其它季节里却满是山雀。这些地方有强风，是因为乳牛吃光了灌木丛。对靠蒸汽取暖的银行家来说，农民在他那里有抵押，而农民需要更多的乳牛，乳牛又需要更多的牧场，因此风并不是一件怎么讨厌人的事……但对山雀来说，冬日的风则限制着它们活动的区域。

书中还写道："有关自然的书籍都很少提到风，只有在提到火炉的时候才顺便提一提。"

又一场雪，下了一整夜，灰头岭雀在争夺一种由油腻的板脂和种子粘在一起的混合物——那本是啄木鸟的野餐。我在想是不是有什么动物死在了悬崖上面。因为我看到金雕正在那里高低起伏地徘徊着，而白头鹰也在那边。记得几年以前我住在森提尼尔的时候，一只鹿闯进了我们的芳草园，不知被什么东西吓坏了，想从仅有6英寸宽的栅栏缝中强行钻过，可它宽大的前胸却被栅栏牢牢地卡住，无法逃脱。那个追赶它的家伙扯走了它的心脏，剩下的尸体仍卡在栅栏上。我们把鹿的尸体拖到了柳树下。几个小时以后，一对金雕发现了那尸体，只用了3天就吃了个精光。如今，我真希望峭壁上那个吸引鹰注意的东西不是驼鹿的尸体。我已经有1个星期没有看见那2头驼鹿了。过了一会儿，一只白头鹰飞回到树上继续捕鱼，6只聒噪的野鸭飞过我的居屋，一只金雕在它们的上空尾随，大概是想在这群野鸭身上碰碰运气。

随着3月份的到来，河流渐深渐宽。我可以从居屋里听到冰面下河水汩汩

[①] 奥尔多·利奥波德,美国作家，科学家，生态学家、林务官和环境保护主义者，代表作《沙乡年鉴》。利奥波德在现代环境伦理的发展与荒野保育运动中都有着重要的影响。

的流动声。正如我所料，红翅黑鹂占据了饲喂器。小岛西岸的柳树林是它们的主要聚集地，在那里上百只黑鹂挤进同一片树丛中，不停地歌唱，炫耀着翅膀上的红色肩章①，然后一同飞去又飞回，继续歌唱，继续炫耀。草原隼在峭壁前方来回巡视，它的颜色和周围灰蒙蒙的岩石很接近，几乎无法辨认它的身影。一只旱獭从腐烂的木堆中钻了出来，在饲喂器下方找到了一个位置，满足地收集着红翅黑鹂丢下的种子。我步行走到农场最东边，蒙蒙细雨中，我看到一只巨大的旱獭正在悬崖顶上朝下面张望。东面几百码以外，我又瞥见一只硕大的草原狼。它马上躲了起来。这两只动物的体型都有些大得不可思议。后来到了春天，我有机会从近距离看清了这对"大猫"。我才知道，我先前看到的那只巨大的旱獭其实是一只美洲狮的幼崽，而那只硕大的草原狼很可能是它的母亲。

在一个温暖宜人的午后，金雕在巢穴上方的峭壁上晒着太阳。它们向外飞起，在空中盘旋，然后飞回到一块突出的岩石上——它们喜欢那里。当金雕在空中飞翔时，它们的影子也同样在峭壁上掠过，很难分清到底哪个是影子，哪个是金雕。体型较大的雌性金雕呆在岩石上，体型较小、颜色较深的雄性金雕则在空中表演着华美的飞行技巧，然后滑翔到爱人身边，献上食物，接着跨上了它的背。在此之前，我从没有见过金雕交配的情景。

每一天"飞鸟云海"都在发生着明显的变化，就连沉闷的泥土也不例外。一些嫩绿的灯心草开始在小岛岸边的土地上萌芽。河面渐渐拓宽，水势也湍急起来。一只驼鹿在消失了2周后再一次出现了。之前它大概是到背面的山坡觅食去了，或许是和它的同伴一起去的。所以我从居屋是看不到它们的。到了这个月的中旬，有那么几天突然转暖，河里所有的冰几乎都融化了。隼、野鸭、鹅、鹰和雕，这些鸟在空中向四面八方急速地飞驰，来来往往。我数了数一共有20只山地知更鸟，我想恐怕没有足够的巢穴来安置它们。但是乌鸦们，由于不堪草原隼一次又一次无情的侵袭，不得不弃旧巢而去。关于它们，我就只剩下了一些回忆。记得在一年前的一个下午，4只小乌鸦蹒跚地步行，笨拙地拍打着翅膀，然后终于离开巢穴，试着学习飞行。那天是阵亡将士纪念日②那一周的周末，夏季的第一场雷暴即将来临。小乌鸦们拍打着翅膀跳来跳去，时而抓住时而落下，或是飞出一小段距离，却也是紧贴着千疮百孔的悬崖峭壁。我们饶有兴致地看着这些小乌鸦，但它们飞飞停停、甚不娴熟的样子引起了周围

---

① Epaulette，肩章，这里是指雄性红翅黑鹂肩上鲜红色色块，雄鸟在飞翔的时候或是在做炫耀动作的时候便会亮出该色块，似红色肩章一样。

② 阵亡将士纪念日是美国的一个公共假期，每年5月的最后一个星期一。起源于美国南北战争时期，后来延伸到纪念各战争中阵亡的官兵。甚至一些美国人借该节日追思死去的亲人。现在，不少活动都会由该星期的周末开始，比如购物，家庭团聚，海滩旅行等。该节日通常标志夏季的开始。

其它鸟类的注意。白头鹰、红尾鵟、隼这些猛禽，在空中盘旋，或是飞上高处准备俯冲式攻击。大雕鸮的鸣叫声从小岛上传来。雷暴终于来了，先是雨声噼啪，接着冷雨倾盆，扑灭了我们的篝火。我肯定小乌鸦们这下是完了。看样子它们回不到岩石壁架的巢穴里了，不能挤在狭窄的岩石架子上或完全暴露在雨中的圆石块上。我们伤心地回到屋里，不敢想明天会发生什么。这些小家伙们能否逃脱那些伺机而动的掠食者的围捕呢？它们又是否会遭到雷暴的重创呢？

拂晓揭示着芳香明媚的一天，雨后的无风和焕然一新，在怀俄明真是难得一见。我们都带着双筒望远镜冲向悬崖边，想去看看是否有小乌鸦能幸免于难。"我看到一只！"有人喊道。接着又有一只湿漉漉的小乌鸦从藏身的洞里来到了阳光下，满身泥污。最后的两只也从峭壁的裂缝中飞了出来。它们全都聚集在一起，在阳光下梳理羽毛，伶俐、活泼、充满生机。它们花了一整天的时间来练习躲避敌人的飞行技巧，而我再也不必为它们担心了。

清晨在海岛上散步，我有机会面对面地看到了柳树林中的一只大雕鸮。奇怪的是，它的左眼是明亮的黄色，而右眼则是铁锈般的棕色，很可能是因为受过伤的缘故。它飞进了一片棉白杨林，在那里呆了整整一天。如今，迁徙的鸟类时常飞过这里，沿着河流的方向前进。一天下午，有6只金雕在飞往其它地方的路上途经这里，忍不住在悬崖上方随气流玩了好一阵子。野鸭、秋沙鸭、河乌来了，随后，黑海番鸭、1对北扑翅䴕、1只白尾鹞和1只西美草地鹨也纷纷赶来。河水因为吸饱了融雪水而暴涨，水位持续上升。3月19日，河水高得足以抬起了桥，将桥身抛到了小岛一侧的河岸，切断了其与陆地的联系。温热的日子持续着，令人烦恼，因为周围的一切都变得非常干燥。天气预报中提到的降雨也没有如期而至。当雨水最终到来时，却将我们的道路变成了冰冷湿滑的一片。

有一只加拿大雁，显然自认为很聪明，将窝高高地筑在了峭壁的东侧，不远处就是一座游隼的巢穴。我在想它是否就是我一年前看到的那只愚蠢的大雁。当时的那只大雁把窝筑在一棵大树的树冠上，完完全全地暴露在天空之下，而两边分别是金雕和草原隼的巢穴。那对大雁为此失去了所有的幼鸟——全部葬身掠食鸟之腹，之后它们不得不重新选择筑巢的位置繁育幼鸟。它们将巢穴建在了树下的土地上，而雄雁则时刻在巢边守卫着。

3月末，一场冬季的暴风雪持续了一天一夜。尽管风雪交加，一群角云雀还是在鼠尾草与一枝黄的草丛间采集着草籽。草原隼不知从什么地方呼啸着向角云雀们俯冲下来，云雀们瞬时炸开，像火箭一般四散逃离。其它的食肉鸟类，特别是蓝知更鸟，沮丧地落在栅栏上，等待春天的到来。待暴风雪过去，地上落满了一英尺深的积雪。寒冷的黎明时分，河面上升腾起一片浓雾，四散弥漫，遮天蔽日。厚厚的积雪下面覆盖着潮湿、几乎冻结的淤泥。为了开辟出一条路，我开着车在车道上来回驶过，将厚厚的积雪压平。雪还把门柱顶端的黑色金属乌鸦装点成了一只喜鹊。

4月份到来时天气多风而又温暖。我在向东漫步的路上发现了一只死去的鱼鹰，它灰色的爪子蜷曲着，仿佛想抓住什么。很难说到底是谁杀死了它。这附近生活着很多拼命守护自己领地的鸟类——半英里的范围内就有两对金雕、红尾鹭和一对游隼，向西再远一点的地方就是乌鸦和草原隼的领地。所有这些鸟都有可能将这只鱼鹰当作入侵者而对它发动攻击。春天是死亡的季节。一具小牛的尸体被冲到小岛的河岸边，这对喜鹊来说是一件相当值得高兴的事，或许对鹰们也是这样。

我还不是很清楚白头鹰一家是如何安排自己的时间的。它们在去年的12月份就已经开始修整巢穴了，这项工作可能持续了好几个月。巢穴看上去超过6英尺宽。但我推测在4月初的那个星期，白头鹰很可能在巢穴中孵出了幼鹰。这主要是因为我发现一只白头鹰在巢穴附近对一只红尾鹭紧追不舍。这只红尾鹭已经在悬崖的西侧徘徊了数日。这样推测，白头鹰产卵的时间大约在2月最后一周或是在3月最初的一周。通常雌鹰在1周内会产下2至3枚卵。产卵完成后，雄鹰和雌鹰需要轮流孵卵。尽管雌鹰在孵化的过程中会承担较多的工作，但雄鹰和雌鹰的腹部都会有孵卵斑①——温热裸露的，直接贴在卵上的皮肤。当一只鹰在孵卵，另一只则负责去觅食。如果天气温暖晴朗，那么雄鹰和雌鹰就都可以稍稍地休息一会儿。整个孵化过程会持续35天左右。一旦幼鹰孵化出来，接下来的工作将会更加辛苦。如果天气仍然很冷，那么必须有一只鹰留下来设法为幼鹰保暖。而当春日的阳光变得过于炎热和猛烈，雄鹰和雌鹰就会张开羽翼，像阳伞一样为幼鹰遮挡阳光。在开始的几天，雄鹰会忙于外出捕猎，然后将食物带回巢穴，一天大概需要捕食4至8次。几周后，雌鹰也开始出去觅食。而到了哺育幼鸟的后期，雌鹰将担负起绝大部分的捕食工作。

4月份的第三个星期，出现了一群美国白鹈鹕。喙上巨大的皮囊，表明它们正处于繁殖期。鹈鹕是极佳的飞行能手，在多风的日子里它们常常在空中疾速地上升和俯冲，上演精彩的飞行表演。但鹈鹕却常遭到怀俄明捕鱼者们的枪杀，因为捕鱼者坚信鹈鹕会和他们抢夺并吃光所有的鱼。在"飞鸟云海"度过的第一个春天令我十分震惊，无数只巨大的毛绒绒的鹈鹕的白色尸体浮荡在水

---

① 孵卵斑是指大多数鸟在孵卵期间腹部羽毛脱落形成的一块裸露的皮肤。由于血管丰富，有利于将腹部热量传导给卵。

面上，顺流而下。

5月，各种杂草开始滋生。我花了几个小时拔掉那些可恶的群心菜，竭力从土里挖出它们繁茂的白色根茎。天空中点缀着数以万计的飞燕。有几只固执的红翎粗腿燕想要在屋檐下筑巢。为了防止豪猪四处筑巢，我开始在小岛上将朽木和枯枝堆积在一起，打算在雨天生起一堆篝火。而河对岸有大片闲置的地方可以做豪猪的巢穴。一只深色小巧的莺鹪鹩在小岛上找到了一间大小合适的鸟舍，便开始搬家了，它衔来小捆的枯草和牙签大小的细小嫩枝来装扮新巢。

我看见一只白脸彩鹮出现在大门前，那里有一片灌溉溢出的水滩。我激动极了。它在这里逗留了几个星期。几天后，我正坐在河边，看到2只鹭飞到了白头鹰捕鱼时的那棵树上。它们体型很小，不像是大蓝鹭，也不像是小蓝鹭。我用几分钟翻查了有关鹭的书籍，终于找到了答案：它们其实是三色鹭，这是我第一次见到这种鸟。到了月底，天气又转冷了，但是美国金丝雀仍然在空中飞来飞去，像被掷来掷去的金币。

很快就到了6月中旬，乳浆草、旱雀草、加拿大蓟，以及大片的群心菜，这些有害的杂草四处生长。随处可见巢穴中的幼鸟，这让那些已经孵化完幼鸟的食肉鸟们捞到了不少油水。就算是外出捕食的大蓝鹭也会被其它体型较小的掠食鸟追捕。我一直不敢靠近正对着巨大巢穴的栅栏，害怕受惊的金雕会因此弃巢而去，但是我仍然可以看到巢中有两只体型很大的小金雕。6月份也带来了一种我从未见过的昆虫——*Eremobates pallipes*，又名避日蛛，分布于沙漠地带以及美国西部大盆地地区。避日蛛身色淡黄，体长四分之三英寸，外形酷似蝎子，但没有毒性，受到侵扰时会咬人。避日蛛以小型昆虫为食，于是我抓了一只，养在屋外，希望它能够帮着捉蚊子。但它更有可能成为外面那些游荡着的饥饿的鸟的点心。

7月4日，天气炎热，尘土飞扬。我沿着公路向农场东面走去，很高兴今天没有受到那对金雕的打扰。一只小金雕在离巢不远的峭壁上找到了一处带有屋檐的壁架，就一直坐在那里，但却一直受到侵扰。被谁侵扰呢？还会有谁？不就是草原隼。但即便是小金雕也不是好惹的，草原隼只得灰溜溜地离开了。等我散步回来，发现不知是哪只鸟在居屋的露天平台上丢下了一只雏鸟的尸体，那雏鸟体型很大，身上长着白色的绒毛，双翼尚未丰满，头已经不知所踪。我猜想这应该是一只大蓝鹭或是山丘鹤的雏鸟。干旱到了非常严重的程度，一天又一天，天气炎热而干燥，好久没有下雨了。草坪一踏上去就会干裂破碎，天气热得即便在夜晚也难以入睡。这真是适合避日蛛生存的天气。

猛烈且炎热的风不断地吹过，风干了园子里的莴苣，扯下所有花的花瓣—

一只要它不是钢打的。那些幼鹰们——白头鹰和金雕的幼鹰,却非常钟爱炎热的风。它们和父母一起腾空而起,在空中疾速地飞行,表演各种特技飞行,不断攀升,然后乘气流而下。有时我可以同时看到 7 只鹰在不同的高度翱翔,有些飞得太高,看上去像是折弯了的回形针。

几天后的一个清晨,我被一种美得无法形容的鸟鸣声唤醒。我不知道那是什么鸟,卧室的窗户太高,我看不到它。我想在记录着鸟鸣声的 CD 中寻找答案,却徒劳无功。但那鸟鸣声却预示着一小场恼人的霜冻,我完全没有想到,霜冻毁了蕃茄和豆荚的枝叶,密生西葫芦和黄瓜也枯萎了。我当时并不知道,在"飞鸟云海",这场令我吃惊的 8 月中旬的霜降每年都会发生,并且总是在园子里的植物快要成熟时来临。

9 月 1 日,我在厨房里煮咖啡的时候,瞥了一眼窗外的峭壁,发现一只硕大的茶红色的美洲狮正在峭壁顶端行走。美洲狮向下走到了一处位于 2 块巨大方形岩石的右上方的地表岩层上,那两块大方岩石就几乎悬在峭壁的边缘。3 个星期后的一天,我趁着天色未晚,透过望远镜向对面的峭壁和下面的崩积岩张望,发现在碎石堆上有一块大圆石,我不记得曾经见过这块石头。从望远镜里仔细观察,我发现那其实是一只死去的鹿,很显然它是从悬崖顶端掉下去而丧了命。可即便是最愚蠢的鹿也不可能从悬崖上掉下去。我推测一定是美洲狮追赶那只鹿,它受了惊,才跌落悬崖。于是我透过望远镜仔细地看着尸体所在的地方,等着看那只美洲狮来认领它的猎物。可是一直到天黑,美洲狮也没有出现。第二天清晨,鹿的尸体上落着 2 只乌鸦。当我煮咖啡的时候,乌鸦已经离开了,取而代之的是 30 只喜鹊和 2 只草原狼。草原狼费了半小时的劲才把鹿皮啃开。白头鹰落在一旁,等着有机会也可以分一杯羹。几只乌鸦也在旁边等待着。其中一只草原狼走开了。还是不见美洲狮的踪影。上午过半,留下的那只草原狼在一阵狼吞虎咽之后,带着满嘴的血迹大摇大摆地离开了。喜鹊又冲了上来。最谨慎的食客当属白头鹰和乌鸦,它们一直等到 11 点钟之后才围拢到鹿的尸体旁。最先离开的那只草原狼带着它的 2 个朋友回到了这里,它们 3 个一起把尸体拖到崩积岩的边上,那里有一段大约 10 英尺高的陡坡。到了下午,鹿的尸体已经彻底不见了踪迹,应该是落到了那片崩积岩下方的灌木丛里,或许美洲狮会去那认领猎物。我忽然恨起了美洲狮,前一年邻居家的那头牛,或许就是被那只美洲狮追赶落下山崖而死的吧。

草原隼离开了,1 个星期后乌鸦又回来了。一只暗背金翅雀撞上了一扇窗户。我把它留在了露天阳台上。第二天清晨它已经不见了——我希望它是自己醒来后飞走的。很多鸟都会把自己撞晕,表面看上去像是死了,过会儿又会恢复过来——尽管醒来后仍然会虚弱无力、迷迷糊糊，但至少还活着。健硕的北扑翅䴕是一种极好斗的猛禽，它们经常会朝着玻璃窗上映射出来的自己的身影猛扑过去，撞上后像石头一样重重地落下去，仰面朝天、双爪蜷曲地躺在地上好一阵，然后睁开一只眼，颤巍巍地站起来，摇摇晃晃地飞到附近的树枝上，花上一两个小时从头晕目眩的状态中清醒过来——然后再次冲向窗户。

9月底，大部分的迁徙鸟类都离开了。记得以前，也是在9月份，我和几个朋友在绿山山顶上露营，向下俯望红色沙漠的美景，依稀辨认出旧时马车驶过的道路，以及一小群野马。我们在四处漫步观光，注意到几只鹰在出没。上午过半的时候，我们才意识到鹰们正在进行大规模的迁徙。那天，有几百只鹰从我们的头顶飞过，快速地、全神贯注地飞过。同样这样忙着飞来飞去的还有灰噪鸦，它们不是忙着离开，而是忙着觅食，要把它们的大谷仓装满松子。它们将松子一粒接一粒地吞到嗉囊中，然后把这些食物运到它们秘密的储藏室。有一只灰噪鸦塞入的食物太多，嗉囊容纳不下了，它很聪明，拖着沉沉的身子，蹦到一块大圆石顶端，那有一小滩水，它轻啜几口水，润湿口中的松子，就又继续它的采集工作。

到了10月中旬，大部分鸟类都已经迁徙到南方去了。草地鹨是最后离开的。金雕也不知道去了哪里，或许还在这一区域内。白头鹰们则忙于一项重要的工作——在距离河岸更近的棉白杨林中建造一座新巢，这样距离我的居屋就更近了。一只白头鹰飞了回来，2只尖爪抓着一捆干草，那很可能是从一座牧牛场的大捆干草中偷来的。新巢和旧巢不同，能够非常清楚地被观察到。我开始为夏季乘船在河面上漂流的乘客感到担忧了。当然，这对白头鹰很早就对河面上往来的船只，以及我们在居屋附近的活动表现出极大的兴趣，而不是与人类隔离并严守自己的领地。就像我们人类一样，在鸟类的世界中，也有着形形色色的不同个体。几个星期以来，它们不停地拖回各种材料，主要是一些树枝，还有一根橘黄色捆扎用的麻绳，绳子长得有些危险，足以把巢穴中步履笨拙的雏鸟们绊倒并缠在一起。白头鹰夫妇会在建造巢穴之余，飞到峭壁东面一带去捕鱼——当金雕还住在那里的时候，它们是不会这么做的。但是金雕真的已经离开了吗？几日以来持续的雨雪天气已经把道路变成了湿滑的泥沼。

11月1日的晚上，我沿着河岸散步。当我走到一座大巢的正对面时，仿佛一声怒吼从悬崖那边传了过来："滚开，你这个傻瓜。"原来那对金雕正呆在它们峭壁壁龛中的卧室里。

天气愈来愈冷，晴朗而平静无风，自从我在新英格兰的童年，我就爱上了这种天气。一只毛脚䴕——这里的生客，也飞到这里来觅食。白头鹰对此表现得有些反常——它们愤怒地驱赶着毛脚䴕，极力维护自己的领地权。毛脚䴕最后还是逃走了。新巢看起来又大又宽敞。感恩节的第二天，一只北美星鸦只出现了一小会儿。它的样子有些像灰噪鸦，但脸上有一些深色的斑纹，像戴着一张小小的黑色面具。而身体和翅膀则完全符合北美星鸦的特征。我只看了它几秒钟，它就弹开飞走了。不过似乎我所看到的鸟经常和西伯利①所描述的样子有细微的差异。

临近月末，温暖的风吹来了一片云堆。一只白尾鹞飞过牧场，仅仅擦着牧场草坪低空地掠过，缓缓地一直向前滑翔，然后降落在远处，从我的视线中消失了。再一次，它腾身而起，乘着风的气流，越飞越高。一天清晨，一只白头鹰带着一根粗重的木棍回到了新巢。这根木棍又长又笨重，为了把它摆好，白头鹰绕到了巢穴的后面，在爱侣的帮助下将木棍从后面踩了进去。那巢可真是大。几个小时以后，一只大胆的乌鸦飞了过来，就落在白头鹰捕鱼时栖身的那棵树西侧的树枝上，在距离雄鹰大约20英尺远的地方。它俩看上去都非常不自在。乌鸦装作毫不在意的样子，伸了伸翅膀。白头鹰在一旁换了条腿站立，好像在嘟囔着："这个小丑跑到我的树上来想要干什么？"体型较大的雌鹰也飞了过来，落在丈夫的身边。当她落稳的时候，乌鸦灰溜溜地飞走了。

下午的时候，风势在保持了4天的宁静后，开始猛烈起来，而金雕们则非常地享受，飞入高高的天空深处，直到它们的身影消融在蓝色的天幕中。这让我想起了《一千零一夜》中的一个故事，不过却和那个故事恰恰相反。故事所讲的是一个逃跑的人不断地回头张望追赶他的东西，起初那个东西就像砂粒一样大小。过了一阵等他再向后看的时候，那东西已经成了扁豆大小。那人不停地向后张望，那东西先是看上去像一只甲虫，然后又像是一只兔子，最后他看到的是一个流着口水的形似恶魔的东西，正骑在一头疯狂的骆驼上一路追赶着他。但是我此时看到的却恰好相反，金雕先是缩小成知更鸟，然后是鹩鹩，再然后又成了蜂鸟，最后它变成了一只小昆虫，或是流动在天空中的一粒尘埃。在灰色的暮霭降临前，一只白尾鹞归巢而来，但却在峭壁上方误入了敌人的领空。一时间，4只乌鸦紧跟在这只白尾鹞的后面追赶并撕咬着。多出来的那一对乌鸦不知是从什么地方冒出来的，如同魔术大师指缝间凭空出现的黑色纸鸢一般。当黑暗自东边涌出，一轮满月渐渐升起，照亮了大片大片的薄云，如同一块块的织物遮挡在月亮苍白斑驳的面庞上。

11月降下了帷幕，而12月带来了刺冷、清新的雪。地上落了七八英寸的积雪。我原本希望这个月不会有雪的，但如今希望破灭了。我可能会因此收不

---

① 大卫·西伯利，美国鸟类学家，作家。他精心绘制的《西伯利鸟类图鉴》被认为是研究北美鸟类的最为详尽的图鉴。

到邮包或是补给品。有积雪的日子里，我通常都可以驾驶着那辆旧的陆地巡洋舰①慢慢地辗轧过路面上厚厚的积雪。可现在，到处都是风筑起的坚不可摧的雪堆，我被完完全全地困在了公路上。我试图加速冲过一座 5 英尺高的雪堆，那堆雪看起来还算松软，而且比冬季晚些时候形成的大雪堆要小得多。但结果是，我的车子驶上了一个坚硬的雪块，整个车子悬空而起，4 只轮子完全离开了地面。就在圣诞节到来前，又下了一场雪，厚厚的美丽的雪，在难得的无风的日子里静静地躺着。英雄般的太阳终于露出了云端，但仅仅坚持了一刻钟，就负伤败下阵来。只有鹰和鹊鸭还留在这里。黄昏时，我滑雪来到了杰克溪桥。雾气在河面上升腾开来，在雾气的映衬下，峭壁仿佛正在消融一般，而峭壁的顶端则好像漂浮在颤动的泡沫之上。

终于，我坚持到了 12 月的最后几天。气温到了华氏零下 15 度，积雪踩上去吱吱地响。上午晚些时候，我看到那对金雕在峭壁上的高空中飞翔，在寒冷的空气中尽情玩耍。又开始下雪了，我决定明天要想办法离开这个地方。车道已经被大雪封了一半了。我知道，如果明天我不离开，我将会被困在这里很长一段时间，被封在无法通行的路的尽头。于是，我把行李装上我那辆旧的陆地巡洋舰，逃向了新墨西哥州。

（曲美茹 译　张慧芳 校）

---

① 陆地巡洋舰是由日本丰田汽车公司生产的一款四轮驱动汽车。因其高可靠性和耐用性受到广泛欢迎。

后　记

　　应出版社朋友的邀约，《美国游记文学名篇导读与翻译》终于能够按期完稿付梓。搁笔的一刻，感到久违的快乐与轻松：欣赏、咀嚼、标注、翻译众多名篇佳作，仿佛自己亲历一般，时而行走荒漠沙丘，时而穿越热带丛林，时而置身冰天雪地，仿佛这些感觉隐藏在内心深处很多年，不曾发觉，此刻却一股脑儿被激活了。

　　游记是聆听自然的回音。

　　生态文明是人类挖掘不尽的宝藏，她拥有的深邃是无法用几篇游记展现的。没有一种哲学，不是从生态环境中得到启迪；没有一种宗教，不是以生态环境作为载体；没有一种文学艺术，不是把它当作永恒的主题和灵感的源泉。我国北宋文学家王安石曾言："世之奇伟、瑰怪非常之观，常在于险远，而人迹所罕至焉。"编者一直在想，本书所选文章的原作者不论来自哪里，不论旅行何处，都始终紧贴大自然，始终朝向静谧、自由、没有人迹的地方搜寻、探索。究竟原因何在？难道他们不眷恋人群中的繁华与喧嚣？难道他们不感叹日新月异的社会变迁？难道他们对象征"人类文明进步"的工业文明当真嗤之以鼻吗？译罢这些名篇佳作，编者的疑问全都烟消云散了。同时编者也知道，敬畏自然、理解自然、遵从自然，所有这一切，都源于聆听自然的回音。人与人之间有缘份，人与自然之间也有缘份。这种缘份，一半倚赖上天，一半事在人为。

　　生态文明是一种理解方式，是人类对于相比自身更伟大的意义的一种洞悉。原文作者笔下一位位鲜活的人物由敬畏自然转化为信仰自然，进而邀请自然和谐地融入社会组织和物质生活中，一个眼神、一句话语、一抹微笑，细微之处见"文明"。然而作者的亲眼所见，译者的痛心记录，也有令人潸然泪下的场面：青山绿水沦为沙漠，飞禽走兽濒临灭绝，贫穷落后不断蔓延，试图将生态环境引向深渊，企图让生态文明万劫不复。

　　编者希望这本书能达到两个目的，其一是让读者领略美国作家笔下的万千生态文明景观，其二是帮助读者增添一点对自然的敬畏，对生态环保的兴趣，果能如此，编者就十分满足了。那么，就请暂且放下这本无足轻重的书，戴上遮阳帽，背上旅行包，穿上运动鞋，向远方的自然行进，不在山高水远，不在酷夏严冬，不在极地大漠，不在雨林草原，只请将生态文明怀揣在心中，只愿将环境保护放在心间。

  最后，对于本书所选文章的翻译，只是一得之见，一家之言，不敢斗胆说能够完全畅达的表现原文的意旨。惟愿本书能开此生态文明游记翻译之先，作为引玉之砖。希望学界及各位同仁、朋友批评指正，期待更完善的译文出现，以期为文学鉴赏、翻译研究、学术探讨贡献绵薄之力。

COPYRIGHT NOTES

All the texts included in this textbook are selected from *The Best American Travel Writing* series (2000 - 2011) published by Houghton Mifflin. We have tried all the ways to contact the copyright holder of each essay. We have been granted the written reprint permissions as the following listed:

"Lost in the Amazon" by Matthew Power from *Men's Journal*, issue June 9, 2009 © Men's Journal LLC 2009 All Rights Reserved. Reprinted by Permission of *Men's Journal*.

"Thirteen Ways of Looking at a Void" by Michael Finkel. First published by in *National Geographic Adventure*, September/October 2001. Copyright © 2001 by Michael Finkel. Reprinted by permission of National Geographic Stock.

"The Two Faces of Tourism" by Jonathan Tourtellot. First published in *National Geographic Travelers*; July-August 1999. Copyright © 1999 by *National Geographic Traveler*. Reprinted by permission of *National Geographic Stock*.

"The Vanishing Point" by Verlyn Klinkenborg. First published in *The New York Times Magazine*, March 28, 2010. Copyright © 2010 by Verlyn Klinkenborg. Reprinted by permission of *The New York Times*.

"Winter Rules" by Steve Rushin. First published in *Sports Illustrated*, May 17, 1999. Copyright © 1999 by Time Inc. Reprinted by permission of Sports Illustrated.

"Lost in the Arctic" by Lawrence Millman. First published in *National Geographic Adventure*, September 2002. Copyright © by Lawrence Millman. Reprinted by permission of the author.

"Eco-touring in Honduras by Elisabeth Eaves". Copyright © by Elisabeth Eaves. Reprinted by permission of the author.

However, for some reasons, some of our Reprint Permission Requests have not been replied. Here we sincerely and seriously state: we have by no means any intention to misuse or infringe your copyright. We highly appreciate your writing and our only purpose is to introduce your concerned essay to Chinese students. Your essay is used in its entirety without any editorial change. We have footnoted and translated the essay to make it more easily understood by Chinese readers. If you happen to read your essay included in this textbook, please contact us, and we will happily pay the fee as it deserves. The contact information is:

Zhang Huifang
Tianjin University of Finance & Economics
Foreign Languages Department
No. 25, Zhujiang Road, Hexi District
Tianjin 300222
CHINA
shandudu@hotmail.com